Praise for *Teach Yourself Java*

"If you get only one Java book, it should be *Teach Yourself Java in 21 Days*. Authors Laura Lemay and Charles L. Perkins cover all aspects of Java programming in an easy-to-read guide organized around daily lesson plans."

—Jay Munro, *PC Magazine*

"…this is where to begin. Java in all its gory details: classes to applets, methods to multithreading."

—Thom Gillespie, *Library Journal*

"*Teach Yourself Java* gives a thoughtful treatment to under-the-hood issues of Java's implementation."

—Peter Coffee, *PC Week*

"If you buy one book on Java, this is the one to buy. *Teach Yourself Java* is one of the best introductions to hands-on Java programming. The setup of the book is extremely well thought out."

—Scott Sidel, *Independent Web Review*

"This is the best introduction to object-oriented programming ever written. This book does not assume that you know C or C++, but it offers tips for those who do. Laura Lemay is my favorite tech author.…If you can afford only *one* Java book, then this is the one to get."

—David Geary

What's New in This Edition

Given the explosion of tools for building Java applications and the wide variety of things that people are doing with Java, for the Web and for general-purpose applications, there is no shortage of new things to talk about when it comes to Java.

This edition, therefore, is a fully revised and extended edition of the original *Teach Yourself Java in 21 Days*. It has been greatly expanded and enhanced, with all the original content updated, the weak parts fixed, and more examples added. This edition also contains a bonus week that adds further depth and detail about existing topics such as images, animation, and networking, as well as information about tools, debugging, and advanced data structures. In the bonus week you'll also learn about the following:

- ☐ Day 22 describes tools and utilities for programming in Java, including debugging techniques, Java development environments such as Symantec Café and Visual J++, the javadoc documentation system, and other tips and tricks.

- ☐ Day 23 covers creating structures for modeling various forms of data, both with the classes in the java.util package and by creating new classes.

- ☐ Day 24 goes into even more detail about animation in Java, building on the simple techniques covered in Week 2.

- ☐ Sun's java.awt.image package provides a set of classes for working with images. Day 25 covers these classes in detail, explaining the image filter architecture and how you can use it in your own Java programs.

- ☐ Day 26 takes a further look at client/server networking, with extensive examples of networking applets and applications and working with live data sent from a server, as well as connecting to databases from Java applets.

- ☐ Days 27 and 28 move into the future and describe what are known as the standard extension APIs. Many of the features you'll learn about on Day 27 will be part of Java 1.1. Day 28 finishes up with more future topics, including Sun's Java Beans API, Java chips, and the JavaOS.

The bonus week goes into great detail about upcoming features in Java 1.1 and the extension APIs. And with more than 250 pages of reference material in the appendixes, there's little you won't be able to discover using this book.

About This Book

This book teaches you all about the Java language and how to use it to create applets for the World Wide Web, as well as standalone applications. By the time you get through with this book, you'll know enough about Java and about the Java class libraries to do just about anything, inside an applet or out.

Who Should Read This Book

This book is intended for people with at least some basic programming background, which includes people with years of programming experience and people with only a small amount of experience. If you understand what variables, loops, and functions are, you'll be just fine for this book. The sorts of people who might want to read this book include you, if

- ☐ You're a real whiz at HTML, understand CGI programming (in Perl, AppleScript, Visual Basic, or some other popular CGI language) pretty well, and want to move on to the next level in Web page design.
- ☐ You had some BASIC or Pascal in school and you have a basic grasp of what programming is, but you've heard Java is easy to learn, really powerful, and very cool.
- ☐ You've programmed C and C++ for many years, you've heard this Java thing is becoming really popular, and you're wondering what all the fuss is about.
- ☐ You've heard that Java is really good for Web-based applets, and you're curious about how good it is for creating more general applications.

What if you know programming, but you don't know object-oriented programming? Fear not. This book assumes no background in object-oriented design. If you know object-oriented programming, in fact, the first couple days will be easy for you.

What if you're a rank beginner? This book might move a little fast for you. Java is a good language to start with, though, and if you take it slow and work through all the examples, you may still be able to pick up Java and start creating your own applets.

How This Book Is Structured

This book is intended to be read and absorbed over the course of four weeks. During each week, you'll read seven chapters that present concepts related to the Java language and the creation of applets and applications.

Conventions

NOTE

A note box presents interesting pieces of information related to the surrounding discussion.

TECHNICAL NOTE

A technical note presents specific technical information related to the surrounding discussion.

TIP

A tip box offers advice or teaches an easier way to do something.

WARNING

A warning box advises you about potential problems and helps you steer clear of disaster.

NEW TERM New terms are introduced in new term boxes, with the new term in italics.

TYPE A type icon identifies some new Java code that you can type in. You can also get the code from the CD-ROM that accompanies this book.

OUTPUT An output icon shows the output from a Java program.

ANALYSIS An analysis icon alerts you to the author's line-by-line analysis.

Teach
Yourself
JAVA™

in 21 Days,
Professional
Reference Edition

Teach Yourself
JAVA™
in 21 Days, Professional
Reference Edition

Laura Lemay
Charles L. Perkins
Michael Morrison

201 West 103rd Street
Indianapolis, Indiana 46290

President, Sams Publishing   Richard K. Swadley
Publishing Manager   Mark Taber
Managing Editor   Cindy Morrow
Director of Marketing   John Pierce
Assistant Marketing Managers   Kristina Perry
Rachel Wolfe

Acquisitions Editor
Mark Taber

Development Editor
Fran Hatton

Software Development Specialist
Bob Correll

Senior Editor
Kitty Wilson

Copy Editors
Kimberly K. Hannel
Colleen Williams

Indexer
Johnna VanHoose

Technical Reviewers
Brad Birnbaum
Pratip Banerji
Jeff Bankston
Jeff Shockley

Editorial Coordinator
Bill Whitmer

Technical Edit Coordinator
Lorraine Schaffer

Editorial Assistants
Carol Ackerman
Andi Richter
Rhonda Tinch-Mize

Cover Designer
Tim Amrhein

Book Designer
Gary Adair

Copy Writer
Peter Fuller

Production Team Supervisor
Brad Chinn

Production
Cynthia Davis, Elizabeth Deeter,
Sonja Hart, Lousia Klucznik,
Polly Lavrick, Paula Lowell,
Andrew Stone

Overview

Contents

Appendixes

Preface to the Professional Reference Edition

I first saw Java running in May of 1995, and was immediately struck by what it offered to the Web. What I saw seems almost quaint in this day and age of multimedia Web pages—a small animation of a character doing cartwheels across the screen—but at the time it was a revolution. My friend Jim Graham, a programmer on the Java team, showed me various aspects of the Java language and the HotJava browser, and I sat with my mouth agape, unable to say much of anything except for "that is so cool." At the time, I was just finishing up a book about HTML and looking for something else to do. I immediately knew that this had to be it. I had to write a book on Java.

It took somewhat longer to actually produce the book, between needing to finish a number of other projects, having to wait for a new version of Java itself, and coming down with a number of bad cases of the flu, but the book was written and shipped in early 1996. That book was the original *Teach Yourself Java in 21 Days*.

While not the first book available on the Java language, it was widely regarded as the first *good* book and the first one that wasn't either too vague or that assumed too much knowledge of programming. Written for an intermediate programmer, *Teach Yourself Java* continues to be one of the few books available that offers a basic tutorial in Java, enough to get you started and enough to move beyond the basics. *Teach Yourself Java* continues to be popular and continues to be recommended as one of the best books on getting started in Java.

Which brings us to this hefty tome that you're holding in your hands. Since early 1996 Java itself has not changed overly much. The current 1.0.2 release has added few features since 1.0; for the new features we'll have to wait for 1.1 (due out in late 1996). But given the explosion of tools for building Java applications and the wide variety of things that people are doing with Java out there for the Web and for general-purpose applications, there is no shortage of things to talk about when it comes to Java.

This book, therefore, is an extension of the original *Teach Yourself Java*. It has been greatly expanded and enhanced, with all the original content updated, the weak parts fixed, and more examples added. This book also contains a bonus week that adds further depth and detail about existing topics such as images, animation, and networking; it includes information about tools, debugging, and advanced data structures; and it goes into great detail about upcoming features in Java 1.1 and the extension APIs. With more than 250 pages of reference material, there's little you won't be able to discover using this book.

If you haven't yet worked with Java, this is the book to start with. If you have worked with Java but are looking for more information, this is the book to continue with. And even if you've read the original *Teach Yourself Java*, you'll find enough new in this edition to merit putting aside the original and adding this one to the stack of programming books on your desk.

Good luck and enjoy!

Laura Lemay
August 1996

Acknowledgments

From Laura Lemay:

To Sun's Java team, for all their hard work on Java, the language, and on the browser, and particularly to Jim Graham, who demonstrated Java and HotJava to me on very short notice in May and planted the idea for this book.

To everyone who bought my previous books and liked them: Buy this one, too.

From Charles L. Perkins:

To Patrick Naughton, who first showed me the power and the promise of Oak (Java) in early 1993.

To Mark Taber, who shepherded this lost sheep through his first book.

From Mike Morrison:

Thanks to Mark Taber for giving me the opportunity to contribute to such a cool project, and to Fran Hatton for being so enormously positive and helpful.

About the Authors

Laura Lemay

Laura Lemay is a technical writer and a nerd. After spending six years writing software documentation for various computer companies in Silicon Valley, she decided that writing books would be much more fun (but has still not yet made up her mind). In her spare time she collects computers, e-mail addresses, interesting hair colors, and nonrunning motorcycles. She is also the perpetrator of *Teach Yourself Web Publishing with HTML in 14 Days*.

You can visit her home page at `http://www.lne.com/lemay/`.

Charles L. Perkins

Charles L. Perkins is the founder of Virtual Rendezvous, a company building a Java-based service that will foster socially focused, computer-mediated, real-time filtered interactions between people's personas in the virtual environments of the near future. In previous lives, he has evangelized NeXTSTEP, SmallTalk, and UNIX, and has degrees in both physics and computer science. Before attempting this book, he was an amateur columnist and author. He's done research in speech recognition, neural nets, gestural user interfaces, computer graphics, and language theory, but had the most fun working at Thinking Machines and Xerox PARC's SmallTalk group. In his spare time, he reads textbooks for fun.

You can reach him via e-mail at `virtual@rendezvous.com`, or visit his Java page at `http://rendezvous.com/java`.

Michael Morrison

Michael Morrison is the author of *Teach Yourself Internet Game Programming with Java in 21 Days*, and a contributing author to *Tricks of the Java Programming Gurus, Java Unleashed,* and *Game Developer* magazine. Michael lives in Scottsdale, Arizona, with his (now legally recognized) female cohort, Mahsheed. In his spare time, Michael enjoys testing his threshold for pain on skateboard ramps. You can reach Michael via e-mail at `mmorrison@thetribe.com`, or check out his Web site at `http://www.thetribe.com`.

Dedications

To Eric, for all the usual reasons (moral support, stupid questions, comfort in dark times, brewing big pots of coffee).

—L.L.

For RKJP, ARL, and NMH, the three most important people in my life.

—C.L.P.

To Mahsheed, who saw the potential in a dorky teenager way back when.

—M.M.

Tell Us What You Think!

As a reader, you are the most important critic and commentator of our books. We value your opinion and want to know what we're doing right, what we could do better, what areas you'd like to see us publish in, and any other words of wisdom you're willing to pass our way. You can help us make strong books that meet your needs and give you the computer guidance you require.

Do you have access to CompuServe or the World Wide Web? Then check out our CompuServe forum by typing GO SAMS at any prompt. If you prefer the World Wide Web, check out our site at http://www.mcp.com.

NOTE

> If you have a technical question about this book, call the technical support line at 800-571-5840, ext. 3668.

As the team leader of the group that created this book, I welcome your comments. You can fax, e-mail, or write me directly to let me know what you did or didn't like about this book—as well as what we can do to make our books stronger. Here's the information:

FAX: 317-581-4669

E-mail: newtech_mgr@sams.mcp.com

Mail: Mark Taber
            Publishing Manager
            Sams.net Publishing
            201 W. 103rd Street
            Indianapolis, IN 46290

Introduction

The World Wide Web, for much of its existence, has been a method for distributing passive information to a widely distributed number of people. The Web has, indeed, been exceptionally good for that purpose. With the addition of forms and image maps, Web pages began to become interactive—but the interaction was often simply a new way to get at the same information. The limitations of Web distribution were all too apparent once designers began to try to stretch the boundaries of what the Web can do. Even other innovations, such as Netscape's server push to create dynamic animations, were merely clever tricks layered on top of a framework that wasn't built to support much other than static documents with images and text.

Enter Java, and the capability for Web pages to contain Java applets. Applets are small programs that create animations, multimedia presentations, real-time (video) games, multiuser networked games, and real interactivity—in fact, most anything a small program can do, Java applets can. Downloaded over the Net and executed inside a Web page by a browser that supports Java, applets are an enormous step beyond standard Web design.

The disadvantage of Java is that to create Java applets right now, you need to write them in the Java language. Java is a programming language, and therefore, creating Java applets is more difficult than creating a Web page or a form using HTML. Soon there will be tools and programs that will make creating Java applets easier—they may be available by the time you read this. For now, however, the only way to delve into Java is to learn the language and start playing with the raw Java code. Even when the tools come out, you may want to do more with Java than the tools can provide, and you're back to learning the language.

That's where *Teach Yourself Java in 21 Days* comes in. This book teaches you all about the Java language and how to use it to create not only applets, but also applications, which are more general Java programs that don't need to run inside a Web browser. By the time you get through with this book, you'll know enough about Java to do just about anything, inside an applet or out.

How This Book Is Organized

Teach Yourself Java in 21 Days covers the Java language and its class libraries in 21 days, organized as three separate weeks. In addition, this edition contains a bonus week that's chock full of new and advanced information. Each week covers a different broad area of developing Java applets and applications.

In the first week you'll learn about the Java language itself:

- ☐ Day 1 is the basic introduction: what Java is, why it's cool, and how to get the software. You'll also create your first Java applications and applets.

- ☐ On Day 2 you'll explore basic object-oriented programming concepts as they apply to Java.

- ☐ On Day 3 you'll start getting down to details with the basic Java building blocks: data types, variables, and expressions, such as arithmetic and comparisons.

- ☐ Day 4 goes into detail about how to deal with objects in Java: how to create them, how to access their variables and call their methods, and how to compare and copy them. You'll also get your first glance at the Java class libraries.

- ☐ On Day 5 you'll learn more about Java, with arrays, conditional statements, and loops.

- ☐ Day 6 is the best one yet. You'll learn how to create classes, the basic building blocks of any Java program, and how to put together a Java application (a Java program that can run on its own without a Web browser).

- ☐ Day 7 builds on what you learned on Day 6. You'll learn more about how to create and use methods, including overriding and overloading methods and creating constructors.

Week 2 is dedicated to applets and the Java class libraries:

- ☐ Day 8 provides the basics of applets—how they're different from applications, how to create them, and about the most important parts of an applet's life cycle. You'll also learn how to create HTML pages that contain Java applets.

- ☐ On Day 9 you'll learn about the Java classes for drawing shapes and characters to the screen—in black, white, or any other color.

- ☐ On Day 10 you'll start animating those shapes you learned about on Day 9, including learning about threads and their uses.

- ☐ Day 11 covers more detail about animation, adding bitmap images and audio to the soup.

- ☐ Day 12 delves into interactivity—handling mouse and keyboard clicks from the user in your Java applets.

- ☐ Day 13 is ambitious; you'll learn about using Java's Abstract Windowing Toolkit to create a user interface in your applet, including menus, buttons, check boxes, and other elements.

- ☐ On Day 14 you'll explore the last of the main Java class libraries for creating applets: windows and dialogs, networking, and a few other tidbits.

Week 3 includes advanced topics for when you start doing larger and more complex Java programs or when you want to learn more:

☐ On Day 15 you'll learn more about the Java language's modifiers—for abstract and final methods and classes as well as for protecting a class's private information from the prying eyes of other classes.

☐ Day 16 covers interfaces and packages, useful for abstracting protocols of methods to aid reuse and for the grouping and categorization of classes.

☐ Day 17 covers exceptions: errors and warnings and other abnormal conditions, generated either by the system or by you in your programs.

☐ Day 18 builds on the thread basics you learned on Day 10 to give a broad overview of multithreading and how to use it to allow different parts of your Java programs to run in parallel.

☐ On Day 19 you'll learn all about the input and output streams in Java's I/O library.

☐ Day 20 teaches you about native code—how to link C code into your Java programs to provide missing functionality or to gain performance.

☐ On Day 21 you'll get an overview of some of the behind-the-scenes technical details of how Java works: the bytecode compiler and interpreter, the techniques Java uses to ensure the integrity and security of your programs, and the Java garbage collector.

This Professional Reference Edition also includes a bonus week that contains more depth about some of the topics previously mentioned in the book, lots more sample programs, and coverage of the various tools and utilities currently available for writing with Java. It also gives you a preview of the features coming up in Java 1.1:

☐ Day 22 describes tools and utilities for programming in Java, including debugging techniques, Java development environments such as Symantec Café and Visual J++, the javadoc documentation system, and other tips and tricks.

☐ On Day 23 you'll learn about creating structures for modeling various forms of data, both with the classes in the java.util package and by creating new classes.

☐ Day 24 goes into even more detail about animation in Java, building on the simple techniques covered in Week 2. On this day you'll learn about creating sprite-based animation and coordinating image and media loading with your programs.

☐ Sun's java.awt.image package provides a set of classes for working with images. Day 25 covers these classes in detail, explaining the image filter architecture and how you can use it in your own Java programs.

☐ Day 14 gives a very basic introduction to networking in Java. Day 26 takes it further, with extensive examples of networking applets and applications, working with "live" data sent from a server, and connecting to databases from Java applets.

□ On Day 27 we move into the future and describe what are known as the standard extension APIs. Sun is developing these APIs in conjunction with other interested parties, and many of the features you'll learn about in this chapter will be part of the 1.1 Java API.

□ Day 28 finishes up with more future topics, including Sun's Java Beans API, Java chips, and the JavaOS. How will these technologies affect how you work in Java and how Java will affect you? Learn about it here as you finish up the book.

Preparing for the Future: The Upcoming Java 1.1 Release

At the time this book is being written, the current version of Java is known as the 1.0 API (or, more exactly, the 1.0.2 version of the JDK). A new version of Java is on the horizon, one that will add a significant number of new features to Java while still being backward compatible with the original version. This new version of Java, called Java 1.1, is expected to be available in a prerelease form in late 1996.

This book covers the Java 1.0 API in intimate detail. Where information about an upcoming feature of 1.1 is available, we have attempted to explain that new feature, how it will affect what you have already learned about the 1.0 API, and where to look for further information. In addition, the last two chapters of this book cover the more advanced features of 1.1 and how they will be used. These notes and comments will help you prepare for when 1.1 is released and help you migrate the code you may have already written quickly and easily to the new API.

Features expected to be in the 1.1 JDK include

□ JDBC (the Java Database Connectivity interface) provides a mechanism for connecting Java applications and applets to SQL databases such as Oracle and Sybase. The JDBC, available in a prerelease form at this time from `http://splash.javasoft.com/jdbc/`, is covered on Day 27.

□ RMI (Remote Method Invocation) is the ability to call a Java method from an object running elsewhere (for example, in a different Java environment running on the same machine or on any machine on the network). RMI is closely related to object serialization, which allows objects to be encoded into a stream of bytes, which can then be sent over a network or saved to a file. The result can then also be decoded back into a Java object at the other end. Object serialization is an extension of the stream classes discussed on Day 19. RMI is discussed in greater detail on Day 27. Information about both of these topics can be found at `http://chatsubo.javasoft.com/current/`.

☐ The Java native methods interface is the ability for Java to call system-specific libraries such as DLLs or loadable libraries written in C. Writing native methods is described on Day 20; enhancement in Java 1.1 will include a better API for making sure native method libraries are compatible with every implementation of the Java runtime across platforms.

☐ JIT compilers are tools that convert Java bytecode to native machine code. You'll learn about JIT compilers throughout this book, but particularly on Days 21 and 22. In Java 1.1 there will be better specifications for writing your own JIT or other tool that generates native code from Java bytecodes.

☐ Changes to the AWT. Probably some of the more significant changes to Java will be in the area of the Abstract Windowing Toolkit, or AWT, the portion of Java that controls drawing to the screen, creating user interface elements such as buttons and windows, and handling painting and user input between all those elements. This book covers the AWT primarily in Week 2. Enhancements to the AWT in Java 1.1 include printing, pop-up menus, supports for clipboards (copy and paste), internationalization for fonts, better scrolling capabilities, and delegation-based events. You'll learn more about these changes throughout Week 2.

☐ Security enhancements. JDK 1.1 will provide many features for implementing security in Java applications, including signatures, access control, key management, and message digests (MD5 hashes, for example). These additions won't affect much of 1.0 because they are new enhancements. You'll learn all about 1.1's security features on Day 27.

☐ Networking enhancements. Java 1.0 provides the `java.net` classes, which provide simple network connections, URL management, and simple client and server sockets. Java 1.1 provides more flexibility for the existing socket classes, a new `MulticastSocket` class, and BSD-style socket options. Learn about all these new features on Day 14 or from the URL `http://java.sun.com/products/JDK/1.1/designspecs/net/index.html`.

☐ Adapter classes allow you to implement an API defined by an interface or a class and have the flow of control move from the adapter class back to an enclosing object. Java 1.1 provides Java syntax for nesting class definitions inside other class definitions to more easily create adapter classes. You'll learn more on Day 6.

☐ Object reflection is the ability for Java to inspect an object and find out its methods and variables (and call and change them). Object reflection is useful for class browsers or other tools that need to find out information about an object on-the-fly, as well as component object systems that need defined ways of referring to other objects' contents. Java 1.1 provides many features for handling object reflection, including a number of new classes. You'll find out more on Day 4 or from `http://java.sun.com/products/JDK/1.1/designspecs/reflection/index.html`.

☐ Java 1.1 provides a number of new features for internationalization, particularly language-specific features such as strings, character set conversions, Unicode character display, and support for definable "locales."

☐ Java archives (JAR files) provide a mechanism for combining several classes into a single file for faster downloading over the Net. Netscape provides a single archive file mechanism for applets, but JAR files provide a more cross-platform file format, compression, and the ability to include media files in the archive. The capability to store Java classes in JAR files, and to use them with Java-enabled browsers, will be in Java 1.1. The current JAR file format specification is available from `http://java.sun.com/security/codesign/jar-format.html`.

You can learn more about all these features via information throughout this book or from the Java 1.1 preview page at `http://www.java.sun.com/products/JDK/1.1/designspecs/`.

Conventions Used in This Book

Text that you type and text that should appear on your screen is presented in `monospace` type:

```
It will look like this.
```

It mimics the way text looks on your screen. Placeholders for variables and expressions appear in `monospace italic`.

The end of each chapter offers common questions asked about that day's subject matter, with answers from the authors.

Sources for Further Information

Before, while, and after you read this book, there are several Web sites that may be of interest to you as a Java developer.

The official Java Web site is at `http://java.sun.com/`. At this site, you'll find the Java development software and online documentation for all aspects of the Java language, including the previously mentioned Java 1.1 preview page. It has several mirror sites that it lists online, and you should probably use the site "closest" to you on the Internet for your downloading and Java Web browsing.

There is also an excellent site for developer resources, called Gamelan, at `http://www.gamelan.com/`, which contains an enormous number of applets and applications, with sample code, help, and plenty of information about Java and Java development.

This book also has a companion Web site at `http://www.lne.com/Web/JavaProf/`. Information at that site includes examples, more information, and background for this book, corrections to this book, and other tidbits that are not included here.

For discussion about the Java language and the tools to develop in it, check out the Usenet newsgroups for `comp.lang.java`. This set of newsgroups—which includes `comp.lang.java.programming`, `comp.lang.java.api`, `comp.lang.java.misc`, `comp.lang.java.security`, and `comp.lang.java.tech`—is a terrific source for getting questions answered and for keeping up on new Java developments.

WEEK 1

At a Glance

1

2

3

4

5

6

7

☐ **Arrays, Conditionals, and Loops**

Conditional tests, iteration, block statements

☐ **Creating Classes and Applications in Java**

Defining constants, instance and class variables, and methods

☐ **More About Methods**

Overloading methods, constructor methods, and overriding methods

Day 1

An Introduction to Java Programming

by Laura Lemay

Hello and welcome to *Teach Yourself Java in 21 Days*! Starting today and for the next few weeks you'll learn all about the Java language and how to use it to create programs that run inside Web pages (called applets) and programs that can run on their own (called applications).

That's the overall goal for the next couple weeks. Today, the goals are somewhat more modest, and you'll learn about the following:

- ☐ What exactly Java is, and its current status
- ☐ Why you should learn Java—its various features and advantages over other programming languages

☐ Getting started programming in Java—what you'll need in terms of software and background, as well as some basic terminology

☐ How to create your first Java programs—to close this day, you'll create both a simple Java application and a simple Java applet!

What Is Java?

Based on the enormous amount of press Java is getting and the amount of excitement it has generated, you may get the impression that Java will save the world—or at least solve all the problems of the Internet. Not so. Java's hype has run far ahead of its capabilities, and while Java is indeed new and interesting, it really is another programming language with which you write programs that run on the Internet. In this respect, Java is closer to popular programming languages such as C, C++, Visual Basic, or Pascal, than it is to a page description language such as HTML, or a very simple scripting language such as JavaScript.

More specifically, Java is an object-oriented programming language developed by Sun Microsystems, a company best known for its high-end UNIX workstations. Modeled after C++, the Java language was designed to be small, simple, and portable across platforms and operating systems, both at the source and at the binary level, which means that Java programs (applets and applications) can run on any machine that has the Java virtual machine installed (you'll learn more about this later).

Java is usually mentioned in the context of the World Wide Web, where browsers such as Netscape's Navigator and Microsoft's Internet Explorer claim to be "Java enabled." *Java enabled* means that the browser in question can download and play Java programs, called *applets*, on the reader's system. Applets appear in a Web page much the same way as images do, but unlike images, applets are dynamic and interactive. Applets can be used to create animation, figures, forms that immediately respond to input from the reader, games, or other interactive effects on the same Web pages among the text and graphics. Figure 1.1 shows an applet running in Netscape 3.0. (This applet, at `http://prominence.com/java/poetry/`, is an electronic version of the refrigerator magnets that you can move around to create poetry or messages.)

 Applets are programs that are downloaded from the World Wide Web by a Web browser and run inside an HTML Web page. You'll need a Java-enabled browser such as Netscape Navigator or Microsoft's Internet Explorer to run applets.

To create an applet, you write it in the Java language, compile it using a Java compiler, and refer to that applet in your HTML Web pages. You put the resulting HTML and Java files on a Web site in the same way that you make ordinary HTML and image files available. Then, when someone using a Java-enabled browser views your page with the embedded applet, that

browser downloads the applet to the local system and executes it, allowing your reader to view and interact with your applet in all its glory. (Readers using other browsers may see text, a static graphic, or nothing.) You'll learn more about how applets, browsers, and the World Wide Web work together later in this book.

Figure 1.1.

Netscape running a Java applet.

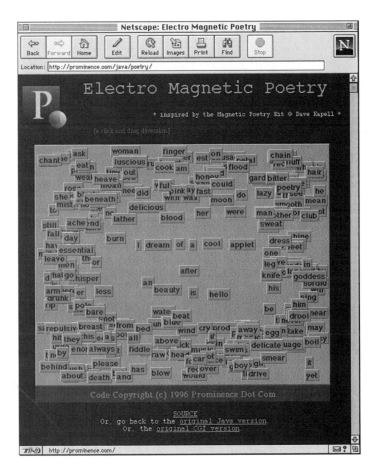

While applets are probably the most popular use of Java, the important thing to understand about Java is that you can do so much more with it than create and use applets. Java was written as a full-fledged general-purpose programming language in which you can accomplish the same sorts of tasks and solve the same sorts of problems that you can in other programming languages, such as C or C++.

Java's Past, Present, and Future

The Java language was developed at Sun Microsystems in 1991 as part of a research project to develop software for consumer electronics devices—television sets, VCRs, toasters, and the other sorts of machines you can buy at any department store. Java's goals at that time were to be small, fast, efficient, and easily portable to a wide range of hardware devices. Those same goals made Java an ideal language for distributing executable programs via the World Wide Web and also a general-purpose programming language for developing programs that are easily usable and portable across different platforms.

The Java language was used in several projects within Sun (under the name Oak), but did not get very much commercial attention until it was paired with HotJava. HotJava, an experimental World Wide Web browser, was written in 1994 in a matter of months, both as a vehicle for downloading and running applets and also as an example of the sort of complex application that can be written in Java. Although HotJava got a lot of attention in the Web community, it wasn't until Netscape incorporated HotJava's ability to play applets into its own browser that Java really took off and started to generate the excitement that it has both on and off the World Wide Web. Java has generated so much excitement, in fact, that inside Sun the Java group spun off into its own subsidiary called JavaSoft.

Versions of Java itself, or, as it's most commonly called, the Java API, correspond to versions of Sun's Java Developer's Kit, or JDK. As of this writing, the current version of the JDK is 1.0.2. Previously released versions of the JDK (alphas and betas) did not have all the features or had a number of security-related bugs. Most Java tools and browsers conform to the features in the 1.0.2 JDK, and all the examples in this book run on that version as well.

The next major release of the JDK and therefore of the Java API will be 1.1, with a prerelease version available sometime in the later part of 1996. This release will have few changes to the language, but a number of additional capabilities and features added to the class library. Throughout this book, if a feature will change or will be enhanced in 1.1, we'll let you know, and in the last two days of this book you'll find out more about new Java features for 1.1 and for the future.

Currently, to program in Java, you'll need a Java development environment of some sort for your platform. Sun's JDK works just fine for this purpose and includes tools for compiling and testing Java applets and applications. In addition, a wide variety of excellent Java development environments have been developed, including Sun's own Java Workshop, Symantec's Café, Microsoft's Visual J++ (which is indeed a Java tool, despite its name), and Natural Intelligence's Roaster, with more development tools appearing all the time.

1

To run and view Java applets, you'll need a Java-enabled browser or other tool. As mentioned before, recent versions of Netscape Navigator (2.0 and higher) and Internet Explorer (3.0) can both run Java applets. (Note that for Windows you'll need the 32-bit version of Netscape, and for Macintosh you'll need Netscape 3.0.) You can also use Sun's own HotJava browser to view applets, as long as you have the 1.0 prebeta version (older versions are not compatible with newer applets, and vice versa). Even if you don't have a Java-enabled browser, many development tools provide simple viewers with which you can run your applets. The JDK comes with one of these; it's called the `appletviewer`.

NOTE

> If you're running Windows 3.*x* as your main system, very few tools exist for you to be able to work with Java. As I write this, the only Java tool available for writing and running Java applets is a version of the JDK from IBM called the ADK. You can write applets using this tool, and view them using the applet viewer that comes with that package (neither Netscape nor Internet Explorer will run Java applets on Windows 3.1). See `http://www.alphaWorks.ibm.com/` for more information.

What's in store for Java in the future? A number of new developments have been brewing (pardon the pun):

☐ Sun is developing a number of new features for the Java environment, including a number of new class libraries for database integration, multimedia, electronic commerce, and other uses. Sun also has a Java-based Web server, a Java-based hardware chip (with which you can write Java-specific systems), and a Java-based operating system. You'll learn about all these things later in this book. The 1.1 release of the JDK will include many of these features; others will be released as separate packages.

☐ Sun is also developing a framework called Java Beans, which will allow the development of component objects in Java, similarly to Microsoft's ActiveX (OLE) technology. These different components can then be easily combined and interact with each other using standard component assembly tools. You'll learn more about Java Beans later in this book.

☐ Java capabilities will be incorporated into a wide variety of operating systems, including Solaris, Windows 95, and MacOS. This means that Java applications (as opposed to applets) can run nearly anywhere without needing additional software to be installed.

☐ Many companies are working on performance enhancements for Java programs, including the aforementioned Java chip and what are called *just-in-time compilers*.

Why Learn Java?

At the moment, probably the most compelling reason to learn Java—and probably the reason you bought this book—is that applets are written in Java. Even if that were not the case, Java as a programming language has significant advantages over other languages and other environments that make it suitable for just about any programming task. This section describes some of those advantages.

Java Is Platform Independent

Platform independence—that is, the ability of a program to move easily from one computer system to another—is one of the most significant advantages that Java has over other programming languages, particularly if your software needs to run on many different platforms. If you're writing software for the World Wide Web, being able to run the same program on many different systems is crucial to that program's success. Java is platform independent at both the source and the binary level.

 Platform independence means that a program can run on any computer system. Java programs can run on any system for which a Java virtual machine has been installed.

At the source level, Java's primitive data types have consistent sizes across all development platforms. Java's foundation class libraries make it easy to write code that can be moved from platform to platform without the need to rewrite it to work with that platform. When you write a program in Java, you don't need to rely on features of that particular operating system to accomplish basic tasks. Platform independence at the source level means that you can move Java source files from system to system and have them compile and run cleanly on any system.

Platform independence in Java doesn't stop at the source level, however. Java compiled binary files are also platform independent and can run on multiple platforms (if they have a Java virtual machine available) without the need to recompile the source.

Normally, when you compile a program written in C or in most other languages, the compiler translates your program into machine code or processor instructions. Those instructions are specific to the processor your computer is running—so, for example, if you compile your code on an Intel-based system, the resulting program will run only on other Intel-based systems. If you want to use the same program on another system, you have to go back to your original source code, get a compiler for that system, and recompile your code so that you have a program specific to that system. Figure 1.2 shows the result of this system: multiple executable programs for multiple systems.

Figure 1.2.

Traditional compiled programs.

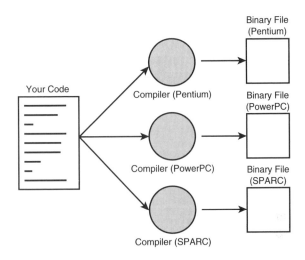

Things are different when you write code in Java. The Java development environment actually has two parts: a Java compiler and a Java interpreter. The Java compiler takes your Java program and, instead of generating machine codes from your source files, it generates *bytecodes*. Bytecodes are instructions that look a lot like machine code, but are not specific to any one processor.

To execute a Java program, you run a program called a bytecode interpreter, which in turn reads the bytecodes and executes your Java program (see Figure 1.3). The Java bytecode interpreter is often also called the Java virtual machine or the Java runtime.

> **NEW TERM** Java *bytecodes* are a special set of machine instructions that are not specific to any one processor or computer system. A platform-specific *bytecode interpreter* executes the Java bytecodes. The bytecode interpreter is also called the Java virtual machine or the Java runtime interpreter.

Where do you get the bytecode interpreter? For applets, the bytecode interpreter is built into every Java-enabled browser, so you don't have to worry about it—Java applets just automatically run. For more general Java applications, you'll need to have the interpreter installed on your system in order to run that Java program. Right now, you can get the Java interpreter as part of your development environment, or if you buy a Java program, you'll get it with that package. In the future, however, the Java bytecode interpreter will most likely come with every new operating system—buy a Windows machine, and you'll get Java for free.

Why go through all the trouble of adding this extra layer of the bytecode interpreter? Having your Java programs in bytecode form means that instead of being specific to any one system, your programs can be run on any platform and any operating or window system as long as the Java interpreter is available. This capability of a single binary file to be executable across platforms is crucial to what makes applets work because the World Wide Web itself is also platform independent. Just as HTML files can be read on any platform, so can applets be executed on any platform that has a Java-enabled browser.

Figure 1.3.

Java programs.

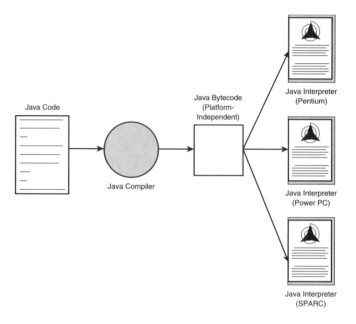

The disadvantage of using bytecodes is in execution speed. Because system-specific programs run directly on the hardware for which they are compiled, they run significantly faster than Java bytecodes, which must be processed by the interpreter. For many basic Java programs, speed may not be an issue. If you write programs that require more execution speed than the Java interpreter can provide, you have several solutions available to you, including being able to link native code into your Java program or using special tools (called *just-in-time compilers*) to convert your Java bytecodes into native code and speed up their execution. Note that by using any of these solutions, you lose the portability that Java bytecodes provide. You'll learn about each of these mechanisms on Day 20, "Using Native Methods and Libraries."

Java Is Object Oriented

To some, the object-oriented programming (OOP) technique is merely a way of organizing programs, and it can be accomplished using any language. Working with a real object-oriented language and programming environment, however, enables you to take full advantage of object-oriented methodology and its capabilities for creating flexible, modular programs and reusing code.

Many of Java's object-oriented concepts are inherited from C++, the language on which it is based, but it borrows many concepts from other object-oriented languages as well. Like most object-oriented programming languages, Java includes a set of class libraries that provide basic data types, system input and output capabilities, and other utility functions. These basic libraries are part of the standard Java environment, which also includes simple libraries, form networking, common Internet protocols, and user interface toolkit functions. Because these class libraries are written in Java, they are portable across platforms as all Java applications are.

You'll learn more about object-oriented programming and Java tomorrow.

Java Is Easy to Learn

In addition to its portability and object orientation, one of Java's initial design goals was to be small and simple, and therefore easier to write, easier to compile, easier to debug, and, best of all, easy to learn. Keeping the language small also makes it more robust because there are fewer chances for programmers to make mistakes that are difficult to fix. Despite its size and simple design, however, Java still has a great deal of power and flexibility.

Java is modeled after C and C++, and much of the syntax and object-oriented structure is borrowed from the latter. If you are familiar with C++, learning Java will be particularly easy for you because you have most of the foundation already. (In fact, you may find yourself skipping through the first week of this book fairly rapidly. Go ahead; I won't mind.)

Although Java looks similar to C and C++, most of the more complex parts of those languages have been excluded from Java, making the language simpler without sacrificing much of its power. There are no pointers in Java, nor is there pointer arithmetic. Strings and arrays are real objects in Java. Memory management is automatic. To an experienced programmer, these omissions may be difficult to get used to, but to beginners or programmers who have worked in other languages, they make the Java language far easier to learn.

However, while Java's design makes it easier to learn than other programming languages, working with a programming language is still a great deal more complicated than, say, working in HTML. If you have no programming language background at all, you may find Java difficult to understand and to grasp. But don't be discouraged! Learning programming is a valuable skill for the Web and for computers in general, and Java is a terrific language to start out with.

Getting Started Programming in Java

Enough background! For the second half of this day let's actually dive into simple Java programming and create two Java programs: a standalone Java application and an applet that you can view in a Java-enabled browser. Although both these programs are extremely simple, they will give you an idea of what a Java program looks like and how to compile and run it.

Getting a Java Development Environment

 In order to write Java programs, you will, of course, need a Java development environment. (Although browsers such as Netscape allow you to play Java applets, they don't let you write them. For that you'll need a separate tool.) Sun's JDK, which is available for downloading at the JavaSoft Web site (http://www.javasoft.com/) and included on the CD for this book, will do just fine. It runs on Solaris, Windows 95 and NT, and Macintosh. However, despite the JDK's popularity, it is not the easiest development tool to use. If you're used to using a graphical user interface–based development tool with an integrated editor and debugger, you'll most likely find the JDK's command-line interfaces rather primitive. Fortunately, the JDK is not the only tool in town.

As mentioned earlier, a number of third-party development environments (called *integrated development environments*, or IDEs) are also available for developing in Java. These include Sun's Java Workshop for Solaris, Windows NT and Windows 95 (you can get more information about it at http://www.sun.com/developer-products/java/); Symantec's Café for Windows 95, Windows NT, and Macintosh (http://cafe.symantec.com/); Microsoft's Visual J++ for Windows 95 and Windows NT (http://www.microsoft.com/visualj/); and Natural Intelligence's Roaster (http://www.natural.com/pages/products/roaster/index.html). All three are commercial programs, but you might be able to download trial or limited versions of these programs to try them out. You'll learn more about the features and capabilities of the various Java IDEs on Day 22, "Java Programming Tools."

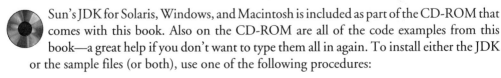

NOTE

I find the graphical development environments far easier to use than the standard JDK. If you have the money and the time to invest in one of these tools, I highly recommend you do so. It'll make your Java development experience much more pleasant.

Installing the JDK and Sample Files

 Sun's JDK for Solaris, Windows, and Macintosh is included as part of the CD-ROM that comes with this book. Also on the CD-ROM are all of the code examples from this book—a great help if you don't want to type them all in again. To install either the JDK or the sample files (or both), use one of the following procedures:

NOTE

> If you don't have access to a CD-ROM drive, you can also get access to these files over the World Wide Web. You can download the JDK itself from http://java.sun.com/products/JDK/1.0.2/ and install it per the instructions on those pages. The sample files from this book are available on the Web site for this book: http://www.lne.com/Web/JavaProf/.
>
> If you download the JDK and source files, as opposed to getting them off the CD-ROM, make sure you read the section "Configuring the JDK" to make sure everything is set up right.

WINDOWS   Sun's JDK runs on Windows 95 and Windows NT. It does not run on Windows 3.x.

To install the JDK or the sample files on Windows, run the Setup program on the CD-ROM (double-clicking the CD icon will do this automatically). By default, the package will be installed into C:\Java; you can install it anywhere on your hard disk that you'd like. You'll be given options to install the JDK, the sample files, and various other extra files; choose the options you want and those files will be installed.

If you've installed the JDK, note that in the directory JDK\lib there is a file called classes.zip. Do *not* unzip this file; it needs to remain in zip form for it to work correctly. The file JDK\src.zip contains the source code for many of the JDK libraries; you can unzip this one if you like. Make sure if you do that you have a zip program that supports long filenames, or it will not work correctly!

MACINTOSH   Sun's JDK for Macintosh runs on System 7 (MacOS) for 68KB or Power Mac.

To install the JDK or the sample files on the Macintosh, double-click the installation program on the CD-ROM. By default, the package will be installed into the folder Java on your hard disk; you can install it anywhere on your disk that you'd like. You'll be given options to install the JDK, the sample files, and various other extra files; choose the options you want and those files will be installed.

SOLARIS   Sun's JDK for Solaris runs on Solaris 2.3, 2.4, and 2.5, as well as the x86 version of Solaris.

The CD-ROM for this book contains the tarred and zipped JDK in the directory jdk/solaris/jdk1.02.tgz. Using the utilities gunzip and tar, you can extract the contents of that file anywhere on the file system you would like. For example, if you copy the .tgz file to your home directory and use the following commands to extract it, you'll end up with a `java` directory that contains the full JDK:

```
gunzip ./jdk1.02.tgz
tar xvf ./jdk1.02.tar
```

Note that in the directory `java\lib` there is a file called `classes.zip`. Do *not* unzip this file; it needs to remain in zip form for it to work correctly. The file `java\src.zip` contains the source code for many of the JDK libraries; you can unzip this one if you're interested in the source code.

The sample files are also contained on the CD-ROM in `authors/authors.tar`. Create a directory where the sample files will live (for example, a directory called `javasamples` in your home directory), copy the `authors.tar` file there, and then use the `tar` command to extract it, like this:

```
mkdir ~/javasamples
cp /cdrom/authors/authors.tar
tar xvf authors.tar
```

Configuring the JDK

If you've installed the JDK using the setup programs from the CD-ROM, chances are good that it has been correctly configured for you. However, because most common problems with Java result from configuration errors, I recommend that you double-check your configuration to make sure everything is right. And if you've installed the JDK from a source other than the CD-ROM, you'll definitely want to read this section to make sure you're all set up.

 The JDK needs two important modifications to your `autoexec.bat` file in order to work correctly: The `JDK\bin` directory must be in your execution path, and you must have the `CLASSPATH` variable set up.

Edit your `autoexec.bat` file using your favorite editor (Notepad will do just fine). Look for a line that looks something like this:

```
PATH C:\WINDOWS;C:\WINDOWS\COMMAND;C:\DOS; ...
```

Somewhere in that line you should see an entry for the JDK; if you installed the JDK from CD-ROM, it'll look something like this (the dots are there to indicate that there may be other stuff on this line):

```
PATH C:\WINDOWS; ... C:\TEACHY~1\JDK\BIN; ...
```

If you cannot find any reference to `JDK\BIN` or `JAVA\BIN` in your `PATH`, you'll need to add it.

Simply include the full pathname to your JDK installation to the end of that line, starting with C: and ending with BIN; for example, C:\JAVA\BIN or C:\Java\JDK\BIN.

NOTE

The directories Teach Yourself Java and TEACHY~1 are actually the same thing; the former is how the directory appears in Windows 95, and the latter is how it appears in DOS. Either one will work fine; there's no need to change it if one or the other appears. Note, however, that if the pathname contains spaces, it must be in quotes.

The second thing you'll need to add to the autoexec.bat file (if it isn't already there) is a CLASSPATH variable. Look for a line that looks something like this:

```
SET CLASSPATH=C:\TEACHY~1\JDK\lib\classes.zip;.;
```

The CLASSPATH variable may also have other entries in it for Netscape or Internet Explorer, but the one you're most interested in is a reference to the classes.zip file in the JDK, and to the current directory (.). If your autoexec.bat file does not include either of these locations, add a line to the file that contains both these things (the line shown above will work just fine).

After saving your autoexec.bat file, you'll need to restart Windows for the changes to take effect.

 The JDK for Macintosh should need no further configuration after installation.

SOLARIS To configure the JDK for Solaris, all you need to do is add the java/bin or jdk/bin directory to your execution path. Usually a line something like this in your .cshrc, .login, or .profile files will work:

```
set path= (~/java/bin/ $path)
```

This line assumes that you've installed the JDK (as the directory java) into your home directory; if you've installed it somewhere else, you'll want to substitute that pathname.

Make sure you use the source command with the name of the appropriate file to make sure the changes take effect (or log out and log back in again):

```
source ~/.login
```

Creating a Java Application

Now let's actually get to work. We'll start by creating a simple Java application: the classic Hello World example that many programming language books use to begin.

Java applications are different from Java applets. Applets, as you have learned, are Java programs that are downloaded over the World Wide Web and executed by a Web browser on the reader's machine. Applets depend on a Java-enabled browser in order to run.

Java applications, however, are more general programs written in the Java language. Java applications don't require a browser to run; in fact, Java can be used to create all the kinds of applications that you would normally use a more conventional programming language to create.

 Java applications are standalone Java programs that do not require a Web browser to run. Java applications are more general-purpose programs such as you'd find on any computer.

A single Java program can be an applet or an application, or both, depending on how you write that program and the capabilities that program uses. Throughout this first week as you learn the Java language, you'll be writing mostly applications; then you'll apply what you've learned to write applets in Week 2. If you're eager to get started with applets, be patient. Everything that you learn while you're creating simple Java applications will apply to creating applets, and it's easier to start with the basics before moving onto the hard stuff. You'll be creating plenty of applets in Week 2.

Creating the Source File

As with all programming languages, your Java source files are created in a plain text editor, or in an editor that can save files in plain ASCII without any formatting characters. On UNIX, emacs, pico, and vi will work; on Windows, Notepad or DOS Edit are both text editors that will work (although I prefer to use the shareware TextPad). On the Macintosh, SimpleText (which came with your Mac) or the shareware BBedit will work. If you're using a development environment like Café or Roaster, it'll have its own built-in text editor you can use.

 If you're using Windows to do your Java development, you may have to make sure Windows understands the .java file extension before you start; otherwise, your text editor may insist on giving all your files a .txt extension. The easiest way to do this is to go to any Windows

Explorer window, choose View|Options|File Types, choose New Type, and add `Java Source File` and `.java` to the Description of Type and Associated Extension boxes, respectively.

Fire up your editor of choice and enter the Java program shown in Listing 1.1. Type this program, as shown, in your text editor. Be careful that all the parentheses, braces, and quotes are there, and that you've used all the correct upper- and lowercase letters.

 NOTE

 You can also find the code for these examples on the CD-ROM as part of the sample code. However, it's a good idea to actually type these first few short examples in so that you get a feel for what Java code actually looks like.

TYPE **Listing 1.1. Your first Java application.**

```
1: class HelloWorld {
2:     public static void main (String args[]) {
3:         System.out.println("Hello World!");
4:     }
5: }
```

WARNING

The number before each line is part of the listing and not part of the program; the numbers are there so I can refer to specific line numbers when I explain what's going on in the program. Do not include them in your own file.

After you've finished typing in the program, save the file somewhere on your disk with the name `HelloWorld.java`. This is very important. Java source files must have the same name as the class they define (including the same upper- and lowercase letters), and they must have the extension `.java`. Here, the class definition has the name `HelloWorld`, so the filename must be `HelloWorld.java`. If you name your file something else (even something like `helloworld.java` or `Helloworld.java`), you won't be able to compile it. Make absolutely certain the name is `HelloWorld.java`.

You can save your Java files anywhere you like on your disk, but I like to have a central directory or folder to keep them all in. For the examples in this chapter, I've put my files into a directory called TYJtests (short for Teach Yourself Java Tests).

Compiling and Running the Source File

Now it's time to compile the file. If you're using the JDK, you can use the instructions for your computer system contained in the next few pages. If you're using a graphical development environment, there will most likely be a button or option to compile the file (check with the documentation that came with your program).

 To compile the Java source file, you'll use the command-line Java compiler that comes with the JDK. To run the compiler, you'll need to first start up a DOS shell. In Windows 95, the DOS shell is under the Programs menu (it's called MS-DOS Prompt).

From inside DOS, change directories to the location where you've saved your HelloWorld.java file. I put mine into the directory TYJtests, so to change directories I'd use this command:

```
CD C:\TYJtests
```

Once you've changed to the right directory, use the javac command as follows, with the name of the file *as you saved it in Windows* (javac stands for *Java compiler*). Note that you have to make sure you type all the same upper- and lowercase here as well:

```
javac HelloWorld.java
```

NOTE

The reason that I've emphasized using the original filename is that once you're inside the DOS shell, you might notice that your nice long filenames have been truncated to old-style 8.3 names and that, in fact, HelloWorld.java actually shows up as HELLOW~1.jav. Don't panic; this is simply a side effect of Windows 95 and how it manages long filenames. Ignore the fact that the file appears to be HELLOW~1.jav and just use the filename you originally used when you saved the file.

Figure 1.4 shows what I've done in the DOS shell so you can make sure you're following along.

If all goes well, you'll end up with a file called HelloWorld.class (or at least that's what it'll be called if you look at it outside the DOS shell; from inside DOS its called HELLOW~1.cla). That's your Java bytecode file. If you get any errors, go back to your original source file and make sure you typed it exactly as it appears in Listing 1.1 with the same upper- and lowercase.

Figure 1.4.

Compiling Java in the DOS shell.

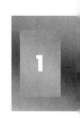

Also make sure the filename has exactly the same upper- and lowercase as the name of the class (that is, both should be HelloWorld).

Once you have a class file, you can run that file using the Java bytecode interpreter. The Java interpreter is called simply java, and you run it from the DOS shell as you did javac. Run your Hello World program like this from the command line, with all the same upper- and lowercase (and note that the argument to the java program does *not* have a .class extension):

```
java HelloWorld
```

If your program was typed and compiled correctly, you should get the phrase Hello World! printed to your screen as a response. Figure 1.5 shows how I did it.

Figure 1.5.

Running Java applications in the DOS shell.

NOTE

Remember, the Java compiler and the Java interpreter are different things. You use the Java compiler (javac) for your Java source files to create .class files, and you use the Java interpreter (java) to actually run your class files.

MACINTOSH The JDK for the Mac comes with an application called Java Compiler. To compile your Java source file, simply drag and drop it on top of the Java Compiler icon. The program will compile your Java file and, if there are no errors, create a file called HelloWorld.class in the same folder as your original source file.

TIP

Putting an alias for Java Compiler on the desktop makes it easy to drag and drop Java source files.

If you get any errors, go back to your original source file and make sure you typed it exactly as it appears in Listing 1.1, with the same upper- and lowercase. Also make sure the filename has exactly the same upper- and lowercase as the name of the class (that is, both should be HelloWorld).

Once you've successfully generated a HelloWorld.class file, simply double-click it to run it. The application Java Runner, part of the Mac JDK, will start, and the program will ask you for command-line arguments. Leave that screen blank and click OK. A window labeled stdout will appear with the message Hello World!. Figure 1.6 shows that window.

Figure 1.6.

Running Java applications on the Mac using Java Runner.

That's it! Keep in mind as you work that you use the Java Compiler application to compile your .java files into .class files, which you can then run using Java Runner.

SOLARIS To compile the Java source file in Solaris, you'll use the command-line Java compiler that comes with the JDK. From a UNIX command line, cd to the directory that contains your Java source file. I put mine in the directory TYJtests, so to change directories I'd use this command:

```
cd ~/TYJtests
```

Once you're in the right directory, use the javac command with the name of the file, like this:

```
javac HelloWorld.java
```

If all goes well, you'll end up with a file called HelloWorld.class in the same directory as your source file. That's your Java bytecode file. If you get any errors, go back to your original source file and make sure you typed it exactly as it appears in Listing 1.1, with the same upper- and lowercase letters. Also make sure the filename has exactly the same upper- and lowercase letters as the name of the class (that is, both should be HelloWorld).

Once you have a class file, you can run that file using the Java bytecode interpreter. The Java interpreter is called simply java, and you run it from the command line as you did javac, like this (and note that the argument to the java program does *not* have a .class extension):

```
java HelloWorld
```

If your program was typed and compiled correctly, you should get the phrase Hello World! printed to your screen as a response. Figure 1.7 shows a listing of all the commands I used to get to this point (the part with [desire]~[1] is my system prompt).

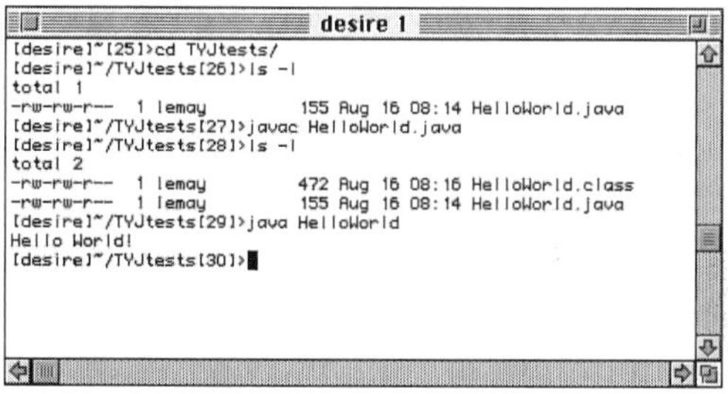

Figure 1.7.

Compiling and running a Java application on Solaris.

```
                            desire 1
[desire]~[25]>cd TVJtests/
[desire]~/TVJtests[26]>ls -l
total 1
-rw-rw-r--   1 lemay            155 Aug 16 08:14 HelloWorld.java
[desire]~/TVJtests[27]>javac HelloWorld.java
[desire]~/TVJtests[28]>ls -l
total 2
-rw-rw-r--   1 lemay            472 Aug 16 08:16 HelloWorld.class
-rw-rw-r--   1 lemay            155 Aug 16 08:14 HelloWorld.java
[desire]~/TVJtests[29]>java HelloWorld
Hello World!
[desire]~/TVJtests[30]>
```

NOTE

Remember that the Java compiler and the Java interpreter are different things. You use the Java compiler (javac) for your Java source files to create .class files, and you use the Java interpreter (java) to actually run your class files.

Creating a Java Applet

Creating applets is different from creating a simple application. Java applets run and are displayed inside a Web page with other page elements, and therefore have special rules for how they behave. Because of these special rules for applets, creating an applet may in many cases be more complex than creating an application.

For example, to create a simple Hello World applet, instead of merely being able to print a message as a set of characters, you have to make space for your message on the Web pages and then use special font and graphics operations to paint the message to the screen.

NOTE

Actually, you can run a plain Java application as an applet, but the `Hello World` message will print to a special window or to a log file, depending on how the browser has its output set up. You'll learn more about this next week.

Creating the Source File

In this example, you'll create a simple Hello World applet, place it inside a Web page, and view the result. As with the Hello World application, you'll first create the source file in a plain text editor. Listing 1.2 shows the code for the example.

TYPE   **Listing 1.2. The Hello World applet.**

```
1: import java.awt.Graphics;
2:
3: public class HelloWorldApplet extends java.applet.Applet {
4:
5:     public void paint(Graphics g) {
6:         g.drawString("Hello world!", 5, 25);
7:     }
8:}
```

Save that file just as you did the Hello World application, with the filename exactly the same as the name of the class. In this case the class name is `HelloWorldApplet`, so the filename you save it to would be `HelloWorldApplet.java`. As with the application, I put the file in a directory called `TYJch01`, but you can save it anywhere you like.

Compiling the Source File

The next step is to compile the Java applet file. Despite the fact that this is an applet, you compile the file exactly the same way you did the Java application, using one of the following procedures:

WINDOWS From inside a DOS shell, `cd` to the directory containing your applet source file, and use the `javac` command to compile it (watch those upper- and lowercase letters):

```
javac HelloWorldApplet.java
```

Drag and drop the HelloWorldApplet.java file onto the Java Compiler icon.

 From a command line, cd to the directory containing your applet source file and use the javac command to compile it:

```
javac HelloWorldApplet.java
```

Including the Applet in a Web Page

If you've typed the file correctly, you should end up with a file called HelloWorldApplet.class in the same directory as your source file. That's your Java applet file; to have the applet run inside a Web page you must refer to that class file inside the HTML code for that page using the <APPLET> tag. Listing 1.3 shows a simple HTML file you can use.

TYPE **Listing 1.3. The HTML with the applet in it.**

```
1: <HTML>
2: <HEAD>
3: <TITLE>Hello to Everyone!</TITLE>
4: </HEAD><BODY>
5: <P>My Java applet says:
6: <APPLET CODE="HelloWorldApplet.class" WIDTH=150 HEIGHT=25>
7: </APPLET>
8: </BODY>
9: </HTML>
```

You'll learn more about <APPLET> later in this book, but here are two things to note about it:

- [ ] Use the CODE attribute to indicate the name of the class that contains your applet, here HelloWorldApplet.Class.

- [ ] Use the WIDTH and HEIGHT attributes to indicate the size of the applet on the page. The browser uses these values to know how big a chunk of space to leave for the applet on the page. Here, a box 150 pixels wide and 25 pixels high is created.

Save the HTML file in the same directory as your class file, with a descriptive name and an .html extension (for example, you might name your HTML file the same name as your applet—HelloWorldApplet.html).

NOTE

As mentioned earlier with the Java source files, your text editor may insist on naming your HTML files with a .txt extension if Windows does not understand what the .html extension is used for. Select

View|Options|File Types from any Windows Explorer window to add a new file type for HTML files to solve this problem.

Now you're ready for the final test—actually viewing the result of running your applet. To view the applet, you need one of the following:

☐ A browser that supports Java applets, such as Netscape 2.0 or Internet Explorer 3.0. If you're running on the Macintosh, you'll need Netscape 3.0 or later. If you're running on Windows 95 or NT, you'll need the 32-bit version of Netscape. And if you're using Internet Explorer, you'll need the 3.0 beta 5 or later (the final version will do just fine).

☐ The `appletviewer` application, which is part of the JDK. The `appletviewer` is not a Web browser and won't let you to see the entire Web page, but it's acceptable for testing to see how an applet will look and behave if there is nothing else available.

☐ An applet viewer or runner tool that comes with your development environment.

If you're using a Java-enabled browser such as Netscape to view your applet files, you can use the Open File... item under the File menu to navigate to the HTML file containing the applet (make sure you open the HTML file and not the class file). In Internet Explorer, select File|Open and then Browse to find the file on your disk. You don't need to install anything on a Web server yet; all this works on your local system. Note that the Java applet may take a while to start up after the page appears to be done loading; be patient. Figure 1.8 shows the result of running the applet in Netscape.

Figure 1.8.

The applet running in Netscape.

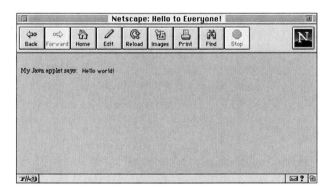

If you don't have a Web browser with Java capabilities built into it, you can use the JDK's `appletviewer` program to view your Java applet.

To run the `appletviewer` in Windows or Solaris versions of the JDK, `cd` to the directory where your HTML and class files are contained and use the `appletviewer` command with the name of the HTML file you just created:

```
appletviewer HTML/HelloWorldApplet.html
```

The `appletviewer` will show you only the applet itself, not the HTML text around the applet. Although the `appletviewer` is a good way to do simple tests of Java applets, it's a better idea to get a Java-enabled browser so that you can see your applet on its page in its full glory.

Troubleshooting

If you've run into any problems with the previous examples, this section can help. Here are some of the most common problems and how to fix them:

☐ `Bad command or filename` or `Command not found`

These errors result when you do not have the JDK's `bin` directory in your execution path, or the path to that directory is wrong. On Windows, double-check your `autoexec.bat` file; on UNIX, check the system file with your path commands in it (`.cshrc`, `.login`, `.profile`, or some similar file).

☐ `javac: invalid argument`

Make sure the name of the file you're giving to the `javac` command is exactly the same name as the file. In particular, in the DOS shell you want to use the Windows filename with a `.java` extension, *not* the DOS equivalent (`HELLOW~1.jav`, for example).

☐ `Warning: public class HelloWorldApplet must be defined in a file called HelloWorldApplet.java`

This error most often happens if there is a mismatch between the name of the class as defined in the Java file itself (the name following the word *class*) and the name of the `java` source file. Both the filenames must match, including upper- and lowercase letters (this particular error implies that the filename had lowercase letters). Rename either the filename or the class name, and this error will go away.

☐ Insufficient-memory errors

The JDK is not the most efficient user of memory. If you're getting errors about memory, consider closing larger programs before running Java compiles, turn on virtual memory, or install more RAM.

☐ Other code errors

If you're unable to compile the Java source files because of other errors I haven't mentioned here, be sure that you've typed them in exactly as they appear, including all upper- and lowercase letters. Java is case sensitive, meaning that upper- and lowercase letters are treated differently, so you will need to make sure that everything is capitalized correctly. If all else fails, try comparing your source files to the files on the CD-ROM.

Summary

Today you've gotten a basic introduction to the Java language and its goals and features. Java is a programming language, similar to C or C++, in which you can develop a wide range of programs. The most common use of Java at the moment is in creating applets for HotJava, an advanced World Wide Web browser also written in Java. Applets are Java programs that are downloaded and run as part of a Web page. Applets can create animation, games, interactive programs, and other multimedia effects on Web pages.

Java's strengths lie in its portability—both at the source and at the binary level, in its object-oriented design—and in its simplicity. Each of these features helps make applets possible, but they also make Java an excellent language for writing more general-purpose programs that do not require a Java-enabled browser to run. These general-purpose Java programs are called applications.

To end this day, you experimented with an example of an applet and an example of an application, getting a feel for the differences between the two and how to create, compile, and run Java programs—or, in the case of applets, how to include them in Web pages. From here, you now have the foundation to create more complex applications and applets. Onward to Day 2, "Object-Oriented Programming and Java"!

Q&A

Q I know a lot about HTML, but not much about computer programming. Can I still write Java programs?

A If you have no programming experience whatsoever, you most likely will find programming Java significantly more difficult than HTML. However, Java is an excellent language to learn programming with, and if you patiently work through the examples and the exercises in this book, you should be able to learn enough to get started with Java.

Q What's the relationship between JavaScript and Java?

A They have the same first four letters.

A common misconception in the Web world today is that Java and JavaScript have more in common than they actually do. Java is the general-purpose programming language that you'll learn about in this book; you use it to create applets. JavaScript

is a Netscape-invented scripting language that looks sort of like Java; with it you can do various nifty things in Web pages. They are independent languages, used for different purposes. If you're interested in JavaScript programming, you'll want to pick up another book, such as *Teach Yourself JavaScript in a Week* or *Laura Lemay's Web Workshop: JavaScript*, both also available from Sams.net Publishing.

Q **According to today's lesson, Java applets are downloaded via a Java-enabled browser such as Netscape and run on the reader's system. Isn't that an enormous security hole? What stops someone from writing an applet that compromises the security of my system—or worse, that damages my system?**

A Sun's Java team has thought a great deal about the security of applets within Java-enabled browsers and has implemented several checks to make sure applets cannot do nasty things:

- ☐ Java applets cannot read or write to the disk on the local system.
- ☐ Java applets cannot execute any programs on the local system.
- ☐ Java applets cannot connect to any machines on the Web except for the server from which they are originally downloaded.

Note that some of these restrictions may be allowed in some browsers or may be turned on in the browser configuration. However, you cannot expect any of these capabilities to be available.

In addition, the Java compiler and interpreter check both the Java source code and the Java bytecodes to make sure that the Java programmer has not tried any sneaky tricks (for example, overrunning buffers or stack frames).

These checks obviously cannot stop every potential security hole (no system can promise that!), but they can significantly reduce the potential for hostile applets. You'll learn more about security issues for applets on Day 8, "Java Applet Basics," and in greater detail on Day 21, "Under the Hood."

Q **I followed all the directions you gave for creating a Java applet. I loaded it into HotJava, but Hello World didn't show up. What did I do wrong?**

A Don't use HotJava to view applets you've created in this book; get a more up-to-date browser such as Netscape or Internet Explorer. HotJava was an experimental browser and has not been updated since soon after its original release. The steps you take to define and write an applet have changed since then, and the applets you write now will not run on HotJava.

Q You've mentioned Solaris, Windows, and Macintosh in this chapter. What about other operating systems?

A If you use a flavor of UNIX other than Solaris, chances are good that the JDK has been ported to your system. Here are some examples:

☐ SGI's version of the JDK can be found at `http://www.sgi.com/Products/cosmo/cosmo_instructions.html`.

☐ Information about Java for Linux can be found at `http://www.blackdown.org/java-linux/`.

☐ IBM has ported the JDK to OS/2 and AIX. Find out more from `http://www.ncc.hurley.ibm.com/javainfo/`.

☐ OSF is porting the JDK to HP/UX, Unixware, Sony NEWS, and Digital UNIX. See `http://www.osf.org/mall/web/javaport.htm`.

(Thanks to Elliote Rusty Harold's Java FAQ at `http://www.sunsite.unc.edu/javafaq/javafaq/html` for this information.)

Q Why doesn't Java run on Windows 3.1?

A Technical limitations in Windows 3.1 make porting Java to Windows 3.1 particularly difficult. Rumor has it that both IBM and Microsoft are working on ports, but no real information is forthcoming.

Q I'm using Notepad on Windows to edit my Java files. The program insists on adding a `.txt` extension to all my files, regardless of what I name them (so I always end up with files like `HelloWorld.java.txt`). Short of renaming them before I compile them, what else can I do to fix this?

A Although you can rename the files just before you compile them, that can get to be a pain, particularly when you have a lot of files. The problem here is that Windows doesn't understand the `.java` extension (you may also have this problem with HTML's `.html` extension as well).

To fix this, go into any Windows Explorer window and select View|Options|File Types. From that panel, select New Type. Enter `Java Source Files` in the Description of Type box and `.java` into the Associated Extension box. Then click OK. Do the same with HTML files if you need to, and click OK again. You should now be able to use Notepad (or any other text editor) to create and save Java and HTML files.

Q   **Where can I learn more about Java and find applets and applications to play with?**

A   You can read the rest of this book! Here are some other places to look for Java information and Java applets:

☐ The Java home page at `http://www.java.sun.com/` is the official source for Java information, including information about the JDK, about the upcoming 1.1 release, and about developer tools such as the Java Workshop, as well as extensive documentation.

☐ Gamelan, at `http://www.gamelan.com/`, is a repository of applets and Java information, organized into categories. If you want to play with applets or applications, this is the place to look.

☐ For Java discussion, check out the `comp.lang.java` newsgroups, including `comp.lang.java.programmer`, `comp.lang.java.tech`, `comp.lang.java.advocacy`, and so on. (You'll need a Usenet newsreader to access these newsgroups.)

Day 2

Object-Oriented Programming and Java

by Laura Lemay

Object-oriented programming (OOP) is one of the biggest programming ideas of recent years, and you might worry that you must spend years learning all about object-oriented programming methodologies and how they can make your life easier than The Old Way of programming. It all comes down to organizing your programs in ways that echo how things are put together in the real world.

Today you'll get an overview of object-oriented programming concepts in Java and how they relate to how you structure your own programs:

☐ What classes and objects are and how they relate to each other

☐ The two main parts of a class or object: its behaviors and its attributes

☐ Class inheritance and how inheritance affects the way you design your programs

☐ Some information about packages and interfaces

If you're already familiar with object-oriented programming, much of today's lesson will be old hat to you. You may want to skim it and go to a movie today instead. Tomorrow, you'll get into more specific details.

Thinking in Objects: An Analogy

Consider, if you will, Legos. Legos, for those who do not spend much time with children, are small plastic building blocks in various colors and sizes. They have small round bits on one side that fit into small round holes on other Legos so that they fit together snugly to create larger shapes. With different Lego parts (Lego wheels, Lego engines, Lego hinges, Lego pulleys), you can put together castles, automobiles, giant robots that swallow cities, or just about anything else you can imagine. Each Lego part is a small object that fits together with other small objects in predefined ways to create other larger objects. That is roughly how object-oriented programming works: putting together smaller elements to build larger ones.

Here's another example. You can walk into a computer store and, with a little background and often some help, assemble an entire PC computer system from various components: a motherboard, a CPU chip, a video card, a hard disk, a keyboard, and so on. Ideally, when you finish assembling all the various self-contained units, you have a system in which all the units work together to create a larger system with which you can solve the problems you bought the computer for in the first place.

Internally, each of those components may be vastly complicated and engineered by different companies with different methods of design. But you don't need to know how the component works, what every chip on the board does, or how, when you press the A key, an *A* gets sent to your computer. As the assembler of the overall system, each component you use is a self-contained unit, and all you are interested in is how the units interact with each other. Will this video card fit into the slots on the motherboard, and will this monitor work with this video card? Will each particular component speak the right commands to the other components it interacts with so that each part of the computer is understood by every other part? Once you know what the interactions are between the components and can match the interactions, putting together the overall system is easy.

What does this have to do with programming? Everything. Object-oriented programming works in exactly this same way. Using object-oriented programming, your overall program is made up of lots of different self-contained components (objects), each of which has a specific role in the program and all of which can talk to each other in predefined ways.

Objects and Classes

Object-oriented programming is modeled on how, in the real world, objects are often made up of many kinds of smaller objects. This capability of combining objects, however, is only one very general aspect of object-oriented programming. Object-oriented programming provides several other concepts and features to make creating and using objects easier and more flexible, and the most important of these features is classes.

When you write a program in an object-oriented language, you don't define actual objects. You define classes of objects, where a *class* is a template for multiple objects with similar features. Classes embody all the features of a particular set of objects. For example, you might have a Tree class that describes the features of all trees (has leaves and roots, grows, creates chlorophyll). The Tree class serves as an abstract model for the concept of a tree—to reach out and grab, or interact with, or cut down a tree you have to have a concrete instance of that tree. Of course, once you have a tree class, you can create lots of different *instances* of that tree, and each different tree instance can have different features (short, tall, bushy, drops leaves in autumn), while still behaving like and being immediately recognizable as a tree (see Figure 2.1).

Figure 2.1.

The Tree *class and several* Tree *instances.*

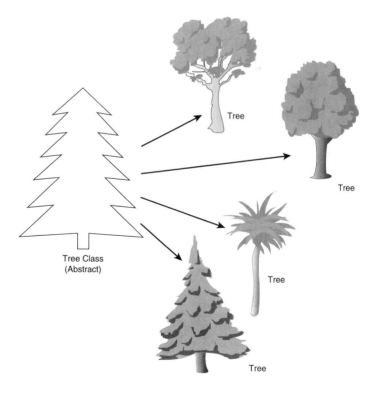

NEW TERM   A *class* is a generic template for a set of objects with similar features.

An *instance* of a class is another word for an actual object. If class is the general (generic) representation of an object, an instance is its concrete representation. So what, precisely, is the difference between an instance and an object? Nothing, really. Object is the more general term, but both instances and objects are the concrete representation of a class. In fact, the terms instance and object are often used interchangeably in OOP lingo. An instance of a tree and a tree object are both the same thing.

NEW TERM   An *instance* is the specific concrete representation of a class. Instances and objects are the same thing.

What about an example closer to the sort of things you might want to do in Java programming? You might create a class for the user interface element called a button. The Button class defines the features of a button (its label, its size, its appearance) and how it behaves. (Does it need a single-click or a double-click to activate it? Does it change color when it's clicked? What does it do when it's activated?) After you define the Button class, you can then easily create instances of that button—that is, button objects—that all take on the basic features of the button as defined by the class, but may have different appearances and behavior based on what you want that particular button to do. By creating a Button class, you don't have to keep rewriting the code for each individual button you want to use in your program, and you can reuse the Button class to create different kinds of buttons as you need them in this program and in other programs.

> **TIP**   If you're used to programming in C, you can think of a class as sort of creating a new composite data type by using struct and typedef. Classes, however, can provide much more than just a collection of data, as you'll discover in the rest of today's lesson.

When you write a Java program, you design and construct a set of classes. Then when your program runs, instances of those classes are created and discarded as needed. Your task, as a Java programmer, is to create the right set of classes to accomplish what your program needs to accomplish.

Fortunately, you don't have to start from the very beginning: The Java environment comes with a standard set of classes (called a *class library*) that implement a lot of the basic behavior you need—not only for basic programming tasks (classes to provide basic math functions, arrays, strings, and so on), but also for graphics and networking behavior. In many cases, the Java class libraries may be enough so that all you have to do in your Java program is create

2

a single class that uses the standard class libraries. For complicated Java programs, you may have to create a whole set of classes with defined interactions between them.

 A *class library* is a collection of classes intended to be reused repeatedly in different programs. The standard Java class libraries contain quite a few classes for accomplishing basic programming tasks in Java.

Behavior and Attributes

Every class you write in Java has two basic features: attributes and behavior. In this section you'll learn about each one as it applies to a theoretical simple class called `Motorcycle`. To finish up this section, you'll create the Java code to implement a representation of a motorcycle.

Attributes

Attributes are the individual things that differentiate one object from another and determine the appearance, state, or other qualities of that object. Let's create a theoretical class called `Motorcycle`. A motorcycle class might include the following attributes and have these typical values:

- ☐ `Color`: red, green, silver, brown
- ☐ `Style`: cruiser, sport bike, standard
- ☐ `Make`: Honda, BMW, Bultaco

Attributes of an object can also include information about its state; for example, you could have features for engine condition (off or on) or current gear selected.

Attributes are defined in classes by variables. Those variables' types and names are defined in the class, and each object can have its own values for those variables. Because each instance of a class can have different values for its variables, these variables are often called *instance variables*.

 An *instance variable* defines the attributes of the object. Instance variables' types and names are defined in the class, but their values are set and changed in the object.

Instance variables may be initially set when an object is created and stay constant throughout the life of the object, or they may be able to change at will as the program runs. Change the value of the variable, and you change an object's attributes.

In addition to instance variables, there are also class variables, which apply to the class itself and to all its instances. Unlike instance variables, whose values are stored in the instance, class variables' values are stored in the class itself. You'll learn about class variables later on this week and more specifics about instance variables tomorrow.

Behavior

A class's behavior determines how an instance of that class operates; for example, how it will "react" if asked to do something by another class or object or if its internal state changes. Behavior is the only way objects can do anything to themselves or have anything done to them. For example, to go back to the theoretical `Motorcycle` class, here are some behaviors that the `Motorcycle` class might have:

- ☐ Start the engine
- ☐ Stop the engine
- ☐ Speed up
- ☐ Change gear
- ☐ Stall

To define an object's behavior, you create *methods*, a set of Java statements that accomplish some task. Methods look and behave just like functions in other languages but are defined and accessible solely inside a class. Java does not have functions defined outside classes (as C++ does).

NEW TERM   *Methods* are functions defined inside classes that operate on instances of those classes.

While methods can be used solely to operate on an individual object, methods are also used between objects to communicate with each other. A class or an object can call methods in another class or object to communicate changes in the environment or to ask that object to change its state.

Just as there are instance and class variables, there are also instance and class methods. Instance methods (which are so common that they're usually just called methods) apply and operate on an instance of a class; class methods apply and operate on the class itself. You'll learn more about class methods later on this week.

Creating a Class

Up to this point, today's lesson has been pretty theoretical. In this section, you'll create a working example of the `Motorcycle` class so that you can see how instance variables and methods are defined in a class in Java. You'll also create a Java application that creates a new instance of the `Motorcycle` class and shows its instance variables.

NOTE

I'm not going to go into a lot of detail about the actual syntax of this example here. Don't worry too much about it if you're not really sure what's going on; it will become clear to you later on this week. All you really need to worry about in this example is understanding the basic parts of this class definition.

Ready? Let's start with a basic class definition. Open the text editor you've been using to create Java source code and enter the following (remember, upper- and lowercase matters):

```
class Motorcycle {

}
```

Congratulations! You've now created a class. Of course, it doesn't do very much at the moment, but that's a Java class at its very simplest.

First, let's create some instance variables for this class—three of them, to be specific. Just below the first line, add the following three lines:

```
String make;
String color;
boolean engineState = false;
```

Here you've created three instance variables: Two, make and color, can contain String objects (a string is the generic term for a series of characters; String, with a capital *S*, is part of that standard class library mentioned earlier). The third, engineState, is a boolean variable that refers to whether the engine is off or on; a value of false means that the engine is off, and true means that the engine is on. Note that boolean is lowercase *b*.

NEW TERM A *boolean* is a value of either true or false.

TECHNICAL NOTE

boolean in Java is a real data type that can have the values true or false. Unlike in C, booleans are not numbers. You'll hear about this again tomorrow so that you won't forget.

Now let's add some behavior (methods) to the class. There are all kinds of things a motorcycle can do, but to keep things short, let's add just one method—a method that starts the engine. Add the following lines below the instance variables in your class definition:

```
void startEngine() {
    if (engineState == true)
        System.out.println("The engine is already on.");
    else {
```

```
        engineState = true;
        System.out.println("The engine is now on.");
    }
}
```

The startEngine() method tests to see whether the engine is already running (in the part engineState == true) and, if it is, merely prints a message to that effect. If the engine isn't already running, it changes the state of the engine to true (turning the engine on) and then prints a message. Finally, because the startEngine() method doesn't return a value, its definition includes the word void at the beginning. (You can also define methods to return values; you'll learn more about method definitions on Day 6, "Creating Classes and Applications in Java.")

TIP

Here and throughout this book, whenever I refer to the name of a method, I'll add empty parentheses to the end of the name (for example, as I did in the first sentence of the previous paragraph: "The startEngine() method..." This is a convention used in the programming community at large to indicate that a particular name is a method and not a variable. The parentheses are silent.

With your methods and variables in place, save the program to a file called Motorcycle.java (remember that you should always name your Java source files the same names as the class they define). Listing 2.1 shows what your program should look like so far.

TYPE   **Listing 2.1. The Motorcycle.java file.**

```
1:class Motorcycle {
2:
3: String make;
4: String color;
5: boolean engineState = false;
6:
7: void startEngine() {
8:     if (engineState == true)
9:         System.out.println("The engine is already on.");
10:    else {
11:        engineState = true;
12:        System.out.println("The engine is now on.");
13:    }
14: }
15:}
```

TIP

The indentation of each part of the class isn't important to the Java compiler. Using some form of indentation, however, makes your class definition easier for you and other people to read. The indentation used here, with instance variables and methods indented from the class definition, is the style used throughout this book. The Java class libraries use a similar indentation. You can choose any indentation style that you like.

Before you compile this class, let's add one more method just below the `startEngine()` method (that is, between lines 14 and 15). The `showAtts()` method is used to print the current values of all the instance variables in an instance of your `Motorcycle` class. Here's what it looks like:

```java
void showAtts() {
    System.out.println("This motorcycle is a "
        + color + " " + make);
    if (engineState == true)
        System.out.println("The engine is on.");
    else System.out.println("The engine is off.");
}
```

The `showAtts()` method prints two lines to the screen: the `make` and `color` of the motorcycle object and whether the engine is on or off.

Now you have a Java class with three instance variables and two methods defined. Save that file again, and compile it using one of the following methods:

 NOTE

After this point, I'm going to assume you know how to compile and run Java programs. I won't repeat this information after this.

 WINDOWS

From inside a DOS shell, CD to the directory containing your Java source file, and use the `javac` command to compile it:

```
javac Motorcycle.java
```

MACINTOSH

Drag and drop the `Motorcycle.java` file onto the Java Compiler icon.

 SOLARIS

From a command line, CD to the directory containing your Java source file, and use the `javac` command to compile it:

```
javac Motorcycle.java
```

When you run this little program using the java or Java Runner programs, you'll get an error. Why? When you run a compiled Java class directly, Java assumes that the class is an application and looks for a main() method. Because we haven't defined a main() method inside the class, the Java interpreter (java) gives you an error something like one of these two errors:

```
In class Motorcycle: void main(String argv[]) is not defined
Exception in thread "main":  java.lang.UnknownError
```

To do something with the Motorcycle class—for example, to create instances of that class and play with them—you're going to need to create a separate Java applet or application that uses this class or add a main() method to this one. For simplicity's sake, let's do the latter. Listing 2.2 shows the main() method you'll add to the Motorcycle class. You'll want to add this method to your Motorcycle.java source file just before the last closing brace (}), underneath the startEngine() and showAtts() methods.

TYPE   **Listing 2.2. The main() method for Motorcycle.java.**

```
 1: public static void main (String args[]) {
 2:     Motorcycle m = new Motorcycle();
 3:     m.make = "Yamaha RZ350";
 4:     m.color = "yellow";
 5:     System.out.println("Calling showAtts...");
 6:     m.showAtts();
 7:     System.out.println("--------");
 8:     System.out.println("Starting engine...");
 9:     m.startEngine();
10:     System.out.println("--------");
11:     System.out.println("Calling showAtts...");
12:     m.showAtts();
13:     System.out.println("--------");
14:     System.out.println("Starting engine...");
15:     m.startEngine();
16:}
```

With the main() method in place, the Motorcycle class is now an official application, and you can compile it again and this time it'll run. Here's how the output should look:

OUTPUT
```
Calling showAtts...
This motorcycle is a yellow Yamaha RZ350
The engine is off.
--------
Starting engine...
The engine is now on.
--------
Calling showAtts...
This motorcycle is a yellow Yamaha RZ350
The engine is on.
--------
Starting engine...
The engine is already on.
```

ANALYSIS The contents of the main() method are all going to look very new to you, so let's go through it line by line so that you at least have a basic idea of what it does (you'll get details about the specifics of all of this tomorrow and the day after).

The first line declares the main() method. The first line of the main() method always looks like this; you'll learn the specifics of each part later this week.

Line 2, Motorcycle m = new Motorcycle();, creates a new instance of the Motorcycle class and stores a reference to it in the variable m. Remember, you don't usually operate directly on classes in your Java programs; instead, you create objects from those classes and then call methods in those objects.

Lines 3 and 4 set the instance variables for this Motorcycle object: The make is now a Yamaha RZ350 (a very pretty motorcycle from the mid-1980s), and the color is yellow.

Lines 5 and 6 call the showAtts() method, defined in your Motorcycle object. (Actually, only 6 does; 5 just prints a message that you're about to call this method.) The new motorcycle object then prints out the values of its instance variables—the make and color as you set in the previous lines—and shows that the engine is off.

Line 7 prints a divider line to the screen; this is just for prettier output.

Line 9 calls the startEngine() method in the motorcycle object to start the engine. The engine should now be on.

Line 11 prints the values of the instance variables again. This time, the report should say the engine is now on.

Line 15 tries to start the engine again, just for fun. Because the engine is already on, this should print the message The engine is already on.

 Listing 2.3 shows the final Motorcycle class, in case you've been having trouble compiling and running the one you've got (and remember, this example and all the examples in this book are available on the CD that accompanies the book):

TYPE **Listing 2.3. The final version of Motorcycle.java.**

```
1: class Motorcycle {
2:
3:     String make;
4:     String color;
5:     boolean engineState;
6:
7:     void startEngine() {
8:         if (engineState == true)
9:             System.out.println("The engine is already on.");
10:        else {
```

continues

Listing 2.3. continued

```
11:            engineState = true;
12:            System.out.println("The engine is now on.");
13:        }
14:    }
15:
16:    void showAtts() {
17:        System.out.println("This motorcycle is a "
18:            + color + " " + make);
19:        if (engineState == true)
20:          System.out.println("The engine is on.");
21:        else System.out.println("The engine is off.");
22:    }
23:
24:    public static void main (String args[]) {
25:        Motorcycle m = new Motorcycle();
26:        m.make = "Yamaha RZ350";
27:        m.color = "yellow";
28:        System.out.println("Calling showAtts...");
29:        m.showAtts();
30:      System.out.println("------");
31:        System.out.println("Starting engine...");
32:        m.startEngine();
33:        System.out.println("------");
34:        System.out.println("Calling showAtts...");
35:        m.showAtts();
36:        System.out.println("------");
37:        System.out.println("Starting engine...");
38:        m.startEngine();
39:    }
40:}
```

Inheritance, Interfaces, and Packages

Now that you have a basic grasp of classes, objects, methods, variables, and how to put them all together in a Java program, it's time to confuse you again. Inheritance, interfaces, and packages are all mechanisms for organizing classes and class behaviors. The Java class libraries use all these concepts, and the best class libraries you write for your own programs will also use these concepts.

Inheritance

Inheritance is one of the most crucial concepts in object-oriented programming, and it has a very direct effect on how you design and write your Java classes. Inheritance is a powerful mechanism that means when you write a class you only have to specify how that class is different from some other class; inheritance will give you automatic access to the information contained in that other class.

With inheritance, all classes—those you write, those from other class libraries that you use, and those from the standard utility classes as well—are arranged in a strict hierarchy (see Figure 2.2). Each class has a superclass (the class above it in the hierarchy), and each class can have one or more subclasses (classes below that class in the hierarchy). Classes further down in the hierarchy are said to *inherit from* classes further up in the hierarchy.

Figure 2.2.

A class hierarchy.

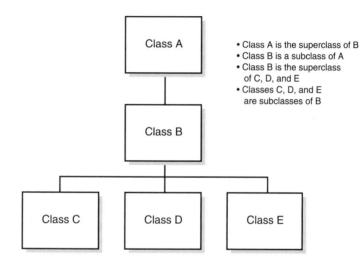

- Class A is the superclass of B
- Class B is a subclass of A
- Class B is the superclass of C, D, and E
- Classes C, D, and E are subclasses of B

Subclasses inherit all the methods and variables from their superclasses—that is, in any particular class, if the superclass defines behavior that your class needs, you don't have to redefine it or copy that code from some other class. Your class automatically gets that behavior from its superclass, that superclass gets behavior from its superclass, and so on all the way up the hierarchy. Your class becomes a combination of all the features of the classes above it in the hierarchy.

NEW TERM *Inheritance* is a concept in object-oriented programming where all classes are arranged in a strict *hierarchy*. Each class in the hierarchy has *superclasses* (classes above it in the hierarchy) and any number of *subclasses* (classes below it in the hierarchy). Subclasses inherit attributes and behavior from their superclasses.

At the top of the Java class hierarchy is the class Object; all classes inherit from this one superclass. Object is the most general class in the hierarchy; it defines behavior inherited by all the classes in Java. Each class further down in the hierarchy adds more information and becomes more tailored to a specific purpose. In this way, you can think of a class hierarchy as defining very abstract concepts at the top of the hierarchy and those ideas becoming more concrete the farther down the chain of superclasses you go.

Most of the time when you write new Java classes, you'll want to create a class that has all the information some other class has, plus some extra information. For example, you may want a version of a Button with its own built-in label. To get all the Button information, all you have to do is define your class to inherit from Button. Your class will automatically get all the behavior defined in Button (and in Button's superclasses), so all you have to worry about are the things that make your class different from Button itself. This mechanism for defining new classes as the differences between them and their superclasses is called *subclassing*.

Subclassing involves creating a new class that inherits from some other class in the class hierarchy. Using subclassing, you only need to define the differences between your class and its parent; the additional behavior is all available to your class through inheritance.

NEW TERM   *Subclassing* is the process of creating a new class that inherits from some other already-existing class.

What if your class defines an entirely new behavior and isn't really a subclass of another class? Your class can also inherit directly from Object, which still allows it to fit neatly into the Java class hierarchy. In fact, if you create a class definition that doesn't indicate its superclass in the first line, Java automatically assumes you're inheriting from Object. The Motorcycle class you created in the previous section inherited from Object.

Creating a Class Hierarchy

If you're creating a larger set of classes for a very complex program, it makes sense for your classes not only to inherit from the existing class hierarchy, but also to make up a hierarchy themselves. This may take some planning beforehand when you're trying to figure out how to organize your Java code, but the advantages are significant once it's done:

☐ When you develop your classes in a hierarchy, you can factor out information common to multiple classes in superclasses, and then reuse that superclass's information over and over again. Each subclass gets that common information from its superclass.

☐ Changing (or inserting) a class further up in the hierarchy automatically changes the behavior of its subclasses—no need to change or recompile any of the lower classes because they get the new information through inheritance and not by copying any of the code.

For example, let's go back to that Motorcycle class and pretend you created a Java program to implement all the features of a motorcycle. It's done, it works, and everything is fine. Now, your next task is to create a Java class called Car.

Car and Motorcycle have many similar features—both are vehicles driven by engines. Both have transmissions, headlamps, and speedometers. So your first impulse may be to open your Motorcycle class file and copy over a lot of the information you already defined into the new class Car.

A far better plan is to factor out the common information for Car and Motorcycle into a more general class hierarchy. This may be a lot of work just for the classes Motorcycle and Car, but once you add Bicycle, Scooter, Truck, and so on, having common behavior in a reusable superclass significantly reduces the amount of work you have to do overall.

Let's design a class hierarchy that might serve this purpose. Starting at the top is the class Object, which is the root of all Java classes. The most general class to which a motorcycle and a car both belong might be called Vehicle. A vehicle, generally, is defined as a thing that propels someone from one place to another. In the Vehicle class, you define only the behavior that enables someone to be propelled from point a to point b, and nothing more.

Below Vehicle? How about two classes: PersonPoweredVehicle and EnginePoweredVehicle? EnginePoweredVehicle is different from Vehicle because it has an engine, and the behaviors might include stopping and starting the engine, having certain amounts of gasoline and oil, and perhaps the speed or gear in which the engine is running. Person-powered vehicles have some kind of mechanism for translating people motion into vehicle motion—pedals, for example. Figure 2.3 shows what you have so far.

Figure 2.3.

The basic vehicle hierarchy.

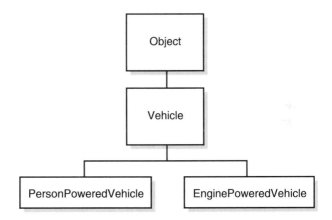

Now let's become even more specific. With EnginePoweredVehicle, you might have several classes: Motorcycle, Car, Truck, and so on. Or you can factor out still more behavior and have intermediate classes for TwoWheeled and FourWheeled vehicles, with different behaviors for each (see Figure 2.4).

Finally, with a subclass for the two-wheeled engine-powered vehicles, you can have a class for motorcycles. Alternatively, you could additionally define scooters and mopeds, both of which are two-wheeled engine-powered vehicles but have different qualities from motorcycles.

Figure 2.4.
Two-wheeled and four-wheeled vehicles.

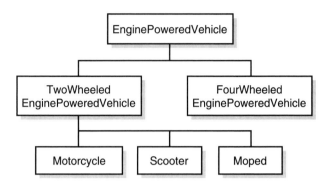

Where do qualities such as make or color come in? Wherever you want them to go—or, more usually, where they fit most naturally in the class hierarchy. You can define the make and color on Vehicle, and all the subclasses will have those variables as well. The point to remember is that you have to define a feature or a behavior only once in the hierarchy; it's automatically reused by each subclass.

How Inheritance Works

How does inheritance work? How is it that instances of one class can automatically get variables and methods from the classes further up in the hierarchy?

For instance variables, when you create a new instance of a class, you get a "slot" for each variable defined in the current class and for each variable defined in all its superclasses. In this way, all the classes combine to form a template for the current object, and then each object fills in the information appropriate to its situation.

Methods operate similarly: New objects have access to all the method names of its class and its superclasses, but method definitions are chosen dynamically when a method is called. That is, if you call a method on a particular object, Java first checks the object's class for the definition of that method. If it's not defined in the object's class, it looks in that class's superclass, and so on up the chain until the method definition is found (see Figure 2.5).

Things get complicated when a subclass defines a method that has the same signature (name, number, and type of arguments) as a method defined in a superclass. In this case, the method definition that is found first (starting at the bottom and working upward toward the top of the hierarchy) is the one that is actually executed. Therefore, you can intentionally define a method in a subclass that has the same signature as a method in a superclass, which then "hides" the superclass's method. This is called *overriding* a method. You'll learn all about methods on Day 7, "More About Methods."

Figure 2.5.
How methods are located.

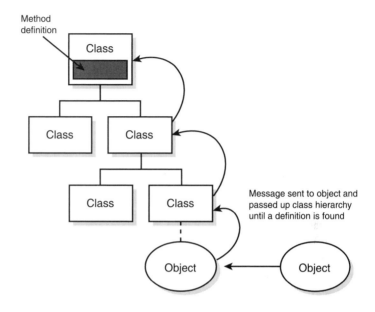

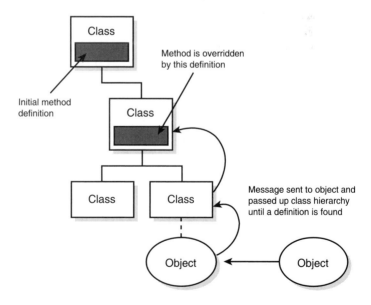

NEW TERM   *Overriding* a method is creating a method in a subclass that has the same signature (name, number, and type of arguments) as a method in a superclass. That new method then hides the superclass's method (see Figure 2.6).

Figure 2.6.
Overriding methods.

Single and Multiple Inheritance

Java's form of inheritance, as you learned in the previous sections, is called *single inheritance*. Single inheritance means that each Java class can have only one superclass (although any given superclass can have multiple subclasses).

In other object-oriented programming languages, such as C++, classes can have more than one superclass, and they inherit combined variables and methods from all those classes. This is called *multiple inheritance*. Multiple inheritance can provide enormous power in terms of being able to create classes that factor just about all imaginable behavior, but it can also significantly complicate class definitions and the code to produce them. Java makes inheritance simpler by being only singly inherited.

Interfaces and Packages

There are two remaining concepts to discuss here: packages and interfaces. Both are advanced topics for implementing and designing groups of classes and class behavior. You'll learn about both interfaces and packages on Day 16, "Packages and Interfaces," but they are worth at least introducing here.

Recall that each Java class has only a single superclass, and it inherits variables and methods from that superclass and all its superclasses. Although single inheritance makes the relationship between classes and the functionality those classes implement easy to understand and to design, it can also be somewhat restrictive—in particular, when you have similar behavior that needs to be duplicated across different "branches" of the class hierarchy. Java solves this problem of shared behavior by using the concept of interfaces, which collect method names into one place and then allow you to add those methods as a group to the various classes that need them. Note that interfaces contain only method names and interfaces (arguments, for example), not actual definitions.

Although a single Java class can have only one superclass (due to single inheritance), that class can also implement any number of interfaces. By implementing an interface, a class provides method implementations (definitions) for the method names defined by the interface. If two very disparate classes implement the same interface, they can both respond to the same method calls (as defined by that interface), although what each class actually does in response to those method calls may be very different.

 NEW TERM   An *interface* is a collection of method names, without definitions, that can be added to classes to provide additional behavior not included with those methods the class defined itself or inherited from its superclasses.

You don't need to know very much about interfaces right now. You'll learn more as the book progresses, so if all this is very confusing, don't panic!

The final new Java concept for today is packages. *Packages* in Java are a way of grouping together related classes and interfaces in a single library or collection. Packages enable modular groups of classes to be available only if they are needed and eliminate potential conflicts between class names in different groups of classes.

You'll learn all about packages, including how to create and use them, in Week 3. For now, there are only a few things you need to know:

☐ The class libraries in the Java Developer's Kit are contained in a package called java. The classes in the java package are guaranteed to be available in any Java implementation and are the *only* classes guaranteed to be available across different implementations. The java package itself contains other packages for classes that define the language, the input and output classes, some basic networking, the window toolkit functions, and classes that define applets. Classes in other packages (for example, classes in the sun or netscape packages) may be available only in specific implementations.

☐ By default, your Java classes have access to only the classes in java.lang (the base language package inside the java package). To use classes from any other package, you have to either refer to them explicitly by package name or import them into your source file.

☐ To refer to a class within a package, list all the packages that class is contained in and the class name, all separated by periods (.). For example, take the Color class, which is contained in the awt package (awt stands for Abstract Windowing Toolkit). The awt package, in turn, is inside the java package. To refer to the Color class in your program, you use the notation java.awt.Color.

Creating a Subclass

To finish up today, let's create a class that is a subclass of another class and override some methods. You'll also get a basic feel for how packages work in this example.

Probably the most typical instance of creating a subclass, at least when you first start programming in Java, is creating an applet. All applets are subclasses of the class Applet (which is part of the java.applet package). By creating a subclass of Applet, you automatically get all the behavior from the window toolkit and the layout classes that enable your applet to be drawn in the right place on the page and to interact with system operations, such as keypresses and mouse clicks.

In this example, you'll create an applet similar to the Hello World applet from yesterday, but one that draws the Hello string in a larger font and a different color. To start this example, let's first construct the class definition itself. Let's go to your text editor, and enter the following class definition:

```
public class HelloAgainApplet extends java.applet.Applet {

}
```

Here, you're creating a class called `HelloAgainApplet`. Note the part that says `extends java.applet.Applet`—that's the part that says your applet class is a subclass of the `Applet` class. Note that because the `Applet` class is contained in the `java.applet` package, you don't have automatic access to that class, and you have to refer to it explicitly by package and class name.

The other part of this class definition is the `public` keyword. Public means that your class is available to the Java system at large once it is loaded. Most of the time you need to make a class `public` only if you want it to be visible to all the other classes in your Java program, but applets, in particular, must be declared to be public. (You'll learn more about `public` classes in Week 3.)

A class definition with nothing in it doesn't really have much of a point; without adding or overriding any of its superclasses' variables or methods, there's no reason to create a subclass at all. Let's add some information to this class, inside the two enclosing braces, to make it different from its superclass.

First, add an instance variable to contain a `Font` object:

```
Font f = new Font("TimesRoman", Font.BOLD, 36);
```

The `f` instance variable now contains a new instance of the class `Font`, part of the `java.awt` package. This particular `Font` object is a Times Roman font, boldface, 36 points high. In the previous Hello World applet, the font used for the text was the default font: 12-point Times Roman. Using a `Font` object, you can change the font of the text you draw in your applet.

By creating an instance variable to hold this font object, you make it available to all the methods in your class. Now let's create a method that uses it.

When you write applets, there are several "standard" methods defined in the applet superclasses that you will commonly override in your applet class. These include methods to initialize the applet, to make it start running, to handle operations such as mouse movements or mouse clicks, or to clean up when the applet stops running. One of those standard methods is the `paint()` method, which actually displays your applet onscreen. The default definition of `paint()` doesn't do anything—it's an empty method. By overriding `paint()`, you tell the applet just what to draw on the screen. Here's a definition of `paint()`:

```
public void paint(Graphics g) {
    g.setFont(f);
    g.setColor(Color.red);
    g.drawString("Hello again!", 5, 40);
}
```

There are two things to know about the paint() method. First, note that this method is declared public, just as the applet itself was. The paint() method is actually public for a different reason—because the method it's overriding is also public. If a superclass's method is defined as public, your override method also has to be public, or you'll get an error when you compile the class.

Second, note that the paint() method takes a single argument: an instance of the Graphics class. The Graphics class provides platform-independent behavior for rendering fonts, colors, and behavior for drawing basic lines and shapes. You'll learn a lot more about the Graphics class in Week 2, when you create more extensive applets.

Inside your paint() method, you've done three things:

☐ You've told the graphics object that the default drawing font will be the one contained in the instance variable f.

☐ You've told the graphics object that the default color is an instance of the Color class for the color red.

☐ Finally, you've drawn your "Hello Again!" string onto the screen, at the x and y positions of 5 and 25. The string will be rendered in the new font and color.

For an applet this simple, this is all you need to do. Here's what the applet looks like so far:

```
public class HelloAgainApplet extends java.applet.Applet {

  Font f = new Font("TimesRoman",Font.BOLD,36);

  public void paint(Graphics g) {
    g.setFont(f);
    g.setColor(Color.red);
    g.drawString("Hello again!", 5, 40);
  }
}
```

If you've been paying close attention, you'll notice that something is wrong with this example up to this point. If you don't know what it is, try saving this file (remember, save it to the same name as the class: HelloAgainApplet.java) and compiling it. You should get a bunch of errors similar to this one:

```
HelloAgainApplet.java:7: Class Graphics not found in type declaration.
```

Why are you getting these errors? Because the classes you're referring to in this class, such as Graphics and Font, are part of a package that isn't available by default. Remember that the only package you have access to automatically in your Java programs is java.lang. You referred to the Applet class in the first line of the class definition by referring to its full package name (java.applet.Applet). Further on in the program, however, you referred to all kinds of other classes as if they were available. The compiler catches this and tells you that you don't have access to those other classes.

There are two ways to solve this problem: Refer to all external classes by full package name or import the appropriate class or package at the beginning of your class file. Which one you choose to do is mostly a matter of choice, although if you find yourself referring to a class in another package lots of times, you may want to import it to cut down on the amount of typing.

In this example, you'll import the classes you need. There are three of them: Graphics, Font, and Color. All three are part of the java.awt package. Here are the lines to import these classes. These lines go at the top of your program, before the actual class definition:

```
import java.awt.Graphics;
import java.awt.Font;
import java.awt.Color;
```

TIP

> You also can import an entire package of public classes by using an asterisk (*) in place of a specific class name. For example, to import all the classes in the awt package, you can use this line:
>
> ```
> import java.awt.*;
> ```

Now, with the proper classes imported into your program, HelloAgainApplet.java should compile cleanly to a class file. Listing 2.4 shows the final version to double-check.

TYPE **Listing 2.4. The final version of HelloAgainApplet.java.**

```
 1:import java.awt.Graphics;
 2:import java.awt.Font;
 3:import java.awt.Color;
 4:
 5:public class HelloAgainApplet extends java.applet.Applet {
 6:
 7:  Font f = new Font("TimesRoman",Font.BOLD,36);
 8:
 9:  public void paint(Graphics g) {
10:     g.setFont(f);
11:     g.setColor(Color.red);
12:     g.drawString("Hello again!", 5, 40);
13:  }
14:}
```

To test it, create an HTML file with the <APPLET> tag as you did yesterday. Here's an HTML file to use:

```
<HTML>
<HEAD>
```

```
<TITLE>Another Applet</TITLE>
</HEAD>
<BODY>
<P>My second Java applet says:
<BR><APPLET CODE="HelloAgainApplet.class" WIDTH=200 HEIGHT=50>
</APPLET>
</BODY>
</HTML>
```

For this HTML example, your Java class file is in the same directory as this HTML file. Save the file to `HelloAgainApplet.html` and fire up your Java-enabled browser or the Java applet viewer. Figure 2.7 shows the result you should be getting (the `"Hello Again!"` string is red).

Figure 2.7.

The `HelloAgain` *applet.*

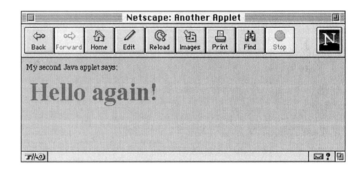

Summary

If this is your first encounter with object-oriented programming, a lot of the information in this lesson is going to seem really theoretical and overwhelming. Fear not—the further along in this book you get, and the more Java classes and applications you create, the easier it is to understand.

One of the biggest hurdles of object-oriented programming is not necessarily the concepts; it's their names. OOP has lots of jargon surrounding it. To summarize today's material, here's a glossary of terms and concepts you learned today:

class: A template for an object, which contains variables and methods representing behavior and attributes. Classes can inherit variables and methods from other classes.

class method: A method defined in a class, which operates on the class itself and can be called via the class or any of its instances.

class variable: A variable that is "owned" by the class and all its instances as a whole and is stored in the class.

instance: The same thing as an object; each object is an instance of some class.

instance method: A method defined in a class, which operates on an instance of that class. Instance methods are usually called just *methods.*

instance variable: A variable that is owned by an individual instance and whose value is stored in the instance.

interface: A collection of abstract behavior specifications that individual classes can then implement.

object: A concrete instance of some class. Multiple objects that are instances of the same class have access to the same methods, but often have different values for their instance variables.

package: A collection of classes and interfaces. Classes from packages other than java.lang must be explicitly imported or referred to by full package name.

subclass: A class lower in the inheritance hierarchy than its parent, the superclass. When you create a new class, it's often called *subclassing*.

superclass: A class further up in the inheritance hierarchy than its child, the subclass.

Q&A

Q Methods are effectively functions that are defined inside classes. If they look like functions and act like functions, why aren't they called functions?

A Some object-oriented programming languages do call them functions (C++ calls them member functions). Other object-oriented languages differentiate between functions inside and outside a body of a class or object, where having separate terms is important to understanding how each works. Because the difference is relevant in other languages and because the term method is now in such common use in object-oriented technology, Java uses the word as well.

Q I understand instance variables and methods, but not the idea of class variables and methods.

A Most everything you do in a Java program will be with objects. Some behaviors and attributes, however, make more sense if they are stored in the class itself rather than in the object. For example, to create a new instance of a class, you need a method that is defined and available in the class itself. (Otherwise, how can you create an object? You need an object to call the method, but you don't have an object yet.) Class variables, on the other hand, are often used when you have an attribute whose value you want to share with all the instances of a class.

Most of the time, you'll use instance variables and methods. You'll learn more about class variables and methods later this week.

Day 3

Java Basics

by Laura Lemay

Already this week you've learned about Java programming in very broad terms—what a Java program and an executable look like, and how to create simple classes. For the remainder of this week, you're going to get down to details and deal with the specifics of what the Java language looks like.

Today you won't define any classes or objects or worry about how any of them communicate inside a Java program. Rather, you'll draw closer and examine simple Java statements—the basic things you can do in Java within a method definition such as main().

Today you'll learn about the following:

☐ Java statements and expressions

☐ Variables and data types

☐ Comments

☐ Literals

☐ Arithmetic

☐ Comparisons

☐ Logical operators

TECHNICAL NOTE

> Java looks a lot like C++, and—by extension—like C. Much of the syntax will be very familiar to you if you are used to working in these languages. If you are an experienced C or C++ programmer, you may want to pay special attention to the technical notes (such as this one), because they provide information about the specific differences between these and other traditional languages and Java.

Statements and Expressions

A statement indicates the simplest tasks you can accomplish in Java; a statement forms a single Java operation. All the following are simple Java statements:

```
int i = 1;
import java.awt.Font;
System.out.println("This motorcycle is a "
    + color + " " + make);
m.engineState = true;
```

Statements sometimes return values—for example, when you add two numbers together or test to see whether one value is equal to another. These kind of statements are called *expressions*. You'll learn about these later today.

White space in Java statements, as with C, is unimportant. A statement can be contained on a single line or on multiple lines, and the Java compiler will be able to read it just fine. The most important thing to remember about Java statements is that each one ends with a semicolon (;). Forget the semicolon, and your Java program won't compile.

Java also has compound statements, or blocks, which can be placed wherever a single statement can. Block statements are surrounded by braces ({}). You'll learn more about blocks on Day 5, "Arrays, Conditionals, and Loops."

Variables and Data Types

Variables are locations in memory in which values can be stored. Each one has a name, a type, and a value. Before you can use a variable, you have to declare it. After it is declared, you can then assign values to it (you can also declare and assign a value to a variable at the same time, as you'll learn in this section).

Java actually has three kinds of variables: instance variables, class variables, and local variables.

Instance variables, as you learned yesterday, are used to define the attributes of a particular object. Class variables are similar to instance variables, except their values apply to all that class's instances (and to the class itself) rather than having different values for each object.

Local variables are declared and used inside method definitions, for example, for index counters in loops, as temporary variables, or to hold values that you need only inside the method definition itself. They can also be used inside blocks, which you'll learn about on Day 5. Once the method (or block) finishes executing, the variable definition and its value cease to exist. Use local variables to store information needed by a single method and instance variables to store information needed by multiple methods in the object.

Although all three kinds of variables are declared in much the same ways, class and instance variables are accessed and assigned in slightly different ways from local variables. Today you'll focus on variables as used within method definitions; tomorrow you'll learn how to deal with instance and class variables.

NOTE

> Unlike other languages, Java does not have global variables—that is, variables that are global to all parts of a program. Instance and class variables can be used to communicate global information between and among objects. Remember that Java is an object-oriented language, so you should think in terms of objects and how they interact, rather than in terms of programs.

Declaring Variables

To use any variable in a Java program, you must first declare it. Variable declarations consist of a type and a variable name:

```
int myAge;
String myName;
boolean isTired;
```

Variable definitions can go anywhere in a method definition (that is, anywhere a regular Java statement can go), although they are most commonly declared at the beginning of the definition before they are used:

```
public static void main (String args[]) {
    int count;
    String title;
    boolean isAsleep;
...
}
```

You can string together variable names with the same type on one line:

```
int x, y, z;
String firstName, LastName;
```

You can also give each variable an initial value when you declare it:

```
int myAge, mySize, numShoes = 28;
String myName = "Laura";
boolean isTired = true;
int a = 4, b = 5, c = 6;
```

If there are multiple variables on the same line with only one initializer (as in the first of the previous examples), the initial value applies to only the last variable in a declaration. You can also group individual variables and initializers on the same line using commas, as with the last example.

Local variables must be given values before they can be used (your Java program will not compile if you try to use an unassigned local variable). For this reason, it's a good idea always to give local variables initial values. Instance and class variable definitions do not have this restriction. (Their initial value depends on the type of the variable: `null` for instances of classes, `0` for numeric variables, `'\0'` for characters, and `false` for booleans.)

Notes on Variable Names

Variable names in Java can start with a letter, an underscore (_), or a dollar sign ($). They cannot start with a number. After the first character, your variable names can include any letter or number. Symbols, such as `%`, `*`, `@`, and so on, are often reserved for operators in Java, so be careful when using symbols in variable names.

In addition, the Java language uses the Unicode character set. Unicode is a character set definition that not only offers characters in the standard ASCII character set, but also includes several thousand other characters for representing most international alphabets. This means that you can use accented characters and other glyphs as legal characters in variable names, as long as they have a Unicode character number above `00C0`.

WARNING

The Unicode specification is a two-volume set of lists of thousands of characters. If you don't understand Unicode, or don't think you have a use for it, it's safest just to use plain numbers and letters in your variable names. You'll learn a little more about Unicode later.

Finally, note that the Java language is case sensitive, which means that uppercase letters are different from lowercase letters. This means that the variable X is different from the variable x, and a rose is not a Rose is not a ROSE. Keep this in mind as you write your own Java programs and as you read Java code other people have written.

By convention, Java variables have meaningful names, often made up of several words combined. The first word is lowercase, but all following words have an initial uppercase letter:

```
Button theButton;
long reallyBigNumber;
boolean currentWeatherStateOfPlanetXShortVersion;
```

Variable Types

In addition to the variable name, each variable declaration must have a type, which defines what values that variable can hold. The variable type can be one of three things:

☐ One of the eight primitive data types

☐ The name of a class or interface

☐ An array

You'll learn about how to declare and use array variables on Day 5; this lesson focuses on the primitive and class types.

Primitive Types

The eight primitive data types handle common types for integers, floating-point numbers, characters, and boolean values (true or false). They're called *primitive* because they're built into the system and are not actual objects, which makes them more efficient to use. Note that these data types are machine-independent, which means that you can rely on their sizes and characteristics to be consistent across your Java programs.

There are four Java integer types, each with a different range of values (as listed in Table 3.1). All are signed, which means they can hold either positive or negative numbers. Which type you choose for your variables depends on the range of values you expect that variable to hold; if a value becomes too big for the variable type, it is silently truncated.

Table 3.1. Integer types.

Type	Size	Range
byte	8 bits	-128 to 127
short	16 bits	-32,768 to 32,767
int	32 bits	-2,147,483,648 to 2,147,483,647
long	64 bits	-9,223,372,036,854,775,808 to 9,223,372,036,854,775,807

Floating-point numbers are used for numbers with a decimal part. Java floating-point numbers are compliant with IEEE 754 (an international standard for defining floating-point numbers and arithmetic). There are two floating-point types: float (32 bits, single precision) and double (64 bits, double precision).

The char type is used for individual characters. Because Java uses the Unicode character set, the char type has 16 bits of precision, unsigned.

Finally, the boolean type can have one of two values, true or false. Note that unlike in other C-like languages, boolean is not a number, nor can it be treated as one. All tests of boolean variables should test for true or false.

Note that all the primitive types are in lowercase. Be careful when you use them in your programs that you do use the lowercase, because there are also classes with the same names (and an initial capital letter) that have different behavior—so, for example, the primitive type boolean is different from the Boolean class. You'll learn more about these special classes and what they're used for on Day 4, "Working with Objects."

Class Types

In addition to the eight primitive data types, variables in Java can also be declared to hold an instance of a particular class:

```
String LastName;
Font basicFont;
OvalShape myOval;
```

Each of these variables can hold instances of the named class or of any of its subclasses. The latter is useful when you want a variable to be able to hold different instances of related classes. For example, let's say you had a set of fruit classes—Apple, Pear, Strawberry, and so on— all of which inherited from the general class Fruit. By declaring a variable of type Fruit, that variable can then hold instances of any of the Fruit classes. Declaring a variable of type Object means that variable can hold any object.

TECHNICAL NOTE

> Java does not have a typedef statement (as in C and C++). To declare new types in Java, you declare a new class; then variables can be declared to be of that class's type.

Assigning Values to Variables

Once a variable has been declared, you can assign a value to that variable by using the assignment operator =, like this:

```
size = 14;
tooMuchCaffiene = true;
```

Comments

Java has three kinds of comments: two for regular comments in source code and one for the special documentation system javadoc.

The symbols /* and */ surround multiline comments, as in C or C++. All text between the two delimiters is ignored:

```
/* I don't know how I wrote this next part; I was working
   really late one night and it just sort of appeared. I
   suspect the code elves did it for me. It might be wise
   not to try and change it.
*/
```

These comments cannot be nested; that is, you cannot have a comment inside a comment.

Double-slashes (//) can be used for a single line of comment. All the text up to the end of the line is ignored:

```
int vices = 7; // are there really only 7 vices?
```

The final type of comment begins with /** and ends with */. The contents of these special comments are used by the javadoc system, but are otherwise used identically to the first type of comment. javadoc is used to generate API documentation from the code. You'll learn more about javadoc on Day 22, "Java Programming Tools."

Literals

Literal is a programming language term that essentially means that what you type is what you get. For example, if you type 4 in a Java program, you automatically get an integer with the value 4. If you type 'a', you get a character with the value a. Literals are used to indicate simple values in your Java programs.

A *literal* is a simple value where "what you type is what you get." Numbers, characters, and strings are all examples of literals.

Literals may seem intuitive most of the time, but there are some special cases of literals in Java for different kinds of numbers, characters, strings, and boolean values.

Number Literals

There are several integer literals. 4, for example, is a decimal integer literal of type `int` (although you can assign it to a variable of type `byte` or `short` because it's small enough to fit into those types). A decimal integer literal larger than an `int` is automatically of type `long`. You also can force a smaller number to a `long` by appending an `L` or `l` to that number (for example, `4L` is a `long` integer of value 4). Negative integers are preceded by a minus sign— for example, `-45`.

Integers can also be expressed as octal or hexadecimal: A leading `0` indicates that a number is octal—for example, `0777` or `0004`. A leading `0x` (or `0X`) means that it is in hex (`0xFF`, `0XAF45`). Hexadecimal numbers can contain regular digits (0-9) or upper- or lowercase hex digits (a–f or A–F).

Floating-point literals usually have two parts, the integer part and the decimal part—for example, `5.77777`. A floating-point literal results in a floating-point number of type `double`, regardless of the precision of the number. You can force the number to the type `float` by appending the letter `f` (or `F`) to that number—for example, `2.56F`.

You can use exponents in floating-point literals using the letter `e` or `E` followed by the exponent (which can be a negative number): `10e45` or `.36E-2`.

Boolean Literals

Boolean literals consist of the keywords `true` and `false`. These keywords can be used anywhere you need a test or as the only possible values for boolean variables.

Character Literals

Character literals are expressed by a single character surrounded by single quotes: `'a'`, `'#'`, `'3'`, and so on. Characters are stored as 16-bit Unicode characters. Table 3.2 lists the special codes that can represent nonprintable characters, as well as characters from the Unicode character set. The letter `d` in the octal, hex, and Unicode escapes represents a number or a hexadecimal digit (a–f or A–F).

Table 3.2. Character escape codes.

Escape	Meaning
\n	Newline
\t	Tab
\b	Backspace
\r	Carriage return
\f	Formfeed
\\	Backslash
\'	Single quote
\"	Double quote
\ddd	Octal
\xdd	Hexadecimal
\udddd	Unicode character

TECHNICAL NOTE

C and C++ programmers should note that Java does not include character codes for \a (bell) or \v (vertical tab).

String Literals

A combination of characters is a string. Strings in Java are instances of the class `String`. Strings are not simply arrays of characters as they are in C or C++, although they do have many array-like characteristics (for example, you can test their length, and access and change individual characters). Because string objects are real objects in Java, they have methods that enable you to combine, test, and modify strings very easily.

String literals consist of a series of characters inside double quotes:

```
"Hi, I'm a string literal."
"" //an empty string
```

Strings can contain character constants such as newline, tab, and Unicode characters:

```
"A string with a \t tab in it"
"Nested strings are \"strings inside of\" other strings"
"This string brought to you by Java\u2122"
```

In the last example, the Unicode code sequence for \u2122 produces a trademark symbol (™).

> Just because you can represent a character using a Unicode escape does not mean your computer can display that character—the computer or operating system you are running may not support Unicode, or the font you're using may not have a glyph (picture) for that character. All that Unicode escapes in Java provide is a way to encode Unicode characters for systems that support Unicode.
>
> Java 1.1 will provide better capabilities for the display of Unicode characters and for handling international character sets.

When you use a string literal in your Java program, Java automatically creates an instance of the class `String` for you with the value you give it. Strings are unusual in this respect; the other literals do not behave in this way (none of the primitive data types are actual objects), and usually creating a new object involves explicitly creating a new instance of a class. You'll learn more about strings, the `String` class, and the things you can do with strings later today and tomorrow.

Expressions and Operators

Expressions are the simplest form of statement in Java that actually accomplishes something: All expressions, when evaluated, return a value (other statements don't necessarily do so). Arithmetic and tests for equality and magnitude are common examples of expressions. Because they return a value, you can assign that result to a variable or test that value in other Java statements.

Most of the expressions in Java use operators. Operators are special symbols for things like arithmetic, various forms of assignment, increment and decrement, and logical operations.

 Expressions are statements that return a value.

 Operators are special symbols that are commonly used in expressions.

Arithmetic

Java has five operators for basic arithmetic (see Table 3.3).

Table 3.3. Arithmetic operators.

Operator	Meaning	Example
+	Addition	3 + 4
-	Subtraction	5 - 7
*	Multiplication	5 * 5
/	Division	14 / 7
%	Modulus	20 % 7

Each operator takes two operands, one on either side of the operator. The subtraction operator (-) can also be used to negate a single operand.

Integer division results in an integer. Because integers don't have decimal fractions, any remainder is ignored. The expression 31 / 9, for example, results in 3 (9 goes into 31 only 3 times).

Modulus (%) gives the remainder once the operands have been evenly divided. For example, 31 % 9 results in 4 because 9 goes into 31 three times, with 4 left over.

Note that the result type of most arithmetic operations involving integers is an int regardless of the original type of the operands (shorts and bytes are both automatically converted to int). If either or both operands is of type long, the result is of type long. If one operand is an integer and another is a floating-point number, the result is a floating point. (If you're interested in the details of how Java promotes and converts numeric types from one type to another, you may want to check out the Java Language Specification on Sun's official Java Web site at http://java.sun.com/; that's more detail than I want to cover here.)

Listing 3.1 is an example of simple arithmetic in Java.

TYPE **Listing 3.1. Simple arithmetic.**

```
1: class ArithmeticTest {
2: public static void main (String args[]) {
3:     short x = 6;
4:     int y = 4;
5:     float a = 12.5f;
6:     float b = 7f;
7:
8:     System.out.println("x is " + x + ", y is " + y);
9:     System.out.println("x + y = " + (x + y));
10:     System.out.println("x - y = " + (x - y));
11:     System.out.println("x / y = " + (x / y));
12:     System.out.println("x % y = " + (x % y));
```

continues

Listing 3.1. continued

```
13:
14:        System.out.println("a is " + a + ", b is " + b);
15:        System.out.println("a / b = " + (a / b));
16: }
17: }
```

OUTPUT

```
x is 6, y is 4
x + y = 10
x - y = 2
x / y = 1
x % y = 2
a is 12.5, b is 7
a / b = 1.78571
```

ANALYSIS   In this simple Java application (note the `main()` method), you initially define four variables in lines 3 through 6: x and y, which are integers (type `int`), and a and b, which are floating-point numbers (type `float`). Keep in mind that the default type for floating-point literals (such as `12.5`) is `double`, so to make sure these are numbers of type `float`, you have to use an f after each one (lines 5 and 6).

The remainder of the program merely does some math with integers and floating-point numbers and prints out the results.

There is one other thing to mention about this program: the method `System.out.println()`. You've seen this method on previous days, but you haven't really learned exactly what it does. The `System.out.println()` method merely prints a message to the standard output of your system—to the screen, to a special window, or maybe just to a special log file, depending on your system and the development environment you're running. The `System.out.println()` method takes a single argument—a string—but you can use + to concatenate multiple values into a single string, as you'll learn later today.

More About Assignment

Variable assignment is a form of expression; in fact, because one assignment expression results in a value, you can string them together like this:

```
x = y = z = 0;
```

In this example, all three variables now have the value `0`.

The right side of an assignment expression is always evaluated before the assignment takes place. This means that expressions such as x = x + 2 do the right thing; 2 is added to the value of x, and then that new value is reassigned to x. In fact, this sort of operation is so common that Java has several operators to do a shorthand version of this, borrowed from C and C++. Table 3.4 shows these shorthand assignment operators.

Table 3.4. Assignment operators.

Expression	Meaning
x += y	x = x + y
x -= y	x = x - y
x *= y	x = x * y
x /= y	x = x / y

TECHNICAL NOTE

Technically, the shorthand assignment and longhand expressions are not exactly equivalent, particularly in cases where x or y may themselves be complicated expressions and your code relies on side effects of those expressions. In most instances, however, they are functionally equivalent. For more information about very complicated expressions, evaluation order, and side effects, you may want to consult the Java Language Specification.

Incrementing and Decrementing

As in C and C++, the ++ and -- operators are used to increment or decrement a variable's value by 1. For example, x++ increments the value of x by 1 just as if you had used the expression x = x + 1. Similarly x-- decrements the value of x by 1. (Unlike C and C++, Java allows x to be floating point.)

These increment and decrement operators can be prefixed or postfixed; that is, the ++ or -- can appear before or after the value it increments or decrements. For simple increment or decrement expressions, which one you use isn't overly important. In complex assignments, where you are assigning the result of an increment or decrement expression, which one you use makes a difference.

Take, for example, the following two expressions:

```
y = x++;
y = ++x;
```

These two expressions yield very different results because of the difference between prefix and postfix. When you use postfix operators (x++ or x--), y gets the value of x before x is changed; using prefix, the value of x is assigned to y after the change has occurred. Listing 3.2 is a Java example of how all this works.

TYPE | **Listing 3.2. Test of prefix and postfix increment operators.**

```
 1: class PrePostFixTest {
 2:
 3: public static void main (String args[]) {
 4:      int x = 0;
 5:      int y = 0;
 6:
 7:      System.out.println("x and y are " + x + " and " + y );
 8:      x++;
 9:      System.out.println("x++ results in " + x);
10:      ++x;
11:      System.out.println("++x results in " + x);
12:      System.out.println("Resetting x back to 0.");
13:      x = 0;
14:      System.out.println("------------");
15:      y = x++;
16:      System.out.println("y = x++ (postfix) results in:");
17:      System.out.println("x is " + x);
18:      System.out.println("y is " + y);
19:      System.out.println("------------");
20:
21:      y = ++x;
22:      System.out.println("y = ++x (prefix) results in:");
23:      System.out.println("x is " + x);
24:      System.out.println("y is " + y);
25:      System.out.println("------------");
26:
27: }
28: }
```

OUTPUT
```
x and y are 0 and 0
x++ results in 1
++x results in 2
Resetting x back to 0.
------------
y = x++ (postfix) results in:
x is 1
y is 0
------------
y = ++x (prefix) results in:
x is 2
y is 2
------------
```

In the first part of this example, you increment x alone using both prefix and postfix increment operators. In each, x is incremented by 1 each time. In this simple form, using either prefix or postfix works the same way.

In the second part of this example, you use the expression y = x++, in which the postfix increment operator is used. In this result, the value of x is incremented *after* that value is assigned to y. Hence the result: y is assigned the original value of x (0), and then x is incremented by 1.

3

In the third part, you use the `prefix` expression y = ++x. Here, the reverse occurs: x is incremented before its value is assigned to y. Because x is 1 from the previous step, its value is incremented (to 2), and then that value is assigned to y. Both x and y end up being 2.

TECHNICAL NOTE

> Technically, this description is not entirely correct. In reality, Java *always* completely evaluates all expressions on the right of an expression before assigning that value to a variable, so the concept of "assigning x to y before x is incremented" isn't precisely right. Instead, Java takes the value of x and "remembers" it, evaluates (increments) x, and *then* assigns the original value of x to y. Although in most simple cases this distinction may not be important, for more complex expressions with side effects, it may change the behavior of the expression overall. See the Language Specification for many more details about expression evaluation in Java.

Comparisons

Java has several expressions for testing equality and magnitude. All of these expressions return a boolean value (that is, `true` or `false`). Table 3.5 shows the comparison operators.

Table 3.5. Comparison operators.

Operator	Meaning	Example
==	Equal	x == 3
!=	Not equal	x != 3
<	Less than	x < 3
>	Greater than	x > 3
<=	Less than or equal to	x <= 3
>=	Greater than or equal to	x >= 3

Logical Operators

Expressions that result in boolean values (for example, the comparison operators) can be combined by using logical operators that represent the logical combinations AND, OR, XOR, and logical NOT.

For AND combinations, use either the & or && operators. The entire expression will be true only if both expressions on either side of the operator are also true; if either expression is false, the entire expression is false. The difference between the two operators is in expression evaluation. Using &, both sides of the expression are evaluated regardless of the outcome. Using &&, if the left side of the expression is false, the entire expression is assumed to be false (the value of the right side doesn't matter), so the expression returns false, and the right side of the expression is never evaluated. (This is often called a "short-circuited" expression.)

For OR expressions, use either ¦ or ¦¦. OR expressions result in true if either or both of the expressions on either side is also true; if both expression operands are false, the expression is false. As with & and &&, the single ¦ evaluates both sides of the expression regardless of the outcome; and ¦¦ is short-circuited: If the left expression is true, the expression returns true and the right side is never evaluated.

In addition, there is the XOR operator ^, which returns true only if its operands are different (one true and one false, or vice versa) and false otherwise (even if both are true).

In general, only the && and ¦¦ are commonly used as actual logical combinations. &, ¦, and ^ are more commonly used for bitwise logical operations.

For NOT, use the ! operator with a single expression argument. The value of the NOT expression is the negation of the expression; if x is true, !x is false.

Bitwise Operators

Finally, here's a short summary of the bitwise operators in Java. Most of these expressions are inherited from C and C++ and are used to perform operations on individual bits in integers. This book does not go into bitwise operations; it's an advanced topic covered better in books on C or C++. Table 3.6 summarizes the bitwise operators.

Table 3.6. Bitwise operators.

Operator	Meaning
&	Bitwise AND
¦	Bitwise OR
^	Bitwise XOR
<<	Left shift
>>	Right shift
>>>	Zero fill right shift
~	Bitwise complement

Operator	Meaning
<<=	Left shift assignment (x = x << y)
>>=	Right shift assignment (x = x >> y)
>>>=	Zero fill right shift assignment (x = x >>> y)
x&=y	AND assignment (x = x & y)
x¦=y	OR assignment (x = x ¦ y)
x^=y	XOR assignment (x = x ^ y)

Operator Precedence

Operator precedence determines the order in which expressions are evaluated. This, in some cases, can determine the overall value of the expression. For example, take the following expression:

```
y = 6 + 4 / 2
```

Depending on whether the 6 + 4 expression or the 4 / 2 expression is evaluated first, the value of y can end up being 5 or 8. Operator precedence determines the order in which expressions are evaluated, so you can predict the outcome of an expression. In general, increment and decrement are evaluated before arithmetic, arithmetic expressions are evaluated before comparisons, and comparisons are evaluated before logical expressions. Assignment expressions are evaluated last.

Table 3.7 shows the specific precedence of the various operators in Java. Operators further up in the table are evaluated first; operators on the same line have the same precedence and are evaluated left to right based on how they appear in the expression itself. For example, given that same expression y = 6 + 4 / 2, you now know, according to this table, that division is evaluated before addition, so the value of y will be 8.

Table 3.7. Operator precedence.

Operator	Notes
. [] ()	Parentheses (()) are used to group expressions; dot (.) is used for access to methods and variables within objects and classes (discussed tomorrow); square brackets ([]) are used for arrays (this is discussed later on in the week)
++ —— ! ~ instanceof	The instanceof operator returns true or false based on whether the object is an instance of the named class or any of that class's subclasses (discussed tomorrow)

continues

Table 3.7. continued

Operator	Notes
new (type)expression	The new operator is used for creating new instances of classes; () in this case is for casting a value to another type (you'll learn about both of these tomorrow)
* / %	Multiplication, division, modulus
+ —	Addition, subtraction
<< >> >>>	Bitwise left and right shift
< > <= >=	Relational comparison tests
== !=	Equality
&	AND
^	XOR
¦	OR
&&	Logical AND
¦¦	Logical OR
? :	Shorthand for if...then...else (discussed on Day 5)
= += —= *= /= %= ^=	Various assignments
&= ¦= <<= >>= >>>=	More assignments

You can always change the order in which expressions are evaluated by using parentheses around the expressions you want to evaluate first. You can nest parentheses to make sure expressions evaluate in the order you want them to (the innermost parenthetic expression is evaluated first). The following expression results in a value of 5, because the 6 + 4 expression is evaluated first, and then the result of that expression (10) is divided by 2:

```
y = (6 + 4) / 2
```

Parentheses also can be useful in cases where the precedence of an expression isn't immediately clear—in other words, they can make your code easier to read. Adding parentheses doesn't hurt, so if they help you figure out how expressions are evaluated, go ahead and use them.

String Arithmetic

One special expression in Java is the use of the addition operator (+) to create and concatenate strings. In most of the examples shown today and in earlier lessons, you've seen lots of lines that looked something like this:

```
System.out.println(name + " is a " + color + " beetle");
```

The output of that line (to the standard output) is a single string, with the values of the variables (name and color), inserted in the appropriate spots in the string. So what's going on here?

The + operator, when used with strings and other objects, creates a single string that contains the concatenation of all its operands. If any of the operands in string concatenation is not a string, it is automatically converted to a string, making it easy to create these sorts of output lines.

TECHNICAL NOTE

An object or type can be converted to a string if you implement the method toString(). All objects have a default string representation, but most classes override toString() to provide a more meaningful printable representation.

String concatenation makes lines such as the previous one especially easy to construct. To create a string, just add all the parts together—the descriptions plus the variables—and print it to the standard output, to the screen, to an applet, or anywhere.

The += operator, which you learned about earlier, also works for strings. For example, take the following expression:

```
myName += " Jr.";
```

This expression is equivalent to this:

```
myName = myName + " Jr.";
```

just as it would be for numbers. In this case, it changes the value of myName, which might be something like John Smith to have a Jr. at the end (John Smith Jr.).

Summary

As you have learned in the last two lessons, a Java program is made up primarily of classes and objects. Classes and objects, in turn, are made up of methods and variables, and methods are made up of statements and expressions. It is those last two things that you've learned about today; the basic building blocks that enable you to create classes and methods and build them up to a full-fledged Java program.

Today, you have learned about variables, how to declare them and assign values to them; literals for easily creating numbers, characters, and strings; and operators for arithmetic, tests, and other simple operations. With this basic syntax, you can move on tomorrow to learning about working with objects and building simple, useful Java programs.

To finish up this summary, Table 3.8 is a list of all the operators you have learned about today so that you can refer back to them.

Table 3.8. Operator summary.

Operator	Meaning
+	Addition
—	Subtraction
*	Multiplication
/	Division
%	Modulus
<	Less than
>	Greater than
<=	Less than or equal to
>=	Greater than or equal to
==	Equal
!=	Not equal
&&	Logical AND
¦¦	Logical OR
!	Logical NOT
&	AND
¦	OR
^	XOR
<<	Left shift
>>	Right shift
>>>	Zero fill right shift
~	Complement
=	Assignment
++	Increment
- - - -	Decrement

3

Operator	Meaning
+=	Add and assign
—=	Subtract and assign
*=	Multiply and assign
/=	Divide and assign
%=	Modulus and assign
&=	AND and assign
¦=	OR and assign
<<=	Left shift and assign
^=	XOR and assign
>>=	Right shift and assign
>>>=	Zero fill right shift and assign

3

Q&A

Q I didn't see any way to define constants.

A You can't create local constants in Java; you can create only constant instance and class variables. You'll learn how to do this tomorrow.

Q What happens if you assign an integer value to a variable that is too large for that variable to hold?

A Logically, you would think that the variable is just converted to the next larger type, but this isn't what happens. What does happen is called *overflow*. This means that if a number becomes too big for its variable, that number wraps around to the smallest possible negative number for that type and starts counting upward toward zero again.

Because this can result in some very confusing (and wrong) results, make sure that you declare the right integer type for all your numbers. If there's a chance a number will overflow its type, use the next larger type instead.

Q How can you find out the type of a given variable?

A If you're using any of the primitive types (int, float, boolean), and so on, you can't. If you care about the type, you can convert the value to some other type by using casting. (You'll learn about this tomorrow.)

If you're using class types, you can use the `instanceof` operator, which you'll learn more about tomorrow.

Q Why does Java have all these shorthand operators for arithmetic and assignment? It's really hard to read that way.

A The syntax of Java is based on C++, and therefore on C. One of C's implicit goals is the capability of doing very powerful things with a minimum of typing. Because of this, shorthand operators, such as the wide array of assignments, are common.

There's no rule that says you have to use these operators in your own programs, however. If you find your code to be more readable using the long form, no one will come to your house and make you change it.

Q You covered simple math in this section using operators. I'm assuming that Java has ways of doing more complex math operations?

A You assume correctly. A special class in the `java.lang` package, called `java.lang.Math`, has a number of methods for exponential, trigonometric, and other basic math operations. In fact, because you call these methods using the `Math` class itself, these are prime examples of class methods. You'll learn more about this tomorrow.

Day **4**

Working with Objects

by Laura Lemay

Let's start today's lesson with an obvious statement: Because Java is an object-oriented language, you're going to be dealing with a lot of objects. You'll create them, modify them, move them around, change their variables, call their methods, combine them with other objects—and, of course, develop classes and use your own objects in the mix.

Today, therefore, you'll learn all about the Java object in its natural habitat. Today's topics include

☐ Creating instances of classes

☐ Testing and modifying class and instance variables in your new instance

☐ Calling methods in that object

☐   Casting (converting) objects and other data types from one class to another

☐   Other odds and ends about working with objects

☐   An overview of the Java class libraries

Creating New Objects

When you write a Java program, you define a set of classes. As you learned on Day 2, "Object-Oriented Programming and Java," classes are templates for objects; for the most part, you merely use the class to create instances and then work with those instances. In this section, therefore, you'll learn how to create a new object from any given class.

Remember strings from yesterday? You learned that using a string literal—a series of characters enclosed in double-quotes—creates a new instance of the class String with the value of that string.

The String class is unusual in that respect—although it's a class, there's an easy way to create instances of that class using a literal. The other classes don't have that shortcut; to create instances of those classes you have to do so explicitly by using the new operator.

NOTE

> What about the literals for numbers and characters? Don't they create objects, too? Actually, they don't. The primitive data types for numbers and characters create numbers and characters, but for efficiency, they aren't actually objects. You can put object wrappers around them if you need to treat them like objects (you'll learn how to do this in "Casting and Converting Objects and Primitive Types").

Using new

To create a new object, you use the new operator with the name of the class you want to create an instance of, then parentheses after that. The following examples create new instances of the classes String, Random, and Motorcycle, and store those new instances in variables of the appropriate types:

```
String str = new String();

Random r = new Random();

Motorcycle m2 = new Motorcycle();
```

The parentheses are important; don't leave them off. The parentheses can be empty (as in these examples), in which case the most simple, basic object is created; or the parentheses can contain arguments that determine the initial values of instance variables or other initial qualities of that object:

```
Date dt = new Date(90, 4, 1, 4, 30);

Point pt = new Point(0,0);
```

The number and type of arguments you can use inside the parentheses with new are defined by the class itself using a special method called a constructor (you'll learn more about constructors later today). If you try and create a new instance of a class with the wrong number or type of arguments (or if you give it no arguments and it needs some), then you'll get an error when you try to compile your Java program.

Here's an example of creating several different types of objects using different numbers and types of arguments. The Date class, part of the java.util package, creates objects that represent the current date. Listing 4.1 is a Java program that shows three different ways of creating a Date object using new.

TYPE **Listing 4.1. Laura's Date program.**

```
 1: import java.util.Date;
 2:
 3: class CreateDates {
 4:
 5:     public static void main(String args[]) {
 6:         Date d1, d2, d3;
 7:
 8:         d1 = new Date();
 9:         System.out.println("Date 1: " + d1);
10:
11:         d2 = new Date(71, 7, 1, 7, 30);
12:         System.out.println("Date 2: " + d2);
13:
14:         d3 = new Date("April 3 1993 3:24 PM");
15:         System.out.println("Date 3: " + d3);
16:     }
17: }
```

OUTPUT
```
Date 1: Tue Feb 13 09:36:56 PST 1996
Date 2: Sun Aug 01 07:30:00 PDT 1971
Date 3: Sat Apr 03 15:24:00 PST 1993
```

ANALYSIS In this example, three different date objects are created using different arguments to the class listed after new. The first instance (line 8) uses new Date() with no arguments, which creates a Date object for today's date (the first line of the output shows a sample; your output will, of course, read the current date and time for you).

The second Date object you create in this example has five integer arguments. The arguments represent a date: year, month, day, hours, and minutes. And, as the output shows, this creates a Date object for that particular date: Sunday, August 1, 1971, at 7:30 a.m.

NOTE

> Java numbers months starting from 0. So although you might expect the seventh month to be July, month 7 in Java is indeed August.

The third version of Date takes one argument, a string, representing the date as a text string. When the Date object is created, that string is parsed, and a Date object with that date and time is created (see the third line of output). The date string can take many different formats; see the API documentation for the Date class (part of the java.util package) for information about what strings you can use.

What new **Does**

When you use the new operator, the new instance of the given class is created, and memory is allocated for it. In addition (and most importantly), a special method defined in the given class is called to initialize the object and set up any initial values it needs. This special method is called a constructor. *Constructors* are special methods, defined in classes, that create and initialize new instances of classes.

Constructors are special methods that initialize a new object, set its variables, create any other objects that object needs, and generally perform any other operations the object needs to initialize itself.

Multiple constructor definitions in a class can each have a different number or type of arguments—then, when you use new, you can specify different arguments in the argument list, and the right constructor for those arguments will be called. That's how each of those different versions of new that you used in the CreateDates class can create different Date objects.

When you create your own classes, you can define as many constructors as you need to implement that class's behavior. You'll learn how to create constructors on Day 7, "More About Methods."

A Note on Memory Management

Memory management in Java is dynamic and automatic. When you create a new object in Java, Java automatically allocates the right amount of memory for that object in the heap. You don't have to allocate any memory for any objects explicitly; Java does it for you.

What happens when you're finished with that object? How do you de-allocate the memory that object uses? The answer, again, is that memory management is automatic. Once you're done with an object, you reassign all the variables that might hold that object and remove it from any arrays, thereby making the object unusable. Java has a "garbage collector" that looks for unused objects and reclaims the memory that those objects are using. You don't have to do any explicit freeing of memory; you just have to make sure you're not still holding onto an object you want to get rid of. You'll learn more specific details about the Java garbage collector and how it works on Day 21, "Under the Hood."

 A *garbage collector* is a special thing built into the Java environment that looks for unused objects. If it finds any, it automatically removes those objects and frees the memory those objects were using.

Accessing and Setting Class and Instance Variables

Now you have your very own object, and that object may have class or instance variables defined in it. How do you work with those variables? Easy! Class and instance variables behave in exactly the same ways as the local variables you learned about yesterday; you just refer to them slightly differently than you do regular variables in your code.

Getting Values

To get to the value of an instance variable, you use an expression in what's called *dot notation*. With dot notation, the reference to an instance or class variable has two parts: the object on the left side of the dot and the variable on the right side of the dot.

 Dot notation is an expression used to get at instance variables and methods inside a given object.

For example, if you have an object assigned to the variable myObject, and that object has a variable called var, you refer to that variable's value like this:

```
myObject.var;
```

This form for accessing variables is an expression (it returns a value), and both sides of the dot can also be expressions. This means that you can nest instance variable access. If that var instance variable itself holds an object and that object has its own instance variable called state, you could refer to it like this:

```
myObject.var.state;
```

Dot expressions are evaluated left to right, so you start with myObject's variable var, which points to another object with the variable state. You end up with the value of that state variable after the entire expression is done evaluating.

Changing Values

Assigning a value to that variable is equally easy—just tack an assignment operator on the right side of the expression:

```
myObject.var.state = true;
```

Listing 4.2 is an example of a program that tests and modifies the instance variables in a Point object. Point is part of the java.awt package and refers to a coordinate point with an x and a y value.

TYPE   **Listing 4.2. The TestPoint Class.**

```
 1: import java.awt.Point;
 2:
 3: class TestPoint {
 4: public static void main(String args[]) {
 5:     Point thePoint = new Point(10,10);
 6:
 7:     System.out.println("X is " + thePoint.x);
 8:     System.out.println("Y is " + thePoint.y);
 9:
10:     System.out.println("Setting X to 5.");
11:     thePoint.x = 5;
12:     System.out.println("Setting Y to 15.");
13:     thePoint.y = 15;
14:
15:     System.out.println("X is " + thePoint.x);
16:     System.out.println("Y is " + thePoint.y);
17:
18:  }
19:}
```

OUTPUT
```
X is 10
Y is 10
Setting X to 5.
Setting Y to 15.
X is 5
Y is 15
```

ANALYSIS   In this example, you first create an instance of Point where X and Y are both 10 (line 6). Lines 8 and 9 print out those individual values, and you can see dot notation at work there. Lines 11 through 14 change the values of those variables to 5 and 15, respectively. Finally, lines 16 and 17 print out the values of X and Y again to show how they've changed.

Class Variables

Class variables, as you've already learned, are variables that are defined and stored in the class itself. Their values, therefore, apply to the class and to all its instances.

With instance variables, each new instance of the class gets a new copy of the instance variables that class defines. Each instance can then change the values of those instance variables without affecting any other instances. With class variables, there is only one copy of that variable. Every instance of the class has access to that variable, but there is only one value. Changing the value of that variable changes it for all the instances of that class.

You define class variables by including the `static` keyword before the variable itself. You'll learn more about this on Day 6, "Creating Classes and Applications in Java." For example, take the following partial class definition:

```
class FamilyMember {
    static String surname = "Johnson";
    String name;
    int age;
    ...
}
```

Instances of the class `FamilyMember` each have their own values for name and age. But the class variable `surname` has only one value for all family members. Change `surname`, and all the instances of `FamilyMember` are affected.

To access class variables, you use the same dot notation as you do with instance variables. To get or change the value of the class variable, you can use either the instance or the name of the class on the left side of the dot. Both of the lines of output in this example print the same value:

```
FamilyMember dad = new FamilyMember();
System.out.println("Family's surname is: " + dad.surname);
System.out.println("Family's surname is: " + FamilyMember.surname);
```

Because you can use an instance to change the value of a class variable, it's easy to become confused about class variables and where their values are coming from (remember that the value of a class variable affects all the instances). For this reason, it's a good idea to use the name of the class when you refer to a class variable—it makes your code easier to read and strange results easier to debug.

Calling Methods

Calling a method is similar to referring to an object's instance variables: Method calls to objects also use dot notation. The object itself whose method you're calling is on the left side of the dot; the name of the method and its arguments are on the right side of the dot:

```
myObject.methodOne(arg1, arg2, arg3);
```

Note that all calls to methods must have parentheses after them, even if that method takes no arguments:

```
myObject.methodNoArgs();
```

If the method you've called returns an object that itself has methods, you can nest methods as you would variables. This next example calls the getName() method, which is defined in the object returned by the getClass() method, which was defined in myObject. Got it?

```
myObject.getClass().getName();
```

You can combine nested method calls and instance variable references as well (in this case you're calling the methodTwo() method, which is defined in the object stored by the var instance variable, which in turn is part of the myObject object):

```
myObject.var.methodTwo(arg1, arg2);
```

System.out.println(), the method you've been using through the book this far to print out bits of text, is a great example of nesting variables and methods. The System class (part of the java.lang package) describes system-specific behavior. System.out is a class variable that contains an instance of the class PrintStream that points to the standard output of the system. PrintStream instances have a println() method that prints a string to that output stream.

Listing 4.3 shows an example of calling some methods defined in the String class. Strings include methods for string tests and modification, similar to what you would expect in a string library in other languages.

TYPE   **Listing 4.3. Several uses of String methods.**

```
 1: class TestString {
 2:
 3:     public static void main(String args[]) {
 4:         String str = "Now is the winter of our discontent";
 5:
 6:         System.out.println("The string is: " + str);
 7:         System.out.println("Length of this string: "
 8:                 + str.length());
 9:         System.out.println("The character at position 5: "
10:                 + str.charAt(5));
11:         System.out.println("The substring from 11 to 17: "
12:                 + str.substring(11, 17));
13:         System.out.println("The index of the character d: "
14:                 + str.indexOf('d'));
15:         System.out.print("The index of the beginning of the ");
16:         System.out.println("substring \"winter\": "
17:                 + str.indexOf("winter"));
18:         System.out.println("The string in upper case: "
19:                 + str.toUpperCase());
20:     }
21: }
```

OUTPUT

```
The string is: Now is the winter of our discontent
Length of this string: 35
The character at position 5: s
The substring from positions 11 to 17: winter
The index of the character d: 25
The index of the beginning of the substring "winter": 11
The string in upper case: NOW IS THE WINTER OF OUR DISCONTENT
```

ANALYSIS In line 4, you create a new instance of String by using a string literal (it's easier that way than using new and then putting the characters in individually). The remainder of the program simply calls different string methods to do different operations on that string:

☐ Line 6 prints the value of the string we created in line 4: "Now is the winter of our discontent".

☐ Line 7 calls the length() method in the new String object. This string has 35 characters.

☐ Line 9 calls the charAt() method, which returns the character at the given position in the string. Note that string positions start at 0, so the character at position 5 is s.

☐ Line 11 calls the substring() method, which takes two integers indicating a range and returns the substring at those starting and ending points. The substring() method can also be called with only one argument, which returns the substring from that position to the end of the string.

☐ Line 13 calls the indexOf() method, which returns the position of the first instance of the given character (here, 'd').

☐ Line 15 shows a different use of the indexOf() method, which takes a string argument and returns the index of the beginning of that string.

☐ Finally, line 19 uses the toUpperCase() method to return a copy of the string in all uppercase.

Class Methods

Class methods, like class variables, apply to the class as a whole and not to its instances. Class methods are commonly used for general utility methods that may not operate directly on an instance of that class, but fit with that class conceptually. For example, the String class contains a class method called valueOf(), which can take one of many different types of arguments (integers, booleans, other objects, and so on). The valueOf() method then returns a new instance of String containing the string value of the argument it was given. This method doesn't operate directly on an existing instance of String, but getting a string from another object or data type is definitely a String-like operation, and it makes sense to define it in the String class.

Class methods can also be useful for gathering general methods together in one place (the class). For example, the Math class, defined in the java.lang package, contains a large set of mathematical operations as class methods—there are no instances of the class Math, but you can still use its methods with numeric or boolean arguments. For example, the class method Math.max() takes two arguments and returns the larger of the two. You don't need to create a new instance of Math; just call the method anywhere you need it, like this:

```
in biggerOne = Math.max(x, y);
```

To call a class method, you use dot notation as you do with instance methods. As with class variables, you can use either an instance of the class or the class itself on the left site of the dot. However, for the same reasons noted in the discussion on class variables, using the name of the class for class methods makes your code easier to read. The last two lines in this example produce the same result (the string "5"):

```
String s, s2;
s = "foo";
s2 = s.valueOf(5);
s2 = String.valueOf(5);
```

References to Objects

As you work with objects, one important thing going on behind the scenes is the use of references to those objects. When you assign objects to variables, or pass objects as arguments to methods, you are passing references to those objects, not the objects themselves or copies of those objects.

An example should make this clearer. Examine Listing 4.4, which shows a simple example of how references work.

TYPE   **Listing 4.4. A references example.**

```
 1: import java.awt.Point;
 2:
 3: class ReferencesTest {
 4:     public static void main (String args[]) {
 5:         Point pt1, pt2;
 6:         pt1 = new Point(100, 100);
 7:         pt2 = pt1;
 8:
 9:         pt1.x = 200;
10:         pt1.y = 200;
11:         System.out.println("Point1: " + pt1.x + ", " + pt1.y);
12:         System.out.println("Point2: " + pt2.x + ", " + pt2.y);
13:     }
14: }
```

`Point1: 200, 200`
`Point2: 200, 200`

 In the first part of this program, you declare two variables of type `Point` (line 5), create a new `Point` object to pt1 (line 6), and finally, assign the value of pt1 to pt2 (line 7).

Now, here's the challenge. After changing pt1's x and y instance variables in lines 9 and 10, what will pt2 look like?

As you can see, pt2's x and y instance variables were also changed, even though you never explicitly changed them. When you assign the value of pt1 to pt2, you actually create a reference from pt2 to the same object to which pt1 refers (see Figure 4.1). Change the object that pt2 refers to, and you also change the object that pt1 points to, because both are references to the same object.

NOTE

> If you actually do want pt1 and pt2 to point to separate objects, you should use new `Point()` for both lines to create separate objects.

Figure 4.1.

References to objects.

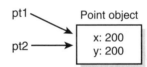

The fact that Java uses references becomes particularly important when you pass arguments to methods. You'll learn more about this later today, but keep these references in mind.

TECHNICAL NOTE

> There are no explicit pointers or pointer arithmetic in Java as there are in C-like languages—just references. However, with these references, and with Java arrays, you have most of the capabilities that you have with pointers without the confusion and lurking bugs that explicit pointers can create.

Casting and Converting Objects and Primitive Types

Sometimes in your Java programs you may have a value stored somewhere that is the wrong type for what you want to do with it. Maybe it's an instance of the wrong class, or perhaps it's a `float` and you want it to be an `int`. To convert the value of one type to another, you use casting. Casting is a programming term that means, effectively, converting a value or an object from one type to another. The result of a cast is a new value or object; casting does not change the original object or value.

New Term   *Casting* converts the value of an object or primitive type into another type.

Although the concept of casting is a simple one, the rules for what types in Java can be converted to what other types are complicated by the fact that Java has both primitive types (`int`, `float`, `boolean`), and object types (`String`, `Point`, `Window`, and so on). There are three forms of casts and conversions to talk about in this section:

- [ ] Casting between primitive types: `int` to `float` or `float` to `double`
- [ ] Casting between object types: an instance of a class to an instance of another class
- [ ] Converting primitive types to objects and then extracting primitive values back out of those objects

Casting Primitive Types

Casting between primitive types allows you to "convert" the value of one type to another primitive type—for example, to assign a number of one type to a variable of another type. Casting between primitive types most commonly occurs with the numeric types; boolean values cannot be cast to any other primitive type.

Often, if the type you are casting to is "larger" than the type of the value you're converting, you may not have to use an explicit cast. You can often automatically treat a byte or a character as an `int`, for example, or an `int` as a `long`, an `int` as a `float`, or anything as a `double` automatically. In most cases, because the larger type provides more precision than the smaller, no loss of information occurs when the value is cast. The exception is casting integers to floating-point values; casting an `int` or a `long` to a `float` or a `long` to a `double` may cause some loss of precision.

To convert a large value to smaller type, you must use an explicit cast, because converting that value may result in a loss of precision. Explicit casts look like this:

`(typename)value`

In this form, `typename` is the name of the type you're converting to (for example: `short`, `int`, float, boolean), and *value* is an expression that results in the value you want to convert. So, for example, in this expression the value of x is divided by the value of y and the result is cast to an int:

```
(int) (x / y);
```

Note that because the precedence of casting is higher than that of arithmetic, you have to use parentheses here; otherwise, the value of x would be cast first and then divided by y (which might very well be a very different result).

Casting Objects

Instances of classes can also be cast to instances of other classes, with one restriction: The class of the object you're casting and the class you're casting it to must be related by inheritance; that is, you can cast an object only to an instance of its class's sub- or superclass—not to any random class.

Analogous to converting a primitive value to a larger type, some objects may not need to be cast explicitly. In particular, because subclasses contain all the same information as their superclass, you can use an instance of a subclass anywhere a superclass is expected. (Did you just have to read that sentence four times before you understood it? I had to rewrite it a whole lot of times before it became even that simple. Bear with me, its not that bad. Let's try an example.) Suppose you have a method that takes two arguments: one of type Object, and one of type Number. You don't have to pass instances of those particular classes to that method. For the Object argument, you can pass any subclass of Object (any object, in other words), and for the Number argument you can pass in any instance of any subclass of Number (Integer, Boolean, Float, and so on); you don't have to explicitly convert them first.

Casting downward in the class hierarchy is automatic, but casting upward is not. Converting an instance of a subclass to an instance of a superclass loses the information the original subclass provided and requires an explicit cast. To cast an object to another class, you use the same casting operation that you used for base types:

```
(classname)object
```

In this case, *classname* is the name of the class you want to cast the object to, and *object* is a reference to the object you're casting. Note that casting creates a reference to the old object of the type *classname*; the old object still continues to exist as it did before.

Here's a (fictitious) example of a cast of an instance of the class GreenApple to an instance of the class Apple (where GreenApple is theoretically a subclass of Apple with more information to define the apple as green):

```
GreenApple a;
Apple a2;
a = new GreenApple();
a2 = (Apple) a;
```

In addition to casting objects to classes, you can also cast objects to interfaces—but only if that object's class or one of its superclasses actually implements that interface. Casting an object to an interface means that you can call one of that interface's methods even if that object's class does not actually implement that interface. You'll learn more about interfaces in Week 3.

Converting Primitive Types to Objects and Vice Versa

Now you know how to cast a primitive type to another primitive type and how to cast between classes. How can you cast one to the other?

You can't! Primitive types and objects are very different things in Java and you can't automatically cast or convert between the two. However, the java.lang package includes several special classes that correspond to each primitive data type: Integer for ints, Float for floats, Boolean for booleans, and so on. Note that the class names have an initial capital letter, and the primitive types are lowercase. Java treats these names very differently, so don't confuse them, or your methods and variables won't behave the way you expect.

Using class methods defined in these classes, you can create an object-equivalent for all the primitive types using new. The following line of code creates an instance of the Integer class with the value 35:

```
Integer intObject = new Integer(35);
```

Once you have actual objects, you can treat those values as objects. Then, when you want the primitive values back again, there are methods for that as well—for example, the intValue() method extracts an int primitive value from an Integer object:

```
int theInt = intObject.intValue();   // returns 35
```

See the Java API documentation for these special classes for specifics on the methods for converting primitives to and from objects.

NOTE

In Java 1.0 there are special type classes for Boolean, Character, Double, Float, Integer, and Long. Java 1.1 adds classes for Byte and Short, as well as a special wrapper class for Void. The latter classes are used primarily for object reflection.

Odds and Ends

This section is a catchall for other information about working with objects, particularly the following:

- ☐ Comparing objects
- ☐ Finding out the class of any given object
- ☐ Testing to see whether an object is an instance of a given class

Comparing Objects

Yesterday you learned about operators for comparing values: equals, not equals, less than, and so on. Most of these operators work only on primitive types, not on objects. If you try to use other values as operands, the Java compiler produces errors.

The exception to this rule is with the operators for equality: == (equal) and != (not equal). These operators, when used with objects, test whether the two operands refer to exactly the same object in memory.

What should you do if you want to be able to compare instances of your class and have meaningful results? You have to implement special methods in your class, and you have to call those methods using those method names.

TECHNICAL NOTE

> Java does not have the concept of operator overloading—that is, the ability to redefine the behavior of the built-in operators using methods in your own classes. The built-in operators remain defined only for numbers.

A good example of this is the String class. It is possible to have two strings, two independent objects in memory with the same values—that is, the same characters in the same order. According to the == operator, however, those two String objects will not be equal, because, although their contents are the same, they are not the same object.

The String class, therefore, defines a method called equals() that tests each character in the string and returns true if the two strings have the same values. Listing 4.5 illustrates this.

TYPE   **Listing 4.5. A test of string equality.**

```
 1: class EqualsTest {
 2: public static void main(String args[]) {
 3:         String str1, str2;
 4:         str1 = "she sells sea shells by the sea shore.";
 5:         str2 = str1;
 6:
 7:       System.out.println("String1: " + str1);
 8:        System.out.println("String2: " + str2);
 9:        System.out.println("Same object? " + (str1 == str2));
10:
11:       str2 = new String(str1);
12:
13:       System.out.println("String1: " + str1);
14:        System.out.println("String2: " + str2);
15:        System.out.println("Same object? " + (str1 == str2));
16:        System.out.println("Same value? " + str1.equals(str2));
17:    }
18:  }
```

OUTPUT
```
String1: she sells sea shells by the sea shore.
String2: she sells sea shells by the sea shore.
Same object? true
String1: she sells sea shells by the sea shore.
String2: she sells sea shells by the sea shore.
Same object? false
Same value? true
```

ANALYSIS   The first part of this program (lines 4 through 6) declares two variables (str1 and str2) assigns the literal she sells sea shells by the sea shore. to str1, and then assigns that value to str2. As you learned earlier when we talked about object references, now str1 and str2 point to the same object, and the equality test at line 10 proves that.

In the second part, you create a new string object with the same value as str1 and assign str2 to that new string object. Now you have two different string objects in str1 and str2, both with the same value. Testing them to see whether they're the same object by using the == operator (line 16) returns the expected answer (false—they are not the same object in memory), as does testing them using the equals() method (line 17) (true—they have the same values).

TECHNICAL NOTE   Why can't you just use another literal when you change str2, rather than using new? String literals are optimized in Java—if you create a string using a literal, and then use another literal with the same characters, Java knows enough to give you the first String object back. Both strings are the same objects—to create two separate objects you have to go out of your way.

Determining the Class of an Object

Want to find out the class of an object? Here's the way to do it for an object assigned to the variable obj:

```
String name = obj.getClass().getName();
```

What does this do? The getClass() method is defined in the Object class, and as such is available for all objects. The result of that method is a Class object (where Class is itself a class), which has a method called getName(). getName() returns a string representing the name of the class.

Another test that might be useful to you is the instanceof operator. instanceof has two operands: an object on the left and the name of a class on the right. The expression returns true or false based on whether the object is an instance of the named class or any of that class's subclasses:

```
"foo" instanceof String // true
Point pt = new Point(10, 10);
pt instanceof String // false
```

The instanceof operator can also be used for interfaces; if an object implements an interface, the instanceof operator with that interface name on the right side returns true. You'll learn all about interfaces in Week 3.

Class and Object Reflection (Java 1.1)

Reflection, also known as introspection, is a somewhat lofty term to describe the ability to "look inside" a class or an object and get information about that object's variables and methods as well as actually set and get the values of those variables and to call methods. Object reflection is useful for tools such as class browsers or debuggers, where getting at the information of an object on-the-fly allows you to explore what that object can do, or for component-based programs such as Java Beans, where the ability for one object to query another object about what it can do (and then ask it to do something) is useful to building larger applications.

The classes that support reflection of Java classes and objects will be part of the core Java 1.1 API (they are not available in the 1.0.2 version of the JDK). A new package, java.lang.reflect, will contain new classes to support reflection, which include the following:

- ☐ Field, for managing and finding out information about class and instance variables
- ☐ Method, for managing class and instance methods
- ☐ Constructor, for managing the special methods for creating new instances of classes (you'll learn more about constructors on Day 7)

☐ `Array`, for managing arrays

☐ `Modifier`, for decoding modifier information about classes, variables and methods (more about modifiers on Day 15, "Modifiers, Access Control, and Class Design")

In addition, there will be a number of new methods available in the `Class` class to help tie together the various reflection classes.

You can find out more about the new reflection classes and methods from `http://java.sun.com/products/JDK/1.1/designspecs/reflection/`.

The Java Class Library

To finish up today, let's look at the Java class library. Actually, you've had some experience with some of the Java classes already, so they shouldn't seem that strange.

The Java class library provides the set of classes that are guaranteed to be available in any commercial Java environment (for example, in any Java development environment or in browsers such as Netscape). Those classes are in the `java` package and include all the classes you've seen so far in this book, plus a whole lot more classes you'll learn about later on in this book (and more you may not learn about at all).

The Java Developer's Kit comes with documentation for all of the Java class library, which includes descriptions of each class's instance variables, methods, constructors, interfaces, and so on. You can get to this documentation (called the Java Application Programmer's Interface, or API) via the Web at `http://java.sun.com:80/products/JDK/CurrentRelease/api/packages.html`. A shorter summary of the Java API is in Appendix C as well. Exploring the Java class library and its methods and instance variables is a great way to figure out what Java can and cannot do, as well as how it can become a starting point for your own development.

Here are the class packages that are part of the Java class library:

☐ `java.lang`—Classes that apply to the language itself, including the `Object` class, the `String` class, and the `System` class. It also contains the special classes for the primitive types (`Integer`, `Character`, `Float`, and so on). You'll get at least a glance at most of the classes in this package in this first week.

☐ `java.util`—Utility classes, such as `Date`, as well as simple collection classes, such as `Vector` and `Hashtable`. You'll learn more about these classes in the Bonus Week.

☐ `java.io`—Input and output classes for writing to and reading from streams (such as standard input and output) and for handling files. Day 19, "Streams and I/O," describes the classes in this package.

☐ `java.net`—Classes for networking support, including `Socket` and `URL` (a class to represent references to documents on the World Wide Web). You'll learn a little about networking on Day 14, "Windows, Networking, and Other Tidbits," and then on Day 26, "Client/Server Networking in Java."

☐ `java.awt`—This is the Abstract Windowing Toolkit. It contains classes to implement graphical user interface features, including classes for `Window`, `Menu`, `Button`, `Font`, `CheckBox`, and so on. It also includes mechanisms for managing system events and for processing images (in the `java.awt.Image` package). You'll learn all about the AWT in Week 2.

☐ `java.applet`—Classes to implement Java applets.

In addition to the Java classes, your development environment may also include additional classes that provide other utilities or functionality. Although these classes may be useful, because they are not part of the standard Java library, they may not be available to other people trying to run your Java program unless you explicitly include those classes with your program. This is particularly important for applets, because applets are expected to be able to run on any platform, using any Java-enabled browser. Only classes inside the `java` package are guaranteed to be available on all browsers and Java environments.

Summary

Objects, objects everywhere. Today, you've learned all about how to deal with objects: how to create them, how to find out and change the values of their variables, and how to call their methods. You have also learned how to copy and compare them and how to convert them into other objects. Finally, you have learned a bit about the Java class libraries—which give you a whole slew of classes to play with in your own programs.

You now have the fundamentals of how to deal with most simple things in the Java language. All you have left are arrays, conditionals, and loops, which you'll learn about tomorrow. Then you'll learn how to define and use classes in Java applications on Day 6, and launch directly into applets next week. With just about everything you do in your Java programs, you'll always come back to objects.

Q&A

Q I'm confused about the differences between objects and the primitive data types, such as `int` and `boolean`.

A The primitive types in the language (`byte`, `short`, `int`, `long`, `float`, `double`, `boolean`, and `char`) represent the smallest things in the language. They are not objects, although in many ways they can be handled like objects—they can be assigned to variables and passed in and out of methods. Most of the operations that work exclusively on objects, however, will not work with primitive types.

Objects are instances of classes and, as such, are usually much more complex data types than simple numbers and characters, often containing numbers and characters as instance or class variables.

Q **No pointers in Java? If you don't have pointers, how are you supposed to do something like linked lists, where you have a pointer from one nose to another so you can traverse them?**

A Java doesn't have no pointers at all; it has no *explicit* pointers. Object references are, effectively, pointers. So to create something like a linked list, you would create a class called Node, which would have an instance variable also of type Node. Then to link together node objects all you need to do is assign a node object to the instance variable of the object just before it in the list. Because object references are pointers, linked lists set up this way will behave as you would expect them to.

Q **In the section on calling methods, you had examples of calling a method with a different number of arguments each time—and it gave a different kind of result. How is that possible?**

A That's called *method overloading*. Overloading means that the same method can have different behavior based on the arguments it's called with—and the number and type of arguments can vary. When you define methods in your own classes, you define separate method signatures with different sets of arguments and different definitions. When a method is called, Java figures out which definition to execute based on the number and type of arguments with which you called it.

You'll learn all about this on Day 6.

Q **No operator overloading in Java? Why not? I thought Java was based on C++, and C++ has operator overloading.**

A Java was indeed based on C++, but it was also designed to be simple, so many of C++'s features have been removed. The argument against operator overloading is that because the operator can be defined to mean anything; it makes it very difficult to figure out what any given operator is doing at any one time. This can result in entirely unreadable code. When you use a method, you know it can mean many things to many classes, but when you use an operator you would like to know that it always means the same thing. Given the potential for abuse, the designers of Java felt it was one of the C++ features that was best left out.

4

Day 5

Arrays, Conditionals, and Loops

by Laura Lemay

Although you could write Java programs using what you've learned so far, those programs would be pretty dull. Much of the good stuff in Java or in any programming language results when you have arrays to store values in and control-flow constructs (loops and conditionals) to execute different bits of a program based on tests. Today, you'll find out about the following:

☐ Arrays, one of the most useful objects in Java, which enable you to collect objects or primitive types into an easy-to-manage list

☐ Block statements, for grouping together related statements

☐ `if` and `switch`, for conditional tests

☐ `for` and `while` loops, for iteration or repeating a statement or statements multiple times

Arrays

Arrays in Java, as in other languages, are a way to store collections of items into a single unit. The array has some number of *slots*, each of which holds an individual item. You can add and delete items to those slots as needed. Unlike in other languages, however, arrays in Java are actual objects that can be passed around and treated just like other objects.

 An *array* is a collection of items. Each slot in the array can hold an object or a primitive value. Arrays in Java are objects that can be treated just like other objects in the language.

Arrays can contain any type of element value (primitive types or objects), but you can't store different types in a single array. You can have an array of integers or an array of strings or an array of arrays, but you can't have an array that contains, for example, both strings and integers.

To create an array in Java, you use three steps:

1. Declare a variable to hold the array.
2. Create a new array object and assign it to the array variable.
3. Store things in that array.

Declaring Array Variables

The first step in creating an array is creating a variable that will hold the array, just as you would any other variable. Array variables indicate the type of object the array will hold (just as they do for any variable) and the name of the array, followed by empty brackets ([ ]). The following are all typical array variable declarations:

```
String difficultWords[];

Point hits[];

int temps[];
```

An alternate method of defining an array variable is to put the brackets after the type instead of after the variable. They are equivalent, but this latter form is often much more readable. So, for example, these three declarations could be written like this:

```
String[] difficultWords;

Point[] hits;

int[] temps;
```

Creating Array Objects

The second step is to create an array object and assign it to that variable. There are two ways to do this:

- ☐ Using new
- ☐ Directly initializing the contents of that array

The first way is to use the new operator to create a new instance of an array:

```
String[] names = new String[10];
```

That line creates a new array of Strings with 10 slots (sometimes called elements). When you create a new array object using new, you must indicate how many slots that array will hold. This line does not put actual String objects in the slots—you'll have to do that later.

Array objects can contain primitive types such as integers or booleans, just as they can contain objects:

```
int[] temps = new int[99];
```

When you create an array object using new, all its slots are initialized for you (0 for numeric arrays, false for boolean, '\0' for character arrays, and null for objects). You can then assign actual values or objects to the slots in that array. You can also create an array and initialize its contents at the same time. Instead of using new to create the new array object, enclose the elements of the array inside braces, separated by commas:

```
String[] chiles = { "jalapeno", "anaheim", "serrano",
    "habanero", "thai" };
```

TECHNICAL NOTE | Note that the Java keyword null refers to a null object (and can be used for any object reference). It is not equivalent to zero or the '\0' character as the NULL constant is in C.

Each of the elements inside the braces must be of the same type and must be the same type as the variable that holds that array (the Java compiler will complain if they're not). An array the size of the number of elements you've included will be automatically created for you. This example creates an array of String objects named chiles that contains five elements.

Accessing Array Elements

Once you have an array with initial values, you can test and change the values in each slot of that array. To get at a value stored within an array, use the array subscript expression ([ ]):

```
myArray[subscript];
```

The myArray part of this expression is a variable holding an array object, although it can also be an expression that results in an array. The subscript part of the expression, inside the brackets, specifies the number of the slot within the array to access. Array subscripts start with 0, as they do in C and C++. So, an array with 10 elements has 10 array slots accessed using subscript 0 to 9.

Note that all array subscripts are checked when your Java program is run to make sure that they are inside the boundaries of the array (greater than or equal to 0 but less than the array's length). Unlike in C, it is impossible in Java to access or assign a value to an array slot outside the boundaries of the array (thereby avoiding a lot of the common problems and bugs that result from overrunning the bounds of an array in C-like languages). Note the following two statements, for example:

```
String[] arr = new String[10];
arr[10] = "eggplant";
```

A program with that last statement in it produces an error at that line when you try to run it. (Actually, to be more technically correct, it throws an exception. You'll learn more about exceptions on Day 18, "Multithreading.") The array stored in arr has only 10 slots numbered from 0, the element at subscript 10 doesn't exist.

If the array subscript is calculated at runtime (for example, as part of a loop) and ends up outside the boundaries of the array, the Java interpreter also produces an error.

How can you keep from accidentally overrunning the end of an array in your own programs? You can test for the length of the array in your programs using the length instance variable—it's available for all array objects, regardless of type:

```
int len = arr.length // returns 10
```

However, just to reiterate: The length of the array is 10, but its subscript can only go up to 9. Arrays start numbering from 0. Whenever you work with arrays, keep this in mind and subtract 1 from the length of the array to get its largest element.

Changing Array Elements

To assign an element value to a particular array slot, merely put an assignment statement after the array access expression:

```
myarray[1] = 15;
sentence[0] = "The";
sentence[10] = sentence[0];
```

An important thing to note is that an array of objects in Java is an array of references to those objects (similar in some ways to an array of pointers in C or C++). When you assign a value to a slot in an array, you're creating a reference to that object, just as you do for a plain variable. When you move values around inside arrays (as in that last line), you just reassign the reference; you don't copy the value from one slot to another. Arrays of primitive types such as ints or floats do copy the values from one slot to another.

Arrays of references to objects, as opposed to the objects themselves, are particularly useful because you can have multiple references to the same objects both inside and outside arrays. For example, you can assign an object contained in an array to a variable and refer to that same object by using either the variable or the array position.

Got it? Arrays are pretty simple to create and modify, but they provide an enormous amount of functionality for Java. You'll find yourself running into arrays a lot the more you use Java.

To finish up the discussion on arrays, here's a simple program that shows how to create, initialize, modify, and examine parts of an array. Listing 5.1 has the code.

TYPE   **Listing 5.1. Various simple array operations.**

```
 1: class ArrayTest {
 2:
 3:     String[] firstNames = { "Dennis", "Grace", "Bjarne", "James" };
 4:     String[] lastNames = new String[firstNames.length];
 5:
 6:     void printNames() {
 7:       int i = 0;
 8:        System.out.println(firstNames[i]
 9:           + " " + lastNames[i]);
10:        i++;
11:        System.out.println(firstNames[i]
12:           + " " + lastNames[i]);
13:        i++;
14:        System.out.println(firstNames[i]
15:           + " " + lastNames[i]);
16:        i++;
```

continues

Listing 5.1. continued

```
17:      System.out.println(firstNames[i]
18:          + " " + lastNames[i]);
19:    }
20:
21:    public static void main (String args[]) {
22:      ArrayTest a = new ArrayTest();
23:       a.printNames();
24:       System.out.println("----------");
25:       a.lastNames[0] = "Ritchie";
26:       a.lastNames[1] = "Hopper";
27:     a.lastNames[2] = "Stroustrup";
28:       a.lastNames[3] = "Gosling";
29:       a.printNames();
30:    }
31:}
```

OUTPUT
```
Dennis null
Grace null
Bjarne null
James null
----------
Dennis Ritchie
Grace Hopper
Bjarne Stroustrup
James Gosling
```

ANALYSIS This somewhat verbose example shows you how to create and use arrays. The class we've created here, ArrayTest, has two instance variables that hold arrays of String objects. The first, called firstNames, is declared and initialized in the same line (line 3) to contain four strings. The second instance variable, lastNames, is declared and created in line 4, but no initial values are placed in the slots. Note also that we created the lastNames array to have exactly the same number of slots as the firstNames array by using the firstNames.length variable as the initial array index. The length instance variable on array objects returns the number of slots in the array.

The ArrayTest class also has two methods: printNames() and main(). printNames(), defined in lines 6 through 19, is a utility method that does nothing but go through the firstNames and lastNames arrays sequentially, printing the values of each slot, one name per line. Note that the array index we've defined here (i) is initially set to 0 because Java array slots all start numbering from 0.

Finally, there is main(), which performs the actual actions of this example. The main() method here does four things:

- Line 22 creates an initial instance of `ArrayTest`, so we can set and modify its instance variables and call its methods.

- Line 23 calls `printNames()` to show what the object looks like initially. The result is the first four lines of the output; note that the `firstNames` array was initialized, but the values in `lastNames` are all `null`. If you don't initialize an array when you declare it, the values of the initial slots will be empty (or, actually, `null` for object arrays, `0` for numbers, and `false` for booleans).

- Lines 25 through 28 set the values of each of the slots in the `lastNames` array to actual strings.

- Finally, line 29 calls `printNames()` once again to show that the `lastNames` array is now full of values, and each first and last name prints as you would expect. The results are shown in the last four lines of the output.

NOTE

> Who are the people in this example? They're inventors of computer programming languages. Dennis Ritchie is the inventor of C, Bjarne Stroustrup did C++, Grace Hopper is credited with COBOL, and, finally, James Gosling is the principal designer of Java.

One other note I should make about Listing 5.1 is that it's a terrible example of programming style. Usually when you deal with arrays you do not hard code the number of elements into the code as we have here; instead you use a loop to go through each element of the array in turn. This makes the code a lot shorter and, in many cases, easier to read. You'll learn about loops later in this section, and we'll rewrite this example so that it works more flexibly.

Multidimensional Arrays

One last thing to note about arrays before we move on to the rest of this lesson is about multidimensional arrays. Java does not directly support multidimensional arrays. However, you can declare and create an array of arrays (and those arrays can contain arrays, and so on, for however many dimensions you need) and access the arrays as you would C-style multidimensional arrays:

```
int coords[][] = new int[12][12];
coords[0][0] = 1;
coords[0][1] = 2;
```

Block Statements

Before we launch into the last two-thirds of this lesson, let's take a small detour into a topic I haven't mentioned a whole lot up to this point (but that will be important later on): block statements.

A block statement is simply a group of Java statements surrounded by braces ({}). You've seen blocks a whole lot already; you've used a block statement to contain the variables and methods in a class definition, and inside that block you've also used blocks to hold the body of a method definition. The opening brace opens the block, and the closing brace closes the nearest closing block. Easy, right?

You can also use blocks even further, inside method definitions. The rule is that you can use a block anywhere a single statement would go. Each statement inside the block is then executed sequentially.

NEW TERM   A *block statement* is a group of individual Java statements enclosed in braces ({}). You can put a block statement anywhere a single statement can go.

So what's the difference between using a group of individual statements and using a block? The block creates a new local variable scope for the statements inside it. This means that you can declare and use local variables inside a block, and those variables will cease to exist after the block is finished executing. For example, here's a block inside a method definition that declares a new variable y. You cannot use y outside the block in which it's declared:

```
void testblock() {
    int x = 10;
    { // start of block
      int y = 50;
      System.out.println("inside the block:");
      System.out.println("x:" + x);
      System.out.println("y:" + y);
    } // end of block
}
```

Blocks are not usually used in this way—alone in a method definition, with random variable declarations inside them. You've mostly seen blocks up to this point surrounding class and method definitions, but another very common use of block statements is in the control flow constructs you'll learn about in the remainder of today's lesson.

`if` Conditionals

The `if` conditional statement is used when you want to execute different bits of code based on a simple test. `if` conditions are nearly identical to `if` statements in C: They contain the keyword `if`, followed by a boolean test, followed by either a single statement or a block statement to execute if the test is `true`. Here's a simple example that prints the message `x is smaller than y` only if the value of x is less than the value of y:

```
if (x < y)
    System.out.println("x is smaller than y");
```

An optional `else` keyword provides the alternative statement to execute if the test is `false`:

```
if (x < y)
    System.out.println("x is smaller than y");
else System.out.println("y is bigger");
```

NEW TERM The `if` *conditional* executes different bits of code based on the result of a single boolean test.

TECHNICAL NOTE The difference between `if` conditionals in Java and C or C++ is that the test must return a boolean value (`true` or `false`). Unlike in C, the test cannot return an integer.

Using `if`, you can only include a single statement as the code to execute after the test (in this case, the `System.out.println()` method for each one). But because a block can appear anywhere a single statement can, if you want to do more than just one thing (as you usually will), you can enclose those statements inside a block:

```
if (engineState == true )
    System.out.println("Engine is already on.");
else {
    System.out.println("Now starting Engine.");
    if (gasLevel >= 1)
        engineState = true;
    else System.out.println("Low on gas! Can't start engine.");
}
```

This example uses the test (`engineState == true`). For boolean tests of this type, a common shortcut is merely to include the first part of the expression rather than explicitly test its value against `true` or `false`. Because it's a boolean variable, it automatically returns `true` or `false` all by itself, so you don't have to explicitly test it for that value. Here's a shorter version of the previous code, with the test replaced with the shorthand version:

```
if (engineState)
    System.out.println("Engine is on.");
else System.out.println("Engine is off.");
```

Listing 5.2 shows another simple example—this one in full application form. The `Peeper` class contains one utility method called `peepMe()`, which tests a value to see if it's even. If it is, it prints `Peep!` to the screen.

TYPE **Listing 5.2. The Peeper class.**

```
1: class Peeper {
2:
3:     void peepMe(int val) {
4:         System.out.println("Value is "
5:             + val + ". ");
6:         if (val % 2 == 0)
7:             System.out.println("Peep!");
8:     }
9:
10:     public static void main (String args[]) {
11:         Peeper p = new Peeper();
12:
13:         p.peepMe(1);
14:         p.peepMe(2);
15:          p.peepMe(54);
16:         p.peepMe(77);
17:         p.peepMe(1346);
18:     }
19: }
```

OUTPUT
```
Value is 1.
Value is 2.
Peep!
Value is 54.
Peep!
Value is 77.
Value is 1346.
Peep!
```

ANALYSIS The heart of the Peeper class is the peepMe() method (lines 3 through 8), where values are tested and an appropriate message is printed. Unlike the methods you've defined in previous examples, note that the definition of peepMe() includes a single integer argument (see line 3). The peepMe() method starts by printing out the value that was passed to it. Then that argument is tested, using an if conditional, to see if it's an even number. (The modulus test, as you'll remember from Day 3, "Java Basics," returns the remainder of the division of its operands. So if the remainder of a number divided by 2 is 0, it's an even number.) If the number is even, Peep! is printed (you'll learn more about defining methods with arguments tomorrow).

We'll use a main() method, as always, in this application to create a new instance of Peeper and test it, calling the peepMe() method repeatedly with different values. In the output, only the values that are even get a Peep! message.

The Conditional Operator

An alternative to using the `if` and `else` keywords in a conditional statement is to use the *conditional operator*, sometimes called the *ternary operator* (*ternary* means three; the conditional operator has three parts).

The conditional operator is an expression, meaning that it returns a value (unlike the more general `if`, which can only result in a statement or block being executed). The conditional operator is most useful for very short or simple conditionals and looks like this:

```
test ? trueresult : falseresult;
```

test is a boolean expression that returns `true` or `false`, just like the test in the `if` statement. If the test is `true`, the conditional operator returns the value of *trueresult*; if it's `false`, it returns the value of *falseresult*. For example, the following conditional tests the values of x and y, returns the smaller of the two, and assigns that value to the variable `smaller`:

```
int smaller = x < y ? x : y;
```

The conditional operator has a very low precedence; that is, it's usually evaluated only after all its subexpressions are evaluated. The only operators lower in precedence are the assignment operators. See the precedence chart in Day 3's lesson for a refresher on precedence of all the operators.

`switch` Conditionals

A common programming practice in any language is to test a variable against some value, and if it doesn't match that value, to test it again against a different value, and if it doesn't match that one to make yet another test, and so on until it matches with the right result. Using only `if` statements, this can become unwieldy, depending on how it's formatted and how many different options you have to test. For example, you might end up with a set of `if` statements something like this or longer:

```
if (oper == '+')
  addargs(arg1, arg2);
else if (oper == '-')
   subargs(arg1, arg2);
else if (oper == '*')
   multargs(arg1, arg2);
else if (oper == '/')
   divargs(arg1, arg2);
```

This form of `if` statement is called a *nested* `if` because each `else` statement in turn contains yet another `if`, and so on, until all possible tests have been made.

5

Many languages have a shorthand version of the nested `if` that is (somewhat) easier to read and allows you to group the tests and actions. Called a `switch` or `case` statement, in Java it's called `switch` and behaves as it does in C:

```
switch (test) {
    case valueOne:
      resultOne;
      break;
    case valueTwo:
      resultTwo;
      break;
    case valueThree:
      resultThree;
      break;
    ...
    default: defaultresult;
}
```

In the `switch` statement, the *test* (a variable or expression that evaluates to a `byte`, `char`, `short`, or `int`) is compared with each of the case values (`valueOne`, `valueTwo`, and so on) in turn. If a match is found, the statement (or statements) after the test is executed. If no match is found, the `default` statement is executed. The `default` is optional, so if there isn't a match in any of the cases and `default` doesn't exist, the `switch` statement completes without doing anything.

Note that the significant limitation of the `switch` in Java is that the tests and values can be only simple primitive types (and then only primitive types that are automatically castable to `int`). You cannot use larger primitive types (`long`, `float`), strings, or other objects within a `switch`, nor can you test for any relationship other than simple equality. This limits the usefulness of `switch`; nested `ifs` can work for any kind of test on any type.

Here's a simple example of a `switch` statement similar to the nested `if` shown earlier:

```
switch (oper) {
    case '+':
        addargs(arg1, arg2);
        break;
    case '-':
        subargs(arg1, arg2);
        break;
    case '*':
        multargs(arg1, arg2);
        break;
    case '/':
        divargs(arg1, arg2);
        break;
 }
```

There are two things to be aware of in this example: The first is that after each case, you can include a single result statement or as many as you need. Unlike with `if`, you don't need to surround multiple statements with braces for it to work. The second thing to note about this example is the `break` statement included at the end of every case. Without the explicit break, once a match is made, the statements for that match (*and also* all the statements further down in the `switch` for all the other cases) are executed until a `break` or the end of the `switch` is found. In some cases, this may be exactly what you want to do, but in most cases, you'll want to make sure to include the `break` so that only the statements you want to be executed are actually executed (break, which you'll learn about in the section "Breaking Out of Loops," stops execution at the current point and jumps to the code outside of the next closing bracket (`}`)).

One handy use of allowing a `switch` to continue processing statements after a match is found occurs when you want multiple values to match to the same statements. In this instance, you can use multiple case lines with no result, and the `switch` will execute the first statement it finds. For example, in the following `switch` statement, the string `"x is an even number."` is printed if x has a value of 2, 4, 6, or 8. All other values of x print the string `"x is an odd number."`:

```
switch (x) {
    case 2:
    case 4:
    case 6:
    case 8:
        System.out.println("x is an even number.");
        break;
    default: System.out.println("x is an odd number.");
}
```

Listing 5.3 shows yet another example of a `switch`. This class, called `NumberReader`, converts integer values to their actual English word equivalents using a method called `convertIt()`.

TYPE   **Listing 5.3. The `NumberReader` class.**

```
 1: class NumberReader {
 2:
 3:     String convertNum(int val) {
 4:         switch (val) {
 5:             case 0: return "zero ";
 6:             case 1: return "one ";
 7:             case 2: return "two ";
 8:             case 3: return "three ";
 9:             case 4: return "four ";
10:             case 5: return "five ";
11:             case 6: return "six ";
12:             case 7: return "seven ";
13:             case 8: return "eight ";
14:             case 9: return "nine ";
15:             default: return " ";
16:         }
17:     }
18:
```

continues

Listing 5.3. continued

```
19:    public static void main (String args[]) {
20:       NumberReader n = new NumberReader();
21:       String num = n.convertNum(4) + n.convertNum(1)  + n.convertNum(5);
22:       System.out.println("415 converts to " + num);
23:    }
24:}
```

OUTPUT 415 converts to four one five

ANALYSIS The heart of this example is, of course, the main switch statement in the middle of the convertNum() method in lines 4 through 16. This switch statement takes the integer argument that was passed into convertNum() and, when it finds a match, returns the appropriate string value. (Note that this method is defined to return a string as opposed to the other methods you've defined up to this point, which didn't return anything. You'll learn more about this tomorrow.)

So where are the break statements? You don't need them here because you're using return instead. return is similar to break except that it breaks out of the entire method definition and returns a single value. Again, you'll learn more about this tomorrow when you learn all about how to define methods.

At this point you've probably seen enough main() methods to know what's going on, but let's run through this one quickly.

Line 20 creates a new instance of the NumberReader class.

Line 21 defines a string called num that will be the concatenation of the string values of three numbers. Each number is converted using a call to the convertNum() method.

Finally, line 22 prints out the result.

for **Loops**

The for loop, as in C, repeats a statement or block of statements until a condition is matched. for loops are frequently used for simple iterations in which you repeat a block of statements a certain number of times and then stop, but you can use for loops for just about any kind of loop.

The for loop in Java looks roughly like this:

```
for (initialization; test; increment) {
    statements;
}
```

5

The start of the `for` loop has three parts:

- [ ] `initialization` is an expression that initializes the start of the loop. If you have a loop index variable to keep track of how many times the loop has occurred, this expression might declare and initialize it—for example, `int i = 0`. Variables that you declare in this part of the `for` loop are local to the loop itself; they cease existing after the loop is finished executing.

- [ ] `test` is the test that occurs before each pass of the loop. The test must be a boolean expression or function that returns a boolean value—for example, `i < 10`. If the test is `true`, the loop executes. Once the test is `false`, the loop stops executing.

- [ ] `increment` is any expression or function call. Commonly, the increment is used to change the value of the loop index to bring the state of the loop closer to returning `false` and completing.

The statement part of the `for` loop is the statements that are executed each time the loop iterates. Just as with `if`, you can only include one statement, although a block will work just fine as well.

Remember the example in the section on arrays where I said that iterating over the contents of an array is usually done with a loop? Here's an example of a `for` loop that does just that—it initializes all the values of a `String` array to null strings:

```
String strArray[] = new String[10]; \\ the array
int i; // loop index

for (i = 0; i < strArray.length; i++)
    strArray[i] = "";
```

In this example, the variable I keeps track of the number of times the loop has occurred; it also makes a convenient index for the array itself. Here, we start the `for` loop with an index of I. The test for when the `for` loop will end is whether the current index is less than the length of the array (once the index is bigger than the array, you should stop), and the increment is simply to add 1 to the index each time. Then, for every loop you can put a null string (`""`) into the array at the given slot.

Any of the parts of the `for` loop can be empty statements; that is, you can simply include a semicolon with no expression or statement, and that part of the `for` loop will be ignored. Note that if you do use a null statement in your `for` loop, you may have to initialize or increment any loop variables or loop indices yourself elsewhere in the program.

You can also have an empty statement for the body of your `for` loop, if everything you want to do is in the first line of that loop. For example, here's one that finds the first prime number higher than 4000 (it calls a method called `notPrime()`, which will theoretically have a way of figuring that out):

5

```
for (i = 4001; notPrime(i); i += 2)
    ;
```

Note that a common mistake in C that also occurs in Java is to accidentally put a semicolon after the first line of the `for` loop:

```
for (i = 0; i < 10; i++);
    System.out.println("Loop!");
```

Because the first semicolon ends the loop with an empty statement, the loop doesn't actually do anything. The `println()` function will be printed only once because it's actually outside the `for` loop entirely. Be careful not to make this mistake in your own Java programs.

To finish up `for` loops, let's rewrite that example with the names from the array section. The original example is long and repetitive and only works with an array four elements long. This version, shown in Listing 5.4, is shorter and more flexible (but it returns the same output).

TYPE   **Listing 5.4. A modified array test with loops.**

```
 1: class NamesLoop {
 2:
 3:     String[] firstNames = { "Dennis", "Grace", "Bjarne", "James" };
 4:     String[] lastNames = new String[firstNames.length];
 5:
 6:     void printNames() {
 7:       for (int i = 0; i < firstNames.length; i++)
 8:           System.out.println(firstNames[i] + " " + lastNames[i]);
 9:     }
10:
11:   public static void main (String args[]) {
12:       ArrayTest a = new ArrayTest();
13:       a.printNames();
14:       System.out.println("----------");
15:       a.lastNames[0] = "Ritchie";
16:       a.lastNames[1] = "Hopper";
17:     a.lastNames[2] = "Stroustrup";
18:       a.lastNames[3] = "Gosling";
19:
20:       a.printNames();
21:}
22:}
```

OUTPUT
```
Dennis null
Grace null
Bjarne null
James null
----------
Dennis Ritchie
Grace Hopper
Bjarne Stroustrup
James Gosling
```

5

ANALYSIS The only difference between this example and Listing 5.1 is in the `printNames()` method. Instead of going through the array slots one by one, this example uses a `for` loop to iterate through the array one slot at a time, stopping at the last element in the array. Using a more general-purpose loop to iterate over an array allows you to use `printNames()` for any array of any size and still have it print all the elements.

`while` and `do` Loops

Finally, there are `while` and `do` loops. `while` and `do` loops, like `for` loops, repeat the execution of a block of Java code until a specific condition is met. Whether you use a `for` loop, a `while`, or a `do` is mostly a matter of your programming style.

`while` and `do` loops are exactly the same as in C and C++ except that their test conditions must be booleans.

`while` Loops

The `while` loop is used to repeat a statement or block of statements as long as a particular condition is `true`. `while` loops look like this:

```
while (condition) {
    bodyOfLoop;
}
```

The `condition` is a boolean test because it is in the `if` and `for` constructions. If the test returns `true`, the `while` loop executes the statements in `bodyOfLoop` and then tests the condition again, repeating until the condition is `false`. I've shown the `while` loop here with a block statement because it's most commonly used, although you can use a single statement in place of the block.

Listing 5.5 shows an example of a `while` loop that copies the elements of an array of integers (in `array1`) to an array of `float`s (in `array2`), casting each element to a `float` as it goes. The one catch is that if any of the elements in the first array is 0, the loop will immediately exit at that point.

TYPE **Listing 5.5. `while` loops to copy array elements.**

```
1: class CopyArrayWhile {
2:   public static void main (String args[]) {
3:       int[] array1 = { 5, 7, 3, 6, 0, 3, 2, 1 };
4:       float[] array2 = new float[array1.length];
5:
6:        System.out.print("array1: [ ");
```

continues

Listing 5.5. continued

```
 7:          for (int i = 0; i < array1.length; i++) {
 8:              System.out.print(array1[i] + " ");
 9:          }
10:          System.out.println("]");
11:
12:          System.out.print("array2: [ ");
13:          int count = 0;
14:          while ( count < array1.length && array1[count] != 0) {
15:                  array2[count] = (float) array1[count];
16:                  System.out.print(array2[count++] + " ");
17:          }
18:            System.out.println("]");
19:      }
20:}
```

OUTPUT   array1: [5 7 3 6 0 3 2 1]
              array2: [5 7 3 6]

ANALYSIS   I've done all the work here in main() to make things shorter. Here's what's going
               on here:

Lines 3 and 4, declare the arrays; array1 is an array of ints, which I've initialized to some
suitable numbers. array2, or floats, is the same length as array1, but doesn't have any initial
values.

Lines 6 through 10 are for output purposes; they simply iterate through array1 using a for
loop to print out its values.

Lines 13 through 17 are where the interesting stuff happens. This bunch of statements both
assigns the values of array2 (converting the numbers to floats along the array) and prints it
out at the same time. We start with a count variable, which keeps track of the array index
elements. The test in the while loop keeps track of the two conditions for existing the loop,
where those two conditions are running out of elements in array1 or encountering a 0 in
array1 (remember, that was part of the original description of what this program does). We
can use the logical conditional && to keep track of the test; remember that && makes sure both
conditions are true before the entire expression is true. If either one is false, the expression
returns false and the loop exits.

So what goes on in this particular example? The output shows that the first four elements in
array1 were copied to array2, but there was a 0 in the middle that stopped the loop from going
any further. Without the 0, array2 should end up with all the same elements as array1.

Note that if the while loop's test is initially false the first time it is tested (for example, if the
first element in that first array is 0), the body of the while loop will never be executed. If you
need to execute the loop at least once, you can do one of two things:

☐ Duplicate the body of the loop outside the `while` loop.

☐ Use a do loop (which is described in the following section).

The do loop is considered the better solution of the two.

do...while **Loops**

The do loop is just like a `while` loop, except that do executes a given statement or block until the condition is `false`. The main difference is that `while` loops test the condition before looping, making it possible that the body of the loop will never execute if the condition is `false` the first time it's tested. do loops run the body of the loop at least once before testing the condition. do loops look like this:

```
do {
    bodyOfLoop;
} while (condition);
```

Here, the `bodyOfLoop` part is the statements that are executed with each iteration. It's shown here with a block statement because it's most commonly used that way, but you can substitute the braces for a single statement as you can with the other control-flow constructs. The condition is a boolean test. If it returns `true`, the loop is run again. If it returns `false`, the loop exits. Keep in mind that with do loops, the body of the loop executes at least once.

Listing 5.6 shows a simple example of a do loop that prints a message each time the loop iterates (10 times, for this example):

TYPE | **Listing 5.6. A simple do loop.**

```
 1: class DoTest {
 2:     public static void main (String args[]) {
 3:         int x = 1;
 4:
 5:         do {
 6:             System.out.println("Looping, round " + x);
 7:             x++;
 8:         } while (x <= 10);
 9:     }
10: }
```

OUTPUT
```
Looping, round 1
Looping, round 2
Looping, round 3
Looping, round 4
Looping, round 5
Looping, round 6
Looping, round 7
Looping, round 8
Looping, round 9
Looping, round 10
```

Breaking Out of Loops

In all the loops (`for`, `while`, and `do`), the loop ends when the condition you're testing for is met. What happens if something odd occurs within the body of the loop and you want to exit the loop early? For that, you can use the `break` and `continue` keywords.

You've already seen `break` as part of the `switch` statement; it stops execution of the `switch`, and the program continues. The `break` keyword, when used with a loop, does the same thing—it immediately halts execution of the current loop. If you've nested loops within loops, execution picks up in the next outer loop; otherwise, the program merely continues executing the next statement after the loop.

For example, take that `while` loop that copied elements from an integer array into an array of floats until the end of the array or until a `0` is reached. You can instead test for that latter case inside the body of the `while` and then use a `break` to exit the loop:

```
int count = 0;
while (count < array1.length) {
    if (array1[count] == 0) {
        break;
    }
    array2[count] = (float) array1[count++];
}
```

`continue` is similar to `break` except that instead of halting execution of the loop entirely, the loop starts over at the next iteration. For `do` and `while` loops, this means that the execution of the block starts over again; for `for` loops, the increment and test expressions are evaluated and then the block is executed. `continue` is useful when you want to special-case elements within a loop. With the previous example of copying one array to another, you can test for whether the current element is `0` and restart the loop if you find it so that the resulting array will never contain zero. Note that because you're skipping elements in the first array, you now have to keep track of two different array counters:

```
int count1 = 0;
int count2 = 0;
while (count < array1.length) {
    if (array1[count1] == 0)  {
        continue;
        count1++
    }
    array2[count2++] = (float)array1[count1++];
}
```

Labeled Loops

Both `break` and `continue` can have an optional label that tells Java where to break to. Without a label, `break` jumps outside the nearest loop (to an enclosing loop or to the next statement outside the loop), and `continue` restarts the enclosing loop. Using labeled `break`s and `continues`, you can break to specific points outside nested loops or continue a loop outside the current loop.

To use a labeled loop, add the label before the initial part of the loop, with a colon between them. Then, when you use `break` or `continue`, add the name of the label after the keyword itself:

```
out:
    for (int i = 0; i <10; i++) {
        while (x < 50) {
            if (i * x == 400)
                break out;
            ...
        }
        ...
    }
```

In this snippet of code, the label `out` labels the outer loop. Then, inside both the `for` and the `while` loops, when a particular condition is met, a `break` causes the execution to break out of both loops and continue executing any code after both loops.

Here's another example: The program shown in Listing 5.7 contains a nested `for` loop. Inside the innermost loop, if the summed values of the two counters is greater than 4, both loops exit at once.

TYPE **Listing 5.7. A labeled loop example.**

```
 1: class LabelTest {
 2:     public static void main (String arg[]) {
 3:
 4:       foo:
 5:       for (int i = 1; i <= 5; i++)
 6:         for (int j = 1; j <= 3; j++) {
 7:             System.out.println("i is " + i + ", j is " + j);
 8:             if (( i + j) > 4)
 9:             break foo;
10:         }
11:       System.out.println("end of loops");
12:     }
13:}
```

OUTPUT
```
i is 1, j is 1
i is 1, j is 2
i is 1, j is 3
i is 2, j is 1
i is 2, j is 2
i is 2, j is 3
end of loops
```

As you can see, the loop iterated until the sum of i and j was greater than 4, and then both loops exited back to the outer block and the final message was printed.

Summary

Today you have learned about three main topics that you'll most likely use quite often in your own Java programs: arrays, conditionals, and loops.

You have learned how to declare an array variable, create and assign an array object to that variable, and access and change elements within that array.

Conditionals include the if and switch statements, with which you can branch to different parts of your program based on a boolean test.

Finally, you have learned about the for, while, and do loops, each of which enable you to execute a portion of your program repeatedly until a given condition is met.

Now that you've learned the small stuff, all that's left is to go over the bigger issues of declaring classes and creating methods within which instances of those classes can communicate with each other by calling methods. Get to bed early tonight, because tomorrow is going to be a wild ride.

Q&A

Q If arrays are objects, and you use new to create them, and they have an instance variable length, where is the Array class? I didn't see it in the Java class libraries.

A Arrays are implemented kind of weirdly in Java. The Array class is constructed automatically when your Java program runs; Array provides the basic framework for arrays, including the length variable. Additionally, each primitive type and object has an implicit subclass of Array that represents an array of that class or object. When you create a new array object, it may not have an actual class, but it behaves as if it does.

Q When you create an array, you have to give it the number of slots that the array has. What happens if you get halfway through your program and you've run out of slots in the array? Does the array get bigger automatically?

A No, arrays stay the same size throughout their existence. And, as I noted in the part of this lesson on arrays, you cannot access slots outside the bounds of the array, so adding extra elements to a full array will cause an error.

So what do you do if an array is full? You have to do it the hard way: Create a new array that's bigger than the initial one and copy all the elements from the old array to the new.

Optionally, you can use a data structure other than an array if you expect to have widely varying numbers of elements in the array. The Vector class, part of the java.util package, is a growable collection you can use in place of an array.

Q Does Java have gotos?

A The Java language defines the keyword goto, but it is not currently used for anything. In other words, no—Java does not have gotos.

Q I declared a variable inside a block statement for an if. When the if was done, the definition of that variable vanished. Where did it go?

A In technical terms, block statements form a new lexical scope. What this means is that if you declare a variable inside a block, it's only visible and usable inside that block. When the block finishes executing, all the variables you declared go away.

It's a good idea to declare most of your variables in the outermost block in which they'll be needed—usually at the top of a block statement. The exception might be very simple variables, such as index counters in for loops, where declaring them in the first line of the for loop is an easy shortcut.

Q Why can't you use switch with strings?

A Strings are objects, and switch in Java works only for the primitive types byte, char, short, and int. To compare strings, you have to use nested ifs, which enable more general expression tests, including string comparison.

Q It seems to me that a lot of for loops could be written as while loops, and vice versa.

A True. The for loop is actually a special case of while that enables you to iterate a loop a specific number of times. You could just as easily do this with a while and then increment a counter inside the loop. Either works equally well. This is mostly just a question of programming style and personal choice.

5

Day **6**

Creating Classes and Applications in Java

by Laura Lemay

In just about every lesson up to this point you've been creating Java applications—writing classes, creating instance variables and methods, and running those applications to perform simple tasks. Also up to this point, you've focused either on the very broad (general object-oriented theory) or the very minute (arithmetic and other expressions). Today you'll pull it all together and learn how and why to create classes by using the following basics:

☐ The parts of a class definition

☐ Declaring and using instance variables

☐ Defining and using methods

☐ Creating Java applications, including the main() method and how to pass arguments to a Java program from a command line

Defining Classes

Defining classes is pretty easy; you've seen how to do it a bunch of times in previous lessons. To define a class, use the `class` keyword and the name of the class:

```
class MyClassName {
...
}
```

By default, classes inherit from the `Object` class. If this class is a subclass of another specific class (that is, inherits from another class), use `extends` to indicate the superclass of this class:

```
class myClassName extends mySuperClassName {
...
}
```

NOTE
Java 1.1 will give you the ability to nest a class definition inside other classes—a useful construction when you're defining "adapter classes" that implement an interface. The flow of control from the inner class then moves automatically to the outer class. For more details (beyond this sketchy description), see the information at the 1.1 Preview Page at `http://java.sun.com/products/JDK/1.1/designspecs/`.

Creating Instance and Class Variables

A class definition with nothing in it is pretty dull; usually, when you create a class, you have something you want to add to make that class different from its superclasses. Inside each class definition are declarations and definitions for variables or methods or both—for the class *and* for each instance. In this section, you'll learn all about instance and class variables; the next section talks about methods.

Defining Instance Variables

On Day 3, "Java Basics," you learned how to declare and initialize local variables—that is, variables inside method definitions. Instance variables, fortunately, are declared and defined in almost exactly the same way as local variables; the main difference is their location in the class definition. Variables are considered instance variables if they are declared outside a method definition. Customarily, however, most instance variables are defined just after the first line of the class definition. For example, Listing 6.1 shows a simple class definition for the class `Bicycle`, which inherits from the class `PersonPoweredVehicle`. This class definition contains five instance variables:

- [ ] `bikeType`—The kind of bicycle this bicycle is—for example, `Mountain` or `Street`
- [ ] `chainGear`—The number of gears in the front
- [ ] `rearCogs`—The number of minor gears on the rear axle
- [ ] `currentGearFront` and `currentGearRear`—The gear the bike is currently in, both front and rear

TYPE **Listing 6.1. The `Bicycle` class.**

```
1: class Bicycle extends PersonPoweredVehicle {
2:     String bikeType;
3:     int chainGear;
4:     int rearCogs;
5:     int currentGearFront;
6:     int currentGearRear;
7: }
```

Constants

A *constant variable* or *constant* is a variable whose value never changes (which may seem strange given the meaning of the word *variable*). Constants are useful for defining shared values for all the methods of an object—for giving meaningful names to objectwide values that will never change. In Java, you can create constants only for instance or class variables, not for local variables.

NEW TERM A *constant* is a variable whose value never changes.

To declare a constant, use the `final` keyword before the variable declaration and include an initial value for that variable:

```
final float pi = 3.141592;
final boolean debug = false;
final int maxsize = 40000;
```

TECHNICAL NOTE

The only way to define constants in Java is by using the `final` keyword. Neither the C and C++ constructs for `#define` nor `const` are available in Java, although the `const` keyword is reserved to prevent you from accidentally using it.

Constants can be useful for naming various states of an object and then testing for those states. For example, suppose you have a test label that can be aligned left, right, or center. You can define those values as constant integers:

```
final int LEFT = 0;
final int RIGHT = 1;
final int CENTER = 2;
```

The variable alignment is then also declared as an `int`:

```
int alignment;
```

Then, later in the body of a method definition, you can either set the alignment:

```
this.alignment = CENTER;
```

or test for a given alignment:

```
switch (this.alignment) {
    case LEFT: // deal with left alignment
            ...
            break;
    case RIGHT: // deal with right alignment
            ...
            break;
    case CENTER: // deal with center alignment
            ...
            break;
}
```

Class Variables

As you have learned in previous lessons, class variables are global to a class and to all that class's instances. You can think of class variables as being even more global than instance variables. Class variables are good for communicating between different objects with the same class, or for keeping track of global states among a set of objects.

To declare a class variable, use the `static` keyword in the class declaration:

```
static int sum;
static final int maxObjects = 10;
```

Creating Methods

Methods, as you learned on Day 2, "Object-Oriented Programming and Java," define an object's behavior—what happens when that object is created and the various operations that object can perform during its lifetime. In this section, you'll get a basic introduction to method definition and how methods work; tomorrow, you'll go into more detail about advanced things you can do with methods.

Defining Methods

Method definitions have four basic parts:

- ☐ The name of the method
- ☐ The type of object or primitive type the method returns
- ☐ A list of parameters
- ☐ The body of the method

NOTE

To keep things simple today, I've left off two optional parts of the method definition: a modifier such as `public` or `private`, and the `throws` keyword, which indicates the exceptions a method can throw. You'll learn about these parts of a method definition in Week 3.

The first three parts of the method definition form what's called the method's *signature* and indicate the most important information about the method itself.

In other languages, the name of the method (or function, subroutine, or procedure) is enough to distinguish it from other methods in the program. In Java, you can have different methods that have the same name but a different return type or argument list, so all these parts of the method definition are important. This is called *method overloading*, and you'll learn more about it tomorrow.

NEW TERM A method's *signature* is a combination of the name of the method, the type of object or primitive data type this method returns, and a list of parameters.

Here's what a basic method definition looks like:

```
returntype methodname(type1 arg1, type2 arg2, type3 arg3..) {
    ...
}
```

The *returntype* is the type of value this method returns. It can be one of the primitive types, a class name, or `void` if the method does not return a value at all.

Note that if this method returns an array object, the array brackets can go either after the return type or after the parameter list; because the former way is considerably easier to read, it is used in the examples today (and throughout this book):

```
int[] makeRange(int lower, int upper) {...}
```

The method's parameter list is a set of variable declarations, separated by commas, inside parentheses. These parameters become local variables in the body of the method, whose values are the objects or values of primitives passed in when the method is called.

Inside the body of the method you can have statements, expressions, method calls to other objects, conditionals, loops, and so on—everything you've learned about in the previous lessons.

If your method has a real return type (that is, it has not been declared to return void), somewhere inside the body of the method you need to explicitly return a value. Use the return keyword to do this. Listing 6.2 shows an example of a class that defines a makeRange() method. makeRange() takes two integers—a lower bound and an upper bound—and creates an array that contains all the integers between those two boundaries (inclusive).

TYPE   **Listing 6.2. The RangeClass class.**

```
1: class RangeClass {
2:     int[] makeRange(int lower, int upper) {
3:         int arr[] = new int[ (upper - lower) + 1 ];
4:
5:         for (int i = 0; i < arr.length; i++) {
6:             arr[i] = lower++;
7:         }
8:         return arr;
9:     }
10:
11:     public static void main(String arg[]) {
12:         int theArray[];
13:         RangeClass theRange = new RangeClass();
14:
15:         theArray = theRange.makeRange(1, 10);
16:         System.out.print("The array: [ ");
17:         for (int i = 0; i < theArray.length; i++) {
18:             System.out.print(theArray[i] + " ");
19:         }
20:         System.out.println("]");
21:     }
22:
23: }
```

OUTPUT   The array: [1 2 3 4 5 6 7 8 9 10]

ANALYSIS   The main() method in this class tests the makeRange() method by creating a range where the lower and upper boundaries of the range are 1 and 10, respectively (see line 6), and then uses a for loop to print the values of the new array.

The this Keyword

In the body of a method definition, you may want to refer to the current object—the object in which the method is contained in the first place—to refer to that object's instance variables or to pass the current object as an argument to another method. To refer to the current object in these cases, you can use the `this` keyword. `this` can be used anywhere the current object might appear—in dot notation to refer to the object's instance variables, as an argument to a method, as the return value for the current method, and so on. Here's an example:

```
t = this.x;            // the x instance variable for this object
this.myMethod(this);   // call the myMethod method, defined in
                       // this class, and pass it the current
                       // object
return this;           // return the current object
```

In many cases you may be able to omit the `this` keyword entirely. You can refer to both instance variables and method calls defined in the current class simply by name; the `this` is implicit in those references. So the first two examples could be written like this:

```
t = x              // the x instance variable for this object
myMethod(this)     // call the myMethod method, defined in this
                   // class
```

NOTE

> Omitting the `this` keyword for instance variables depends on whether there are no variables of the same name declared in the local scope. See the next section for more details on variable scope.

Keep in mind that because `this` is a reference to the current *instance* of a class, you should only use it inside the body of an instance method definition. Class methods—that is, methods declared with the static keyword—cannot use `this`.

Variable Scope and Method Definitions

When you declare a variable, that variable always has a limited scope. Variable scope determines where that variable can be used. Variables with a local scope, for example, can only be used inside the block in which they were defined. Instance variables have a scope that extends to the entire class so they can be used by any of the methods within that class.

NEW TERM *Variable scope* determines where a variable can be used.

When you refer to a variable within your method definitions, Java checks for a definition of that variable first in the current scope (which may be a block, for example, inside a loop), then in the outer scopes up to the current method definition. If that variable is not a local variable, Java then checks for a definition of that variable as an instance or class variable in the current class, and then, finally, in each superclass in turn.

Because of the way Java checks for the scope of a given variable, it is possible for you to create a variable in a lower scope such that a definition of that same variable "hides" the original value of that variable. This can introduce subtle and confusing bugs into your code.

For example, note the small Java program in Listing 6.3.

TYPE **Listing 6.3. A variable scope example.**

```
 1: class ScopeTest {
 2:     int test = 10;
 3:
 4:     void printTest () {
 5:         int test = 20;
 6:         System.out.println("test = " + test);
 7:     }
 8:
 9:     public static void main (String args[]) {
10:         ScopeTest st = new ScopeTest();
11:         st.printTest();
12:     }
13: }
```

ANALYSIS In this class, you have two variables with the same name and definition: The first, an instance variable, has the name `test` and is initialized to the value `10`. The second is a local variable with the same name, but with the value `20`. Because the local variable hides the instance variable, the `println()` method will print that `test` is `20`.

The easiest way to get around this problem is to make sure you don't use the same names for local variables as you do for instance variables. Another way to get around this particular problem, however, is to use `this.test` to refer to the instance variable, and just `test` to refer to the local variable. By referring explicitly to the instance variable by its object scope you avoid the conflict.

A more insidious example of this variable naming problem occurs when you redefine a variable in a subclass that already occurs in a superclass. This can create very subtle bugs in your code—for example, you may call methods that are intended to change the value of an instance variable, but that change the wrong one. Another bug might occur when you cast an object from one class to another—the value of your instance variable may mysteriously change (because it was getting that value from the superclass instead of from your class). The best way to avoid this behavior is to make sure that when you define variables in a subclass you're aware of the variables in each of that class's superclasses and you don't duplicate what is already there.

Passing Arguments to Methods

When you call a method with object parameters, the variables you pass into the body of the method are passed by reference, which means that whatever you do to those objects inside the method affects the original objects as well. This includes arrays and all the objects that arrays contain; when you pass an array into a method and modify its contents, the original array is affected. (Note that primitive types are passed by value.)

Listing 6.4 is an example to demonstrate how this works.

TYPE **Listing 6.4. The** PassByReference **class.**

```
1: class PassByReference {
2:      int onetoZero(int arg[]) {
3:          int count = 0;
4:
5:          for (int i = 0; i < arg.length; i++) {
6:              if (arg[i] == 1) {
7:                  count++;
8:                  arg[i] = 0;
9:              }
10:         }
11:         return count;
12:     }
13:     public static void main (String arg[]) {
14:       int arr[] = { 1, 3, 4, 5, 1, 1, 7 };
15:         PassByReference test = new PassByReference();
16:         int numOnes;
17:
18:         System.out.print("Values of the array: [ ");
19:         for (int i = 0; i < arr.length; i++) {
20:             System.out.print(arr[i] + " ");
21:         }
22:         System.out.println("]");
23:
24:       numOnes = test.onetoZero(arr);
25:         System.out.println("Number of Ones = " + numOnes);
26:         System.out.print("New values of the array: [ ");
27:         for (int i = 0; i < arr.length; i++) {
28:             System.out.print(arr[i] + " ");
29:         }
30:         System.out.println("]");
31:     }
32:}
```

6

OUTPUT
```
Values of the array: [ 1 3 4 5 1 1 7 ]
Number of Ones = 3
New values of the array: [ 0 3 4 5 0 0 7 ]
```

ANALYSIS Note the method definition for the onetoZero() method in lines 2 to 12, which takes a single array as an argument. The onetoZero() method does two things:

☐ It counts the number of 1s in the array and returns that value.

☐ If it finds a 1, it substitutes a 0 in its place in the array.

The `main()` method in the `PassByReference` class tests the use of the `onetoZero()` method. Let's go over the `main()` method line by line so that you can see what is going on and why the output shows what it does.

Lines 14 through 16 set up the initial variables for this example. The first one is an array of integers; the second one is an instance of the class `PassByReference`, which is stored in the variable test. The third is a simple integer to hold the number of ones in the array.

Lines 18 through 22 print out the initial values of the array; you can see the output of these lines in the first line of the output.

Line 24 is where the real work takes place; this is where you call the `onetoZero()` method, defined in the object test, and pass it the array stored in `arr`. This method returns the number of ones in the array, which you'll then assign to the variable numOnes.

Got it so far? Line 25 prints out the number of 1s (that is, the value you got back from the `onetoZero()` method). It returns 3, as you would expect.

The last bunch of lines print out the array values. Because a reference to the array object is passed to the method, changing the array inside that method changes that original copy of the array. Printing out the values in lines 27 through 30 proves this—that last line of output shows that all the 1s in the array have been changed to 0s.

Class Methods

Just as you have class and instance variables, you also have class and instance methods, and the differences between the two types of methods are analogous. Class methods are available to any instance of the class itself and can be made available to other classes. Therefore, some class methods can be used anywhere, regardless of whether an instance of the class exists.

For example, the Java class libraries include a class called `Math`. The `Math` class defines a whole set of math operations that can be used in any program or the various number types:

```
float root = Math.sqrt(453.0);
System.out.print("The larger of x and y is " + Math.max(x, y));
```

To define class methods, use the `static` keyword in front of the method definition, just as you would create a class variable. For example, that max class method might have a signature like this:

```
static int max(int arg1, int arg2) { ... }
```

Java supplies "wrapper" classes for each of the primitive data types—for example, classes for `Integer`, `Float`, and `boolean`. Using class methods defined in those classes, you can convert to and from objects and primitive types. For example, the parseInt() class method in the Integer class takes a string and a radix (base) and returns the value of that string as an integer:

```
int count = Integer.parseInt("42", 10) // returns 42
```

Most methods that operate on a particular object, or that affect that object, should be defined as instance methods. Methods that provide some general utility but do not directly affect an instance of that class are better declared as class methods.

Creating Java Applications

Now that you know how to create classes, objects, and class and instance variables and methods, all that's left is to put it together into something that can actually run—in other words, to create a Java application.

Applications, to refresh your memory, are Java programs that run on their own. Applications are different from applets, which require a Java-enabled browser to view them. Much of what you've been creating up to this point have been Java applications; next week you'll dive into how to create applets. (Applets require a bit more background in order to get them to interact with the browser and draw and update with the graphics system. You'll learn all of this next week.)

A Java application consists of one or more classes and can be as large or as small as you want it to be. While all the Java applications you've created up to this point do nothing but output some characters to the screen or to a window, you can also create Java applications that use windows, graphics, and user interface elements, just as applets do (you'll learn how to do this next week). The only thing you need to make a Java application run, however, is one class that serves as the "jumping-off" point for the rest of your Java program. If your program is small enough, it may need only the one class.

The jumping-off class for your application needs only one thing: a main() method. When you run your compiled Java class (using the Java interpreter), the main() method is the first thing that gets called. None of this should be much of a surprise to you at this point; you've been creating Java applications with main() methods all along.

The signature for the main() method always looks like this:

```
public static void main(String args[]) {...}
```

Here's a run-down of the parts of the main() method:

- [ ] `public` means that this method is available to other classes and objects. The `main()` method must be declared `public`. You'll learn more about `public` and `private` methods in Week 3.
- [ ] `static` means that this is a class method.
- [ ] `void` means that the `main()` method doesn't return anything.
- [ ] `main()` takes one parameter: an array of strings. This argument is used for command-line arguments, which you'll learn about in the next section.

The body of the `main()` method contains any code you need to get your application started: initializing variables or creating instances of any classes you may have declared.

When Java executes the `main()` method, keep in mind that `main()` is a class method—the class that holds it is not automatically instantiated when your program runs. If you want to treat that class as an object, you have to instantiate it in the `main()` method yourself (all the examples up to this point have done this).

Helper Classes

Your Java application can have only one class, or, in the case of most larger programs, it may be made up of several classes, where different instances of each class are created and used while the application is running. You can create as many classes as you want for your program, and as long as they are in the same directory or listed in your `CLASSPATH`, Java will be able to find them when your program runs. Note, however, that only the one jumping-off class, only the class you use with the Java bytecode interpreter needs a `main()` method. Remember, `main()` is used only so that Java can start up the program and create an initial object; after that, the methods inside the various classes and objects take over. While you can include `main()` methods in helper classes, they will be ignored when the program actually runs.

Java Applications and Command-Line Arguments

Because Java applications are standalone programs, it's useful to be able to pass arguments or options to a program to determine how the program is going to run, or to enable a generic program to operate on many different kinds of input. Command-line arguments can be used for many different purposes—for example, to turn on debugging input, to indicate a filename to read or write from, or for any other information that you might want your Java program to know.

Passing Arguments to Java Programs

How you pass arguments to a Java application varies based on the platform you're running Java on. On Windows and UNIX, you can pass arguments to the Java program via the command line; in the Macintosh, the Java Runner gives you a special window to type those arguments in.

  To pass arguments to a Java program on Windows or Solaris, append them to the command line when you run your Java program:

```
java Myprogram argumentOne 2 three
```

 To pass arguments to a Java program on the Macintosh, double-click the compiled Java class file. The Java Runner will start up, and you'll get the dialog box shown in Figure 6.1.

Figure 6.1.

Java Runner arguments.

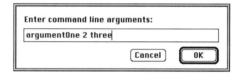

Enter your arguments, separated by spaces, into this box.

In these examples, you've passed three arguments to your program: argumentOne, the number 2, and three. Note that a space separates arguments, so if you use the phrase Java is cool as your arguments, you'll get three of them.

To group arguments, surround them with double-quotes. So, for example, the argument "Java is cool" produces one argument for your program to deal with. The double-quotes are stripped off before the argument gets to your Java program.

Handling Arguments in Your Java Program

How does Java handle arguments? It stores them in an array of strings, which is passed to the main() method in your Java program. Remember the signature for main():

```
public static void main (String args[]) {...}
```

Here, args is the name of the array of strings that contains the list of arguments. You can actually call it anything you want.

Inside your main() method, you can then handle the arguments your program was given by iterating over the array of arguments and handling those arguments any way you want. For example, Listing 6.5 is a really simple class that prints out the arguments it gets, one per line.

6

Listing 6.5. The EchoArgs class.

```
1: class EchoArgs {
2:     public static void main(String args[]) {
3:         for (int i = 0; i < args.length; i++) {
4:             System.out.println("Argument " + i + ": " + args[i]);
5:         }
6:     }
7: }
```

The following is some sample input and output from this program:

INPUT

```
java EchoArgs 1 2 3 jump
```

OUTPUT

```
Argument 0: 1
Argument 1: 2
Argument 2: 3
Argument 3: jump
```

INPUT

```
java EchoArgs "foo bar" zap twaddle 5
```

OUTPUT

```
Argument 0: foo bar
Argument 1: zap
Argument 2: twaddle
Argument 3: 5
```

Note how the arguments are grouped in the second input example; putting quotes around foo bar causes that argument to be treated as one unit inside the argument array.

TECHNICAL NOTE

> The array of arguments in Java is not analogous to argv in C and UNIX. In particular, arg[0], the first element in the array of arguments, is the first command-line argument after the name of the class—*not* the name of the program as it would be in C. Be careful of this as you write your Java programs.

An important thing to note about the arguments you pass into a Java program is that those arguments will be stored in an array of strings. This means that any arguments you pass to your Java program are strings stored in the argument array. To treat them as non-strings, you'll have to convert them to whatever type you want them to be.

For example, suppose you have a very simple Java program called SumAverage that takes any number of numeric arguments and returns the sum and the average of those arguments. Listing 6.6 shows a first pass at this program. Don't try compiling this one; just look at the code and see if you can figure out what it does.

TYPE
Listing 6.6. A first try at the SumAverage **class.**

```
 1: class SumAverage {
 2:     public static void main (String args[]) {
 3:         int sum = 0;
 4:
 5:         for (int i = 0; i < args.length; i++) {
 6:             sum += args[i];
 7:         }
 8:
 9:         System.out.println("Sum is: " + sum);
10:         System.out.println("Average is: " +
11:             (float)sum / args.length);
12:     }
13: }
```

At first glance, this program seems rather straightforward—a `for` loop iterates over the array of arguments, summing them, and then the sum and the average are printed out as the last step.

What happens when you try and compile this? You get an error similar to this one:

```
SumAverage.java:6: Incompatible type for +=.
Can't convert java.lang.String to int.
    sum += args[i];
```

You get this error because the argument array is an array of strings. Even though you passed integers into the program from the command line, those integers were converted to strings before they were stored in the array. To be able to sum those integers, you have to convert them back from strings to integers. There's a class method for the `Integer` class, called `parseInt`, that does just this. If you change line 6 to use that method, everything works just fine:

```
sum += Integer.parseInt(args[i]);
```

Now, compiling the program produces no errors and running it with various arguments returns the expected results. For example, `java SumAverage 1 2 3` returns the following output:

```
Sum is: 6
Average is: 2
```

Summary

Today you put together everything you've come across in the preceding days of this week about how to create Java classes and use them in Java applications. This includes the following:

☐ Instance and class variables, which hold the attributes of the class and its instances. You have learned how to declare them, how they are different from regular local variables, and how to declare constants.

☐ Instance and class methods, which define a class's behavior. You have learned how to define methods, including the parts of a method's signature, how to return values from a method, how arguments are passed in and out of methods, and how to use the this keyword to refer to the current object.

☐ Java applications—all about the main() method and how it works, as well as how to pass arguments into a Java application from a command line.

Q&A

Q **I tried creating a constant variable inside a method, and I got a compiler error when I tried it. What was I doing wrong?**

A You can create only constant (final) class or instance variables; local variables cannot be constant.

Q **static and final are not exactly the most descriptive words for creating class variables, class methods, and constants. Why not use class and const?**

A static comes from Java's C++ heritage; C++ uses the static keyword to retain memory for class variables and methods (and, in fact, they aren't called class methods and variables in C++: static member functions and variables are more common terms).

final, however, is new. final is used in a more general way for classes and methods to indicate that those things cannot be subclassed or overridden. Using the final keyword for variables is consistent with that behavior. final variables are not quite the same as constant variables in C++, which is why the const keyword is not used.

Q **In my class, I have an instance variable called origin. I also have a local variable called origin in a method, which, because of variable scope, gets hidden by the local variable. Is there any way to get hold of the instance variable's value?**

A The easiest way is not to name your local variables the same names as your instance variables. If you feel you must, you can use this.origin to refer to the instance variable and origin to refer to the local variable.

Q **I want to pass command-line arguments to an applet. How do I do this?**

A You're writing applets already? Been skipping ahead, have you? The answer is that you use HTML attributes to pass arguments to an applet, not the command line (you don't have a command line for applets). You'll learn how to do this next week.

Q **I wrote a program to take four arguments, but if I give it too few arguments, it crashes with a runtime error.**

A Testing for the number and type of arguments your program expects is up to you in your Java program; Java won't do it for you. If your program requires four arguments, test that you have indeed been given four arguments, and return an error message if you haven't.

6

Day 7

More About Methods

by Laura Lemay

Methods are arguably the most important part of any object-oriented language. Whereas classes and objects provide the framework, and class and instance variables provide a way of holding that class's or object's attributes, the methods actually provide an object's behavior and define how that object interacts with other objects in the system.

Yesterday you learned a little about defining methods. With what you learned yesterday, you could create lots of Java programs, but you'd be missing some of the features of methods that make them really powerful and that make your objects and classes more efficient and easier to understand. Today you'll learn about these additional features, including the following:

- ☐ Overloading methods—that is, creating methods with multiple signatures and definitions but with the same name

- ☐ Creating constructor methods—methods that enable you to initialize objects to set up their initial state when created

☐ Overriding methods—creating a different definition for a method that has been defined in a superclass

☐ Using finalizer methods—a way for an object to clean up after itself before it is removed from the system

Creating Methods with the Same Name, Different Arguments

Yesterday you learned how to create methods with a single name and a single signature. Methods in Java can also be overloaded—that is, you can create methods that have the same name, but different signatures and different definitions. Method overloading allows instances of your class to have a simpler interface to other objects (no need for entirely different methods with different names that do essentially the same thing) and to behave differently based on the input to that method. For example, an overloaded draw() method could be used to draw just about anything, whether it were a circle or a point or an image. The same method name, with different arguments, could be used for all cases.

When you call a method in an object, Java matches up the method name and the number and type of arguments to choose which method definition to execute.

 Method overloading is creating multiple methods with the same name but with different signatures and definitions. Java uses the number and type of arguments to choose which method definition to execute.

To create an overloaded method, all you need to do is create several different method definitions in your class, all with the same name, but with different parameter lists (either in number or type of arguments). Java allows method overloading as long as each parameter list is unique for the same method name.

Note that Java differentiates overloaded methods based on the number and type of parameters to that method, not on the method's return type. That is, if you try to create two methods with the same name and same parameter list, but different return types, you'll get a compiler error. Also, the variable names you choose for each parameter to the method are irrelevant—all that matters is the number and the type.

Here's an example of creating an overloaded method. Listing 7.1 shows a simple class definition for a class called MyRect, which defines a rectangular shape. The MyRect class has four instance variables to define the upper-left and lower-right corners of the rectangle: x1, y1, x2, and y2.

NOTE

Why did I call it MyRect instead of just Rectangle? The java.awt package has a class called Rectangle that implements much of this same behavior. I called this class MyRect to prevent confusion between the two classes.

TYPE **Listing 7.1. The MyRect class.**

```
1: class MyRect {
2:     int x1 = 0;
3:     int y1 = 0;
4:     int x2 = 0;
5:     int y2 = 0;
6: }
```

NOTE

Don't try to compile this example yet. Actually, it'll compile just fine, but it won't run because it doesn't (yet) have a main() method. When you're finished building this class definition, the final version can be compiled and run.

When a new instance of the myRect class is initially created, all its instance variables are initialized to 0. Let's define a buildRecpt() method that takes four integer arguments and "resizes" the rectangle to have the appropriate values for its corners, returning the resulting rectangle object (note that because the arguments have the same names as the instance variables, you have to make sure to use this to refer to them):

```
MyRect buildRect(int x1, int y1, int x2, int y2) {
    this.x1 = x1;
    this.y1 = y1;
    this.x2 = x2;
    this.y2 = y2;
    return this;
}
```

What if you want to define a rectangle's dimensions in a different way—for example, by using Point objects rather than individual coordinates? You can overload buildRect() so that its parameter list takes two Point objects (note that you'll also need to import the java.awt.Point class at the top of your source file so Java can find it):

```
MyRect buildRect(Point topLeft, Point bottomRight) {
    x1 = topLeft.x;
    y1 = topLeft.y;
```

```
        x2 = bottomRight.x;
        y2 = bottomRight.y;
        return this;
}
```

Perhaps you want to define the rectangle using a top corner and a width and height. You can do that, too. Just create a different definition for buildRect():

```
MyRect buildRect(Point topLeft, int w, int h) {
        x1 = topLeft.x;
        y1 = topLeft.y;
        x2 = (x1 + w);
        y2 = (y1 + h);
        return this;
}
```

To finish up this example, let's create a method—called printRect()—to print out the rectangle's coordinates, and a main() method to test it all (just to prove that this does indeed work). Listing 7.2 shows the completed class definition with all its methods: three buildRect() methods, one printRect(), and one main().

TYPE   **Listing 7.2. The complete MyRect class.**

```
 1:import java.awt.Point;
 2:
 3:class MyRect {
 4:    int x1 = 0;
 5:    int y1 = 0;
 6:    int x2 = 0;
 7:    int y2 = 0;
 8:
 9:    MyRect buildRect(int x1, int y1, int x2, int y2) {
10:        this.x1 = x1;
11:        this.y1 = y1;
12:        this.x2 = x2;
13:        this.y2 = y2;
14:        return this;
15:    }
16:
17:    MyRect buildRect(Point topLeft, Point bottomRight) {
18:        x1 = topLeft.x;
19:        y1 = topLeft.y;
20:        x2 = bottomRight.x;
21:        y2 = bottomRight.y;
22:        return this;
23:    }
24:
25:    MyRect buildRect(Point topLeft, int w, int h) {
26:        x1 = topLeft.x;
27:        y1 = topLeft.y;
28:        x2 = (x1 + w);
29:        y2 = (y1 + h);
30:        return this;
31:    }
32:
```

```
33:     void printRect(){
34:         System.out.print("MyRect: <" + x1 + ", " + y1);
35:         System.out.println(", " + x2 + ", " + y2 + ">");
36:     }
37:
38:     public static void main(String args[]) {
39:         MyRect rect = new MyRect();
40:
41:         System.out.println("Calling buildRect with coordinates 25,25
            ➥50,50:");
42:         rect.buildRect(25, 25, 50, 50);
43:         rect.printRect();
44:         System.out.println("----------");
45:
46:         System.out.println("Calling buildRect w/points (10,10), (20,20):");
47:         rect.buildRect(new Point(10,10), new Point(20,20));
48:         rect.printRect();
49:         System.out.println("----------");
50:
51:         System.out.print("Calling buildRect w/1 point (10,10),");
52:         System.out.println(" width (50) and height (50):");
53:
54:         rect.buildRect(new Point(10,10), 50, 50);
55:         rect.printRect();
56:         System.out.println("----------");
57:     }
58: }
```

OUTPUT
```
Calling buildRect with coordinates 25,25 50,50:
MyRect: <25, 25, 50, 50>
----------
Calling buildRect w/points (10,10), (20,20):
MyRect: <10, 10, 20, 20>
----------
Calling buildRect w/1 point (10,10), width (50) and height (50):
MyRect: <10, 10, 60, 60>
----------
```

As you can see from this example, all the buildRect() methods work based on the arguments with which they are called. You can define as many versions of a method as you need to in your own classes to implement the behavior you need for that class.

Constructor Methods

In addition to regular methods, you can also define constructor methods in your class definition. Constructor methods are used to initialize new objects when they're created. Unlike regular methods, you can't call a constructor method by calling it directly; instead, constructor methods are called by Java automatically when you create a new object. As you learned on Day 4, "Working with Objects," when you use new, Java does three things:

☐ Allocates memory for the new object

☐ Initializes that object's instance variables, either to their initial values or to a default (0 for numbers, null for objects, false for booleans, '\0' for characters)

☐ Calls the class's constructor method (which may be one of several methods)

NEW TERM *Constructor methods* are special methods that are called automatically by Java to initialize a new object.

If a class doesn't have any special constructor methods defined, you'll still end up with a new object, but you might have to set its instance variables or call other methods that the object needs to initialize itself. All the examples you've created up to this point have behaved like this.

By defining constructor methods in your own classes, you can set initial values of instance variables, call methods based on those variables or on other objects, or calculate initial properties of your object. You can also overload constructors, as you would regular methods, to create an object that has specific properties based on the arguments you give in the new expression.

Basic Constructors

Constructors look a lot like regular methods, with two basic differences:

☐ Constructors always have the same name as the class.

☐ Constructors don't have a return type.

For example, Listing 7.3 shows a simple class called Person. The constructor method for Person takes two arguments: a string object representing a person's name and an integer for the person's age.

TYPE   **Listing 7.3. The Person class.**

```
 1: class Person {
 2:     String name;
 3:     int age;
 4:
 5:     Person(String n, int a) {
 6:         name = n;
 7:         age = a;
 8:     }
 9:
10:     void printPerson() {
11:         System.out.print("Hi, my name is " + name);
12:         System.out.println(". I am " + age + " years old.");
13:     }
14:
15:     public static void main (String args[]) {
```

```
16:        Person p;
17:        p = new Person("Laura", 20);
18:        p.printPerson();
19:        System.out.println("--------");
20:        p = new Person("Tommy", 3);
21:        p.printPerson();
22:        System.out.println("--------");
23:   }
24:}
```

OUTPUT
```
Hi, my name is Laura. I am 20 years old.
--------
Hi, my name is Tommy. I am 3 years old.
--------
```

The person class has three methods: The first is the constructor method, defined in lines 5 to 8, which initializes the class's two instance variables based on the arguments to new. The Person class also includes a method called printPerson() so that the object can "introduce" itself, and a main() method to test each of these things.

Calling Another Constructor

Some constructors you write may be supersets of other constructors defined in your class; that is, they might have the same behavior plus a little bit more. Rather than duplicating identical behavior in multiple constructor methods in your class, it makes sense to be able to just call that first constructor from inside the body of the second constructor. Java provides a special syntax for doing this. To call a constructor defined on the current class, use the this keyword as if it were a method name, with the arguments just after it, like this:

```
this(arg1, arg2, arg3...);
```

The arguments to this() are, of course, the arguments to the constructor.

Overloading Constructors

Like regular methods, constructors can also take varying numbers and types of parameters, enabling you to create your object with exactly the properties you want it to have, or for it to be able to calculate properties from different kinds of input.

For example, the buildRect() methods you defined in the MyRect class earlier today would make excellent constructors because they're initializing an object's instance variables to the appropriate values. So, for example, instead of the original buildRect() method you had defined (which took four parameters for the coordinates of the corners), you could create a constructor instead. Listing 7.4 shows a new class, MyRect2, that has all the same functionality of the original MyRect, except with overloaded constructor methods instead of the overloaded buildRect() method. The output shown at the end is also the same output as for the previous MyRect class; only the code to produce it has changed.

7

Listing 7.4. The MyRect2 class (with constructors).

```
1: import java.awt.Point;
2:
3: class MyRect2 {
4:     int x1 = 0;
5:     int y1 = 0;
6:     int x2 = 0;
7:     int y2 = 0;
8:
9:     MyRect2(int x1, int y1, int x2, int y2) {
10:         this.x1 = x1;
11:         this.y1 = y1;
12:         this.x2 = x2;
13:         this.y2 = y2;
14:     }
15:
16:     MyRect2(Point topLeft, Point bottomRight) {
17:         x1 = topLeft.x;
18:         y1 = topLeft.y;
19:         x2 = bottomRight.x;
20:         y2 = bottomRight.y;
21:     }
22:
23:     MyRect2(Point topLeft, int w, int h) {
24:         x1 = topLeft.x;
25:         y1 = topLeft.y;
26:         x2 = (x1 + w);
27:         y2 = (y1 + h);
28:     }
29:
30:     void printRect() {
31:         System.out.print("MyRect: <" + x1 + ", " + y1);
32:         System.out.println(", " + x2 + ", " + y2 + ">");
33:     }
34:
35:     public static void main(String args[]) {
36:         MyRect2 rect;
37:
38:         System.out.println("Calling MyRect2 with coordinates 25,25 50,50:");
39:         rect = new MyRect2(25, 25, 50,50);
40:         rect.printRect();
41:         System.out.println("----------");
42:
43:         System.out.println("Calling MyRect2 w/points (10,10), (20,20):");
44:         rect= new MyRect2(new Point(10,10), new Point(20,20));
45:         rect.printRect();
46:         System.out.println("----------");
47:
48:         System.out.print("Calling MyRect2 w/1 point (10,10)");
49:         System.out.println(" width (50) and height (50):");
50:         rect = new MyRect2(new Point(10,10), 50, 50);
51:         rect.printRect();
52:         System.out.println("----------");
53:
54:     }
55: }
```

```
OUTPUT   Calling MyRect2 with coordinates 25,25 50,50:
         MyRect: <25, 25, 50, 50>
         - - - - - - - - - -
         Calling MyRect2 w/points (10,10), (20,20):
         MyRect: <10, 10, 20, 20>
         - - - - - - - - - -
         Calling MyRect2 w/1 point (10,10), width (50) and height (50):
         MyRect: <10, 10, 60, 60>
         - - - - - - - - - -
```

Overriding Methods

When you call an object's method, Java looks for that method definition in the class of that object, and if it doesn't find a match with the right signature, it passes the method call up the class hierarchy until a definition is found. Method inheritance means that you can use methods in subclasses without having to duplicate the code.

However, there may be times when you want an object to respond to the same methods but have different behavior when that method is called. In this case, you can override that method. Overriding a method involves defining a method in a subclass that has the same signature as a method in a superclass. Then, when that method is called, the method in the subclass is found and executed instead of the one in the superclass.

Creating Methods That Override Existing Methods

To override a method, all you have to do is create a method in your subclass that has the same signature (name, return type, and parameter list) as a method defined by one of your class's superclasses. Because Java executes the first method definition it finds that matches the signature, this effectively "hides" the original method definition. Here's a simple example; Listing 7.5 shows a simple class with a method called `printMe()`, which prints out the name of the class and the values of its instance variables.

TYPE **Listing 7.5. The `PrintClass` class.**

```
 1: class PrintClass {
 2:     int x = 0;
 3:     int y = 1;
 4:
 5:     void printMe() {
 6:         System.out.println("x is " + x + ", y is " + y);
 7:         System.out.println("I am an instance of the class " +
 8:             this.getClass().getName());
 9:     }
10: }
```

7

Listing 7.6 shows a class called `PrintSubClass` that is a subclass of (extends) `PrintClass`. The only difference between `PrintClass` and `PrintSubClass` is that the latter has a z instance variable.

 Listing 7.6. The `PrintSubClass` class.

```
1: class PrintSubClass extends PrintClass {
2:     int z = 3;
3:
4:     public static void main(String args[]) {
5:         PrintSubClass obj = new PrintSubClass();
6:         obj.printMe();
7:     }
8: }
```

OUTPUT

```
x is 0, y is 1
I am an instance of the class PrintSubClass
```

In the `main()` method of `PrintSubClass`, you create a `PrintSubClass` object and call the `printMe()` method. Note that `PrintSubClass` doesn't define this method, so Java looks for it in each of `PrintSubClass`'s superclasses—and finds it, in this case, in `PrintClass`. Unfortunately, because `printMe()` is still defined in `PrintClass`, it doesn't print the z instance variable.

NOTE

> There's an important feature of `PrintClass` I should point out: It doesn't have a `main()` method. It doesn't need one; it isn't an application. `PrintClass` is simply a utility class for the `PrintSubClass` class, which is an application and therefore has a `main()` method. Only the class that you're actually executing the Java interpreter on needs a `main()` method.

Now, let's create a third class. `PrintSubClass2` is nearly identical to `PrintSubClass`, but you override the `printMe()` method to include the z variable. Listing 7.7 shows this class.

TYPE **Listing 7.7. The `PrintSubClass2` class.**

```
1: class PrintSubClass2 extends PrintClass {
2:     int z = 3;
3:
4:     void printMe() {
5:         System.out.println("x is " + x + ", y is " + y +
6:                 ", z is " + z);
7:         System.out.println("I am an instance of the class " +
8:                 this.getClass().getName());
```

```
 9:     }
10:
11:     public static void main(String args[]) {
12:         PrintSubClass2 obj = new PrintSubClass2();
13:         obj.printMe();
14:     }
15: }
```

Now when you instantiate this class and call the printMe() method, the version of printMe() you defined for this class is called instead of the one in the superclass PrintClass (as you can see in this output):

OUTPUT
```
x is 0, y is 1, z is 3
I am an instance of the class PrintSubClass2
```

Calling the Original Method

Usually, there are two reasons why you want to override a method that a superclass has already implemented:

☐ To replace the definition of that original method completely

☐ To augment the original method with additional behavior

You've already learned about the first one; by overriding a method and giving that method a new definition, you've hidden the original method definition. But sometimes you may just want to add behavior to the original definition rather than erase it altogether. This is particularly useful where you end up duplicating behavior in both the original method and the method that overrides it; by being able to call the original method in the body of the overridden method, you can add only what you need.

To call the original method from inside a method definition, use the super keyword to pass the method call up the hierarchy:

```
void myMethod (String a, String b) {
    // do stuff here
    super.myMethod(a, b);
    // maybe do more stuff here
}
```

The super keyword, somewhat like the this keyword, is a placeholder for this class's superclass. You can use it anywhere you can use this, but to refer to the superclass rather than to the current class.

For example, Listing 7.8 shows the two different printMe() methods used in the previous example.

7

Listing 7.8. The `printMe()` methods.

```
 1: // from PrintClass
 2: void printMe() {
 3:         System.out.println("x is " + x + ", y is " + y);
 4:         System.out.println("I am an instance of the class" +
 5:                     this.getClass().getName());
 6:     }
 7: }
 8:
 9: //from PrintSubClass2
10:     void printMe() {
11:         System.out.println("x is " + x + ", y is " + y + ", z is " + z);
12:         System.out.println("I am an instance of the class " +
13:                     this.getClass().getName());
14:     }
```

Rather than duplicating most of the behavior of the superclass's method in the subclass, you can rearrange the superclass's method so that additional behavior can easily be added:

```
// from PrintClass
void printMe() {
    System.out.println("I am an instance of the class" +
                this.getClass().getName());
    System.out.println("x is " + x);
    System.out.println("y is " + y);
}
```

Then, in the subclass, when you override `printMe()`, you can merely call the original method and then add the extra stuff:

```
// From PrintSubClass2
void printMe() {
    super.printMe();
    System.out.println("z is " + z);
}
```

Here's the output of calling `printMe()` on an instance of the subclass:

```
I am an instance of the class PrintSubClass2
X is 0
Y is 1
Z is 3
```

Overriding Constructors

Because constructors have the same name as the current class, you cannot technically override a superclass's constructors. If you want a constructor in a subclass with the same number and type of arguments as in the superclass, you'll have to define that constructor in your own class.

However, when you create your constructors you will almost always want to call your superclass's constructors to make sure that the inherited parts of your object get initialized

the way your superclass intends them to be. By explicitly calling your superclasses constructors in this way you can create constructors that effectively override or overload your
superclass's constructors.

To call a regular method in a superclass, you use the form `super.methodname(arguments)`.
Because with constructors you don't have a method name to call, you have to use a different
form:

```
super(arg1, arg2, ...);
```

Note that Java has a specific rule for the use of `super()`: It must be the very first thing in your
constructor definition. If you don't call `super()` explicitly in your constructor, Java will do
it for you—using `super()` with no arguments.

Similar to using `this(...)` in a constructor, `super(...)` calls a constructor method for the
immediate superclass with the appropriate arguments (which may, in turn, call the constructor of its superclass, and so on). Note that a constructor with that signature has to exist in the
superclass in order for the call to `super()` to work. The Java compiler will check this when
you try to compile the source file.

Note that you don't have to call the constructor in your superclass that has exactly the same
signature as the constructor in your class; you only have to call the constructor for the values
you need initialized. In fact, you can create a class that has constructors with entirely different
signatures from any of the superclass's constructors.

Listing 7.9 shows a class called `NamedPoint`, which extends the class `Point` from Java's `awt`
package. The `Point` class has only one constructor, which takes an `x` and a `y` argument and
returns a `Point` object. `NamedPoint` has an additional instance variable (a string for the name)
and defines a constructor to initialize `x`, `y`, and the name.

TYPE   **Listing 7.9. The `NamedPoint` class.**

```
1: import java.awt.Point;
2: class NamedPoint extends Point {
3:     String name;
4:
5:     NamedPoint(int x, int y, String name) {
6:         super(x,y);
7:         this.name = name;
8:     }
9:     public static void main (String arg[]) {
10:        NamedPoint np = new NamedPoint(5, 5, "SmallPoint");
11:        System.out.println("x is " + np.x);
12:        System.out.println("y is " + np.y);
13:        System.out.println("Name is " + np.name);
14:     }
15:}
```

7

```
x is 5
y is 5
name is SmallPoint
```

The constructor defined here for NamedPoint (lines 5 through 8) calls Point's constructor method to initialize Point's instance variables (x and y). Although you can just as easily initialize x and y yourself, you may not know what other things Point is doing to initialize itself, so it's always a good idea to pass constructors up the hierarchy to make sure everything is set up correctly.

Finalizer Methods

Finalizer methods are almost the opposite of constructor methods; whereas a constructor method is used to initialize an object, finalizer methods are called just before the object is garbage-collected and its memory reclaimed.

The finalizer method is named simply finalize(). The Object class defines a default finalizer method, which does nothing. To create a finalizer method for your own classes, override the finalize() method using this signature:

```
protected void finalize() throws Throwable {
    super.finalize();
}
```

NOTE

> The throws Throwable part of this method definition refers to the errors that might occur when this method is called. Errors in Java are called *exceptions*; you'll learn more about them on Day 17, "Exceptions." For now, all you need to do is include these keywords in the method definition.

Inside the body of that finalize() method, include any cleaning up you want to do for that object. You can also call super.finalize() to allow your class's superclasses to finalize your object, if necessary (it's a good idea to do so just to make sure that everyone gets a chance to deal with the object if they need to).

You can always call the finalize() method yourself at any time; it's just a plain method like any other. However, calling finalize() does not trigger an object to be garbage-collected. Only removing all references to an object will cause it to be marked for deleting.

Finalizer methods are best used for optimizing the removal of an object—for example, by removing references to other objects, by releasing external resources that have been acquired (for example, external files), or for other behaviors that may make it easier for that object to be removed. In most cases, you will not need to use finalize() at all. See Day 21, "Under the Hood," for more about garbage collection and finalize().

Summary

Today you have learned all kinds of techniques for using, reusing, defining, and redefining methods. You have learned how to overload a method name so that the same method can have different behaviors based on the arguments with which it's called. You've learned about constructor methods, which are used to initialize a new object when it's created. You have learned about method inheritance and how to override methods that have been defined in a class's superclasses. Finally, you have learned about finalizer methods, which can be used to clean up after an object just before that object is garbage-collected and its memory reclaimed.

Congratulations on completing your first week of *Teach Yourself Java in 21 Days*! Starting next week, you'll apply everything you've learned this week to writing Java applets and to working with more advanced concepts in putting together Java programs and working with the standard Java class libraries.

Q&A

Q **I created two methods with the following signatures:**

```
int total(int arg1, int arg2, int arg3) {...}
float total(int arg1, int arg2, int arg3) {...}
```

The Java compiler complains when I try to compile the class with these method definitions. But their signatures are different. What have I done wrong?

A Method overloading in Java works only if the parameter lists are different—either in number or type of arguments. Return type is not relevant for method overloading. Think about it—if you had two methods with exactly the same parameter list, how would Java know which one to call?

Q **Can I overload overridden methods (that is, can I create methods that have the same name as an inherited method, but a different parameter list)?**

A Sure! As long as parameter lists vary, it doesn't matter whether you've defined a new method name or one that you've inherited from a superclass.

7

WEEK 2

8

9

10

11

12

13

14

At a Glance

☐ **Java Applet Basics**

Including an applet on a Web page, passing parameters

☐ **Graphics, Fonts, and Color**

Graphics primitives, the Color class

☐ **Simple Animation and Threads**

paint() and repaint(), reducing animation flicker, stop and start

☐ **More Animation, Images, and Sound**

Scaling options, executing sound effectively, double-buffering

☐ **Managing Simple Events and Interactivity**

MouseDown and MouseUp, the Java event handler

☐ **Creating User Interfaces with the AWT**

Canvases, text components, grid bag layouts, window construction components

☐ **Windows, Networking, and Other Tidbits**

Programming menus and creating links inside applets

Day 8

Java Applet Basics

by Laura Lemay

Much of Java's current popularity has come about because of Java-enabled World Wide Web browsers and their support for *applets*—Java programs that run on Web pages and can be used to create dynamic, interactive Web sites. Applets, as noted at the beginning of this book, are written in the Java language, and can be viewed in any browser that supports Java, including Netscape's Navigator and Microsoft's Internet Explorer. Learning how to create applets is most likely the reason you bought this book, so let's waste no more time.

Last week, you focused on learning about the Java language itself, and most of the little programs you created were Java applications. This week, now that you have the basics down, you'll move on to creating and using applets, which includes a discussion of many of the classes in the standard Java class library.

Today you'll start with the basics:

☐ A small review of differences between Java applets and applications

☐ Getting started with applets: the basics of how an applet works and how to create your own simple applets

☐ Including an applet on a Web page by using the <APPLET> tag, including the various features of that tag

☐ Passing parameters to applets

How Applets and Applications Are Different

Although you explored the differences between Java applications and Java applets in the early part of this book, let's review them.

In short, Java applications are standalone Java programs that can be run by using just the Java interpreter, for example, from a command line. Most everything you've used up to this point in the book has been a Java application, albeit a simple one.

Java applets, however, are run from inside a World Wide Web browser. A reference to an applet is embedded in a Web page using a special HTML tag. When a reader, using a Java-enabled browser, loads a Web page with an applet in it, the browser downloads that applet from a Web server and executes it on the local system (the one the browser is running on). (The Java interpreter is built into the browser and runs the compiled Java class file from there.)

Because Java applets run inside a Java browser, they have access to the structure the browser provides: an existing window, an event-handling and graphics context, and the surrounding user interface. Java applications can also create this structure (allowing you to create graphical applications), but they don't require it (you'll learn how to create Java applications that use applet-like graphics and user interface (UI) features on Day 14, "Windows, Networking, and Other Tidbits").

Note that a single Java program can be written to operate as both a Java application and a Java applet. While you use different procedures and rules to create applets and applications, none of those procedures or rules conflict with each other. The features specific to applets are ignored when the program runs as an application, and vice versa. Keep this in mind as you design your own applets and applications.

One final significant difference between Java applets and applications—probably the biggest difference—is the set of restrictions placed on how applets can operate in the name of security. Given the fact that Java applets can be downloaded from any site on the World Wide

8

Web and run on a client's system, Java-enabled browsers and tools limit what can be done to prevent a rogue applet from causing system damage or security breaches. Without these restrictions in place, Java applets could be written to contain viruses or trojan horses (programs that seem friendly but do some sort of damage to the system), or be used to compromise the security of the system that runs them. The restrictions on applets include the following:

☐ Applets can't read or write to the reader's file system, which means they cannot delete files or test to see what programs you have installed on the hard drive.

☐ Applets can't communicate with any network server other than the one that had originally stored the applet, to prevent the applet from attacking another system from the reader's system.

☐ Applets can't run any programs on the reader's system. For UNIX systems, this includes forking a process.

☐ Applets can't load programs native to the local platform, including shared libraries such as DLLs.

All these rules are true for Java applets running Netscape Navigator or Microsoft Internet Explorer. Other Java-enabled browsers or tools may allow you to configure the level of security you want—for example, the `appletviewer` tool in the JDK allows you to set an access control list for which directories an applet can read or write. However, as an applet developer, it's safe to assume that most of your audience is going to be viewing your applets in a browser that implements the strictest rules for what an applet can do. Java applications have none of these restrictions.

NOTE

> The security restrictions imposed on applets are sometimes called "the sandbox" (as in applets are only allowed to play in the sandbox and can go no further). Work is being done by Sun and by the Java community to find ways for applets to be able to break out of the sandbox, including digital signatures and encryption. On Day 21, "Under the Hood," you'll learn more details on Java and applet security.

In addition to the applet restrictions listed, Java itself includes various forms of security and consistency checking in the Java compiler and interpreter for all Java programs to prevent unorthodox use of the language (you'll learn more about this on Day 21). This combination of restrictions and security features makes it more difficult for a rogue Java applet to do damage to the client's system.

NOTE

> These restrictions prevent all of the traditional ways of causing damage to a client's system, but it's impossible to be absolutely sure that a clever programmer cannot somehow work around these restrictions, violate privacy, use CPU resources, or just plain be annoying. Sun has asked the Net at large to try to break Java's security and to create an applet that can work around the restrictions imposed on it, and, in fact, several problems have been unearthed and fixed, usually relating to loading classes and to connecting to unauthorized sites. You'll learn about more issues in Java security on Day 21.

Creating Applets

For the most part, all the Java programs you've created up to this point have been Java applications—simple programs with a single `main()` method that create objects, set instance variables, and run methods. Today and in the next few days you'll be creating applets exclusively, so you will need a good grasp of how an applet works, the sorts of features an applet has, and where to start when you first create your own applets.

To create an applet, you create a subclass of the class `Applet`. The `Applet` class, part of the `java.applet` package, provides much of the behavior your applet needs to work inside a Java-enabled browser. Applets also take strong advantage of Java's Abstract Windowing Toolkit (AWT), which provides behavior for creating graphical user interface (GUI)-based applets and applications: drawing to the screen; creating windows, menu bars, buttons, check boxes, and other UI elements; and managing user input such as mouse clicks and keypresses. The AWT classes are part of the `java.awt` package.

NEW TERM   Java's Abstract Windowing Toolkit (AWT) provides classes and behavior for creating GUI-based applications in Java. Applets make use of many of the capabilities in the AWT.

Although your applet can have as many additional "helper" classes as it needs, it's the main applet class that triggers the execution of the applet. That initial applet class always has a signature like this:

```
public class myClass extends java.applet.Applet {
    ...
}
```

Note the `public` keyword. Java requires that your applet subclass be declared `public`. Again, this is true only of your main applet class; any helper classes you create do not necessarily need

8

to be public. public, private, and other forms of access control are described on Day 15, "Modifiers, Access Control, and Class Design."

When a Java-enabled browser encounters your applet in a Web page, it loads your initial applet class over the network, as well as any other helper classes that first class uses, and runs the applet using the browser's built-in bytecode interpreter. Unlike with applications, where Java calls the main() method directly on your initial class, when your applet is loaded, Java creates an instance of the applet class, and a series of special applet methods are called on that instance. Different applets that use the same class use different instances, so each one can behave differently from the other applets running in the same browser.

Major Applet Activities

To create a basic Java application, your class has to have one method, main(), with a specific signature. Then, when your application runs, main() is found and executed, and from main() you can set up the behavior that your program needs to run. Applets are similar but more complicated—and, in fact, applets don't need a main() method at all. Applets have many different activities that correspond to various major events in the life cycle of the applet— for example, initialization, painting, and mouse events. Each activity has a corresponding method, so when an event occurs, the browser or other Java-enabled tool calls those specific methods.

The default implementations of these activity methods do nothing; to provide behavior for an event you must override the appropriate method in your applet's subclass. You don't have to override all of them, of course; different applet behavior requires different methods to be overridden.

You'll learn about the various important methods to override as the week progresses, but, for a general overview, here are five of the most important methods in an applet's execution: initialization, starting, stopping, destroying, and painting.

Initialization

Initialization occurs when the applet is first loaded (or reloaded), similarly to the main() method in applications. The initialization of an applet might include reading and parsing any parameters to the applet, creating any helper objects it needs, setting up an initial state, or loading images or fonts. To provide behavior for the initialization of your applet, override the init() method in your applet class:

```
public void init() {
    ...
}
```

Starting

After an applet is initialized, it is started. Starting is different from initialization because it can happen many different times during an applet's lifetime, whereas initialization happens only once. Starting can also occur if the applet was previously stopped. For example, an applet is stopped if the reader follows a link to a different page, and it is started again when the reader returns to this page. To provide startup behavior for your applet, override the start() method:

```
public void start() {
    ...
}
```

Functionality that you put in the start() method might include creating and starting up a thread to control the applet, sending the appropriate messages to helper objects, or in some way telling the applet to begin running. You'll learn more about starting applets on Day 10, "Simple Animation and Threads."

Stopping

Stopping and starting go hand in hand. Stopping occurs when the reader leaves the page that contains a currently running applet, or you can stop the applet yourself by calling stop(). By default, when the reader leaves a page, any threads the applet had started will continue running. You'll learn more about threads on Day 10. By overriding stop(), you can suspend execution of these threads and then restart them if the applet is viewed again:

```
public void stop() {
    ...
}
```

Destroying

Destroying sounds more violent than it is. Destroying enables the applet to clean up after itself just before it is freed or the browser exits—for example, to stop and remove any running threads, close any open network connections, or release any other running objects. Generally, you won't want to override destroy() unless you have specific resources that need to be released—for example, threads that the applet has created. To provide clean-up behavior for your applet, override the destroy() method:

```
public void destroy() {
    ...
}
```

TECHNICAL NOTE

How is `destroy()` different from `finalize()`, which was described on Day 7, "More About Methods"? First, `destroy()` applies only to applets. `finalize()` is a more general-purpose way for a single object of any type to clean up after itself.

Painting

Painting is how an applet actually draws something on the screen, be it text, a line, a colored background, or an image. Painting can occur many thousands of times during an applet's life cycle (for example, after the applet is initialized, if the browser is placed behind another window on the screen and then brought forward again, if the browser window is moved to a different position on the screen, or perhaps repeatedly, in the case of animation). You override the `paint()` method if your applet needs to have an actual appearance on the screen (that is, most of the time). The `paint()` method looks like this:

```
public void paint(Graphics g) {
    ...
}
```

Note that unlike the other major methods in this section, `paint()` takes an argument, an instance of the class `Graphics`. This object is created and passed to `paint` by the browser, so you don't have to worry about it. However, you will have to make sure that the `Graphics` class (part of the `java.awt` package) gets imported into your applet code, usually through an `import` statement at the top of your Java file:

```
import java.awt.Graphics;
```

A Simple Applet

Way back on Day 2, "Object-Oriented Programming and Java," you created a simple applet called `HelloAgainApplet` (this was the one with the big red `Hello Again`). There, you created and used that applet as an example of creating a subclass. Let's go over the code for that applet again, this time looking at it slightly differently in light of the things you just learned about applets. Listing 8.1 shows the code for that applet.

TYPE   **Listing 8.1. The Hello Again applet.**

```
1:  import java.awt.Graphics;
2:  import java.awt.Font;
3:  import java.awt.Color;
```

continues

Listing 8.1. continued

```
 4:
 5:   public class HelloAgainApplet extends java.applet.Applet {
 6:
 7:       Font f = new Font("TimesRoman", Font.BOLD, 36);
 8:
 9:       public void paint(Graphics g) {
10:           g.setFont(f);
11:           g.setColor(Color.red);
12:           g.drawString("Hello again!", 5, 40);
13:       }
14: }
```

ANALYSIS   This applet implements the paint() method, one of the major methods described in the previous section (actually, it overrides the default implementation of paint(), which does nothing). Because the applet doesn't actually do much (all it does is print a couple words to the screen), and there's not really anything to initialize, you don't need a start(), stop(), init(), or destroy() method.

The paint method is where the real work of this applet (what little work goes on) really occurs. The Graphics object passed into the paint() method holds the graphics state for the applet—that is, the current features of the drawing surface, such as foreground and background colors or clipping area. Lines 10 and 11 set up the font and color for this graphics state (here, the font object held in the f instance variable, and a Color object representing the color red).

Line 12 draws the string "Hello Again!" by using the current font and color at the position 5, 40. Note that the 0 point for x, y is at the top left of the applet's drawing surface, with positive y moving downward, so 50 is actually at the bottom of the applet. Figure 8.1 shows how the applet's bounding box and the string are drawn on the page.

Figure 8.1.

Drawing the applet.

If you've been following along with all the examples up to this point, you might notice that there appears to be something missing in this class: a main() method. As mentioned in the section on the differences between applets and applications, applets don't need a `main()` method. By implementing the right applet methods in your class (`init()`, `start()`, `stop()`, `paint()`, and so on), your applet just seamlessly works without needing an explicit jumping-off point.

Including an Applet on a Web Page

After you create a class or classes that contain your applet and compile them into class files as you would any other Java program, you have to create a Web page that will hold that applet by using the HTML language. There is a special HTML tag for including applets in Web pages; Java-enabled browsers use the information contained in that tag to locate the compiled class files and execute the applet itself. In this section, you'll learn about how to put Java applets in a Web page and how to serve those files to the Web at large.

NOTE

> The following section assumes that you have at least a passing under-
> standing of writing HTML pages. If you need help in this area, you
> may find the book *Teach Yourself Web Publishing with HTML in 14
> Days* useful. It is also from Sams.net and also by Laura Lemay, the
> author of much of this book.

The `<APPLET>` Tag

To include an applet on a Web page, use the `<APPLET>` tag. `<APPLET>` is a special extension to HTML for including applets in Web pages. Listing 8.2 shows a very simple example of a Web page with an applet included in it.

TYPE   **Listing 8.2. A simple HTML page.**

```
 1:   <HTML>
 2:   <HEAD>
 3:   <TITLE>This page has an applet on it</TITLE>
 4:   </HEAD>
 5:   <BODY>
 6:   <P>My second Java applet says:
 7:   <BR><APPLET CODE="HelloAgainApplet.class" WIDTH=200 HEIGHT=50>
 8:   Hello Again!
 9:   </APPLET>
10:   </BODY>
11:   </HTML>
```

Analysis There are three things to note about the `<APPLET>` tag in this page:

☐ The `CODE` attribute indicates the name of the class file that contains this applet, including the `.class` extension. In this case, the class file must be in the same directory as this HTML file. To indicate applets are in a specific directory, use `CODEBASE`, described later today.

☐ `WIDTH` and `HEIGHT` are required and are used to indicate the bounding box of the applet—that is, how big a box to draw for the applet on the Web page. Be sure you set `WIDTH` and `HEIGHT` to be an appropriate size for the applet; depending on the browser, if your applet draws outside the boundaries of the space you've given it, you may not be able to see or get to those parts of the applet outside the bounding box.

☐ The text between the `<APPLET>` and `</APPLET>` tags is displayed by browsers that do not understand the `<APPLET>` tag (which includes most browsers that are not Java aware). Because your page may be viewed in many different kinds of browsers, it is a very good idea to include some sort of alternate text or HTML tags here so that readers of your page who don't have Java will see something other than a blank line. For example, you might show just an image or some other element. Here, you include a simple statement that says `Hello Again!`.

Note that the `<APPLET>` tag, like the `<IMG>` tag itself, is not a paragraph, so it should be enclosed inside a more general text tag, such as `<P>` or one of the heading tags (`<H1>`, `<H2>`, and so on).

Testing the Result

Now with a class file and an HTML file that refers to your applet, you should be able to load that HTML file into your Java-enabled browser from your local disk (in Netscape, use Open File from the File menu; in Internet Explorer, use Open from the File menu and then choose Browse to find the right file on your disk). The browser loads and parses your HTML file, and then loads and executes your applet class.

If you don't have a Java-enabled browser, there are often tools that come with your development environment to help you test applets. In the JDK, the `appletviewer` application will test your applets. You won't see the Web page the applet is running on, but you can figure out if the applet is indeed running the way you expect it to.

Figure 8.2 shows the Hello Again applet running in Netscape.

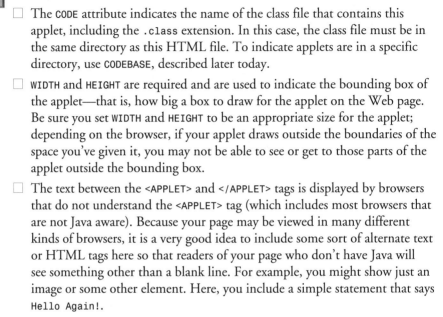

Figure 8.2.

The Hello Again applet.

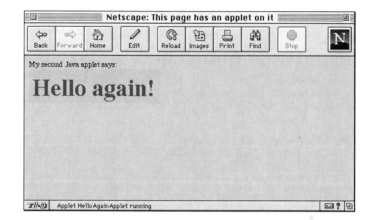

Making Java Applets Available to the Web

After you have an applet and an HTML file, and you've verified that everything is working correctly on your local system, the last step is to make that applet available to the World Wide Web at large so that anyone with a Java-enabled browser can view that applet.

Java applets are served by a Web server the same way that HTML files, images, and other media are. You don't need special server software to make Java applets available to the Web; you don't even need to configure your server to handle Java files. If you have a Web server up and running, or space on a Web server available to you, all you have to do is move your HTML and compiled class files to that server, as you would any other file.

If you don't have a Web server, you have to rent space on one or set one up yourself. (Web server setup and administration, as well as other facets of Web publishing in general, are outside the scope of this book.)

More About the <APPLET> Tag

In its simplest form, by using CODE, WIDTH, and HEIGHT, the <APPLET> tag merely creates a space of the appropriate size and then loads and runs the applet in that space. The <APPLET> tag, however, does include several attributes that can help you better integrate your applet into the overall design of your Web page.

NOTE

The attributes available for the <APPLET> tag are almost identical to those for the HTML <IMG> tag.

ALIGN

The ALIGN attribute defines how the applet will be aligned on the page. This attribute can have one of nine values: LEFT, RIGHT, TOP, TEXTTOP, MIDDLE, ABSMIDDLE, BASELINE, BOTTOM, or ABSBOTTOM.

In the case of ALIGN=LEFT and ALIGN=RIGHT, the applet is placed at the left or right margin of the page, respectively, and all text following that applet flows in the space to the right or left of that applet. The text will continue to flow in that space until the end of the applet, or you can use a line break tag (<BR>) with the CLEAR attribute to start the left line of text below that applet. The CLEAR attribute can have one of three values: CLEAR=LEFT starts the text at the next clear left margin, CLEAR=RIGHT does the same for the right margin, and CLEAR=ALL starts the text at the next line where both margins are clear.

 NOTE

> In Netscape Navigator for Windows, the use of the ALIGN attribute prevents the applet from actually being loaded (this is a bug; it works fine in the UNIX and Macintosh versions of Netscape, as well as in Internet Explorer). If you're using alignment extensively in your Web pages with applets, you might want to enclose them in tables and align the tables themselves rather than use ALIGN.

For example, here's a snippet of HTML code that aligns an applet against the left margin, has some text flowing alongside it, and then breaks at the end of the paragraph so that the next bit of text starts below the applet:

```
<P><APPLET CODE="HelloAgainApplet.class" WIDTH=200 HEIGHT=50
ALIGN=LEFT>Hello Again!</APPLET>
To the left of this paragraph is an applet. It's a
simple, unassuming applet, in which a small string is
printed in red type, set in 36 point Times bold.
<BR CLEAR=ALL>
<P>In the next part of the page, we demonstrate how
under certain conditions, styrofoam peanuts can be
used as a healthy snack.
```

Figure 8.3 shows how this applet and the text surrounding it might appear in a Java-enabled browser (I've lightened the default page background so you can see where the applet begins and the background ends).

Figure 8.3.

An applet aligned left.

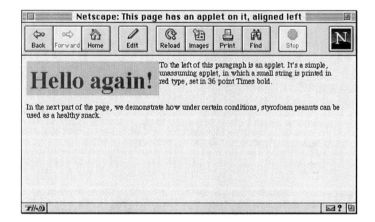

For smaller applets, you might want to include your applet within a single line of text. To do this, there are seven values for ALIGN that determine how the applet is vertically aligned with the text:

☐ ALIGN=TEXTTOP aligns the top of the applet with the top of the tallest text in the line.

☐ ALIGN=TOP aligns the applet with the topmost item in the line (which may be another applet, or an image, or the top of the text).

☐ ALIGN=ABSMIDDLE aligns the middle of the applet with the middle of the largest item in the line.

☐ ALIGN=MIDDLE aligns the middle of the applet with the middle of the baseline of the text.

☐ ALIGN=BASELINE aligns the bottom of the applet with the baseline of the text. ALIGN=BASELINE is the same as ALIGN=BOTTOM, but ALIGN=BASELINE is a more descriptive name.

☐ ALIGN=ABSBOTTOM aligns the bottom of the applet with the lowest item in the line (which may be the baseline of the text or another applet or image).

Figure 8.4 shows the various alignment options, where the line is an image and the arrow is a small applet.

Figure 8.4.

Applet alignment options.

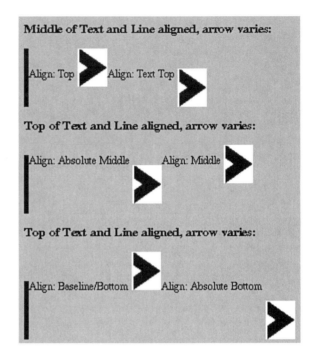

HSPACE **and** VSPACE

The HSPACE and VSPACE attributes are used to set the amount of space, in pixels, between an applet and its surrounding text. HSPACE controls the horizontal space (the space to the left and right of the applet). VSPACE controls the vertical space (the space above and below). For example, here's that sample snippet of HTML with vertical space of 50 and horizontal space of 10:

```
<P><APPLET CODE="HelloAgainApplet.class" WIDTH=300 HEIGHT=200
ALIGN=LEFT VSPACE=50 HSPACE=10>Hello Again!</APPLET>
To the left of this paragraph is an applet. Its a
simple, unassuming applet, in which a small string is
printed in red type, set in 36 point Times bold.
<BR CLEAR=ALL>
<P>In the next part of the page, we demonstrate how
under certain conditions, styrofoam peanuts can be
used as a healthy snack.
```

The result in a typical Java browser might look like that in Figure 8.5.

8

Figure 8.5.

Vertical and horizontal space.

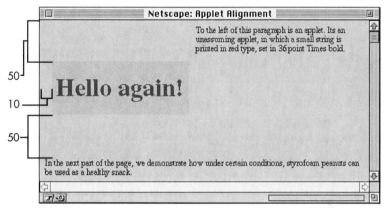

CODE and CODEBASE

The final two attributes to note in <APPLET> are CODE and CODEBASE. Unlike the other attributes, neither of these has anything to do with the applet's appearance on the page; these two refer to the actual location of the Java applet file so that the Java-enabled browser can find it.

CODE is used to indicate the name of the class file that holds the current applet. If CODE is used alone in the <APPLET> tag, the class file is searched for in the same directory as the HTML file that references it. Note that class filenames used in CODE have the .class extension; this is different from in the Java command-line interpreter, which doesn't use the extension.

If you want to store your class files in a different directory on your Web server than that of your HTML files, you have to tell the browser where to find those class files. To do this, you use CODEBASE. CODE contains only the name of the class file; CODEBASE contains an alternate pathname (actually a URL or relative pathname) where classes are contained. For example, if you store your class files in a directory called classes, which is in the same directory as your HTML files, CODEBASE is the following:

```
<APPLET CODE="myclass.class" CODEBASE="classes"
    WIDTH=100 HEIGHT=100></APPLET>
```

If you store all your Java classes in some central location, you can also use a URL in CODEBASE:

```
<APPLET CODE="myclass.class" CODEBASE="http://myserver.com/javaclasses"
    WIDTH=100 HEIGHT=100></APPLET>
```

What if your class files are actually stored on an entirely different server altogether? You can use that URL in CODEBASE as well:

```
<APPLET CODE="myclass.class" CODEBASE="http://www.joesserver.com/javaclasses"
    WIDTH=100 HEIGHT=100></APPLET>
```

Java Archives

Normally, using the standard way of indicating Java applets in Web pages, you use <APPLET> to point to the primary applet class for your applet. Your Java-enabled browser will then download and run that applet. That applet may use other classes or media files, all of which are also downloaded from the Web server as they are needed.

The problem with running applets in this way is that every single file an applet needs—be it another helper class, image, audio file, text file, or anything else—is a separate connection the browser has to make to the server. Because there's a fair amount of time needed just to make the connection itself, this can increase the amount of time it takes to download your applet and everything it needs.

The solution to this problem is a Java archive. A Java archive is a collection of Java classes and other files contained in a single file. By using a Java archive, the browser only makes one connection to the server, rather than several. By reducing the number of files the browser has to load from the server, your applet can be downloaded and run that much faster. Java archives may also be compressed, making the overall file size smaller and therefore faster to download as well (although it may take some time on the browser side for the files to be decompressed before they can run).

Right now only Netscape supports the use of Java archives, and only for Java class files (not for media). Within Netscape, you can use the ARCHIVE attribute to indicate the name of the archive, like this:

```
<APPLET CODE="MyApplet.class" ARCHIVE="appletstuff.zip" WIDTH=100 HEIGHT=100>
...
</APPLET>
```

The archive itself is an uncompressed zip file. Standard zip files, which use some form of compression to make the file smaller, are not recognized. Also, helper classes may be contained inside or outside the zip file; Netscape will look in either place.

The ARCHIVE attribute is ignored by browsers or applet viewers that may run across this Web page. If you do use Java archives for Netscape, it's a good idea to store both the archive and the individual files on your Web server so that all the Java-enabled browsers who visit your Web page can view your applet.

In addition to Netscape's simple archive scheme, Java 1.1 will include support for JAR files. JAR files are Java archives, with or without compression, that can contain both classes and media. In addition, JAR files are platform independent, and the tools to create them will be available on any platform that supports the JDK. JAR files and their individual components can also be digitally signed, meaning that their creator can be reliably identified (a form of

8

security). For more information about JAR files, including the specifications for the actual file format, see the JDK 1.1 Preview Page at http://java.sun.com/products/JDK/1.1/ designspecs/.

Passing Parameters to Applets

With Java applications, you pass parameters to your main() routine by using arguments on the command line, or, for Macintoshes, in the Java Runner's dialog box. You can then parse those arguments inside the body of your class, and the application acts accordingly, based on the arguments it is given.

Applets, however, don't have a command line. How do you pass in different arguments to an applet? Applets can get different input from the HTML file that contains the <APPLET> tag through the use of applet parameters. To set up and handle parameters in an applet, you need two things:

☐ A special parameter tag in the HTML file

☐ Code in your applet to parse those parameters

Applet parameters come in two parts: a parameter name, which is simply a name you pick, and a value, which is the actual value of that particular parameter. So, for example, you can indicate the color of text in an applet by using a parameter with the name color and the value red. You can determine an animation's speed using a parameter with the name speed and the value 5.

In the HTML file that contains the embedded applet, you indicate each parameter using the <PARAM> tag, which has two attributes for the name and the value, called (surprisingly enough) NAME and VALUE. The <PARAM> tag goes inside the opening and closing <APPLET> tags:

```
<APPLET CODE="MyApplet.class" WIDTH=100 HEIGHT=100>
<PARAM NAME=font VALUE="TimesRoman">
<PARAM NAME=size VALUE="36">
A Java applet appears here.</APPLET>
```

This particular example defines two parameters to the MyApplet applet: one whose name is font and whose value is TimesRoman, and one whose name is size and whose value is 36.

Parameters are passed to your applet when it is loaded. In the init() method for your applet, you can then get hold of those parameters by using the getParameter() method. getParameter() takes one argument—a string representing the name of the parameter you're looking for—and returns a string containing the corresponding value of that parameter. (Like arguments in Java applications, all the parameter values are strings.) To get the value of the font parameter from the HTML file, you might have a line such as this in your init() method:

```
String theFontName = getParameter("font");
```

NOTE

> The names of the parameters as specified in `<PARAM>` and the names of the parameters in `getParameter()` must match identically, including having the same case. In other words, `<PARAM NAME="name">` is different from `<PARAM NAME="Name">`. If your parameters are not being properly passed to your applet, make sure the parameter cases match.

Note that if a parameter you expect has not been specified in the HTML file, `getParameter()` returns `null`. Most often, you will want to test for a `null` parameter in your Java code and supply a reasonable default:

```
if (theFontName == null)
    theFontName = "Courier"
```

Keep in mind that `getParameter()` returns strings—if you want a parameter to be some other object or type, you have to convert it yourself. To parse the `size` parameter from that same HTML file and assign it to an integer variable called `theSize`, you might use the following lines:

```
int theSize;
String s = getParameter("size");
if (s == null)
    theSize = 12;
else theSize = Integer.parseInt(s);
```

Get it? Not yet? Let's create an example of an applet that uses this technique. You'll modify the Hello Again applet so that it says hello to a specific name, for example, `"Hello Bill"` or `"Hello Alice"`. The name is passed into the applet through an HTML parameter.

Let's start by copying the original `HelloAgainApplet` class and calling it `MoreHelloAgain` (see Listing 8.3).

TYPE **Listing 8.3. The More Hello Again applet.**

```
 1:import java.awt.Graphics;
 2:import java.awt.Font;
 3:import java.awt.Color;
 4:
 5:public class MoreHelloApplet extends java.applet.Applet {
 6:
 7:    Font f = new Font("TimesRoman", Font.BOLD, 36);
 8:
 9:    public void paint(Graphics g) {
10:        g.setFont(f);
11:        g.setColor(Color.red);
12:        g.drawString("Hello Again!", 5, 40);
13:    }
14:}
```

The first thing you need to add to this class is a place to hold the name of the person you're saying hello to. Because you'll need that name throughout the applet, let's add an instance variable for the name, just after the variable for the font in line 7:

```
String name;
```

To set a value for the name, you have to get that parameter from the HTML file. The best place to handle parameters to an applet is inside an `init()` method. The `init()` method is defined similarly to `paint()` (`public`, with no arguments, and a return type of `void`). Make sure when you test for a parameter that you test for a value of `null`. The default, in this case, if a name isn't indicated, is to say hello to `"Laura"`. Add the `init()` method in between your instance variable definitions and the definition for `paint()`, just before line 9:

```
public void init() {
    name = getParameter("name");
    if (name == null)
        name = "Laura";
}
```

Now that you have the name from the HTML parameters, you'll need to modify it so that it's a complete string—that is, to tack the word `Hello` with a space onto the beginning, and an exclamation point onto the end. You could do this in the `paint()` method just before printing the string to the screen, but that would mean creating a new string every time the applet is painted. It would be much more efficient to do it just once, right after getting the name itself, in the `init()` method. Add this line to the `init()` method just before the last brace:

```
name = "Hello " + name + "!";
```

And now, all that's left is to modify the `paint()` method to use the new name parameter. The original `drawString()` method looked like this:

```
g.drawString("Hello Again!", 5, 40);
```

To draw the new string you have stored in the `name` instance variable, all you need to do is substitute that variable for the literal string:

```
g.drawString(name, 5, 40);
```

Listing 8.4 shows the final result of the `MoreHelloApplet` class. Compile it so that you have a class file ready.

TYPE | **Listing 8.4. The `MoreHelloApplet` class.**

```
1:  import java.awt.Graphics;
2:  import java.awt.Font;
3:  import java.awt.Color;
4:
```

continues

Listing 8.4. continued

```
 5:  public class MoreHelloApplet extends java.applet.Applet {
 6:
 7:      Font f = new Font("TimesRoman", Font.BOLD, 36);
 8:      String name;
 9:
10:      public void init() {
11:          name = getParameter("name");
12:          if (name == null)
13:              name = "Laura";
14:
15:          name = "Hello " + name + "!";
16:      }
17:
18:      public void paint(Graphics g) {
19:          g.setFont(f);
20:          g.setColor(Color.red);
21:          g.drawString(name, 5, 40);
22:      }
23: }
```

Now let's create the HTML file that contains this applet. Listing 8.5 shows a new Web page for the MoreHelloApplet applet.

TYPE   **Listing 8.5. The HTML file for the MoreHelloApplet applet.**

```
 1:  <HTML>
 2:  <HEAD>
 3:  <TITLE>Hello!</TITLE>
 4:  </HEAD>
 5:  <BODY>
 6:  <P>
 7:  <APPLET CODE="MoreHelloApplet.class" WIDTH=200 HEIGHT=50>
 8:  <PARAM NAME=name VALUE="Bonzo">
 9:  Hello to whoever you are!
10:  </APPLET>
11:  </BODY>
12:  </HTML>
```

ANALYSIS   Note the <APPLET> tag, which points to the class file for the applet and has the appropriate width and height (200 and 50). Just below it (line 8) is the <PARAM> tag, which you use to pass in the value for the name. Here, the NAME parameter is simply name, and the VALUE is the string "Bonzo".

Loading up this HTML file in Netscape produces the result shown in Figure 8.6.

Let's try a second example. Remember that in the code for MoreHelloApplet, if no name is specified in a parameter, the default is the name Laura. Listing 8.6 creates an HTML file with no parameter tag for name.

Figure 8.6.

The result of using
MoreHelloApplet *the first
time.*

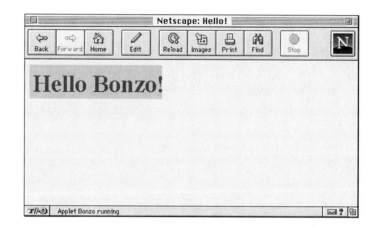

TYPE **Listing 8.6. Another HTML file for the MoreHelloApplet applet.**

```
 1: <HTML>
 2: <HEAD>
 3: <TITLE>Hello!</TITLE>
 4: </HEAD>
 5: <BODY>
 6: <P>
 7: <APPLET CODE="MoreHelloApplet.class" WIDTH=200 HEIGHT=50>
 8: Hello to whoever you are!
 9: </APPLET>
10: </BODY>
11: </HTML>
```

Here, because no name was supplied, the applet uses the default, and the result is what you might expect (see Figure 8.7).

Figure 8.7.

The result of using
MoreHelloApplet *the
second time.*

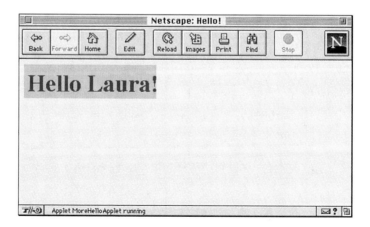

Summary

Applets are probably the most common use of the Java language today. Applets are more complicated than many Java applications because they are executed and drawn inline within Web pages, but they can access the graphics, user interface, and event structure provided by the Web browser itself. Today you learned the basics of creating applets, including the following things:

☐ All applets you develop using Java inherit from the Applet class, which is part of the java.applet package. The Applet class provides basic behavior for how the applet will be integrated with and react to the browser and various forms of input from that browser and the person running it. By subclassing Applet, you have access to all that behavior.

☐ Applets have five main methods, which are used for the basic activities an applet performs during its life cycle: init(), start(), stop(), destroy(), and paint(). Although you don't need to override all these methods, these are the most common methods you'll see repeated in many of the applets you'll create in this book and in other sample programs.

☐ To run a compiled applet class file, you include it in an HTML Web page by using the <APPLET> tag. When a Java-capable browser comes across <APPLET>, it loads and runs the applet described in that tag. Note that to publish Java applets on the World Wide Web alongside HTML files you do not need special server software; any plain old Web server will do just fine.

☐ Unlike applications, applets do not have a command line on which to pass arguments, so those arguments must be passed into the applet through the HTML file that contains it. You indicate parameters in an HTML file by using the <PARAM> tag inside the opening and closing <APPLET> tags. <PARAM> has two attributes: NAME for the name of the parameter, and VALUE for its value. Inside the body of your applet (usually in init()), you can then gain access to those parameters using the getParameter() method.

Q&A

Q **In the first part of today's lesson, you say that applets are downloaded from random Web servers and run on the client's system. What's to stop an applet developer from creating an applet that deletes all the files on that system, or in some other way compromises the security of the system?**

A Recall that Java applets have several restrictions that make it difficult for all of the more obvious malicious behavior to take place. For example, because Java applets cannot read or write files on the client system, they cannot delete files or read system files that might contain private information. Because they cannot run programs on the client's system without your express permission, they cannot, for example, pretend to be you and run system programs. Nor can they run so many programs that your system crashes.

In addition, Java's very architecture makes it difficult to circumvent these restrictions. The language itself, the Java compiler, and the Java interpreter all have checks to make sure that no one has tried to sneak in bogus code or play games with the system itself. You'll learn more about these checks at the end of this book.

Of course, no system can claim to be 100 percent secure, and the fact that Java applets are run on your system should make you suspicious—see Day 21 for more on security.

Q Wait a minute. If I can't read or write files or run programs on the system the applet is running on, doesn't that mean I basically can't do anything other than simple animation and flashy graphics? How can I save state in an applet? How can I create, say, a word processor or a spreadsheet as a Java applet?

A For everyone who doesn't believe that Java is secure enough, there is someone who believes that Java's security restrictions are too severe for just these reasons. Yes, Java applets are limited because of the security restrictions. But, given the possibility for abuse, I believe that it's better to err on the side of being more conservative as far as security is concerned. Consider it a challenge.

Keep in mind, also, that Java applications have none of the restrictions that Java applets do, but because they are also compiled to bytecode, they are portable across platforms. It may be that the thing you want to create would make a much better application than an applet.

If the thing you want to create has to be an applet, the only solution you have for saving state or implementing something like a word processor in a Java applet is to allow your readers to save the state back to your server.

Q Will applets be like this forever—confined to the sandbox and unable to do anything other than whizzy animation and simple toys?

A Sun is working on future models for applet security that will allow applets to break out of the sandbox in some instances. One of the solutions being discussed is for the applet class file to be digitally signed, which is a way to identify without a doubt where an applet came from (for example, if an applet is signed by Sun, you can be sure it was Sun that actually created it, and therefore trust it more than some other random applet need). You'll learn more about applet security on Day 21.

Q I have an older version of the HotJava browser. I followed all the examples in this section, but HotJava cannot read my applets (it seems to ignore them). What's going on?

A You most likely have an alpha version of HotJava. Recall that significant changes were made to the Java API and how Java applets are written between alpha and the 1.0 release. The result of these changes is that browsers that support alpha applets cannot read beta applets, and vice versa. The HTML tags are even different, so an older browser just skips over newer applets, and vice versa.

By the time you read this, there may be a new version of HotJava with support for 1.0. If not, you can use Netscape, Internet Explorer, or the JDK's `appletviewer` to view applets written to the beta specification.

Q **I noticed in my documentation that the `<APPLET>` tag also has a `NAME` attribute. You didn't discuss it here.**

A `NAME` is used when you have multiple applets on a page that need to communicate with each other. You'll learn about this on Day 12, "Managing Simple Events and Interactivity."

Q **Lots of the applet examples I've seen on the Web have an `init()` method that does nothing to call a `resize()` method with the same values as in the `<APPLET>` tag's `WIDTH` and `HEIGHT`. I asked a friend about that and he said that you have to have `resize()` in there to make sure the applet's the right size. You don't mention `resize()`.**

A The call to the `resize()` method in `init()` is left over from the early days of applets when you did need `resize()` to set the initial size of the applet. These days only the `WIDTH` and `HEIGHT` attributes do that; calling `resize()` isn't necessary.

Q **I have an applet that takes parameters and an HTML file that passes it those parameters. But when my applet runs, all I get are `null` values. What's going on here?**

A Do the names of your parameters (in the `NAME` attribute) match exactly with the names you're testing for in `getParameter()`? They must be exact, including case, for the match to be made. Make sure also that your `<PARAM>` tags are inside the opening and closing `<APPLET>` tags, and that you haven't misspelled anything.

Q **Since applets don't have a command line or a `stdout` stream, how can you do simple debugging output like `System.out.println()` in an applet?**

A You can. Depending on your browser or other Java-enabled environment, there may be a console window where debugging output (the result of `System.out.println()`) appears, or it may be saved to a log file (Netscape has a Java Console under the Options menu; Internet Explorer uses a Java log file that you must enable using Options | Advanced). You can continue to print messages using `System.out.println()` in your applets—just remember to remove them once you're done so they don't confuse your actual readers!

Day 9

Graphics, Fonts, and Color

by Laura Lemay

Knowing the basics of how applets work is only the first step. The next step is to become familiar with the capabilities Java gives you for drawing to the screen, performing dynamic updating, managing mouse and keyboard events, and creating user interface elements. You'll do all these things this week. You'll start today with how to draw to the screen—that is, how to produce lines and shapes with the built-in graphics primitives, how to print text using fonts, and how to use and modify color in your applets. Today you'll learn, specifically, the following:

☐ How the graphics system works in Java: the Graphics class, the coordinate system used to draw to the screen, and how applets paint and repaint

☐ How to use the Java graphics primitives, including drawing and filling lines, rectangles, ovals, and arcs

☐ How to create and use fonts, including how to draw characters and strings and how to find out the metrics of a given font for better layout

☐ All about color in Java, including the Color class and how to set the foreground (drawing) and background color for your applet

NOTE

Today and for the rest of this week, you'll get an introduction to many of the classes that make up the Java class libraries, in particular the classes in the java.awt package. Keep in mind, however, that I only have the space to give you an introduction to these classes—there are many other capabilities available to you in these classes that you can use in your own programs, depending on what you're trying to accomplish. After you finish this book (and perhaps after each of these lessons), you'll want to familiarize yourself with the classes themselves and what they can do. Be sure to check out the Java API documentation for more details; you can find that API documentation on the Java Web site at `http://java.sun.com/products/JDK/1.0.2/api/packages.html`.

The Graphics Class

With the basic graphics capabilities built into Java's class libraries, you can draw lines, shapes, characters, and images to the screen inside your applet. Most of the graphics operations in Java are methods defined in the Graphics class. You don't have to create an instance of Graphics in order to draw something in your applet; in your applet's paint() method (which you learned about yesterday), you are given a Graphics object. By drawing on that object, you draw onto your applet and the results appear onscreen.

The Graphics class is part of the java.awt package, so if your applet does any painting (as it usually will), make sure you import that class at the beginning of your Java file:

```
import java.awt.Graphics;

public class MyClass extends java.applet.Applet {
...
}
```

The Graphics Coordinate System

To draw an object on the screen, you call one of the drawing methods available in the Graphics class. All the drawing methods have arguments representing endpoints, corners, or starting locations of the object as values in the applet's coordinate system—for example, a line starts at the point 10,10 and ends at the point 20,20.

Java's coordinate system has the origin (0,0) in the top-left corner. Positive x values are to the right and positive y values are down. All pixel values are integers; there are no partial or fractional pixels. Figure 9.1 shows how you might draw a simple square by using this coordinate system.

Figure 9.1.

The Java graphics coordinate system.

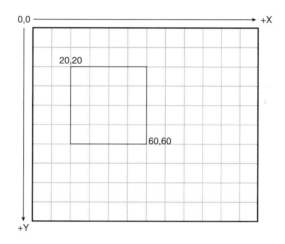

Java's coordinate system is different from that of many painting and layout programs, which have their x and y in the bottom left. If you're not used to working with this upside-down graphics system, it may take some practice to get familiar with it.

Drawing and Filling

The Graphics class provides a set of simple built-in graphics primitives for drawing, including lines, rectangles, polygons, ovals, and arcs.

NOTE

> Bitmap images, such as GIF files, can also be drawn by using the Graphics class. You'll learn about this tomorrow.

Lines

To draw straight lines, use the drawLine() method. drawLine() takes four arguments: the x and y coordinates of the starting point and the x and y coordinates of the ending point. So, for example, the following `MyLine` class draws a line from the point 25,25 to the point 75,75. Note that the `drawLine()` method is defined in the `Graphics` class (as are all the other graphics methods you'll learn about today). Here we're using that method for the current graphics context stored in the variable g:

```
import java.awt.Graphics;

public class MyLine extends java.applet.Applet {
    public void paint(Graphics g) {
        g.drawLine(25,25,75,75);
    }
}
```

Figure 9.2 shows how the simple `MyLine` class looks in a Java-enabled browser such as Netscape.

Figure 9.2.

Drawing lines.

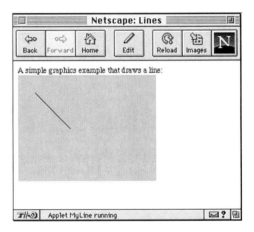

Rectangles

The Java graphics primitives provide not just one, but three kinds of rectangles:

☐ Plain rectangles

☐ Rounded rectangles, which are rectangles with rounded corners

☐ Three-dimensional rectangles, which are drawn with a shaded border

For each of these rectangles, you have two methods to choose from: one that draws the rectangle in outline form and one that draws the rectangle filled with color.

To draw a plain rectangle, use either the `drawRect()` or `fillRect()` methods. Both take four arguments: the x and y coordinates of the top-left corner of the rectangle, and the width and height of the rectangle to draw. For example, the following class (`MyRect`) draws two squares: The left one is an outline and the right one is filled (Figure 9.3 shows the result):

```
import java.awt.Graphics;

public class MyRect extends java.applet.Applet {
    public void paint(Graphics g) {
        g.drawRect(20,20,60,60);
        g.fillRect(120,20,60,60);
    }
}
```

Figure 9.3.

Rectangles.

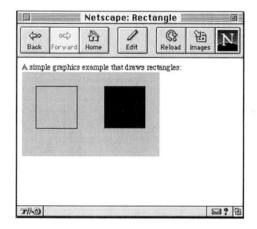

Rounded rectangles are, as you might expect, rectangles with rounded corners. The drawRoundRect() and fillRoundRect() methods to draw rounded rectangles are similar to regular rectangles except that rounded rectangles have two extra arguments for the width and height of the angle of the corners. Those two arguments determine how far along the edges of the rectangle the arc for the corner will start; the first for the angle along the horizontal plane, the second for the vertical. Larger values for the angle width and height make the overall rectangle more rounded; values equal to the width and height of the rectangle itself produce a circle. Figure 9.4 shows some examples of rounded corners.

The following is a paint() method inside a class called MyRRect that draws two rounded rectangles: one as an outline with a rounded corner 10 pixels square; the other, filled, with a rounded corner 20 pixels square (Figure 9.5 shows the resulting squares):

```
import java.awt.Graphics;

public class MyRRect extends java.applet.Applet {
    public void paint(Graphics g) {
        g.drawRoundRect(20,20,60,60,10,10);
        g.fillRoundRect(120,20,60,60,20,20);
    }
}
```

Figure 9.4.

Rounded corners.

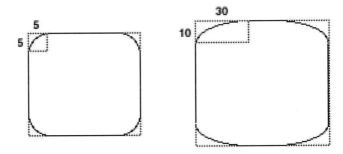

Figure 9.5.

Rounded rectangles.

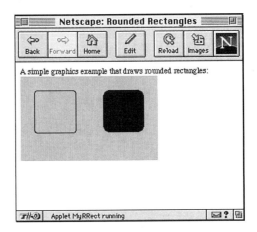

Finally, there are three-dimensional rectangles. These rectangles aren't really 3D; instead, they have a slight shadow effect that makes them appear either raised or indented from the surface of the applet. Three-dimensional rectangles have four arguments for the x and y of the start position and the width and height of the rectangle. The fifth argument is a boolean indicating whether the 3D effect is to raise the rectangle (`true`) or indent it (`false`). As with the other rectangles, there are also different methods for drawing and filling: `draw3DRect()` and `fill3DRect()`. The following is a class called `My3DRect`, which produces two 3D squares—the left one raised, the right one indented (Figure 9.6 shows the result):

```
import java.awt.Graphics;

public class My3DRect extends java.applet.Applet {
    public void paint(Graphics g) {
        g.draw3DRect(20,20,60,60,true);
        g.draw3DRect(120,20,60,60,false);
    }
}
```

Figure 9.6.

*Three-dimensional
rectangles.*

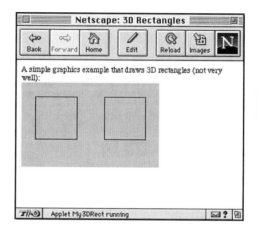

NOTE

The 3D rectangles in Figure 9.6 don't look very 3D, do they? In the
current version of the Java Developer's Kit, it is extremely difficult to
see the 3D effect on 3D rectangles, due to a very small line width. If
you are having troubles with 3D rectangles, this may be why. Drawing
3D rectangles in any color other than black makes them easier to see.

Polygons

Polygons are shapes with an unlimited number of sides. To draw a polygon, you need a set
of x and y coordinates. The polygon is then drawn as a set of straight lines from the first point
to the second, the second to the third, and so on.

As with rectangles, you can draw an outline or a filled polygon (using the drawPolygon() and
fillPolygon() methods, respectively). You also have a choice of how you want to indicate
the list of coordinates—either as arrays of x and y coordinates or as an instance of the Polygon
class.

Using the first way of drawing polygons, the drawPolygon() and fillPolygon() methods take three arguments:

☐ An array of integers representing x coordinates

☐ An array of integers representing y coordinates

☐ An integer for the total number of points

The x and y arrays should, of course, have the same number of elements.

Here's an example of drawing a polygon's outline using this method (Figure 9.7 shows the result):

```
import java.awt.Graphics;

public class MyPoly extends java.applet.Applet {
    public void paint(Graphics g) {
        int exes[] = { 39,94,97,142,53,58,26 };
        int whys[] = { 33,74,36,70,108,80,106 };
        int pts = exes.length;

        g.drawPolygon(exes,whys,pts);
    }
}
```

Figure 9.7.

A polygon.

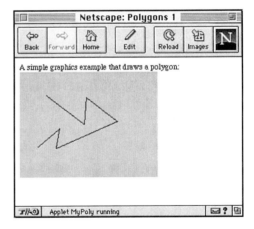

Note that Java does not automatically close the polygon; if you want to complete the shape, you have to include the starting point of the polygon at the end of the array. Drawing a filled polygon, however, joins the starting and ending points.

The second way of calling drawPolygon() and fillPolygon() is to use a Polygon object to store the individual points of the polygon. The Polygon class is useful if you intend to add points to the polygon or if you're building the polygon on-the-fly. Using the Polygon class, you can treat the polygon as an object rather than having to deal with individual arrays.

To create a polygon object, you can either first create an empty polygon:

```
Polygon poly = new Polygon();
```

or create a polygon from a set of points using integer arrays, as in the previous example:

```
int exes[] = { 39,94,97,142,53,58,26 };
int whys[] = { 33,74,36,70,108,80,106 };
int pts = exes.length;
Polygon poly = new Polygon(exes,whys,pts);
```

Once you have a polygon object, you can add points to the polygon as you need to:

```
poly.addPoint(20,35);
```

Then, to draw the polygon, just use the polygon object as an argument to `drawPolygon()` or `fillPolygon()`. Here's that previous example, rewritten this time with a `Polygon` object. You'll also fill this polygon rather than just drawing its outline (Figure 9.8 shows the output):

```
import java.awt.Graphics;

public class MyPoly2 extends java.applet.Applet {
    public void paint(Graphics g) {
        int exes[] = { 39,94,97,142,53,58,26 };
        int whys[] = { 33,74,36,70,108,80,106 };
        int pts = exes.length;
        Polygon poly = new Polygon(exes,whys,pts);
        g.fillPolygon(poly);
    }
}
```

Figure 9.8.

Another polygon.

Ovals

You use ovals to draw ellipses or circles. Ovals are just like rectangles with overly rounded corners. You draw them using four arguments: the x and y of the top corner, and the width and height of the oval itself. Note that because you're drawing an oval, the starting point is some distance to the left and up from the actual outline of the oval itself. Again, if you think of it as a rectangle, it's easier to place.

As with the other drawing operations, the drawOval() method draws an outline of an oval, and the fillOval() method draws a filled oval.

The following example draws two ovals—a circle and an ellipse (Figure 9.9 shows how these two ovals appear onscreen):

```
import java.awt.Graphics;

public class MyOval extends java.applet.Applet {
    public void paint(Graphics g) {
        g.drawOval(20,20,60,60);
        g.fillOval(120,20,100,60);
    }
}
```

Figure 9.9.

Ovals.

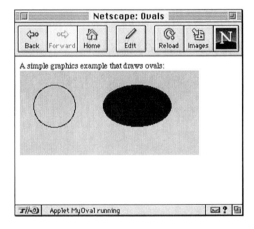

Arcs

Of all the shapes you can construct using methods in the Graphics class, arcs are the most complex to construct, which is why I saved them for last. An arc is a part of an oval; in fact, the easiest way to think of an arc is as a section of a complete oval. Figure 9.10 shows some arcs.

Figure 9.10.

Arcs.

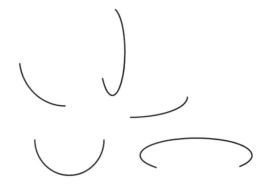

9

The drawArc() method takes six arguments: the starting corner, the width and height, the angle at which to start the arc, and the degrees to draw it before stopping. Once again, there is a drawArc method to draw the arc's outline and the fillArc() method to fill the arc. Filled arcs are drawn as if they were sections of a pie; instead of joining the two endpoints, both endpoints are joined to the center of the circle.

The important thing to understand about arcs is that you're actually formulating the arc as an oval and then drawing only some of that. The starting corner and width and height are not the starting point and width and height of the actual arc as drawn on the screen; they're the width and height of the full ellipse of which the arc is a part. Those first points determine the size and shape of the arc; the last two arguments (for the degrees) determine the starting and ending points.

Let's start with a simple arc, a C shape on a circle, as shown in Figure 9.11.

Figure 9.11.

A C arc.

To construct the method to draw this arc, the first thing you do is think of it as a complete circle. Then you find the x and y coordinates and the width and height of that circle. Those four values are the first four arguments to the drawArc() or fillArc() methods. Figure 9.12 shows how to get those values from the arc.

Figure 9.12.

Constructing a circular arc.

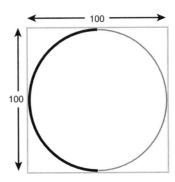

To get the last two arguments, think in degrees around the circle, going counterclockwise. Zero degrees is at 3 o'clock, 90 degrees is at 12 o'clock, 180 at 9 o'clock, and 270 at 6 o'clock. The start of the arc is the degree value of the start of the arc. In this example, the starting point is the top of the C at 90 degrees; 90 is the fifth argument.

The sixth and last argument is another degree value indicating how far around the circle to sweep and the direction to go in (it's *not* the ending degree angle, as you might think). In this case, because you're going halfway around the circle, you're sweeping 180 degrees—and 180 is therefore the last argument in the arc. The important part is that you're sweeping 180 degrees counterclockwise, which is in the positive direction in Java. If you are drawing a backwards C, you sweep 180 degrees in the negative direction, and the last argument is -180. See Figure 9.13 for the final illustration of how this works.

Figure 9.13.

Arcs on circles.

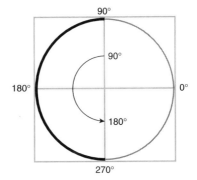

NOTE

It doesn't matter which side of the arc you start with. Because the shape of the arc has already been determined by the complete oval it's a section of, starting at either endpoint will work.

Here's the code for this example; you'll draw an outline of the C and a filled C to its right, as shown in Figure 9.14:

```
import java.awt.Graphics;

public class MyOval extends java.applet.Applet {
    public void paint(Graphics g) {
        g.drawArc(20,20,60,60,90,180);
        g.fillArc(120,20,60,60,90,180);
    }
}
```

Figure 9.14.

Two circular arcs.

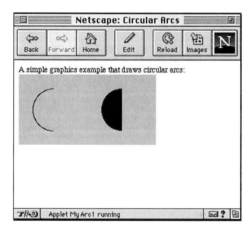

Circles are an easy way to visualize arcs on circles; arcs on ellipses are slightly more difficult. Let's go through this same process to draw the arc shown in Figure 9.15.

Figure 9.15.

An elliptical arc.

Like the arc on the circle, this arc is a piece of a complete oval, in this case, an elliptical oval. By completing the oval that this arc is a part of, you can get the starting points and the width and height arguments for the `drawArc()` or `fillArc()` method (see Figure 9.16).

Figure 9.16.

Arcs on ellipses.

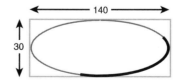

Then all you need is to figure out the starting angle and the angle to sweep. This arc doesn't start on a nice boundary such as 90 or 180 degrees, so you'll need some trial and error. This arc starts somewhere around 25 degrees, and then sweeps clockwise about 130 degrees (see Figure 9.17).

Figure 9.17.

Starting and ending points.

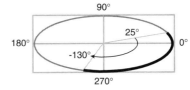

With all portions of the arc in place, you can write the code. Here's the Java code for this arc, both drawn and filled (note in the filled case how filled arcs are drawn as if they were pie sections):

```
import java.awt.Graphics;

public class MyOval extends java.applet.Applet {
    public void paint(Graphics g) {
        g.drawArc(10,20,150,50,25,-130);
        g.fillArc(10,80,150,50,25,-130);
    }
}
```

Figure 9.18 shows the two elliptical arcs.

Figure 9.18.

Two elliptical arcs.

To summarize, here are the steps to take to construct arcs in Java:

1. Think of the arc as a slice of a complete oval.

2. Construct the full oval with the starting point and the width and height (it often helps to draw the full oval on the screen to get an idea of the right positioning).

3. Determine the starting angle for the beginning of the arc.

4. Determine how far to sweep the arc and in which direction (counterclockwise indicates positive values, clockwise indicates negative).

A Simple Graphics Example

Here's an example of an applet that uses many of the built-in graphics primitives to draw a rudimentary shape. In this case, it's a lamp with a spotted shade (or a sort of cubist mushroom, depending on your point of view). Listing 9.1 has the complete code for the lamp; Figure 9.19 shows the resulting applet.

TYPE **Listing 9.1. The Lamp class.**

```
 1: import java.awt.*;
 2:
 3: public class Lamp extends java.applet.Applet {
 4:
 5:     public void paint(Graphics g) {
 6:         // the lamp platform
 7:         g.fillRect(0,250,290,290);
 8:
 9:         // the base of the lamp
10:         g.drawLine(125,250,125,160);
11:         g.drawLine(175,250,175,160);
12:
13:         // the lamp shade, top and bottom edges
14:         g.drawArc(85,157,130,50,-65,312);
15:         g.drawArc(85,87,130,50,62,58);
16:
17:         // lamp shade, sides
18:         g.drawLine(85,177,119,89);
19:         g.drawLine(215,177,181,89);
20:
21:         // dots on the shade
22:         g.fillArc(78,120,40,40,63,-174);
23:         g.fillOval(120,96,40,40);
24:         g.fillArc(173,100,40,40,110,180);
25:     }
26: }
```

Figure 9.19.

The Lamp applet.

Copying and Clearing

Once you've drawn a few things on the screen, you may want to move them around or clear the entire applet. The Graphics class provides methods for doing both these things.

The copyArea() method copies a rectangular area of the screen to another area of the screen. copyArea() takes six arguments: the x and y of the top corner of the rectangle to copy, the width and the height of that rectangle, and the distance in the x and y directions to which to copy it. For example, this line copies a square area 100 pixels on a side 100 pixels directly to its right:

```
g.copyArea(0,0,100,100,100,0);
```

To clear a rectangular area, use the clearRect() method. clearRect(), which takes the same four arguments as the drawRect() and fillRect() methods, fills the given rectangle with the current background color of the applet (you'll learn how to set the current background color later today).

To clear the entire applet, you can use the size() method, which returns a Dimension object representing the width and height of the applet. You can then get to the actual values for width and height by using the width and height instance variables:

```
g.clearRect(0,0,size().width,size().height);
```

Text and Fonts

Using the Graphics class, you can also print text on the screen, in conjunction with the Font class (and, sometimes, the FontMetrics class). The Font class represents a given font—its name, style, and point size—and FontMetrics gives you information about that font (for example, the actual height or width of a given character) so that you can precisely lay out text in your applet.

Note that the text here is drawn to the screen once and intended to stay there. You'll learn about entering text from the keyboard later this week.

Creating Font Objects

To draw text to the screen, first you need to create an instance of the Font class. Font objects represent an individual font—that is, its name, style (bold, italic), and point size. Font names are strings representing the family of the font, for example, "TimesRoman", "Courier", or "Helvetica". Font styles are constants defined by the Font class; you can get to them using class variables—for example, Font.PLAIN, Font.BOLD, or Font.ITALIC. Finally, the point size is the size of the font, as defined by the font itself; the point size may or may not be the height of the characters.

To create an individual font object, use these three arguments to the Font class's new constructor:

```
Font f = new Font("TimesRoman", Font.BOLD, 24);
```

This example creates a font object for the TimesRoman BOLD font, in 24 points. Note that like most Java classes, you have to import the java.awt.Font class before you can use it.

> **TIP**
>
> Font styles are actually integer constants that can be added to create combined styles; for example, Font.BOLD + Font.ITALIC produces a font that is both bold and italic.

The fonts you have available to you in your applets depend on which fonts are installed on the system where the applet is running. If you pick a font for your applet and that font isn't available on the current system, Java will substitute a default font (usually Courier). You can get an array of the names of the current fonts available in the system using this bit of code:

```
String[] fontslist = this.getToolkit().getFontList();
```

From this list, you can then often intelligently decide which fonts you want to use in your applet. For best results, however, it's a good idea to stick with standard fonts such as "TimesRoman", "Helvetica", and "Courier".

Drawing Characters and Strings

With a font object in hand, you can draw text on the screen using the methods drawChars() and drawString(). First, though, you need to set the current font to your font object using the setFont() method.

The current font is part of the graphics state that is kept track of by the Graphics object on which you're drawing. Each time you draw a character or a string to the screen, Java draws that text in the current font. To change the font of the text, therefore, first change the current font. The following paint() method creates a new font, sets the current font to that font, and draws the string "This is a big font.", at the point 10,100:

```
public void paint(Graphics g) {
    Font f = new Font("TimesRoman", Font.PLAIN, 72);
    g.setFont(f);
    g.drawString("This is a big font.", 10, 100);
}
```

This should all look familiar to you; this is how the Hello World and Hello Again applets throughout this book were produced.

The latter two arguments to drawString() determine the point where the string will start. The x value is the start of the leftmost edge of the text; y is the baseline for the entire string.

Similar to drawString() is the drawChars() method that, instead of taking a string as an argument, takes an array of characters. drawChars() has five arguments: the array of characters, an integer representing the first character in the array to draw, another integer for the last character in the array to draw (all characters between the first and last are drawn), and the x and y for the starting point. Most of the time, drawString() is more useful than drawChars().

Listing 9.2 shows an applet that draws several lines of text in different fonts; Figure 9.20 shows the result.

TYPE **Listing 9.2. Many different fonts.**

```
1: import java.awt.Font;
2: import java.awt.Graphics;
3:
4: public class ManyFonts extends java.applet.Applet {
5:
6:     public void paint(Graphics g) {
```

```
 7:          Font f = new Font("TimesRoman", Font.PLAIN, 18);
 8:          Font fb = new Font("TimesRoman", Font.BOLD, 18);
 9:          Font fi = new Font("TimesRoman", Font.ITALIC, 18);
10:          Font fbi = new Font("TimesRoman", Font.BOLD + Font.ITALIC, 18);
11:
12:          g.setFont(f);
13:          g.drawString("This is a plain font", 10, 25);
14:          g.setFont(fb);
15:          g.drawString("This is a bold font", 10, 50);
16:          g.setFont(fi);
17:          g.drawString("This is an italic font", 10, 75);
18:          g.setFont(fbi);
19:          g.drawString("This is a bold italic font", 10, 100);
20:      }
21:
22: }
```

Figure 9.20.

The output of the
ManyFonts *applet.*

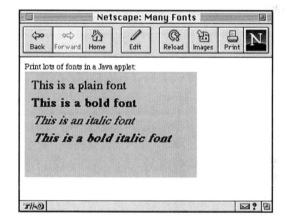

Finding Out Information About a Font

Sometimes you may want to make decisions in your Java program based on the qualities of the current font—for example, its point size and the total height of its characters. You can find out some basic information about fonts and font objects by using simple methods on Graphics and on the Font objects. Table 9.1 shows some of these methods.

Table 9.1. Font methods.

Method Name	In Object	Action
getFont()	Graphics	Returns the current font object as previously set by setFont()
getName()	Font	Returns the name of the font as a string
getSize()	Font	Returns the current font size (an integer)

continues

Table 9.1. continued

Method Name	In Object	Action
getStyle()	Font	Returns the current style of the font (styles are integer constants: 0 is plain, 1 is bold, 2 is italic, 3 is bold italic)
isPlain()	Font	Returns true or false if the font's style is plain
isBold()	Font	Returns true or false if the font's style is bold
isItalic()	Font	Returns true or false if the font's style is italic

For more detailed information about the qualities of the current font (for example, the length or height of given characters), you need to work with font metrics. The FontMetrics class describes information specific to a given font: the leading between lines, the height and width of each character, and so on. To work with these sorts of values, you create a FontMetrics object based on the current font by using the applet method getFontMetrics():

```
Font f = new Font("TimesRoman", Font.BOLD, 36);
FontMetrics fmetrics = getFontMetrics(f);
g.setfont(f);
```

Table 9.2 shows some of the things you can find out using font metrics. All these methods should be called on a FontMetrics object.

Table 9.2. Font metrics methods.

Method Name	Action
stringWidth(string)	Given a string, returns the full width of that string, in pixels
charWidth(char)	Given a character, returns the width of that character
getAscent()	Returns the ascent of the font, that is, the distance between the font's baseline and the top of the characters
getDescent()	Returns the descent of the font—that is, the distance between the font's baseline and the bottoms of the characters (for characters such as p and q that drop below the baseline)
getLeading()	Returns the leading for the font, that is, the spacing between the descent of one line and the ascent of another line
getHeight()	Returns the total height of the font, which is the sum of the ascent, descent, and leading value

As an example of the sorts of information you can use with font metrics, Listing 9.3 shows the Java code for an applet that automatically centers a string horizontally and vertically inside an applet. The centering position is different depending on the font and font size; by using font metrics to find out the actual size of a string, you can draw the string in the appropriate place.

Figure 9.21 shows the result (which is less interesting than if you actually compile and experiment with various applet and font sizes).

TYPE | **Listing 9.3. Centering a string.**

```
 1: import java.awt.Font;
 2: import java.awt.Graphics;
 3: import java.awt.FontMetrics;
 4:
 5: public class Centered extends java.applet.Applet {
 6:
 7:     public void paint(Graphics g) {
 8:         Font f = new Font("TimesRoman", Font.PLAIN, 36);
 9:         FontMetrics fm = getFontMetrics(f);
10:         g.setFont(f);
11:
12:         String s = "This is how the world ends.";
13:         int xstart = (size().width - fm.stringWidth(s)) / 2;
14:         int ystart = size().height / 2;
15:
16:         g.drawString(s, xstart, ystart);
17:     }
18:}
```

Figure 9.21.

The centered text.

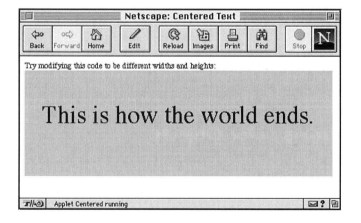

ANALYSIS Note the `size()` method in lines 13 and 14, which returns the width and height of the overall applet area as a `Dimension` object. You can then get to the individual width and height using the `width` and `height` instance variables of that `Dimension`, here by chaining the method call and the variable name. Getting the current applet size in this way is a better idea than hard coding the size of the applet into your code; this code works equally well with an applet of any size.

Note also that the line of text, as shown in Figure 9.21, isn't precisely vertically centered in the applet bounding box. This example centers the baseline of the text inside the applet; using the `getAscent()` and `getDescent()` methods from the `FontMetrics` class (to get the number of pixels from the baseline to the top of the characters and the number of pixels from the baseline to the bottom of the characters), you can figure out exactly the middle of the line of text.

Color

Drawing black lines and text on a gray background is all very nice, but being able to use different colors is much nicer. Java provides methods and behaviors for dealing with color in general through the `Color` class, and also provides methods for setting the current foreground and background colors so that you can draw with the colors you created.

Java's abstract color model uses 24-bit color, wherein a color is represented as a combination of red, green, and blue values. Each component of the color can have a number between `0` and `255`. `0,0,0` is black, `255,255,255` is white, and Java can represent millions of colors between as well.

Java's abstract color model maps onto the color model of the platform Java is running on, which usually has only 256 or fewer colors from which to choose. If a requested color in a color object is not available for display, the resulting color may be mapped to another or dithered, depending on how the browser viewing the color implemented it, and depending on the platform on which you're running. In other words, although Java gives the capability of managing millions of colors, very few may actually be available to you in real life.

Using Color Objects

To draw an object in a particular color, you must create an instance of the `Color` class to represent that color. The `Color` class defines a set of standard color objects, stored in class variables, to quickly get a color object for some of the more popular colors. For example, `Color.red` returns a `Color` object representing red (RGB values of `255`, `0`, and `0`), `Color.white` returns a white color (RGB values of `255`, `255`, and `255`), and so on. Table 9.3 shows the standard colors defined by variables in the `Color` class.

Table 9.3. Standard colors.

Color Name	RGB Value
Color.white	255,255,255
Color.black	0,0,0
Color.lightGray	192,192,192
Color.gray	128,128,128
Color.darkGray	64,64,64
Color.red	255,0,0
Color.green	0,255,0
Color.blue	0,0,255
Color.yellow	255,255,0
Color.magenta	255,0,255
Color.cyan	0,255,255
Color.pink	255,175,175
Color.orange	255,200,0

If the color you want to draw in is not one of the standard Color objects, fear not. You can create a color object for any combination of red, green, and blue, as long as you have the values of the color you want. Just create a new color object:

```
Color c = new Color(140,140,140);
```

This line of Java code creates a color object representing a dark gray. You can use any combination of red, green, and blue values to construct a color object.

Alternatively, you can create a color object using three floats from 0.0 to 1.0:

```
Color c = new Color(0.55,0.55,0.55);
```

Testing and Setting the Current Colors

To draw an object or text using a color object, you have to set the current color to be that color object, just as you have to set the current font to the font in which you want to draw. Use the setColor() method (a method for Graphics objects) to do this:

```
g.setColor(Color.green);
```

After you set the current color, all drawing operations will occur in that color.

In addition to setting the current color for the graphics context, you can also set the background and foreground colors for the applet itself by using the setBackground() and setForeground() methods. Both of these methods are defined in the java.awt.Component class, which Applet—and therefore your classes—automatically inherits.

The setBackground() method sets the background color of the applet, which is usually a light gray (to match the default background of the browser). It takes a single argument, a Color object:

```
setBackground(Color.white);
```

The setForeground() method also takes a single color as an argument, and it affects everything that has been drawn on the applet, regardless of the color in which it has been drawn. You can use setForeground() to change the color of everything in the applet at once, rather than having to redraw everything:

```
setForeground(Color.black);
```

In addition to the setColor(), setForeground(), and setBackground() methods, there are corresponding get methods that enable you to retrieve the current graphics color, background, or foreground. Those methods are getColor() (defined in Graphics objects), getForeground() (defined in Applet), and getBackground() (also in Applet). You can use these methods to choose colors based on existing colors in the applet:

```
setForeground(g.getColor());
```

A Simple Color Example

Listing 9.4 shows the code for an applet that fills the applet's drawing area with square boxes, each of which has a randomly chosen color in it. It's written so that it can handle any size of applet and automatically fill the area with the right number of boxes.

TYPE   **Listing 9.4. Random color boxes.**

```
 1: import java.awt.Graphics;
 2: import java.awt.Color;
 3:
 4: public class ColorBoxes extends java.applet.Applet {
 5:
 6:     public void paint(Graphics g) {
 7:         int rval, gval, bval;
 8:
 9:         for (int j = 30; j < (size().height -25); j += 30)
10:             for (int i = 5; i < (size().width -25); i += 30) {
11:                 rval = (int)Math.floor(Math.random() * 256);
12:                 gval = (int)Math.floor(Math.random() * 256);
```

```
13:                    bval = (int)Math.floor(Math.random() * 256);
14:
15:                    g.setColor(new Color(rval,gval,bval));
16:                    g.fillRect(i, j, 25, 25);
17:                    g.setColor(Color.black);
18:                    g.drawRect(i-1, j-1, 25, 25);
19:                }
20:        }
21: }
```

ANALYSIS The two for loops are the heart of this example; the first one draws the rows, and the second draws the individual boxes within each row. When a box is drawn, the random color is calculated first, and then the box is drawn. A black outline is drawn around each box, because some of them tend to blend into the background of the applet.

Because this `paint` method generates new colors each time the applet is painted, you can regenerate the colors by moving the window around or by covering the applet's window with another one (or by reloading the page). Figure 9.22 shows the final applet (although given that this picture is black and white, you can't get the full effect of the multicolored squares).

Figure 9.22.

The random colors applet.

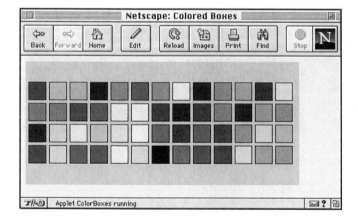

Summary

You present something on the screen by painting inside your applet: shapes, graphics, text, or images. Today you have learned the basics of how to paint, including how to use the graphics primitives to draw rudimentary shapes, how to use fonts and font metrics to draw text, and how to use `Color` objects to change the color of what you're drawing on the screen. It's this foundation in painting that enables you to do animation inside an applet (which basically involves just painting repeatedly to the screen) and to work with images. These are topics you'll learn about tomorrow.

Q&A

Q In all the examples you show, and in all the tests I've made, the graphics primitives, such as `drawLine()` and `drawRect()`, produce lines that are one pixel wide. How can I draw thicker lines?

A In the current state of the Java Graphics class, you can't; no methods exist for changing the default line width. If you really need a thicker line, you have to draw multiple lines one pixel apart to produce that effect.

Q I want to draw a line of text with a boldface word in the middle. I understand that I need two font objects—one for the regular font and one for the bold one—and that I'll need to reset the current font in between. The problem is that `drawString()` requires an x and a y position for the start of each string, and can't find anything that refers to "current point." How can I figure out where to start the boldface word?

A Java's text display capabilities are fairly primitive. There is no concept of the current point, so you'll have to manually figure out where the end of one string was so that you can begin the next string. The `stringWidth()` methods can help you with that, both to find out the width of the string you just drew and to add the space after it.

Q How do I use non-roman fonts such as kanji in Java?

A Java's support for international fonts in the 1.0.2 version of the JDK is sketchy, beyond the encoding of the raw characters as Unicode. Your best bet is to wait for the 1.1 version of the JDK, which will offer much more flexibility in the way of Unicode character display, support for internationalization, and non-roman fonts.

Q I tried out the applet that draws boxes with random colors, but each time it draws, a lot of the boxes are the same color. If the colors are truly random, why is it doing this?

A Two reasons. The first is that the random number generator I used in that code (from the `Math` class) isn't a very good random number generator; in fact, the documentation for that method says as much. For a better random number generator, use the `Random` class from the `java.util` package.

The second, more likely, reason is that there just aren't enough colors available in your browser or on your system to draw all the colors that the applet is generating. If your system can't produce the wide range of colors available using the `Color` class, or if the browser has allocated too many colors for other things, you may end up with duplicate colors in the boxes, depending on how the browser and the system have been written to handle that. Usually your applet won't use quite so many colors, so you won't run into this problem quite so often.

Q **I have a tiled background on my Web page. I can create images with transparent backgrounds so that the tiled page background shows through. Can I create transparent applets?**

A Not with the 1.02 JDK (and perhaps not with 1.1 either). For applets, your best bet is to use a plain-colored background and set your applet's background to be that same color.

Another idea if you use a tile for the page background is to import that image and draw it as the background for your applet (you'll learn about images tomorrow). However, using that mechanism, it is unlikely that the edges of the tile will exactly match up. Unfortunately, there doesn't appear to be a good workaround for this problem.

Day 10

Simple Animation and Threads

by Laura Lemay

The first thing I ever saw Java do was an animation: a large red Hi there! that ran across the screen from the right to left. Even that simple form of animation was enough to make me stop and think, "this is really cool."

That sort of simple animation takes only a few methods to implement in Java, but those few methods are the basis for any Java applet that you want to update the screen dynamically—for something as simple as flashy animation applets, or for more complex applets that may need to be updated based on data they get from the user, from databases connected to over the network, or from any other source.

Animation in Java is accomplished through various interrelated parts of the Java Abstract Windowing Toolkit (AWT). Today you'll learn the fundamentals of animation in Java: how the various parts of the system all work together so that you can create moving figures and dynamically updatable applets. Specifically, you'll explore the following:

- [ ] How to create animation in Java—the paint() and repaint() methods, starting and stopping dynamic applets, and how to use and override these methods in your own applets

- [ ] Threads—what they are and how they can make your applets more well-behaved with other applets and with other parts of the AWT

- [ ] Reducing animation flicker, which is a common problem with animation in Java

Throughout today, you'll also work with lots of examples of real applets that create animation or perform some kind of dynamic movement.

Creating Animation in Java

Animation in Java involves two basic steps: constructing a frame of animation, and then asking Java to paint that frame. You repeat these steps as necessary to create the illusion of movement. The basic, static graphical applets that you created yesterday taught you how to accomplish the first part; all that's left is how to tell Java to paint a frame.

Painting and Repainting

The paint() method, as you learned yesterday, is called whenever an applet needs to be painted—when the applet is initially drawn, when the window containing it is moved, or when another window is moved from over it. You can also, however, ask Java to repaint the applet at a time you choose. So, to change the appearance of what is on the screen, you construct the image or "frame" you want to paint, and then ask Java to paint this frame. If you do this repeatedly, and fast enough, you get animation inside your Java applet. That's all there is to it.

Where does all this take place? Not in the paint() method itself. All paint() does is put dots on the screen. paint(), in other words, is responsible only for the current frame of the animation. The real work of changing what paint() does, of modifying the frame for an animation, actually occurs somewhere else in the definition of your applet.

In that "somewhere else," you construct the frame (set variables for paint() to use, create Color or Font or other objects that paint() will need), and then call the repaint() method. repaint() is the trigger that causes Java to call paint() and causes your frame to get drawn.

TECHNICAL NOTE

Because a Java applet can contain many different components that all need to be painted (as you'll learn later this week), and in fact, applets can be embedded inside a larger Java application that also paints to the screen in similar ways, when you call repaint() (and therefore paint()) you're not actually immediately drawing to the screen as you do in other window or graphics toolkits. Instead, repaint() is a *request* for Java to repaint your applet as soon as it can. Also, if too many repaint() requests are made in a short amount of time, the system may only call repaint() once for all of them. Much of the time, the delay between the call and the actual repaint is negligible. However, for very tight loops, the AWT may collapse several calls to repaint() into one. Keep this in mind as you create your own animation.

Starting and Stopping an Applet's Execution

Remember start() and stop() from Day 8, "Java Applet Basics"? These are the methods that trigger your applet to start and stop running. You didn't use start() and stop() yesterday because the applets on that day did nothing except paint once. With animation and other Java applets that are actually processing and running over time, you'll need to make use of start() and stop() to trigger the start of your applet's execution, and to stop it from running when you leave the page that contains that applet. For many applets, you'll want to override start() and stop() for just this reason.

The start() method triggers the execution of the applet. You can either do all the applet's work inside that method, or you can call other object's methods in order to do so. Usually, start() is used to create and begin execution of a thread so the applet can run in its own time.

stop(), on the other hand, suspends an applet's execution so when you move off the page on which the applet is displaying, it doesn't keep running and using up system resources. Most of the time when you create a start() method, you should also create a corresponding stop().

The Missing Link: Threads

There's one more part to the animation mix that you'll have to know about, and that's threads. I'm going to discuss threads in a lot greater detail later on in this lesson (and in even more detail on Day 18, "Multithreading") but for now here's the basic idea: Anything you do in a Java program that runs continually and takes up a lot of processing time should run in its own thread. Animation is one of these things. To accomplish animation in Java, therefore, you use the start() method to start a thread, and then do all your animation processing inside the thread's run() method. This allows the animation to run on its own without interfering with any other parts of the program.

Putting It Together

Explaining how to do Java animation is more of a task than actually showing you how it works in code. An example will help make the relationship between all these methods clearer.

Listing 10.1 shows a sample applet that uses basic applet animation techniques to display the date and time and constantly updates it every second, creating a very simple animated digital clock (a frame from that clock is shown in Figure 10.1).

This applet uses the paint(), repaint(), start(), and stop() methods. It also uses threads. For this discussion, we'll focus on the animation parts of the applet and won't worry so much about how the threads work. We'll take another look at this applet later, after we've discussed threads in greater detail.

TYPE **Listing 10.1. The `DigitalClock` applet.**

```
 1: import java.awt.Graphics;
 2: import java.awt.Font;
 3: import java.util.Date;
 4:
 5: public class DigitalClock extends java.applet.Applet
 6:    implements Runnable {
 7:
 8:    Font theFont = new Font("TimesRoman",Font.BOLD,24);
 9:  Date theDate;
10:    Thread runner;
11:
12:    public void start() {
13:      if (runner == null) {
14:        runner = new Thread(this);
15:        runner.start();
16:      }
17:    }
18:
19:    public void stop() {
20:      if (runner != null) {
21:        runner.stop();
21:        runner = null;
22:      }
23:    }
24:
25:    public void run() {
26:      while (true) {
27:        theDate = new Date();
28:        repaint();
29:      try { Thread.sleep(1000); }
30:        catch (InterruptedException e) { }
31:      }
32:    }
33:
34:    public void paint(Graphics g) {
```

10

```
35:      g.setFont(theFont);
36:      g.drawString(theDate.toString(),10,50);
37:    }
38:}
```

Figure 10.1.

The digital clock.

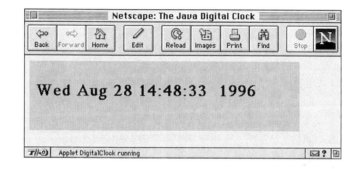

10

ANALYSIS We'll look at this applet from the perspective of the actual animation parts in this section, and deal with the parts that manage threads later on.

Lines 7 and 8 define two basic instance variables: theFont and theDate, which hold objects representing the current font and the current date, respectively. You'll learn more about these later.

The start() and stop() methods here start and stop a thread; the bulk of the applet's work goes on in the run() methods (lines 25 to 32).

Inside run() is where the animation actually takes place. Note the while loop inside this method (line 26); given that the test (true) always returns true, the loop never exits. A single animation frame is constructed inside that while loop, with the following steps:

☐ The Date class represents a date and time (Date is part of the java.util package—note that it was specifically imported in line 3). Line 27 creates a new instance of the Date class, which holds the current date and time, and assigns it to the theDate instance variable.

☐ The repaint() method is called (line 28) to repaint the applet.

☐ Lines 14 and 15, as complicated as they look, do nothing except pause for 1000 milliseconds (1 second) before the loop repeats. The sleep() method there, part of the Thread class, is what causes the applet to pause. Without a specific sleep() method, the applet would run as fast as it possibly could, which, for most computer systems, would be too fast for the eye to see. The sleep() method controls exactly how fast the animation takes place. The try and catch stuff around it enables Java to manage errors if they occur. try and catch handle exceptions and are described on Day 17, "Exceptions."

On to the `paint()` method in lines 34 through 37. Here, inside `paint()`, all that happens is that the current font (in the variable `theFont`) is set, and the date itself is printed to the screen (note that you have to call the `toString()` method to convert the date to a string). Because `paint()` is called repeatedly with whatever value happens to be in `theDate`, the string is updated every second to reflect the new date.

There are a few things to note about this example. First, you might think it would be easier to create the new `Date` object inside the `paint()` method. That way you could use a local variable and not need an instance variable to pass the `Date` object around. Although doing things that way creates cleaner code, it also results in a less efficient program. The `paint()` method is called every time a frame needs to be changed. In this case, it's not that important, but in an animation that needs to change frames very quickly, the `paint()` method has to pause to create that new object every time. By leaving `paint()` to do what it does best—painting the screen—and calculating new objects beforehand, you can make painting as efficient as possible. This is precisely the same reason why the `Font` object is also in an instance variable.

Threads: What They Are and Why You Need Them

So what are these threads all about? Why are they important to animation?

Threads are a very important part of Java and of programming Java. The larger your Java programs get and the more things they do, the more likely it is that you'll want to use threads. Depending on your experience with operating systems and with environments within those systems, you may or may not have run into the concept of threads, so let's start from the beginning.

First, the analogy. A group of students is on a bus, on a field trip somewhere. To pass the time, the teachers are leading a sing-along. As the trip progresses, the students sing one song, then when that song is done, they sing another song. While different parts of the bus could sing different songs, it wouldn't sound very good, so the singing of one song monopolizes the time until its done, at which time another song can start.

Now let's say you have two busses; both are on the same route to the field trip, both are going at the same speed, and both are full of students singing songs. But the songs being sung by the students in the second bus don't interfere with the songs being sung in the first bus; in this way you can get twice as many songs sung in the same amount of time by singing them in parallel.

Threads are like that. In a regular single-threaded program, the program starts executing, runs its initialization code, calls methods or procedures, and continues running and processing until it's complete or until the program is exited. That program runs in a single thread—it's the one bus with all the students.

Multithreading, as in Java, means that several different parts of the same program can run at the same time, in parallel, without interfering with each other. Multiple threads, each running by itself, are like multiple busses with different things going on in each bus.

Here's a simple example. Suppose you have a long computation near the start of a program's execution. This long computation may not be needed until later in the program's execution—it's actually tangential to the main point of the program, but it needs to get done eventually. In a single-threaded program, you have to wait for that computation to finish before the rest of the program can continue running. In a multithreaded system, you can put that computation into its own thread, and the rest of the program can continue to run independently.

Animation is an example of the kind of task that needs its own thread. Take, for example, that digital clock applet, which has an endless `while()` loop. If you didn't use threads, `while()` would run in the default Java system thread, which is also responsible for handling painting the screen, dealing with user input like mouse clicks, and keeping everything internally up-to-date. Unfortunately, however, if you run that `while()` loop in the main system thread, it will monopolize all Java's resources and prevent anything else—including painting—from happening. You'd never actually see anything on the screen because Java would be sitting and waiting for the `while()` loop to finish before it did anything else. And that's not what you want.

Using threads in Java, you can create parts of an applet (or application) that run in their own threads, and those parts will happily run all by themselves without interfering with anything else. Depending on how many threads you have, you may eventually tax the system so that all of them will run slower, but all of them will still run independently.

Even if you don't use lots of them, using threads in your applets is a good Java programming practice. The general rule of thumb for well-behaved applets: Whenever you have any bit of processing that is likely to continue for a long time (such as an animation loop, or a bit of code that takes a long time to execute), put it in a thread.

Writing Applets with Threads

Creating applets that use threads is very easy. In fact, many of the basic things you need to do to use threads are just boilerplate code that you can copy and paste from one applet to another. Because it's so easy, there's almost no reason *not* to use threads in your applets, given the benefits.

There are four modifications you need to make to create an applet that uses threads:

- ☐ Change the signature of your applet class to include the words `implements Runnable`.
- ☐ Include an instance variable to hold the applet's thread object.
- ☐ Create a `start()` method that does nothing but create a thread and start it running.
- ☐ Create a `stop()` method that stops the thread.
- ☐ Create a `run()` method that contains the actual code that controls the applet.

The first change is to the first line of your class definition. You've already got something like this:

```
public class MyAppletClass extends java.applet.Applet {
...
}
```

You need to change it to the following:

```
public class MyAppletClass extends java.applet.Applet  implements Runnable {
...
}
```

What does this do? It includes support for the `Runnable` interface in your applet. If you think way back to Day 2, "Object-Oriented Programming and Java," you'll remember that interfaces are a way to collect method names common to different classes, which can then be mixed in and implemented inside different classes that need to implement that behavior. Here, the `Runnable` interface defines the behavior your applet needs to run a thread; in particular, it gives you a default definition for the `run()` method. By implementing `Runnable`, you tell others that they can call the `Run()` method on your instances.

The second step is to add an instance variable to hold this applet's thread. Call it anything you like; it's a variable of the type `Thread` (`Thread` is a class in `java.lang`, so you don't have to import it):

```
Thread runner;
```

Third, add a `start()` method or modify the existing one so that it does nothing but create a new thread and start it running. Here's a typical example of a `start()` method:

```
public void start() {
    if (runner == null) {
        runner = new Thread(this);
        runner.start();
    }
}
```

If you modify `start()` to do nothing but spawn a thread, where does the code that drives your applet go? It goes into a new method, `run()`, which looks like this:

```
public void run() {
    // what your applet actually does
}
```

Your `run()` method actually overrides the default version of `run()`, which you get when you include the `Runnable` interface with your applet. `run()` is one of those standard methods, like `start()` and `paint()`, that you override in your own classes to get standard behavior.

`run()` can contain anything you want to run in the separate thread: initialization code, the actual loop for your applet, or anything else that needs to run in its own thread. You also can create new objects and call methods from inside `run()`, and they'll also run inside that thread. The `run()` method is the real heart of your applet.

Finally, now that you've got threads running and a `start()` method to start them, you should add a `stop()` method to suspend execution of that thread (and therefore whatever the applet is doing at the time) when the reader leaves the page. `stop()`, like `start()`, is usually something along these lines:

```
public void stop() {
  if (runner != null) {
      runner.stop();
      runner = null;
  }
}
```

The `stop()` method here does two things: It stops the thread from executing and also sets the thread's variable `runner` to `null`. Setting the variable to `null` makes the `Thread` object it previously contained available for garbage collection so that the applet can be removed from memory after a certain amount of time. If the reader comes back to this page and this applet, the `start()` method creates a new thread and starts up the applet once again.

And that's it! Four basic modifications, and now you have a well-behaved applet that runs in its own thread.

Another Look at the Digital Clock

Let's take another look at that `DigitalClock` applet, this time from the standpoint of threads. Listing 10.2 shows that applet's code once again.

Type **Listing 10.2. The `DigitalClock` applet, revisited.**

```
1: import java.awt.Graphics;
2: import java.awt.Font;
3: import java.util.Date;
4:
5: public class DigitalClock extends java.applet.Applet
```

continues

Listing 10.2. continued

```
 6:    implements Runnable {
 7:
 8:    Font theFont = new Font("TimesRoman",Font.BOLD,24);
 9:   Date theDate;
10:    Thread runner;
11:
12:    public void start() {
13:      if (runner == null) {
14:        runner = new Thread(this);
15:        runner.start();
16:      }
17:    }
18:
19:    public void stop() {
20:      if (runner != null) {
21:        runner.stop();
21:        runner = null;
22:      }
23:    }
24:
25:    public void run() {
26:      while (true) {
27:        theDate = new Date();
28:        repaint();
29:        try { Thread.sleep(1000); }
30:        catch (InterruptedException e) { }
31:      }
32:    }
33:
34:    public void paint(Graphics g) {
35:      g.setFont(theFont);
36:      g.drawString(theDate.toString(),10,50);
37:    }
38:}
```

ANALYSIS Let's look at the lines of this applet that create and manage threads. First, look at the class definition itself in lines 5 and 6; note that the class definition includes the Runnable interface. Any classes you create that use threads must include Runnable.

Line 10 defines a third instance variable for this class called runner of type Thread, which will hold the thread object for this applet.

Lines 12 through 23 define the boilerplate start() and stop() methods that do nothing except create and destroy threads. These method definitions can essentially be exactly the same from class to class because all they do is set up the infrastructure for the thread itself.

And, finally, the bulk of your applet's work goes on inside the run() method in lines 25 through 32, as we already discussed the last time we looked at this applet. Inside this method is the endless while loop, the calls to repaint(), and the sleep() method, which pauses things so they only run once a second.

10

Reducing Animation Flicker

If you've been following along with this lesson and trying the examples as you go, rather than reading this book on an airplane or in the bathtub, you may have noticed that when the digital clock program runs, every once in a while there's an annoying flicker in the animation. (Not that there's anything wrong with reading this book in the bathtub, but you won't see the flicker if you do that, so just trust me—there's a flicker.) This isn't a mistake or an error in the program; in fact, that flicker is a side effect of creating animation in Java. Because it is really annoying, you'll learn how to reduce flicker in this part of today's lesson so that your animations run cleaner and look better on the screen.

Flicker and How to Avoid It

Flicker is caused by the way Java paints and repaints each frame of an applet. At the beginning of today's lesson, you learned that when you call the repaint() method, repaint() calls paint(). That's not precisely true. A call to paint() does indeed occur in response to a repaint(), but what actually happens are the following steps:

1. The call to repaint() results in a call to the method update().

2. The update() method clears the screen of any existing contents (in essence, fills it with the current background color), and then calls paint().

3. The paint() method then draws the contents of the current frame.

It's step 2, the call to update(), that causes animation flicker. Because the screen is cleared between frames, the parts of the screen that don't change alternate rapidly between being painted and being cleared. Hence, flickering.

There are two major ways to avoid flicker in your Java applets:

☐ Override update() either not to clear the screen at all, or to clear only the parts of the screen you've changed.

☐ Override both update() and paint(), and use double-buffering.

If the second way sounds complicated, that's because it is. Double-buffering involves drawing to an offscreen graphics surface and then copying that entire surface to the screen. Because it's more complicated, you'll explore that one tomorrow. Today let's cover the easier solution: overriding update().

How to Override update()

The cause of flickering lies in the update() method. To reduce flickering, therefore, override update(). Here's what the default version of update() does (comes from the Component class, is part of the AWT, and is one of the superclasses of the applet class. You'll learn more about it on Day 13, "Creating User Interfaces with the AWT"):

```
public void update(Graphics g) {
    g.setColor(getBackground());
    g.fillRect(0, 0, width, height);
    g.setColor(getForeground());
    paint(g);
}
```

Basically, update() clears the screen (or, to be exact, fills the applet's bounding rectangle with the background color), sets things back to normal, and then calls paint(). When you override update(), you have to keep these two things in mind and make sure that your version of update() does something similar. In the next two sections, you'll work through some examples of overriding update() in different cases to reduce flicker.

Solution One: Don't Clear the Screen

The first solution to reducing flicker is not to clear the screen at all. This works only for some applets, of course. Here's an example of an applet of this type. The ColorSwirl applet prints a single string to the screen ("All the Swirly Colors"), but that string is presented in different colors that fade into each other dynamically. This applet flickers terribly when it's run. Listing 10.3 shows the initial source for this applet, and Figure 10.2 shows the result.

TYPE   **Listing 10.3. The ColorSwirl applet.**

```
 1:   import java.awt.Graphics;
 2:   import java.awt.Color;
 3:   import java.awt.Font;
 4:
 5:  public class ColorSwirl extends java.applet.Applet
 6:       implements Runnable {
 7:
 8:       Font f = new Font("TimesRoman",Font.BOLD,48);
 9:       Color colors[] = new Color[50];
10:       Thread runThread;
11:
12:       public void start() {
13:           if (runThread == null) {
14:               runThread = new Thread(this);
15:               runThread.start();
16:           }
17:       }
18:
19:       public void stop() {
20:           if (runThread != null) {
21:               runThread.stop();
22:               runThread = null;
23:           }
```

10

```
24:     }
25:
26:     public void run() {
27:
28:         // initialize the color array
29:         float c = 0;
30:         for (int i = 0; i < colors.length; i++) {
31:             colors[i] =
32:             Color.getHSBColor(c, (float)1.0,(float)1.0);
33:             c += .02;
34:         }
35:
36:         // cycle through the colors
37:         int i = 0;
38:         while (true) {
39:             setForeground(colors[i]);
40:             repaint();
41:             i++;
42:             try { Thread.sleep(50); }
43:             catch (InterruptedException e) { }
44:             if (i == colors.length ) i = 0;
45:         }
46:     }
47:
48:     public void paint(Graphics g) {
49:         g.setFont(f);
50:         g.drawString("All the Swirly Colors", 15, 50);
51:     }
52: }
```

Figure 10.2.

The ColorSwirl *applet.*

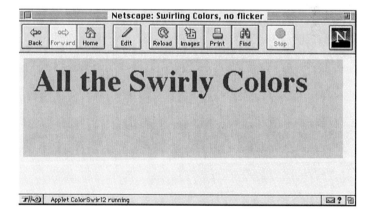

ANALYSIS There are three new things to note about this applet that might look strange to you:

☐ Line 9 defines an instance variable Colors, which is an array of 50 elements. When the applet starts, the first thing you do in the run() method (in lines 28 through 34) is to fill up that array with color objects. By creating all the colors beforehand, you can then jusxt draw text in that color, one at a time; it's easier to precompute all the colors at once (and, in fact, this `for` loop might make more sense in an `init()` method because it only needs to happen once). Note that I arbitrarily picked the number 50 for the number of colors we'll be using; we could just as easily cycle through 20 or 250 colors.

☐ To create the different color objects, we used a method in the `Color` class called `getHSBColor()`, rather than just using new with various RGB values. The `getHSBColor()` class method creates a color object based on values for hue, saturation, and brightness, rather than the standard red, green, and blue. HSB is simply a different way of looking at colors, and by incrementing the hue value and keeping saturation and brightness constant, you can create a range of colors without having to know the RGB for each one. If you don't understand this, don't worry about it; it's just a quick and easy way to create the color array.

☐ To create the animation, the applet cycles through the array of colors, setting the foreground color to each color object in turn and calling `repaint()`. When it gets to the end of the array, it starts over again (line 44), so the process repeats over and over ad infinitum.

Now that you understand what the applet does, let's fix the flicker. Flicker here results because each time the applet is painted, there's a moment where the screen is cleared. Instead of the text cycling neatly from red to a nice pink to purple, it's going from red to gray, to pink to gray, to purple to gray, and so on—not very nice looking at all.

Because the screen clearing is all that's causing the problem, the solution is easy: Override `update()` and remove the part where the screen gets cleared. It doesn't really need to get cleared anyhow, because nothing is changing except the color of the text. With the screen clearing behavior removed from `update()`, all update needs to do is call `paint()`. Here's what the `update()` method looks like in this applet (you'll want to add it after the `paint()` method after line 51):

```
public void update(Graphics g) {
    paint(g);
}
```

With that—with one small three-line addition—no more flicker. Wasn't that easy?

NOTE

If you're following along with the examples on the CD, the `ColorSwirl.java` file contains the original applet with the flicker; `ColorSwirl2.java` has the fixed version.

Solution Two: Redraw Only What You Have To

For some applets, it won't be quite as easy as just not clearing the screen. With some kinds of animation, clearing the screen is necessary for the animation to work properly. Here's another example. In this applet, called Checkers, a red oval (a checker piece) moves from a black square to a white square, as if on a checkerboard. Listing 10.4 shows the code for this applet, and Figure 10.3 shows the applet itself.

TYPE **Listing 10.4. The Checkers applet.**

```
 1:   import java.awt.Graphics;
 2:     import java.awt.Color;
 3:
 4:   public class Checkers extends java.applet.Applet
 5:       implements Runnable {
 6:
 7:       Thread runner;
 8:       int xpos;
 9:
10:       public void start() {
11:           if (runner == null) {
12:               runner = new Thread(this);
13:               runner.start();
14:           }
15:       }
16:
17:       public void stop() {
18:           if (runner != null) {
19:               runner.stop();
20:               runner = null;
21:           }
22:       }
23:
24:   public void run() {
25:       setBackground(Color.blue);
26:       while (true) {
27:           for (xpos = 5; xpos <= 105; xpos+=4) {
28:               repaint();
29:               try { Thread.sleep(100); }
30:               catch (InterruptedException e) { }
31:           }
32:           xpos = 5;
33:       }
34:   }
35:
36:       public void paint(Graphics g) {
37:           // Draw background
38:           g.setColor(Color.black);
39:           g.fillRect(0, 0, 100, 100);
40:           g.setColor(Color.white);
41:           g.fillRect(101, 0, 100, 100);
42:
```

continues

Listing 10.4. continued

```
43:            // Draw checker
44:            g.setColor(Color.red);
45:            g.fillOval(xpos, 5, 90, 90);
46:        }
47:    }
```

ANALYSIS Here's a quick run-through of what this applet does: An instance variable, xpos, keeps track of the current starting position of the checker (because it moves horizontally, the y stays constant and only the x changes; we don't need to keep track of the y position). In the run() method, you change the value of x and repaint, waiting 100 milliseconds between each move. The checker then appears to move from the left side of the screen to the right, resetting back at its original position once it hits the right side of the screen.

Figure 10.3.

The Checkers *applet.*

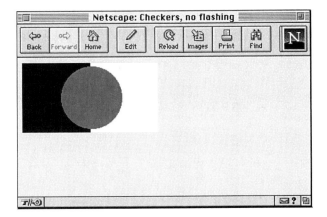

In the actual paint() method, the background squares are painted (one black and one white), and then the checker is drawn at its current position.

This applet, like the ColorSwirl applet, also has a terrible flicker. (In line 25, I changed the background color to blue to emphasize it, so if you run this applet, you'll definitely see the flicker.)

However, the solution to solving the flicker problem for this applet is more difficult than for the last one, because you actually do want to clear the screen before the next frame is drawn. Otherwise, the red checker won't have the appearance of leaving one position and moving to another; it'll just leave a red smear from one side of the checkerboard to the other.

How do you get around this? You still clear the screen, in order to get the animation effect, but, rather than clearing the entire screen each time, you clear only the part that has actually changed from one frame to the next. By limiting the redraw to only a small area, you can eliminate some of the flicker you get from redrawing the entire screen.

To limit what gets redrawn, you need a couple things. First, you need a way to restrict the drawing area so that each time paint() is called, only the part that needs to get redrawn actually gets redrawn. Fortunately, this is easy by using a mechanism called clipping. *Clipping*, part of the graphics class, enables you to restrict the drawing area to a small portion of the full screen; although the entire screen may get instructions to redraw, only the portions inside the clipping area are actually drawn.

NEW TERM *Clipping* restricts the drawing area to some smaller portion of the screen.

The second thing you need is a way to keep track of the actual area to redraw. Both the left and right edges of the drawing area change for each frame of the animation (one side to draw the new oval, the other to erase the bit of the oval left over from the previous frame), so to keep track of those two x values, you need instance variables for both the left side and the right.

With those two concepts in mind, let's start modifying the Checkers applet to redraw only what needs to be redrawn. First, you'll add instance variables for the left and right edges of the drawing area. Let's call those instance variables ux1 and ux2 (u for update), where ux1 is the left side of the area to draw and ux2 the right:

```
int ux1,ux2;
```

Now let's modify the run() method so that it keeps track of the actual area to be drawn, which you would think is easy—just update each side for each iteration of the animation. Here, however, things can get complicated because of the way Java uses paint() and repaint().

The problem with updating the edges of the drawing area with each frame of the animation is that for every call to repaint() there may not be an individual corresponding paint(). If system resources get tight (because of other programs running on the system or for any other reason), paint() may not get executed immediately and several calls to paint() may queue up waiting for their turn to change the pixels on the screen. In this case, rather than trying to make all those calls to paint() in order (and be potentially behind all the time), Java catches up by executing only the *most recent* call to paint() and skips all the others.

This poses a difficult problem in the Checkers applet. If you update the edges of the drawing area with each call to repaint(), and a couple calls to paint() are skipped, you end up with bits of the drawing surface not being updated at all or bits of the oval (colloquially called "turds") left behind. Because of how repaint() and paint() work in Java, you cannot guarantee that every single clipping region will eventually get painted—some may be skipped. The way to solve this is not to reset the clipping region to something new every single pass, but instead to reset the region only if that region was indeed updated. This way, if a couple of calls to paint() get skipped, the area to be updated will get larger for each frame, and when paint() finally gets caught up, everything will get repainted correctly.

Yes, this is horrifyingly complex. If I could have written this applet more simply, I would have (and, in fact, I did make it as simple as I could after much rewriting), but without this mechanism the applet will not get repainted correctly (my first try at this applet left turds all over the place). Let's step through it slowly in the code so you can get a better grasp of what's going on at each step.

Let's start with run(), where each frame of the animation takes place. Here's where you calculate each side of the clipping area based on the old position of the oval and the new position of the oval. The value of ux1 (the left side of the drawing area) is the previous oval's x position (xpos), and the value of ux2 is the x position of the current oval plus the width of that oval (90 pixels in this example).

Here's what the old run() method looked like:

```
public void run() {
    setBackground(Color.blue);
    while (true) {
        for (xpos = 5; xpos <= 105; xpos += 4) {
            repaint();
            try { Thread.sleep(100); }
            catch (InterruptedException e) { }
        }
        xpos = 5;
    }
}
```

For each step in which the oval moves toward the right, you first update ux2 (the right edge of the drawing area):

```
ux2 = xpos + 90;
```

Then, after the repaint() has occurred, you can update ux1 to reflect the old x position of the oval. However, you want to update this value *only* if the paint actually happened, so you don't end up skipping bits of the screen. How can you tell if the paint actually happened? You can reset ux1 in paint() to a given value (say 0), and then test inside run() to see whether you can update that value or whether you have to wait for the paint() to occur:

```
if (ux1 == 0) ux1 = xpos;
```

Finally, there's one other change to make. When the oval reaches the right side of the screen and resets back to its original position, there's one frame where you want to redraw the whole screen rather than create a clipping region (otherwise, the image of the oval would remain on the right side of the screen). So, in this one case, you want to set ux2 to be the full width of the applet. Here we'll modify the line we just put in to set the value of ux2, using an if statement to test to see if the oval is at the left side of the screen:

```
if (xpos == 5) ux2 = size().width;
else ux2 = xpos + 90;
```

The size() method is used to get the dimensions of the applet; size().width gives the full width of the applet so that the entire drawing surface will be updated.

Here's the new version of run() with those changes in place:

```
public void run() {
    setBackground(Color.blue);
    while (true) {
      for (xpos = 5; xpos <= 105; xpos+=4) {
          if (xpos == 5) ux2 = size().width;
          else ux2 = xpos + 90;
          repaint();
          try { Thread.sleep(100); }
          catch (InterruptedException e) { }
          if (ux1 == 0) ux1 = xpos;
      }
      xpos = 5;
    }
  }
```

Those are the only modifications run() needs. Let's override update() to limit the region that is being painted to the left and right edges of the drawing area that you set inside run(). To clip the drawing area to a specific rectangle, use the clipRect() method. clipRect(), like drawRect(), fillRect(), and clearRect(), is defined for Graphics objects and takes four arguments: x and y starting positions, and the width and height of the region.

Here's where ux1 and ux2 come into play. ux1 is the x point of the top corner of the region; then use ux2 to get the width of the region by subtracting ux1 from that value. The y values are the standard y values for the oval, which don't vary at all (the oval starts at y position 5 and ends at 95). Finally, to finish update(), you call paint():

```
public void update(Graphics g) {
   g.clipRect(ux1, 5, ux2 - ux1, 95);
   paint(g);
 }
```

Note that with the clipping region in place, you don't have to do anything to the actual paint() method. paint() goes ahead and draws to the entire screen each time, but only the areas inside the clipping region actually get changed onscreen.

You will need to make one change to paint(), however. You need to update the trailing edge of each drawing area inside paint() in case several calls to paint() were skipped. Because you are testing for a value of 0 inside run(), inside paint() you can merely reset ux1 and ux2 to 0 after drawing everything:

```
ux1 = ux2 = 0;
```

Those are the only changes you have to make to this applet in order to draw only the parts of the applet that changed (and to manage the case where some frames don't get updated immediately). Although this doesn't totally eliminate flickering in the animation, it does reduce it a great deal. Try it and see. Listing 10.5 shows the final code for the Checkers applet (called Checkers2.java).

TYPE **Listing 10.5. The final** Checkers **applet.**

```
 1: import java.awt.Graphics;
 2: import java.awt.Color;
 3:
 4: public class Checkers2 extends java.applet.Applet implements Runnable {
 5:
 6:     Thread runner;
 7:     int xpos;
 8:     int ux1,ux2;
 9:
10:     public void start() {
11:         if (runner == null) {
12:             runner = new Thread(this);
13:             runner.start();
14:         }
15:     }
16:
17:     public void stop() {
18:         if (runner != null) {
19:             runner.stop();
20:             runner = null;
21:         }
22:     }
23:
24:     public void run() {
25:         setBackground(Color.blue);
26:         while (true) {
27:           for (xpos = 5; xpos <= 105; xpos+=4) {
28:               if (xpos == 5) ux2 = size().width;
29:               else ux2 = xpos + 90;
30:               repaint();
31:               try { Thread.sleep(100); }
32:               catch (InterruptedException e) { }
33:               if (ux1 == 0) ux1 = xpos;
34:           }
35:           xpos = 5;
36:         }
37:     }
38:
39:     public void update(Graphics g) {
40:         g.clipRect(ux1, 5, ux2 - ux1, 95);
41:         paint(g);
42:     }
43:
44:     public void paint(Graphics g) {
45:         // Draw background
46:         g.setColor(Color.black);
47:         g.fillRect(0, 0, 100, 100);
48:         g.setColor(Color.white);
49:         g.fillRect(101, 0, 100, 100);
50:
51:         // Draw checker
52:         g.setColor(Color.red);
53:         g.fillOval(xpos, 5, 90, 90);
```

10

```
54:
55:            // reset the drawing area
56:            ux1 = ux2 = 0;
57:        }
58:}
```

Summary

Congratulations on getting through Day 10! This day was a bit rough; you've learned a lot, and it all might seem overwhelming. You learned about a plethora of methods to use and override—start(), stop(), paint(), repaint(), run(), and update()—and you got a basic foundation in creating and using threads. Other than handling bitmap images, which you'll learn about tomorrow, you now have the basic background to create just about any animation you want in Java.

10

Q&A

Q **Why all the indirection with paint(), repaint(), update(), and all that? Why not have a simple paint method that puts stuff on the screen when you want it there?**

A The Java AWT enables you to nest drawable surfaces within other drawable surfaces. When a paint() takes place, all the parts of the system are redrawn, starting from the outermost surface and moving downward into the most nested one. Because the drawing of your applet takes place at the same time everything else is drawn, your applet doesn't get any special treatment. Your applet will be painted when everything else is painted. Although with this system you sacrifice some of the immediacy of instant painting, it enables your applet to coexist with the rest of the system more cleanly.

Q **Are Java threads like threads on other systems?**

A Java threads have been influenced by other thread systems, and if you're used to working with threads, many of the concepts in Java threads will be very familiar to you. You learned the basics today; you'll learn more next week on Day 18.

Q **When an applet uses threads, I just have to tell the thread to start and it starts, and tell it to stop and it stops? That's it? I don't have to test anything in my loops or keep track of its state? It just stops?**

A It just stops. When you put your applet into a thread, Java can control the execution of your applet much more readily. By causing the thread to stop, your applet just stops running, and then resumes when the thread starts up again. Yes, it's all automatic. Neat, isn't it?

Q **The `ColorSwirl` applet seems to display only five or six colors, which isn't very swirly. What's going on here?**

A This is the same problem you ran into yesterday. On some systems, there might not be enough colors available to be able to display all of them reliably. If you're running into this problem, besides upgrading your hardware, you might try quitting other applications running on your system that use color. Other browsers or color tools in particular might be hogging colors that Java wants to be able to use.

Q **Even with the changes you made, the `Checkers` applet still flickers.**

A And, unfortunately, it will continue to do so. Reducing the size of the drawing area by using clipping does *reduce* the flickering, but it doesn't stop it entirely. For many applets, using either of the methods described today may be enough to reduce animation flicker to the point where your applet looks good. To get totally flicker-free animation, you'll need to use a technique called double-buffering, which you'll learn about tomorrow.

10

Day 11

More Animation, Images, and Sound

by Laura Lemay

Animation is fun and easy to do in Java, but there's only so much you can do with the built-in Java methods for lines and fonts and colors. For really interesting animation, you have to provide your own images for each frame of the animation—and having sounds is nice, as well. Today you'll do more with animation, incorporating images and sounds into Java applets.

Specifically, you'll explore the following topics:

- ☐ Using bitmap images such as GIF or JPEG files—getting them from the server, loading them into Java, and displaying them in your applet
- ☐ Creating animation using images
- ☐ Using sounds—getting them and playing them at the appropriate times

☐ Using precompiled animator applets—an easy way to organize animation and sounds in Java

☐ Double-buffering—hard-core flicker avoidance

Retrieving and Using Images

Basic image handling in Java is easy. The Image class in the java.awt package provides abstract methods to represent common image behavior, and special methods defined in Applet and Graphics give you everything you need to load and display images in your applet as easily as drawing a rectangle. In this section, you'll learn about how to get and draw images in your Java applets.

Getting Images

To display an image in your applet, you first must load that image over the Net into your Java program. Images are stored as separate files from your Java class files, so you have to tell Java where to find them.

The Applet class provides a method called getImage(), which loads an image and automatically creates an instance of the Image class for you. To use it, all you have to do is import the java.awt.Image class into your Java program, and then give getImage the URL of the image you want to load. There are two ways of doing the latter step:

☐ The getImage() method with a single argument (an object of type URL) retrieves the image at that URL.

☐ The getImage() method with two arguments: the base URL (also a URL object) and a string representing the path or filename of the actual image (relative to the base).

Although the first way may seem easier (just plug in the URL as a URL object), the second is more flexible. Remember, because you're compiling Java files, if you include a hard-coded URL of an image and then move your files around to a different location, you have to recompile all your Java files.

The latter form, therefore, is usually the one to use. The Applet class also provides two methods that will help with the base URL argument to getImage():

☐ The getDocumentBase() method returns a URL object representing the directory of the HTML file that contains this applet. So, for example, if the HTML file is located at http://www.myserver.com/htmlfiles/javahtml/, getDocumentBase() returns a URL pointing to that path.

☐ The `getCodeBase()` method returns a string representing the directory in which this applet is contained—which may or may not be the same directory as the HTML file, depending on whether the `CODEBASE` attribute in `<APPLET>` is set or not.

Whether you use `getDocumentBase()` or `getCodebase()` depends on whether your images are relative to your HTML files or relative to your Java class files. Use whichever one applies better to your situation. Note that either of these methods is more flexible than hard-coding a URL or pathname into the `getImage()` method; using either `getDocumentBase()` or `getCodeBase()` enables you to move your HTML files and applets around and Java can still find your images. (This assumes, of course, that you move the class files and the images around together. If you move the images somewhere else and leave the class files where they are, you'll have to edit and recompile your source.)

Here are a few examples of `getImage`, to give you an idea of how to use it. This first call to `getImage()` retrieves the file at that specific URL (`http://www.server.com/files/image.gif`). If any part of that URL changes, you have to recompile your Java applet to take into account the new path:

```
Image img = getImage(
    new URL("http://www.server.com/files/image.gif"));
```

In the following form of `getImage`, the `image.gif` file is in the same directory as the HTML files that refer to this applet:

```
Image img = getImage(getDocumentBase(), "image.gif")
```

In this similar form, the file `image.gif` is in the same directory as the applet itself:

```
Image img = getImage(getCodeBase(), "image.gif")
```

If you have lots of image files, it's common to put them into their own subdirectory. This form of `getImage()` looks for the file `image.gif` in the directory `images`, which, in turn, is in the same directory as the Java applet:

```
Image img = getImage(getCodeBase(), "images/image.gif")
```

If `getImage()` can't find the file indicated, it returns `null`. `drawImage()` on a `null` image will simply draw nothing. Using a `null` image in other ways will probably cause an error.

NOTE

Currently, Java supports images in the GIF and JPEG formats. Other image formats may be available later; however, for now, your images should be in either GIF or JPEG.

Drawing Images

All that stuff with getImage() does nothing except go off and retrieve an image and stuff it into an instance of the Image class. Now that you have an image, you have to do something with it.

TECHNICAL NOTE

Actually, the loading of images is internally a lot more complex than this. When you retrieve an image using getImage(), that method actually spawns a thread to load the image and returns almost immediately with your Image object. This gives your program the illusion of almost instantaneously having the image there ready to use. It may take some time, however, for the actual image to download and decompress, which may cause your image applets to draw with only partial images, or for the image to be drawn on the screen incrementally as it loads (all the examples in this chapter work like this). You can control how you want your applet to behave given a partial image (for example, if you want it to wait until it's all there before displaying it) by taking advantage of the ImageObserver interface. You'll learn more about ImageObserver later in this lesson in the section "A Note About Image Observers."

The most likely thing you're going to want to do with an image is display it as you would a rectangle or a text string. The Graphics class provides two methods to do just this, both called drawImage().

The first version of drawImage() takes four arguments: the image to display, the x and y positions of the top left corner, and this:

```
public void paint() {
    g.drawImage(img, 10, 10, this);
}
```

This first form does what you would expect it to: It draws the image in its original dimensions with the top-left corner at the given x and y positions. Listing 11.1 shows the code for a very simple applet that loads an image called ladybug.gif and displays it. Figure 11.1 shows the obvious result.

TYPE   **Listing 11.1. The Ladybug applet.**

```
1:import java.awt.Graphics;
2:import java.awt.Image;
3:
4:public class LadyBug extends java.applet.Applet {
```

```
 5:
 6:    Image bugimg;
 7:
 8:    public void init() {
 9:        bugimg = getImage(getCodeBase(),
10:          "images/ladybug.gif");
11:    }
12:
13:    public void paint(Graphics g) {
14:      g.drawImage(bugimg, 10, 10,this);
15:    }
16:}
```

Figure 11.1.

The ladybug image.

ANALYSIS   In this example the instance variable `bugimg` holds the ladybug image, which is loaded in the `init()` method. The `paint()` method then draws that image on the screen.

The second form of `drawImage()` takes six arguments: the image to draw, the x and y coordinates of the top-left corner, a width and height of the image bounding box, and `this`. If the width and height arguments for the bounding box are smaller or larger than the actual image, the image is automatically scaled to fit. By using those extra arguments, you can squeeze and expand images into whatever space you need them to fit in (keep in mind, however, that there may be some image degradation from scaling it smaller or larger than its intended size).

One helpful hint for scaling images is to find out the size of the actual image that you've loaded, so you can then scale it to a specific percentage and avoid distortion in either direction. Two methods defined for the `Image` class can give you that information: `getWidth()` and `getHeight()`. Both take a single argument, an instance of `ImageObserver`, which is used to track the loading of the image (more about this later). Most of the time, you can use just `this` as an argument to either `getWidth()` or `getHeight()`.

If you stored the ladybug image in a variable called `bugimg`, for example, this line returns the width of that image, in pixels:

```
theWidth = bugimg.getWidth(this);
```

TECHNICAL NOTE

Here's another case where, if the image isn't loaded all the way, you may get different results. Calling getWidth() or getHeight() before the image has fully loaded will result in values of -1 for each one. Tracking image loading with image observers can help you keep track of when this information appears.

Listing 11.2 shows another use of the ladybug image, this time scaled several times to different sizes (Figure 11.2 shows the result).

TYPE | **Listing 11.2. More ladybugs, scaled.**

```
 1:  import java.awt.Graphics;
 2: import java.awt.Image;
 3:
 4: public class LadyBug2 extends java.applet.Applet {
 5:
 6:     Image bugimg;
 7:
 8:     public void init() {
 9:         bugimg = getImage(getCodeBase(),
10:             "images/ladybug.gif");
11:     }
12:
13:     public void paint(Graphics g) {
14:         int iwidth = bugimg.getWidth(this);
15:         int iheight = bugimg.getHeight(this);
16:         int xpos = 10;
17:
18:         // 25 %
19:         g.drawImage(bugimg, xpos, 10,
20:             iwidth / 4, iheight / 4, this);
21:
22:         // 50 %
23:         xpos += (iwidth / 4) + 10;
24:         g.drawImage(bugimg, xpos , 10,
25:              iwidth / 2, iheight / 2, this);
26:
27:         // 100%
28:         xpos += (iwidth / 2) + 10;
29:         g.drawImage(bugimg, xpos, 10, this);
30:
31:         // 150% x, 25% y
32:         g.drawImage(bugimg, 10, iheight + 30,
33:              (int)(iwidth * 1.5), iheight / 4, this);
34:     }
35: }
```

Figure 11.2.

The second Ladybug applet.

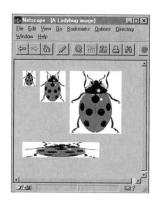

A Note About Image Observers

I've been steadfastly ignoring mentioning that last argument to drawImage(): the mysterious this, which also appears as an argument to getWidth() and getHeight(). Why is this argument used? Its official use is to pass in an object that functions as an ImageObserver (that is, an object that implements the ImageObserver interface). Image observers are used to watch the progress of how far along an image is in the loading process and to make decisions when the image is only fully or partially loaded. So, for example, your applet could pause until all the images are loaded and ready, or display a "loading" message, or do something else while it was waiting.

The Applet class, which your applet inherits from, contains a default behavior for image observation (which it inherits from the Component superclass) that should work in the majority of cases—hence, the this argument to drawImage(), getWidth(), and getHeight(). The only reason you'll want to use an alternate argument in its place is if you want more control over what your applet will do in cases where an image may only be partially loaded, or if tracking lots of images loading asynchronously.

You'll learn more about how to deal with image observers on Day 24, "Advanced Animation and Media."

Modifying Images

In addition to the basics of handling images described in this section, the java.awt.image package provides more classes and interfaces that enable you to modify images and their internal colors, or to create bitmap images by hand. You'll learn more about modifying images on Day 25, "Fun with Image Filters."

11

Creating Animation Using Images

Creating animation with images is much the same as creating animation with fonts, colors, or shapes—you use the same methods and the same procedures for painting, repainting, and reducing flicker that you learned about yesterday. The only difference is that you have a stack of images to flip through rather than a set of painting methods.

Probably the best way to show you how to use images for animation is simply to walk through an example. Here's an extensive one of an animation of a small cat called Neko.

An Example: Neko

Neko was a small Macintosh animation/game written and drawn by Kenji Gotoh in 1989. "Neko" is Japanese for "cat," and the animation is of a small kitten that chases the mouse pointer around the screen, sleeps, scratches, and generally acts cute. The Neko program has since been ported to just about every possible platform, as well as rewritten as a popular screensaver.

For this example, you'll implement a small animation based on the original Neko graphics. Unlike the original Neko the cat, which was autonomous (it could "sense" the edges of the window and turn and run in a different direction), this applet merely causes Neko to run in from the left side of the screen, stop in the middle, yawn, scratch its ear, sleep a little, and then run off to the right.

NOTE

> This is by far the largest of the applets discussed so far in this book, and if I either print it here and then describe it, or build it up line by line, you'll be here for days. Instead, I'm going to describe the parts of this applet independently, and I'm going to leave out the basics—the stuff you learned yesterday about starting and stopping threads, what the run() method does, and so on. All the code is printed later today so that you can put it all together.

Step 1: Collect Your Images

Before you begin writing Java code to construct an animation, you should have all the images that form the animation itself. For this version of Neko there are nine of them (the original has 36), as shown in Figure 11.3.

Figure 11.3.

The images for Neko.

NOTE

The Neko images, as well as the source code for this applet, are available on the CD.

For this example I've stored these images in a directory called, appropriately, images. Where you store your images isn't all that important, but you should take note of where you've put them because you'll need that information later on when you load your images.

Step 2: Organize and Load the Images in Your Applet

Now, on to the applet. The basic idea here is that you have a set of images and you display them one at a time, rapidly, so that they give the appearance of movement. The easiest way to manage this in Java is to store the images in an array of class Image, and then to have a special variable to keep track of the current image. As you iterate over the slots in the array (using a for loop), you can change the value of the current image each time.

For the Neko applet, you'll create instance variables to implement both these things: an array to hold the images, called nekopics, and a variable of type Image called currentimg, to hold the current image being displayed:

```
Image nekopics[] = new Image[9];
Image currentimg;
```

Here the image array has nine slots, as the Neko animation has nine images. If you have a larger or smaller set of images, you'll have a different number of slots.

TECHNICAL NOTE

The java.util class contains a class (HashTable) that implements a hash table. For large numbers of images, a hash table is faster to find and retrieve images from than an array is. Because there's a small number of images here, and because arrays are better for fixed-length, repeating animation, I'll use an array here.

Because the Neko animation draws the cat images in different positions on the screen, you'll also want to keep track of the current x and y positions so that the various methods in this applet know where to start drawing. The y stays constant for this particular applet (Neko runs left to right at the same y position), but the x may vary. Let's add two instance variables for those two positions:

```
int xpos;
int ypos = 50;
```

Now, on to the body of the applet. During the applet's initialization, you'll read in all the images and store them in the nekopics array. This is the sort of operation that works especially well in an init() method.

Given that you have nine images with nine different filenames, you could do a separate call to getImage() for each one. You can save at least a little typing, however, by creating a local array of the file names (nekosrc, an array of strings) and then use a for loop to iterate over each one and load them in turn. Here's the init() method for the Neko applet that loads all the images into the nekopics array:

```
public void init() {

    String nekosrc[] = { "right1.gif", "right2.gif",
            "stop.gif", "yawn.gif", "scratch1.gif",
            "scratch2.gif","sleep1.gif", "sleep2.gif",
            "awake.gif" };
    for (int i=0; i < nekopics.length; i++) {
        nekopics[i] = getImage(getCodeBase(),
            "images/" + nekosrc[i]);
    }
}
```

Note here in the call to getImage() that the directory these images are stored in (the image directory) is included as part of the path.

Step 3: Animate the Images

With the images loaded, the next step is to start animating the bits of the applet. You do this inside the applet's thread's run() method. In this applet, Neko does five main things:

☐ Runs in from the left side of the screen

☐ Stops in the middle and yawns

☐ Scratches four times

☐ Sleeps

☐ Wakes up and runs off to the right side of the screen

Although you could animate this applet by merely painting the right image to the screen at the right time, it makes more sense to write this applet so that many of Neko's activities are contained in individual methods. This way, you can reuse some of the activities (the animation of Neko running, in particular) if you want Neko to do things in a different order.

Let's start by creating a method to make Neko run. Because you're going to be using this one twice, making it generic is a good plan. Let's create a `nekorun()` method, which takes two arguments: the x position to start, and the x position to end. Neko then runs between those two positions (the y remains constant).

```
void nekorun(int start, int end) {
...
}
```

There are two images that represent Neko running; to create the running effect, you need to alternate between those two images (stored in positions 0 and 1 of the image array), as well as move them across the screen. The moving part is a simple `for` loop between the `start` and `end` arguments, setting the x position to the current loop value. Swapping the images means merely testing to see which one is active at any turn of the loop and assigning the other one to the current image. Finally, at each new frame, you'll call `repaint()` and `sleep()` for a bit to pause the animation.

Actually, given that during this animation there will be a lot of pausing of various intervals, it makes sense to create a utility method that does just that—pause for a given amount of time. The `pause()` method, therefore, takes one argument, a number of milliseconds. Here's its definition:

```
void pause(int time) {
    try { Thread.sleep(time); }
    catch (InterruptedException e) { }
}
```

Back to the `nekorun()` method. To summarize, `nekorun()` iterates from the `start` position to the `end` position. For each turn of the loop, it sets the current x position, sets `currentimg` to the right animation frame, calls `repaint()`, and pauses. Got it? Here's the definition of `nekorun`:

```
void nekorun(int start, int end) {
    for (int i = start; i < end; i+=10) {
        xpos = i;
        // swap images
        if (currentimg == nekopics[0])
            currentimg = nekopics[1];
        else currentimg = nekopics[0];
        repaint();
        pause(150);
    }
}
```

Note that in that second line you increment the loop by 10 pixels. Why 10 pixels and not, say, 5 or 8? The answer is determined mostly through trial and error to see what looks right.

Ten seems to work best for the animation. When you write your own animation, you have to play with both the distances and the sleep times until you get an animation you like.

Speaking of repaint(), let's skip over to that paint() method, which paints each frame. Here the paint() method is trivially simple; all paint() is responsible for is painting the current image at the current x and y positions. All that information is stored in instance variables. However, we do want to make sure that the images actually exist before we draw them (the images might be in the process of loading). To catch this and make sure we don't try drawing an image that isn't there (resulting in all kinds of errors), we'll test to make sure currentimg isn't null before calling drawImage() to paint the image:

```
public void paint(Graphics g) {
    if (currentimg != null)
        g.drawImage(currentimg, xpos, ypos, this);
}
```

Now let's back up to the run() method, where the main processing of this animation is happening. You've created the nekorun() method; in run() you'll call that method with the appropriate values to make Neko run from the left edge of the screen to the center:

```
// run from one side of the screen to the middle
nekorun(0, size().width / 2);
```

The second major thing Neko does in this animation is stop and yawn. You have a single frame for each of these things (in positions 2 and 3 in the array), so you don't really need a separate method to draw them. All you need to do is set the appropriate image, call repaint(), and pause for the right amount of time. This example pauses for a second each time for both stopping and yawning—again, using trial and error. Here's the code:

```
// stop and pause
currentimg = nekopics[2];
repaint();
pause(1000);

// yawn
currentimg = nekopics[3];
repaint();
pause(1000);
```

Let's move on to the third part of the animation: Neko scratching. There's no horizontal movement for this part of the animation. You alternate between the two scratching images (stored in positions 4 and 5 of the image array). Because scratching is a distinct action, however, let's create a separate method for it.

The nekoscratch() method takes a single argument: the number of times to scratch. With that argument, you can iterate, and then, inside the loop, alternate between the two scratching images and repaint each time:

```
void nekoscratch(int numtimes) {
    for (int i = numtimes; i > 0; i--) {
        currentimg = nekopics[4];
        repaint();
        pause(150);
        currentimg = nekopics[5];
        repaint();
        pause(150);
    }
}
```

Inside the run method, you can then call nekoscratch() with an argument of (4):

```
// scratch four times
nekoscratch(4);
```

Onward! After scratching, Neko sleeps. Again, you have two images for sleeping (in positions 6 and 7 of the array), which you'll alternate a certain number of times. Here's the nekosleep() method, which takes a single number argument, and animates for that many "turns":

```
void nekosleep(int numtimes) {
    for (int i = numtimes; i > 0; i--) {
        currentimg = nekopics[6];
        repaint();
        pause(250);
        currentimg = nekopics[7];
        repaint();
        pause(250);
    }
}
```

Call nekosleep() in the run() method like this:

```
// sleep for 5 "turns"
nekosleep(5);
```

Finally, to finish off the applet, Neko wakes up and runs off to the right side of the screen. The waking up image is the last image in the array (position 8), and you can reuse the nekorun method to finish:

```
// wake up and run off
currentimg = nekopics[8];
repaint();
pause(500);
nekorun(xpos, size().width + 10);
```

Step 4: Finish Up

There's one more thing left to do to finish the applet. The images for the animation all have white backgrounds. Drawing those images on the default applet background (a medium gray) means an unsightly white box around each image. To get around the problem, merely set the applet's background to white at the start of the run() method:

```
setBackground(Color.white);
```

Got all that? There's a lot of code in this applet, and a lot of individual methods to accomplish a rather simple animation, but it's not all that complicated. The heart of it, as in the heart of all forms of animation in Java, is to set up the frame and then call repaint() to enable the screen to be drawn.

Note that you don't do anything to reduce the amount of flicker in this applet. It turns out that the images are small enough, and the drawing area also small enough, that flicker is not a problem for this applet. It's always a good idea to write your animation to do the simplest thing first, and then add behavior to make it run cleaner.

To finish up this section, Listing 11.3 shows the complete code for the Neko applet.

TYPE | **Listing 11.3. The final Neko applet.**

```
 1:   import java.awt.Graphics;
 2:   import java.awt.Image;
 3:   import java.awt.Color;
 4:
 5:   public class Neko extends java.applet.Applet
 6:        implements Runnable {
 7:
 8:        Image nekopics[] = new Image[9];
 9:        Image currentimg;
10:        Thread runner;
11:        int xpos;
12:        int ypos = 50;
13:
14:        public void init() {
15:              String nekosrc[] = { "right1.gif", "right2.gif",
16:              "stop.gif", "yawn.gif", "scratch1.gif",
17:              "scratch2.gif","sleep1.gif", "sleep2.gif",
18:              "awake.gif" };
19:
20:           for (int i=0; i < nekopics.length; i++) {
21:                nekopics[i] = getImage(getCodeBase(),
22:                "images/" + nekosrc[i]);
23:           }
24:        }
25:        public void start() {
26:           if (runner == null) {
27:                runner = new Thread(this);
28:                runner.start();
29:           }
30:        }
31:
32:        public void stop() {
33:           if (runner != null) {
34:                runner.stop();
35:                runner = null;
36:           }
37:        }
```

```
38:
39:        public void run() {
40:
41:            setBackground(Color.white);
42:
43:            // run from one side of the screen to the middle
44:            nekorun(0, size().width / 2);
45:
46:            // stop and pause
47:            currentimg = nekopics[2];
48:            repaint();
49:            pause(1000);
50:
51:            // yawn
52:            currentimg = nekopics[3];
53:            repaint();
54:            pause(1000);
55:
56:            // scratch four times
57:            nekoscratch(4);
58:
59:            // sleep for 5 "turns"
60:            nekosleep(5);
61:
62:            // wake up and run off
63:            currentimg = nekopics[8];
64:            repaint();
65:            pause(500);
66:            nekorun(xpos, size().width + 10);
67:        }
68:
69:        void nekorun(int start, int end) {
70:            for (int i = start; i < end; i += 10) {
71:                xpos = i;
72:                // swap images
73:                if (currentimg == nekopics[0])
74:                    currentimg = nekopics[1];
75:                else currentimg = nekopics[0];
76:                repaint();
77:                pause(150);
78:            }
79:        }
80:
81:        void nekoscratch(int numtimes) {
82:            for (int i = numtimes; i > 0; i--) {
83:                currentimg = nekopics[4];
84:                repaint();
85:                pause(150);
86:                currentimg = nekopics[5];
87:                repaint();
88:                pause(150);
89:            }
90:        }
91:
```

continues

Listing 11.3. continued

```
 92:        void nekosleep(int numtimes) {
 93:            for (int i = numtimes; i > 0; i--) {
 94:                currentimg = nekopics[6];
 95:                repaint();
 96:                pause(250);
 97:                currentimg = nekopics[7];
 98:                repaint();
 99:                pause(250);
100:            }
101:
102:        void pause(int time) {
103:            try { Thread.sleep(time); }
104:            catch (InterruptedException e) { }
105:        }
106:
107:        public void paint(Graphics g) {
108:            if (currentimg != null)
109:                g.drawImage(currentimg, xpos, ypos, this);
110:        }
111: }
```

Retrieving and Using Sounds

Java has built-in support for playing sounds in conjunction with running animation or for sounds on their own. In fact, support for sound, like support for images, is built into the Applet and awt classes, so using sound in your Java applets is as easy as loading and using images.

Currently, the only sound format that Java supports is Sun's AU format, sometimes called μ-law format. AU files tend to be smaller than sound files in other formats, but the sound quality is not very good. If you're especially concerned with sound quality, you may want your sound clips to be references in the traditional HTML way (as links to external files) rather than included in a Java applet.

The simplest way to retrieve and play a sound is through the play() method, part of the Applet class and therefore available to you in your applets. The play() method is similar to the getImage() method in that it takes one of two forms:

☐ play() with one argument, a URL object, loads and plays the given audio clip at that URL.

☐ play() with two arguments, one a base URL and one a pathname, loads and plays that audio file. The first argument can most usefully be either a call to getDocumentBase() or getCodeBase().

For example, the following line of code retrieves and plays the sound meow.au, which is contained in the audio directory. The audio directory, in turn, is located in the same directory as this applet:

```
play(getCodeBase(), "audio/meow.au");
```

The play() method retrieves and plays the given sound as soon as possible after it is called. If it can't find the sound, you won't get an error; you just won't get any audio when you expect it.

If you want to play a sound repeatedly, start and stop the sound clip, or run the clip as a loop (play it over and over), things are slightly more complicated—but not much more so. In this case, you use the applet method getAudioClip() to load the sound clip into an instance of the class AudioClip (part of java.applet—don't forget to import it) and then operate directly on that AudioClip object.

Suppose, for example, that you have a sound loop that you want to play in the background of your applet. In your initialization code, you can use this line to get the audio clip:

```
AudioClip clip = getAudioClip(getCodeBase(),
    "audio/loop.au");
```

Then, to play the clip once, use the play() method:

```
clip.play();
```

To stop a currently playing sound clip, use the stop() method:

```
clip.stop();
```

To loop the clip (play it repeatedly), use the loop() method:

```
clip.loop();
```

If the getAudioClip() method can't find the sound you indicate, or can't load it for any reason, it returns null. It's a good idea to test for this case in your code before trying to play the audio clip, because trying to call the play(), stop(), and loop() methods on a null object will result in an error (actually, an exception).

In your applet, you can play as many audio clips as you need; all the sounds you use will mix together properly as they are played by your applet.

Note that if you use a background sound—a sound clip that loops repeatedly—that sound clip will not stop playing automatically when you suspend the applet's thread. This means that even if your reader moves to another page, the first applet's sounds will continue to play. You can fix this problem by stopping the applet's background sound in your stop() method:

```
public void stop() {
    if (runner != null) {
        if (bgsound != null)
            bgsound.stop();
        runner.stop();
        runner = null;
    }
}
```

Listing 11.4 shows a simple framework for an applet that plays two sounds: The first, a background sound called loop.au, plays repeatedly. The second, a horn honking (beep.au), plays every 5 seconds. (I won't bother giving you a picture of this applet because it doesn't actually display anything other than a simple string to the screen.)

TYPE **Listing 11.4. The** AudioLoop **applet.**

```
1: import java.awt.Graphics;
2: import java.applet.AudioClip;
3:
4: public class AudioLoop extends java.applet.Applet
5:  implements Runnable {
6:
7:     AudioClip bgsound;
8:     AudioClip beep;
9:     Thread runner;
10:
11:     public void start() {
12:         if (runner == null) {
13:             runner = new Thread(this);
14:             runner.start();
15:         }
16:     }
17:
18:     public void stop() {
19:         if (runner != null) {
20:             if (bgsound != null) bgsound.stop();
21:             runner.stop();
22:             runner = null;
23:         }
24:     }
25:
26:     public void init() {
27:         bgsound = getAudioClip(getCodeBase(),"audio/loop.au");
28:         beep = getAudioClip(getCodeBase(), "audio/beep.au");
29:     }
30:
31:     public void run() {
32:         if (bgsound != null) bgsound.loop();
33:         while (runner != null) {
34:             try { Thread.sleep(5000); }
35:             catch (InterruptedException e) { }
36:             if (beep != null) beep.play();
37:         }
38:     }
39:
```

```
40:     public void paint(Graphics g) {
41:         g.drawString("Playing Sounds....", 10, 10);
42:     }
43: }
```

ANALYSIS There are only a few things to note about this applet. First, note the `init()` method in lines 26 to 29, which loads both the `loop.au` and the `beep.au` sound files. We've made no attempt here to make sure these files actually load as expected, so the possibility exists that the `bgsound` and `beep` instance variables may end up with the null values if the file cannot load. In that case, we won't be able to call `loop()`, `stop()`, or any other methods, so we should make sure we test for that elsewhere in the applet.

And we have tested for null several places here, particularly in the `run()` method in lines 32 and 36. These lines start the sounds looping and playing, but only if the values of the `bgsound` and `beep` variables are something other than null.

Finally, note line 20, which explicitly turns off the background sound if the thread is also being stopped. Because background sounds do not stop playing even when the thread has been stopped, you have to explicitly stop them here.

Using Animation Packages

Up until this point, I've described animation in a fair amount of detail, in order to help explain other topics that you can use in applets that aren't necessarily animation (for example, graphics, threads, managing bitmap images).

If the purpose of your applet is animation, however, in many cases writing your own applet is overkill. General-purpose applets that do nothing but animation exist, and you can use those applets in your own Web pages with your own set of images—all you need to do is modify the HTML files to give different parameters to the applet itself. Using these packages makes creating simple animation in Java far easier, particularly for Java developers who aren't as good at the programming side of Java.

Two animation packages are particularly useful in this respect: Sun's Animator applet and Dimension X's Liquid Motion.

Sun's Animator Applet

Sun's Animator applet, one of the examples in the 1.0.2 JDK, provides a simple, general-purpose applet for creating animation with Java. You compile the code and create an HTML file with the appropriate parameters for the animation. Using the Animator applet, you can do the following:

     ☐ Create an animation loop, that is, an animation that plays repeatedly.

     ☐ Add a soundtrack to the applet.

     ☐ Add sounds to be played at individual frames.

     ☐ Indicate the speed at which the animation is to occur.

     ☐ Specify the order of the frames in the animation—which means that you can reuse frames that repeat during the course of the animation.

Even if you don't intend to use Sun's Animator for your own animation, you might want to look at the code. The Animator applet is a great example of how animation works in Java and the sorts of clever tricks you can use in a Java applet.

Dimension X's Liquid Motion

While Sun's Animator applet is a simple (and free) example of a general-purpose animation tool, Liquid Motion from Dimension X is much more ambitious. Liquid Motion is an entire GUI application, running in Java, with which you build animation (they call them scenes) given a set of media files (images and sound). If you've ever used Macromedia Director to create multimedia presentations (or Shockwave presentations for the Web), you're familiar with the approach. To use Liquid Motion, you import your media files, and then you can arrange images on the screen, arrange them in frames over points in time, have them move along predefined paths, and add colors and backgrounds and audio tracks simply by clicking buttons. Figure 11.4 shows the main Liquid Motion screen.

Figure 11.4.

Liquid Motion.

When you save a Liquid Motion scene as HTML, the program saves all the Java class files you'll need to run the presentation and writes an HTML file, complete with the appropriate <APPLET> tags and parameters, to run that scene. All you need to do is move the files to your Web server and you're done—there's no Java programming involved whatsoever. But even if you are a Java programmer (as you will be by the time you finish this book), you can extend the Liquid Motion framework to include new behavior and features.

Because Liquid Motion is a Java application, it runs on any platform that Java runs on (Windows, UNIX, Mac). It is a commercial application, costing $149.99 for the Windows and UNIX versions (the Mac version exists, but does not appear to cost anything). Demonstration copies of the Solaris and Windows versions, which allow you to play with the interface but not to publish the files on the Web, are available at Dimension X's Web site.

Liquid Motion is worth checking out if you intend to do a lot of animation-type applets in your Web pages; using Liquid Motion its fairly easy to get up and running, far faster than working directly with the code. Check out `http://www.dimensionx.com/products/lm/` for more information and demonstration versions.

More About Flicker: Double-Buffering

Yesterday you learned two simple ways to reduce flickering in Java animation. Although you learned specifically about animation using drawing, flicker can also result from animation using images. In addition to the two flicker-reducing methods described yesterday, there is one other way to reduce flicker: double-buffering.

With *double-buffering*, you create a second surface (offscreen, so to speak), do all your painting to that offscreen surface, and then draw the whole surface at once onto the actual applet (and onto the screen) at the end—rather than drawing to the applet's actual graphics surface. Because all the work actually goes on behind the scenes, there's no opportunity for interim parts of the drawing process to appear accidentally and disrupt the smoothness of the animation.

 Double-buffering is the process of doing all your drawing to an offscreen buffer and then displaying that entire screen at once. It's called double-buffering because there are two drawing buffers and you switch between them.

Double-buffering isn't always the best solution. If your applet is suffering from flicker, try overriding `update()` and drawing only portions of the screen first; that may solve your problem. Double-buffering is less efficient than regular buffering and also takes up more memory and space, so, if you can avoid it, make an effort to do so. In terms of nearly eliminating animation flicker, however, double-buffering works exceptionally well.

Creating Applets with Double-Buffering

To create an applet that uses double-buffering, you need two things: an offscreen image to draw on and a graphics context for that image. Those two together mimic the effect of the applet's drawing surface: the graphics context (an instance of `Graphics`) to provide the drawing methods, such as `drawImage` (and `drawString`), and the `Image` to hold the dots that get drawn.

There are four major steps to adding double-buffering to your applet. First, your offscreen image and graphics context need to be stored in instance variables so that you can pass them to the paint() method. Declare the following instance variables in your class definition:

```
Image offscreenImage;
Graphics offscreenGraphics;
```

Second, during the initialization of the applet, you'll create an Image and a Graphics object and assign them to these variables (you have to wait until initialization so you know how big they're going to be). The createImage() method gives you an instance of Image, which you can then send the getGraphics() method in order to get a new graphics context for that image:

```
offscreenImage = createImage(size().width,
    size().height);
offscreenGraphics = offscreenImage.getGraphics();
```

Now, whenever you have to draw to the screen (usually in your paint() method), rather than drawing to paint's graphics, draw to the offscreen graphics. For example, to draw an image called img at position 10,10, use this line:

```
offscreenGraphics.drawImage(img, 10, 10, this);
```

Finally, at the end of your paint method, after all the drawing to the offscreen image is done, add the following line to place the offscreen buffer on to the real screen:

```
g.drawImage(offscreenImage, 0, 0, this);
```

Of course, you most likely will want to override update() so that it doesn't clear the screen between paintings:

```
public void update(Graphics g) {
    paint(g);
}
```

Let's review those four steps:

1. Add instance variables to hold the image and graphics contexts for the offscreen buffer.

2. Create an image and a graphics context when your applet is initialized.

3. Do all your applet painting to the offscreen buffer, not the applet's drawing surface.

4. At the end of your paint() method, draw the offscreen buffer to the real screen.

A Note on Disposing Graphics Contexts

If you make extensive use of graphics contexts in your applets or applications, be aware that those contexts will often continue to stay around after you're done with them, even if you no longer have any references to them. Graphics contexts are special objects in the AWT that map to the native operating system; Java's garbage collector cannot release those contexts by itself. If you use multiple graphics contexts or use them repeatedly, you'll want to explicitly get rid of those contexts once you're done with them.

Use the `dispose()` method to explicitly clean up a graphics context. A good place to put this might be in the applet's `destroy()` method (which you learned about on Day 8, "Java Applet Basics"; it was one of the primary applet methods, along with `init()`, `start()`, and `stop()`):

```
public void destroy() {
  offscreenGraphics.dispose();
}
```

An Example: Checkers Revisited

Yesterday's example featured the animated moving red oval to demonstrate animation flicker and how to reduce it. Even with the operations you did yesterday, however, the Checkers applet still flashed occasionally. Let's revise that applet to include double-buffering.

First, add the instance variables for the offscreen image and its graphics context:

```
Image offscreenImg;
Graphics offscreenG;
```

Second, add an `init` method to initialize the offscreen buffer:

```
public void init() {
    offscreenImg = createImage(size().width, size().height);
    offscreenG = offscreenImg.getGraphics();
}
```

Third, modify the `paint()` method to draw to the offscreen buffer instead of to the main graphics buffer:

```
public void paint(Graphics g) {
    // Draw background
    offscreenG.setColor(Color.black);
    offscreenG.fillRect(0, 0, 100, 100);
    offscreenG.setColor(Color.white);
    offscreenG.fillRect(100, 0, 100, 100);

    // Draw checker
    offscreenG.setColor(Color.red);
    offscreenG.fillOval(xpos, 5, 90, 90);

    g.drawImage(offscreenImg, 0, 0, this);
}
```

Note that you're still clipping the main graphics rectangle in the `update()` method, as you did yesterday; you don't have to change that part. The only part that is relevant is that final line in the `paint()` method wherein everything is drawn offscreen before finally being displayed.

Finally, in the applet's destroy() method we'll explicitly dispose of the graphics context stored in offscreenG:

```
public void destroy() {
   offscreenG.dispose();
}
```

Listing 11.5 shows the final code for the Checkers applet (Checkers3.java), which includes double-buffering.

TYPE **Listing 11.5. Checkers revisited, with double-buffering.**

```
 1: import java.awt.Graphics;
 2: import java.awt.Color;
 3: import java.awt.Image;
 4:
 5: public class Checkers3 extends java.applet.Applet implements Runnable {
 6:
 7:    Thread runner;
 8:    int xpos;
 9:    int ux1,ux2;
10:    Image offscreenImg;
11:    Graphics offscreenG;
12:
13:    public void init() {
14:       offscreenImg = createImage(this.size().width, this.size().height);
15:       offscreenG = offscreenImg.getGraphics();
16:    }
17:
18:    public void start() {
19:       if (runner == null); {
20:          runner = new Thread(this);
21:          runner.start();
22:       }
23:    }
24:
25:    public void stop() {
26:       if (runner != null) {
27:          runner.stop();
28:          runner = null;
29:       }
30:    }
31:
32:    public void run() {
33:       setBackground(Color.blue);
34:       while (true) {
35:          for (xpos = 5; xpos <= 105; xpos+=4) {
36:             if (xpos == 5) ux2 = size().width;
37:             else ux2 = xpos + 90;
38:             repaint();
39:             try { Thread.sleep(100); }
40:             catch (InterruptedException e) { }
41:             if (ux1 == 0) ux1 = xpos;
```

11

```
42:         }
43:            xpos = 5;
44:         }
45:    }
46:
47:    public void update(Graphics g) {
48:        g.clipRect(ux1, 5, ux2 - ux1, 95);
49:        paint(g);
50:    }
51:
52:    public void paint(Graphics g) {
53:        // Draw background
54:        offscreenG.setColor(Color.black);
55:        offscreenG.fillRect(0,0,100,100);
56:        offscreenG.setColor(Color.white);
57:        offscreenG.fillRect(100,0,100,100);
58:
59:        // Draw checker
60:        offscreenG.setColor(Color.red);
61:        offscreenG.fillOval(xpos,5,90,90);
62:
63:        g.drawImage(offscreenImg,0,0,this);
64:
65:        // reset the drawing area
66:        ux1 = ux2 = 0;
67:    }
68:
69:    public void destroy() {
70:        offscreenG.dispose();
71:    }
72: }
```

11

Summary

Three major topics are the focus of today's lesson. First, you learned about using images in your applets—locating them, loading them, and using the `drawImage()` method to display them, either at their normal size or scaled to different sizes. You also learned how to create animation in Java using images.

Second, you learned how to use sounds, which can be included in your applets any time you need them—at specific moments or as background sounds that can be repeated while the applet executes. You learned how to locate, load, and play sounds using both the `play()` and the `getAudioClip()` methods.

Finally, you learned about double-buffering, a technique that enables you to virtually eliminate flicker in your animation, at some expense of animation efficiency and speed. Using images and graphics contexts, you can create an offscreen buffer to draw to, the result of which is then displayed to the screen at the last possible moment.

Q&A

Q In the Neko program, you put the image loading into the `init()` method. It seems to me that it might take Java a long time to load all those images, and because `init()` isn't in the main thread of the applet, there's going to be a distinct pause there. Why not put the image loading at the beginning of the `run()` method instead?

A There are sneaky things going on behind the scenes. The `getImage()` method doesn't actually load the image; in fact, it returns an `Image` object almost instantaneously, so it isn't taking up a large amount of processing time during initialization. The image data that `getImage()` points to isn't actually loaded until the image is needed. This way, Java doesn't have to keep enormous images around in memory if the program is going to use only a small piece. Instead, it can just keep a reference to that data and retrieve what it needs later.

Q I compiled and ran the Neko applet. Something weird is going on; the animation starts in the middle and drops frames. It's as if only some of the images have loaded when the applet is run.

A That's precisely what's going on. Because image loading doesn't actually load the image right away, your applet may be merrily animating blank screens while the images are still being loaded. Depending on how long it takes those images to load, your applet may appear to start in the middle, to drop frames, or to not work at all.

There are three possible solutions to this problem. The first is to have the animation loop (that is, start over from the beginning once it stops). Eventually the images will load and the animation will work correctly. The second solution, and not a very good one, is to sleep for a while before starting the animation, to pause while the images load. The third, and best solution, is to use image observers to make sure no part of the animation plays before its images have loaded. You'll learn more about image observers on Day 24.

Q I wrote an applet to do a background sound using the `getAudioClip()` and `loop()` methods. The sound works great, but it won't stop. I've tried suspending the current thread and killing the thread together, but the sound goes on.

A I mentioned this as a small note in the section on sounds; background sounds don't run in the main thread of the applet, so if you stop the thread, the sound keeps going. The solution is easy—in the same method where you stop the thread, also stop the sound, like this:

```
runner.stop()  //stop the thread
bgsound.stop() //also stop the sound
```

Q **If I use double-buffering, do I still have to clip to a small region of the screen? Because double-buffering eliminates flicker, it seems easier to draw the whole frame every time.**

A Easier, yes, but less efficient. Drawing only part of the screen not only reduces flicker, it often also limits the amount of work your applet has to do in the paint() method. The faster the paint() method works, the faster and smoother your animation will run. Using clip regions and drawing only what is necessary is a good practice to follow in general—not just if you have a problem with flicker.

Day 12

Managing Simple Events and Interactivity

by Laura Lemay

Java events are part of the Java AWT (Abstract Windowing Toolkit) package. An event is the way that the AWT communicates to you, as the programmer, and to other Java AWT components that *something* has happened. That something can be input from the user (mouse movements or clicks, keypresses), changes in the system environment (a window opening or closing, the window being scrolled up or down), or a host of other things that might, in some way, affect the operation of the program.

In other words, whenever just about anything happens to a Java AWT component, including an applet, an event is generated. Some events are handled by the AWT or by the environment your applet is running in (the browser) without you needing to do anything. paint() methods, for example, are generated and handled by the environment—all you have to do is tell the AWT what you want painted when it gets to your part of the window. However, you may need to know about some events, such as a mouse click inside the boundaries of your applet. By writing your Java programs to handle these kinds of events, you can get input from the user and have your applet change its behavior based on that input.

Today you'll learn about managing simple events, including the following basics:

- ☐ Mouse clicks
- ☐ Mouse movements, including mouse dragging
- ☐ Keyboard actions

You'll also learn about the `handleEvent()` method, which is the basis for collecting, handling, and passing on events of all kinds from your applet to other components of the window or of your applet itself. Tomorrow you'll learn how to combine events with other AWT components to create a complete interface for your applet.

Mouse Clicks

Let's start with the most common event you might be interested in: mouse clicks. Mouse-click events occur when your user clicks the mouse somewhere in the body of your applet. You can intercept mouse clicks to do very simple things—for example, to toggle the sound on and off in your applet, to move to the next slide in a presentation, or to clear the screen and start over—or you can use mouse clicks in conjunction with mouse movements to perform more complex motions inside your applet.

Mouse Down and Mouse Up Events

When you click the mouse once, the AWT generates two events: a mouse down event when the mouse button is pressed and a mouse up event when the button is released. Why two individual events for a single mouse action? Because you may want to do different things for the "down" and the "up." For example, look at a pull-down menu. The mouse down extends the menu, and the mouse up selects an item (with mouse drags between—but you'll learn about that one later). If you have only one event for both actions (mouse up and mouse down), you cannot implement that sort of user interaction.

Handling mouse events in your applet is easy—all you have to do is override the right method definition in your applet. That method will be called when that particular event occurs. Here's an example of the method signature for a mouse down event:

```
public boolean mouseDown(Event evt, int x, int y) {
...
}
```

The `mouseDown()` method (and the `mouseUp()` method as well) takes three parameters: the event itself and the x and y coordinates where the mouse down or mouse up event occurred.

The evt argument is an instance of the class Event. All system events generate an instance of the Event class, which contains information about where and when the event took place, the kind of event it is, and other information that you might want to know about this event. Sometimes having a handle to that Event object is useful, as you'll discover later in this section.

The x and the y coordinates of the event, as passed in through the x and y arguments to the mouseDown() method, are particularly nice to know because you can use them to determine precisely where the mouse click took place. So, for example, if the mouse down event were over a graphical button, you could activate that button.

For example, here's a simple method that prints out information about a mouse down when it occurs:

```
public boolean mouseDown(Event evt, int x, int y) {
    System.out.println("Mouse down at " + x + "," + y);
    return true;
```

By including this method in your applet, every time your user clicks the mouse inside your applet, this message will get printed. The AWT system calls each of these methods when the actual event takes place.

NOTE

Unlike with Java applications, where System.out.println() outputs to the screen, the output that appears in applets varies from system to system and browser to browser. Netscape has a special window called the *Java console* that must be visible for you to see the output. Internet Explorer logs Java output to a separate file. Check with your environment to see where Java output from applets is sent.

Note that this method, unlike the other system methods you've studied this far, returns a boolean value instead of not returning anything (void). This will become important tomorrow when you create user interfaces and then manage input to these interfaces; having an event handler method return true or false determines whether a given component can intercept an event or whether it needs to pass it on to the enclosing component. The general rule is that if your method intercepts and does something with the event, it should return true. If for any reason the method doesn't do anything with that event, it should return false so that other components in the system can have a chance to see that event. In most of the examples in today's lesson, you'll be intercepting simple events, so most of the methods here will return true. Tomorrow you'll learn about nesting components and passing events up the component hierarchy.

12

The second half of the mouse click is the mouseUp() method, which is called when the mouse button is released. To handle a mouse up event, add the mouseUp() method to your applet: mouseUp() looks just like mouseDown():

```
public boolean mouseUp(Event evt, int x, int y) {
    ....
}
```

An Example: Spots

In this section you'll create an example of an applet that uses mouse events—mouse down events in particular. The Spots applet starts with a blank screen and then sits and waits. When you click the mouse on that screen, a blue dot is drawn. You can place up to 10 dots on the screen. Figure 12.1 shows the Spots applet.

Figure 12.1.

The Spots applet.

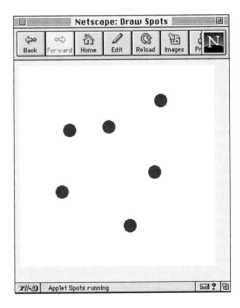

Let's start from the beginning and build this applet, starting from the initial class definition:

```
import java.awt.Graphics;
import java.awt.Color;
import java.awt.Event;

public class Spots extends java.applet.Applet {

    final int MAXSPOTS = 10;
    int xspots[] = new int[MAXSPOTS];
    int yspots[] = new int[MAXSPOTS];
    int currspots = 0;

}
```

12

This class uses three other AWT classes: Graphics, Color, and Event. That last class, Event, needs to be imported in any applets that use events. The class has four instance variables: a constant to determine the maximum number of spots that can be drawn, two arrays to store the x and y coordinates of the spots that have already been drawn, and an integer to keep track of the number of the current spot.

NOTE

This class doesn't include the implements Runnable words in its definition. As you'll see later as you build this applet, it also doesn't have a run() method. Why not? Because it doesn't actually do anything on its own—all it does is wait for input and then do stuff when input happens. There's no need for threads if your applet isn't actively doing something all the time.

Let's start by adding the init() method, which does only one thing: set the background color to white:

```
public void init() {
    setBackground(Color.white);
}
```

We've set the background here in init() instead of in paint() as you have in past examples because you need to set the background only once. Because paint() is called repeatedly each time a new spot is added, setting the background in the paint() method unnecessarily slows down that method. Putting it here is a much better idea.

The main action of this applet occurs with the mouseDown() method, so let's add that one now:

```
public boolean mouseDown(Event evt, int x, int y) {
    if (currspots < MAXSPOTS) {
        addspot(x,y);
        return true;
    }
    else {
        System.out.println("Too many spots.");
        return false;
    }
}
```

When the mouse click occurs, the mouseDown() method tests to see whether there are fewer than 10 spots. If so, it calls the addspot() method (which you'll write soon) and returns true (the mouse down event was intercepted and handled). If not, it just prints an error message and returns false.

What does addspot() do? It adds the coordinates of the spot to the arrays that store the coordinates, increments the currspots variable, and then calls repaint():

```
void addspot(int x, int y) {
    xspots[currspots] = x;
    yspots[currspots] = y;
    currspots++;
    repaint();
}
```

You may be wondering why you have to keep track of all the past spots in addition to the current spot. It's because of repaint(): Each time you paint the screen, you have to paint all the old spots in addition to the newest spot. Otherwise, each time you painted a new spot, the older spots would get erased. Now, on to the paint() method:

```
public void paint(Graphics g) {
    g.setColor(Color.blue);
    for (int i = 0; i < currspots; i++) {
        g.fillOval(xspots[i] -10, yspots[i] - 10, 20, 20);
    }
}
```

Inside paint(), you just loop through the spots you've stored in the xspots and yspots arrays, painting each one (actually, painting them a little to the right and upward so that the spot is painted around the mouse pointer rather than below and to the right).

That's it! That's all you need to create an applet that handles mouse clicks. Everything else is handled for you. You have to add the appropriate behavior to mouseDown() or mouseUp() to intercept and handle that event. Listing 12.1 shows the full text for the Spots applet.

TYPE   **12.1. The Spots applet.**

```
 1: import java.awt.Graphics;
 2: import java.awt.Color;
 3: import java.awt.Event;
 4:
 5: public class Spots extends java.applet.Applet {
 6:
 7:     final int MAXSPOTS = 10;
 8:     int xspots[] = new int[MAXSPOTS];
 9:     int yspots[] = new int[MAXSPOTS];
10:     int currspots = 0;
11:
12:     public void init() {
13:         setBackground(Color.white);
14:     }
15:
16:     public boolean mouseDown(Event evt, int x, int y) {
17:         if (currspots < MAXSPOTS) {
18:             addspot(x,y);
19:             return true;
20:         }
21:         else {
22:             System.out.println("Too many spots.");
23:             return false;
24:         }
25:     }
```

12

```
26:
27:     void addspot(int x,int y) {
28:          xspots[currspots] = x;
29:          yspots[currspots] = y;
30:          currspots++;
31:          repaint();
32:     }
33:
34:     public void paint(Graphics g) {
35:          g.setColor(Color.blue);
36:          for (int i = 0; i < currspots; i++) {
37:              g.fillOval(xspots[i] - 10, yspots[i] - 10, 20, 20);
38:          }
39:     }
40: }
```

Double-Clicks

What if the mouse event you're interested in is more than a single mouse click—what if you want to track double- or triple-clicks? The Java Event class provides a variable for tracking this information, called clickCount. clickCount is an integer representing the number of consecutive mouse clicks that have occurred (where "consecutive" is usually determined by the operating system or the mouse hardware). If you're interested in multiple mouse clicks in your applets, you can test this value in the body of your mouseDown() method, like this:

```
public boolean mouseDown(Event evt, int x, int y) {
    switch (evt.clickCount) {
      case 1:  // single-click
      case 2:  // double-click
      case 3:  // triple-click
      ....
    }
}
```

12

Mouse Movements

Every time the mouse is moved a single pixel in any direction, a mouse move event is generated. There are two mouse movement events: mouse drags, where the movement occurs with the mouse button pressed down, and plain mouse movements, where the mouse button isn't pressed.

To manage mouse movement events, use the mouseDrag() and mouseMove() methods.

Mouse Drag and Mouse Move Events

The mouseDrag() and mouseMove() methods, when included in your applet code, intercept and handle mouse movement events. Mouse move and move drag events are generated for every pixel change the mouse moves, so a mouse movement from one side of the applet to the other may generate hundreds of events. The `mouseMove()` method, for plain mouse pointer movements without the mouse button pressed, looks much like the mouse-click methods:

```
public boolean mouseMove(Event evt, int x, int y) {
    ...
}
```

The `mouseDrag()` method handles mouse movements made with the mouse button pressed down (a complete dragging movement consists of a mouse down event, a series of mouse drag events for each pixel the mouse is moved, and a mouse up when the button is released). The `mouseDrag()` method looks like this:

```
public boolean mouseDrag(Event evt, int x, int y) {
    ...
}
```

Note that for both the `mouseMove()` and `mouseDrag()` methods, the arguments for the x and y coordinates are the new location of the mouse, not its starting location.

Mouse Enter and Mouse Exit Events

Finally, there are the `mouseEnter()` and `mouseExit()` methods. These two methods are called when the mouse pointer enters or exits an applet or a portion of that applet. (In case you're wondering why you might need to know this, it's more useful on AWT components that you might put inside an applet. You'll learn more about the AWT tomorrow.)

Both `mouseEnter()` and `mouseExit()` have signatures similar to the mouse click methods—three arguments: the event object and the x and y coordinates of the point where the mouse entered or exited the applet. These examples show the signatures for `mouseEnter()` and `mouseExit()`:

```
public boolean mouseEnter(Event evt, int x, int y) {
    ...
}

public boolean mouseExit(Event evt, int x, int y) {
    ...
}
```

An Example: Drawing Lines

Examples always help to make concepts more concrete. In this section you'll create an applet that enables you to draw straight lines on the screen by dragging from the startpoint to the endpoint. Figure 12.2 shows the applet at work.

Figure 12.2.

Drawing lines.

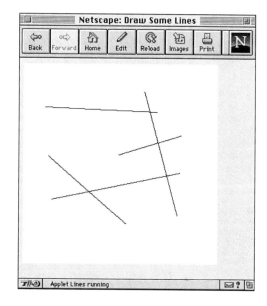

As with the Spots applet (on which this applet is based), let's start with the basic definition and work our way through it, adding the appropriate methods to build the applet. Here's a simple class definition for the Lines applet, with a number of initial instance variables and a simple init() method:

```
import java.awt.Graphics;
import java.awt.Color;
import java.awt.Event;
import java.awt.Point;

public class Lines extends java.applet.Applet {

    final int MAXLINES = 10;
    Point starts[] = new Point[MAXLINES]; // starting points
    Point ends[] = new Point[MAXLINES];   // ending points
    Point anchor;     // start of current line
    Point currentpoint; // current end of line
    int currline = 0; // number of lines

    public void init() {
        setBackground(Color.white);
    }
}
```

This applet adds a few more things than Spots. Unlike Spots, which keeps track of individual integer coordinates, this one keeps track of Point objects. Points represent an x and a y coordinate, encapsulated in a single object. To deal with points, you import the Point class and set up a bunch of instance variables that hold points:

☐ The starts array holds points representing the starts of lines already drawn.

☐ The ends array holds the endpoints of those same lines.

☐ anchor holds the starting point of the line currently being drawn.

☐ currentpoint holds the current endpoint of the line currently being drawn.

☐ currline holds the current number of lines (to make sure you don't go over MAXLINES, and to keep track of which line in the array to access next).

Finally, the init() method, as in the Spots applet, sets the background of the applet to white.

The three main events this applet deals with are mouseDown(), to set the anchor point for the current line, mouseDrag(), to animate the current line as it's being drawn, and mouseUp(), to set the ending point for the new line. Given that you have instance variables to hold each of these values, it's merely a matter of plugging the right variables into the right methods. Here's mouseDown(), which sets the anchor point (but only if we haven't exceeded the maximum number of lines):

```
public boolean mouseDown(Event evt, int x, int y) {
    if (currline < MAXLINES) {
        anchor = new Point(x,y);
        return true;
    }
    else {
        System.out.println("Too many lines.");
        return false;
    }
}
```

While the mouse is being dragged to draw the line, the applet animates the line being drawn. As you drag the mouse around, the new line moves with it from the anchor point to the tip of the mouse. The mouseDrag() event contains the current point each time the mouse moves, so use that method to keep track of the current point (and to repaint for each movement so the line "animates"). Note that if we've exceeded the maximum number of lines, we won't want to do any of this. Here's the mouseDrag() method to do all those things:

```
public boolean mouseDrag(Event evt, int x, int y) {
    if (currline < MAXLINES) {
        currentpoint = new Point(x,y);
        repaint();
        return true;
    }
    else return false;
}
```

The new line doesn't get added to the arrays of old lines until the mouse button is released. Here's mouseUp(), which tests to make sure you haven't exceeded the maximum number of lines before calling the addline() method (described next):

```
public boolean mouseUp(Event evt, int x, int y) {
    if (currline < MAXLINES) {
        addline(x,y);
        return true;
    }
    else return false;
}
```

The addline() method is where the arrays of starting and ending points get updated and where the applet is repainted to take the new line into effect:

```
void addline(int x,int y) {
    starts[currline] = anchor;
    ends[currline] = new Point(x,y);
    currline++;
    currentpoint = null;
    anchor = null;
    repaint();
}
```

Note that in this method you also set currentpoint and anchor to null. Why? Because the current line you were drawing is over. By setting these variables to null, you can test for that value in the paint() method to see whether you need to draw a current line.

Painting the applet means drawing all the old lines stored in the starts and ends arrays, as well as drawing the current line in progress (whose endpoints are in anchor and currentpoint, respectively). To show the animation of the current line, draw it in blue. Here's the paint() method for the Lines applet:

```
public void paint(Graphics g) {

    // Draw existing lines
    for (int i = 0; i < currline; i++) {
        g.drawLine(starts[i].x, starts[i].y,
            ends[i].x, ends[i].y);
    }

    // Draw current line
    g.setColor(Color.blue);
    if (currentpoint != null)
        g.drawLine(anchor.x, anchor.y,
            currentpoint.x, currentpoint.y);
}
```

12

In paint(), when you're drawing the current line, you test first to see whether currentpoint is null. If it is, the applet isn't in the middle of drawing a line, so there's no reason to try drawing a line that doesn't exist. By testing for currentpoint (and by setting currentpoint to null in the addline() method), you can paint only what you need.

That's it—just 60 lines of code and a few basic methods, and you have a very basic drawing application in your Web browser. Listing 12.2 shows the full text of the Lines applet so that you can put the pieces together.

Listing 12.2. The Lines applet.

```
 1: import java.awt.Graphics;
 2: import java.awt.Color;
 3: import java.awt.Event;
 4: import java.awt.Point;
 5:
 6: public class Lines extends java.applet.Applet {
 7:
 8:     final int MAXLINES = 10;
 9:     Point starts[] = new Point[MAXLINES]; // starting points
10:     Point ends[] = new Point[MAXLINES];    // endingpoints
11:     Point anchor;    // start of current line
12:     Point currentpoint; // current end of line
13:     int currline = 0; // number of lines
14:
15:     public void init() {
16:         setBackground(Color.white);
17:     }
18:
19:     public boolean mouseDown(Event evt, int x, int y) {
20:         if (currline < MAXLINES) {
21:             anchor = new Point(x,y);
22:             return true;
23:         }
24:         else  {
25:             System.out.println("Too many lines.");
26:             return false;
27:         }
28:     }
29:
30:     public boolean mouseUp(Event evt, int x, int y) {
31:         if (currline < MAXLINES) {
32:             addline(x,y);
33:             return true;
34:         }
35:         else return false;
36:     }
37:
38:     public boolean mouseDrag(Event evt, int x, int y) {
39:         if (currline < MAXLINES) {
40:             currentpoint = new Point(x,y);
41:             repaint();
42:             return true;
43:         }
44:         else return false;
45:     }
46:
47:     void addline(int x,int y) {
48:         starts[currline] = anchor;
49:         ends[currline] = new Point(x,y);
50:         currline++;
51:         currentpoint = null;
52:         anchor = null;
53:         repaint();
54:     }
```

12

```
55:
56:    public void paint(Graphics g) {
57:
58:        // Draw existing lines
59:        for (int i = 0; i < currline; i++) {
50:            g.drawLine(starts[i].x, starts[i].y,
51:                    ends[i].x, ends[i].y);
52:        }
53:
54:        // draw current line
55:        g.setColor(Color.blue);
56:        if (currentpoint != null)
57:            g.drawLine(anchor.x,anchor.y,
58:                currentpoint.x,currentpoint.y);
59:    }
60:}
```

Keyboard Events

A keyboard event is generated whenever a user presses a key on the keyboard. By using keyboard events, you can get hold of the values of the keys the user pressed to perform an action or merely to get character input from the users of your applet.

The `keyDown()` and `keyUp()` Methods

To capture a keyboard event, use the `keyDown()` method:

```
public boolean keyDown(Event evt, int key) {
    ...
}
```

The keys generated by key down events (and passed into `keyDown()` as the key argument) are integers representing Unicode character values, which include alphanumeric characters, function keys, tabs, returns, and so on. To use them as characters (for example, to print them), you need to cast them to characters:

```
currentchar = (char)key;
```

Here's a simple example of a `keyDown()` method that does nothing but print the key you just typed in both its Unicode and character representation (it can be fun to see which key characters produce which values):

```
public boolean keyDown(Event evt, int key) {
    System.out.println("ASCII value: " + key);
    System.out.println("Character: " + (char)key);
    return true;
}
```

12

As with mouse clicks, each key down event also has a corresponding key up event. To intercept key up events, use the keyUp() method:

```
public booklean keyUp(Event evt, int key)  {
    ...
}
```

Default Keys

The Event class provides a set of class variables that refer to several standard nonalphanumeric keys, such as the arrow and function keys. If your applet's interface uses these keys, you can provide more readable code by testing for these names in your keyDown() method rather than testing for their numeric values (and you're also more likely to be cross-platform if you use these variables). For example, to test whether the up arrow was pressed, you might use the following snippet of code:

```
if (key == Event.UP) {
    ...
}
```

Because the values these class variables hold are integers, you also can use the switch statement to test for them.

Table 12.1 shows the standard event class variables for various keys and the actual keys they represent.

Table 12.1. Standard keys defined by the Event class.

Class Variable	Represented Key
Event.HOME	The Home key
Event.END	The End key
Event.PGUP	The Page Up key
Event.PGDN	The Page Down key
Event.UP	The up arrow
Event.DOWN	The down arrow
Event.LEFT	The left arrow
Event.RIGHT	The right arrow
Event.F1	The F1 key
Event.F2	The F2 key
Event.F3	The F3 key
Event.F4	The F4 key

12

Class Variable	Represented Key
Event.F5	The F5 key
Event.F6	The F6 key
Event.F7	The F7 key
Event.F8	The F8 key
Event.F9	The F9 key
Event.F10	The F10 key
Event.F11	The F11 key
Event.F12	The F12 key

An Example: Entering, Displaying, and Moving Characters

Let's look at an applet that demonstrates keyboard events. With this applet, you type a character, and that character is displayed in the center of the applet window. You then can move that character around on the screen with the arrow keys. Typing another character at any time changes the character as it's currently displayed. Figure 12.3 shows an example.

Figure 12.3.

The Keys applet.

NOTE

To get this applet to work, you might have to click once with the
mouse on it in order for the keys to show up. This is to make sure the
applet has the keyboard focus (that is, that its actually listening when
you type characters on the keyboard).

This applet is actually less complicated than the previous applets you've used. This one has
only three methods: `init()`, `keyDown()`, and `paint()`. The instance variables are also simpler
because the only things you need to keep track of are the x and y positions of the current
character and the values of that character itself. Here's the initial class definition:

```
import java.awt.Graphics;
import java.awt.Event;
import java.awt.Font;
import java.awt.Color;

public class Keys extends java.applet.Applet {

    char currkey;
    int currx;
    int curry;
}
```

Let's start by adding an `init()` method. Here, `init()` is responsible for three things: setting
the background color, setting the applet's font (here, 36-point Helvetica bold), and setting
the beginning position for the character (the middle of the screen, minus a few points to
nudge it up and to the right):

```
public void init() {
    currx = (size().width / 2) - 8;
    curry = (size().height / 2) - 16;
    setBackground(Color.white);
    setFont(new Font("Helvetica", Font.BOLD, 36));
}
```

Because this applet's behavior is based on keyboard input, the `keyDown()` method is where
most of the work of the applet takes place:

```
public boolean keyDown(Event evt, int key) {
    switch (key) {
        case Event.DOWN:
            curry += 5;
            break;
        case Event.UP:
            curry -= 5;
            break;
        case Event.LEFT:
            currx -= 5;
            break;
        case Event.RIGHT:
            currx += 5;
            break;
```

```
        default:
            currkey = (char)key;
        }
        repaint();
        return true;
    }
```

In the center of the keyDown() applet is a switch statement that tests for different key events. If the event is an arrow key, the appropriate change is made to the character's position. If the event is any other key, the character itself is changed (that's the default part of the switch). The method finishes up with a repaint() and returns true.

The paint() method here is almost trivial; just display the current character at the current position. However, note that when the applet starts up, there's no initial character and nothing to draw, so you have to take that into account. The currkey variable is initialized to 0, so you paint the applet only if currkey has an actual value:

```
public void paint(Graphics g) {
    if (currkey != 0) {
        g.drawString(String.valueOf(currkey), currx,curry);
    }
}
```

Listing 12.3 shows the complete source code for the Keys applet.

TYPE **Listing 12.3. The Keys applet.**

```
 1: import java.awt.Graphics;
 2: import java.awt.Event;
 3: import java.awt.Font;
 4: import java.awt.Color;
 5:
 6: public class Keys extends java.applet.Applet {
 7:
 8:     char currkey;
 9:     int currx;
10:    int curry;
11:
12:     public void init() {
13:         currx = (size().width / 2) -8;  // default
14:         curry = (size().height / 2) -16;
15:
16:         setBackground(Color.white);
17:         setFont(new Font("Helvetica",Font.BOLD,36));
18:     }
19:
20:     public boolean keyDown(Event evt, int key) {
21:         switch (key) {
22:         case Event.DOWN:
23:             curry += 5;
24:             break;
```

continues

Listing 12.3. continued

```
25:            case Event.UP:
26:                curry -= 5;
27:                break;
28:            case Event.LEFT:
29:                currx -= 5;
30:                break;
31:            case Event.RIGHT:
32:                currx += 5;
33:                break;
34:            default:
35:                currkey = (char)key;
36:            }
37:
38:            repaint();
39:            return true;
40:        }
41:
42:        public void paint(Graphics g) {
43:            if (currkey != 0) {
44:                g.drawString(String.valueOf(currkey), currx,curry);
45:            }
46:        }
47: }
```

Testing for Modifier Keys and Multiple Mouse Buttons

Shift, Control (Ctrl), and Meta are modifier keys. They don't generate key events themselves, but when you get an ordinary mouse or keyboard event, you can test to see whether those modifier keys were held down when the event occurred. Sometimes it may be obvious—shifted alphanumeric keys produce different key events than unshifted ones, for example. For other events, however—mouse events in particular—you may want to handle an event with a modifier key held down differently from a regular version of that event.

NOTE   The Meta key is commonly used on UNIX systems; it's usually mapped
              to Alt on PC keyboards and Command (apple) on Macintoshes.

The Event class provides three methods for testing whether a modifier key is held down: shiftDown(), metaDown(), and controlDown(). All return boolean values based on whether that modifier key is indeed held down. You can use these three methods in any of the event-handling methods (mouse or keyboard) by calling them on the event object passed into that method:

```
public boolean mouseDown(Event evt, int x, int y ) {
    if (evt.shiftDown())
        // handle shift-click
    else // handle regular click
}
```

One other significant use of these modifier key methods is to test for which mouse button generated a particular mouse event on systems with two or three mouse buttons. By default, mouse events (such as mouse down and mouse drag) are generated regardless of which mouse button is used. However, Java events internally map left and middle mouse actions to meta and Control (Ctrl) modifier keys, respectively, so testing for the key tests for the mouse button's action. By testing for modifier keys, you can find out which mouse button was used and execute different behavior for those buttons than you would for the left button. Use an if statement to test each case, like this:

```
public boolean mouseDown(Event evt, int x, int y ) {
    if (evt.metaDown())
        // handle a right-click
    else if (evt.controlDown())
        // handle a middle-click
    else // handle a regular click
}
```

Note that because this mapping from multiple mouse buttons to keyboard modifiers happens automatically, you don't have to do a lot of work to make sure your applets or applications work on different systems with different kinds of mouse devices. Because left-button or right-button mouse clicks map to modifier key events, you can use those actual modifier keys on systems with fewer mouse buttons to generate exactly the same results. So, for example, holding down the Ctrl key and clicking the mouse on Windows or holding the Control key on the Macintosh is the same as clicking the middle mouse button on a three-button mouse; holding down the Command (apple) key and clicking the mouse on the Mac is the same as clicking the right mouse button on a two- or three-button mouse.

Consider, however, that the use of different mouse buttons or modifier keys may not be immediately obvious if your applet or application runs on a system with fewer buttons than you're used to working with. Consider restricting your interface to a single mouse button or to providing help or documentation to explain the use of your program in this case.

The AWT Event Handler

The default methods you've learned about today for handling basic events in applets are actually called by a generic event handler method called handleEvent(). The handleEvent() method is how the AWT generically deals with events that occur between application components and events based on user input.

In the default `handleEvent()` method, basic events are processed and the methods you learned about today are called. To handle events other than those mentioned here (for example, events for scrollbars or for other user interface elements—which you'll learn about on Day 13, "Creating User Interfaces with the AWT"), to change the default event handling behavior, or to create and pass around your own events, you need to override `handleEvent()` in your own Java programs. The `handleEvent()` method looks like this:

```
public boolean handleEvent(Event evt) {
    ...
}
```

To test for specific events, examine the `id` instance variable of the `Event` object that gets passed in to `handleEvent()`. The event ID is an integer, but fortunately the `Event` class defines a whole set of event IDs as class variables whose names you can test for in the body of `handleEvent()`. Because these class variables are integer constants, a `switch` statement works particularly well. For example, here's a simple `handleEvent()` method to print out debugging information about mouse events:

```
public boolean handleEvent(Event evt) {
    switch (evt.id) {
    case Event.MOUSE_DOWN:
        System.out.println("MouseDown: " +
                evt.x + "," + evt.y);
        return true;
    case Event.MOUSE_UP:
        System.out.println("MouseUp: " +
                evt.x + "," + evt.y);
        return true;
    case Event.MOUSE_MOVE:
        System.out.println("MouseMove: " +
                evt.x + "," + evt.y);
        return true;
    case Event.MOUSE_DRAG:
        System.out.println("MouseDrag: " +
                evt.x + "," + evt.y);
        return true;
    default:
        return false;
    }
}
```

You can test for the following keyboard events:

- [ ] `Event.KEY_PRESS` is generated when a key is pressed (the same as the `keyDown()` method).

- [ ] `Event.KEY_RELEASE` is generated when a key is released.

- [ ] `Event.KEY_ACTION` and `Event.KEY_ACTION_RELEASE` are generated when an action key (a function key, an arrow key, Page Up, Page Down, or Home) is pressed or released.

12

You can test for these mouse events:

- [ ] `Event.MOUSE_DOWN` is generated when the mouse button is pressed (the same as the `mouseDown()` method).

- [ ] `Event.MOUSE_UP` is generated when the mouse button is released (the same as the `mouseUp()` method).

- [ ] `Event.MOUSE_MOVE` is generated when the mouse is moved (the same as the `mouseMove()` method).

- [ ] `Event.MOUSE_DRAG` is generated when the mouse is moved with the button pressed (the same as the `mouseDrag()` method).

- [ ] `Event.MOUSE_ENTER` is generated when the mouse enters the applet (or a component of that applet). You can also use the `mouseEnter()` method.

- [ ] `Event.MOUSE_EXIT` is generated when the mouse exits the applet. You can also use the `mouseExit()` method.

In addition to these events, the `Event` class has a whole suite of methods for handling AWT components. You'll learn more about these events tomorrow.

Note that if you override `handleEvent()` in your class, none of the default event-handling methods you learned about today will get called unless you explicitly call them in the body of `handleEvent()`, so be careful if you decide to do this. One way to get around this is to test for the event you're interested in, and if that event isn't it, call `super.handleEvent()` so that the superclass that defines `handleEvent()` can process things. Here's an example of how to do this:

```
public boolean handleEvent(Event evt) {
    if (evt.id == Event.MOUSE_DOWN) {
        // process the mouse down
        return true;
    } else {
        return super.handleEvent(evt);
    }
}
```

Also, note that like the individual methods for individual events, `handleEvent()` also returns a boolean. The value you return here is particularly important; if you pass handling of the event to another method, you must return `false`. If you handle the event in the body of this method, return `true`. If you pass the event up to a superclass, that method will return `true` or `false`; you don't have to yourself.

Summary

Handling events in Java's Abstract Windowing Toolkit is easy. Most of the time all you need to do is stick the right method in your applet code, and your applet intercepts and handles that event at the right time. Here are some of the basic events you can manage in this way:

- ☐ Mouse clicks—mouseUp() and mouseDown() methods for each part of a mouse click.
- ☐ Mouse movements—mouseMove() and mouseDrag() for mouse movement with the mouse button released and pressed, respectively, as well as mouseEnter() and mouseExit() for when the mouse enters and exits the applet area.
- ☐ keyDown() and keyUp() for when a key on the keyboard is pressed.

All events in the AWT generate an Event object; inside that object, you can find out information about the event, when it occurred, and its x and y coordinates (if applicable). You can also test that event to see whether a modifier key was pressed when the event occurred, by using the shiftDown(), controlDown(), and metaDown() methods.

Finally, there is the handleEvent() method, the "parent" of the individual event methods. The handleEvent() method is actually what the Java system calls to manage events; the default implementation calls the individual method events where necessary. To override how methods are managed in your applet, override handleEvent().

Q&A

Q In the Spots applet, the spot coordinates are stored in arrays, which have a limited size. How can I modify this applet so that it will draw an unlimited number of spots?

A You can do one of a couple things:

The first thing to do is test, in your addspot() method, whether the number of spots has exceeded MAXSPOTS. Then create a bigger array, copy the elements of the old array into that bigger array (use the System.arraycopy() method to do that), and reassign the x and y arrays to that new, bigger array.

The second thing to do is to use the Vector class. Vector, part of the java.util package, implements an array that is automatically growable—sort of like a linked list is in other languages. The disadvantage of Vector is that to put something into Vector, it has to be an actual object. This means you'll have to cast integers to Integer objects, and then extract their values from Integer objects to treat them as integers again. The Vector class allows you to access and change elements in the Vector just as you can in an array (by using method calls, rather than array syntax). Check it out.

Q What's a Meta key?

A It's popular in UNIX systems, and often mapped to Alt on most keyboards (Option on Macs). Because Shift and Control (Ctrl) are much more popular and widespread, it's probably a good idea to base your interfaces on those modifier keys if you can.

Q How do I test to see whether the Return key has been pressed?

A Return (line feed) is character 10; Enter (carriage return) is character 13. Note that different platforms may send different keys for the actual key marked Return. In particular, UNIX systems send line feeds, Macintoshes send carriage returns, and DOS systems send both. So to provide cross-platform behavior, you may want to test for both line feed and carriage return.

The word from the Java team is that a Return is a Return is a Return, regardless of the platform. However, at the time of this writing, it is questionable whether this is currently true in the Java Developer's Kit. You may want to check the API documentation for the Event class to see whether this has changed in the interim.

Q I looked at the API for the Event class, and there are many more event types listed there than the ones you mention today.

A Yes. The Event class defines many different kinds of events, both for general user input, such as the mouse and keyboard events you learned about here, and also events for managing changes to the state of user interface components, such as windows and scrollbars. Tomorrow you'll learn about those other events.

12

Day 13

Creating User Interfaces with the AWT

by Laura Lemay

For the past five days you've concentrated on creating applets that do very simple things: display text, play an animation or a sound, or interact with the user. When you get past that point, however, you may want to start creating more complex applets that behave like real applications embedded in a Web page—applets that start to look like real GUI applications with buttons, menus, text fields, and other elements.

It's this sort of real work in Java applets and applications for which Java's *Abstract Windowing Toolkit*, or AWT, was designed. You've actually been using the AWT all along, as you might have guessed from the classes you've been importing. The Applet class and most of the classes you've been using this week are all integral parts of the AWT.

The AWT provides the following:

☐ A full set of user interface (UI) widgets and other components, including windows, menus, buttons, check boxes, text fields, scrollbars, and scrolling lists

☐ Support for UI containers, which can contain other embedded containers or UI widgets

☐ An event system for managing system and user events among parts of the AWT

☐ Mechanisms for laying out components in a way that enables platform-independent UI design

Today you'll learn about how to use all these things in your Java applets. Tomorrow you'll learn about creating windows, menus, and dialog boxes, which enable you to pop up separate windows from the browser window. In addition, you can use the AWT in standalone applications, so everything you've learned so far this week can still be used. If you find the framework of the Web browser too limiting, you can take your AWT background and start writing full-fledged Java applications.

Today, however, you'll continue focusing on applets.

NOTE

This is by far the most complex lesson so far, and it's a long chapter as well. There's a lot to cover and a lot of code to go through today, so if it starts becoming overwhelming, you might want to take two days (or more) for this one.

An AWT Overview

The basic idea behind the AWT is that a graphical Java program is a set of nested components, starting from the outermost window all the way down to the smallest UI component. Components can include things you can actually see on the screen, such as windows, menu bars, buttons, and text fields, and they can also include containers, which in turn can contain other components. Figure 13.1 shows how a sample page in a Java browser might include several different components, all of which are managed through the AWT.

This nesting of components within containers within other components creates a hierarchy of components, from the smallest check box inside an applet to the overall window on the screen. The hierarchy of components determines the arrangement of items on the screen and inside other items, the order in which they are painted, and how events are passed from one component to another.

Figure 13.1.

AWT components.

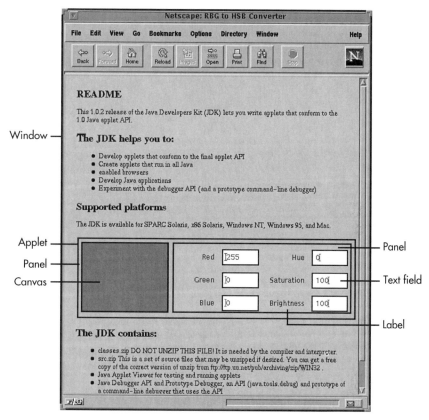

These are the major components you can work with in the AWT:

☐ *Containers.* Containers are generic AWT components that can contain other components, including other containers. The most common form of container is the *panel*, which represents a container that can be displayed onscreen. Applets are a form of panel (in fact, the `Applet` class is a subclass of the `Panel` class).

☐ *Canvases.* A canvas is a simple drawing surface. Although you can draw on panels (as you've been doing all along), canvases are good for painting images or performing other graphics operations.

☐ *UI components.* These can include buttons, lists, simple pop-up menus, check boxes, test fields, and other typical elements of a user interface.

☐ *Window construction components.* These include windows, frames, menu bars, and dialog boxes. They are listed separately from the other UI components because you'll use these less often—particularly in applets. In applets, the browser provides the main window and menu bar, so you don't have to use these. Your applet may create a new window, however, or you may want to write your own Java application that uses these components. (You'll learn about these tomorrow.)

13

The classes inside the `java.awt` package are written and organized to mirror the abstract structure of containers, components, and individual UI components. Figure 13.2 shows some of the class hierarchy that makes up the main classes in the AWT. The root of most of the AWT components is the class `Component`, which provides basic display and event-handling features. The classes `Container`, `Canvas`, `TextComponent`, and many of the other UI components inherit from `Component`. Inheriting from the `Container` class are objects that can contain other AWT components—the `Panel` and `Window` classes, in particular. Note that the `java.applet.Applet` class, even though it lives in its own package, inherits from `Panel`, so your applets are an integral part of the hierarchy of components in the AWT system.

Figure 13.2.

A partial AWT class hierarchy.

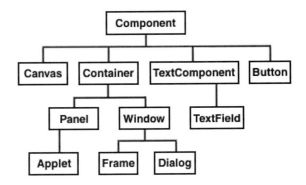

A graphical user interface–based application that you write by using the AWT can be as complex as you like, with dozens of nested containers and components inside each other. The AWT was designed so that each component can play its part in the overall AWT system without needing to duplicate or keep track of the behavior of other parts in the system.

In addition to the components themselves, the AWT also includes a set of layout managers. Layout managers determine how the various components are arranged when they are displayed onscreen, and their various sizes relative to each other. Because Java applets and applications that use the AWT can run on different systems with different displays, different fonts, and different resolutions, you cannot just stick a particular component at a particular spot on the window. Layout managers help you create UI layouts that are dynamically arranged and can be displayed anywhere the applet or application might be run.

The Basic User Interface Components

The simplest form of AWT component is the basic UI component. You can create and add these to your applet without needing to know anything about creating containers or panels—your applet, even before you start painting and drawing and handling events, is already an AWT container. Because an applet is a container, you can put other AWT components—such as UI components or other containers—into it.

In this section, you'll learn about the basic UI components: labels, buttons, check boxes, choice menus, and text fields. In each case, the procedure for creating the component is the same—you first create the component and then add it to the panel that holds it, at which point it is displayed on the screen. To add a component to a panel (such as your applet, for example), use the add() method:

```
public void init() {
    Button b = new Button("OK");
    add(b);
}
```

Here the add() method refers to the current applet—in other words, it means "add this element to me." You can also add elements to other containers, as you'll learn later.

Note that where the component appears in the panel depends on the layout manager that panel is defined to have. In these examples I've used both flow layouts and grid layouts, depending on which makes the applet look better. You'll learn more about panels and layouts in the next section.

Note also that each of these components has an action associated with it—that is, something that component does when it's activated. *Actions* generally trigger events or other activities in your applet (they are often called *callbacks* in other window toolkits). In this section, you'll focus on creating the components themselves; you'll learn about adding actions to them later in today's lesson.

On to the components!

Labels

The simplest form of UI component is the label, which is, effectively, a text string that you can use to label other UI components. Labels are not editable; they just label other components on the screen.

The advantages that a label has over an ordinary text string (that you'd draw using drawString() in the paint() method) are

☐ You don't have to redraw labels yourself. Labels are an AWT element, and the AWT keeps track of drawing them.

☐ Labels follow the layout of the panel in which they're contained and can be aligned with other UI components. Panel layout is determined by the layout manager, which you'll learn about later, in the section "Panels and Layout."

NEW TERM A *label* is an uneditable text string that acts as a description for other AWT components.

13

To create a label, use one of the following constructors:

☐ Label() creates an empty label, with its text aligned left.

☐ Label(*String*) creates a label with the given text string, also aligned left.

☐ Label(*String*, *int*) creates a label with the given text string and the given alignment. The available alignment numbers are stored in class variables in Label, making them easier to remember: Label.RIGHT, Label.LEFT, and Label.CENTER.

You can change the label's font with the setFont() method, either called on the label itself to change the individual label, or on the enclosing component to change all the labels. Here's some simple code to create a few labels in Helvetica Bold (Figure 13.3 shows how this looks onscreen):

NOTE

This code uses the setLayout method to create a new layout manager. Don't worry about that line right now; you'll learn more about layout managers in the next section.

```java
import java.awt.*;

public class LabelTest extends java.applet.Applet {

  public void init() {
    setFont(new Font ("Helvetica", Font.BOLD, 14));
    setLayout(new GridLayout(3,1));
    add(new Label("aligned left", Label.LEFT));
    add(new Label("aligned center", Label.CENTER));
    add(new Label("aligned right", Label.RIGHT));
  }
}
```

Figure 13.3.

Three labels with various alignments.

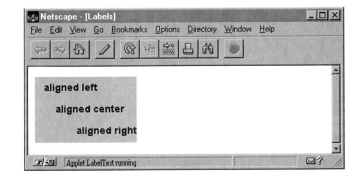

When you have a `Label` object, you can use methods defined in the `Label` class to get and set the values of the text, as shown in Table 13.1.

Table 13.1. Label methods.

Method	Action
getText()	Returns a string containing this label's text
setText(String)	Changes the text of this label
getAlignment()	Returns an integer representing the alignment of this label: 0 is Label.LEFT 1 is Label.CENTER 2 is Label.RIGHT
setAlignment(int)	Changes the alignment of this label to the given integer— use the class variables listed in the getAlignment() method

Buttons

The second user interface component to explore is the button. Buttons are simple UI components that trigger some action in your interface when they are pressed. For example, a calculator applet might have buttons for each number and operator, or a dialog box might have buttons for OK and Cancel.

 A *button* is a UI component that, when "pressed" (selected) with the mouse, triggers some action.

To create a button, use one of the following constructors:

- `Button()` creates an empty button with no label.
- `Button(String)` creates a button with the given string as a label.

Once you have a `Button` object, you can get the value of the button's label by using the `getLabel()` method and set the label using the `setLabel(String)` method.

Figure 13.4 shows some simple buttons, created using the following code:

```
public class ButtonTest extends java.applet.Applet {

  public void init() {
    add(new Button("Rewind"));
    add(new Button("Play"));
    add(new Button("Fast Forward"));
    add(new Button("Stop"));
  }
}
```

13

Figure 13.4.

Four buttons in Netscape.

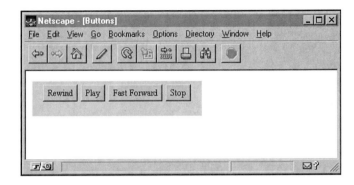

Check Boxes

Check boxes are user-interface components that have two states: on and off (or checked and unchecked, selected and unselected, true and false, and so on). Unlike buttons, check boxes usually don't trigger direct actions in a UI, but instead are used to indicate optional features of some other action.

Check boxes can be used in two ways:

☐ Nonexclusive: Given a series of check boxes, any of them can be selected.

☐ Exclusive: Given a series, only one check box can be selected at a time.

The latter kind of check boxes are called radio buttons or check box groups, and are described in the next section.

 Check boxes are UI components that can be selected or deselected (checked or unchecked) to provide options. Nonexclusive check boxes can be checked or unchecked independently of other check boxes.

Exclusive check boxes, sometimes called *radio buttons*, exist in groups; only one in the group can be checked at one time.

Nonexclusive check boxes can be created by using the Checkbox class. You can create a check box using one of the following constructors:

☐ Checkbox() creates an empty check box, unselected.

☐ Checkbox(*String*) creates a check box with the given string as a label.

☐ Checkbox(*String, null, boolean*) creates a check box that is either selected or deselected based on whether the boolean argument is true or false, respectively. (The null is used as a placeholder for a group argument. Only radio buttons have groups, as you'll learn in the next section.)

13

Figure 13.5 shows a few simple check boxes (only Underwear is selected) generated using the following code:

```java
import java.awt.*;

public class CheckboxTest extends java.applet.Applet {

  public void init() {
    setLayout(new FlowLayout(FlowLayout.LEFT));
    add(new Checkbox("Shoes"));
    add(new Checkbox("Socks"));
    add(new Checkbox("Pants"));
    add(new Checkbox("Underwear", null, true));
    add(new Checkbox("Shirt"));
  }

}
```

Figure 13.5.

Five check boxes, one selected.

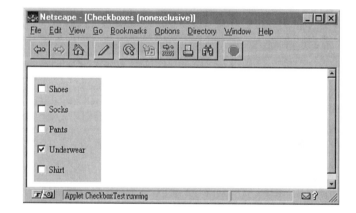

Table 13.2 lists some of the check box methods.

Table 13.2. Check box methods.

Method	Action
getLabel()	Returns a string containing this check box's label
setLabel(String)	Changes the text of the check box's label
getState()	Returns true or false, based on whether the check box is selected
setState(boolean)	Changes the check box's state to selected (true) or unselected (false)

13

Radio Buttons

Radio buttons have the same appearance as check boxes, but only one in a series can be selected at a time. To create a series of radio buttons, first create an instance of CheckboxGroup:

```
CheckboxGroup cbg = new CheckboxGroup();
```

Then create and add the individual check boxes using the constructor with three arguments (the first is the label, the second is the group, and the third is whether that check box is selected). Note that because radio buttons, by definition, have only one in the group selected at a time, the last true to be added will be the one selected by default:

```
add(new Checkbox("Yes", cbg, true);
add(new Checkbox("No", cbg, false);
```

Here's a simple example (the results of which are shown in Figure 13.6):

```
import java.awt.*;

public class CheckboxGroupTest extends java.applet.Applet {

  public void init() {
    setLayout(new FlowLayout(FlowLayout.LEFT));
    CheckboxGroup cbg = new CheckboxGroup();

    add(new Checkbox("Red", cbg, false));
    add(new Checkbox("Blue", cbg, false));
    add(new Checkbox("Yellow", cbg, false));
    add(new Checkbox("Green", cbg, true));
    add(new Checkbox("Orange", cbg, false));
    add(new Checkbox("Purple", cbg, false));
  }

}
```

Figure 13.6.

Six radio buttons (exclusive check boxes), one selected.

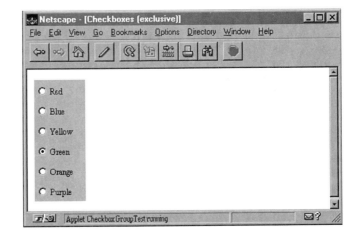

All the check box methods shown in Table 13.2 in the previous section can be used with the check boxes in the group. In addition, you can use the getCheckboxGroup() and setCheckboxGroup() methods (defined in the Checkbox() class) to access and change the group of any given check box.

Finally, the getCurrent() and setCurrent(Checkbox) methods, defined in CheckboxGroup, can be used to get or set the currently selected check box.

Choice Menus

The choice menu is a more complex UI component than labels, buttons, or check boxes. Choice menus are pop-up (or pull-down) menus from which you can select an item. The menu then displays that choice on the screen. The function of a choice menu is the same across platforms, but its actual appearance may vary from platform to platform.

Note that choice menus can have only one item selected at a time. If you want to be able to choose multiple items from the menu, use a scrolling list instead (you'll learn more about scrolling lists later today, in the section "More UI Components").

NEW TERM   *Choice menus* are pop-up menus of items from which you can choose one item.

To create a choice menu, create an instance of the Choice class and then use the addItem() method to add individual items to it in the order in which they should appear. Finally, add the entire choice menu to the panel in the usual way. Here's a simple program that builds a choice menu of fruits; Figure 13.7 shows the result (with the menu pulled down):

```java
import java.awt.*;

public class ChoiceTest extends java.applet.Applet {

  public void init() {
    Choice c = new Choice();

    c.addItem("Apples");
    c.addItem("Oranges");
    c.addItem("Strawberries");
    c.addItem("Blueberries");
    c.addItem("Bananas");

    add(c);
  }
}
```

13

Figure 13.7.

A choice menu.

Even after your choice menu has been added to a panel, you can continue to add items to that menu with the addItem() method. Table 13.3 shows some other methods that may be useful in working with choice menus.

Table 13.3. Choice menu methods.

Method	Action
getItem(int)	Returns the string item at the given position (items inside a choice begin at 0, just like arrays)
countItems()	Returns the number of items in the menu
getSelectedIndex()	Returns the index position of the item that's selected
getSelectedItem()	Returns the currently selected item as a string
select(int)	Selects the item at the given position
select(String)	Selects the item with the given string

Text Fields

Unlike the UI components up to this point, which only enable you to select among several options to perform an action, text fields allow you to enter and edit text. Text fields are generally only a single line and do not have scrollbars; text areas, which you'll learn about later today, are better for larger amounts of text.

Text fields are different from labels in that they can be edited; labels are good for just displaying text, text fields for getting text input from the user.

NEW TERM   *Text fields* provide an area where you can enter and edit a single line of text.

To create a text field, use one of the following constructors:

- ☐ `TextField()` creates an empty `TextField` that is 0 characters wide (it will be resized by the current layout manager).
- ☐ `TextField(int)` creates an empty text field. The integer argument indicates the minimum number of characters to display.
- ☐ `TextField(String)` creates a text field initialized with the given string. The field will be automatically resized by the current layout manager.
- ☐ `TextField(String, int)` creates a text field some number of characters wide (the integer argument) containing the given string. If the string is longer than the width, you can select and drag portions of the text within the field, and the box will scroll left or right.

For example, the following line creates a text field 30 characters wide with the string `"Enter Your Name"` as its initial contents:

```
TextField tf = new TextField("Enter Your Name", 30);
add(tf);
```

TIP

Text fields include only the editable field itself. You usually need to include a label with a text field to indicate what belongs in that text field.

You can also create a text field that obscures the characters typed into it—for example, for password fields. To do this, first create the text field itself; then use the `setEchoCharacter()` method to set the character that is echoed on the screen. Here is an example:

```
TextField tf = new TextField(30);
tf.setEchoCharacter('*');
```

Figure 13.8 shows three text boxes (and labels) that were created using the following code:

```
add(new Label("Enter your Name"));
add(new TextField("your name here", 45));
add(new Label("Enter your phone number"));
add(new TextField(12));
add(new Label("Enter your password"));
TextField t = new TextField(20);
t.setEchoCharacter('*');
add(t);
```

The text in the first field (`your name here`) was initialized in the code; I typed the text in the remaining two boxes just before taking the snapshot.

13

Figure 13.8.

Three text fields to allow input from the user.

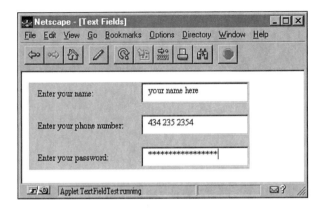

Text fields inherit from the class `TextComponent` and have a whole suite of methods, both inherited from that class and defined in their own class, that may be useful to you in your Java programs. Table 13.4 shows a selection of those methods.

Table 13.4. Text field methods.

Method	Action
`getText()`	Returns the text this text field contains (as a string)
`setText(String)`	Puts the given text string into the field
`getColumns()`	Returns the width of this text field
`select(int, int)`	Selects the text between the two integer positions (positions start from 0)
`selectAll()`	Selects all the text in the field
`isEditable()`	Returns `true` or `false` based on whether the text is editable
`setEditable(boolean)`	`true` (the default) enables text to be edited; `false` freezes the text
`getEchoChar()`	Returns the character used for masking input
`echoCharIsSet()`	Returns `true` or `false` based on whether the field has a masking character

NOTE

The descriptions of the `getEchoChar()` and `echoCharIsSet()` methods refer to masking user input. User input masking is a technique of limiting user input to a specific type, such as a number. Other types of user input masking include dates and phone numbers, where there are a specific number of numeric digits arranged in a constant format.

13

Panels and Layout

AWT panels can contain UI components or other panels. The question now is how those components are actually arranged and displayed onscreen.

In other windowing systems, UI components are often arranged using hard-coded pixel measurements—put a text field at the position 10,30, for example—the same way you used the graphics operations to paint squares and ovals on the screen. In the AWT, your UI design may be displayed on many different window systems on many different screens and with many different kinds of fonts with different font metrics. Therefore, you need a more flexible method of arranging components on the screen so that a layout that looks nice on one platform isn't a jumbled, unusable mess on another.

For just this purpose, Java has layout managers, insets, and hints that each component can provide to help dynamically lay out the screen.

Note that the nice thing about AWT components and user-interface items is that you don't have to paint them—the AWT system manages all that for you. If you have graphical components or images, or you want to create animation inside panels, you still have to do that by hand, but for most of the basic components, all you have to do is put them on the screen and Java will handle the rest.

Layout Managers: An Overview

The actual appearance of the AWT components on the screen is usually determined by two things: how those components are added to the panel that holds them (either the order or through arguments to add()) and the layout manager that panel is currently using to lay out the screen. The layout manager determines how portions of the screen will be sectioned and how components within that panel will be placed.

 The *layout manager* determines how AWT components are dynamically arranged on the screen.

Each panel on the screen can have its own layout manager. By nesting panels within panels, and using the appropriate layout manager for each one, you can often arrange your UI to group and arrange components in a way that is functionally useful and that looks good on a variety of platforms and windowing systems. You'll learn about nesting panels in a later section.

The AWT provides five basic layout managers: FlowLayout, GridLayout, BorderLayout, CardLayout, and GridBagLayout. To create a layout manager for a given panel, create an instance of that layout manager and then use the `setLayout()` method for that panel. This example sets the layout manager of the entire enclosing applet panel:

```
public void init() {
    setLayout(new FlowLayout());
}
```

Setting the default layout manager, like creating user-interface components, is best done during the applet's initialization, which is why it's included here.

After the layout manager is set, you can start adding components to the panel. The order in which components are added or the arguments you use to add those components is often significant, depending on which layout manager is currently active. Read on for information about the specific layout managers and how they present components within the panel to which they apply.

The following sections describe the five basic Java AWT layout managers.

The `FlowLayout` Class

The `FlowLayout` class is the most basic of layouts. Using flow layout, components are added to the panel one at a time, row by row. If a component doesn't fit onto a row, it's wrapped onto the next row. The flow layout also has an alignment, which determines the alignment of each row. By default, each row is centered.

NEW TERM *Flow layout* arranges components from left to right in rows. The rows are aligned left, right, or centered.

To create a basic flow layout with a centered alignment, use the following line of code in your panel's initialization (because this is the default pane layout, you don't need to include this line if that is your intent):

```
setLayout(new FlowLayout());
```

With the layout set, the order in which you add elements to the layout determines their position. The following code creates a simple row of six buttons in a centered flow layout (Figure 13.9 shows the result):

```
import java.awt.*;

public class FlowLayoutTest extends java.applet.Applet {

  public void init() {
    setLayout(new FlowLayout());
    add(new Button("One"));
    add(new Button("Two"));
    add(new Button("Three"));
    add(new Button("Four"));
```

```
        add(new Button("Five"));
        add(new Button("Six"));
    }
}
```

Figure 13.9.

*Six buttons, arranged
using a flow layout
manager.*

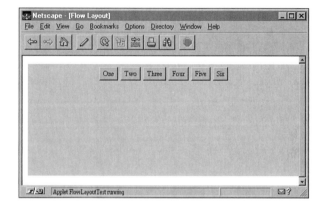

To create a flow layout with an alignment other than centered, add the FlowLayout.RIGHT or FlowLayout.LEFT class variable as an argument:

```
setLayout(new FlowLayout(FlowLayout.LEFT));
```

You can also set horizontal and vertical gap values by using flow layouts. The *gap* is the number of pixels between components in a panel; by default, the horizontal and vertical gap values are three pixels, which can be very close indeed. Horizontal gap spreads out components to the left and to the right; vertical gap spreads them to the top and bottom of each component. Add integer arguments to the flow layout constructor to increase the gap. Figure 13.10 shows the result of adding a gap of 30 points in the horizontal and 10 in the vertical directions, like this:

```
setLayout(new FlowLayout(FlowLayout.LEFT, 30, 10));
```

Figure 13.10.

*Flow layout with a gap of
10 points.*

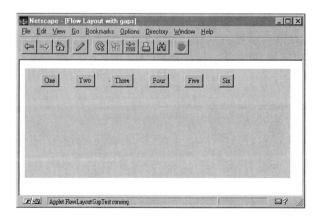

13

Grid Layouts

Grid layouts offer more control over the placement of components inside a panel. Using a grid layout, you portion off the display area of the panel into rows and columns. Each component you then add to the panel is placed in a *cell* of the grid, starting from the top row and progressing through each row from left to right (here's where the order of calls to the add() method are very relevant to how the screen is laid out).

To create a grid layout, indicate the number of rows and columns you want the grid to have when you create a new instance of the GridLayout class. Here's a grid layout with three rows and two columns (Figure 13.11 shows the result):

```
import java.awt.*;

public class GridLayoutTest extends java.applet.Applet {

  public void init() {
    setLayout(new GridLayout(3,2);
    add(new Button("One"));
    add(new Button("Two"));
    add(new Button("Three"));
    add(new Button("Four"));
    add(new Button("Five"));
    add(new Button("Six"));
  }
}
```

Figure 13.11.

Six buttons, displayed using a grid layout of three rows and two columns.

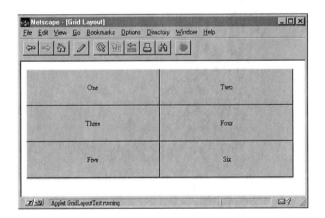

Grid layouts can also have a horizontal and vertical gap between components. To create gaps, add those pixel values:

```
setLayout(new GridLayout(3, 3, 10, 30));
```

Figure 13.12 shows a grid layout with a 10-pixel horizontal gap and a 30-pixel vertical gap.

Figure 13.12.

A grid layout with horizontal and vertical gaps.

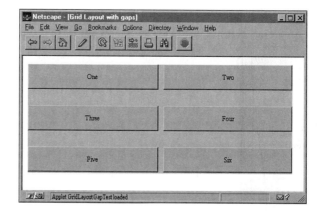

Border Layouts

Border layouts behave differently from flow and grid layouts. When you add a component to a panel that uses a border layout, you indicate its placement as a geographic direction: north, south, east, west, or center. (See Figure 13.13.) The components around all the edges are laid out with as much size as they need; the component in the center, if any, gets any space left over.

Figure 13.13.

Where components go in a border layout.

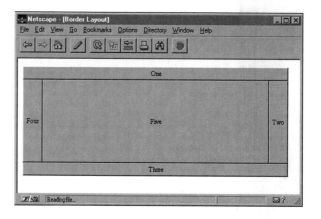

To use a border layout, you create it as you do the other layouts; then you add the individual components with a special add() method that has two arguments. The first argument is a string indicating the position of the component within the layout, and the second is the component to add:

```
add("North", new TextField("Title", 50));
```

You can also use this form of add() for the other layout managers; the string argument will just be ignored if it's not needed.

Here's the code to generate the border layout shown in Figure 13.13:

```
import java.awt.*;

public class BorderLayoutTest extends java.applet.Applet {

  public void init() {
    setLayout(new BorderLayout());
    add("North", new Button("One"));
    add("East", new Button("Two"));
    add("South", new Button("Three"));
    add("West", new Button("Four"));
    add("Center", new Button("Five"));
    add(new Button("Six"));
  }
}
```

Border layouts can also have horizontal and vertical gaps. Note that the north and south components extend all the way to the edge of the panel, so the gap will result in less vertical space for the east, right, and center components. To add gaps to a border layout, include those pixel values in the constructor as with the other layout managers:

```
setLayout(new BorderLayout(10, 10));
```

Card Layouts

Card layouts behave much differently from the other layouts. When you add components to one of the other layout managers, all those components appear on the screen at once. Card layouts are used to produce slide shows of components, one at a time. If you've ever used the HyperCard program on the Macintosh, or seen dialog boxes on windows with several different tabbed pages, you've worked with the same basic idea.

When you create a card layout, the components you add to the outer panel will be other container components—usually other panels. You can then use different layouts for those individual cards so that each screen has its own look.

NEW TERM   *Cards,* in a card layout, are different panels added one at a time and displayed one at a time. If you think of a card file, you'll get the idea; only one card can be displayed at once, but you can switch between cards.

When you add each card to the panel, you can give it a name. Then, to flip between the container cards, you can use methods defined in the CardLayout class to move to a named card, move forward or back, or move to the first card or to the last card. Typically you'll have a set of buttons that call these methods to make navigating the card layout easier.

13

Here's a simple snippet of code that creates a card layout containing three cards:

```
setLayout(new CardLayout());
//add the cards
Panel one = new Panel()
add("first", one);
Panel two = new Panel()
add("second", two);
Panel three = new Panel()
add("third", three);

// move around
show(this, "second"); //go to the card named "second"
show(this, "third");  //go to the card named "third"
previous(this);       //go back to the second card
first(this);          // got to the first card
```

Grid Bag Layouts

I've saved grid bag layouts for last because although they are the most powerful way of managing AWT layout, they are also extremely complicated.

Using one of the other four layout managers, it can sometimes be difficult to get the exact layout you want without doing a lot of nesting of panels within panels. Grid bags provide a more general-purpose solution. Like grid layouts, *grid bag layouts* allow you to arrange your components in a grid-like layout. However, grid bag layouts also allow you to control the span of individual cells in the grid, the proportions between the rows and columns, and the arrangement of components inside cells in the grid.

To create a grid bag layout, you actually use two classes: GridBagLayout, which provides the overall layout manager, and GridBagConstraints, which defines the properties of each component in the grid—its placement, dimensions, alignment, and so on. It's the relationship between the grid bag, the constraints, and each component that defines the overall layout.

In its most general form, creating a grid bag layout involves the following steps:

☐ Creating a GridBagLayout object and defining it as the current layout manager, as you would any other layout manager

☐ Creating a new instance of GridBagConstraints

☐ Setting up the constraints for a component

☐ Telling the layout manager about the component and its constraints

☐ Adding the component to the panel

13

Here's some simple code that sets up the layout and then creates constraints for a single button (don't worry about the various values for the constraints; I'll cover these later on in this section):

```
// set up layout
GridBagLayout gridbag = new GridBagLayout();
GridBagConstraints constraints = new GridBagConstraints();
setLayout(gridbag);

// define constraints for the button
Button b = new Button("Save");
constraints.gridx = 0;
constraints.gridy = 0;
constraints.gridwidth = 1;
constraints.gridheight = 1;
constraints.weightx = 30;
constraints.weighty = 30;
constraints.fill = GridBagConstraints.NONE;
constraints.anchor = GridBagConstraints.CENTER;

// attach constraints to layout, add button
gridbag.setConstraints(b, constraints);
add(b);
```

By far, the most tedious part of this process is setting up the constraints for each component (as you can see from this example, you have to set all those constraints for every component you want to add to the panel). In addition to the tedium, constraints aren't all that easy to understand; they have many different values, many of which are interrelated, which means that changing one may have strange effects on others.

Given the numerous constraints, it helps to have a plan and to deal with each kind of constraint one at a time. There are four steps I like to follow in this process. Let's walk through each of them.

Step One: Design the Grid

The first place to start in the grid bag layout is on paper. Sketching out your UI design beforehand—before you write even a single line of code—will help enormously in the long run with trying to figure out where everything goes. So put your editor aside for a second, pick up a piece of paper and a pencil, and let's build the grid.

Figure 13.14 shows the panel layout we'll be building in this example. Figure 13.15 shows the same layout with a grid imposed on top of it. Your layout will have a grid similar to this one, with rows and columns forming individual cells.

Keep in mind as you draw your grid that each component must have its own cell. You cannot put more than one component into the same cell. The reverse is not true, however; one component can span multiple cells in the x or y directions (as in the OK button in the bottom row, which spans two columns). Note in Figure 13.15 that the labels and text fields have their own grids and that the button spans two column cells.

Figure 13.14.

A grid bag layout.

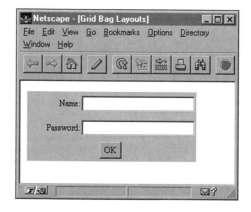

Figure 13.15.

The grid bag layout from Figure 13.14, with grid imposed.

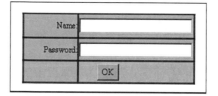

While you're still working on paper, something that will help you later is to label the cells with their x and y coordinates. These aren't pixel coordinates; rather, they're cell coordinates. The top-left cell is 0,0. The next cell to the right of that in the top row is 1,0. The cell to the right of that is 2,0. Moving to the next row, the leftmost cell is 1,0, the next cell in the row is 1,1, and so on. Label your cells on the paper with these numbers; you'll need them later when we do the code for this example. Figure 13.16 shows the numbers for each of the cells in this example.

Figure 13.16.

The grid bag layout from Figure 13.14, with cell coordinates.

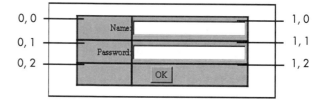

Step Two: Create the Grid in Java

Let's go back to Java and start implementing the layout you've just drawn on paper. Initially we're going to focus exclusively on the layout—getting the grid and the proportions right. For that, it helps to not work with actual UI elements. I like to use buttons as placeholders for the actual elements in the layout until I can get everything set up right, and then change the buttons to the right elements.

To cut down on the amount of typing we have to do to set up all those constraints, I'm going to start by defining a helper method that takes several values and sets the constraints for those values. `buildConstraints()` takes seven arguments: a `GridBagConstraints` object and six integers representing the `GridBagConstraints` instance variables `gridx`, `gridy`, `gridwidth`, `gridheight`, `weightx`, and `weighty`. You'll learn what these actually do soon; for now, here's the code to the helper method that we'll use further on in this example:

```
void buildConstraints(GridBagConstraints gbc, int gx, int gy,
  int gw, int gh, int wx, int wy) {
    gbc.gridx = gx;
    gbc.gridy = gy;
    gbc.gridwidth = gw;
    gbc.gridheight = gh;
    gbc.weightx = wx;
    gbc.weighty = wy;
  }
```

Now let's move on to the `init()` method, where all the layout actually occurs. Here's the basic method definition, where we'll define the `GridBagLayout` to be the initial layout manager and create a `constraints` object (an instance of `GridBagConstraints`):

```
public void init() {
    GridBagLayout gridbag = new GridBagLayout();
    GridBagConstraints constraints = new GridBagConstraints();
    setLayout(gridbag);

    constraints.fill = GridBagConstraints.BOTH;
}
```

One more small note of explanation: That last line, which sets the value of `constraints.fill`, will be removed (and explained) later. It's there so that the components will fill the entire cell in which they're contained, which makes it easier to see what's going on. Add it for now and you'll get a clearer idea of what it's for later.

Now we'll add the button placeholders to the layout (remember, we're focusing on basic grid organization at the moment, so we'll use buttons as placeholders for the actual UI elements you'll add later). Let's start with a single button so you can get a feel for setting its constraints. This code will go into the `init()` method just after the `setLayout` line:

```
// Name label
buildConstraints(constraints, 0, 0, 1, 1, 100, 100);
Button label1 = new Button("Name:");
gridbag.setConstraints(label1, constraints);
add(label1);
```

These four lines set up the constraints for an object, create a new button, attach those constraints to that button, and then add it to the panel. Note that constraints for a component are stored in the `GridBagConstraints` object, so the component doesn't even have to exist to set up its constraints.

Now let's get down to details: Just what are the values for the constraints that we've plugged into the helper method `buildConstraints`?

The first two integer arguments are the gridx and gridy values of the constraints. These are the cell coordinates of the cell that contains this component. Remember how you wrote these down on the paper in step one? With the cells nearly numbered on paper, all you have to do is plug in the right values. Note that if you have a component that spans multiple cells, the cell coordinates are those of the cell in the top-left corner.

Here this button is in the top-left corner, so its gridx and gridy (the first two arguments to buildConstraints()) are 0 and 0, respectively.

The second two integer arguments are the gridwidth and gridheight. These are not the pixel widths and heights of the cells; rather, they are the number of cells this component spans: gridwidth for the columns and gridheight for the rows. Here this component spans only one cell, so the values for both are 1.

The last two integer arguments are for weightx and weighty. These are used to set up the proportions of the rows and columns—that is, how wide or deep they will be. Weights can become very confusing, so for now just set both values to 100. You'll deal with weights in step three.

After the constraints have been built, you can attach them to an object using the setConstraints() method. setConstraints90, which is a method defined in GridBagLayout, takes two arguments: the component (here a button) and the constraints for that button. Finally, you can add the button to the panel.

After you've set and assigned the constraints to one component, you can reuse that GridBagConstraints object to set up the constraints for the next object. This effectively means duplicating those four lines for each component in the grid, with different values for the buildConstraints() method. To save space, I'm just going to show you the buildConstraints() methods for the last four cells.

The second cell we'll add is the one that will hold the text box for the name. The cell coordinates for this one are 1,0 (second column, first row); it too spans only one cell, and the weights (for now) are also both 100:

```
buildConstraints(constraints, 1, 0, 1, 1, 100, 100);
```

The next two components, which will be a label and a text field, are nearly exactly the same as the previous two; the only difference is in their cell coordinates. The password label is at 0,1 (first column, second row), and the password text field is at 1,1 (second column, second row):

```
buildConstraints(constraints, 0, 1, 1, 1, 100, 100);
buildConstraints(constraints, 1, 1, 1, 1, 100, 100);
```

And, finally, there is the OK button, which is a component that spans two cells in the bottom row of the panel. Here the cell coordinates are the left and topmost cell where the span starts (0,2). Here, unlike the previous components, we'll set gridwidth and gridheight to be something other than 1 because this cell spans multiple columns. The `gridweight` is 2 (it spans two cells), and the `gridheight` is 1 (it spans only one row):

```
buildConstraints(constraints, 0, 2, 2, 1, 100, 100);
```

Got it? Those are the placement constraints for all the components that you'll add to the grid layout. You will also need to assign each component's constraints to the layout manager and then add each component to the panel. Figure 13.17 shows the result so far. Note that you're not concerned about exact proportions here, or about making sure everything lines up. What you should keep track of at this point is making sure the grid is working, that there are the right number of rows and columns, that the spans are correct, and that nothing strange is going on (cells in the wrong place, cells overlapping, that kind of thing).

Figure 13.17.

Grid bag layout, first pass.

Step Three: Determine the Proportions

The next step is to determine the proportions of the rows and columns in relation to other rows and columns. For example, in this case you'll want the labels (name and password) to take up less space than the text boxes. And you might want the OK button at the bottom to be only half the height of the two text boxes above it. You arrange the proportions of the cells within your layout using the `weightx` and `weighty` constraints.

The easiest way to think of `weightx` and `weighty` is that their values are either percentages of the total width and height of the panel, or 0 if the weight or height has been set by some other cell. The values of `weightx` and `weighty` for all your components, therefore, should sum to 100.

TECHNICAL NOTE

Actually, the `weightx` and `weighty` values are not percentages; they're simply proportions—they can have any value whatsoever. When the proportions are calculated, all the values in a direction are summed so that each individual value is in proportion to that total (in other words,

13

divided into the total to actually get a percentage). Because this is incredibly non-intuitive, I find it far easier to look at the weights as percentages and to make sure they all sum up to 100 to make sure it's all coming out right.

So which cells get values and which cells get 0? Cells that span multiple rows or columns should always be 0 in the direction they span. Beyond that, it's simply a question of picking a cell to have a value, and then all the other cells in that row or columns should be 0.

Let's look at the five calls to `buildConstraints()` we made in the last step:

```
buildConstraints(constraints, 0, 0, 1, 1, 100, 100); //name
buildConstraints(constraints, 1, 0, 1, 1, 100, 100); //name text
buildConstraints(constraints, 0, 1, 1, 1, 100, 100); //password
buildConstraints(constraints, 1, 1, 1, 1, 100, 100); //password text
buildConstraints(constraints, 0, 2, 2, 1, 100, 100); //OK button
```

We'll be changing those last two arguments in each call to `buildConstraints` to be either a value or 0. Let's start with the x direction (the proportions of the columns), which is the second-to-last argument in that list.

If you look back to Figure 13.15 (the picture of the panel with the grid imposed), you'll note that the second column is much larger than the first. If you were going to pick theoretical percentages for those columns, you might say that the first is 10 percent and the second is 90 percent (I'm making a guess here; that's all you need to do as well). With those two guesses, let's assign them to cells. We don't want to assign any values to the cell with the OK button because that cell spans both columns, and percentages there wouldn't work. So let's add them to the first two cells, the name label and the name text field:

```
buildConstraints(constraints, 0, 0, 1, 1, 10, 100); //name
buildConstraints(constraints, 1, 0, 1, 1, 90, 100); //name text
```

And what about the values of the remaining two cells, the password label and text field? Because the proportions of the columns have already been set up by the name label and field, we don't have to reset them here. We'll give both of these cells and the one for the OK box 0 values:

```
buildConstraints(constraints, 0, 1, 1, 1, 0, 100); //password
buildConstraints(constraints, 1, 1, 1, 1, 0, 100); //password text
buildConstraints(constraints, 0, 2, 2, 1, 0, 100); //OK button
```

Note here that a 0 value does *not* mean that the cell has 0 width. These are proportions, not pixel values. A 0 simply means that the proportion has been set somewhere else; all 0 says is "stretch it to fit."

13

Now that the totals of all the weightx constraints are 100, let's move onto the weightys. Here there are three rows; glancing over the grid we drew, it looks like the button has about 20 percent and the text fields have the rest (40 percent each). As with the x values, we only have to set the value of one cell per row (the two labels and the button), with all the other cells having a weightx of 0.

Here are the final five calls to buildConstraints() with the weights in place:

```
buildConstraints(constraints, 0, 0, 1, 1, 10, 40); //name
buildConstraints(constraints, 1, 0, 1, 1, 90, 0); //name text
buildConstraints(constraints, 0, 1, 1, 1, 0, 40); //password
buildConstraints(constraints, 1, 1, 1, 1, 0, 0); //password text
buildConstraints(constraints, 0, 2, 2, 1, 0, 20); //OK button
```

Figure 13.18 shows the result with the correct proportions.

Figure 13.18.

Grid bag layout, second pass.

At this step, the goal here is to try to come up with some basic proportions for how the rows and cells will be spaced on the screen. You can make some basic estimates based on how big you expect the various components to be, but chances are you're going to use a lot of trial and error in this part of the process.

Step Four: Add and Arrange the Components

With the layout and the proportions in place, now you can replace the button placeholders with actual labels and text fields. And because you set everything up already, it should all work perfectly, right? Well, almost. Figure 13.19 shows what you get if you use the same constraints as before and replace the buttons with actual components.

13

Figure 13.19.

Grid bag layout, almost there.

It's close, but it's weird. The text boxes are too tall, and the OK button stretches the width of the cell.

What's missing are the constraints that arrange the components inside the cell. There are two of them: `fill` and `anchor`.

The `fill` constraint determines, for components that can stretch in either direction (like text boxes and buttons), in which direction to stretch. `fill` can have one of four values, defined as class variables in the `GridBagConstraints` class:

☐ `GridBagConstraints.BOTH`, which stretches the component to fill the cell in both directions.

☐ `GridBagConstraints.NONE`, which causes the component to be displayed in its smallest size.

☐ `GridBagConstraints.HORIZONTAL`, which stretches the component in the horizontal direction.

☐ `GridBagConstraints.VERTICAL`, which stretches the component in the vertical direction.

NOTE

Keep in mind that this is dynamic layout. You're not going to set up the actual pixel dimensions of any components; rather, you're telling these elements in which direction they can grow given a panel that can be of any size.

By default, the `fill` constraint for all components is `NONE`. So why are those text fields and labels filling the cells? If you remember way back to the start of the code for this example, I added this line to the `init()` method:

```
constraints.fill = GridBagConstraints.BOTH;
```

Now you know what it does. For the final version of this applet, you'll want to remove that line and add `fill` values for each independent component.

The second constraint that affects how a component appears in the cell is `anchor`. This constraint applies only to components that aren't filling the whole cell, and it tells the AWT where inside the cell to place the component. The possible values for the `anchor` constraint are `GridBagConstraints.CENTER`, which aligns the component both vertically and horizontally inside the cell, or one of eight direction values: `GridBagConstraints.NORTH`, `GridBagConstraints.NORTHEAST`, `GridBagConstraints.EAST`, `GridBagConstraints.SOUTHEAST`, `GridBagConstraints.SOUTH`, `GridBagConstraints.SOUTHWEST`, `GridBagConstraints.WEST`, or `GridBagConstraints.NORTHWEST`. The default value of `anchor` is `GridBagConstraints.CENTER`.

You set these constraints in the same way you did all the other ones: by changing instance variables in the `GridBagConstraints` object. Here you can change the definition of `buildConstraints()` to take two more arguments (they're `int`s), or you could just set them in the body of the `init()` method. I prefer the latter way.

Be careful with defaults. Keep in mind that because you're reusing the same `GridBagConstraints` object for each component, there may be some values left over after you're done with one component. On the other hand, if a `fill` or `anchor` from one object is the same as the one before it, you don't have to reset that object.

For this example, I'm going to make three changes to the `fill`s and `anchor`s of the components:

☐ The labels will have no fill and will be aligned east (so they hug the right side of the cell)

☐ The text fields will be filled horizontally (so they start one line high, but stretch to the width of the cell)

☐ The button will have no fill and will be center aligned

I'm not going to show you all the code for this here; the full code for the example is at the end of this section. You can see the changes I've made there.

Step Five: Futz with It

I added this step to the list because in my own experimentation with grid bag layouts, I found that even by following all the steps, usually the resulting layout wasn't *quite* right, and I needed to do a considerable amount of tinkering and playing with various values of the constraints in order to get it to come out right (that's what *futzing* means) There's nothing wrong with that; the goal of the previous three steps was to get things fairly close to their final positions, not to come out with a perfect layout each and every time.

13

The Code

Listing 13.1 shows the complete code for the panel layout we've been building up in this section. If you had trouble following the discussion up to this point, you might find it useful to go through this code line by line to make sure you understand the various bits.

TYPE **Listing 13.1. The panel with the final grid bag layout.**

```
 1:import java.awt.*;
 2:
 3:public class GridBagTestFinal extends java.applet.Applet {
 4:
 5:  void buildConstraints(GridBagConstraints gbc, int gx, int gy,
 6:       int gw, int gh,
 7:       int wx, int wy) {
 8:       gbc.gridx = gx;
 9:       gbc.gridy = gy;
10:       gbc.gridwidth = gw;
11:       gbc.gridheight = gh;
12:       gbc.weightx = wx;
13:       gbc.weighty = wy;
14:  }
15:
16:  public void init() {
17:       GridBagLayout gridbag = new GridBagLayout();
18:       GridBagConstraints constraints = new GridBagConstraints();
19:       setLayout(gridbag);
20:
21:       // Name label
22:       buildConstraints(constraints, 0, 0, 1, 1, 10, 40);
23:       constraints.fill = GridBagConstraints.NONE;
24:       constraints.anchor = GridBagConstraints.EAST;
25:       Label label1 = new Label("Name:", Label.LEFT);
26:       gridbag.setConstraints(label1, constraints);
27:       add(label1);
28:
29:       // Name text field
30:       buildConstraints(constraints, 1, 0, 1, 1, 90, 0);
31:       constraints.fill = GridBagConstraints.HORIZONTAL;
32:       TextField tfname = new TextField();
33:       gridbag.setConstraints(tfname, constraints);
34:       add(tfname);
35:
36:       // password label
37:       buildConstraints(constraints, 0, 1, 1, 1, 0, 40);
38:       constraints.fill = GridBagConstraints.NONE;
39:       constraints.anchor = GridBagConstraints.EAST;
40:       Label label2 = new Label("Password:", Label.LEFT);
41:       gridbag.setConstraints(label2, constraints);
42:       add(label2);
43:
44:       // password text field
45:       buildConstraints(constraints, 1, 1, 1, 1, 0, 0);
46:       constraints.fill = GridBagConstraints.HORIZONTAL;
```

continues

Listing 13.1. continued

```
47:        TextField tfpass = new TextField();
48:        tfpass.setEchoCharacter('*');
49:        gridbag.setConstraints(tfpass, constraints);
50:        add(tfpass);
51:
52:        // OK Button
53:        buildConstraints(constraints, 0, 2, 2, 1, 0, 20);
54:        constraints.fill = GridBagConstraints.NONE;
55:        constraints.anchor = GridBagConstraints.CENTER;
56:        Button okb = new Button("OK");
57:        gridbag.setConstraints(okb, constraints);
58:        add(okb);
59:    }
60:}
```

`ipadx` **and** `ipady`

Before finishing up with grid bag layouts (isn't it over *yet?*), there are a two more constraints that deserve mentioning: `ipadx` and `ipady`. These two constraints control the *padding*—that is, the extra space around an individual component. By default, no components have extra space around them (which is easiest to see in components that fill their cells).

`ipadx` adds space to either side of the component, and `ipady` adds it above and below.

Insets

Horizontal and vertical gap, created when you create a new layout manager (using `ipadx` and `ipady` in grid bag layouts), are used to determine the amount of space between components in a panel. *Insets*, however, are used to determine the amount of space around the panel itself. The `Insets` class includes values for the top, bottom, left, and right insets, which are then used when the panel itself is drawn.

> **NEW TERM** *Insets* determine the amount of space between the edges of a panel and that panel's components.

To include an inset, override the `insets()` method in your class (your `Applet` class or other class that serves as a panel). Inside the `insets()` method, create a new `Insets` object, where the constructor to the `Insets` class takes four integer values representing the insets on the top, left, bottom, and right of the panel. The `insets()` method should then return that `Insets` object. Here's some code to add insets for a grid layout, `10` to the top and bottom, and `30` to the left and right. (Figure 13.20 shows the inset):

```
public Insets insets() {
    return new Insets(10, 30, 10, 30);
}
```

Figure 13.20.

A panel with insets of 10 pixels on the top and bottom and 30 pixels to the left and right.

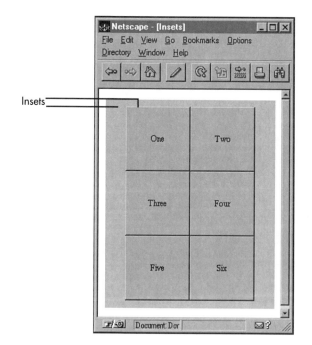

The arguments to the Insets constructor provide pixel insets for the top, bottom, left, and right edges of the panel, respectively. This particular example provides an inset of 10 pixels on all four sides of the panel.

Handling UI Actions and Events

If you stopped reading today's lesson right now, you could go out and create an applet that had lots of little UI components, nicely laid out on the screen with the proper layout manager, gap, and insets. If you did stop right here, however, your applet would be really dull, because none of your UI components would actually do anything when they were pressed, typed into, or selected.

For your UI components to do something when they are activated, you need to hook up the UI's action with an operation. Actions are a form of event, and testing for an action by a UI component involves event management. Everything you learned yesterday about events will come in handy here.

NEW TERM   *UI actions* are events that occur when a UI component is activated—pressed, selected, typed into, and so on.

13

To intercept an action event generated by any UI component, you define an `action()` method in your applet or class:

```
public boolean action(Event evt, Object arg) {
    ...
}
```

The `action()` method should look similar to the basic mouse and keyboard event methods. Like those methods, it gets passed the event object that represents this event. It also gets an extra object (in this code, the parameter `arg`), which can be of any class type.

What kind of object that second argument to the action method is depends on the UI component that's generating the action. The basic definition is that it's any arbitrary argument—when a component generates an event, it can pass along any extra information that might be useful for you to use in processing that action.

All the basic UI components (except for labels, which have no action) have different actions and arguments:

☐ Buttons create actions when they are pressed and released with the mouse, and a button's extra argument is the label string of that button.

☐ Check boxes, both exclusive and nonexclusive, generate actions when a box is checked. The extra argument is always `true`.

☐ Choice menus generate an action when a menu item is selected, and the extra argument is the label string of that item.

☐ Text fields create actions when the user presses Return or Enter inside that text field. Note that if the user tabs to a different text field or uses the mouse to change the input focus, an action is *not* generated. Pressing Return or Enter is the only thing that triggers the action.

Note that with actions, unlike with ordinary events, you can have many different kinds of objects generating the action event, as opposed to a single movement (a mouse press) generating a single event (such as a `mouseDown`). To deal with those different UI components and the actions they generate, you have to test for the type of object that sent/created the event in the first place inside the body of your `action()` method. That object is stored in the event's `target` instance variable, and you can use the `instanceof` operator to find out what kind of UI component sent it:

```
public boolean action(Event evt, Object arg) {
    if (evt.target instanceof TextField)
        return handleText(evt.target);
    else if (evt.target instanceof Choice)
        return handleChoice(arg);
    ...
}
```

13

Although you can handle UI actions in the body of the action() method, it's much more common simply to define a special method in your action() method and call that method instead. Here, there are two special methods: one to handle the action on the text field (handleText()) and one to handle the action on the choice menu (handleChoice()). Depending on the action you want to handle, you may also want to pass on the argument from the action, the UI component that sent it, or any other information that the event might contain.

As with the other event methods, action() returns a boolean value. As with all the event methods, you should return true if action() itself deals with the method, or false if it passes the method on somewhere else (or ignores it).

Listing 13.2 shows a simple applet that has five buttons labeled with colors. The action() method tests for a button action and then passes control to a method called changeColor(), which changes the background color of the applet based on which button was pressed (see Figure 13.21 to see the applet in action).

TYPE **Listing 13.2. The** `ButtonActionsTest` **applet.**

```
 1:import java.awt.*;
 2:
 3:public class ButtonActionsTest extends java.applet.Applet {
 4:
 5:   public void init() {
 6:     setBackground(Color.white);
 7:
 8:     add(new Button("Red"));
 9:     add(new Button("Blue"));
10:     add(new Button("Green"));
11:     add(new Button("White"));
12:     add(new Button("Black"));
13:   }
14:
15:   public boolean action(Event evt, Object arg) {
16:     if (evt.target instanceof Button) {
17:       changeColor((String)arg);
18:       return true;
19:     } else return false;
20:   }
21:
22:   void changeColor(String bname) {
23:     if (bname.equals("Red")) setBackground(Color.red);
24:     else if (bname.equals("Blue")) setBackground(Color.blue);
25:     else if (bname.equals("Green")) setBackground(Color.green);
26:     else if (bname.equals("White")) setBackground(Color.white);
27:     else setBackground(Color.black);
28:
29:     repaint();
30:   }
31:}
```

13

Figure 13.21.

The ButtonAction *applet.*

ANALYSIS   As with most AWT-based applets, this one starts with an init() method that initializes the applet's state and creates and adds components to the layout. The init() method defined in lines 8 through 13 here sets the applet's background color to white and creates five new buttons with color labels. Here we'll use the default layout manager, which is a FlowLayout. The buttons will appear all in a row at the top of the screen.

With the buttons in place, the second step is to attach actions to those buttons. The action() method, defined in lines 15 through 20, does this. The first thing to check is to make sure it's a button action that's been generated (line 16) and, if so, to pass the extra argument (cast to a string) to the changeColor() method, which will do all the work to change the color. If the event is indeed a button action, we'll return true to intercept that event. Otherwise, we'll return false and let some other component handle the event.

The changeColor() method is where all the work goes on. Here we test for each of the button labels in turn to see which button it was that was pressed and to set the background to the appropriate color. A final repaint at the end does the actual change (setting the background color does not automatically trigger a repaint; you'll have to do it yourself).

Nesting Panels and Components

Adding UI components to individual panels or applets is fun, but working with the AWT begins to turn into lots of fun when you start working with nested panels. By nesting different panels inside your applet, and panels inside those panels, you can create different layouts for different parts of the overall applet area, isolate background and foreground colors and fonts to individual parts of an applet, and manage the design of your UI components individually and in distinct groups. The more complex the layout of your applet, the more likely you're going to want to use nested panels.

Nested Panels

Panels, as you've already learned, are components that can be actually displayed onscreen; Panel's superclass Container provides the generic behavior for holding other components inside it. The Applet class, from which your applets all inherit, is a subclass of Panel. To nest other panels inside an applet, you merely create a new panel and add it to the applet, just as you would add any other UI component:

```
setLayout(new GridLayout(1, 2, 10, 10));
Panel panel1 = new Panel();
Panel panel2 = new Panel();
add(panel1);
add(panel2);
```

You can then set up an independent layout for those subpanels and add AWT components to them (including still more subpanels) by calling the add() method in the appropriate panel:

```
panel1.setLayout(new FlowLayout());
panel1.add(new Button("Up"));
panel1.add(new Button("Down"));
```

Although you can do all this in a single class, it's common in graphical applets and applications that make heavy use of subpanels to factor out the layout and behavior of the subpanels into separate classes and to communicate between the panels by using methods. You'll look at an extensive example of this later in today's lesson in the section "A Complete Example: RGB-to-HSB Converter."

Events and Nested Panels

When you create applets with nested panels, those panels form a hierarchy from the outermost panel (the applet, usually) to the innermost UI component. This hierarchy is important to how each component in the interface interacts with other components; for example, the component hierarchy determines the order in which those components are painted to the screen.

More importantly, however, the hierarchy also affects event handling, particularly for user-input events such as mouse and keyboard events.

Events are received by the innermost component in the component hierarchy and passed up the chain to the applet's panel (or to the root window in Java applications). Suppose, for example, that you have an applet with a subpanel that can handle mouse events (using the mouseDown() and mouseUp() methods), and that panel contains a button. Clicking the button means that the button receives the event before the panel does; if the button isn't interested in that mouseDown(), the event gets passed to the panel, which can then process it or pass it further up the hierarchy.

13

Remember the discussion about the basic event methods yesterday? You learned that the basic event methods all return boolean values. Those boolean values become important when you're talking about handling events or passing them on.

An event-handling method, whether it is the set of basic event methods or the more generic `handleEvent()`, can do one of three things, given any random event:

☐ Ignore the event entirely, if the event doesn't match whatever criteria the event-handling method set—for example, the `mouseDown` wasn't in the right area, or the action wasn't a button action. If this is the case, the event handler should return `false` so the event is passed up the hierarchy until a component processes it (or it is ignored altogether).

☐ Intercept the event, process it, and return `true`. In this case, the event stops with that event method.

☐ Intercept the method, process it, and pass it on to another, more specific event handler—for example, as `handleEvent` passes events onto `mouseDown()`.

More UI Components

After you master the basic UI components and how to add them to panels, organize their layout, and manage their events, you can add more UI components. In this section, you'll learn about text areas, scrolling lists, scrollbars, and canvases.

Note that most of the components in this section do not produce actions, so you can't use the `action()` method to handle their behavior. Instead, you have to use a generic `handleEvent()` method to test for specific events that these UI components generate. You'll learn more about this in the next section.

Text Areas

Text areas are like text fields, except they have more functionality for handling large amounts of text. Because text fields are limited in size and don't scroll, they are better for one-line responses and simple data entry; text areas can be any given width and height and have scrollbars by default, so you can deal with larger amounts of text more easily.

NEW TERM   *Text areas* are larger, scrollable text-entry components. Whereas text fields only provide one line of text, text areas can hold any amount of editable text.

To create a text area, use one of the following constructors:

☐ `TextArea()` creates an empty text area 0 rows long and 0 characters wide (the text area will be automatically resized based on the layout manager).

- ☐ TextArea(int, int) creates an empty text area with the given number of rows and columns (characters).

- ☐ TextArea(String) creates a text area displaying the given string, which will be sized according to the current layout manager.

- ☐ TextArea(String, int, int) creates a text area displaying the given string and with the given dimensions.

Figure 13.22 shows a simple text area generated from the following code:

```java
import java.awt.*;

public class TextAreaTest extends java.applet.Applet {

  public void init() {
    String str = "Once upon a midnight dreary, while I pondered, weak and
weary,\n" +
      "Over many a quaint and curious volume of forgotten lore,\n" +
      "While I nodded, nearly napping, suddenly there came a tapping,\n" +
      "As of some one gently rapping, rapping at my chamber door.\n" +
      "\"'Tis some visitor,\" I muttered, \"tapping at my chamber door-\n" +
      "Only this, and nothing more.\"\n\n";
      // more text deleted for space

    add(new TextArea(str,10,50));
  }
}
```

Figure 13.22.

A text area.

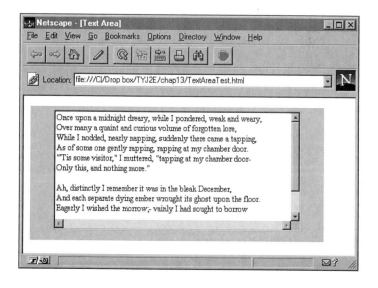

Both text areas and text fields inherit from the TextComponent class, so a lot of the behavior for text fields (particularly getting and setting text and selections) is usable on text areas as well (refer to Table 13.4). Text areas also have a number of their own methods that you may find useful. Table 13.5 shows a sampling of those methods.

Table 13.5. Text area methods.

Method	Action
getColumns()	Returns the width of the text area, in characters or columns
getRows()	Returns the number of rows in the text area (not the number of rows of text that the text area contains)
insertText(String, int)	Inserts the string at the given position in the text (text positions start at 0)
replaceText(String, int, int)	Replaces the text between the given integer positions with the new string

Scrolling Lists

Remember the choice menu, with which you could choose one of several different options? A scrolling list is functionally similar to a choice menu in that it lets you pick several options from a list, but scrolling lists differ in two significant ways:

☐ Scrolling lists are not pop-up menus. They're displayed as a list of items from which you can choose one or more items. If the number of items is larger than the list box, a scrollbar is automatically provided so that you can see the other items.

☐ You can choose more than one item in the list (if the list has been defined to allow it).

NEW TERM *Scrolling lists* provide a menu of items that can be selected or deselected. Unlike choice menus, scrolling lists are not pop-up menus and can be defined to allow multiple selections.

To create a scrolling list, create an instance of the List class and then add individual items to that list. The List class has two constructors:

☐ List() creates an empty scrolling list that enables only one selection at a time.

☐ List(int, boolean) creates a scrolling list with the given number of visible lines on the screen (you're unlimited as to the number of actual items you can add to the list). The boolean argument indicates whether this list enables multiple selections (true) or not (false).

13

After creating a List object, add items to it using the addItem() method and then add the list itself to the panel that contains it. Here's an example that creates a list five items high that allows multiple selections (the result of this code is shown in Figure 13.23):

```java
import java.awt.*;

public class ListsTest extends java.applet.Applet {

  public void init() {
    List lst = new List(5, true);

    lst.addItem("Hamlet");
    lst.addItem("Claudius");
    lst.addItem("Gertrude");
    lst.addItem("Polonius");
    lst.addItem("Horatio");
    lst.addItem("Laertes");
    lst.addItem("Ophelia");

    add(lst);
  }
}
```

Figure 13.23.

A scrolling list.

Scrolling lists generate actions when the user double-clicks a list item (single-clicking generates a LIST_SELECT or LIST_DESELECT event ID; you'll learn more about these in the section "More UI Events"). A scrolling list action has the argument of the string of the item that was double-clicked.

Table 13.6 shows some of the methods available to scrolling lists. See the API documentation for a complete set.

Table 13.6. Scrolling list methods.

Method	Action
`getItem(int)`	Returns the string item at the given position
`countItems()`	Returns the number of items in the menu
`getSelectedIndex()`	Returns the index position of the item that's selected (used for lists that allow only single selections)
`getSelectedIndexes()`	Returns an array of index positions (used for lists that allow multiple selections)
`getSelectedItem()`	Returns the currently selected item as a string
`getSelectedItems()`	Returns an array of strings containing all the selected items
`select(int)`	Selects the item at the given position
`select(String)`	Selects the item with that string

Scrollbars and Sliders

Text areas and scrolling lists come with their own scrollbars, which are built into those UI components and enable you to manage both the body of the area or the list and its scrollbar as a single unit. You can also create individual scrollbars, or *sliders*, to manipulate a range of values.

Scrollbars are used to select a value between a maximum and a minimum value. To change the current value of that scrollbar, you can use three different parts of the scrollbar (see Figure 13.24):

☐ Arrows on either end, which increment or decrement the values by some small unit (`1` by default).

☐ A range in the middle, which increments or decrements the value by a larger amount (`10` by default).

☐ A box in the middle, often called an *elevator* or *thumb*, whose position shows where in the range of values the current value is located. Moving this box with the mouse causes an absolute change in the value, based on the position of the box within the scrollbar.

Choosing any of these visual elements causes a change in the scrollbar's value; you don't have to update anything or handle any events. All you have to do is give the scrollbar a maximum and minimum, and Java will handle the rest.

  A *scrollbar* is a visual UI element that allows you to choose a value between some minimum and some maximum. Scrollbars are sometimes called *sliders*.

Figure 13.24.

Scrollbar parts.

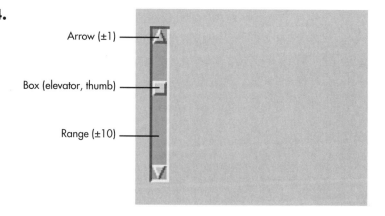

Arrow (±1)

Box (elevator, thumb)

Range (±10)

To create a scrollbar, you can use one of three constructors:

☐ `Scrollbar()` creates a scrollbar with its initial maximum and minimum values both 0, in a vertical orientation.

☐ `Scrollbar(int)` creates a scrollbar with its initial maximum and minimum values both 0. The argument represents an orientation, for which you can use the class variables `Scrollbar.HORIZONTAL` and `Scrollbar.VERTICAL`.

☐ `Scrollbar(int, int, int, int, int)` creates a scrollbar with the following arguments (each one is an integer, and they must be presented in this order):

The first argument is the orientation of the scrollbar: `Scrollbar.HORIZONTAL` and `Scrollbar.VERTICAL`.

The second argument is the initial value of the scrollbar, which should be a value between the scrollbar's maximum and minimum values.

The third argument is the overall width (or height, depending on the orientation) of the scrollbar's box. In user-interface design, a larger box implies that a larger amount of the total range is currently showing (applies best to things such as windows and text areas).

The fourth and fifth arguments are the minimum and maximum values for the scrollbar.

Here's a simple example of a scrollbar that increments a single value (see Figure 13.25). The label to the left of the scrollbar is updated each time the scrollbar's value changes:

```
import java.awt.*;

public class SliderTest extends java.applet.Applet {
  Label l;

  public void init() {
    setLayout(new GridLayout(1,2));
```

13

```
      l = new Label("0", Label.CENTER);
      add(l);
      add(new Scrollbar(Scrollbar.HORIZONTAL,0,0,1,100));
   }

   public Insets insets() {
      return new Insets(15,15,15,15);
   }

   public boolean handleEvent(Event evt) {
      if (evt.target instanceof Scrollbar) {
         int v = ((Scrollbar)evt.target).getValue();
         l.setText(String.valueOf(v));
         repaint();
         return true;
      } else return false;
   }

}
```

Figure 13.25.

A scrollbar.

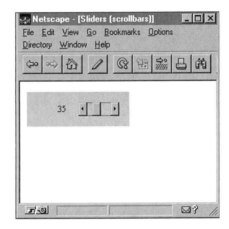

The Scrollbar class provides several methods for managing the values within scrollbars. (See Table 13.7.)

Table 13.7. Scrollbar methods.

Method	Action
getMaximum()	Returns the maximum value.
getMinimum()	Returns the minimum value.
getOrientation()	Returns the orientation of this scrollbar: 0 is Scrollbar.HORIZONTAL; 1 is Scrollbar.VERTICAL.
getValue()	Returns the scrollbar's current value.

Method	Action
setValue(int)	Sets the current value of the scrollbar.
setLineIncrement(int inc)	Change the increment for how far to scroll when the endpoints of the scrollbar are selected. The default is 1.
getLineIncrement()	Returns the increment for how far to scroll when the endpoints of the scrollbar are selected.
setPageIncrement(int inc)	Change the increment for how far to scroll when the inside range of the scrollbar is selected. The default is 10.
getPageIncrement()	Returns the increment for how far to scroll when the inside range of the scrollbar is selected.

Canvases

Although you can draw on most AWT components such as panels using the graphics methods you learned about on Day 11, "More Animation, Images, and Sound," canvases do little *except* let you draw on them. They can't contain other components, but they can accept events, and you can create animation and display images on them. If you have a panel that doesn't need to do anything except display images or animation, a canvas would make a lighter-weight surface than a panel would.

 A *canvas* is a component that you can draw on.

To create a canvas, use the Canvas class and add it to a panel as you would any other component:

```
Canvas can = new Canvas();
add(can);
```

More UI Events

Yesterday, you learned about some basic event types that are generated from user input to the mouse or the keyboard. These event types are stored in the Event object as the event ID, and can be tested for in the body of a handleEvent() method by using class variables defined in Event. For many basic events, such as mouseDown() and keyDown(), you can define methods for those events to handle the event directly. You learned a similar mechanism today for UI actions where creating an action() method handled a specific action generated by a UI component.

The most general way of managing events, however, continues to be the `handleEvent()` method. For events relating to scrollbars and scrolling lists, the only way to intercept these events is to override `handleEvent()`.

To intercept a specific event, test for that event's ID. The available IDs are defined as class variables in the `Event` class, so you can test them by name. You learned about some of the basic events yesterday; Table 13.8 shows additional events that may be useful to you for the components you've learned about today (or that you might find useful in general).

Table 13.8. Additional events.

Event ID	What It Represents
ACTION_EVENT	Generated when a UI component action occurs
GOT_FOCUS	Generated when the user clicks inside a text area
LOST_FOCUS	Generated when the user clicks anywhere outside a text area (after being inside one)
LIST_DESELECT	Generated when an item in a scrolling list is deselected
LIST_SELECT	Generated when an item in a scrolling list is selected
SCROLL_ABSOLUTE	Generated when a scrollbar's box has been moved
SCROLL_LINE_DOWN	Generated when a scrollbar's bottom or left endpoint (button) is selected
SCROLL_LINE_UP	Generated when a scrollbar's top or right endpoint (button) is selected
SCROLL_PAGE_DOWN	Generated when the scrollbar's field below (or to the left of) the box is selected
SCROLL_PAGE_UP	Generated when the scrollbar's field above (or to the right of) the box is selected

Fun with Components

The `Component` class is the root of all the AWT objects: all the UI elements, panels, canvases, even applets. Just about everything you can display, lay out, change the color of, draw to, or interact with using events in the AWT is a component.

Components have a set of methods that allow you to modify their appearance or change their behavior. You've seen the use of a few of these methods already (`setBackground()`, `setFont`, `size()`), applied specifically to applets. But the methods defined in `Component` can be used with any component, allowing you to modify the appearance or the behavior of just about any element in your program. You can also create custom components (classes that inherit from `Panel` or `Canvas`) to make your own special AWT elements or user interface widgets.

Table 13.9 summarizes some of the methods you can use with individual components. For more methods, check out the Java API documentation for the class `Component`. The JDK 1.0.2 documentation is online at

```
http://java.sun.com:80/products/JDK/CurrentRelease/api/
```

Table 13.9. `Component` methods.

`getBackground()`	Returns a `Color` object representing the component's background color.
`setBackground(Color)`	Sets the component's background color.
`getForeground()`	Returns a `Color` object representing the component's current foreground color.
`setForeground(Color)`	Sets the component's foreground color
`getFont()`	Returns a `Font` object representing the component's current font.
`setFont(Font)`	Changes the component's current font.
`size()`	Returns a `Dimension` object representing the component's current size. You can then get to the individual width and height using `size().width()` and `size().height()`.
`minimumSize()`	The component's smallest possible size as a `Dimension` object. `minimumSize()` is usually only used by layout managers to determine how small it can draw a component; if you create a custom component you'll want to override this method to return the minimum size of that component.
`preferredSize()`	The component's preferred size (usually equal to or larger than the component's `minimumSize()`) as a `Dimension` object.
`resize(Dimension)`	Changes the size of the applet to be the current size. For custom components you'll want to also call `validate()` after resizing the applet so that the layout can be redrawn.
`inside(x, y)`	Returns `true` if the given x and y coordinates are inside the component.
`hide()`	Hides the component. Hidden components do not show up onscreen.
`show()`	Shows a component previously hidden.

continues

13

Table 13.9. Component **methods.**

isVisible()	Returns true or false depending on whether this component is visible (not hidden).
disable()	Disables the component—that is, stops generating events. Disabled components cannot be pressed, selected from, typed into, and so on.
enable()	Enables a previously disabled object.
isEnabled()	Returns true or false depending on whether the component is enabled.

A Complete Example: RGB-to-HSB Converter

Let's take a break here from theory and smaller examples to create a larger example that puts together much of what you've learned so far. The following applet example demonstrates layouts, nesting panels, creating user-interface components, and catching and handling actions, as well as using multiple classes to put together a single applet. In short, it's the most complex applet you've created so far.

Figure 13.26 shows the applet you'll be creating in this example. The ColorTest applet enables you to pick colors based on RGB (red, green, and blue) and HSB (hue, saturation, and brightness) values.

NOTE

A very quick summary in case you're not familiar with basic color theory: *RGB* color defines a color by its red, green, and blue values; some combination of these values can produce any color in the spectrum (red, green, and blue are called *additive colors*; that's how your monitor and your TV represent different colors).

HSB stands for hue, saturation, and brightness and is a different way of indicating color. *Hue* is the actual color in the spectrum you're representing (think of it as values along a color wheel). *Saturation* is the amount of that color; low saturation results in pastels; high-saturation colors are more vibrant and "colorful." *Brightness*, finally, is the lightness or darkness of the color. No brightness is black; full brightness is white.

13

A single color can be represented either by its RGB values or by its HSB values, and there are mathematical algorithms to convert between them. The ColorTest applet provides a graphical converter between the two.

Figure 13.26.

The ColorTest *applet.*

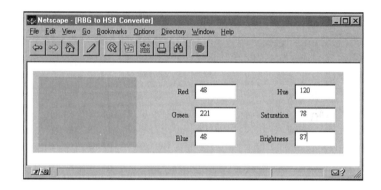

The ColorTest applet has three main parts: a colored box on the left side and two groups of text fields on the right. The first group indicates RGB values; the right, HSB. By changing any of the values in any of the text boxes, the colored box is updated to the new color, as are the values in the other group of text boxes.

NOTE

If you try this applet, be aware that you have to press Enter or Return after changing a number for the updating to occur. Using the Tab key to move between text fields or clicking with the mouse will not cause the applet to update.

This applet uses two classes:

☐ ColorTest, which inherits from Applet. This is the controlling class for the applet itself.

☐ ColorControls, which inherits from Panel. You'll create this class to represent a group of three text fields and to handle actions from those text fields. Two instances of this class, one for the RGB values and one for the HSB ones, will be created and added to the applet.

Let's work through this step by step, because it's very complicated and can get confusing. All the code for this applet will be shown at the end of this section.

13

Designing and Creating the Applet Layout

The best way to start creating an applet that uses AWT components is to worry about the layout first and then worry about the functionality. When dealing with the layout, you should start with the outermost panel first and work inward.

Making a sketch of your UI design can help you figure out how to organize the panels inside your applet or window to best take advantage of layout and space. Paper designs are helpful even when you're not using grid bag layouts, but doubly so when you are (we'll be using a simple grid layout for this applet).

Figure 13.27 shows the `ColorTest` applet with a grid drawn over it so that you can get an idea of how the panels and embedded panels work.

Figure 13.27.

The `ColorTest` *applet panels and components.*

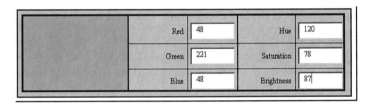

Let's start with the outermost panel—the applet itself. This panel has three parts: the color box on the left, the RGB text fields in the middle, and the HSB fields on the right.

Because the outermost panel is the applet itself, your `ColorTest` class will be the applet class and will inherit from `Applet`. You'll also import the AWT classes here (note that because you use so many of them in this program, it's easiest to just import the entire package):

```
import java.awt.*;

public class ColorTest extends java.applet.Applet {
    ...
}
```

This applet has three main things to keep track of: the color box and the two subpanels. The two subpanels each refer to different things, but they're essentially the same panel and behave in the same ways. Rather than duplicate a lot of code here in this class, this is a perfect opportunity to create another class just for the subpanels, use instances of that class here in the applet, and communicate between everything using methods. In a bit we'll define that new class, called `ColorControls`.

For now, however, we know we need to keep a handle to all three parts of the applet so you can update them when they change. So let's create three instance variables: one of type `Canvas` for the color box, and the other two of type `ColorControls` for the control panels:

```
ColorControls RGBcontrols, HSBcontrols;
Canvas swatch;
```

Now we'll move onto the `init()` method, where all the basic initialization and layout of the applet takes place. There are three steps to initializing this applet:

1. Create the layout for the big parts of the panel. Although a flow layout would work, a grid layout with one row and three columns is a much better idea.

2. Create and initialize the three components of this applet: a canvas for the color box and two subpanels for the text fields.

3. Add those components to the applet.

Step one is the layout. Let's use a grid layout and a gap of 10 points to separate each of the components:

```
setLayout(new GridLayout(1, 3, 5, 15));
```

Step two is creating the components—the canvas first. You have an instance variable to hold that one. Here we'll create the canvas and initialize its background to black:

```
swatch = new Canvas();
swatch.setBackground(Color.black);
```

You need to create two instances of your as-of-yet nonexistent `ColorControls` panels here as well, but because we haven't created the class yet we don't know what the constructors to that class will look like. Let's put in some placeholder constructors here; we'll fill in the details later:

```
RGBcontrols = new ColorControls(...)
HSBcontrols = new ColorControls(...);
```

Step three is adding all three components to the applet panel:

```
add(swatch);
add(RGBcontrols);
add(HSBcontrols);
```

While you're working on layout, let's add insets for the applet: 10 points along all the edges:

```
public Insets insets() {
    return new Insets(10, 10, 10, 10);
}
```

Got it so far? At this point you have three instance variables, an `init()` method with two incomplete constructors, and an `insets()` method in your `ColorTest` class. Let's move on now to creating the subpanel layout in the `ColorControls` class so we can fill in those constructors and finish up the layout.

13

Defining the Subpanels

The `ColorControls` class will have behavior for laying out and handling the subpanels that represent the RGB and HSB values for the color. `ColorControls` doesn't need to be a subclass of `Applet` because it isn't actually an applet; it's just a panel. Define it to inherit from `Panel`:

```
import java.awt.*

class ColorControls extends Panel {
    ...
}
```

NOTE

> I've put the `ColorControls` source code into its own file, called `ColorControls.java`. However, you can put the `ColorControls` class in the same file as the `ColorTest` class. Up to this point, you've only defined one class per file, with the filename the same name as the class. In Java you can have multiple class definitions in a file as long as only one of those classes is declared public (and the name of the source file is the same as that public class). In this case, the `ColorTest` class is public (it's an applet, so it has to be), but the `ColorControls` class isn't public, so it can be in the same source file. When you compile the file, Java will create the appropriate multiple class files for each class definition. You'll learn more about public classes on Day 15, "Modifiers, Access Control, and Class Design," and Day 16, "Packages and Interfaces."
>
> In general, however, I prefer to use separate source files for my classes. It makes it easier for me to find the source for a particular class because I don't have to remember which file I defined it in.

The `ColorControls` class will need a number of instance variables so that information from the panel can get back to the applet. The first of these instance variables is a hook back up to the applet class that contains this panel. Because it's the outer applet class that controls the updating of each panel, this panel will need a way to tell the applet that something has changed. And to call a method in that applet, you need a reference to that object. So, instance variable number one is a reference an instance of the class `ColorTest`:

```
ColorTest applet;
```

If you figure that the applet class is the one that's going to be updating everything, that class if going to be interested in the individual text fields in this subpanel. We'll create instance variables for those text fields:

```
TextField tfield1, tfield2, tfield3;
```

Now let's move on to the constructor for this class. Because this class isn't an applet, we won't use `init()` to initialize it; instead we'll use a constructor method.

Inside the constructor you'll do much of what you did inside `init()`: create the layout for the subpanel, create the text fields, and add them to the panel.

The goal here is to make the `ColorControls` class generic enough so that you can use it for both the RGB fields and the HSB fields. Those two panels differ in only one respect: the labels for the text. That's three values to get before you can create the object. You can pass those three values in through the constructors in `ColorTest`. You also need one more: that reference to the enclosing applet, which you can get from the constructor as well.

You now have four arguments to the basic constructor for the `ColorControls` class. Here's the signature for that constructor:

```
ColorControls(ColorTest parent,
        String l1, String l2, String l3) {
}
```

Let's start this constructor by first setting the value of `parent` to the applet instance variable:

```
applet = parent;
```

Next, create the layout for this panel. You can also use a grid layout for these subpanels, as you did for the applet panel, but this time the grid will have three rows (one for each of the text field and label pairs) and two columns (one for the labels and one for the fields). We'll also define a 10-point gap between the components in the grid:

```
setLayout(new GridLayout(3,2,10,10));
```

Now we can create and add the components to the panel. First, we'll create the text field objects (initialized to the string `"0"`), and assign them to the appropriate instance variables:

```
tfield1 = new TextField("0");
tfield2 = new TextField("0");
tfield3 = new TextField("0");
```

Now we'll add those fields and the appropriate labels to the panel, using the remaining three parameters to the constructor as the text for the labels:

```
add(new Label(l1, Label.RIGHT));
add(tfield1);
add(new Label(l2, Label.RIGHT));
add(tfield2);
add(new Label(l3, Label.RIGHT));
add(tfield3);
```

That finishes up the constructor for the subpanel class `ColorControls`. Are we done with the layout? Not quite. We'll also add an inset around the subpanel—only on the top and bottom edges—to tinker the layout. Add the inset here as you did in the `ColorTest` class, using the `insets()` method:

```
public Insets insets() {
        return new Insets(10, 10, 0, 0);
  }
```

13

You're almost there. You have 98 percent of the basic structure in place and ready to go, but there's one step left: going back to ColorTest and fixing those placeholder constructors for the subpanel so they match the actual constructors for ColorControls.

The constructor for ColorControls that we just created now has four arguments: the ColorTest object and three labels (strings). Remember back to when we created the init() method for ColorTest: We added two placeholders for creating new ColorControls objects; we'll replace those placeholders with the correct versions now. Make sure you add the four arguments that constructor needs to work: the ColorTest object and three strings. To pass the ColorTest object to those constructors, we can use the this keyword:

```
RGBcontrols = new ColorControls(this, "Red", "Green", "Blue");
HSBcontrols = new ColorControls(this, "Hue", "Saturation", "Brightness");
```

NOTE

For the initial values of all the text fields in this example, I used the number 0 (actually, the string "0"). For the color black, both the RGB and the HSB values are 0, which is why I can make this assumption. If you wanted to initialize the applet to be some other color, you might want to rewrite the ColorControls class to use initializer values as well as to initialize labels. This way made for a shorter example.

Handling the Actions

With the layout done, its time to set up event handling and updating between the various components so that when the user interacts with the applet, the applet can respond.

The action of this applet occurs when the user changes a value in any of the text fields and presses Enter. By causing an action in a text field, the color changes, the color box updates to the new color, and the values of the fields in the opposite subpanel change to reflect the new color.

The ColorTest class is responsible for actually doing the updating because it keeps track of all the subpanels. Because the actual event occurs in the subpanel, however, you'll need to track and intercept those events in that subpanel using the action() method in the ColorControls class:

```
public boolean action(Event evt, Object arg) {
    if (evt.target instanceof TextField) {
        applet.update(this);
        return true;
    }
    else return false;
}
```

13

In the action() method, you test to make sure the action was indeed generated by a text field (because there are only text fields available, that's the only action you'll get, but it's a good idea to test for it anyhow). If there was indeed a text field action, we'll call a method to update all the subpanels. That method, which we'll call update(), is defined in the enclosing class, so we'll call it using the object stored in the applet instance variable (and pass along a reference to the panel so that the applet can get at our values). And, finally, we'll return either true or false so that other actions that might occur on this applet can be passed along to enclosing panels or components.

Updating the Result

Now comes the hard part: actually doing the updating based on the new values of whatever text field was changed. For this, you define the update() method in the ColorTest class. This update() method takes a single argument—the ColorControls instance that contains the changed value (you get that argument from the action() method in the ColorControls object).

NOTE

Won't this update() method interfere with the system's update() method? Nope. Remember, methods can have the same name, but different signatures and definitions. Because this update() has a single argument of type ColorControls, it doesn't interfere with the other version of update(). Normally, all methods called update() should mean basically the same thing; it's not true here, but it's only an example.

The update() method is responsible for updating all the panels in the applet. To know which panel to update, you need to know which panel changed. You can find out by testing to see whether the argument you got passed from the panel is the same as the subpanels you have stored in the RGBcontrols and HSBcontrols instance variables:

```
void update(ColorControls controlPanel) {

    if (controlPanel == RGBcontrols) {  // RGB has changed, update HSB
        ...
    } else {  // HSB has changed, update RGB
        ...
    }
}
```

This test is the heart of the update() method. Let's start with that first case—a number has been changed in the RGB text fields. So now, based on those new RGB values, you have to generate a new Color object and update the values on the HSB panel. To reduce some typing, you create a few local variables to hold some basic values. In particular, the values of the text fields are strings whose values you can get to using the getText() method defined in the TextField objects of the ColorControls object. Because most of the time in this method we'll want to deal with those values as integers, we'll get those string values, convert them to integers, and store them in local variables (value1, value2, value3). Here's the code to do this (it looks more complicated than it actually is):

```
int value1 = Integer.parseInt(controlPanel.tfield1.getText());
int value2 = Integer.parseInt(controlPanel.tfield2.getText());
int value3 = Integer.parseInt(controlPanel.tfield3.getText());
```

While we're here defining local variables, we'll also need one for the new Color object:

```
Color c;
```

OK. Let's assume one of the text fields in the RGB side of the applet has changed and add the code to the if part of the update() method. We'll need to create a new Color object and update the HSB side of the panel. That first part is easy; given the three RGB values, you can create a new Color object using those as arguments to the constructor:

```
c = new Color(value1, value2, value3);
```

 NOTE

> This part of the example isn't very robust; it assumes that the user has indeed entered integers from 0 to 255 into the text fields. A better version of this would test to make sure that no data-entry errors had occurred (I was trying to keep this example small).

Now we'll convert the RGB values to HSB. There are standard algorithms to convert an RGB-based color to an HSB color, but we don't have to go look them up. The Color class has a class method we can use called RGBtoHSB() that will do the work for us—or, at least, most of it. There are two problems with the RGBtoHSB() method, however:

☐ The RGBtoHSB() method returns an array of the three HSB values, so we'll have to extract those values from the array.

☐ The HSB values are measured in floating-point values from 0.0 to 1.0. I prefer to think of HSB values as integers, where the hue is a degree value around a color wheel (0 through 360), and saturation and brightness are percentages from 0 to 100.

Neither of these problems is insurmountable; it just means some extra lines of code. Let's start by calling RGBtoHSB() with the new RGB values we have. The return type of that method is an array of floats, so we'll create a local variable (HSB) to store the results of the RBGtoHSB() method. (Note that you'll also need to create and pass in an empty array of floats as the fourth argument to RGBtoHSB()):

```
float[] HSB = Color.RGBtoHSB(value1, value2, value3, (new float[3]));
```

Now we'll convert those floating-point values that range from 0.0 to 1.0 to values that range from 0 and 100 (for the saturation and brightness) and 0 to 360 for the hue by multiplying the appropriate numbers and reassigning the value back to the array:

```
HSB[0] *= 360;
HSB[1] *= 100;
HSB[2] *= 100;
```

Now we have the numbers we want. The last part of the update is to put those values back into the text fields. Of course, those values are still floating-point numbers, so we'll have to cast them to ints before turning them into strings and storing them:

```
HSBcontrols.tfield1.setText(String.valueOf((int)HSB[0]));
HSBcontrols.tfield2.setText(String.valueOf((int)HSB[1]));
HSBcontrols.tfield3.setText(String.valueOf((int)HSB[2]));
```

You're halfway there. The next part of the applet is that part that updates the RGB values where a text field on the HSB side has changed. This is the else in the big if-else that defines this method and determines what to update, given a change.

It's actually easier to generate values from HSB values than it is to do it the other way around. There's a class method in the Color class, called getHSBColor(), that creates a new Color object from three HSB values, and once you have a Color object you can easily pull the RGB values out of there. The catch, of course, is that getHSBColor takes three floating-point arguments, and the values we have are the integer values I prefer to use. So in the call to getHSBColor, we'll have to cast the integer values from the text fields to floats and divide them by the proper conversion factor. The result of getHSBColor is a Color object, so we can simply assign that object to our c local variable so we can use it again later:

```
c = Color.getHSBColor((float)value1 / 360,
    (float)value2 / 100, (float)value3 / 100);
```

With the Color object all set, updating the RGB values involves extracting those values from that Color object. The getRed(), getGreen() and getBlue() methods, defined in the Color class, will do just that:

```
RGBcontrols.tfield1.setText(String.valueOf(c.getRed()));
RGBcontrols.tfield2.setText(String.valueOf(c.getGreen()));
RGBcontrols.tfield3.setText(String.valueOf(c.getBlue()));
```

And finally, regardless of whether the RGB or HSB value has changed, you'll need to update the color box on the left to reflect the new color. Because we have a new Color object stored in the variable c, we can use the setBackground method to change that color. Also note that setBackground doesn't automatically repaint the screen, so you'll want to fire off a repaint() as well:

```
swatch.setBackground(c);
swatch.repaint();
```

That's it! You're done. Compile both the ColorTest and ColorControls classes, create an HTML file to load the ColorTest applet, and check it out.

13

The Complete Source Code

Listing 13.3 shows the complete source code for the applet class `ColorTest`, and Listing 13.4 shows the source for the helper class `ColorControls`. Often it's easier to figure out what's going on in an applet when it's all in one place and you can follow the method calls and how values are passed back and forth. Start with the `init()` method in the `ColorTest` applet and go from there.

TYPE   **Listing 13.3. The `ColorTest` applet.**

```
1:import java.awt.*;
2:
3:public class ColorTest extends java.applet.Applet {
4:   ColorControls RGBcontrols, HSBcontrols;
5:   Canvas swatch;
6:
7:   public void init() {
8:     setLayout(new GridLayout(1,3,5,15));
9:
10:    // The color swatch
11:    swatch = new Canvas();
12:    swatch.setBackground(Color.black);
13:
14:    // the subpanels for the controls
15:    RGBcontrols = new ColorControls(this, "Red", "Green", "Blue");
16:    HSBcontrols = new ColorControls(this, "Hue", "Saturation", "Brightness");
17:
18:    //add it all to the layout
19:    add(swatch);
20:    add(RGBcontrols);
21:    add(HSBcontrols);
22:  }
23:
24:  public Insets insets() {
25:    return new Insets(10,10,10,10);
26:  }
27:
28:  void update(ColorControls controlPanel) {
29:    Color c;
30:    // get string values from text fields, convert to ints
31:    int value1 = Integer.parseInt(controlPanel.tfield1.getText());
32:    int value2 = Integer.parseInt(controlPanel.tfield2.getText());
33:    int value3 = Integer.parseInt(controlPanel.tfield3.getText());
34:
35:    if (controlPanel == RGBcontrols) {  // RGB has changed, update HSB
36:      c = new Color(value1, value2, value3);
37:
38:      // convert RGB values to HSB values
39:      float[] HSB = Color.RGBtoHSB(value1, value2, value3, (new float[3]));
40:      HSB[0] *= 360;
41:      HSB[1] *= 100;
42:      HSB[2] *= 100;
43:
```

13

```
44:         // reset HSB fields
45:         HSBcontrols.tfield1.setText(String.valueOf((int)HSB[0]));
46:         HSBcontrols.tfield2.setText(String.valueOf((int)HSB[1]));
47:         HSBcontrols.tfield3.setText(String.valueOf((int)HSB[2]));
48:
49:     } else {  // HSB has changed, update RGB
50:         c = Color.getHSBColor((float)value1 / 360,
51:             (float)value2 / 100, (float)value3 / 100);
52:
53:         // reset RGB fields
54:         RGBcontrols.tfield1.setText(String.valueOf(c.getRed()));
55:         RGBcontrols.tfield2.setText(String.valueOf(c.getGreen()));
56:         RGBcontrols.tfield3.setText(String.valueOf(c.getBlue()));
57:     }
58:
59:     //update swatch
60:     swatch.setBackground(c);
61: swatch.repaint();
62:}
63:}
```

TYPE **Listing 13.4. The `ColorControls` class.**

```
1:import java.awt.*;
2:
3:class ColorControls extends Panel {
4:   TextField tfield1, tfield2, tfield3;
5:   ColorTest applet;
6:
7:   ColorControls(ColorTest parent,
8:         String l1, String l2, String l3) {
9:
10:     // get hook to outer applet parent
11:     applet = parent;
12:
13:     //do layouts
14:     setLayout(new GridLayout(3,2,10,10));
15:
16:     tfield1 = new TextField("0");
17:     tfield2 = new TextField("0");
18:     tfield3 = new TextField("0");
19:
20:     add(new Label(l1, Label.RIGHT));
21:     add(tfield1);
22:     add(new Label(l2, Label.RIGHT));
23:     add(tfield2);
24:     add(new Label(l3, Label.RIGHT));
25:     add(tfield3);
26:   }
27:
28: public Insets insets() {
29:     return new Insets(10,10,0,0);
30:   }
```

13

continues

Listing 13.4. continued

```
31:
32:  public boolean action(Event evt, Object arg) {
33:    if (evt.target instanceof TextField) {
34:      applet.update(this);
35:      return true;
36:    } else return false;
37:  }
38:}
```

Up and Coming in Java 1.1

Everything you've learned up to this point is available in the 1.0.2 Java API. Java 1.1, however, will add many more features to the AWT, as well as improve performance and robustness across platforms. The goal for the AWT is to move beyond the basics that 1.0.2 provided and make the AWT more suitable for large-scale application development. Note, also, that the 1.1 API will be backward-compatible with the 1.0.2 features; none of the code you write after reading this chapter will be obsolete in 1.1.

Explicit details about the changes to the AWT for 1.1 were not available at the time this book was being written. Sun has announced the following teasers, however for new features in 1.1:

- [ ] New components for pop-up menus, buttons with images on top of them, and menu accelerators
- [ ] Support for clipboard operations (copy and paste), drag and drop, and printing
- [ ] The ability to set a cursor for each component (currently you can have only one cursor per window; you'll learn about this on Day 14, "Windows, Networking, and Other Tidbits")
- [ ] A new set of graphics primitives as part of the new 2D graphics model; you'll learn more about this on Day 27, "The Standard Extension APIs"
- [ ] A new event model that delegates event actions to other objects, as opposed to requiring special methods (`mouseDown()`, `action()`, `handleEvent()`, and so on) to be overridden in the component classes themselves. Those action objects are often called callbacks in other event-driven programming systems.
- [ ] Performance enhancements: a complete rewrite for Windows 95 and NT, improvements in how components are laid out and painted, better scrolling of components, and a "number of bug fixes."

For more information about the Java 1.1 changes to the AWT, check out the 1.1 preview page at `http://java.sun.com/products/JDK/1.1/designspecs/`.

Summary

The Java AWT, or Abstract Windowing Toolkit, is a package of Java classes and interfaces for creating full-fledged access to a window-based graphical user interface system, with mechanisms for graphics display, event management, text and graphics primitives, user-interface components, and cross-platform layout. Applets are also an integral part of the AWT.

Today has been a big day; the lesson has brought together everything you've learned up to this point about simple applet management and added a lot more about creating applets, panels, and user-interface components and managing the interactions between all of them. With the information you got today and the few bits you'll learn tomorrow, you can create cross-platform Java applications that do just about anything you want.

Q&A

Q I really dislike working with layout managers; they're either too simplistic or too complicated (grid bag layout). Even with a whole lot of tinkering, I can never get my applets to look like I want them to. All I want to do is define the sizes of my components and put them at an x and y position on the screen. Can I do this?

A I'm going to tell you how to do this, but not without a lecture.

Java applications and the AWT were designed such that the same graphical user interface could run equally well on different platforms and with different resolutions, different fonts, different screen sizes, and so on. Relying on pixel coordinates in this case is a really bad idea; variations from one platform to another or even from one Java environment to another on the same platform can mess up your careful layouts such that you can easily have components overlapping or obscuring each other, the edges of your applet cut off, or other layout disasters. Just as an example—I found significant differences in the layout of the same applet running in the JDK's `appletviewer` and in Netscape, both on Windows 95, side by side. Can you guarantee that your applet will always be run in precisely the same environment as the one in which you designed it? Layout managers, by dynamically placing elements on the screen, get around these problems. This does mean that your applet may end up looking not quite right on *any* platform—but at least it's *usable* on any platform. New versions of the AWT promise to offer better layout and UI design controls.

Still not convinced? Well, then. To make a component a specific size and to place it at a particular position, use a null layout manager and the `reshape()` method:

13

```
setLayout(null);
Button myButton (new Button("OK");
mybutton.reshape(10, 10, 30, 15);
```

You can find out more about `reshape()` in the `Component` class.

Q I was exploring the AWT classes, and I saw this subpackage called `peer`. There are also references to the peer classes sprinkled throughout the API documentation. What do peers do?

A Peers are responsible for the platform-specific parts of the AWT. For example, when you create a Java AWT window, you have an instance of the `Window` class that provides generic window behavior, and then you have an instance of a class implementing `WindowPeer` that creates the very specific window for that platform—a motif window under X Window, a Macintosh-style window under the Macintosh, or a Windows 95 window under Windows 95. These "peer" classes also handle communication between the window system and the Java window itself. By separating the generic component behavior (the AWT classes) from the actual system implementation and appearance (the peer classes), you can focus on providing behavior in your Java application and let the Java implementation deal with the platform-specific details.

Q There's a whole lot of functionality in the AWT that you haven't talked about here. Why?

A Given that even a basic introduction took this long, I figured that if I put in even more detail than I already have, this book would turn into *Teach Yourself Java in 21 Days Plus a Few Extra for the AWT Stuff.*

As it is, I've left windows, menus, and dialog boxes until tomorrow, so you'll have to wait for those. But you can find out about a lot of the other features of AWT merely by exploring the API documentation. Start with the `Applet` class and examine the sorts of methods you can call. Then look at `Panel`, from which `Applet` inherits—you have all that class's functionality as well. The superclass of `Panel` is `Container`, which provides still more interesting detail. `Component` comes next. Explore the API and see what you can do with it. You might find something interesting.

Q I have a new button class I defined to look different from the standard AWT button objects. I'd like to implement callbacks on this button (that is, to execute an arbitrary function when the button is pressed), but I can't figure out how to get Java to execute an arbitrary method. In C++ I'd just have a pointer to a function. In Smalltalk I'd use `perform:`. How can I do this in Java?

A You can't; Java doesn't have this facility. This is why normal button actions are executed from the generic `action()` method rather than using a mechanism for actions attached to the button itself (which would be more object-oriented, easier to extend, and wouldn't require a whole lot of `if...elses` inside `action()`).

Day **14**

Windows, Networking, and Other Tidbits

by Laura Lemay

Here you are on the last day of the second week, and you're just about finished with applets and the AWT. With the information you'll learn today you can create a wide variety of applets and applications using Java. Next week's lessons provide more of the advanced stuff that you'll need if you start doing really serious work in Java.

Today, to finish up this week, we'll cover three very different topics:

☐ Windows, menus, and dialog boxes—the last of the AWT classes that enable you to pop up real windows and dialog boxes from applets, to add menus to those windows, and to create standalone graphical Java applications that can use all the AWT features you've learned about this week.

□ Networking—how to load new HTML files from a Java-enabled browser, how to retrieve files from Web sites, and some basics on how to work with generic sockets in Java.

□ Extra tidbits—the smaller stuff that didn't fit in anywhere else, but that might be useful to you as you write your Java applets and applications.

Windows, Menus, and Dialog Boxes

Today you'll finish up the last bits of the AWT that didn't fit into yesterday's lesson. In addition to all the graphics, events, user interface, and layout mechanisms that the AWT provides, it also provides windows, menus, and dialog boxes, enabling to you create fully featured applications either as part of your applet or independently for standalone Java applications.

The AWT Window Classes

The Java AWT classes to produce windows and dialogs inherit from a single class: Window. The Window class, which itself inherits from Container (and is therefore a standard AWT component), provides generic behavior for all window-like things. Generally you don't use instances of Window, however; you use instances of Frame or Dialog. Figure 14.1 shows the simple Window class hierarchy.

Figure 14.1.
The Window class hierarchy.

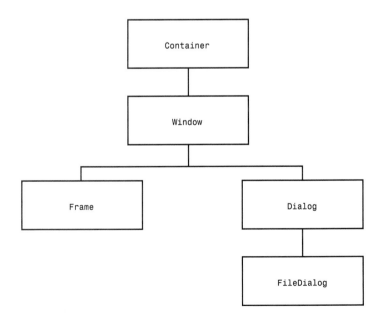

14

The Frame class provides a window with a title bar, close boxes, and other platform-specific window features. Frames also let you add menu bars. Dialog is a more limited form of Frame that typically doesn't have a title. FileDialog, a subclass of Dialog, provides a standard file-picker dialog box (usually only usable from inside Java applications because of security restrictions on applets).

When you want to add a new window or dialog to your applet or application, you'll create subclasses of the Frame and Dialog classes.

Frames

Frames are windows that are independent of an applet and of the browser that contains it—they are separate windows with their own titles, resize handles, close boxes, and menu bars. You can create frames for your own applets to produce windows, or you can use frames in Java applications to hold the contents of that application.

 A *frame* is a platform-specific window with a title, a menu bar, close boxes, resize handles, and other window features.

To create a frame, use one of the following constructors:

☐ new Frame() creates a basic frame without a title.

☐ new Frame(*String*) creates a basic frame with the given title.

Because frames inherit from Window, which inherits from Container, which inherits from Component, frames are created and used much in the same way that other AWT components are created and used. Frames are containers, just like panels are, so you can add other components to them just as you would regular panels, using the add() method. The default layout for frames is BorderLayout. Here's a single example that creates a frame, sets its layout, and adds two buttons:

```
win = new Frame("My Cool Window");
win.setLayout(new BorderLayout(10, 20));
win.add("North", new Button("Start"));
win.add("Center", new Button("Move"));
```

To set a size for the new frame, use the resize() method with the width and height of the new frame. So, for example, this line of code resizes the window to be 100 pixels wide and 200 pixels high:

```
win.resize(100, 200);
```

Note that because different systems have different ideas of what a pixel is and different resolutions for those pixels, it's difficult to create a window that is the "right" size for every platform. Windows that work fine for one may be way too large or too small for another. One

14

way around this is to use the pack() method instead of resize(). The pack() method, which has no arguments, creates a window of the smallest possible size given the current sizes of all the components inside that window and the layout manager and insets in use. Here's an example that creates two buttons, and adds them to a window. The window will then be resized to the smallest possible window that can still hold those buttons:

```
win = new Frame("My Other Cool Window");
win.setLayout(new FlowLayout()));
win.add("North", new Button("OK"));
win.add("Center", new Button("Cancel"));
win.pack();
```

When you initially create a window, it's invisible. You need to use the show() method to make the window appear onscreen (you can use hide() to hide it again):

```
win.show();
```

Note that when you pop up windows from inside applets, the browser may indicate in some way that the window is not a regular browser window—usually with a warning in the window itself. In Netscape, there's a yellow bar at the bottom of every window that says Untrusted Java Window. This warning is intended to let your users know that your window comes from the applet and not from the browser itself (remember that the frame class produces windows that look just like normal system windows). The warning is to prevent you from creating a malicious applet that might, for example, ask the user for his password. There isn't anything you can do to avoid this warning; it's there to stay as long as you want to use windows with applets.

Listings14.1 and 14.2 show examples of a simple applet with a pop-up window frame (both the applet and the window are shown in Figure 14.2). The applet has two buttons: one to show the window, and one to hide the window. The frame itself, created from a subclass I created called BaseFrame, contains a single label: This is a Window. You'll use this basic window and applet all through this section, so the more you understand what's going on here the easier it will be later.

TYPE   **Listing 14.1. A pop-up window.**

```
 1:import java.awt.*;
 2:
 3:public class PopupWindow extends java.applet.Applet {
 4:    Frame window;
 5:
 6:    public void init() {
 7:      add(new Button("Open Window"));
 8:      add(new Button("Close Window"));
 9:
10:      window = new BaseFrame("A Popup Window");
11:      window.resize(150,150);
12:      window.show();
13:    }
```

14

```
14:
15:    public boolean action(Event evt, Object arg) {
16:        if (evt.target instanceof Button) {
17:            String label = (String)arg;
18:            if (label.equals("Open Window")) {
19:                if (!window.isShowing())
20:                    window.show();
21:            }
22:            else if (label.equals("Close Window")) {
23:                if (window.isShowing())
24:                    window.hide();
25:            }
26:            return true;
27:        }
28:        else return false;
29:    }
30:}
```

TYPE **Listing 14.2. The BaseFrame class.**

```
1:import java.awt.*;
2:
3:class BaseFrame extends Frame {
4:    String message = "This is a Window";
5:
6:    BaseFrame1(String title) {
7:        super(title);
8:        setFont(new Font("Helvetica", Font.BOLD, 12));
9:    }
10:
11:    public void paint(Graphics g) {
12:        g.drawString(message, 20, 20);
13:    }
14:}
```

Figure 14.2.

Windows.

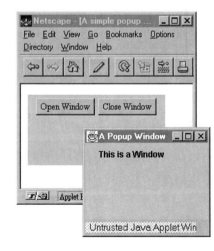

14

ANALYSIS   There are two classes that make up this example: The first, PopupWindow, is the applet class that creates and controls the pop-up window. In the init() method for that class (lines 6 to 13), we added two control buttons to the applet to control the window, and then created, resized, and showed the window itself.

The control in this applet occurs when one of the buttons is pressed. Here, the Open Window button simply shows the window if it's hidden (lines 18 to 21), and hides it if it's showing (lines 22 to 25).

The window itself is a special kind of frame called BaseFrame. In this example, the frame is fairly simple; all it does is paint a text message near the top of the frame. Because frames are components, just like other components, you could have just as easily added a layout manager, buttons, text fields, and so on, to this frame.

Closing Windows

You may have noticed, if you started up that pop-up window applet to play with it, that the new window's close box doesn't work. Nothing happens when you click the mouse on the box. To implement behavior for closing the window—for pop-up windows as in applets to hide them, or to exit the application altogether for applications—you'll have to use a handleEvent() method in your Frame class to test for the WINDOW_DESTROY event.

In the pop-up window example, choosing the close box should hide the window (call the hide() method). You can then show it again using the Open Window button in the applet. This is a very simple fix; just add the following handleEvent() to your BaseFrame1 class:

```
public boolean handleEvent(Event evt) {
   if (evt.id == Event.WINDOW_DESTROY) hide();
   return super.handleEvent(evt);
}
```

Menus

Each new window you create can have its own menu bar along the top of that window. Each menu bar can have a number of menus, and each menu, in turn, can have menu items. The AWT provides classes for all these things called, respectively, MenuBar, Menu, and MenuItem. Figure 14.3 shows the menu classes.

Note that you can have menu bars and individual menus in Java only on components that have title bars—frames in pop-up windows from applets work just fine, as do Java application windows, but you cannot have a menu bar attached to an applet itself.

14

Figure 14.3.

The AWT menu classes.

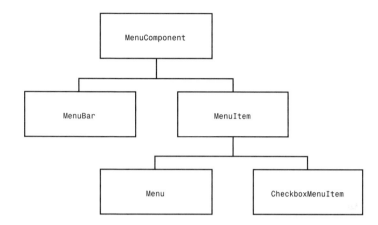

Menus and Menu Bars

To create a menu bar for a given window, create a new instance of the class `MenuBar`:

```
MenuBar mbar = new MenuBar();
```

To set this menu bar as the default menu for the window, use the `setMenuBar()` method (defined in the `Frame` class):

```
window.setMenuBar(mbar);
```

Add individual menus (File, Edit, and so on) to the menu bar by creating them and then adding them to the menu bar using `add()`:

```
Menu myMenu = new Menu("File");
mbar.add(myMenu);
```

Some systems provide a special help menu, which is drawn on the right side of the menu bar as opposed to somewhere in the middle. You can indicate that a specific menu is the help menu with the `setHelpMenu()` method. The given menu should already be added to the menu itself before being made a help menu:

```
Menu helpmenu = new Menu("Help");
mbar.add(helpmenu);
mbar.setHelpMenu(helpmenu);
```

If, for any reason, you want to prevent a user from selecting a menu, you can use the `disable()` command on that menu (and the `enable()` command to make it available again):

```
myMenu.disable();
```

14

Menu Items

There are four kinds of items you can add to individual menus:

☐ Instances of the class `MenuItem`, for regular menu items

☐ Instances of the class `CheckBoxMenuItem`, for toggled menu items

☐ Other menus, with their own menu items

☐ Separators, for lines that separate groups of items on menus

Regular menu items are added by using the `MenuItem` class. Add them to a menu using the `add()` method:

```
Menu myMenu = new Menu("Tools");
myMenu.add(new MenuItem("Info"));
myMenu.add(new MenuItem("Colors"));
```

Submenus can be added simply by creating a new instance of `Menu` and adding it to the first menu. You can then add items to *that* menu:

```
Menu submenu = new Menu("Sizes");
myMenu.add(submenu);
submenu.add(new MenuItem("Small"));
submenu.add(new MenuItem("Medium"));
submenu.add(new MenuItem("Large"));
```

The `CheckBoxMenuItem` class creates a menu item with a check box on it, enabling the menu state to be toggled on and off (selecting it once makes the check box appear selected; selecting it again unselects the check box). Create and add a check box menu item the same way you create and add regular menu items:

```
CheckboxMenuItem coords =
    new CheckboxMenuItem("Show Coordinates");
myMenu.add(coords);
```

Finally, to add a separator to a menu (a line used to separate groups of items in a menu), create and add a menu item with a single dash (-) as the label. That special menu item will be drawn with a separator line. These next two lines of Java code create a separator menu item and add it to the menu `myMenu`:

```
MenuItem msep = new MenuItem("-");
myMenu.add(msep);
```

Any menu item can be disabled by using the `disable()` method and enabled again using `enable()`. Disabled menu items cannot be selected:

```
MenuItem item = new MenuItem("Fill");
myMenu.addItem(item);
item.disable();
```

You'll add a typical menu and menu bar to the pop-up window applet in a bit; but first let's learn about how to activate menu items when they're selected.

Menu Actions

The act of selecting a menu item causes an action event to be generated. You can handle that action the same way you handle other `action` methods—by overriding `action()`. Both regular menu items and check box menu items have actions that generate an extra argument representing the label for that menu. You can use that label to determine which action to take. Note, also, that because `CheckBoxMenuItem` is a subclass of `MenuItem`, you don't have to treat that menu item as a special case. In this example, the Show Coordinates menu item is a `CheckBoxMenuItem`, and Fill is a regular menu item:

```
public boolean action(Event evt, Object arg) {
    if (evt.target instanceof MenuItem) {
        String label = (String)arg;
        if (label.equals("Show Coordinates")) toggleCoords();
        else if (label.equals("Fill")) fillcurrentArea();
        return true;
    }
    else return false;
}
```

A Pop-up Window with Menus

Let's add a menu to the pop-up window you created in the previous section. There are two steps here: creating and adding the menu, with all its menu items, to the layout, and then adding an action method to deal with the actions. Here we'll modify the `BaseFrame` class to include both these things; Listing 14.3 shows the new code. Figure 14.4 shows the menu in action.

NOTE

In the sample code on the CD, I created a new class called `BaseFrame2` for this part of the example, and a new class `PopupWindowMenu.java` to be the applet that owns this window. Use `PopupWindowMenu.html` to view it.

  Listing 14.3. `BaseFrame` **with a menu.**

```
1:import java.awt.*;
2:
3:class BaseFrame2 extends Frame {
4:   String message = "This is a Window";
5:
6:   BaseFrame2(String title) {
7:      super(title);
8:      setFont(new Font("Helvetica", Font.BOLD, 12));
9:
10:     MenuBar mb = new MenuBar();
```

continues

Listing 14.3. continued

```
11:    Menu m = new Menu("Colors");
12:    m.add(new MenuItem("Red"));
13:    m.add(new MenuItem("Blue"));
14:    m.add(new MenuItem("Green"));
15:    m.add(new MenuItem("-"));
16:    m.add(new CheckboxMenuItem("Reverse Text"));
17:    mb.add(m);
18:    setMenuBar(mb);
19:  }
20:
21:  public boolean action(Event evt, Object arg) {
22:    String label = (String)arg;
23:    if (evt.target instanceof MenuItem) {
24:       if (label.equals("Red")) setBackground(Color.red);
25:       else if (label.equals("Blue")) setBackground(Color.blue);
26:       else if (label.equals("Green")) setBackground(Color.green);
27:       else if (label.equals("Reverse Text")) {
28:          if (getForeground() == Color.black) {
29:             setForeground(Color.white);
30:          } else setForeground(Color.black);
31:       }
32:       repaint();
33:       return true;
34:    } else return false;
35:  }
36:
37:  public void paint(Graphics g) {
38:     g.drawString(message, 20, 20);
39:  }
40:
41:  public boolean handleEvent(Event evt) {
42:     if (evt.id == Event.WINDOW_DESTROY) hide();
43:        return super.handleEvent(evt);
44:  }
45:}
```

Figure 14.4.

A menu.

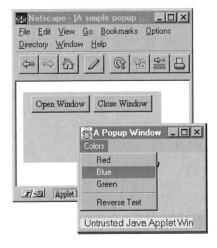

This menu has four items: one each for the colors red, blue, and green (which, when selected, change the background of the window), and one check box menu item for reversing the color of the text (to white). All are added as part of the constructor to this class, in lines 6 to 19.

To handle these menu items when they're chosen, you need an `action()` method. Inside `action()` you test to see if the action came from a menu item (which includes the one check box menu item), and if so, test for each of the menu labels in turn. For the red, blue, and green menu items, all you need to do is set the background. For the Reverse Text toggle, you need to first find out the current color of the text, and then reverse it.

To finish up, call a `repaint()` to make sure the background and the text get updated properly and return the appropriate boolean.

Dialog Boxes

Dialog boxes are functionally similar to frames in that they pop up new windows on the screen. However, dialog boxes are intended to be used for transient windows—for example, windows that let you know about warnings, windows that ask you for specific information, and so on. Dialogs don't usually have title bars or many of the more general features that windows have (although you can create one with a title bar), and they can be made nonresizable or modal (modal dialogs prevent input to any other windows on the screen until they are dismissed).

 Dialogs are transient windows intended to alert the user to some event or to get input from the user. Unlike frames, dialogs do not generally have a title bar or close boxes.

 A *modal dialog* prevents input to any of the other windows on the screen until that dialog is dismissed. (You won't be able to bring other windows to the front or iconify a modal dialog window; you must actually dismiss the modal dialog before being able to do anything else on the system. Warnings and alerts are typically modal dialogs.)

The AWT provides two kinds of dialog boxes: the `Dialog` class, which provides a generic dialog, and `FileDialog`, which produces the platform-specific file browser dialog.

Dialog Objects

Dialogs are created and used in much the same way as windows. To create a generic dialog, use one of these constructors:

- [ ] `Dialog(Frame, boolean)` creates an initially invisible dialog, attached to the current frame, which is either modal (`true`) or not (`false`).
- [ ] `Dialog(Frame, String, boolean)` is the same as the previous constructor, with the addition of a title bar and a title indicated by the string argument.

14

The dialog window, like the frame window, is a panel on which you can lay out and draw user interface components and perform graphics operations, just as you would any other panel. Like other windows, the dialog is initially invisible, but you can show it with show() and hide it with hide().

Let's add a dialog to that same example with the pop-up window. Here we'll modify the BaseFrame class once again to include a dialog, and add a new class, TextDialog, which produces a text entry dialog similar to the one shown in Figure 14.5.

Figure 14.5.

The Enter Text dialog.

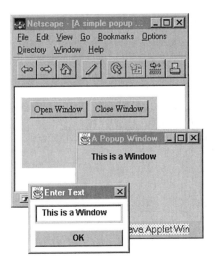

To add the dialog to the BaseFrame class, the changes are minor. First you'll need an instance variable to hold the dialog, since you'll be referring to it throughout this class:

```
TextDialog dl;
```

Next you'll add a menu item to the BaseFrame class's constructor method to change the text the pop-up window displays. This new menu item goes just after the Reverse Text item:

```
...
m.add(new CheckboxMenuItem("Reverse Text"));
m.add(new MenuItem("Set Text..."));
...
```

In that same constructor method, you can create the dialog (an instance of the new class TextDialog you'll create in a bit), assign it to the dl instance variable, and resize it (as shown in the next two lines of code). You don't want to show it yet because it should only appear when the correct menu item is selected:

```
dl = new TextDialog(this, "Enter Text", true);
dl.resize(150,100);
```

14

To get the dialog to appear at the appropriate time, you'll add a line to the `action()` method so that when the Set Text menu item is chosen, the `dl.show()` method is called. You can put this action in the same `if-else` block as the rest of the actions:

```
...
else if (label.equals("Green")) setBackground(Color.green);
else if (label.equals("Set Text...")) dl.show();
else if (label.equals("Reverse Text")) {
...
```

That's the end of the behavior you have to add to the window to create a dialog; the rest of the behavior goes into the `TextDialog` class, the code for which is shown in Listing 14.4.

TYPE **Listing 14.4. The `TextDialog` class.**

```
1:import java.awt.*;
2:
3:class TextDialog extends Dialog {
4:   TextField tf;
5:   BaseFrame3 theFrame;
6:
7:   TextDialog(Frame parent, String title, boolean modal) {
8:      super(parent, title, modal);
9:
10:      theFrame = (BaseFrame3)parent;
11:      setLayout(new BorderLayout(10,10));
12:      setBackground(Color.white);
13:      tf = new TextField(theFrame.message,20);
14:      add("Center", tf);
15:      add("South", new Button("OK"));
16:      resize(150,75);
17:   }
18:
19:   public Insets insets() {
20:      return new Insets(30,10,10,10);
21:   }
22:
23:   public boolean action(Event evt, Object arg) {
24:      String label = (String)arg;
25:      if (evt.target instanceof Button) {
26:        if (label == "OK") {
27:            hide();
28:            theFrame.message = tf.getText();
29:            theFrame.repaint();
30:        }
31:      }
32:      else return false;
33:      return true;
34:   }
35:}
```

14

In many ways this dialog class is very nearly the same as the `BaseFrame` class. It has a constructor that sets up the layout of the components, and an `action()` method to deal with its behavior. This one also has an `insets()` method for more layout information, but that's not a significant difference.

There are a few things to note about this code. First of all, note that the `TextDialog` class has a reference back up to its parent frame. It needs to reference this so it can update that frame with the new text information. Why does the dialog need to update the frame, rather than the frame figuring out when it needs updating? Because only the dialog knows when it's been dismissed. It's the dialog that deals with the change when the user presses OK, not the frame. So the dialog needs to be able to reach back to the original frame. Line 5 defines an instance variable to hold that reference.

The text dialog gets a reference to the parent frame through its constructor. This is actually the standard constructor for dialogs, so nothing new needs to be created here. You can simply call `super()` to initialize the dialog, and then add other bits to it. The first argument to the constructor is the frame argument. This is that hookup to the frame. But since you're getting a frame object, and you want a `BaseFrame` object, you'll have to cast it before you can assign it to the `theFrame` instance variable. Do this in line 10.

The remainder of the constructor for this dialog class simply creates the layout: a text field and a button in a border layout.

The `action()` method is what tells the dialog to hide itself. Mouse actions are broadcast to the window on which they occur; they do not percolate across windows, which is why you can't test to see if the OK button in the dialog was pressed from inside the `BaseFrame` class. Here you'll create an `action()` method to do two things when the OK button is pressed: hide the dialog and update the text message in the frame. Here's where that frame reference is important; in line 28 you're extracting the text that was entered into the dialog's text field and putting it into the frame's message instance variable. The next time the frame goes to paint (and you tell it to `repaint()` in line 29), the text message will get updated.

Attaching Dialogs to Applets

Dialogs can only be attached to frames; to create a dialog you have to pass an instance of the `Frame` class to one of the dialog's constructor methods.

This would imply that you cannot create dialog boxes that are attached to applets. Because applets don't have explicit frames, you cannot give the `Dialog` class a frame argument. Through a bit of sneaky code, however, you can get ahold of the frame object that contains that applet (often the browser or applet viewer window itself) and then use that object as the dialog's frame.

This sneaky code makes use of the `getParent()` method, defined for all AWT components. The `getParent()` method returns the object that contains this object. The parent of all AWT applications, then, must be a frame. Applets behave in this same way; by calling `getParent()` repeatedly, eventually you should be able to get ahold of an instance of `Frame`. Here's the sneaky code to do this that you can put inside your applet:

```
Object anchorpoint = getParent()
while (! (anchorpoint instanceof Frame))
    anchorpoint = ((Component)anchorpoint).getParent();
```

In the first line of this code, you create a local variable, called `anchorpoint`, to hold the eventual frame for this applet. The object assigned to `anchorpoint` may be one of many classes, so we'll declare its type to be `Object`.

The second two lines of this code are a `while` loop that calls `getParent()` on each different object up the chain until it gets to an actual `Frame` object. Note here that since the `getParent()` method is only defined on objects that inherit from `Component`, we have to cast the value of `anchorpoint` to `Component` each time for the `getParent()` method to work.

After the loop exits, the object contained in the `anchorpoint` variable will be an instance of the `Frame` class (or one of its subclasses). You can then create a `Dialog` object attached to that frame, casting the `anchorpoint` one more time to make sure you've got a `Frame` object:

```
TextDialog dl = new TextDialog((Frame)anchorpoint,
    "Enter Text", true);
```

File Dialog Objects

The `FileDialog` class provides a basic file open/save dialog box that enables you to access the file system. The `FileDialog` class is system-independent, but depending on the platform, the standard Open File or Save File dialog is brought up.

NOTE

> For applets, whether or not you can even use instances of `FileDialog` is dependent on the browser (Netscape simply produces an error). `FileDialog` is much more useful in standalone applications.

To create a file dialog, use the following constructors:

- ☐ `FileDialog(Frame, String)` creates an Open File dialog, attached to the given frame, with the given title. This form creates a dialog to load a file.

- ☐ `FileDialog(Frame, String, int)` also creates a file dialog, but that integer argument is used to determine whether the dialog is for loading a file or saving a file (the only difference is the labels on the buttons; the file dialog does not actually open or save anything). The possible options for the mode argument are `FileDialog.LOAD` and `FileDialog.SAVE`.

14

After you create a `FileDialog` instance, use `show()` to display it:

```
FileDialog fd = new FileDialog(this, "FileDialog");
fd.show();
```

When the reader chooses a file in the File dialog and dismisses it, you can then access the filename they chose by using the `getDirectory()` and `getFile()` methods; both return strings indicating the values the reader chose. You can then open that file by using the stream and file handling methods (which you'll learn about next week) and then read from or write to that file.

Cursors

If you use frames in your applets or applications, you can also set the cursor's icon at given moments in your program's execution, to signal wait conditions or other events happening in your program.

The `getCursorType()` and `setCursor()` methods are defined in the `Frame` class. If you can get at a `Frame` object, you can set the cursor (you'll typically set cursors for windows, but you can also set cursors for applets using the `getParent()` method that I explained in the section "Attaching Dialogs to Applets"). Both of these methods use a set of predefined cursor types in the `Frame` class. Table 14.1 shows the cursor types you can use (and test for) in your windows.

NOTE   Keep in mind that not all platforms use the same cursors. For example, cursors for resizing windows do not exist on Macintoshes.

Table 14.1. Cursor types.

Class Variable	Cursor
`Frame.CROSSHAIR_CURSOR`	A cross-hair (plus-shaped) cursor
`Frame.DEFAULT_CURSOR`	The default cursor (usually a pointer or arrow)
`Frame.E_RESIZE_CURSOR`	A cursor to indicate something is being resized
`Frame.HAND_CURSOR`	A hand-shaped cursor (to move an object or the background)
`Frame.MOVE_CURSOR`	A cursor to indicate that something is being moved
`Frame.N_RESIZE_CURSOR`	The top edge of a window is being resized
`Frame.NE_RESIZE_CURSOR`	The top-right corner of a window is being resized

Class Variable	Cursor
Frame.NW_RESIZE_CURSOR	The top-left corner of a window is being resized
Frame.S_RESIZE_CURSOR	The bottom edge of a window is being resized
Frame.SE_RESIZE_CURSOR	The bottom-right corner of the window is being resized
Frame.SW_RESIZE_CURSOR	The bottom-left corner of the window is being resized
Frame.TEXT_CURSOR	A text-entry cursor (sometimes called an I-beam)
Frame.W_RESIZE_CURSOR	The left edge of a window is being resized
Frame.WAIT_CURSOR	A long operation is taking place (usually an icon for a watch or an hourglass)

Window Events

Yesterday you learned about writing your own event handler methods, and you noted that the Event class defines many standard events for which you can test. Window events are part of that list, so if you use windows, these events may be of interest to you, (for example, to hide a window when it's closed, to stop a thread from running when the window is iconified, or to perform some operation when a file is loaded or saved).

You can test the id instance variable of the event object in your handleEvent() method to see if any of these events have occurred:

```
if (evt.id == Event.WINDOW_DESTROY) hide();
```

Table 14.2. shows the various Window events.

Table 14.2. Window events from the Event class.

WINDOW_DESTROY	Generated when a window is destroyed using the close box or the Close menu item
WINDOW_EXPOSE	Generated when the window is brought forward from behind other windows
WINDOW_ICONIFY	Generated when the window is iconified
WINDOW_DEICONIFY	Generated when the window is restored from an icon
WINDOW_MOVED	Generated when the window is moved

14

Standalone AWT Applications

After all the space and time I've devoted to creating applets up to this point, you may be surprised that I'm sticking a description of graphical Java applications here at the end, and in a fairly small section at that. The reason for this is that other than a few simple lines of code and in the environment each runs in, there's not a lot of difference between a Java applet and a graphical Java application. Everything you've learned up to this point about the AWT including the graphics methods, animation techniques, events, UI components, and windows and dialogs, can be used the same way in Java applications as they can in applets. And applications have the advantage of being "outside the sandbox"—they have none of the security restrictions that applets have. You can do just about anything you want to with an application.

So how do you go about creating a graphical Java application? The code to do it is almost trivial. Your main application class should inherit from Frame. If it uses threads (for animation or other processing), it should also implement Runnable:

```
class MyAWTApplication extends Frame implements Runnable {
...
}
```

Inside the main() method for your application, you create a new instance of your class—because your class extends Frame, that'll give you a new AWT window that you can then resize and show as you would any AWT window. Inside the constructor method for your class you'll set up the usual AWT features for a window that you might usually do in an init() method for an applet: Set the title, add a layout manager, create and add components such as a menu bar or other UI elements, start up a thread, and so on. Here's a simple example:

```
class MyAWTApplication extends Frame implements Runnable {

    MyAWTApplication(String title) {
        super(title);

        setLayout(new FlowLayout());
        add(new Button("OK"));
        add(new Button("Reset"));
        add(new Button("Cancel"));
    }

    public static void main(String args[]) {
        MyAWTApplications app = new MyAWTApplication("Hi!  I'm an application");
        app.resize(300,300);
        app.show();
    }
}
```

For the most part, you can use any of the methods you've learned about this week to control and manage your application. The only methods you cannot use are those specific to applets

14

(that is, those defined in `java.applet.Applet`, which includes methods for retrieving URL information and playing audio clips—see the API documentation for that class for more details).

Networking in Java

Networking is the capability of making connections from your applet or application to a system over the network. Networking in Java involves classes in the `java.net` package, which provide cross-platform abstractions for simple networking operations, including connecting and retrieving files by using common Web protocols and creating basic UNIX-like sockets. Used in conjunction with input and output streams (which you'll learn much more about next week), reading and writing files over the network becomes as easy as reading or writing to files on the local disk.

There are restrictions, of course. Java applets usually cannot read or write from the disk on the machine where the browser is running. Java applets cannot connect to systems other than the one on which they were originally stored. Even given these restrictions, you can still accomplish a great deal and take advantage of the Web to read and process information over the Net.

This section describes three ways you can communicate with systems on the Net:

- [ ] `showDocument()`, which enables an applet to tell the browser to load and link to another page on the Web
- [ ] `openStream()`, a method that opens a connection to a URL and enables you to extract data from that connection
- [ ] The socket classes, `Socket` and `ServerSocket`, which enable you to open standard socket connections to hosts and read to and write from those connections

Creating Links Inside Applets

Probably the easiest way to use networking inside an applet is to tell the browser running that applet to load a new page. You can use this, for example, to create animated image maps that, when clicked, load a new page.

To link to a new page, you create a new instance of the class URL. You saw some of this when you worked with images, but let's go over it a little more thoroughly here.

The URL class represents a uniform resource locator. To create a new URL, you can use one of four different forms:

14

☐ `URL(String, String, int, String)` creates a new URL object, given a protocol (http, ftp, gopher, file), a hostname (`www.lne.com`, `ftp.netcom.com`), a port number (`80` for http), and a filename or pathname.

☐ `URL(String, String, String)` does the same thing as the previous form, minus the port number.

☐ `URL(URL, String)` creates a URL, given a base path and a relative path. For the base, you can use `getDocumentBase()` for the URL of the current HTML file, or `getCodeBase()` for the URL of the Java applet class file. The relative path will be tacked onto the last directory in those base URLs (just like with images and sounds).

☐ `URL(String)` creates a URL object from a URL string (which should include the protocol, hostname, optional port name, and filename).

For the last one (creating a URL from a string), you have to catch a malformed URL exception, so surround the URL constructor with a `try...catch`:

```
String url = "http://www.yahoo.com/";
try { theURL = new URL(url); }
catch ( MalformedURLException e) {
    System.out.println("Bad URL: " + theURL);
}
```

Getting a URL object is the hard part. Once you have one, all you have to do is pass it to the browser. Do this by using this single line of code, where `theURL` is the URL object to link to:

```
getAppletContext().showDocument(theURL);
```

The browser that contains the Java applet with this code will then load and display the document at that URL.

Listing 14.5 shows two classes: `ButtonLink` and its helper class `Bookmark`. `ButtonLink` is a simple applet that displays three buttons that represent important Web locations (the buttons are shown in Figure 14.6). Clicking on the buttons causes the document to be loaded from the locations to which those buttons refer.

TYPE   **Listing 14.5. Bookmark buttons.**

```
1: // Buttonlink.java starts here
2: import java.awt.*;
3: import java.net.*;
4:
5: public class ButtonLink extends java.applet.Applet {
6:
7:     Bookmark bmlist[] = new Bookmark[3];
8:
9:     public void init() {
```

14

```
10:          bmlist[0] = new Bookmark("Laura's Home Page",
11:              "http://www.lne.com/lemay/");
12:          bmlist[1] = new Bookmark("Gamelan",
13:              "http://www.gamelan.com");
14:          bmlist[2]= new Bookmark("Java Home Page",
15:              "http://java.sun.com");
16:
17:          setLayout(new GridLayout(bmlist.length,1, 10, 10));
18:          for (int i = 0; i < bmlist.length; i++) {
19:              add(new Button(bmlist[i].name));
20:          }
21:      }
22:
23:      public boolean action(Event evt, Object arg) {
24:          if (evt.target instanceof Button) {
25:              linkTo((String)arg);
26:              return true;
27:          }
28:          else return false;
29:      }
30:
31:      void linkTo(String name) {
32:          URL theURL = null;
33:          for (int i = 0; i < bmlist.length; i++) {
34:              if (name.equals(bmlist[i].name))
35:                  theURL = bmlist[i].url;
36:          }
37:          if (theURL != null)
38:              getAppletContext().showDocument(theURL);
39:      }
40: } //ButtonLink.java ends here
41:
42: //Bookmark.java starts here
43: import java.net.URL;
44: import java.net.MalformedURLException;
45:
46: class Bookmark {
47:     String name;
48:     URL url;
49:
50:     Bookmark(String name, String theURL) {
51:         this.name = name;
52:         try { this.url = new URL(theURL); }
53:         catch ( MalformedURLException e) {
54:         System.out.println("Bad URL: " + theURL);
55:     }
56: }
57:} //Bookmark.java ends here
```

ANALYSIS Two classes make up this applet: The first, ButtonLink, implements the actual applet itself; the second, Bookmark, is a class representing a bookmark. Bookmarks have two parts: a name and a URL.

14

Figure 14.6.

Bookmark buttons.

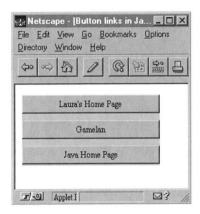

This particular applet creates three bookmark instances (lines 10 through 15) and stores them in an array of bookmarks (this applet could be easily modified to accept bookmarks as parameters from an HTML file). For each bookmark, a button is created whose label is the value of the bookmark's name.

When the buttons are pressed, the linkTo() method is called. linkTo(), defined in lines 31 to 38, extracts the name of the button from the event, uses it to look up the actual URL from the bookmark object, and then tells the browser to load the URL referenced by that bookmark.

Opening Web Connections

Rather than asking the browser to just load the contents of a file, sometimes you might want to get hold of that file's contents so that your applet can use them. If the file you want to grab is stored on the Web, and can be accessed using the more common URL forms (http, ftp, and so on), your applet can use the URL class to get it.

Note that for security reasons, applets can by default connect back only to the same host from which they originally loaded. This means that if you have your applets stored on a system called www.myhost.com, the only machine your applet can open a connection to will be that same host (and that same host *name*, so be careful with host aliases). If the file the applet wants to retrieve is on that same system, using URL connections is the easiest way to get it.

This security restriction will change how you've been writing and testing applets up to this point. Because we haven't been dealing with network connections, we've been able to do all our testing on the local disk simply by opening the HTML files in a browser or with the appletviewer tool. You cannot do this with applets that open network connections. In order for those applets to work correctly, you must do one of two things:

☐ Run your browser on the same machine that your Web server is running on. If you don't have access to your Web server, you can often install and run a Web server on your local machine.

☐ Upload your class and HTML files to your Web server each time you want to test them. Then, instead of using Open File to test your applets, use the actual URL of the HTML file instead.

You'll know when you're not doing things right in regard to making sure your applet, and the connection it's opening, are on the same server. If you try to load an applet or a file from different servers, you'll get a security exception along with a lot of other scary error messages printed to your screen or to the Java console.

That said, let's move on to the methods and classes for retrieving files from the Web.

openStream()

The URL class defines a method called openStream(), which opens a network connection using the given URL (an HTTP connection for Web URLs, an FTP connection for FTP URLs, and so on) and returns an instance of the class InputStream (part of the java.io package). If you convert that stream to a DataInputStream (with a BufferedInputStream in the middle for better performance), you can then read characters and lines from that stream (you'll learn all about streams on Day 19, "Streams and I/O"). For example, these lines open a connection to the URL stored in the variable theURL, and then read and echo each line of the file to the standard output:

```
try {
    InputStream in = theURL.openStream();
    DataInputStream data = new DataInputStream(new BufferedInputStream(in);

    String line;
    while ((line = data.readLine()) != null) {
        System.out.println(line);
    }
}
catch (IOException e) {
    System.out.println("IO Error: " + e.getMessage());
}
```

 NOTE You need to wrap all those lines in a try...catch statement to catch IOExceptions generated. You'll learn more about IOExceptions and the try and catch statements on Day 17, "Exceptions."

14

Here's an example of an applet that uses the openStream() method to open a connection to a Web site, reads a file from that connection (Edgar Allen Poe's poem "The Raven"), and displays the result in a text area. Listing 14.6 shows the code; Figure 14.7 shows the result after the file has been read.

An important note: If you compile this code as written, it won't work—you'll get a security exception. The reason is that this applet opens a connection to the server www.lne.com to get the file raven.txt. When you compile and run this applet, that applet isn't running on www.lne.com (unless you're me, and I already know about this problem). Before you compile this applet, make sure you change line 18 to point to a copy of raven.txt on your server, and install your applet and your HTML files on that same server (you can get raven.txt from the CD or from that very URL).

Alternately, you can use your browser to point to the URL http://www.lne.com/Web/ JavaProf/GetRaven.html. That Web page loads this very applet and downloads the file correctly. Because both the applet and the text file are on the same server, it works just fine.

TYPE   **Listing 14.6. The GetRaven class.**

```
 1: import java.awt.*;
 2: import java.io.DataInputStream;
 3: import java.io.BufferedInputStream;
 4: import java.io.IOException;
 5: import java.net.URL;
 6: import java.net.URLConnection;
 7: import java.net.MalformedURLException;
 8:
 9: public class GetRaven extends java.applet.Applet implements Runnable {
10:   URL theURL;
11:   Thread runner;
12:   TextArea ta = new TextArea("Getting text...");
13:
14:   public void init() {
15:     setLayout(new GridLayout(1,1));
16:
17:     // CHANGE THIS NEXT LINE BEFORE COMPILING!!!
18:     String url = "http://www.lne.com/Web/JavaProf/raven.txt";
19:     try { this.theURL = new URL(url); }
20:     catch ( MalformedURLException e) {
21:       System.out.println("Bad URL: " + theURL);
22:     }
23:     add(ta);
24:   }
25:
26:   public Insets insets() {
27:     return new Insets(10,10,10,10);
28:   }
29:
30:   public void start() {
31:     if (runner == null) {
```

```
32:        runner = new Thread(this);
33:        runner.start();
34:      }
35:  }
36:
37:  public void stop() {
38:      if (runner != null) {
39:        runner.stop();
40:        runner = null;
41:      }
42:  }
43:
44:  public void run() {
45:      URLConnection conn = null;
46:      DataInputStream data = null;
47:      String line;
48:     StringBuffer buf = new StringBuffer();
49:
50:      try {
51:        conn = this.theURL.openConnection();
52:        conn.connect();
53:       ta.setText("Connection opened...");
54:        data = new DataInputStream(new BufferedInputStream(
55:          conn.getInputStream()));
56:        ta.setText("Reading data...");
57:        while ((line = data.readLine()) != null) {
58:          buf.append(line + "\n");
59:        }
60:        ta.setText(buf.toString());
61:      }
62:      catch (IOException e) {
63:        System.out.println("IO Error:" + e.getMessage());
64:      }
65:}
66:}
```

ANALYSIS The init() method (lines 14 to 24) sets up the URL and the text area in which that file will be displayed. The URL could be easily passed into the applet via an HTML parameter; here, it's just hard coded for simplicity.

Because it might take some time to load the file over the network, you put that routine into its own thread and use the familiar start(), stop(), and run() methods to control that thread.

Inside run() (lines 44 to 64), the work takes place. Here, you initialize a bunch of variables and then open the connection to the URL (using the openStream() method in line 50). Once the connection is open, you set up an input stream in lines 51 to 55 and read from it, line by line, putting the result into an instance of StringBuffer (a string buffer is a modifiable string). I put all this work into a thread because it may take some time for the connection to

14

open and for the file to be read—particularly across slower connections. There may be other things going on in the applet that need to take place concurrently to the file loading.

Figure 14.7.

The GetRaven *applet.*

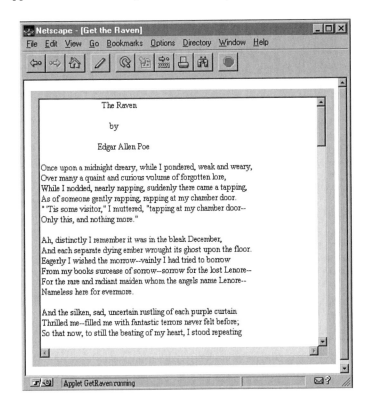

Once all the data has been read, line 60 converts the StringBuffer object into a real string and then puts that result in the text area.

One other thing to note about this example is that the part of the code that opened a network connection, read from the file, and created a string is surrounded by a try and catch statement. If any errors occur while you're trying to read or process the file, these statements enable you to recover from them without the entire program crashing (in this case, the program exits with an error, because there's little else to be done if the applet can't read the file). try and catch give you the capability of handling and recovering from errors. You'll learn more about exceptions on Day 17.

Sockets

For networking applications beyond what the URL and URLconnection classes offer (for example, for other protocols or for more general networking applications), Java provides the Socket and ServerSocket classes as an abstraction of standard socket programming techniques. You'll learn more about working with Java sockets on Day 26, "Client/Server Networking in Java," but for now here's a very short rundown of the socket capabilities in Java.

The Socket class provides a client-side socket interface similar to standard UNIX sockets. To open a connection, create a new instance of Socket (where *hostname* is the host to connect to, and *portnum* is the port number):

```
Socket connection = new Socket(hostname, portnum);
```

NOTE

> If you use sockets in an applet, you are still subject to the applet security restrictions that prevent you from connecting to any system other than the same one the applet came from.

Once the socket is open, you can use input and output streams to read and write from that socket (you'll learn all about input and output streams on Day 19):

```
DataInputStream in = new DataInputStream(
    new BufferedInputStream(connection.getInputStream()));
DataOutputStream out= new DataOutputStream(
    new BufferedOutputStream(connection.getOutputStream()));
```

Once you're done with the socket, don't forget to close it (this also closes all the input and output streams you may have set up for that socket):

```
connection.close();
```

Server-side sockets work similarly, with the exception of the accept() method. A server socket listens on a TCP port for a connection from a client; when a client connects to that port, the accept() method accepts a connection from that client. By using both client and server sockets, you can create applications that communicate with each other over the network.

To create a server socket and bind it to a port, create a new instance of ServerSocket with the port number:

```
ServerSocket sconnection = new ServerSocket(8888);
```

14

To listen on that port (and to accept a connection from any clients if one is made), use the `accept()` method:

```
sconnection.accept();
```

Once the socket connection is made, you can use input and output streams to read from and write to the client.

See the `java.net` package for more information about Java sockets.

Changes to Sockets for Java 1.1

In the 1.0.2 version of Java, the `Socket` and `ServerSocket` classes provide a basic abstract socket implementation. You can create new instances of these classes to make or accept connections and to pass data back and forth from a client to a server.

The problem comes when you try to extend or change Java's socket behavior. The `Socket` and `ServerSocket` classes in the `java.net` package are final classes, which means you cannot create subclasses of those classes (you'll learn more about finalizing classes on Day 15, "Modifiers, Access Control, and Class Design"). To extend the behavior of the socket classes— for example, to allow network connections to work across a firewall or a proxy, you can use the abstract classes `SocketImpl` and the interface `SocketImplFactory` to create a new transport-layer socket implementation. This design fits with the original goal of Java's socket classes: to allow those classes to be portable to other systems with different transport mechanisms.

The problem with this mechanism is that while it works for simple cases, it prevents you from adding other protocols on top of TCP (for example, to implement an encryption mechanism such as SSL) or for having multiple socket implementations per Java runtime.

For these reasons, in Java 1.1 sockets will change such that the `Socket` and `ServerSocket` classes are nonfinal and extendable. You will be able to create subclasses of these classes in Java 1.1, which use either the default socket implementation or one of your own making. This will allow much more flexible network capabilities to Java in 1.1.

In addition, Java 1.1 has added several other new features to the `java.net` package:

- [ ] New options for sockets, based on BSD's socket options (for example, `TCP_NODELAY`, `IP_MULTICAST_LOOP`, `SO_BINDADDR`)
- [ ] Many new subclasses of the `SocketException` class, to represent network errors on a finer level of granularity than in Java 1.0.2 (for example, `NoRouteToHostException` or `ConnectException`)

For more information about all the networking changes between Java 1.02 and 1.1, see the pages at `http://java.sun.com/products/JDK/1.1/designspecs/net/index.html`.

Other Applet Hints

On this, the last section of the last day of the second week, let's finish with some small hints that didn't fit in anywhere else: using showStatus() to print messages in the browser status window, providing applet information, and communicating between multiple applets on the same page.

The showStatus() Method

The showStatus() method, available in the Applet class, enables you to display a string in the status bar of the browser, which contains the applet. You can use this for printing error, link, help, or other status messages:

```
getAppletContext().showStatus("Change the color");
```

The getAppletContext() method enables your applet to access features of the browser that contains it. You already saw a use of this with links, wherein you could use the showDocument() method to tell the browser to load a page. showStatus() uses that same mechanism to print status messages.

NOTE

showStatus() may not be supported in all browsers, so do not depend on it for your applet's functionality or interface. It is a useful way of communicating optional information to your user—if you need a more reliable method of communication, set up a label in your applet and update it to reflect changes in its message.

Applet Information

The AWT gives you a mechanism for associating information with your applet. Usually, there is a mechanism in the browser viewing the applet to view display information. You can use this mechanism to sign your name or your organization to your applet, or to provide contact information so that users can get hold of you if they want.

To provide information about your applet, override the getAppletInfo() method:

```
public String getAppletInfo() {
    return "GetRaven copyright 1995 Laura Lemay";
}
```

14

Communicating Between Applets

Sometimes you want to have an HTML page that has several different applets on it. To do this, all you have to do is include several different iterations of the applet tag. The browser will create different instances of your applet for each one that appears on the HTML page.

What if you want to communicate between those applets? What if you want a change in one applet to affect the other applets in some way? The best way to do this is to use the applet context to get to different applets on the same page.

NOTE

Be forewarned that before you do extensive work with inter-applet communication, the mechanism described in this section is implemented differently (and often unreliably) in different browsers and different Java environments. If you need to rely on communicating between applets for your Web pages, make sure you test those applets extensively in different browsers on different platforms.

The applet context is defined in a class called, appropriately, AppletContext. To get an instance of this class for you applet, you use the getAppletContext() method. You've already seen the use of the getAppletContext() method for other uses; you can also use it to get hold of the other applets on the page. For example, to call a method named sendMessage() on all the applets on a page (including the current applet), use the getApplets() method and a for loop that looks something like this:

```
for (Enumeration e = getAppletContext().getApplets();
        e.hasMoreElements();) {
    Applet current = (MyAppletSubclass)(e.nextElement());
    current.sendMessage();
}
```

The getApplets() method returns an Enumeration object with a list of the applets on the page. Iterating over the Enumeration object in this way enables you to access each element in the Enumeration in turn. Note that each element in the Enumeration object is an instance of the Object class; to get that applet to behave the way you want it to (and accept messages from other applets), you'll have to cast it to be an instance of your applet subclass (here, the class MyAppletSubclass).

If you want to call a method in a specific applet, it's slightly more complicated. To do this, you give your applets a name and then refer to them by name inside the body of code for that applet.

To give an applet a name, use the NAME attribute to <APPLET> in your HTML file:

```
<P>This applet sends information:
<APPLET CODE="MyApplet.class" WIDTH=100 HEIGHT=150
    NAME="sender"> </APPLET>
<P>This applet receives information from the sender:
<APPLET CODE="MyApplet.class" WIDTH=100 HEIGHT=150
    NAME="receiver"> </APPLET>
```

To get a reference to another applet on the same page, use the getApplet() method from the applet context with the name of that applet. This gives you a reference to the applet of that name. You can then refer to that applet as if it were just another object: call methods, set its instance variables, and so on. Here's some code to do just that:

```
// get ahold of the receiver applet
Applet receiver = (MyAppletSubclass)getAppletContext().getApplet("receiver");
// tell it to update itself.
receiver.update(text, value);
```

In this example you use the getApplet() method to get a reference to the applet with the name receiver. Note that the object returned by getApplet is an instance of the generic Applet class; you'll most likely want to cast that object to an instance of your subclass. Given the reference to the named applet, you can then call methods in that applet as if it were just another object in your own environment. Here, for example, if both applets have an update() method, you can tell receiver to update itself by using the information the current applet has.

Naming your applets and then referring to them by using the methods described in this section enables your applets to communicate and stay in sync with each other, providing uniform behavior for all the applets on your page.

Summary

Congratulations! Take a deep breath—you're finished with Week 2. This week has been full of useful information about creating applets and using the Java AWT classes to display, draw, animate, process input, and create fully fledged interfaces in your applets.

Today you finished exploring applets and the AWT by learning about three concepts.

First, you learned about windows, frames, menus, and dialogs, which enable you to create a framework for your applets—or enable your Java applications to take advantage of applet features.

Second, you had a brief introduction to Java networking through some of the classes in the java.net package. Applet networking includes things as simple as pointing the browser to another page from inside your applet, but can also include retrieving files from the Web by using standard Web protocols (http, ftp, and so on). For more advanced networking capabilities, Java provides basic socket interfaces that can be used to implement many basic network-oriented applets—client/server interactions, chat sessions, and so on.

14

Finally, you finished up with the tidbits—small features of the Java AWT and of applets that didn't fit anywhere else, including showStatus(), providing information about your applet, and communicating between multiple applets on a single page.

Q&A

Q **When I create pop-up windows, they all show up with this big yellow bar that says** Warning: applet window. **What does this mean?**

A The warning is to tell you (and the users of your applet) that the window being displayed was generated by an applet, and not by the browser itself. This is a security feature to keep an applet programmer from popping up a window that masquerades as a browser window and, for example, asks users for their passwords.

There's nothing you can do to hide or obscure the warning.

Q **What good is having a file dialog box if you can't read or write files from the local file system?**

A Applets often can't read or write from the local file system (depending on the browser), but because you can use AWT components in Java applications as well as applets, the file dialog box is also very useful for them.

Q **How can I mimic an HTML form submission in a Java applet?**

A Currently, applets make it difficult to do this. The best (and easiest way) is to use GET notation to get the browser to submit the form contents for you.

HTML forms can be submitted in two ways: by using the GET request, or by using POST. If you use GET, your form information is encoded in the URL itself, something like this:

```
http://www.blah.com/cgi-bin/myscript?foo=1&bar=2&name=Laura
```

Because the form input is encoded in the URL, you can write a Java applet to mimic a form, get input from the user, and then construct a new URL object with the form data included on the end. Then just pass that URL to the browser by using getAppletContext().showDocument(), and the browser will submit the form results itself. For simple forms, this is all you need.

Q **How can I do** POST **form submissions?**

A You'll have to mimic what a browser does to send forms using POST: Open a socket to the server and send the data, which looks something like this (the exact format is determined by the HTTP protocol; this is only a subset of it):

```
POST /cgi-bin/mailto.cgi HTTP/1.0
Content-type: application/x-www-form-urlencoded
```

```
Content-length: 36
```

```
{your encoded form data here}
```

If you've done it right, you get the CGI form output back from the server. It's then up to your applet to handle that output properly. Note that if the output is in HTML, there really isn't a way to pass that output to the browser that is running your applet yet. This capability may end up in future Java releases. If you get back a URL, however, you can redirect the browser to that URL.

Q `showStatus()` doesn't work in my browser. How can I give my readers status information?

A As you learned in the section on `showStatus()`, whether or not a browser supports `showStatus()` is up to that browser. If you must have status-like behavior in your applet, consider creating a status label in the applet itself that is updated with the information you need to present.

Q I've been trying to communicate between two applets in my Web page using the `getAppletContext()` and `getApplet()` methods. My applets keep crashing with `NullPointerException` errors. What does this mean?

A The mechanism I described for communicating between applets is how Sun and the Java class library says it's *supposed* to work. However, like `showStatus()`, whether or not a browser implements that mechanism, or implements it correctly, depends on that browser. Version of Netscape before 3.0 and Internet Explorer both have strange problems with inter-applet communication.

Q It looks like the `openStream()` method and the `Socket` classes implement TCP sockets. Does Java support UDP (User Datagram Protocol, often just called datagram) sockets?

A The JDK 1.0 provides two classes, `DatagramSocket` and `DatagramPacket`, which implement UDP sockets. The `DatagramSocket` class operates similarly to the `Socket` class. Use instances of `DatagramPacket` for each packet you send or receive over the socket.

See the API documentation for the `java.net` package for more information.

14

At a Glance

☐ **Modifiers, Access Control, and Class Design**
Methods and variable access control

☐ **Packages and Interfaces**
Hiding classes, design and implementation, inheritance

☐ **Exceptions**
`throw` statements, the `finally` clause

☐ **Multithreading**
Synchronization problems, more about `Point`

☐ **Streams and I/O**
Input and output, `flush()` and `close()`

☐ **Using Native Methods and Libraries**

Built-in optimizations, generating header and stub files

☐ **Under the Hood**

Security and consistency checking, garbage collection

Day 15

Modifiers, Access Control, and Class Design

by Laura Lemay and Charles L. Perkins

Here at the start of Week 3, you've probably grasped the basics of the Java language from Week 1, and you've applied them fairly often to create applets in Week 2. You can stop here, if you like, and go on your merry way, knowing enough Java to get by.

Week 3 extends what you already know. In this week you'll learn more about advanced Java concepts such as access control and packages, and you'll learn techniques for structuring large programs in an efficient object-oriented way so your code can be more easily maintained and extended or, if you so choose, easily reused by other people.

Today we'll start with advanced Java language concepts for organizing and designing individual classes:

☐ What a modifier is and how it's used

☐ Controlling access to methods and variables from outside a class to better encapsulate your code

☐ Using a special case of controlling access to methods and variables: instance variable accessor methods

☐ Using Class variables and methods to store class-specific attributes and behavior

☐ Finalizing classes, methods, and variables so their values or definitions cannot be subclasses or overridden

☐ Creating abstract classes and methods for factoring common behavior into super-classes

Modifiers

The techniques for programming you'll learn today involve different strategies and ways of thinking about how a class is organized. But the one thing all these techniques have in common is that they all use special modifier keywords in the Java language.

In Week 1 you learned how to define classes, methods, and variables in Java. Modifiers are keywords you add to those definitions to change their meaning. Classes, methods, and variables with modifiers are still classes, methods, and variables, but the modifiers change their behavior or how Java treats those elements.

 Modifiers are special language keywords that modify the definition (and the behavior) of a class, method, or variable.

 You've already learned about a few of these modifiers earlier in the book, but here we'll talk about them in detail so you can get the bigger picture of why modifiers work the way they do.

The Java language has a wide variety of modifiers, including

☐ Modifiers for controlling access to a class, method, or variable: public, protected, and private

☐ The static modifier for creating class methods and variables

☐ The abstract modifier, for creating abstract classes and methods

☐ The final modifier, for finalizing the implementations of classes, methods, and variables

☐ The synchronized and volatile modifiers, which are used for threads and which you'll learn more about on Day 18, "Multithreading"

☐ The native modifier, which is used for creating native methods, which you'll learn about on Day 21, "Under the Hood"

Some modifiers, as you can see, can apply only to classes and methods or only to methods and variables. For each of the modifiers, however, to use them you put them just previous to the class, method, or variable definition, as in the following examples:

```
public class MyApplet extends Java.applet.Applet { ... }

private boolean engineState;

static final double pi = 3.141559265

protected static final int MAXNUMELEMENTS = 128;

public static void main(String args[]) { ...}
```

The order of modifiers is irrelevant to their meaning—your order can vary and is really a matter of taste. Pick a style and then be consistent with it throughout all your classes. Here is the usual order:

```
<access> static abstract synchronized volatile final native
```

In this definition, `<access>` can be public, protected, or private (but no more than one of them).

All the modifiers are essentially optional; none have to appear in a declaration. Good object-oriented programming style, however, suggests adding as many as are needed to best describe the intended use of, and restrictions on, the thing you're declaring. In some special situations (inside an interface, for example, as described tomorrow), certain modifiers are implicitly defined for you, and you needn't type them—they will be assumed to be there.

Controlling Access to Methods and Variables

The most important modifiers in the language, from the standpoint of class and object design, are those that allow you to control the visibility of, and access to, variables and methods inside your classes.

Why Access Control Is Important

Why would you care about controlling access to methods and variables inside your classes? If you remember way back to the beginning of this book, I used the analogy of the PC—how you can buy different PC components and put them all together so that they interact to create a larger system.

Each component in that PC system works in a particular way and has a specific way of interacting with the other components in the system. For example, a video card plugs into your motherboard using a standard socket and plug arrangement, as does your monitor to the back of the card. And then your computer can talk the right software language through the card to get bits up on the screen.

The video card itself has a whole lot of other internal features and capabilities beyond this basic hardware and software interface. But as a user or consumer of the card, I don't need to know what every single chip does, nor do I need to touch them in order to get the card to work. Given the standard interfaces, the card figures everything out and does what it needs to do internally. And, in fact, the manufacturer of the card most likely doesn't want me to go in and start mucking with individual chips or capabilities of the card, because I'm likely to screw something up. It's best if I just stick to the defined interface and let the internal workings stay hidden.

Classes and objects are the same way. While a class may define lots of methods and variables, not all of them are useful to a consumer of that class, and some may even be harmful if they're not used in the way they were intended to be used.

Access control is about controlling visibility. When a method or variable is visible to another class, its methods can reference (call, or modify) that method or variable. Protecting those methods and instance variables limits the visibility and the use of those methods and variables (and also limits what you have to document!). As a designer of a class or an entire hierarchy of classes, therefore, it's a good idea to define what the external appearance of a class is going to be, which variables and methods will be accessible for other users of that class, and which ones are for internal use only. This is called *encapsulation* and is an important feature of object-oriented design.

NEW TERM   *Encapsulation* is the process of hiding the internal parts of an object's implementation and allowing access to that object only through a defined interface.

You may note that up to this point we haven't done very much of this in any of the examples; in fact, just about every variable and method we've created has been fairly promiscuous and had no access control whatsoever. The reason I approached the problem in this way is that it makes for simpler examples. As you become a more sophisticated programmer and create Java programs with lots of interrelated classes, you'll find that adding features such as encapsulation and protecting access to the internal workings of your classes makes for better-designed programs overall.

15

The Four Ps of Protection

The Java language provides four levels of protection for methods and instance variables: `public`, `private`, `protected`, and `package` (actually, the latter isn't an explicit form of Java protection, but I've included it here because it's nicely alliterative). Before applying protection levels to your own code, you should know what each form means and understand the fundamental relationships that a method or variable within a class can have to the other classes in the system.

NOTE You can also protect entire classes using these modifiers. But class protection applies better once you know what packages are, so we'll postpone talking about that until tomorrow.

Package Protection

The first form of protection we'll talk about is the one you've been unconsciously using all this time: what's called *package protection*. In C, there's the notion of hiding a name so that only the functions within a given source file can see it. Java doesn't have this kind of control; names will be happily found in other source files as long as Java knows where to find them. Instead of file-level protection, Java has the concept of packages, which, as you learned on Day 2, "Object-Oriented Programming and Java," and will learn a whole lot more about tomorrow, are a group of classes related by purpose or function.

Methods and variables with package protection are visible to all other classes in the same package, but not outside that package. This is the kind of protection you've been using up to this point, and it's not much protection at all. Much of the time you'll want to be more explicit when you define the protection for that class's methods and variables.

NEW TERM *Package protection*, the default level of protection, means that your methods and variables are accessible to all the other classes in the same package.

Package protection isn't an explicit modifier you can add to your method or variable definitions; instead, it's the default protection you get when you don't add any protection modifiers to those definitions.

NOTE You may not think you've been using packages at all up to this point, but actually, you have. In Java, if you don't explicitly put a class into a package, it'll be included in a default package that also includes all the other classes that aren't in a specific package. While not defining a class to be in a package works for simple examples, it's better if you just create packages instead.

Private

From the default protection you get with package protection, you can either become more restrictive or more loose in how you control the visibility and access to your methods and variables. The most restrictive form of protection is private, which limits the visibility of methods and instance variables to the class in which they're defined. A private instance variable, for example, can be used by methods inside the same class, but cannot be seen or used by any other class or object. Private methods, analogously, can be called by other methods inside that same class, but not by any other classes. In addition, neither private variables nor private methods are inherited by subclasses.

NEW TERM   *Private protection* means that your methods and variables are accessible only to other methods in the same class.

To create a private method or instance variable, add the private modifier to its definition:

```
class  Writer {
    private boolean writersBlock = true;
    private String mood;
    private int income = 0;

    private void getIdea(Inspiration in) {
        . . .
    }

    Book createBook(int numDays, long numPages) {
        ...
    }
}
```

In this code example, the internal data to the class Writer (the variables writersBlock, mood, and income and the method getIdea()) is all private. The only method accessible from outside the Writer class is the createBook() method. createBook() is the only thing other objects (editor objects, perhaps?) can ask the Writer object to do; the other bits of data are implementation details that may affect how the book is written, but don't otherwise need to be visible or accessible from other sources.

The rule of thumb for private protection is that any data or behavior internal to the class that other classes or subclasses should not be touching should be private. Judicious use of private variables and methods is how you limit the functionality of a class to only those features you

15

want visible outside that class—as with the example of the PC components. Remember that an object's primary job is to encapsulate its data—to hide it from the world's sight and limit its manipulation. Encapsulation separates design from implementation, minimizes the amount of information one class needs to know about another to get its job done, and reduces the extent of the code changes you need to make if your internal implementation changes. Also, by separating the public interface from the private implementation, your class's interface becomes more abstract—that is, more general purpose and more easily used for other purposes. Subclasses of your class can override the more abstract behavior of your public interface with their own private implementations.

In addition to picking and choosing which methods you'll want to keep private and which will be accessible to others, a general rule of thumb is that all the instance variables in a class should be private, and you should create special nonprivate methods to get or change those variables. You'll learn more about this rule and why it's important a little later, in the section "Instance Variable Protection and Accessor Methods."

Public

The diametric opposite of private protection, and the least restrictive form of protection, is `public`. A method or variable that is declared with the `public` modifier is accessible to the class in which it's defined, all the subclasses of that class, all the classes in the package, and any other classes outside that package, anywhere in the entire universe of Java classes.

 Public protection means that your methods and variables are accessible to other methods anywhere inside or outside the current class or package.

Indicating that a method or variable is `public` isn't necessarily a bad thing. Just as hiding the data that is internal to your class using `private` helps encapsulate an object, using public methods defines precisely what the interface to instances of your class is. If you expect your classes to be reused by other programmers in other programs, the methods that they'll be using to use your class should be public.

In many ways, public protection is very similar to the default package protection. Both allow methods and variables to be accessed by other classes in the same package. The difference occurs when you create packages of classes. Variables and methods with package protection can be used in classes that exist in the same package. But if someone imports your class into his own program from outside your package, those methods and variables will not be accessible unless they have been declared public. Once again, you'll learn more about packages tomorrow.

Public declarations work just like private ones; simply substitute the word `public` for `private`.

Protected

The final form of protection available in Java concerns the relationship between a class and its present and future subclasses declared inside or outside a package. These subclasses are much closer to a particular class than to any other "outside" classes for the following reasons:

- ☐ Subclasses usually "know" more about the internal implementation of a superclass.
- ☐ Subclasses are often written by you or by someone to whom you've given your source code.
- ☐ Subclasses frequently need to modify or enhance the representation of the data within a parent class.

To support a special level of visibility reserved for subclasses somewhat less restrictive than private, Java has an intermediate level of access between package and private called, appropriately, *protected*. Protected methods and variables are accessible to any class inside the package, as they would be if they were package protected, but those methods and variables are *also* available to any subclasses of your class that have been defined outside your package.

 NEW TERM *Protected protection* means that your methods and variables are accessible to all classes inside the package, but only to subclasses outside the package.

 TECHNICAL NOTE
> In C++, the `protected` modifier means that only subclasses can access a method or variable, period. Java's meaning of protected is slightly different, also allowing any class inside the package to access those methods and variables.

Why would you need to do this? You may have methods in your class that are specific to its internal implementation—that is, not intended to be used by the general public—but that would be useful to subclasses for their own internal implementations. In this case, the developer of the subclass—be it you or someone else—can be trusted to be able to handle calling or overriding that method.

For example, let's say you had a class called `AudioPlayer`, which plays a digital audio file. `AudioPlayer` has a method called `openSpeaker()`, which is an internal method that interacts with the hardware to prepare the speaker for playing. `openSpeaker()` isn't important to anyone outside the `AudioPlayer` class, so at first glance you might want to make it private. A snippet of `AudioPlayer` might look something like this:

```
class AudioPlayer {

    private boolean openSpeaker(Speaker sp_ {
        // implementation details
    }
}
```

This works fine if AudioPlayer isn't going to be subclassed. But what if you were going to create a class called StereoAudioPlayer that is a subclass of AudioPlayer? This class would want access to the openSpeaker() method so that it can override it and provide stereo-specific speaker initialization. You still don't want the method generally available to random objects (and so it shouldn't be public), but you want the subclass to have access to it—so protected is just the solution.

TECHNICAL NOTE

In versions of Java and the JDK up to 1.0.1, you could use private and protected together to create yet another form of protection that would restrict access to methods or variables solely to subclasses of a given class. As of 1.0.2, this capability has been removed from the language.

A Summary of Protection Forms

The differences between the various protection types can become very confusing, particularly in the case of protected methods and variables. Table 15.1, which summarizes exactly what is allowed where, will help clarify the differences from the least restrictive (public) to the most restrictive (private) forms of protection.

Table 15.1. Different protection schemes.

Visibility	public	protected	package	private
From the same class	yes	yes	yes	yes
From any class in the same package	yes	yes	yes	no
From any class outside the package	yes	no	no	no
From a subclass in the same package	yes	yes	yes	no
From a subclass outside the same package	yes	yes	no	no

Method Protection and Inheritance

Setting up protections in new classes with new methods is easy; you make your decisions based on your design and apply the right modifiers. When you create subclasses and override other methods, however, you have to take into account the protection of the original method.

The general rule in Java is that you cannot override a method and make the new method more private than the original method (you can, however, make it more public). More specifically, the following rules for inherited methods are enforced by Java:

- Methods declared `public` in a superclass must also be `public` in all subclasses (this, by the way, is the reason most of the applet methods are `public`).

- Methods declared `protected` in a superclass must either be `protected` or `public` in subclasses; they cannot be `private`.

- Methods declared `private` are not inherited and therefore this rule doesn't apply.

- Methods declared without protection at all (the implicit package protection) can be declared more `private` in subclasses.

Instance Variable Protection and Accessor Methods

A good rule of thumb in object-oriented programming is that unless an instance variable is constant it should almost certainly be `private`. But, I hear you say, if instance variables are private, how can they be changed from outside the class? They can't. That's precisely the point. Instead, if you create special methods that indirectly read or change the value of that instance variable, you can much better control the interface of your classes and how those classes behave. You'll learn about how to do this later in this section.

Why Nonprivate Instance Variables Are a Bad Idea

In most cases, having someone else accessing or changing instance variables inside your object isn't a good idea. Take, for example, a class called circle, whose partial definition looks like this:

```
class Circle {
    int x, y, radius;

    Circle(int x, int y, int radius) {
        ...
    }

    void draw() {
        ...
    }
}
```

The `Circle` class has three instance variables: for the x and y position of the center point, and of the radius. A constructor builds the circle from those three values, and the `draw()` method draws the circle on the screen. So far, so good, right?

So let's say you have a `Circle` object created and drawn on the screen. Then some other object comes along and changes the value of `radius`. Now what? Your circle doesn't know that the radius has changed. It doesn't know to redraw itself to take advantage of the new size of the circle. Changing the value of an instance variable doesn't in itself trigger any methods. You have to rely on the same random object that changed the radius to also call the draw() method. And that overly complicates the interface of your class, making it more prone to errors.

Another example of why it's better not to make instance variables publicly accessible is that it's not possible to prevent a nonconstant instance variable from being changed. In other words, you could create a variable that you'd intended to be read-only, and perhaps your program was well mannered and didn't go about changing that variable randomly—but because the variable is there and available someone else may very well change it without understanding your methodology.

Why Accessor Methods Are a Better Idea

If all your instance variables are private, how do you give access to them to the outside world? The answer is to write special methods to read and change that variable (one for reading the value of the variable, one for changing it) rather than allowing it to be read and changed directly. These methods are sometimes called accessor methods, mutator methods (for changing the variable) or simply getters and setters.

 Accessor methods are special methods you implement to indirectly modify otherwise private instance variables.

Having a method to change a given instance variable means you can control both the value that variable is set to (to make sure it's within the boundaries you expect), as well as perform any other operations that may need to be done if that variable changes, for example, to redraw the circle.

Having two methods for reading and changing the variable also allows you to set up different protections for each. The method to read the value, for example, could be public, whereas the method to change the value can be private or protected, effectively creating a variable that's read-only except in a few cases (which is different from constant, which is read-only in all cases).

Using methods to access an instance variable is one of the most frequently used idioms in object-oriented programs. Applying it liberally throughout all your classes repays you numerous times with more robust and reusable programs.

Creating Accessor Methods

Creating accessor methods for your instance variables simply involves creating two extra methods for each variable. There's nothing special about accessor methods; they're just like any other method. So, for example, here's a modified Circle class that has three private instance variables: x, y, and radius. The public getRadius() method is used to retrieve the value of the radius variable, and the setRadius() method is used to set it (and update other parts of the class that need to be updated at the same time):

```
class Circle {
   private int x, y radius;

   public int getRadius() {
     return radius;
   }

   public int setRadius(int value) {
       radius = value;
       draw();
       doOtherStuff();
       return radius;
   }

   ....
}
```

In this modified example of the Circle class the accessor methods for the instance variable radius have the words set and get appended with the name of the variable. This is a naming convention popular among many programmers for accessor methods, so you always know which methods do what and to which variable. To access or change the value of the instance variable, therefore, you'd just call the methods setRadius() and getRadius(), respectively:

```
theCircle.getRadius(); //get the value
theCircle.setRadius(4); //set the value (and redraw, etc)
```

Another convention for naming accessor methods is to use the same name for the methods as for the variable itself. In Java it is legal for instance variables and methods to have the same name; Java knows from how they are used to perform the right operation. While this does make accessor methods shorter to type (no extra "set" or "get" to type at the beginning of each variable), there are two problems with using this convention:

☐ The fact that methods and variables can have the same names is a vague point in the Java specification. If someday this becomes more clarified and they cannot have the same names, you will have to change your code to fix the problem.

☐ I find that using the same name for instance variables and methods makes my code more difficult to read and understand than using a more explicit name.

Which convention you use is a question of personal taste. The most important thing is to choose a convention and stick with it throughout all your classes so that your interfaces are consistent and understandable.

Using Accessor Methods

The idea behind declaring instance variables private and creating accessor methods is so that external users of your class will be forced to use the methods you choose to modify your class's data. But the benefit of accessor methods isn't just for use by objects external to yours; they're also there for *you*. Just because you have access to the actual instance variable inside your own class doesn't mean you can avoid using accessor methods.

Consider that one of the good reasons to make instance variables private is to hide implementation details from outside your object. Protecting a variable with accessor methods means that other objects don't need to know about anything other than the accessor methods—you can happily change the internal implementation of your class without wreaking havoc on everyone who's used your class. The same is true of your code inside that class; by keeping variables separate from accessors, if you must change something about a given instance variable all you have to change are the accessor methods and not every single reference to the variable itself. In terms of code maintenance and reuse, what's good for the goose (external users of your class) is generally also good for the gander (you, as a user of your own class).

Class Variables and Methods

You learned about class variables and methods early last week, so I won't repeat a long description of them here. Because they use modifiers, however, they deserve a cursory mention.

To create a class variable or method, simply include the word `static` in front of the method name. The `static` modifier typically comes after any protection modifiers, like this:

```
public class  Circle {
    public static float  pi = 3.14159265F;

    public float  area(float r) {
        return  pi * r * r;
    }
}
```

NOTE

> The word `static` comes from C and C++. While `static` has a specific meaning for where a method or variable is stored in a program's runtime memory in those languages, `static` simply means that it's stored in the class in Java. Whenever you see the word `static`, remember to mentally substitute the word *class*.

Both class variables and methods can be accessed using standard dot notation with either the class name or an object on the left side of the dot. However, the convention is to always use the name of the class, to clarify that a class variable is being used, and to help the reader to know instantly that the variable is global to all instances. Here are a few examples:

```
float circumference = 2 * Circle.pi * getRadius();

float randomNumer = Math.random();
```

TIP   Class variables, for the same reasons as instance variables, can also benefit from being declared `private` and having accessor methods get or set their values.

Listing 15.1 shows a class called `CountInstances` that uses class and instance variables to keep track of how many instances of that class have been created.

Listing 15.1. The `CountInstances` class, which uses class and

TYPE   **instance variables.**

```
 1: public class  CountInstances {
 2:     private static int    numInstances = 0;
 3:
 4:     protected static int getNumInstances() {
 5:          return numInstances;
 6:     }
 7:
 8:     private static void  addInstance() {
 9:          numInstances++;
10:     }
11:
12:     CountInstances() {
13:          CountInstances.addInstance();
14:     }
15:
16:     public static void  main(String args[]) {
17:          System.out.println("Starting with " +
18:            CountInstances.getNumInstances() + " instances");
19:          for (int  i = 0;  i < 10;  ++i)
20:              new CountInstances();
21:        System.out.println("Created " +
22:            CountInstances.getNumInstances() + " instances");
23:     }
24:}
```

OUTPUT
```
Started with 0 instances
Creates 10 instances
```

ANALYSIS   This example has a number of features, so let's go through it line by line. In line 2 we declare a `private` class variable to hold the number of instances (called `numInstances`). This is a class variable (declared `static`) because the number of instances is relevant to the class as a whole, not to any one instance. And it's `private` so that it follows the same rules as instance variables accessor methods.

Note the initialization of `numInstances` to `0` in that same line. Just as an instance variable is initialized when its instance is created, a class variable is initialized when its class is created.

15

This class initialization happens essentially before anything else can happen to that class, or its instances, so the class in the example will work as planned.

In lines 4 through 6, we created a get method for that private instance variable to get its value (getNumInstances()). This method is also declared as a class method, as it applies directly to the class variable. The getNumInstances() method is declared protected, as opposed to public, because only this class and perhaps subclasses will be interested in that value; other random classes are therefore restricted from seeing it.

Note that there's no accessor method to set the value. The reason is that the value of the variable should be incremented only when a new instance is created; it should not be set to any random value. Instead of creating an accessor method, therefore, we'll create a special private method called addInstance() in lines 8 through 10 that increments the value of numInstances by 1.

Lines 12 through 14 have the constructor method for this class. Remember, constructors are called when a new object is created, which makes this the most logical place to call addInstance() and to increment the variable.

And finally, the main() method indicates that we can run this as a Java application and test all the other methods. In the main() method we create 10 instances of the CountInstances class, reporting after we're done the value of the numInstances class variable (which, predictably, prints 10).

Finalizing Classes, Methods, and Variables

Although it's not the final modifier I'll discuss today, the final modifier is used to finalize classes, methods, and variables. Finalizing a thing effectively "freezes" the implementation or value of that thing. More specifically, here's how final works with classes, variables, and methods:

☐ When the final modifier is applied to a class, it means that the class cannot be subclassed.

☐ When applied to a variable, final means that the variable is constant.

☐ When applied to a method, final means that the method cannot be overridden by subclasses.

NEW TERM *Finalization* (using the final modifier) freezes the implementation of a class, method, or variable.

Finalizing Classes

To finalize a class, add the `final` modifier to its definition. `final` typically goes after any protection modifiers such as `private` or `public`:

```
public final class  AFinalClass {
    . . .
}
```

You declare a class `final` for only two reasons:

- ☐ To prevent others from subclassing your class. If your class has all the capabilities it needs, and no one else should be able to extend its capabilities, then that class should be `final`.
- ☐ For better efficiency. With `final` classes you can rely on instances of only that one class (and no subclasses) being around in the system, and optimize for those instances.

The Java class library uses `final` classes extensively. Classes that have been finalized to prevent their being subclassed include `java.lang.System`, `java.net.InetAddress`, and `java.net.Socket` (although, as you learned on Day 14, "Windows, Networking, and Other Tidbits," the latter will no longer be `final` as of Java 1.1). A good example of a class being declared `final` for efficiency reasons is `java.lang.String`. Strings are so common in Java, and so central to it that Java handles them specially.

In most cases, it will be a rare event for you to create a `final` class yourself since extendible classes are so much more useful than finalized classes, and the efficiency gains are minimal. You will, however, most likely have plenty of opportunity to be upset at certain system classes being `final` (making it more difficult to extend them).

Finalizing Variables

A finalized variable means its value cannot be changed. This is effectively a constant, which you learned about early in Week 1. To declare constants in Java, use `final` variables with initial values:

```
public class  AnotherFinalClass {
    public static final int aConstantInt    = 123;
    public final String aConstantString = "Hello world!";
}
```

Local variables (those inside blocks of code surrounded by braces, for example, in `while` or `for` loops) can't be declared `final`.

Finalizing Methods

Finalized methods are methods that cannot be overridden; that is, their implementations are frozen and cannot be redefined in subclasses.

```
public class  ClassWithFinalMethod {

    public final void  noOneGetsToDoThisButMe() {
        . . .
    }
}
```

The only reason to declare a method `final` is efficiency. Normally, method signatures and implementations are matched up when your Java program runs, not when it's compiled. Remember that when you call a method, Java dynamically checks the current class and each superclass in turn for that method's definition. Although this makes methods very flexible to define and use, it's not very fast.

If you declare a method `final`, however, the compiler can then "in-line" it (stick its definition) right in the middle of methods that call it because it "knows" that no one else can ever subclass and override the method to change its meaning. Although you might not use `final` right away when writing a class, as you tune the system later, you may discover that a few methods have to be `final` to make your class fast enough. Almost all your methods will be fine, however, just as they are.

If you use accessor methods a lot (as recommended), changing your accessor methods to be `final` can be a quick way of speeding up your class. Because subclasses will rarely want to change the definitions of those accessor methods, there's little reason those methods should not be final.

The Java class library declares a lot of commonly used methods `final` so that you'll benefit from the speed-up. In the case of classes that are already `final`, this makes perfect sense and is a wise choice. The few `final` methods declared in non-`final` classes will annoy you—your subclasses can no longer override them. When efficiency becomes less of an issue for the Java environment, many of these `final` methods can be "unfrozen" again, restoring this lost flexibility to the system.

NOTE

Private methods are effectively `final`, as are all methods declared in a `final` class. Marking these latter methods `final` (as the Java library sometimes does) is legal, but redundant; the compiler already treats them as `final`.

It's possible to use `final` methods for some of the same security reasons you use `final` classes, but it's a much rarer event.

Abstract Classes and Methods

Whenever you arrange classes into an inheritance hierarchy, the presumption is that "higher" classes are more abstract and general, whereas "lower" subclasses are more concrete and specific. Often, as you design hierarchies of classes, you factor out common design and implementation into a shared superclass. That superclass won't have any instances; its sole reason for existing is to act as a common, shared repository for information that its subclasses use. These kinds of classes are called *abstract classes,* and you declare them using the `abstract` modifier. For example, the following skeleton class definition for the `Fruit` class declared that class to be both `public` and `abstract`:

```
public abstract class Fruit {
...
}
```

Abstract classes can never be instantiated (you'll get a compiler error if you try), but they can contain anything a normal class can contain, including class and instance variables and methods with any kind of protection or finalization modifiers. In addition, abstract classes can also contain abstract methods. An abstract method is a method signature with no implementation; subclasses of the abstract class are expected to provide the implementation for that method. Abstract methods, in this way, provide the same basic concept as abstract classes; they're a way of factoring common behavior into superclasses and then providing specific concrete uses of those behaviors in subclasses.

 Abstract classes are classes whose sole purpose is to provide common information for subclasses. Abstract classes can have no instances.

 Abstract methods are methods with signatures, but no implementation. Subclasses of the class which contains that abstract method must provide its actual implementation.

Like abstract classes, abstract methods give you the ability to factor common information into a general superclass and then reuse that class in different ways.

The opposite of abstract is concrete: Concrete classes are classes that can be instantiated; concrete methods are those that have actual implementations.

Abstract methods are declared with the `abstract` modifier, which usually goes after the protection modifiers but before either `static` or `final`. In addition, they have no body. Abstract methods can only exist inside abstract classes; even if you have a class full of concrete methods, with only one abstract method, the whole class must be abstract. This is because abstract methods cannot be called; they have no implementation, so calling them would produce an error. Rather than worry about special-case abstract methods inside otherwise concrete instances, it's easier just to insist that abstract methods be contained only inside abstract classes.

15

Listing 15.2 shows two simple classes. One, appropriately called MyFirstAbstractClass, has an instance variable and two methods. One of those methods, subclassesImplementMe(), is abstract. The other, doSomething(), is concrete and has a normal definition.

The second class is AConcreteSubclass, which is a subclass of MyFirstAbstractClass. It provides the implementation of subclassesImplementMe(), and inherits the remaining behavior from MyFirstAbstractClass.

NOTE

> Because both these classes are public, they must be defined in separate source files.

TYPE **Listing 15.2. Two classes: one abstract, one concrete.**

```
 1:ipublic abstract class  MyFirstAbstractClass {
 2:    int  anInstanceVariable;
 3:p
 4:      public abstract int  subclassesImplementMe(); // note no definition
 5:
 6:      public void  doSomething() {
 7:          . . .    // a normal method
 8:      }
 9:}
10:
11:public class  AConcreteSubClass extends MyFirstAbstractClass {
12:    public int  subclassesImplementMe() {
13:        . . .    // we *must* implement this method here
14:    }
15:}
```

Here are some attempted uses of these classes:

```
Object  a = new MyFirstAbstractClass();    // illegal, is abstract

Object  c = new AConcreteSubClass();       // OK, a concrete subclass
```

Using an abstract class with nothing but abstract methods—that is, one that provides nothing but a template for behavior—is better accomplished in Java by using an *interface* (discussed tomorrow). Whenever a design calls for an abstraction that includes instance state and/or a partial implementation, however, an abstract class is your only choice.

Summary

Today you have learned how variables and methods can control their visibility and access by other classes via the four Ps of protection: `public`, `package`, `protected`, and `private`. You have also learned that although instance variables are most often declared `private`, declaring accessor methods allows you to control the reading and writing of them separately. Protection levels allow you, for example, to separate cleanly your public abstractions from their concrete representations.

You have also learned how to create class variables and methods, which are associated with the class itself, and how to declare `final` variables, methods, and classes to represent constants and fast or secure methods and classes.

Finally, you have discovered how to declare and use `abstract` classes, which cannot be instantiated, and `abstract` methods, which have no implementation and must be overridden in subclasses. Together, they provide a template for subclasses to fill in and act as a variant of the powerful interfaces of Java that you'll study tomorrow.

Q&A

Q Why are there so many different levels of protection in Java?

A Each level of protection, or visibility, provides a different view of your class to the outside world. One view is tailored for everyone, one for classes in your own package, another for your class and its subclasses only, one combining these last two and the final one for just within your class. Each is a logically well-defined and useful separation that Java supports directly in the language (as opposed to, for example, accessor methods, which are a convention you must follow).

Q Won't using accessor methods everywhere slow down my Java code?

A Not always. As Java compilers improve and can create more optimizations, they'll be able to make them fast automatically, but if you're concerned about speed, you can always declare accessor methods to be `final`, and they'll be just as fast as direct instance variable accesses.

Q Are class (`static`) methods inherited just like instance methods?

A No. `static` (class) methods are now `final` by default. How, then, can you ever declare a non-`final` class method? The answer is that you can't! Inheritance of class methods is not allowed, breaking the symmetry with instance methods.

Q Based on what I've learned, it seems like `private abstract` methods and `final` `abstract` methods or classes don't make sense. Are they legal?

15

A Nope, they're compile-time errors, as you have guessed. To be useful, `abstract` methods must be overridden, and `abstract` classes must be subclassed, but neither of those two operations would be legal if they were also `private` or `final`.

Q **What about the `transient` modifier? I saw that mentioned in the Java Language Specification.**

A The `transient` modifier is reserved by the designers of Java for use in future versions of the Java language (beyond 1.0.2 and 1.1); it will be used to create persistent object store systems (the ability to save a set of classes and objects and restore their state later on). It, like other modifiers such as `byvalue`, `future`, and `generic`, are not currently used but are reserved words in the language.

Q **I tried creating a private variable inside a method definition. It didn't work. What did I do wrong?**

A Nothing. All the modifiers in this chapter, when you can use them with variables, only apply to class and instance variables. Local variables—those that appear inside the body of a method or loop—cannot use any of these modifiers.

Day 16

Packages and Interfaces

by Laura Lemay and Charles L. Perkins

Packages and interfaces are two capabilities that allow you greater control and flexibility in designing sets of interrelated classes. Packages allow you to combine groups of classes and control which of those classes are available to the outside world; interfaces provide a way of grouping abstract method definitions and sharing them among classes that may not necessarily acquire those methods through inheritance.

Today you'll learn how to design with, use, and create your own packages and interfaces. Specific topics you'll learn about today include

☐ A discussion of designing classes versus coding classes and how to approach each

☐ What packages are and why they are useful for class design

☐ Using other people's packages in your own classes
☐ Creating your own packages
☐ What interfaces buy you in terms of code reuse and design
☐ Designing and working with interfaces

Programming in the Large and Programming in the Small

When you examine a new language feature, you should ask yourself two questions:

☐ How can I use it to better organize the methods and classes of my Java program?
☐ How can I use it while writing the actual Java code?

The first is often called programming in the large, and the second, programming in the small. Bill Joy, a founder of Sun Microsystems, likes to say that Java feels like C when programming in the small and like Smalltalk when programming in the large. What he means by that is that Java is familiar and powerful like any C-like language while you're coding individual lines, but has the extensibility and expressive power of a pure object-oriented language like Smalltalk while you're designing.

The separation of "designing" from "coding" was one of the most fundamental advances in programming in the past few decades, and object-oriented languages such as Java implement a strong form of this separation. The first part of this separation has already been described on previous days: When you develop a Java program, first you design the classes and decide on the relationships between these classes, and then you implement the Java code needed for each of the methods in your design. If you are careful enough with both these processes, you can change your mind about aspects of the design without affecting anything but small, local pieces of your Java code, and you can change the implementation of any method without affecting the rest of the design.

As you begin to explore more advanced Java programming, however, you'll find that this simple model becomes too limiting. Today you'll explore these limitations, for programming in the large and in the small, to motivate the need for packages and interfaces. Let's start with packages.

What Are Packages?

Packages, as mentioned a number of times in this book so far, are a way of organizing groups of classes. A package contains any number of classes that are related in purpose, in scope, or by inheritance.

Why bother with packages? If your programs are small and use a limited number of classes, you may find that you don't need to explore packages at all. But the more Java programming you do, the more classes you'll find you have. And although those classes may be individually well designed, reusable, encapsulated, and with specific interfaces to other classes, you may find the need for a bigger organizational entity that allows you to group your packages.

Packages are useful for several broad reasons:

- ☐ They allow you to organize your classes into units. Just as you have folders or directories on your hard disk to organize your files and applications, packages allow you to organize your classes into groups so that you only use what you need for each program.

- ☐ They reduce problems with conflicts in names. As the number of Java classes grows, so does the likelihood that you'll use the same class name as someone else, opening up the possibility of naming clashes and errors if you try to integrate groups of classes into a single program. Packages allow you to "hide" classes so that conflicts can be avoided.

- ☐ They allow you to protect classes, variables, and methods in larger ways than on a class-by-class basis, as you learned yesterday. You'll learn more about protections with packages later today.

- ☐ They can be used to identify your classes. For example, if you implemented a set of classes to perform some purpose, you could name a package of those classes with a unique identifier that identifies you or your organization.

Although a package is most typically a collection of classes, packages can also contain other packages, forming yet another level of organization somewhat analogous to the inheritance hierarchy. Each "level" usually represents a smaller, more specific grouping of classes. The Java class library itself is organized along these lines. The top level is called java; the next level includes names such as io, net, util, and awt. The last of these has an even lower level, which includes the package image.

NOTE   By convention, the first level of the hierarchy specifies the (globally unique) name to identify the author or owner of those packages. For example, Sun Microsystems's classes, which are not part of the standard Java environment, all begin with the prefix sun. Classes that Netscape includes with its implementation are contained in the netscape package. The standard package, java, is an exception to this rule because it is so fundamental and because it might someday be implemented by multiple companies.

> I'll tell you more about package-naming conventions later when you create your own packages.

Using Packages

You've been using packages all along in this book. Every time you use the `import` command, and every time you refer to a class by its full package name (`java.awt.Color`, for example), you've used packages. Let's go over the specifics of how to use classes from other packages in your own programs to make sure you've got it and to go into greater depth than we have in previous lessons.

To use a class contained in a package, you can use one of three mechanisms:

☐ If the class you want to use is in the package `java.lang` (for example, `System` or `Date`), you can simply use the class name to refer to that class. The `java.lang` classes are automatically available to you in all your programs.

☐ If the class you want to use is in some other package, you can refer to that class by its full name, including any package names (for example, `java.awt.Font`).

☐ For classes that you use frequently from other packages, you can import individual classes or a whole package of classes. After a class or a package has been imported, you can refer to that class by its class name.

What about your own classes in your own programs that don't belong to any package? The rule is that if you don't specifically define your classes to belong to a package, they're put into an unnamed default package. You can refer to those classes simply by class name from anywhere in your code.

Full Package and Class Names

To refer to a class in some other package, you can use its full name: the class name preceded by any package names. You do not have to import the class or the package to use it this way:

```
java.awt.Font f = new java.awt.Font()
```

For classes that you use only once or twice in your program, using the full name makes the most sense. If, however, you use that class multiple times, or if the package name is really long with lots of subpackages, you'll want to import that class instead to save yourself some typing.

16

The `import` Command

To import classes from a package, use the `import` command, as you've used throughout the examples in this book. You can either import an individual class, like this:

```
import java.util.Vector;
```

or you can import an entire package of classes, using an asterisk (*) to replace the individual class names:

```
import java.awt.*
```

NOTE

Actually, to be technically correct, this command doesn't import all the classes in a package—it only imports the classes that have been declared `public`, and even then only imports those classes that the code itself refers to. You'll learn more on this in the section titled "Packages and Class Protection."

Note that the asterisk (*) in this example is not like the one you might use at a command prompt to specify the contents of a directory or to indicate multiple files. For example, if you ask to list the contents of the directory `classes/java/awt/*`, that list includes all the `.class` files and subdirectories, such as `image` and `peer`. Writing `import java.awt.*` imports all the public classes in that package, but does *not* import subpackages such as `image` and `peer`. To import all the classes in a complex package hierarchy, you must explicitly import each level of the hierarchy by hand. Also, you cannot indicate partial class names (for example, `L*` to import all the classes that begin with L). It's all the classes in a package or a single class.

The `import` statements in your class definition go at the top of the file, before any class definitions (but after the package definition, as you'll see in the next section).

So should you take the time to import classes individually or just import them as a group? It depends on how specific you want to be. Importing a group of classes does not slow down your program or make it any larger; only the classes you actually use in your code are loaded as they are needed. But importing a package does make it a little more confusing for readers of your code to figure out where your classes are coming from. Using individual `imports` or importing packages is mostly a question of your own coding style.

TECHNICAL NOTE

Java's `import` command is not at all similar to the `#include` command in C-like languages, although they accomplish similar functions. The C preprocessor takes the contents of all the included files (and, in turn, the files they include, and so on) and stuffs them in at the spot where the `#include` was. The result is an enormous hunk of code that has far more lines than the original program did. Java's `import` behaves more like a linker; it tells the Java compiler and interpreter where (in which files) to find classes, variables, method names, and method definitions. It doesn't bring anything into the current Java program.

Name Conflicts

After you have imported a class or a package of classes, you can usually refer to a class name simply by its name, without the package identifier. I say "usually" because there's one case where you may have to be more explicit: when there are multiple classes with the same name from different packages.

Here's an example. Let's say you import the classes from two packages from two different programmers (Joe and Eleanor):

```
import joesclasses.*;
import eleanorsclasses.*;
```

Inside Joe's package is a class called `Name`. Unfortunately, inside Eleanor's package there is also a class called `Name` that has an entirely different meaning and implementation. You would wonder whose version of `Name` would end up getting used if you referred to the `Name` class in your own program like this:

```
Name myName = new Name("Susan");
```

The answer is neither; the Java compiler will complain about a naming conflict and refuse to compile your program. In this case, despite the fact that you imported both classes, you still have to refer to the appropriate `Name` class by full package name:

```
joesclasses.Name myName = new joesclasses.Name("Susan");
```

A Note About CLASSPATH and Where Classes Are Located

Before I go on to explain how to create your own packages of classes, I'd like to make a note about how Java finds packages and classes when it's compiling and running your classes.

For Java to be able to use a class, it has to be able to find it on the file system. Otherwise, you'll get an error that the class does not exist. Java uses two things to find classes: the package name itself and the directories listed in your CLASSPATH variable.

16

First, the package names. Package names map to directory names on the file system, so the class java.applet.Applet will actually be found in the applet directory, which in turn will be inside the java directory (java/applet/Applet.class, in other words).

Java looks for those directories, in turn, inside the directories listed in your CLASSPATH variable. If you remember back to Day 1, "An Introduction to Java Programming," when you installed the JDK, you had to set up a CLASSPATH variable to point to the various places where your Java classes live. CLASSPATH usually points to the java/lib directory in your JDK release, a class directory in your development environment if you have one, perhaps some browser-specific classes, and to the current directory. When Java looks for a class you've referenced in your source, it looks for the package and class name in each of those directories and returns an error if it can't find the class file. Most "cannot load class" errors result because of missed CLASSPATH variables.

NOTE

If you're using the Macintosh version of the JDK, you're probably wondering what I'm talking about. The Mac JDK doesn't use a CLASSPATH variable; it knows enough to be able to find the default classes and those contained in the current directory. However, if you do a lot of Java development, you may end up with classes and packages in other directories. The Java compiler contains a Preferences dialog box that lets you add directories to Java's search path.

Creating Your Own Packages

Creating your own packages is a difficult, complex process, involving many lines of code, long hours late at night with lots of coffee, and the ritual sacrifice of many goats. Just kidding. To create a package of classes, you have three basic steps to follow, which I'll explain in the following sections.

Pick a Package Name

The first step is to decide what the name of your package is going to be. The name you choose for your package depends on how you are going to be using those classes. Perhaps your package will be named after you, or perhaps after the part of the Java system you're working on (like graphics or hardware_interfaces). If you're intending your package to be distributed to the Net at large, or as part of a commercial product, you'll want to use a package name (or set of package names) that uniquely identifies you or your organization or both.

One convention for naming packages that has been recommended by Sun is to use your Internet domain name with the elements reversed. So, for example, if Sun were following its own recommendation, its packages would be referred to using the name com.sun.java rather than just java. If your Internet domain name is fooblitzky.eng.nonsense.edu, your package name might be edu.nonsense.eng.fooblitzky (and you might add another package name onto the end of that to refer to the product or to you, specifically).

The idea is to make sure your package name is unique. Although packages can hide conflicting class names, the protection stops there. There's no way to make sure your package won't conflict with someone else's package if you both use the same package name.

By convention, package names tend to begin with a lowercase letter to distinguish them from class names. Thus, for example, in the full name of the built-in String class, java.lang.String, it's easier to separate the package name from the class name visually. This convention helps reduce name conflicts.

Create the Directory Structure

Step two in creating packages is to create a directory structure on your disk that matches the package name. If your package has just one name (mypackage), you'll only have to create a directory for that one name. If the package name has several parts, however, you'll have to create directories within directories. For the package name edu.nonsense.eng.fooblitzky, you'll need to create an edu directory and then create a nonsense directory inside edu, an eng directory inside nonsense, and a fooblitzky directory inside eng. Your classes and source files can then go inside the fooblitzky directory.

Use package to Add Your Class to a Package

The final step to putting your class inside packages is to add the package command to your source files. The package command says "this class goes inside this package," and is used like this:

```
package myclasses;
package edu.nonsense.eng.fooblitzky;
package java.awt;
```

The single package command, if any, must be the first line of code in your source file, after any comments or blank lines and before any import commands.

As mentioned before, if your class doesn't have a package command in it, that class is contained in the default package and can be used by any other class. But once you start using packages, you should make sure all your classes belong to some package to reduce the chance of confusion about where your classes belong.

16

Packages and Class Protection

Yesterday you learned all about the four Ps of protection and how they apply (primarily) to methods and variables and their relationship to other classes. When referring to classes and their relationship to other classes in other packages, you only have two Ps to worry about: package and public.

By default, classes have package protection, which means that the class is available to all the other classes in the same package but is not visible or available outside that package—not even to subpackages. It cannot be imported or referred to by name; classes with package protection are hidden inside the package in which they are contained.

Package protection comes about when you define a class as you have throughout this book, like this:

```
class TheHiddenClass extends AnotherHiddenClass {
...
}
```

To allow a class to be visible and importable outside your package, you'll want to give it public protection by adding the `public` modifier to its definition:

```
public class TheVisibleClass {
...
}
```

Classes declared as `public` can be imported by other classes outside the package.

Note that when you use an `import` statement with an asterisk, you import only the public classes inside that package. Hidden classes remain hidden and can be used only by the other classes in that package.

Why would you want to hide a class inside a package? For the same reason you want to hide variables and methods inside a class: so you can have utility classes and behavior that are useful only to your implementation, or so you can limit the interface of your program to minimize the effect of larger changes. As you design your classes, you'll want to take the whole package into consideration and decide which classes will be declared `public` and which will be hidden.

Listing 16.1 shows two classes that illustrate this point. The first is a public class that implements a linked list; the second is a private node of that list.

TYPE **Listing 16.1. The public class** `LinkedList`.

```
1: package  collections;
2:
3: public class  LinkedList {
4:     private Node  root;
```

continues

Listing 16.1. continued

```
 5:
 6:     public  void  add(Object o) {
 7:         root = new Node(o, root);
 8:     }
 9:     . . .
10: }
11:
12: class  Node {    // not public
13:     private Object  contents;
14:     private Node    next;
15:
16:     Node(Object o, Node n) {
17:         contents = o;
18:         next     = n;
19:     }
20:     . . .
21: }
```

NOTE Notice here that I'm including two class definitions in one file. I mentioned this briefly on Day 13, "Creating User Interfaces with the AWT," and it bears mentioning here as well: You can include as many class definitions per file as you want, but only one of them can be declared `public`, and that filename must have the same name as the one public class. When Java compiles the file, it'll create separate `.class` files for each class definition inside the file. In reality, I find the one-to-one correspondence of class definition to file much more easily maintained because I don't have to go searching around for the definition of a class.

The public `LinkedList` class provides a set of useful public methods (such as `add()`) to any other classes that might want to use them. These other classes don't need to know about any support classes `LinkedList` needs to get its job done. `Node`, which is one of those support classes, is therefore declared without a `public` modifier and will not appear as part of the public interface to the `collections` package.

NOTE Just because `Node` isn't public doesn't mean `LinkedList` won't have access to it once it's been imported into some other class. Think of protections not as hiding classes entirely, but more as checking the permissions of a given class to use other classes, variables, and methods. When you import and use `LinkedList`, the `Node` class will also be loaded into the system, but only instances of `LinkedList` will have permission to use it.

One of the great powers of hidden classes is that even if you use them to introduce a great deal of complexity into the implementation of some public class, all the complexity is hidden when that class is imported or used. Thus, creating a good package consists of defining a small, clean set of public classes and methods for other classes to use, and then implementing them by using any number of hidden (package) support classes. You'll see another use for hidden classes later today.

What Are Interfaces?

Interfaces, like the abstract classes and methods you saw yesterday, provide templates of behavior that other classes are expected to implement. Interfaces, however, provide far more functionality to Java and to class and object design than do simple abstract classes and methods. The rest of this lesson explores interfaces: what they are, why they're crucial to getting the most out of the Java language for your own classes, and how to use and implement them.

The Problem of Single Inheritance

When you first begin to design object-oriented programs, the concept of the class hierarchy can seem almost miraculous. Within that single tree you can express a hierarchy of different types of objects, many simple to moderately complex relationships between objects and processes in the world, and any number of points along the axis from abstract/general to concrete/specific. The strict hierarchy of classes appears, at first glance, to be simple, elegant, and easy to use.

After some deeper thought or more complex design experience, however, you may discover that the pure simplicity of the class hierarchy is restrictive, particularly when you have some behavior that needs to be used by classes in different branches of the same tree.

Let's look at a few examples that will make the problems clearer. Way back on Day 2, "Object-Oriented Programming and Java," when you first learned about class hierarchies, we discussed the `Vehicle` hierarchy, as shown in Figure 16.1.

Figure 16.1.

The Vehicle *hierarchy.*

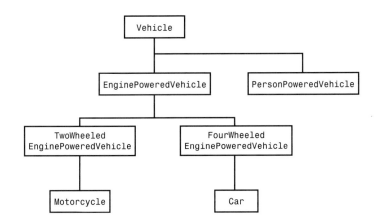

Now let's add to that hierarchy and create the classes BritishCar and BritishMotorcycle underneath Car and Motorcycle, respectively. The behavior that makes a car or motorcycle British (which might include methods for leakOil() or electricalSystemFailure()) is common to both these classes, but because they are in very different parts of the class hierarchy, you can't create a common superclass for both of them. And you can't put the British behavior further up in the hierarchy because that behavior isn't common to all motorcycles and cars. Other than physically copying the behavior between the two classes (which breaks the object-oriented programming [OOP] rules of code reuse and shared behavior), how can you create a hierarchy like this?

Let's look at an even thornier example. Say you have a biological hierarchy with Animal at the top, and the classes Mammal and Bird underneath. Things that define a mammal include bearing live young and having fur. Behavior or features of birds include having a beak and laying eggs. So far, so good, right? So how do you go about creating a class for the platypus, which has fur, has a beak, and lays eggs? You'd need to combine behavior from two classes to form the Platypus class. And, because classes can have only one immediate superclass in Java, this sort of problem simply cannot be solved elegantly.

Other OOP languages include the concept of *multiple inheritance*, which solves this problem. With multiple inheritance, a class can inherit from more than one superclass and get behavior and attributes from all its superclasses at once. Using multiple inheritance, you could simply factor the common behavior of BritishCar and BritishMotorcycle into a single class (BritishThing) and then create new classes that inherit from both their primary superclass *and* the British class.

The problem with multiple inheritance is that it makes a programming language far more complex to learn, to use, and to implement. Questions of method invocation and how the class hierarchy is organized become far more complicated with multiple inheritance, and more open to confusion and ambiguity. And because one of the goals for Java was that it be simple, multiple inheritance was rejected in favor of the simpler single inheritance.

So how do you solve the problem of needing common behavior that doesn't fit into the strict class hierarchy? Java, borrowing from Objective-C, has another hierarchy altogether separate from the main class hierarchy, a hierarchy of mixable behavior classes. Then, when you create a new class, that class has only one primary superclass, but it can pick and choose different common behaviors from the other hierarchy.

This other hierarchy is the *interface hierarchy*. A Java *interface* is a collection of abstract behavior that can be mixed into any class to add to that class behavior that is not supplied by its superclasses. Specifically, a Java interface contains nothing but abstract method definitions and constants—no instance variables and no method implementations.

Interfaces are implemented and used throughout the Java class library whenever a behavior is expected to be implemented by a number of disparate classes. The Java class hierarchy, for example, defines and uses the interfaces `java.lang.Runnable`, `java.util.Enumeration`, `java.util.Observable`, `java.awt.image.ImageConsumer`, and `java.awt.image.ImageProducer`. Some of these interfaces you've seen before; others you'll see later in this book. Still others may be useful to you in your own programs, so be sure to examine the API to see what's available to you.

Abstract Design and Concrete Implementation

Throughout this book you've gotten a taste of the difference between design and implementation in object-oriented programming, where the design of a thing is its abstract representation and its implementation is the concrete counterpart of the design. You saw this with methods, where a method's signature defines how it's used, but the method implementation can occur anywhere in the class hierarchy. You saw this with abstract classes, where the class's design provides a template for behavior, but that behavior isn't implemented until further down in the hierarchy.

This distinction between the design and the implementation of a class or a method is a crucial part of object-oriented programming theory. Thinking in terms of design when you organize your classes allows you to get the big picture without being bogged down in implementation details. And having the overall design already defined when you actually start implementing allows you to concentrate on those details solely for the class you're working on. This programming version of "think globally, act locally" provides a powerful way of thinking about how your classes and your programs and your overall designs are organized and how they interrelate.

An interface is made up of a set of method signatures with no implementations, making it the embodiment of pure design. By mixing an interface in with your class, you're encompassing that design into your implementation. That design can then be safely included anywhere in the class hierarchy because there are no class-specific details of how an interface behaves—nothing to override, nothing to keep track of, just the name and arguments for a method.

What about abstract classes? Don't abstract classes provide this same behavior? Yes and no. Abstract classes and the abstract methods inside them do provide a separation of design and implementation, allowing you to factor common behavior into an abstract superclass. But abstract classes can, and often do, contain some concrete data (such as instance variables), and you can have an abstract superclass with both abstract and regular methods, thereby confusing the distinction.

Even a pure abstract class with only abstract methods isn't as powerful as an interface. An abstract class is simply another class; it inherits from some other class and has its place in the hierarchy. Abstract classes cannot be shared across different parts of the class hierarchy the way interfaces can, nor can they be mixed into other classes that need their behavior. To attain the sort of flexibility of shared behavior across the class hierarchy, you need an interface.

You can think of the difference between the design and the implementation of any Java class as the difference between the interface hierarchy and the design hierarchy. The singly inherited class hierarchy contains the implementations where the relationships between classes and behavior are rigidly defined. The multiply inherited mixable interface hierarchy, however, contains the design and can be freely used anywhere it's needed in the implementation. This is a powerful way of thinking about the organization of your program, and although it takes a little getting used to, it's also a highly recommended one.

Interfaces and Classes

Classes and interfaces, despite their different definitions, have an awful lot in common. Interfaces, like classes, are declared in source files, one interface to a file. Like classes, they also are compiled using the Java compiler into .class files. And, in most cases, anywhere you can use a class (as a data type for a variable, as the result of a cast, and so on), you can also use an interface.

Almost everywhere that this book has a class name in any of its examples or discussions, you can substitute an interface name. Java programmers often say "class" when they actually mean "class or interface." Interfaces complement and extend the power of classes, and the two can be treated almost exactly the same. One of the few differences between them is that an interface cannot be instantiated: new can only create an instance of a class.

16

Implementing and Using Interfaces

Now that you've grasped what interfaces are and why they're powerful (the "programming in the large" part), let's move on to actual bits of code ("programming in the small"). There are two things you can do with interfaces: use them in your own classes and define your own. Let's start with the former.

The `implements` Keyword

To use an interface, you include the `implements` keyword as part of your class definition. You did this back on Day 11, "More Animation, Images, and Sound," when you learned about threads and included the `Runnable` interface in your applet definition:

```
// java.applet.Applet is the superclass
public class Neko extends java.applet.Applet
    implements Runnable {  // but it also has Runnable behavior
...
}
```

Because interfaces provide nothing but abstract method definitions, you then have to implement those methods in your own classes, using the same method signatures from the interface. Note that once you include an interface, you have to implement *all* the methods in that interface—you can't pick and choose the methods you need. By implementing an interface you're telling users of your class that you support *all* of that interface. (Note that this is another difference between interfaces and abstract classes—subclasses of the latter can pick which methods to implement or override and can ignore others.)

After your class implements an interface, subclasses of your class will inherit those new methods (and can override or overload them) just as if your superclass had actually defined them. If your class inherits from a superclass that implements a given interface, you don't have to include the `implements` keyword in your own class definition.

Let's examine one simple example—creating the new class `Orange`. Suppose you already have a good implementation of the class `Fruit` and an interface, `Fruitlike`, that represents what `Fruit`s are expected to be able to do. You want an orange to be a fruit, but you also want it to be a spherical object that can be tossed, rotated, and so on. Here's how to express it all (don't worry about the definitions of these interfaces for now; you'll learn more about them later today):

```
interface  Fruitlike {
    void  decay();
    void  squish();
    . . .
}
```

16

```
class  Fruit implements Fruitlike {
    private Color  myColor;
    private int    daysTilIRot;
    . . .
}

interface  Spherelike {
    void  toss();
    void  rotate();
    . . .
}

class  Orange extends Fruit implements Spherelike {
    . . .  // toss()ing may squish() me (unique to me)
}
```

Note that the class `Orange` doesn't have to say `implements Fruitlike` because, by extending `Fruit`, it already has! One of the nice things about this structure is that you can change your mind about what class `Orange` extends (if a really great `Sphere` class is suddenly implemented, for example), yet class `Orange` will still understand the same two interfaces:

```
class  Sphere implements Spherelike {   // extends Object
    private float  radius;
    . . .
}

class  Orange extends Sphere implements Fruitlike {
    . . .       // users of Orange never need know about the change!
}
```

Implementing Multiple Interfaces

Unlike the singly inherited class hierarchy, you can include as many interfaces as you need in your own classes, and your class will implement the combined behavior of all the included interfaces. To include multiple interfaces in a class, just separate their names with commas:

```
public class Neko extends java.applet.Applet
    implements Runnable, Eatable, Sortable, Observable {
...
}
```

Note that complications may arise from implementing multiple interfaces—what happens if two different interfaces both define the same method? There are three ways to solve this:

□ If the methods in each of the interfaces have identical signatures, you implement one method in your class and that definition satisfies both interfaces.

□ If the methods have different parameter lists, it is a simple case of method overloading; you implement both method signatures, and each definition satisfies its respective interface definition.

16

☐ If the methods have the same parameter lists but differ in return type, you cannot create a method that satisfies both (remember, method overloading is triggered by parameter lists, not by return type). In this case, trying to compile a class that implements both interfaces will produce a compiler error. Running across this problem suggests that your interfaces have some design flaws that might need re-examining.

Other Uses of Interfaces

Remember that almost everywhere that you can use a class, you can use an interface instead. So, for example, you can declare a variable to be of an interface type:

```
Runnable aRunnableObject = new MyAnimationClass()
```

When a variable is declared to be of an interface type, it simply means that any object the variable refers to is expected to have implemented that interface—that is, it is expected to understand all the methods that interface specifies. It assumes that a promise made between the designer of the interface and its eventual implementors has been kept. In this case, because aRunnableObject contains an object of the type Runnable, the assumption is that you can call aRunnableObject.run().

The important thing to realize here is that although aRunnableObject is expected to be able to have the run() method, you could write this code long before any classes that qualify are actually implemented (or even created!). In traditional object-oriented programming, you are forced to create a class with "stub" implementations (empty methods, or methods that print silly messages) to get the same effect.

You can also cast objects to an interface, just as you can cast objects to other classes. So, for example, let's go back to that definition of the Orange class, which implemented both the Fruitlike interface (through its superclass, Fruit) and the Spherelike interface. Here we'll cast instances of Orange to both classes and interfaces:

```
Orange      anOrange    = new Orange();
Fruit       aFruit      = (Fruit)anOrange;
Fruitlike   aFruitlike  = (Fruitlike)anOrange;
Spherelike  aSpherelike = (Spherelike)anOrange;


aFruit.decay();         // fruits decay
aFruitlike.squish();    //   and squish

aFruitlike.toss();      // things that are fruitlike do not toss
aSpherelike.toss();     // but things that are spherelike do

anOrange.decay();       // oranges can do it all
anOrange.squish();
anOrange.toss();
anOrange.rotate();
```

Declarations and casts are used in this example to restrict an orange's behavior to acting more like a mere fruit or sphere.

Finally, note that although interfaces are usually used to mix in behavior to other classes (method signatures), interfaces can also be used to mix in generally useful constants. So, for example, if an interface defined a set of constants, and then multiple classes used those constants, the values of those constants could be globally changed without having to modify multiple classes. This is yet another example of where the use of interfaces to separate design from implementation can make your code more general and more easily maintainable.

Creating and Extending Interfaces

After using interfaces for a while, the next step is to define your own interfaces. Interfaces look a lot like classes; they are declared in much the same way and can be arranged into a hierarchy, but there are rules for declaring interfaces that must be followed.

New Interfaces

To create a new interface, you declare it like this:

```
public interface Growable {
...
}
```

This is, effectively, the same as a class definition, with the word `interface` replacing the word `class`. Inside the interface definition you have methods and constants. The method definitions inside the interface are `public` and `abstract` methods; you can either declare them explicitly as such, or they will be turned into `public` and `abstract` methods if you do not include those modifiers. You cannot declare a method inside an interface to be either `private` or `protected`. So, for example, here's a `Growable` interface with one method explicitly declared `public` and `abstract` (`growIt()`) and one implicitly declared as such (`growItBigger()`).

```
public interface Growable {
    public abstract void growIt(); //explicity public and abstract
    void growItBigger();          // effectively public and abstract
}
```

Note that, as with abstract methods in classes, methods inside interfaces do not have bodies. Remember, an interface is pure design; there is no implementation involved.

In addition to methods, interfaces can also have variables, but those variables must be declared `public`, `static`, and `final` (making them constant). As with methods, you can explicitly define a variable to be `public`, `static`, and `final`, or it will be implicitly defined as such if you don't use those modifiers. Here's that same `Growable` definition with two new variables:

```
public interface Growable {
    public static final int increment = 10;
    long maxnum = 1000000;  // becomes public static and final

    public abstract void growIt(); //explicitly public and abstract
    void growItBigger();           // effectively public and abstract
}
```

Interfaces must have either public or package protection, just like classes. Note, however, that interfaces without the public modifier do not automatically convert their methods to public and abstract nor their constants to public. A non-public interface also has non-public methods and constants that can be used only by classes and other interfaces in the same package.

Interfaces, like classes, can belong to a package by adding a package statement to the first line of the class file. Interfaces can also import other interfaces and classes from other packages, just as classes can.

Methods Inside Interfaces

One trick to note about methods inside interfaces: Those methods are supposed to be abstract and apply to any kind of class, but how can you define parameters to those methods? You don't know what class will be using them!

The answer lies in the fact that you use an interface name anywhere a class name can be used, as you learned earlier. By defining your method parameters to be interface types, you can create generic parameters that apply to any class that might use this interface.

So, for example, take the interface Fruitlike, which defines methods (with no arguments) for decay() and squish(). There might also be a method for germinateSeeds(), which has one argument: the fruit itself. Of what type is that argument going to be? It can't be simply Fruit, because there may be a class that's Fruitlike (that is, implements the Fruitlike interface) without actually being a fruit. The solution is to declare the argument as simply Fruitlike in the interface:

```
public interface Fruitlike {
    public abstract germinate(Fruitlike self) {
        ...
    }
}
```

Then, in an actual implementation for this method in a class, you can take the generic Fruitlike argument and cast it to the appropriate object:

```
public class Orange extends Fruit {

    public germinate(Fruitlike self) {
        Orange theOrange = (Orange)self;
```

```
         ...
      }
}
```

Extending Interfaces

As with classes, interfaces can be organized into a hierarchy. When one interface inherits from another interface, that "subinterface" acquires all the method definitions and constants that its "superinterface" defined. To extend an interface, you use the extends keyword just as you do in a class definition:

```
public interface Fruitlike extends Foodlike {
...
}
```

Note that, unlike classes, the interface hierarchy has no equivalent of the Object class; this hierarchy is not rooted at any one point. Interfaces can either exist entirely on their own or inherit from another interface.

Note also that, unlike the class hierarchy, the inheritance hierarchy is multiply inherited. So, for example, a single interface can extend as many classes as it needs to (separated by commas in the extends part of the definition), and the new interface will contain a combination of all its parent's methods and constants. Here's an interface definition for an interface called BusyInterface that inherits from a whole lot of other interfaces:

```
public interface BusyInterface extends Runnable, Growable, Fruitlike, Observable
{
...}
```

In multiply inherited interfaces, the rules for managing method name conflicts are the same as for classes that use multiple interfaces; methods that differ only in return type will result in a compiler error.

An Example: Enumerating Linked Lists

To finish up today's lesson, here's an example that uses packages, package protection, and defines a class that implements the Enumeration interface (part of the java.util package). Listing 16.2 shows the code.

TYPE **Listing 16.2. Packages, classes, and interfaces.**

```
1: package  collections;
2:
3: public class  LinkedList {
4:       private Node  root;
```

```
 5:
 6:        . . .
 7:        public Enumeration  enumerate() {
 8:            return new LinkedListEnumerator(root);
 9:        }
10: }
11:
12: class  Node {
13:     private Object   contents;
14:     private Node     next;
15:
16:        . . .
17:     public  Object  contents() {
18:         return contents;
19:     }
20:
21:     public  Node    next() {
22:         return next;
23:     }
24: }
25:
26: class  LinkedListEnumerator implements Enumeration {
27:     private Node  currentNode;
28:
29:      LinkedListEnumerator(Node  root) {
30:          currentNode = root;
31:     }
32:
33:     public boolean  hasMoreElements() {
34:         return currentNode != null;
35:     }
36:
37:     public Object    nextElement() {
38:         Object  anObject = currentNode.contents();
39:
40:         currentNode = currentNode.next();
41:         return  anObject;
42:     }
43: }
```

Here is a typical use of the enumerator:

```
collections.LinkedList aLinkedList = createLinkedList();
java.util.Enumeration e = aLinkedList.enumerate();

while (e.hasMoreElements()) {
    Object  anObject = e.nextElement();
    // do something useful with anObject
}
```

Notice that, although you are using the Enumeration e as though you know what it is, you actually do not. In fact, it is an instance of a hidden class (LinkedListEnumerator) that you cannot see or use directly. By using a combination of packages and interfaces, the LinkedList class has managed to provide a transparent public interface to some of its most important behavior (via the already defined interface `java.util.Enumeration`) while still encapsulating (hiding) its two implementation (support) classes.

Handing out an object like this is sometimes called *vending*. Often the "vendor" gives out an object that a receiver can't create itself but that it knows how to use. By giving it back to the vendor, the receiver can prove it has a certain capability, authenticate itself, or do any number of useful tasks—all without knowing much about the vended object. This is a powerful metaphor that can be applied in a broad range of situations.

Summary

Today you have learned how packages can be used to collect and categorize classes into meaningful groups. Packages are arranged in a hierarchy, which not only better organizes your programs but allows you and the millions of Java programmers out on the Net to name and share their projects uniquely with one another.

You have also learned how to use packages, both your own and the many preexisting ones in the Java class library.

You then discovered how to declare and use interfaces, a powerful mechanism for extending the traditional single inheritance of Java's classes and for separating design inheritance from implementation inheritance in your programs. Interfaces are often used to call common (shared) methods when the exact class involved is not known. You'll see further uses of interfaces tomorrow and the day after.

Finally, you learned that packages and interfaces can be combined to provide useful abstractions, such as `LinkedList`, that appear simple yet are actually hiding almost all their (complex) implementation from their users. This is a powerful technique.

Q&A

Q Can you use `import some.package.B*` to import all the classes in that package that begin with B?

A No, the import asterisk (*) does not act like a command-line asterisk.

Q Then what exactly does `importing` with an * mean?

A Combining everything said previously, this precise definition emerges: It imports all the public classes you use in your Java code that are *directly* inside the package named, and not inside one of its subpackages. (You can only import exactly this set of classes, or exactly one explicitly named class, from a given package.) By the way, Java only "loads" the information for a class when you actually refer to that class in your code, so the * form of `import` is no less efficient than naming each class individually.

Q Why is full multiple inheritance so complex that Java abandoned it?

A It's not so much that it is too complex, but that it makes the language overly complicated—and as you'll learn on Day 21, "Under the Hood," this can cause larger systems to be less trustworthy and thus less secure. For example, if you were to inherit from two different parents, each having an instance variable with the same name, you would be forced to allow the conflict and explain how the exact same reference to that variable name in each of your superclasses, and in you (all three), are now different. Instead of being able to call "super" methods to get more abstract behavior accomplished, you would always need to worry about which of the (possibly many) identical methods you actually wished to call in which parent. Java's run-time method dispatching would have to be more complex as well. Finally, because so many people would be providing classes for reuse on the Net, the normally manageable conflicts that would arise in your own program would be confounded by millions of users mixing and matching these fully multiply inherited classes at will. In the future, if all these issues are resolved, more powerful inheritance may be added to Java, but its current capabilities are already sufficient for 99 percent of your programs.

Q abstract classes don't have to implement all the methods in an interface themselves, but don't all their subclasses have to?

A Actually, no. Because of inheritance, the precise rule is that an implementation must be provided by some class for each method, but it doesn't have to be your class. This is analogous to when you are the subclass of a class that implements an interface for you. Whatever the `abstract` class doesn't implement, the first non-abstract class below it must implement. Then, any further subclasses need do nothing further.

Q You didn't mention callbacks. Aren't they an important use of interfaces?

A Yes, but I didn't mention them because a good example would be too bulky. Callbacks are often used in user interfaces (such as window systems) to specify what set of methods is going to be sent whenever the user does a certain set of things (such as clicking the mouse somewhere, typing, and so forth). Because the user interface classes should not "know" anything about the classes using them, an interface's ability to specify a set of methods separate from the class tree is crucial in this case. Callbacks using interfaces are not as general as using, for example, the perform: method of Smalltalk, however, because a given object can only request that a user interface object "call it back" using a single method name. Suppose that object wanted two user interface objects of the same class to call it back, using different names to tell them apart? It cannot do this in Java, and it is forced to use special state and tests to tell them apart. (I warned you that it was complicated!) So although interfaces are quite valuable in this case, they are not the ideal callback facility.

Day **17**

Exceptions

by Charles L. Perkins and Laura Lemay

Programmers in any language endeavor to write bug-free programs, programs that never crash, programs that can handle any situation with grace and that can recover from unusual situations without causing the user any undue stress. Good intentions aside, programs like this don't exist.

In real programs, errors occur, either because the programmer didn't anticipate every situation your code would get into (or didn't have the time to test the program enough), or because of situations out of the programmer's control—bad data from users, corrupt files that don't have the right data in them, network connections that don't connect, hardware devices that don't respond, sun spots, gremlins, whatever.

In Java, these sorts of strange events that may cause a program to fail are called *exceptions*. And Java defines a number of language features to deal with exceptions, including

☐ How to handle them in your code and recover gracefully from potential problems

☐ How to tell Java and users of your methods that you're expecting a potential exception

☐ How to create an exception if you detect one

☐ How your code is limited, yet made more robust by them

NEW TERM *Exceptions* are unusual things that can happen in your Java programs outside the normal or desired behavior of that program. Exceptions include errors that could be fatal to your program but also include other unusual situations. By managing exceptions, you can manage errors and possibly work around them.

Exceptions, the Old and Confusing Way

Programming languages have long labored to solve the following common problem:

```
int  status = callSomethingThatAlmostAlwaysWorks();

if (status == FUNNY_RETURN_VALUE) {
    . . .        // something unusual happened, handle it
    switch(someGlobalErrorIndicator) {
        . . . // handle more specific problems
    }
} else {
    . . .        // all is well, go your merry way
}
```

What this bit of code is attempting to do is to run a method that should work, but might not for some unusual reason. The status might end up being some unusual return value, in which case the code attempts to figure out what happened and work around it. Somehow this seems like a lot of work to do to handle a rare case. And if the function you called returns an int as part of its normal answer, you'll have to distinguish one special integer (FUNNY_RETURN_VALUE) as an error. Alternatively, you could pass in a special return value pointer, or use a global variable to store those errors, but then problems arise with keeping track of multiple errors with the same bit of code, or of the original error stored in the global being overwritten by a new error before you have a chance to deal with it.

Once you start creating larger systems, error management can become a major problem. Different programmers may use different special values for handling errors, and may not document them overly well, if at all. You may inconsistently use errors in your own programs. Code to manage these kinds of errors can often obscure the original intent of the program, making that code difficult to read and to maintain. And, finally, if you try dealing with errors in this kludgey way, there's no easy way for the compiler to check for consistency the way it can check to make sure you called a method with the right arguments.

For all these reasons, Java has exceptions to deal with managing, creating, and expecting errors and other unusual situations. Through a combination of special language features, consistency checking at compile time and a set of extensible exception classes, errors and other unusual conditions in Java programs can be much more easily managed. Given these features, you can now add a whole new dimension to the behavior and design of your classes, of your class hierarchy, and of your overall system. Your class and interface definitions describe how your program is supposed to behave given the best circumstances. By integrating exception handling into your program design, you can consistently describe how the program will behave when circumstances are not quite as good, and allow people who use your classes to know what to expect in those cases.

Java Exceptions

At this point in the book, chances are you've run into at least one Java exception—perhaps you mistyped a method name or made a mistake in your code that caused a problem. And chances are that your program quit and spewed a bunch of mysterious errors to the screen. Those mysterious errors are exceptions. When your program quits, it's because an exception was "thrown." Exceptions can be thrown by the system or thrown by you, and they can be caught as well (catching an exception involves dealing with it so your program doesn't crash. You'll learn more about this later). "An exception was thrown" is the proper Java terminology for "an error happened."

 Exceptions don't occur, they are *thrown*. Java throws an exception in response to an unusual situation. You can also throw your own exceptions, or *catch* an exception to gracefully manage errors.

The heart of the Java exception system is the exception itself. Exceptions in Java are actual objects, instances of classes that inherit from the class `Throwable`. When an exception is thrown, an instance of a `Throwable` class is created. Figure 17.1 shows a partial class hierarchy for exceptions.

`Throwable` has two subclasses: `Error` and `Exception`. Instances of `Error` are internal errors in the Java runtime environment (the virtual machine). These errors are rare and usually fatal; there's not much you can do about them (either to catch them or to throw them yourself), but they exist so that Java can use them if it needs to.

The class `Exception` is more interesting. Subclasses of `Exception` fall into two general groups:

- ☐ Runtime exceptions (subclasses of the class `RuntimeException`) such as `ArrayIndexOutofBounds`, `SecurityException`, or `NullPointerException`.
- ☐ Other exceptions such as `EOFException` and `MalformedURLException`.

Figure 17.1.

The exception class hierarchy.

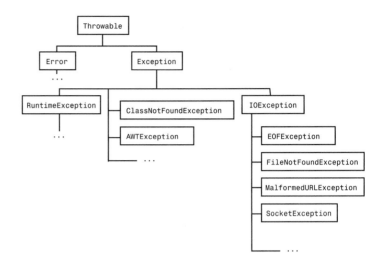

Runtime exceptions usually occur because of code that isn't very robust. An ArrayIndexOutofBounds exception, for example, should never be thrown if you're properly checking to make sure your code doesn't extend past the end of an array. NullPointerException exceptions won't happen if you don't try to reference the values of a variable that doesn't actually hold an object. If your program is causing runtime exceptions under any circumstances whatsoever, you should be fixing those problems before you even begin to deal with exception management.

The final group of exceptions is the most interesting because these are the exceptions that indicate that something very strange and out of control is happening. EOFExceptions, for example, happen when you're reading from a file and the file ends before you expect it to. MalformedURLExceptions happen when a URL isn't in the right format (perhaps your user typed it wrong). This group includes exceptions that you yourself create to signal unusual cases that may occur in your own programs.

Exceptions are arranged in a hierarchy like other classes, where the Exception superclasses are more general errors, and subclasses are more specific errors. This organization will become more important to you as you deal with exceptions in your own code.

Most of the exception classes are part of the java.lang package (including Throwable, Exception, and RuntimeException). But many of the other packages define other exceptions, and those exceptions are used throughout the class library. For example, the java.io package defines a general exception class called IOException, which is subclassed not only in the java.io package for input and output exceptions (EOFException, FileNotFoundException), but also in the java.net classes for networking exceptions such as MalFormedURLException.

Managing Exceptions

So now that you know what an exception is, how do you deal with them in your own code? In many cases, the Java compiler enforces exception management when you try to use methods that use exceptions; you'll need to deal with those exceptions in your own code or it simply won't compile. In this section you'll learn about that consistency checking and how to use the try, catch, and finally language keywords to deal with exceptions that may or may not occur.

Exception Consistency Checking

The more you work with the Java class libraries, the more likely it is that you'll run into a compiler error (an exception!) similar to this one:

```
TestProg.java:32: Exception java.lang.InterruptedException
must be caught or it must be declared in the throws clause
of this method.
```

What on earth does that mean? In Java, a method can indicate the kinds of errors it might possibly throw. For example, methods that read from files might potentially throw IOException errors, so those methods are declared with a special modifier that indicates potential errors. When you use those methods in your own Java programs, you have to protect your code against those exceptions. This rule is enforced by the compiler itself, the same way that the compiler checks to make sure that you're using methods with the right number of arguments and that all your variable types match the thing you're assigning to them.

Why is this check in place? By having methods declare the exceptions they throw, and by forcing you to handle those exceptions in some way, the potential for fatal errors in a program occurring because you simply didn't know they could occur is minimized. You no longer have to carefully read the documentation or the code of an object you're going to use to make sure you've dealt with all the potential problems—Java does the checking for you. And, on the other side, if you define your methods so that they indicate the exceptions they can throw, then Java can tell users of your objects to handle those errors.

Protecting Code and Catching Exceptions

Let's assume that you've been happily coding and during a test compile you ran into that exception message. According to the message, you have to either catch the error or declare that your method throws it. Let's deal with the first case: catching potential exceptions.

To catch an exception, you do two things:

☐ You protect the code that contains the method that might throw an exception inside a `try` block.

☐ You test for and deal with an exception inside a `catch` block.

What `try` and `catch` effectively mean is "try this bit of code that might cause an exception. If it executes okay, go on with the program. If it doesn't, catch the exception and deal with it."

You've seen `try` and `catch` once before, when we dealt with threads. On Day 10, "Simple Animation and Threads," you learned about an applet that created a digital clock, and the animation paused once a second using this bit of code:

```
try { Thread.sleep(1000) }
catch (InterruptedException e) {}
```

While this example uses `try` and `catch`, it's not a very good use of it. Here, the `Thread.sleep()` class method could potentially throw an exception of type `InterruptedException` (for when the thread is interrupted from running). So we've put the call to `sleep()` inside the `try` clause to catch that exception if it happens. And inside `catch` (inside the parentheses), we indicate that we're specifically looking for `InterruptedException` exceptions. The problem here is that there isn't anything inside the `catch` clause—in other words, we'll catch the exception if it happens, but then we'll drop it on the floor and pretend we didn't see it. In all but the simplest cases (such as this one, where the exception really doesn't matter), you're going to want to put something inside the braces after `catch` to try to do something responsible to clean up after the exception happens.

The part of the `catch` clause inside the parentheses is similar to the parameter list of a method definition; it contains the class of the exception to be caught and a variable name (e is very commonly used). Inside the body of the catch clause, you can then refer to the exception object, for example, to get to the detailed error message contained in the `getMessage()` method:

```
catch (InterruptedException e) {
    System.out.println("Ooops.  Error: " + e.getMessage());
}
```

Here's another example. Say you have a program that reads from a file. This program most likely uses one of the streams classes you'll learn about on Day 19, "Streams and I/O," but the basic idea here is that you open a connection to a file and then use the `read()` method to get data from it. What if some strange disk error happens and the `read()` method can't read anything? What if the file is truncated and has fewer bytes in it than you expected? In either of these instances, the `read()` method will throw an `IOException` which, if you didn't catch it, would cause your program to stop executing and possibly crash. By putting your `read()` method inside a `try` clause, you can then deal gracefully with that error inside `catch` to clean up after the error and return to some safe state, to patch things up enough to be able to proceed, or, if all else fails, to save as much of the current program's state as possible and to exit. This example does just that; it tries to read from the file, and catches exceptions if they happen:

```
try {
    while (numbytes <= mybuffer.length) {
        myinputstream.read(mybuffer);
        numbytes;++
    }
} catch (IOException e) {
  System.out.println("Ooops, IO Exception.  Only read " + numbytes.");
  // other cleanup code
}
```

Here, the "other cleanup code" can be anything you want it to be; perhaps you can go on with the program using the partial information you got from the file, or perhaps you want to put up a dialog saying that the file is corrupt and to let the user try to select another file or do some other operation.

Note that because the Exception classes are organized into hierarchies as other classes are, and because of the rule that you can use a subclass anywhere a superclass is expected, you can catch "groups" of exceptions and handle them with the same catch code. For example, although there are several different types of IOExceptions (EOFException, FileNotFoundException, and so on—see the java.io package for examples), by catching IOException you also catch instances of any subclass of IOException.

What if you do want to catch very different kinds of exceptions that aren't related by inheritance? You can use multiple catch clauses for a given try, like this:

```
try {
    // protected code
} catch (OneKindOfException e) {
  ...
} catch (AnotherKindOfException e2) {
  ....
} catch (YetAnotherException e3) {
  ...
} catch (StilMoreException e4) {
  ....
}
```

Note that because the scope of local variables inside catch is the same as the scope of the outer block (the method definition or a loop if you're inside one), you'll have to use different local variables for each individual catch.

Because the first catch clause that matches is executed, you can build chains such as the following:

```
try {
    someReallyExceptionalMethod();
} catch (NullPointerException n) {  // a subclass of RuntimeException
```

17

```
    . . .
} catch (RuntimeException r) {       // a subclass of Exception
    . . .
} catch (IOException i) {             // a subclass of Exception
    . . .
} catch (MyFirstException m) {        // our subclass of Exception
    . . .
} catch (Exception e) {               // a subclass of Throwable
    . . .
} catch (Throwable t) {
    . . .  // Errors, plus anything not caught above are caught here
}
```

By listing subclasses before their parent classes, the parent catches anything it would normally catch that's also *not* one of the subclasses above it. By juggling chains like these, you can express almost any combination of tests.

The `finally` Clause

Suppose there is some action in your code that you absolutely must do, no matter what happens, whether an exception is thrown or not. Usually, this is to free some external resource after acquiring it, to close a file after opening it, or something similar. While you could put that action both inside a `catch` and outside it, that would be duplicating the same code in two different places. Instead, put one copy of that code inside a special optional part of the `try...catch` clause, called `finally`:

```
SomeFileClass  f = new SomeFileClass();

if (f.open("/a/file/name/path")) {
    try {
        someReallyExceptionalMethod();
    { catch (IOException e) {
        // deal with errors
    } finally {
        f.close();
    }
}
```

The `finally` clause is actually useful outside exceptions; you can also use it to execute cleanup code after a return, a break, or a continue inside loops. For the latter cases, you can use a `try` clause with a `finally` but without a `catch` clause.

Here's a fairly complex example of how this might work:

```
int  mysteriousState = getContext();

while (true) {
    System.out.print("Who ");
    try {
        System.out.print("is ");
        if (mysteriousState == 1)
```

17

```
        return;
    System.out.print("that ");
    if (mysteriousState == 2)
        break;
    System.out.print("strange ");
    if (mysteriousState == 3)
        continue;
    System.out.print("but kindly ");
    if (mysteriousState == 4)
        throw new UncaughtException();
    System.out.print("not at all ");
} finally {
    System.out.print("amusing man?\n");
}
System.out.print("I'd like to meet the man");
}
System.out.print("Please tell me.\n");
```

Here is the output produced depending on the value of `mysteriousState`:

```
1    Who is amusing man? Please tell me.
2    Who is that amusing man? Please tell me.
3    Who is that strange amusing man? Who is that strange ....
4    Who is that strange but kindly amusing man? Please tell me.
5    Who is that strange but kindly not at all amusing man?
     I'd like to meet that man. Who is that strange ...
```

NOTE   In cases 3 and 5, the output never ends until you quit the program. In 4, an error message generated by the `UncaughtException` is also printed.

Declaring Methods That Might Throw Exceptions

In the previous example you learned how to deal with methods that might possibly throw exceptions by protecting code and catching any exceptions that occur. The Java compiler will check to make sure you've somehow dealt with a method's exceptions—but how did it know which exceptions to tell you about in the first place?

The answer is that the original method indicated in its signature the exceptions that it might possibly throw. You can use this mechanism in your own methods—in fact, it's good style to do so to make sure that other users of your classes are alerted to the errors your methods may come across.

To indicate that a method may possibly throw an exception, you use a special clause in the method definition called `throws`.

The throws Clause

To indicate that some code in the body of your method may throw an exception, simply add the throws keyword after the signature for the method (before the opening brace) with the name or names of the exception that your method throws:

```
public boolean myMethod (int x, int y) throws AnException {
    ...
}
```

If your method may possibly throw multiple kinds of exceptions, you can put all of them in the throws clause, separated by commas:

```
public boolean myOtherMethod (int x, int y)
    throws AnException, AnotherExeption, AThirdException {
    ...
}
```

Note that as with catch you can use a superclass of a group of exceptions to indicate that your method may throw any subclass of that exception:

```
public void YetAnotherMethod() throws IOException {
...
}
```

Keep in mind that adding a throws method to your method definition simply means that the method might throw an exception if something goes wrong, not that it actually will. The throws clause simply provides extra information to your method definition about potential exceptions and allows Java to make sure that your method is being used correctly by other people.

Think of a method's overall description as a contract between the designer of that method (or class) and the caller of the method (you can be either side of that contract, of course). Usually, the description indicates the types of a method's arguments, what it returns, and the general semantics of what it normally does. Using throws, you add information about the abnormal things it can do as well. This new part of the contract helps to separate and make explicit all the places where exceptional conditions should be handled in your program, and that makes large-scale design easier.

Which Exceptions Should You Throw?

Once you decide to declare that your method might throw an exception, you have to decide which exceptions it might throw (and actually throw them or call a method that will throw them—you'll learn about throwing your own exceptions in the next section). In many instances, this will be apparent from the operation of the method itself. Perhaps you're creating and throwing your own exceptions, in which case you'll know exactly which exceptions to throw.

You don't really have to list all the possible exceptions that your method could throw; some exceptions are handled by the runtime itself and are so common (well, not common, but ubiquitous) that you don't have to deal with them. In particular, exceptions of either class Error or RuntimeException (or any of their subclasses) do not have to be listed in your throws clause. They get special treatment because they can occur anywhere within a Java program and are usually conditions that you, as the programmer, did not directly cause. One good example is OutOfMemoryError, which can happen anywhere, at any time, and for any number of reasons. These two kinds of exceptions are called implicit exceptions, and you don't have to worry about them.

Implicit exceptions are exceptions that are subclasses of the classes RuntimeException and Error. Implicit exceptions are usually thrown by the Java runtime itself. You do not have to declare that your method throws them.

NOTE

You can, of course, choose to list these errors and runtime exceptions in your throws clause if you like, but the callers of your methods will not be forced to handle them; only non-runtime exceptions *must* be handled.

All other exceptions are called explicit exceptions and are potential candidates of a throws clause in your method.

Passing On Exceptions

In addition to declaring methods that throw exceptions, there's one other instance in which your method definition may include a throws clause. In this case, you want to use a method that throws an exception, but you don't want to catch that exception or deal with it. In many cases, it might make more sense for the method that calls your method to deal with that exception rather than for you to deal with it. There's nothing wrong with this; it's a fairly common occurrence that you won't actually deal with an exception, but will pass it back to the method that calls yours. At any rate, it's a better idea to pass on exceptions to calling methods than to catch them and ignore them.

Rather than using the try and catch clauses in the body of your method, you can declare your method with a throws clause such that it, too, might possibly throw the appropriate exception. Then it's the responsibility of the method that calls your method to deal with that exception. This is the other case that will satisfy the Java compiler that you have done something with a given method. Here's another way of implementing an example that reads characters from a stream:

```
public void readTheFile(String filename) throws IO Exception {
    // open the file, init the stream, etc.
    while (numbytes <= mybuffer.length) {
        myinputstream.read(mybuffer);
        numbytes;++
    }
}
```

This example is similar to the example used previously today; remember that the read()
method was declared to throw an IOException, so you had to use try and catch to use it. Once
you declare your method to throw an exception, however, you can use other methods that
also throw those exceptions inside the body of this method, without needing to protect the
code or catch the exception.

NOTE   You can, of course, deal with other exceptions using try and catch in
the body of your method in addition to passing on the exceptions you
listed in the throws clause. You can also both deal with the exception in
some way and then re-throw it so that your method's calling method
has to deal with it anyhow. You'll learn how to throw methods in the
next section.

throws **and Inheritance**

If your method definition overrides a method in a superclass that includes a throws clause,
there are special rules for how your overridden method deals with throws. Unlike with the
other parts of the method signature, your new method does not have to have the same set of
exceptions listed in the throws clause. Because there's a potential that your new method may
deal better with exceptions, rather than just throwing them, your subclass's method can
potentially throw fewer types of exceptions than its superclass's method definition, up to and
including throwing no exceptions at all. That means that you can have the following two class
definitions and things will work just fine:

```
public class Fruit {
    public void ripen() throws RotException {
        ...
    }
}

public class WaxFruit extends Fruit {
    public void ripen() {
        ...
    }
}
```

The converse of this rule is not true; a subclass's method cannot throw more exceptions
(either exceptions of different types or more general exception classes) than its superclass's
method.

Creating and Throwing Your Own Exceptions

There are two sides to every exception: the side that throws the exception and the side that catches it. An exception can be tossed around a number of times to a number of methods before it's caught, but eventually it'll be caught and dealt with.

But who does the actual throwing? Where do exceptions come from? Many exceptions are thrown by the Java runtime, or by methods inside the Java classes themselves. You can also throw any of the standard exceptions that the Java class libraries define, or you can create and throw your own exceptions. This section describes all these things.

Throwing Exceptions

Declaring that your method throws an exception is useful only to users of your method and to the Java compiler, which checks to make sure all your exceptions are being dealt with. But the declaration itself doesn't do anything to actually throw that exception should it occur; you have to do that yourself in the body of the method.

Remember that exceptions are all instances of some exception class, of which there are many defined in the standard Java class libraries. In order to throw an exception, therefore, you'll need to create a new instance of an exception class. Once you have that instance, use the `throw` statement to throw it (could this be any easier?). The simplest way to throw an exception is simply like this:

```
throw new ServiceNOteAvailableException();
```

TECHNICAL NOTE

You can only throw objects that are instances of subclasses of `Throwable`. This is different from C++'s exceptions, which allow you to throw objects of any type.

Depending on the exception class you're using, the exception may also have arguments to its constructor that you can use. The most common of these is a string argument, which lets you describe the actual problem in greater detail (which can be very useful for debugging purposes). Here's an example:

```
throw new ServiceNotAvailableException("Exception:
    service not available, database is offline.");
```

Once an exception is thrown, the method exits immediately, without executing any other code (other than the code inside `finally`, if that clause exists) and without returning a value. If the calling method does not have a `try` or `catch` surrounding the call to your method, the program may very well exit based on the exception you threw.

Creating Your Own Exceptions

Exceptions are simply classes, just like any other classes in the Java hierarchy. Although there are a fair number of exceptions in the Java class library that you can use in your own methods, there is a strong possibility that you may want to create your own exceptions to handle different kinds of errors your programs might run into. Fortunately, creating new exceptions is easy.

Your new exception should inherit from some other exception in the Java hierarchy. Look for an exception that's close to the one you're creating; for example, an exception for a bad file format would logically be an `IOException`. If you can't find a closely related exception for your new exception, consider inheriting from `Exception`, which forms the "top" of the exception hierarchy for explicit exceptions (remember that implicit exceptions, which include subclasses of `Error` and `RuntimeException`, inherit from `Throwable`).

Exception classes typically have two constructors: The first takes no arguments and the second takes a single string as an argument. In the latter case you'll want to call `super()` in that constructor to make sure the string is applied to the right place in the exception.

Beyond those three rules, exception classes look just like other classes. You can put them in their own source files and compile them just as you would other classes:

```java
public class SunSpotException extends Exception {
    public SunSpotException() {}
    public SunSpotExceotion(String msg) {
        super(msg);
    }
}
```

Doing It All: Combining throws, try, and throw

What if you want to combine all the approaches shown so far? In your method, you'd like to handle incoming exceptions yourself, but also you'd like to pass the exception up to your caller. Simply using `try` and `catch` doesn't pass on the exception, and simply adding a `throws` clause doesn't give you a chance to deal with the exception. If you want to both manage the exception and pass it on to the caller, use all three mechanisms: the `throws` clause, the `try` statement, and by explicitly rethrowing the exception:

```java
public void  responsibleExceptionalMethod() throws MyFirstException {
    MyFirstExceptionalClass  aMFEC = new MyFirstExceptionalClass();
```

```
    try {
        aMFEC.anExceptionalMethod();
    } catch (MyFirstException m) {
        . . .           // do something responsible
        throw m;        // re-throw the exception
    }
}
```

This works because exception handlers can be nested. You handle the exception by doing something responsible with it, but decide that it is too important to not give an exception handler that might be in your caller a chance to handle it as well. Exceptions float all the way up the chain of method callers this way (usually not being handled by most of them) until at last the system itself handles any uncaught ones by aborting your program and printing an error message. In a standalone program, this is not such a bad idea; but in an applet, it can cause the browser to crash. Most browsers protect themselves from this disaster by catching all exceptions themselves whenever they run an applet, but you can never tell. If it's possible for you to catch an exception and do something intelligent with it, you should.

When and When Not to Use Exceptions

To finish up today's lesson, here's a quick summary and some advice on when to use exceptions…and when not to use them.

When to Use Exceptions

Because throwing, catching, and declaring exceptions are interrelated concepts and can be very confusing, here's a quick summary of when to do what.

If your method uses someone else's method, and that method has a throws clause, you can do one of three things:

- [ ] Deal with the exception using try and catch statements.
- [ ] Pass the exception up the calling chain by adding your own throws clause to your method definition.
- [ ] Do both of the above by catching the exception using catch and then explicitly rethrowing it using throw.

In cases where a method throws more than one exception, you can, of course, handle each of those exceptions differently. For example, you might catch some of those exceptions while allowing others to pass up the calling chain.

If your method throws its own exceptions, you should declare that it throws those methods using the throws clause. If your method overrides a superclass's method that has a throws clause, you can throw the same types of exceptions or subclasses of those exceptions; you cannot throw any different types of exceptions.

And, finally, if your method has been declared with a `throws` clause, don't forget to actually throw the exception in the body of your method using `throw`.

When Not to Use Exceptions

Exceptions are cool. But they aren't *that* cool. There are several cases in which you should not use exceptions, even though they may seem appropriate at the time.

First, you should not use exceptions if the exception is something that you expect and a simple test to avoid that exceptional condition would make much more sense. For example, although you can rely on an `ArrayIndexOutofBounds` exception to tell you when you've gone past the end of the array, a simple test of the length of the array in your code to make sure you don't get that exception in the first place is a much better idea. Or if your users are going to enter data that you need to be a letter, testing to make sure that data is a letter is a much better idea than throwing an exception and dealing with it somewhere else.

Exceptions take up a lot of processing time for your Java program. Whereas you may find exceptions stylistically interesting for your own code, a simple test or series of tests will run much faster and make your program that much more efficient. Exceptions, as I mentioned earlier, should only be used for truly exceptional cases that are out of your control.

It's also easy to get carried away with exceptions and to try to make sure that all your methods have been declared to throw all the possible exceptions that they can possibly throw. In addition to making your code more complex in general, if other people will be using your code, they'll have to deal with handling all the exceptions that your methods might throw. You're making more work for everyone involved when you get carried away with exceptions. Declaring a method to throw either few or lots of exceptions is a trade-off; the more exceptions your method potentially throws, the more complex that method is to use. Declare only the exceptions that have a reasonably fair chance of happening and that make sense for the overall design of your classes.

Bad Style Using Exceptions

When you first start using exceptions, it might be appealing to work around the compiler errors that result when you use a method that declared a `throws` clause. While it is legal to add an empty catch clause or to add a `throws` clause to your own method (and there are appropriate reasons for doing both of these things), intentionally dropping exceptions on the floor and subverting the checks the Java compiler does for you is very bad style.

The Java exception system was designed so that if a potential error can occur, you're warned about it. Ignoring those warnings and working around them makes it possible for fatal errors to occur in your program—errors that you could have avoided with a few lines of code. And, even worse, adding `throws` clauses to your methods to avoid exceptions means that the users of your methods (objects further up in the calling chain) will have to deal with them. You've just made more work for someone else and made your methods more difficult to use for other people.

Compiler errors regarding exceptions are there to remind you to reflect on these issues. Take the time to deal with the exceptions that may affect your code. This extra care will richly reward you as you reuse your classes in later projects and in larger and larger programs. Of course, the Java class library has been written with exactly this degree of care, and that's one of the reasons it's robust enough to be used in constructing all your Java projects.

Summary

Today you have learned about how exceptions aid your program's design and robustness. Exceptions give you a way of managing potential errors in your programs and of alerting users of your programs that potential errors can occur. The Java class library has a vast array of exceptions defined and thrown, and also allows you to define and throw your own exceptions. Using try, catch, and finally you can protect code that may result in exceptions, catch and handle those exceptions if they occur, and execute code whether or not an exception was generated.

Handling exceptions is only half of the equation; the other half is generating and throwing exceptions yourself. Today you have learned about the throws clause, which tells users of your method that the method might throw an exception. throws can also be used to "pass on" an exception from a method call in the body of your method.

In addition to the information given by the throws clause, you learned how to actually create and throw your own methods be defining new exception classes and by throwing instances of any exception classes using throw.

And, finally, Java's reliance on strict exception handling does place some restrictions on the programmer, but you have learned that these restrictions are light compared to the rewards.

Q&A

Q I'm still not sure I understand the differences between exceptions, errors, and runtime exceptions. Is there another way of looking at them?

A Errors are caused by dynamic linking, or virtual machine problems, and are thus too low-level for most programs to care about—or be able to handle even if they did care about them. Runtime exceptions are generated by the normal execution of Java code, and although they occasionally reflect a condition you will want to handle explicitly, more often they reflect a coding mistake by the programmer and thus simply need to print an error to help flag that mistake. Exceptions that are not runtime exceptions (IOException exceptions, for example) are conditions that, because of their nature, should be explicitly handled by any robust and well-thought-out code. The Java class library has been written using only a few of these, but those few are extremely important to using the system safely and correctly. The compiler helps you handle these exceptions properly via its throws clause checks and restrictions.

Q Is there any way to "get around" the strict restrictions placed on methods by the throws clause?

A Yes. Suppose you have thought long and hard and have decided that you need to circumvent this restriction. This is almost never the case, because the right solution is to go back and redesign your methods to reflect the exceptions that you need to throw. Imagine, however, that for some reason a system class has you in a strait-jacket. Your first solution is to subclass RuntimeException to make up a new, exempt exception of your own. Now you can throw it to your heart's content, because the throws clause that was annoying you does not need to include this new exception. If you need a lot of such exceptions, an elegant approach is to mix in some novel exception interfaces to your new Runtime classes. You're free to choose whatever subset of these new interfaces you want to catch (none of the normal Runtime exceptions need be caught), while any leftover (new) Runtime exceptions are (legally) allowed to go through that otherwise annoying standard method in the library.

Q I'm still a little confused by long chains of catch clauses. Can you label the previous example with which exceptions are handled by each line of code?

A Certainly. Here it is:

```
try {
    someReallyExceptionalMethod();
} catch (NullPointerException n) {
    . . . // handles NullPointerExceptions
} catch (RuntimeException r) {
    . . . // handles RuntimeExceptions
           //that are not NullPointerExceptions
} catch (IOException i) {
    . . . // handles IOExceptions
} catch (MyFirstException m) {
    . . . // handles MyFirstExceptions
} catch (Exception e) {
    . . . // handles Exceptions that are not
           // RuntimeExceptions nor IOExceptions
           // nor MyFirstExceptions
} catch (Throwable t) {
    . . . // handles Throwables that
           // are not Exceptions (i.e., Errors)
}
```

17

Q **Given how annoying it can sometimes be to handle exceptional conditions properly, what's stopping me from surrounding any method as follows:**

```
try { thatAnnoyingMethod(); } catch (Throwable t) { }
```

and simply ignoring all exceptions?

A Nothing, other than your own conscience. In some cases, you *should* do nothing, because it is the correct thing to do for your method's implementation. Otherwise, you should struggle through the annoyance and gain experience. Good style is a struggle even for the best of programmers, but the rewards are rich indeed.

Day 18

Multithreading

by Charles L. Perkins and Michael Morrison

One of the major features in the Java programming environment and runtime system is the multithreaded architecture shared by both. Multithreading, which is a fairly recent construct in the computer science world, is a very powerful means of enhancing and controlling program execution. Today's lesson takes a look at how the Java language supports multithreading through the use of threads. You'll learn all about the different classes that enable Java to be a threaded language, along with many of the issues surrounding the effective use of threads.

To better understand the importance of threads, imagine that you're using your favorite text editor on a large file. When it starts up, does it need to examine the entire file before it lets you begin editing? Does it need to make a copy of the file? If the file is huge, this can be a nightmare. Wouldn't it be nicer for it to show you the first page, allowing you to begin editing, and somehow (in the background) complete the slower tasks necessary for initialization? Threads allow exactly this kind of within-the-program parallelism.

Perhaps the best example of threading (or lack of it) is a Web browser. Can your browser download an indefinite number of files and Web pages at once while still enabling you to continue browsing? While these pages are downloading, can your browser download all the pictures, sounds, and so forth in parallel, interleaving the fast and slow download times of multiple Internet servers? Multithreaded browsers can do all these things by virtue of their internal usage of threads.

Today you'll learn about the following primary issues surrounding threads:

☐ Thread fundamentals

☐ How to "think multithreaded"

☐ How to protect your methods and variables from unintended thread conflicts

☐ How to create, start, and stop threads and threaded classes

☐ How the scheduler works in Java

Let's begin today's lesson by defining what a thread is.

Thread Fundamentals

The multithreading support in Java revolves around the concept of a thread. So what exactly is a thread? Put simply, a *thread* is a single stream of execution within a process. Okay, maybe that wasn't so simple. It might be better to start off by explaining exactly what a process is. A *process* is a program executing within its own address space. Java is a multiprocessing system, meaning that it supports many processes running concurrently in their own address spaces. You may be more familiar with the term multitasking, which describes a scenario very similar to multiprocessing. As an example, consider the variety of applications typically running at once in a graphical environment. Most Windows 95 users typically run a variety of applications together at once, such as Microsoft Word, CD Player, Windows Messaging, Volume Control, and of course Solitaire. These applications are all processes executing within the Windows 95 environment. So you can think of processes as being analogous to applications, or standalone programs; each process in a system is given its own space in memory to execute.

NEW TERM A *process* is a program executing within its own address space.

NEW TERM A *thread* is a single stream of execution within a process.

A thread is a sequence of code executing within the context of a process. As a matter of fact, threads cannot execute on their own; they require the overhead of a parent process to run. Within each of the processes typically running, there are no doubt a variety of threads

18

executing. For example, Word may have a thread in the background automatically checking the spelling of what is being written, while another thread may be automatically saving changes to the document. Like Word, each application (process) can be running many threads that are performing any number of tasks. The significance here is that threads are always associated with a particular process.

Judging by the fact that I've described threads and processes using Windows 95 as an example, you've probably guessed that Java isn't the first system to employ the use of threads. That's true, but Java is the first major programming language to incorporate threads at the heart of the language itself. Typically, threads are implemented at the system level, requiring a platform-specific programming interface separate from the core programming language. Since Java is presented as both a language and a runtime system, the Sun architects were able to integrate threads into both. The end result is that you are able to make use of Java threads in a standard, cross-platform fashion.

The Problem with Parallelism

If threading is so wonderful, why doesn't every system have it? Many modern operating systems have the basic primitives needed to create and run threads, but they are missing a key ingredient: The rest of their environment is not *thread safe*. A thread-safe environment is one that allows threads to safely coexist with each other peacefully. Imagine that you are in a thread, one of many, and each of you is sharing some important data managed by the system. If you were managing that data, you could take steps to protect it (as you'll see later today), but the system is managing it. Now visualize a piece of code in the system that reads some crucial value, thinks about it for a while, and then adds 1 to the value:

```
if (crucialValue > 0) {
    . . .               // think about what to do
    crucialValue += 1;
}
```

Remember that any number of threads may be calling on this part of the system at once. The disaster occurs when two threads have both executed the if test before either has incremented crucialValue. In that case, the value is clobbered by them both with the same crucialValue += 1, and one of the increments has been lost. This may not seem so bad on the surface, but imagine if the crucial value affects the state of the screen as it is being displayed. Now, unfortunate ordering of the threads can cause the screen to be updated incorrectly. In the same way, mouse or keyboard events can be lost, databases can be inaccurately updated, and general havoc can ensue.

This disaster is inescapable if any significant part of the system has not been written with threads in mind. Therein lies the reason why there are few mainstream threaded environments—the large effort required to rewrite existing libraries for thread safety. Luckily, Java

18

was written from scratch with this is mind, and every Java class in its library is thread safe. Thus, you now have to worry only about your own synchronization and thread-ordering problems because you can assume that the Java system will do the right thing.

Synchronized sections of code are called *critical sections*, implying that access to them is critical to the successful threaded execution of the program. Critical sections are also sometimes referred to as *atomic operations*, meaning that they appear to other threads as if they occur at once. In other words, just as an atom is a discrete unit of matter, atomic operations effectively act like a discrete operation to other threads, even though they may really contain many operations inside.

Critical sections, or *atomic operations*, are synchronized sections of code that appear to happen "all at once"—exactly at the same time—to other threads. This results in only one thread being able to access code in a critical section at a time.

Some readers may wonder what the fundamental problem really is. Can't you just make the . . . area in the previous example smaller and smaller to reduce or eliminate the problem? Without atomic operations, the answer is no. Even if the . . . took zero time, you must first look at the value of some variable to make any decision and then change something to reflect that decision. These two steps can never be made to happen at the same time without an atomic operation. Unless you're given one by the system, it's literally impossible to create your own.

Even the one line `crucialValue += 1` involves three steps: get the current value, add one to it, and store it back. (Using `++crucialValue` doesn't help either.) All three steps need to happen "all at once" (atomically) to be safe. Special Java primitives, at the lowest levels of the language, provide you with the basic atomic operations you need to build safe, threaded programs.

Thinking Multithreaded

Getting used to threads takes a little while and a new way of thinking. Rather than imagining that you always know exactly what's happening when you look at a method you've written, you have to ask yourself some additional questions. What will happen if more than one thread calls into this method at the same time? Do you need to protect it in some way? What about your class as a whole? Are you assuming that only one of its methods is running at the same time?

Often you make such assumptions, and a local instance variable will be messed up as a result. Since common wisdom dictates that we learn from our mistakes, let's make a few mistakes and then try to correct them. First, here's the simplest case:

```
public class ThreadCounter {
    int crucialValue;

    public void countMe() {
        crucialValue += 1;
    }

    public int howMany() {
        return crucialValue;
    }
}
```

This code shows a class used to count threads that suffers from the most pure form of the "synchronization problem": The += takes more than one step, and you may miscount the number of threads as a result. (Don't worry about how threads are created yet; just imagine that a whole bunch of them are able to call countMe(), at once, but at slightly different times.) Java allows you to fix this situation:

```
public class SafeThreadCounter {
    int crucialValue;

    public synchronized void countMe() {
        crucialValue += 1;
    }

    public int howMany() {
        return crucialValue;
    }
}
```

The synchronized keyword tells Java to make the block of code in the method thread safe. This means that only one thread will be allowed inside this method at once, and others will have to wait until the currently running thread is finished with it before they can begin running it. This implies that synchronizing a large, long-running method is almost always a bad idea. All your threads would end up stuck at this bottleneck, waiting single file to get their turn at this one slow method.

It's even worse than you might think for unsynchronized variables. Because the compiler can keep them around in CPU registers during computations, and a thread's registers can't be seen by other threads, a variable can be updated in such a way that *no possible order* of thread updates could have produced the result. This is completely incomprehensible to the programmer, but it can happen. To avoid this bizarre case, you can label a variable volatile, meaning that you know it will be updated asynchronously by multiprocessor-like threads. Java then loads and stores it each time it's needed and does not use CPU registers.

18

> All variables are assumed to be thread safe unless you specifically mark them as `volatile`. Keep in mind that using `volatile` is an extremely rare event. In fact, in the 1.0.2 release, the Java API does not use `volatile` anywhere.

Points About Points

The method `howMany()` in the last example doesn't need to be synchronized because it simply returns the current value of an instance variable. A method higher in the call chain—one that uses the value returned from `howMany()`— may need to be synchronized, though. Listing 18.1 contains an example of a thread in need of this type of synchronization.

TYPE | **Listing 18.1. The `Point` class.**

```
 1: public class Point {        //redefines class Point from package java.awt
 2:     private float x, y;     //OK since we're in a different package here
 3:
 4:     public float x() {           // needs no synchronization
 5:         return x;
 6:     }
 7:
 8:     public float y() {           // ditto
 9:         return y;
10:     }
11:     . . .     // methods to set and change x and y
12: }
13:
14: public class UnsafePointPrinter {
15:     public void print(Point p) {
16:         System.out.println("The point's x is " + p.x()
17:                            + " and y is " + p.y() + ".");
18:     }
19: }
```

ANALYSIS The methods analogous to `howMany()` are `x()` and `y()`. They need no synchronization because they just return the values of member variables. It is the responsibility of the caller of `x()` and `y()` to decide whether it needs to synchronize itself—and in this case, it does. Although the method `print()` simply reads values and prints them out, it reads *two* values. This means that there is a chance that some other thread, running between the call to `p.x()` and the call to `p.y()`, could have changed the value of x and y stored inside the `Point` p. Remember, you don't know how many other threads have a way to reach and call methods

18

in this Point object! "Thinking multithreaded" comes down to being careful any time you make an assumption that something has *not* happened between two parts of your program (even two parts of the same line, or the same expression, such as the string + expression in this example).

TryAgainPointPrinter

You could try to make a safe version of print() by simply adding the synchronized keyword modifier to it, but instead, let's try a slightly different approach:

```
public class TryAgainPointPrinter {
    public void print(Point p) {
        float safeX, safeY;

        synchronized(this) {
            safeX = p.x();      // these two lines now
            safeY = p.y();      // happen atomically
        }
        System.out.print("The point's x is " + safeX
                                    + " y is " + safeY);
    }
}
```

The synchronized statement takes an argument that says what object you would like to lock to prevent more than one thread from executing the enclosed block of code at the same time. Here, you use this (the instance itself), which is exactly the object that would have been locked by the synchronized method as a whole if you had changed print() to be like your safe countMe() method. You have an added bonus with this new form of synchronization: You can specify exactly what part of a method needs to be safe, and the rest can be left unsafe.

Notice how you took advantage of this freedom to make the protected part of the method as small as possible, while leaving the String creations, concatenations, and printing (which together take a small but finite amount of time) outside the "protected" area. This is both good style (as a guide to the reader of your code) and more efficient, because fewer threads get stuck waiting to get into protected areas.

SafePointPrinter

The astute reader, though, may still be worried by the last example. It seems as if you made sure that no one executes *your* calls to x() and y() out of order, but have you prevented the Point p from changing out from under you? If the answer is no, you still have not completely solved the problem. It turns out that you really do need the full power of the synchronized statement:

```
public class SafePointPrinter {
    public void print(Point p) {
        float safeX, safeY;
```

```
synchronized(p) {      // no one can change p
    safeX = p.x();     // while these two lines
    safeY = p.y();     // are happening atomically
}
System.out.print("The point's x is " + safeX
                          + " y is " + safeY);
    }
}
```

Now you've got it! You actually needed to protect the Point p from changes, so you lock it by providing it as the argument to your synchronized statement. Now when x() and y() are called together, they can be sure to get the current x and y of the Point p, without any other thread being able to call a modifying method between. You're still assuming, however, that the Point p has properly protected *itself.* You can always assume this about system classes— but *you* wrote this Point class. You can make sure it's okay by writing the only method that can change x and y inside p yourself:

```
public class  Point {
    private float x, y;

    . . .           // the x() and y() methods

    public synchronized void setXAndY(float  newX,  float  newY) {
        x = newX;
        y = newY;
    }
}
```

By making synchronized the only "set" method in Point, you guarantee that any other thread trying to grab the Point p and change it out from under you has to wait. You've locked the Point p with your synchronized(p) statement, and any other thread has to lock the same Point p via the implicit synchronized(this) statement that is executed when p enters setXAndY(). So at last you are thread safe.

NOTE

By the way, if Java had some way of returning more than one value at once, you could write a synchronized getXAndY() method for Point that returns both values safely. In the current Java language, such a method could return a new, unique Point to guarantee to its callers that no one else has a copy that might be changed. This sort of trick can be used to minimize the parts of the system that need to worry about synchronization.

Protecting a Class Variable

Suppose you want a class variable to collect some information across all a class's instances:

```
public class StaticCounter {
    private static int crucialValue;

    public synchronized void countMe() {
        crucialValue += 1;
    }
}
```

Is this safe? If crucialValue were an instance variable, it would be. Because it's a class variable, however, and there is only one copy of it for all instances; you can still have multiple threads modifying it by using different *instances* of the class. (Remember that the synchronized modifier locks the this object—an instance.) Luckily, you now know the technique required to solve this:

```
public class StaticCounter {
    private static int crucialValue;

    public void countMe() {
        synchronized(getClass()) {   // can't directly name StaticCounter
            crucialValue += 1;        // the (shared) class is now locked
        }
    }
}
```

The trick is to "lock" on a different object—not on an instance of the class, but on the class itself. Because a class variable is "inside" a class, just as an instance variable is inside an instance, this shouldn't be all that unexpected. In a similar way, classes can provide global resources that any instance (or other class) can access directly by using the class name and lock by using that same class name. In the last example, crucialValue was used from within an instance of StaticCounter, but if crucialValue were declared public instead, from anywhere in the program, it would be safe to say the following:

```
synchronized(Class.forName("StaticCounter")) {
    StaticCounter.crucialValue += 1;
}
```

NOTE

> The direct use of another class's (object's) member variable is really bad style—it's used here simply to demonstrate a point quickly. StaticCounter would normally provide a countMe()-like class method of its own to do this sort of dirty work.

18

You can now begin to appreciate how much work the Java team has done for you by thinking all these hard thoughts for each and every class (and method!) in the Java class library.

Creating and Using Threads

Now that you understand the power (and the dangers) of having many threads running at once, how are those threads actually created?

WARNING

The system itself always has a few *daemon threads* running, one of which is constantly doing the tedious task of garbage collection for you in the background. There is also a main user thread that listens for events from your mouse and keyboard. If you're not careful, you can sometimes lock up this main thread. If you do, no events are sent to your program and it appears to be dead. A good rule of thumb is that whenever you're doing something that *can* be done in a separate thread, it probably *should* be. Threads in Java are relatively cheap to create, run, and destroy, so don't use them too sparingly.

Because there is a class `java.lang.Thread`, you might guess that you could create a thread of your own by subclassing it—and you are right:

```
public class MyFirstThread extends Thread { // a.k.a., java.lang.Thread
    public void run() {
        . . .                    // do something useful
    }
}
```

You now have a new type of thread called `MyFirstThread`, which does something useful when its `run()` method is called. Of course, no one has created this thread or called its `run()` method, so at this point it is just a class eager to become a thread. To actually create and run an instance of your new thread class, you write the following:

```
MyFirstThread aMFT = new MyFirstThread();
aMFT.start();    // calls our run() method
```

What could be simpler? You create a new instance of your thread class and then ask it to start running. Whenever you want to stop the thread, you do this:

```
aMFT.stop();
```

Besides responding to start() and stop(), a thread can also be temporarily suspended and later resumed:

```
Thread  t = new Thread();
t.suspend();
 . . .            // do something special while t isn't running
t.resume();
```

A thread will automatically suspend() and then resume() when it's first blocked at a synchronized point and then later unblocked (when it's that thread's "turn" to run).

The Runnable Interface

This is all well and good if every time you want to create a thread you have the luxury of being able to place it under the Thread class in the single-inheritance Java class tree. But what if it more naturally belongs under some other class, from which it needs to inherit most of its implementation? The interfaces you learned about on Day 16, "Packages and Interfaces," come to the rescue:

```
public class MySecondThread extends ImportantClass implements Runnable {
    public void run() {
         . . .            // do something useful
    }
}
```

18

By implementing the interface Runnable, you declare your intention to run in a separate thread. In fact, the Thread class is itself an implementation of this interface, as you might expect from the design discussions on Day 16. As you also might guess from the example, the Runnable interface defines only one method: run(). As in MyFirstThread, you expect someone to create an instance of a thread and somehow call your run() method. Here's how this is accomplished using the interface approach to thread creation:

```
MySecondThread  aMST = new MySecondThread();
Thread          aThread = new Thread(aMST);
aThread.start();    // calls our run() method, indirectly
```

First, you create an instance of MySecondThread. Then, by passing this instance to the constructor creating the new thread, you make it the target of that thread. Whenever that new thread starts up, its run() method calls the run() method of the target it was given (assumed by the thread to be an object that implements the Runnable interface). When start() is called on aThread, your run() method is indirectly called. You can stop aThread with stop(). If you don't need to use the Thread object or instance of MySecondThread explicitly, here's a one-line shortcut:

```
new Thread(new MySecondThread()).start();
```

NOTE

> As you can see, the class name MySecondThread is a bit of a misnomer—it does not descend from Thread, nor is it actually the thread that you start() and stop(). It could have been called MySecondThreadedClass or ImportantRunnableClass to be more clear on this point.

ThreadTester

Listing 18.2 contains a longer example of creating and using threads.

TYPE   **Listing 18.2. The SimpleRunnable class.**

```
 1: public class SimpleRunnable implements Runnable {
 2:     public void run() {
 3:         System.out.println("in thread named '"
 4:                             + Thread.currentThread().getName() + "'");
 5:     } // any other methods run() calls are in current thread as well
 6: }
 7:
 8: public class ThreadTester {
 9:     public static void main(String argv[]) {
10:         SimpleRunnable aSR = new SimpleRunnable();
11:
12:         while (true) {
13:             Thread t = new Thread(aSR);
14:
15:             System.out.println("new Thread() " + (t == null ?
16:                                             "fail" : "succeed") + "ed.");
17:             t.start();
18:             try { t.join(); } catch (InterruptedException ignored) { }
19:                         // waits for thread to finish its run() method
20:         }
21:     }
22: }
```

NOTE

> You may be worried that only one instance of the class SimpleRunnable is created, but many new threads are using it. Don't they get confused? Remember to separate in your mind the aSR instance (and the methods it understands) from the various threads of execution that can pass through it. aSR's methods provide a template for execution, and the multiple threads created are sharing that template. Each remembers

18

where it is executing and whatever else it needs to make it distinct from the other running threads. They all share the same instance and the same methods. That's why you need to be so careful, when adding synchronization, to imagine numerous threads running rampant over each of your methods.

ANALYSIS The class method currentThread() can be called to get the thread in which a method is currently executing. If the SimpleRunnable class were a subclass of Thread, its methods would know the answer already (*it* is the thread running). Because SimpleRunnable simply implements the interface Runnable, however, and counts on someone else (ThreadTester's main()) to create the thread, its run() method needs another way to get its hands on that thread. Often, you'll be deep inside methods called by your run() method when suddenly you need to get the current thread. The class method shown in the example works, no matter where you are.

The example then calls getName() on the current thread to get the thread's name (usually something helpful, such as Thread-23) so it can tell the world in which thread run() is running. The final thing to note is the use of the method join(), which, when sent to a thread, means "I'm planning to wait forever for you to finish your run() method." You don't want to use this approach without good reason: If you have anything else important you need to get done in your thread any time soon, you can't count on how long the joined thread might take to finish. In the example, the run() method is short and finishes quickly, so each loop can safely wait for the previous thread to die before creating the next one. Here's the output produced:

```
new Thread() succeeded.
in thread named 'Thread-1'
new Thread() succeeded.
in thread named 'Thread-2'
new Thread() succeeded.
in thread named 'Thread-3'
^C
```

Incidentally, Ctrl+C was pressed to interrupt the program, because it otherwise would continue on forever.

WARNING

You can do some reasonably disastrous things with your knowledge of threads. For example, if you're running in the main thread of the

> system and, because you think you are in a different thread, you accidentally say the following:
>
> ```
> Thread.currentThread().stop();
> ```
>
> it has unfortunate consequences for your (soon-to-be-dead) program!

NamedThreadTester

If you want your threads to have particular names, you can assign them yourself by using another form of Thread's constructor:

```
public class NamedThreadTester {
    public static void main(String argv[]) {
        SimpleRunnable aSR = new SimpleRunnable();

        for (int i = 1; true; ++i) {
            Thread t = new Thread(aSR, "" + (100 - i)
                                        + " threads on the wall...");

            System.out.println("new Thread() " + (t == null ?
                                        "fail" : "succeed") + "ed.");
            t.start();
            try { t.join(); } catch (InterruptedException ignored) { }
        }
    }
}
```

This version of Thread's constructor takes a target object, as before, and a string, which names the new thread. Here's the output:

```
new Thread() succeeded.
in thread named '99 threads on the wall...'
new Thread() succeeded.
in thread named '98 threads on the wall...'
new Thread() succeeded.
in thread named '97 threads on the wall...'
^C
```

Naming a thread is one easy way to pass it some information. This information flows from the parent thread to its new child. It's also useful, for debugging purposes, to give threads meaningful names (such as network input) so that when they appear during an error—in a stack trace, for example—you can easily identify which thread caused the problem. You might also think of using names to help group or organize your threads, but Java actually provides you with a ThreadGroup class to perform this function.

The ThreadGroup class is used to manage a group of threads as a single unit. This provides you with a means to finely control thread execution for a series of threads. For example, the ThreadGroup class provides stop, suspend, and resume methods for controlling the execution of all the threads in the group. Thread groups can also contain other thread groups, allowing for a nested hierarchy of threads. Another benefit to using thread groups is that they can keep threads from being able to affect other threads, which is useful for security.

Knowing When a Thread Has Stopped

Let's imagine a different version of the last example, one that creates a thread and then hands the thread off to other parts of the program. Suppose the program would then like to know when that thread dies so that it can perform some cleanup operation. If SimpleRunnable were a subclass of Thread, you might try to catch stop() whenever it's sent—but look at Thread's declaration of the stop() method:

```
public final void stop() { . . . }
```

The final here means that you can't override this method in a subclass. In any case, SimpleRunnable is *not* a subclass of Thread, so how can this imagined example possibly catch the death of its thread? The answer is to use the following magic:

```
public class SingleThreadTester {
    public static void main(String argv[]) {
        Thread t = new Thread(new SimpleRunnable());

        try {
            t.start();
            someMethodThatMightStopTheThread(t);
        } catch (ThreadDeath aTD) {
            . . .                // do some required cleanup
            throw aTD;           // re-throw the error
        }
    }
}
```

You understand most of this magic from yesterday's lesson. All you need to know is that if the thread created in the example dies, it throws an error of class ThreadDeath. The code catches that error and performs the required cleanup. It then rethrows the error, allowing the thread to die. The cleanup code is not called if the thread exits normally (its run() method completes), but that's fine; you posited that the cleanup was needed only when stop() was used on the thread.

 NOTE

Threads can die in other ways—for example, by throwing exceptions that no one catches. In these cases, stop() is never called and the previous code is not sufficient. Because unexpected exceptions can come out of nowhere to kill a thread, multithreaded programs that carefully catch and handle all their exceptions are more predictable and robust, and they're easier to debug.

Thread Scheduling

You might be wondering how any software system can be truly threaded when running on a machine with a single CPU. If there is only one physical CPU in a computer system, it's impossible for more than one machine code instruction to be executed at a time. This means that no matter how hard you try to rationalize the behavior of a multithreaded system, only one thread is really being executed at a particular time. The reality is that multithreading on a single CPU system, like the systems most of us use, is at best a good illusion. The good news is that the illusion works so well most of the time that we feel pretty comfortable in the fact that multiple threads are really running in parallel.

The illusion of parallel thread execution on a system with a single CPU is often managed by giving each thread an opportunity to execute a little bit of code at regular intervals. This approach is known as *timeslicing*, which refers to the way each thread gets a little of the CPU's time to execute code. When you speed up this whole scenario to millions of instructions per second, the whole effect of parallel execution comes across pretty well.

The general task of managing and executing multiple threads in an environment such as this is known as *scheduling*. Likewise, the part of the system that decides the real-time ordering of threads is called the *scheduler*.

Preemptive Versus Nonpreemptive

Normally, any scheduler has two fundamentally different ways of looking at its job: nonpreemptive scheduling and preemptive time slicing.

With *nonpreemptive scheduling*, the scheduler runs the current thread forever, requiring that thread to explicitly tell it when it is safe to start a different thread. With *preemptive time slicing*, the scheduler runs the current thread until it has used up a certain tiny fraction of a second, and then "preempts" it, suspends it, and resumes another thread for the next tiny fraction of a second.

Nonpreemptive scheduling is very courtly, always asking for permission to schedule, and is quite valuable in extremely time-critical real-time applications where being interrupted at the wrong moment, or for too long, could mean crashing an airplane.

However, most modern schedulers use preemptive time slicing because it generally has made writing multithreaded programs much easier. For one thing, it does not force each thread to decide exactly when it should "yield" control to another thread. Instead, every thread can just run blindly on, knowing that the scheduler will be fair about giving all the other threads their chance to run.

However, it turns out that this approach is still not the ideal way to schedule threads; you've given up a little too much control to the scheduler. The final touch many modern schedulers add is to allow you to assign each thread a priority. This creates a total ordering of all threads, making some threads more "important" than others. Being higher priority often means that a thread gets run more often or for a longer period of time, but it always means that it can interrupt other, lower-priority threads, even before their "time slice" has expired.

A good example of a low-priority thread is the garbage collection thread in the Java runtime system. Even though garbage collection is a very important function, it is not something you want hogging the CPU. Since the garbage collection thread is a low-priority thread, it chugs along in the background, freeing up memory as the processor allows it. This may result in memory being freed a little slower, but it allows more time-critical threads, such as the user input handling thread, full access to the CPU. You may be wondering what happens if the CPU stays busy and the garbage collector never gets to clean up memory. Does the runtime system run out of memory and crash? No. This brings up one of the neat aspects of threads and how they work. If a high-priority thread can't access a resource it needs, such as memory, it enters a wait state until memory becomes available. When all memory is gone, all the threads running will eventually go into a wait state, thereby freeing up the CPU to execute the garbage collection thread, which in turn frees up memory. And the circle of threaded life continues!

The current Java release (1.0.2) does not precisely specify the behavior of its scheduler. Threads can be assigned priorities, and when a choice is made between several threads that all want to run, the highest-priority thread wins. However, among threads that are all the same priority, the behavior is not well defined. In fact, the different platforms on which Java currently runs have different behaviors—some behaving more like a preemptive scheduler, and some more like a nonpreemptive scheduler.

NOTE This incomplete specification of the scheduler is terribly annoying and, presumably, will be corrected in a later release. Not knowing the fine details of how scheduling occurs is perfectly all right, but not knowing whether equal-priority threads must explicitly yield or face running forever is not all right. For example, all the threads you have created so far are equal-priority threads so you don't know their basic scheduling behavior!

Testing Your Scheduler

To find out what kind of scheduler you have on your system, try out the following code:

```
public class RunnablePotato implements Runnable {
    public void run() {
```

```
            while (true)
                System.out.println(Thread.currentThread().getName());
        }
    }

public class PotatoThreadTester {
    public static void main(String argv[]) {
        RunnablePotato aRP = new RunnablePotato();

        new Thread(aRP, "one potato").start();
        new Thread(aRP, "two potato").start();
    }
}
```

If your system employs a nonpreemptive scheduler, this code results in the following output:

```
one potato
one potato
one potato
. . .
```

This output will go on forever or until you interrupt the program. For a preemptive scheduler that uses time slicing, this code will repeat the line one potato a few times, followed by the same number of two potato lines, over and over:

```
one potato
one potato
...
one potato
two potato
two potato
...
two potato
. . .
```

This output will also go on forever or until you interrupt the program. What if you want to be sure the two threads will take turns, regardless of the type of system scheduler? You rewrite RunnablePotato as follows:

```
public class RunnablePotato implements Runnable {
    public void run() {
        while (true) {
            System.out.println(Thread.currentThread().getName());
            Thread.yield();  // let another thread run for a while
        }
    }
}
```

 TIP

Normally you would have to use Thread.currentThread().yield() to get your hands on the current thread, and then call yield(). Because this pattern is so common, however, the Thread class can be used as a shortcut.

The `yield()` method explicitly gives any other threads that want to run a chance to begin running. (If there are no threads waiting to run, the thread that made the `yield()` simply continues.) In our example, there's another thread that's just *dying* to run, so when you now execute the class `ThreadTester`, it should output the following:

```
one potato
two potato
one potato
two potato
one potato
two potato
. . .
```

This output will be the same regardless of the type of scheduler you have.

To see whether thread priorities are working on your system, try this code:

```java
public class PriorityThreadTester {
    public static void main(String argv[]) {
        RunnablePotato aRP = new RunnablePotato();
        Thread         t1  = new Thread(aRP, "one potato");
        Thread         t2  = new Thread(aRP, "two potato");

        t2.setPriority(t1.getPriority() + 1);
        t1.start();
        t2.start();    // at priority Thread.NORM_PRIORITY + 1
    }
}
```

TIP

> The values representing the lowest, normal, and highest priorities that threads can be assigned are stored in constant class members of the `Thread` class: `Thread.MIN_PRIORITY`, `Thread.NORM_PRIORITY`, and `Thread.MAX_PRIORITY`. The system assigns new threads, by default, the priority `Thread.NORM_PRIORITY`. Priorities in Java are currently defined in a range from 1 to 10, with 5 being normal, but you shouldn't depend on these values; use the class variables or tricks like the one shown in this example.

If one `potato` is the first line of output, your system does not preempt using thread priorities. Why? Imagine that the first thread (`t1`) has just begun to run. Even before it has a chance to print anything, along comes a higher-priority thread (`t2`) that wants to run as well. That higher-priority thread should preempt (interrupt) the first and get a chance to print `two potato` before `t1` finishes printing anything. In fact, if you use the `RunnablePotato` class that never `yield()`s, `t2` stays in control forever, printing `two potato` lines, because it's a higher priority than `t1` and it never yields control. If you use the latest `RunnablePotato` class (with yield()), the output is alternating lines of one potato and two potato as before, but starting with two potato.

Listing 18.3 contains a good, illustrative example of how complex threads behave.

TYPE **Listing 18.3. The** `ComplexThread` **class.**

```
1: public class ComplexThread extends Thread {
2:     private int delay;
3:
4:     ComplexThread(String name, float seconds) {
5:         super(name);
6:         delay = (int) seconds * 1000;   // delays are in milliseconds
7:         start();                        // start up ourself!
8:     }
9:
10:     public void run() {
11:         while (true) {
12:             System.out.println(Thread.currentThread().getName());
13:             try {
14:                 Thread.sleep(delay);
15:             } catch (InterruptedException e) {
16:                 return;
17:             }
18:         }
19:     }
20:
21:     public static void main(String argv[]) {
22:         new ComplexThread("one potato",   1.1F);
23:         new ComplexThread("two potato",   1.3F);
24:         new ComplexThread("three potato", 0.5F);
25:         new ComplexThread("four",         0.7F);
26:     }
27: }
```

ANALYSIS This example combines the thread and its tester into a single class. Its constructor takes care of naming and starting itself because it is now a thread. The main() method creates new instances of its own class because the class is a subclass of Thread. The run() method is also more complicated because it now uses, for the first time, a method that can throw an unexpected exception.

The Thread.sleep() method forces the current thread to yield() and then waits for at least the specified amount of time to elapse before allowing the thread to run again. It might be interrupted by another thread, however, while it's sleeping. In such a case, it throws an InterruptedException. Now, because run() is not defined as throwing this exception, you must "hide" the fact by catching and handling it yourself. Because interruptions are usually requests to stop, you should exit the thread, which you can do by simply returning from the run() method.

This program should output a repeating but complex pattern of four different lines, where every once in a great while you see the following:

```
. . .
one potato
two potato
three potato
four
. . .
```

You should study the pattern output to prove to yourself that true parallelism is going on inside Java programs. You may also begin to appreciate that, if even this simple set of four threads can produce such complex behavior, many more threads must be capable of producing near chaos if not carefully controlled. Luckily, Java provides the synchronization and thread-safe libraries you need to control that chaos.

Summary

Today you have learned that multithreading is desirable and powerful, but introduces many new problems—methods and variables now need to be *protected* from thread conflicts—that can lead to chaos if not carefully controlled. By "thinking multithreaded," you can detect the places in your programs that require synchronized statements (or modifiers) to make them thread safe. A series of Point examples demonstrates the various levels of safety you can achieve, and ThreadTesters shows how subclasses of Thread, or classes that implement the Runnable interface, are created and run to generate multithreaded programs.

You have also learned today how to use yield(), start(), stop(), suspend(), and resume() on your threads, and how to catch ThreadDeath whenever it happens. You have learned about preemptive and nonpreemptive scheduling, both with and without priorities, and how to test your Java system to see which of them your scheduler is using.

You are now armed with enough information to write the most complex of programs: multithreaded ones. As you get more comfortable with threads, you may begin to use the ThreadGroup class or the enumeration methods of Thread to get your hands on all the threads in the system and manipulate them. Don't be afraid to experiment; you can't permanently break anything, and you only learn by trying.

18

Q&A

Q If they're so important to Java, why haven't threads appeared throughout the entire book?

A Actually, they have. Every standalone program written so far has "created" at least one thread, the one in which it is running. (Of course the system created that thread for it automatically.)

Q How exactly do these threads get created and run? What about applets?

A When a simple standalone Java program starts up, the system creates a main thread, and its run() method calls your main() method to start your program—you do nothing to get that thread. Likewise, when a simple applet loads into a Java-enabled browser, a thread has already been created by the browser, and its run() method calls your init() and start() methods to start your program. In either case, a new thread of some kind was created somewhere by the Java environment itself.

Q I know the current Java release is still a little fuzzy about the scheduler's behavior, but what's the word from Sun?

A Here's the scoop, as relayed by Arthur van Hoff at Sun: The way Java schedules threads "…depends on the platform. It is usually preemptive, but not always time sliced. Priorities are not always observed, depending on the underlying implementation." This final clause gives you a hint that all this confusion is an implementation problem, and that in some future release, the design and implementation will both be clear about scheduling behavior.

Q My parallel friends tell me I should worry about something called "deadlock." Should I?

A Not for simple multithreaded programs. However, in more complicated programs, one of the biggest worries does become one of avoiding a situation in which one thread has locked an object and is waiting for another thread to finish, while that other thread is waiting for the first thread to release that same object before it can finish. That's a deadlock—both threads will be stuck forever. Mutual dependencies like this involving more than two threads can be quite intricate, convoluted, and difficult to locate, much less rectify. They are one of the main challenges in writing complex multithreaded programs.

Day **19**

Streams and I/O

by Charles L. Perkins and Laura Lemay

The package `java.io`, part of the standard Java class library, provides a large number of classes designed for handling input and output to files, network connections, and other sources. These I/O classes are known as streams, and provide functionality for reading and writing data in various ways. You got a glimpse of these classes on Day 14, "Windows, Networking, and Other Tidbits," when we opened a network connection to a file and read the contents into an applet.

Today you'll explore Java's input and output classes:

☐ Input streams—and how to create, use, and detect the end of them— and filtered input streams, which can be nested to great effect

☐ Output streams, which are mostly analogous to (but the inverse of) input streams

You'll also learn about two stream interfaces that make the reading and writing of typed streams much easier (as well as about several utility classes used to access the file system).

What Are Streams?

A *stream* is a path of communication between the source of some information and its destination. This information can come from a file, the computer's memory, or even from the Internet. In fact, the source and destination of a stream are completely arbitrary producers and consumers of bytes, respectively—you don't need to know about the source of the information when reading from a stream, and you don't need to know about the final destination when writing to one.

 A *stream* is a path of communication between a source of information and its destination. For example, an input stream allows you to read data from a source, and an output stream allows you to write data to a destination.

General-purpose methods that can read from any source accept a stream argument to specify that source; general-purpose methods for writing accept a stream to specify the destination. Arbitrary *processors* of data commonly have two stream arguments. They read from the first, process the data, and write the results to the second. These processors have no idea of either the source *or* the destination of the data they are processing. Sources and destinations can vary widely: from two memory buffers on the same local computer, to the ELF (extremely low frequency) transmissions to and from a submarine at sea, to the real-time data streams of a NASA probe in deep space.

By decoupling the consuming, processing, or producing of data from the sources and destinations of that data, you can mix and match any combination of them at will as you write your program. In the future, when new, previously nonexistent forms of source or destination (or consumer, processor, or producer) appear, they can be used within the same framework, with no changes to your classes. In addition, new stream abstractions, supporting higher levels of interpretation "on top of" the bytes, can be written completely independently of the underlying transport mechanisms for the bytes themselves.

The `java.io` Package

All the classes you will learn about today are part of the package `java.io`. To use any of these classes in your own programs, you will need to import each individual class or to import the entire `java.io` package, like this:

```
import java.io.InputStream;
import java.io.FilteredInputStream;
import java.io.FileOutputStream;

import java.io.*;
```

All the methods you will explore today are declared to throw `IOExceptions`. This new subclass of `Exception` conceptually embodies all the possible I/O errors that might occur while using streams. Several subclasses of it define a few, more specific exceptions that can be thrown as well. For now, it is enough to know that you must either catch an IOException, or be in a method that can "pass it along," to be a well-behaved user of streams.

The foundations of this stream framework in the Java class hierarchy are the two abstract classes, InputStream and OutputStream. Inheriting from these classes is a virtual cornucopia of categorized subclasses, demonstrating the wide range of streams in the system, but also demonstrating an extremely well-designed hierarchy of relationships between these streams—one well worth learning from. Let's begin with the parents, InputStream and OutputStream, and then work our way down this bushy tree.

Input Streams

Input streams are streams that allow you to read data from a source. These include the root abstract class InputStream, filtered streams, buffered streams, and streams that read from files, strings, and byte arrays.

The Abstract Class InputStream

InputStream is an abstract class that defines the fundamental ways in which a destination (consumer) reads a stream of bytes from some source. The identity of the source, and the manner of the creation and transport of the bytes, is irrelevant. When using an input stream, you are the destination of those bytes, and that's all you need to know.

NOTE
> All input streams descend from InputStream. All share in common the few methods described in this section. Thus, the streams used in these examples can be any of the more complex input streams described in the next few sections.

19

read()

The most important method to the consumer of an input stream is the one that reads bytes from the source. This method, read(), comes in many flavors, and each is demonstrated in an example in today's lesson.

Each of these read() methods is defined to "block" (wait) until all the input requested becomes available. Don't worry about this limitation; because of multithreading, you can do as many other things as you like while this one thread is waiting for input. In fact, it is a common idiom to assign a thread to each stream of input (and for each stream of output) that is solely responsible for reading from it (or writing to it). These input threads might then "hand off" the information to other threads for processing. This naturally overlaps the I/O time of your program with its compute time.

Here's the first form of `read()`:

```
InputStream  s      = getAnInputStreamFromSomewhere();
byte[]       buffer = new byte[1024];   // any size will do

if (s.read(buffer) != buffer.length)
    System.out.println("I got less than I expected.");
```

> **NOTE**
>
> Here and throughout the rest of today's lesson, assume that either an `import java.io.*` appears before all the examples or that you mentally prefix all references to `java.io` classes with the prefix `java.io`.

This form of `read()` attempts to fill the entire buffer given. If it cannot (usually due to reaching the end of the input stream), it returns the actual number of bytes that were read into the buffer. After that, any further calls to `read()` return `-1`, indicating that you are at the end of the stream. Note that the `if` statement still works even in this case, because `-1 != 1024` (this corresponds to an input stream with no bytes in it at all).

> **NOTE**
>
> Don't forget that, unlike in C, the `-1` case in Java is not used to indicate an error. Any I/O errors throw instances of `IOException` (which you're not catching yet). You learned on Day 17, "Exceptions," that all uses of distinguished values can be replaced by the use of exceptions, and so they should. The `-1` in the last example is a bit of a historical anachronism. You'll soon see a better approach to indicating the end of the stream using the class `DataInputStream`.

You can also read into a "slice" of your buffer by specifying the offset into the buffer, and the length desired, as arguments to `read()`:

```
s.read(buffer, 100, 300);
```

This example tries to fill in bytes 100 through 399 and behaves otherwise exactly the same as the previous `read()` method.

Finally, you can read in bytes one at a time:

```
InputStream  s = getAnInputStreamFromSomewhere();
byte         b;
int          byteOrMinus1;

while ((byteOrMinus1 = s.read()) != -1) {
    b = (byte) byteOrMinus1;
    . . .      // process the byte b
}
. . .      // reached end of stream
```

NOTE

Because of the nature of integer promotion in Java in general, and because in this case the read() method returns an int, using the byte type in your code may be a little frustrating. You'll find yourself constantly having to explicitly cast the result of arithmetic expressions, or of int return values, back to your size. Because read() really should be returning a byte in this case, we feel justified in declaring and using it as such (despite the pain)—it makes the size of the data being read clearer. In cases where you feel that the range of a variable is naturally limited to a byte (or a short) rather than an int, please take the time to declare it that way and pay the small price necessary to gain the added clarity. By the way, a lot of the Java class library code simply stores the result of read() in an int.

skip()

What if you want to skip over some of the bytes in a stream, or start reading a stream from other than its beginning? A method similar to read() does the trick:

```
if (s.skip(1024) != 1024)
    System.out.println("I skipped less than I expected.");
```

This example skips over the next 1024 bytes in the input stream. However, the implementation of skip() in InputStream may skip fewer bytes than the given argument, and so it returns a long integer representing the number of bytes it actually skipped. In this example, therefore, a message is printed if the actual number of bytes skipped is less than 1024.

NOTE

The API documentation for skip() in the InputStream class says that skip() behaves this way for "a variety of reasons." Subclasses of InputStream should override this default implementation of skip() if they want to handle skipping more properly.

available()

If for some reason you would like to know how many bytes are in the stream right now, you can ask the following:

```
if (s.available() < 1024)
    System.out.println("Too little is available right now.");
```

This tells you the number of bytes that you can read without blocking. Because of the abstract nature of the source of these bytes, streams may or may not be able to tell you a reasonable answer to this question. For example, some streams always return 0. Unless you use specific subclasses of InputStream that you know provide a reasonable answer to this question, it's not a good idea to rely on this method. Remember that multithreading eliminates many of the problems associated with blocking while waiting for a stream to fill again. Thus, one of the strongest rationales for the use of available() goes away.

mark() **and** reset()

Some streams support the notion of marking a position in the stream and then later resetting the stream to that position to reread the bytes there. Clearly, the stream would have to "remember" all those bytes, so there is a limitation on how far apart in a stream the mark and its subsequent reset can occur. There's also a method that asks whether the stream supports the notion of marking at all. Here's an example:

```
InputStream  s = getAnInputStreamFromSomewhere();

if (s.markSupported()) {     // does s support the notion?
    . . .              // read the stream for a while
    s.mark(1024);
    . . .            // read less than 1024 more bytes
    s.reset();
    . . .            // we can now re-read those bytes
} else {
    . . .                    // no, perform some alternative
}
```

When marking a stream, you specify the maximum number of bytes you intend to allow to pass before resetting it. This allows the stream to limit the size of its byte "memory." If this number of bytes goes by and you have not yet used reset(), the mark becomes invalid, and attempting to use reset() will throw an exception.

Marking and resetting a stream is most valuable when you are attempting to identify the type of the stream (or the next part of the stream), but to do so, you must consume a significant piece of it in the process. Often, this is because you have several black-box parsers that you can hand the stream to, but they will consume some (unknown to you) number of bytes before making up their mind about whether the stream is of their type. Set a large size for the limit in mark(), and let each parser run until it either throws an error or completes a successful parse. If an error is thrown, use reset() and try the next parser.

close()

Because you don't know what resources an open stream represents, nor how to deal with them properly when you're finished reading the stream, you should (usually) explicitly close down a stream so that it can release these resources. Of course, garbage collection and a finalization method can do this for you, but what if you need to reopen that stream or those resources before they have been freed by this asynchronous process? At best, this is annoying or confusing; at worst, it introduces an unexpected, obscure, and difficult-to-track-down bug. Because you're interacting with the outside world of external resources, it's safer to be explicit about when you're finished using them:

```
InputStream   s = alwaysMakesANewInputStream();

try {
    . . .      // use s to your heart's content
} finally {
    s.close();
}
```

Get used to this idiom (using `finally`); it's a useful way to be sure something (such as closing the stream) always gets done. Of course, you're assuming that the stream is always successfully created. If this is not always the case, and `null` is sometimes returned instead, here's the correct way to be safe:

```
InputStream   s = tryToMakeANewInputStream();

if (s != null) {
    try {
        . . .
    } finally {
        s.close();
    }
}
```

ByteArrayInputStream

The "inverse" of some of the previous examples would be to create an input stream *from* an array of bytes. This is exactly what `ByteArrayInputStream` does:

```
byte[]   buffer = new byte[1024];

fillWithUsefulData(buffer);

InputStream   s = new ByteArrayInputStream(buffer);
```

Readers of the new stream s see a stream 1024 bytes long, containing the bytes in the array `buffer`. Just as `read()` has a form that takes an offset and a length, so does this class's constructor:

```
InputStream   s = new ByteArrayInputStream(buffer, 100, 300);
```

Here the stream is 300 bytes long and consists of bytes 100–399 from the array `buffer`.

NOTE

Finally, you've seen your first examples of the *creation* of a stream. These new streams are attached to the simplest of all possible sources of data: an array of bytes in the memory of the local computer.

ByteArrayInputStreams simply implement the standard set of methods that all input streams do. Here, however, the available() method has a particularly simple job—it returns 1024 and 300, respectively, for the two instances of ByteArrayInputStream you created previously, because it knows exactly how many bytes are available. Finally, calling reset() on a ByteArrayInputStream resets it to the beginning of the stream (buffer), no matter where the mark is set.

FileInputStream

One of the most common uses of streams, and historically the earliest, is to attach them to files in the file system. Here, for example, is the creation of such an input stream on a UNIX system:

```
InputStream  s = new FileInputStream("/some/path/and/fileName");
```

WARNING

Applets attempting to open, read, or write streams based on files in the file system will usually cause security exceptions to be thrown from the browser. If you're developing applets, you won't be able to depend on files at all, and you'll have to use your server to hold shared information. (Standalone Java programs have none of these problems, of course.)

You also can create the stream from a previously opened file descriptor (an instance of the FileDescriptor class). Usually, you get file descriptors using the getFD() method on FileInputStream or FileOutputStream classes, so, for example, you could use the same file descriptor to open a file for reading and then reopen it for writing:

```
FileDescriptor      fd = someFileStream.getFD();
InputStream  s  = new FileInputStream(fd);
```

In either case, because it's based on an actual (finite length) file, the input stream created can implement available() precisely and can skip like a champ (just as ByteArrayInputStream can, by the way). In addition, FileInputStream knows a few more tricks:

```
FileInputStream  aFIS = new FileInputStream("aFileName");

FileDescriptor  myFD = aFIS.getFD(); // get a file descriptor

 aFIS.finalize();   // will call close() when automatically called by GC
```

TIP

To call these new methods, you must declare the stream variable aFIS to be of type FileInputStream, because plain InputStreams don't know about them.

19

The first is obvious: getFD() returns the file descriptor of the file on which the stream is based. The second, though, is an interesting shortcut that allows you to create FileInputStreams without worrying about closing them later. FileInputStream's implementation of finalize(), a protected method, closes the stream. Unlike in the contrived call in comments, you almost never can nor should call a finalize() method directly. The garbage collector calls it after noticing that the stream is no longer in use, but before actually destroying the stream. Thus, you can go merrily along using the stream, never closing it, and all will be well. The system takes care of closing it (eventually).

You can get away with this because streams based on files tie up very few resources, and these resources cannot be accidentally reused before garbage collection (these were the things worried about in the previous discussion of finalization and close()). Of course, if you were also *writing* to the file, you would have to be more careful. (Reopening the file too soon after writing might make it appear in an inconsistent state because the finalize()—and thus the close()—might not have happened yet.) Just because you don't *have* to close the stream doesn't mean you might not want to do so anyway. For clarity, or if you don't know precisely what type of an InputStream you were handed, you might choose to call close() yourself.

FilterInputStream

This "abstract" class simply provides a "pass-through" for all the standard methods of InputStream. (It's "abstract," in quotes, because it's not technically an abstract class; you can create instances of it. In most cases, however, you'll use one of the more useful subclasses of FilterInputStream instead of FilterInputStream itself.) FilterInputStream holds inside itself another stream, by definition one further "down" the chain of filters, to which it forwards all method calls. It implements nothing new but allows itself to be nested:

```
InputStream          s  = getAnInputStreamFromSomewhere();
FilterInputStream    s1 = new FilterInputStream(s);
FilterInputStream    s2 = new FilterInputStream(s1);
FilterInputStream    s3 = new FilterInputStream(s2);

... s3.read() ...
```

Whenever a read is performed on the filtered stream s3, it passes along the request to s2, then s2 does the same to s1, and finally s is asked to provide the bytes. Subclasses of FilterInputStream will, of course, do some nontrivial processing of the bytes as they flow past. The rather verbose form of "chaining" in the previous example can be made more elegant:

```
s3 = new FilterInputStream(new FilterInputStream(new FilterInputStream(s)));
```

You should use this idiom in your code whenever you can. It clearly expresses the nesting of chained filters, and can easily be parsed and "read aloud" by starting at the innermost stream s and reading outward—each filter stream applying to the one within—until you reach the outermost stream s3.

Now let's examine each of the subclasses of FilterInputStream in turn.

BufferedInputStream

This is one of the most valuable of all streams. It implements the full complement of InputStream's methods, but it does so by using a buffered array of bytes that acts as a cache for future reading. This decouples the rate and the size of the "chunks" you're reading from the more regular, larger block sizes in which streams are most efficiently read (from, for example, peripheral devices, files in the file system, or the network). It also allows smart streams to read ahead when they expect that you will want more data soon.

Because the buffering of BufferedInputStream is so valuable, and it's also the only class to handle mark() and reset() properly, you might wish that every input stream could somehow share its valuable capabilities. Normally, because those stream classes do not implement them, you would be out of luck. Fortunately, you already saw a way that filter streams can wrap themselves "around" other streams. Suppose that you would like a buffered FileInputStream that can handle marking and resetting correctly. Et voilà:

```
InputStream  s = new BufferedInputStream(new FileInputStream("foo"));
```

You have a buffered input stream based on the file foo that can use mark() and reset().

Now you can begin to see the power of nesting streams. Any capability provided by a filter input stream (or output stream, as you'll see soon) can be used by any other basic stream via nesting. Of course, any *combination* of these capabilities, and in any order, can be as easily accomplished by nesting the filter streams themselves.

DataInputStream

All the methods that instances of this class understand are defined in a separate interface, which both DataInputStream and RandomAccessFile (another class in java.io) implement. This interface is general-purpose enough that you might want to use it yourself in the classes you create. It is called DataInput.

The DataInput Interface

When you begin using streams to any degree, you'll quickly discover that byte streams are not a really helpful format into which to force all data. In particular, the primitive types of the Java language embody a rather nice way of looking at data, but with the streams you've been defining thus far in this book, you could not read data of these types. The DataInput interface specifies a higher-level set of methods that, when used for both reading and writing, can support a more complex, typed stream of data. Here are the methods this interface defines:

```
void  readFully(byte[]  buffer)                               throws IOException;
void  readFully(byte[]  buffer, int  offset, int  length) throws IOException;
int   skipBytes(int n)                                        throws IOException;
```

```
boolean   readBoolean()          throws IOException;
byte      readByte()             throws IOException;
int       readUnsignedByte()     throws IOException;
short     readShort()            throws IOException;
int       readUnsignedShort()    throws IOException;
char      readChar()             throws IOException;
int       readInt()              throws IOException;
long      readLong()             throws IOException;
float     readFloat()            throws IOException;
double    readDouble()           throws IOException;

String    readLine()             throws IOException;
String    readUTF()              throws IOException;
```

The first three methods are simply new names for skip() and the two forms of read() you've seen previously. Each of the next 10 methods reads in a primitive type or its unsigned counterpart (useful for using every bit efficiently in a binary stream). These latter methods must return an integer of a wider size than you might think; because integers are signed in Java, the unsigned value does not fit in anything smaller. The final two methods read a newline ('\r', '\n', or "\r\n") terminated string of characters from the stream—the first in ASCII, and the second in Unicode.

Now that you know what the interface that DataInputStream implements looks like, let's see it in action:

```
DataInputStream  s = new DataInputStream(myRecordInputStream());

long  size = s.readLong();    // the number of items in the stream

while (size-- > 0) {
    if (s.readBoolean()) {    // should I process this item?
        int     anInteger    = s.readInt();
        int     magicBitFlags = s.readUnsignedShort();
        double  aDouble      = s.readDouble();

        if ((magicBitFlags & 0100000) != 0) {
            . . .    // high bit set, do something special
        }
        . . .    // process anInteger and aDouble
    }
}
```

Because the class implements an interface for all its methods, you can also use the following interface:

```
DataInput  d = new DataInputStream(new FileInputStream("anything"));
String     line;

while ((line = d.readLine()) != null) {
    . . .    // process the line
}
```

EOFException

One final point about most of `DataInputStream`'s methods: When the end of the stream is reached, the methods throw an `EOFException`. This is tremendously useful and, in fact, allows you to rewrite all the kludgey uses of ·1 you saw earlier today in a much nicer fashion:

```
DataInputStream  s = new DataInputStream(getAnInputStreamFromSomewhere());

try {
    while (true) {
        byte  b = (byte) s.readByte();
        . . .     // process the byte b
    }
} catch (EOFException e) {
    . . .      // reached end of stream
} finally {
    s.close();
}
```

This works just as well for all but the last two of the `read` methods of `DataInputStream`.

WARNING

> `skipBytes()` does nothing at all on end of stream, `readLine()` returns `null`, and `readUTF()` might throw a `UTFDataFormatException`, if it notices the problem at all.

LineNumberInputStream

In an editor or a debugger, line numbering is crucial. To add this valuable capability to your programs, use the filter stream `LineNumberInputStream`, which keeps track of line numbers as its stream "flows through" it. It's even smart enough to remember a line number and later restore it, during a `mark()` and `reset()`. You might use this class as follows:

```
LineNumberInputStream  aLNIS;
aLNIS = new LineNumberInputStream(new FileInputStream("source"));

DataInputStream  s = new DataInputStream(aLNIS);
String           line;

while ((line = s.readLine()) != null) {
    . . .      // process the line
        System.out.println("Did line number: " + aLNIS.getLineNumber());
}
```

Here, two filter streams are nested around the `FileInputStream` actually providing the data—the first to read lines one at a time and the second to keep track of the line numbers of these lines as they go by. You must explicitly name the intermediate filter stream, `aLNIS`, because if you did not, you couldn't call `getLineNumber()` later. Note that if you invert the order of the nested streams, reading from `DataInputStream` does not cause `LineNumberInputStream` to "see" the lines.

You must put any filter streams acting as "monitors" in the middle of the chain and "pull" the data from the outermost filter stream so that the data will pass through each of the monitors in turn. In the same way, buffering should occur as far inside the chain as possible, because the buffered stream won't be able to do its job properly unless most of the streams that need buffering come after it in the flow. For example, here's a silly order:

```
new BufferedInputStream(new LineNumberInputStream(
        _new DataInputStream(new FileInputStream("foo"));
```

and here's a much better order:

```
new DataInputStream(new LineNumberInputStream(
        _new BufferedInputStream(new FileInputStream("foo"));
```

`LineNumberInputStreams` can also be told `setLineNumber()`, for those few times when you know more than they do.

PushbackInputStream

The filter stream class `PushbackInputStream` is commonly used in parsers, to "push back" a single character in the input (after reading it) while trying to determine what to do next—a simplified version of the `mark()` and `reset()` utility you learned about earlier. Its only addition to the standard set of `InputStream` methods is `unread()`, which, as you might guess, pretends that it never read the byte passed in as its argument, and then gives that byte back as the return value of the next `read()`.

Listing 19.1 shows a simple implementation of `readLine()` using this class:

TYPE **Listing 19.1. A simple line reader.**

```
1:import java.io;
2:
3:public class  SimpleLineReader {
4:    private FilterInputStream  s;
5:
6:    public  SimpleLineReader(InputStream  anIS) {
7:        s = new DataInputStream(anIS);
8:    }
9:
10:    . . .    // other read() methods using stream s
11:
12:    public String  readLine() throws IOException {
13:        char[]  buffer = new char[100];
14:        int     offset = 0;
15:        byte    thisByte;
16:
```

continues

Listing 19.1. continued

```
17:          try {
18:loop:         while (offset < buffer.length) {
19:                  switch (thisByte = (byte) s.read()) {
20:                      case '\n':
21:                          break loop;
22:                      case '\r':
23:                          byte  nextByte = (byte) s.read();
24:
25:                          if (nextByte != '\n') {
26:                              if (!(s instanceof PushbackInputStream)) {
27:                                  s = new PushbackInputStream(s);
28:                              }
29:                              ((PushbackInputStream) s).unread(nextByte);
30:                          }
31:                          break loop;
32:                      default:
33:                          buffer[offset++] = (char) thisByte;
34:                          break;
35:                  }
36:              }
37:          } catch (EOFException e) {
38:              if (offset == 0)
39:                  return null;
40:          }
41:          return String.copyValueOf(buffer, 0, offset);
42:      }
43:}
```

ANALYSIS This example demonstrates numerous things. For the purpose of this example, the readLine() method is restricted to reading the first 100 characters of the line. In this respect, it demonstrates how *not* to write a general-purpose line processor (you should be able to read a line of any size). This example does, however, show you how to break out of an outer loop (using the loop label in line 18 and the break statements in lines 21 and 31), and how to produce a String from an array of characters (in this case, from a "slice" of the array of characters). This example also includes standard uses of InputStream's read() for reading bytes one at a time, and of determining the end of the stream by enclosing it in a DataInputStream and catching EOFException.

One of the more unusual aspects of the example is the way PushbackInputStream is used. To be sure that '\n' is ignored following '\r', you have to "look ahead" one character; but if it is not a '\n', you must push back that character. Look at the lines 26 through 29 as if you didn't know much about the stream s. The general technique used is instructive. First, you see whether s is already an instance of some kind of PushbackInputStream. If so, you can simply use it. If not, you enclose the current stream (whatever it is) inside a new PushbackInputStream and use this new stream. Now, let's jump back into the context of the example.

Line 29 following that if statement in line 26 wants to call the method unread(). The problem is that s has a compile-time type of FilterInputStream, and thus doesn't understand that method. The previous three lines (26) have guaranteed, however, that the runtime *type* of the stream in s is PushbackInputStream, so you can safely cast it to that type and then safely call unread().

NOTE

> This example was done in an unusual way for demonstration purposes. You could have simply declared a PushbackInputStream variable and always enclosed the DataInputStream in it. (Conversely, SimpleLineReader's constructor could have checked whether its argument was already of the right class, the way PushbackInputStream did, before creating a new DataInputStream.) The interesting thing about this approach of wrapping a class only when needed is that it works for any InputStream that you hand it, and it does additional work only if it needs to. Both of these are good general design principles.

All the subclasses of FilterInputStream have now been described. It's time to return to the direct subclasses of InputStream.

PipedInputStream

This class, along with its brother class PipedOutputStream, are covered later today (they need to be understood and demonstrated together). For now, all you need to know is that together they create a simple, two-way communication conduit between threads.

SequenceInputStream

Suppose you have two separate streams and you would like to make a composite stream that consists of one stream followed by the other (like appending two Strings together). This is exactly what SequenceInputStream was created for:

```
InputStream  s1 = new FileInputStream("theFirstPart");
InputStream  s2 = new FileInputStream("theRest");

InputStream  s  = new SequenceInputStream(s1, s2);

... s.read() ...    // reads from each stream in turn
```

You could have "faked" this example by reading each file in turn—but what if you had to hand the composite stream s to some other method that was expecting only a single InputStream? Here's an example (using s) that line-numbers the two previous files with a common numbering scheme:

```
LineNumberInputStream  aLNIS = new LineNumberInputStream(s);

... aLNIS.getLineNumber() ...
```

19

NOTE
> Stringing together streams this way is especially useful when the streams are of unknown length and origin and were just handed to you by someone else.

What if you want to string together more than two streams? You could try the following:

```
Vector  v = new Vector();
. . .   // set up all the streams and add each to the Vector
InputStream  s1 = new SequenceInputStream(v.elementAt(0), v.elementAt(1));
InputStream  s2 = new SequenceInputStream(s1, v.elementAt(2));
InputStream  s3 = new SequenceInputStream(s2, v.elementAt(3));
. . .
```

 NOTE
> A Vector is a growable array of objects that can be filled, referenced (with elementAt()), and enumerated.

However, it's much easier to use a different constructor that SequenceInputStream provides:

```
InputStream  s  = new SequenceInputStream(v.elements());
```

This constructor takes one argument—an object of type Enumeration (in this example, we got that object using Vector's elements() method). The resulting SequenceInputStream object contains all the streams you want to combine and returns a single stream that reads through the data of each in turn.

StringBufferInputStream

StringBufferInputStream is exactly like ByteArrayInputStream, but instead of being based on a byte array, it's based on an array of characters (a String):

```
String       buffer = "Now is the time for all good men to come...";
InputStream  s      = new StringBufferInputStream(buffer);
```

All comments that were made about ByteArrayInputStream apply here as well.

 NOTE
> StringBufferInputStream is a bit of a misnomer because this input stream is actually based on a String. It should really be called StringInputStream.

19

Output Streams

An output stream is the reverse of an input stream; whereas with an input stream you read data from the stream, with output streams you write data to the stream. Most of the InputStream subclasses you've already seen have their equivalent OutputStream brother classes. If an InputStream performs a certain operation, the brother OutputStream performs the *inverse* operation. You'll see more of what this means soon.

The Abstract Class OutputStream

OutputStream is the abstract class that defines the fundamental ways in which a source (producer) writes a stream of bytes to some destination. The identity of the destination, and the manner of the transport and storage of the bytes, is irrelevant. When using an output stream, *you* are the source of those bytes, and that's all you need to know.

write()

The most important method to the producer of an output stream is the one that writes bytes to the destination. This method, write(), comes in many flavors, each demonstrated in the following examples:

NOTE

> Every one of these write() methods is defined to block until all the output requested has been written. You don't need to worry about this limitation—see the note under InputStream's read() method if you don't remember why.

```
OutputStream  s      = getAnOutputStreamFromSomewhere();
byte[]        buffer = new byte[1024];    // any size will do

fillInData(buffer);    // the data we want to output
s.write(buffer);
```

You also can write a "slice" of your buffer by specifying the offset into the buffer, and the length desired, as arguments to write():

```
s.write(buffer, 100, 300);
```

This example writes out bytes 100 through 399 and behaves otherwise exactly the same as the previous write() method.

Finally, you can write out bytes one at a time:

```
while (thereAreMoreBytesToOutput()) {
    byte  b = getNextByteForOutput();

    s.write(b);
}
```

flush()

Because you don't know what an output stream is connected to, you might be required to "flush" your output through some buffered cache to get it to be written (in a timely manner, or at all). OutputStream's version of this method does nothing, but it is expected that subclasses that require flushing (for example, BufferedOutputStream and PrintStream) will override this version to do something nontrivial.

close()

Just like for an InputStream, you should (usually) explicitly close down an OutputStream so that it can release any resources it may have reserved on your behalf. (All the same notes and examples from InputStream's close() method apply here, with the prefix In replaced everywhere by Out.)

All output streams descend from the abstract class OutputStream. All share the previous few methods in common.

ByteArrayOutputStream

The inverse of ByteArrayInputStream, which creates an input stream from an array of bytes, is ByteArrayOutputStream, which directs an output stream *into* an array of bytes:

```
OutputStream  s = new ByteArrayOutputStream();

s.write(123);
. . .
```

The size of the (internal) byte array grows as needed to store a stream of any length. You can provide an initial capacity as an aid to the class, if you like:

```
OutputStream  s = new ByteArrayOutputStream(1024 * 1024);  // 1 Megabyte
```

 NOTE

> You've just seen your first examples of the creation of an output stream. These new streams were attached to the simplest of all possible destinations of data, an array of bytes in the memory of the local computer.

Once the ByteArrayOutputStream object, stored in the variable s, has been "filled," it can be output to another output stream:

```
OutputStream          anotherOutputStream = getTheOtherOutputStream();
ByteArrayOutputStream  s = new ByteArrayOutputStream();

fillWithUsefulData(s);
s.writeTo(anotherOutputStream);
```

It also can be extracted as a byte array or converted to a String:

```
byte[]  buffer            = s.toByteArray();
String  bufferString      = s.toString();
String  bufferUnicodeString = s.toString(upperByteValue);
```

NOTE

The last method allows you to "fake" Unicode (16-bit) characters by filling in their lower bytes with ASCII and then specifying a common upper byte (usually 0) to create a Unicode String result.

ByteArrayOutputStreams have two utility methods: One simply returns the current number of bytes stored in the internal byte array, and the other resets the array so that the stream can be rewritten from the beginning:

```
int  sizeOfMyByteArray = s.size();

s.reset();      // s.size() would now return 0
s.write(123);
. . .
```

FileOutputStream

One of the most common uses of streams is to attach them to files in the file system. Here, for example, is the creation of such an output stream on a UNIX system:

```
OutputStream  s = new FileOutputStream("/some/path/and/fileName");
```

WARNING

Applets attempting to open, read, or write streams based on files in the file system will cause security violations. See the note under FileInputStream for more details.

As with FileInputStream, you also can create the stream from a previously opened file descriptor:

```
FileDescriptor          fd = someFileStream.getFD();
OutputStream  s  = new FileOutputStream(fd);
```

`FileOutputStream` is the inverse of `FileInputStream`, and it knows the same tricks:

```
FileOutputStream  aFOS = new FileOutputStream("aFileName");

FileDescriptor  myFD = aFOS.getFD(); // get a file descriptor

aFOS.finalize();  // will call close() when automatically called by GC
```

NOTE

> To call the new methods, you must declare the stream variable aFOS to be of type `FileOutputStream`, because plain `OutputStreams` don't know about them.

The first is obvious: `getFD()` simply returns the file descriptor for the file on which the stream is based. The second, commented, contrived call to `finalize()` is there to remind you that you may not have to worry about closing this type of stream—it is done for you automatically.

FilterOutputStream

This abstract class simply provides a "pass-through" for all the standard methods of `OutputStream`. It holds inside itself another stream, by definition one further "down" the chain of filters, to which it forwards all method calls. It implements nothing new but allows itself to be nested:

```
OutputStream        s  = getAnOutputStreamFromSomewhere();
FilterOutputStream  s1 = new FilterOutputStream(s);
FilterOutputStream  s2 = new FilterOutputStream(s1);
FilterOutputStream  s3 = new FilterOutputStream(s2);

... s3.write(123) ...
```

Whenever a write is performed on the filtered stream s3, it passes along the request to s2. Then s2 does the same to s1, and finally s is asked to output the bytes. Subclasses of `FilterOutputStream`, of course, do some nontrivial processing of the bytes as they flow past. This chain can be tightly nested—see its brother class, `FilterInputStream`, for more.

Now let's examine each of the subclasses of `FilterOutputStream` in turn.

BufferedOutputStream

`BufferedOutputStream` is one of the most valuable of all streams. All it does is implement the full complement of `OutputStream`'s methods, but it does so by using a buffered array of bytes that acts as a cache for writing. This decouples the rate and the size of the "chunks" you're writing from the more regular, larger block sizes in which streams are most efficiently written (to peripheral devices, files in the file system, or the network, for example).

BufferedOutputStream is one of two classes in the Java library to implement flush(), which pushes the bytes you've written through the buffer and out the other side. Because buffering is so valuable, you might wish that every output stream could somehow be buffered. Fortunately, you can surround any output stream in such a way as to achieve just that:

```
OutputStream  s = new BufferedOutputStream(new FileOutputStream("foo"));
```

You now have a buffered output stream based on the file foo that can be flushed.

Just as for filter input streams, any capability provided by a filter output stream can be used by any other basic stream via nesting, and any combination of these capabilities, in any order, can be as easily accomplished by nesting the filter streams themselves.

DataOutputStream

All the methods that instances of this class understand are defined in a separate interface, which both DataOutputStream and RandomAccessFile implement. This interface is general-purpose enough that you might want to use it yourself in the classes you create. It is called DataOutput.

The DataOutput Interface

In cooperation with its brother inverse interface, DataInput, DataOutput provides a higher-level, typed-stream approach to the reading and writing of data. Rather than dealing with bytes, this interface deals with writing the primitive types of the Java language directly:

```
void   write(int i)                                       throws IOException;
void   write(byte[]  buffer)                              throws IOException;
void   write(byte[]  buffer, int  offset, int  length) throws IOException;

void   writeBoolean(boolean b) throws IOException;
void   writeByte(int i)        throws IOException;
void   writeShort(int i)       throws IOException;
void   writeChar(int i)        throws IOException;
void   writeInt(int i)         throws IOException;
void   writeLong(long l)       throws IOException;
void   writeFloat(float f)     throws IOException;
void   writeDouble(double d)   throws IOException;

void   writeBytes(String s) throws IOException;
void   writeChars(String s) throws IOException;
void   writeUTF(String s)   throws IOException;
```

Most of these methods have counterparts in the interface DataInput.

The first three methods mirror the three forms of write() you saw previously. Each of the next eight methods writes out a primitive type. The final three methods write out a string of bytes or characters to the stream: the first one as 8-bit bytes; the second, as 16-bit Unicode characters; and the last, as a special Unicode stream (readable by DataInput's readUTF()).

19

NOTE

The unsigned read methods in `DataInput` have no counterparts here. You can write out the data they need via `DataOutput`'s signed methods because they accept `int` arguments and also because they write out the correct number of bits for the unsigned integer of a given size as a side effect of writing out the signed integer of that same size. It is the method that reads this integer that must interpret the sign bit correctly; the writer's job is easy.

Now that you know what the interface that `DataOutputStream` implements looks like, let's see it in action:

```
DataOutputStream  s    = new DataOutputStream(myRecordOutputStream());
long              size = getNumberOfItemsInNumericStream();

s.writeLong(size);

for (int  i = 0;  i < size;  ++i) {
    if (shouldProcessNumber(i)) {
        s.writeBoolean(true);      // should process this item
        s.writeInt(theIntegerForItemNumber(i));
        s.writeShort(theMagicBitFlagsForItemNumber(i));
        s.writeDouble(theDoubleForItemNumber(i));
    } else
        s.writeBoolean(false);
}
```

This is the exact inverse of the example that was given for `DataInput`. Together, they form a pair that can communicate a particular array of structured primitive types across any stream (or "transport layer"). Use this pair as a jumping-off point whenever you need to do something similar.

In addition to the preceding interface, the class itself implements one (self-explanatory) utility method:

```
int  theNumberOfBytesWrittenSoFar = s.size();
```

Processing a File

One of the most common idioms in file I/O is to open a file, read and process it line-by-line, and output it again to another file. Here's a prototypical example of how that would be done in Java:

```
DataInput   aDI = new DataInputStream(new FileInputStream("source"));
DataOutput  aDO = new DataOutputStream(new FileOutputStream("dest"));
String      line;

while ((line = aDI.readLine()) != null) {
    StringBuffer  modifiedLine = new StringBuffer(line);
```

Besides responding to start() and stop(), a thread can also be temporarily suspended and later resumed:

```
Thread   t = new Thread();
t.suspend();
. . .              // do something special while t isn't running
t.resume();
```

A thread will automatically suspend() and then resume() when it's first blocked at a synchronized point and then later unblocked (when it's that thread's "turn" to run).

The Runnable **Interface**

This is all well and good if every time you want to create a thread you have the luxury of being able to place it under the Thread class in the single-inheritance Java class tree. But what if it more naturally belongs under some other class, from which it needs to inherit most of its implementation? The interfaces you learned about on Day 16, "Packages and Interfaces," come to the rescue:

```
public class MySecondThread extends ImportantClass implements Runnable {
    public void run() {
        . . .              // do something useful
    }
}
```

By implementing the interface Runnable, you declare your intention to run in a separate thread. In fact, the Thread class is itself an implementation of this interface, as you might expect from the design discussions on Day 16. As you also might guess from the example, the Runnable interface defines only one method: run(). As in MyFirstThread, you expect someone to create an instance of a thread and somehow call your run() method. Here's how this is accomplished using the interface approach to thread creation:

```
MySecondThread  aMST = new MySecondThread();
Thread          aThread = new Thread(aMST);
aThread.start();   // calls our run() method, indirectly
```

First, you create an instance of MySecondThread. Then, by passing this instance to the constructor creating the new thread, you make it the target of that thread. Whenever that new thread starts up, its run() method calls the run() method of the target it was given (assumed by the thread to be an object that implements the Runnable interface). When start() is called on aThread, your run() method is indirectly called. You can stop aThread with stop(). If you don't need to use the Thread object or instance of MySecondThread explicitly, here's a one-line shortcut:

```
new Thread(new MySecondThread()).start();
```

NOTE

As you can see, the class name MySecondThread is a bit of a misnomer—it does not descend from Thread, nor is it actually the thread that you start() and stop(). It could have been called MySecondThreadedClass or ImportantRunnableClass to be more clear on this point.

ThreadTester

Listing 18.2 contains a longer example of creating and using threads.

TYPE | **Listing 18.2. The SimpleRunnable class.**

```
 1: public class SimpleRunnable implements Runnable {
 2:     public void run() {
 3:         System.out.println("in thread named '"
 4:                             + Thread.currentThread().getName() + "'");
 5:     } // any other methods run() calls are in current thread as well
 6: }
 7:
 8: public class ThreadTester {
 9:     public static void main(String argv[]) {
10:         SimpleRunnable aSR = new SimpleRunnable();
11:
12:         while (true) {
13:             Thread t = new Thread(aSR);
14:
15:             System.out.println("new Thread() " + (t == null ?
16:                                 "fail" : "succeed") + "ed.");
17:             t.start();
18:             try { t.join(); } catch (InterruptedException ignored) { }
19:                         // waits for thread to finish its run() method
20:         }
21:     }
22: }
```

NOTE

You may be worried that only one instance of the class SimpleRunnable is created, but many new threads are using it. Don't they get confused? Remember to separate in your mind the aSR instance (and the methods it understands) from the various threads of execution that can pass through it. aSR's methods provide a template for execution, and the multiple threads created are sharing that template. Each remembers

18

```
    . . .          // process modifiedLine in place
    aDO.writeBytes(modifiedLine.toString());
}
aDI.close();
aDO.close();
```

If you want to process it byte-by-byte, use this:

```
try {
    while (true) {
        byte  b = (byte) aDI.readByte();

        . . .         // process b in place
        aDO.writeByte(b);
    }
} finally {
    aDI.close();
    aDO.close();
}
```

Here's a cute two-liner that just copies the file:

```
try { while (true) aDO.writeByte(aDI.readByte()); }
finally { aDI.close(); aDO.close(); }
```

WARNING

> Many of the examples in today's lesson (as well as the last two) are assumed to appear inside a method that has IOException in its throws clause, so they don't have to worry about catching those exceptions and handling them more reasonably. Your code should be a little less cavalier.

PrintStream

You may not realize it, but you're already intimately familiar with the use of two methods of the PrintStream class. That's because whenever you use these method calls:

```
System.out.print(. . .)
System.out.println(. . .)
```

you are actually using a PrintStream instance located in System's class variable out to perform the output. System.err is also a PrintStream, and System.in is an InputStream.

NOTE

> On UNIX systems, these three streams will be attached to standard output, standard error, and standard input, respectively.

`PrintStream` is uniquely an output stream class (it has no brother class). Because it is usually attached to a screen output device of some kind, it provides an implementation of `flush()`. It also provides the familiar `close()` and `write()` methods, as well as a plethora of choices for outputting the primitive types and `Strings` of Java:

```
public void  write(int b);
public void  write(byte[]  buffer, int  offset, int  length);
public void  flush();
public void  close();

public void  print(Object o);
public void  print(String s);
public void  print(char[]  buffer);
public void  print(char c);
public void  print(int i);
public void  print(long l);
public void  print(float f);
public void  print(double d);
public void  print(boolean b);

public void  println(Object o);
public void  println(String s);
public void  println(char[]  buffer);
public void  println(char c);
public void  println(int i);
public void  println(long l);
public void  println(float f);
public void  println(double d);
public void  println(boolean b);

public void  println();    // output a blank line
```

`PrintStream` can also be wrapped around any output stream, just like a filter class:

```
PrintStream  s = new PrintStream(new FileOutputStream("foo"));

s.println("Here's the first line of text in the file foo.");
```

If you provide a second argument to the constructor for `PrintStream`, that second argument is a boolean that specifies whether the stream should auto-flush. If `true`, a `flush()` is sent after each newline character is written.

Here's a simple sample program that operates like the UNIX command `cat`, taking the standard input, line-by-line, and outputting it to the standard output:

```
import java.io.*;    // the one time in the chapter we'll say this

public class  Cat {
    public static void  main(String argv[]) {
        DataInput  d = new DataInputStream(System.in);
        String     line;

      try {  while ((line = d.readLine()) != null)
             System.out.println(line);
         } catch (IOException  ignored) { }
    }
}
```

PipedOutputStream

Along with `PipedInputStream`, this pair of classes supports a UNIX-pipe-like connection between two threads, implementing all the careful synchronization that allows this sort of "shared queue" to operate safely. Use the following to set up the connection:

```
PipedInputStream   sIn  = PipedInputStream();
PipedOutputStream  sOut = PipedOutputStream(sIn);
```

One thread writes to `sOut`; the other reads from `sIn`. By setting up two such pairs, the threads can communicate safely in both directions.

Related Classes

The other classes and interfaces in `java.io` supplement the streams to provide a complete I/O system. Three of them are described here.

The `File` class abstracts files in a platform-independent way. Given a filename, it can respond to queries about the type, status, and properties of a file or directory in the file system.

A `RandomAccessFile` is created given a file, a filename, or a file descriptor. It combines in one class implementations of the `DataInput` and `DataOutput` interfaces, both tuned for "random access" to a file in the file system. In addition to these interfaces, `RandomAccessFile` provides certain traditional UNIX-like facilities, such as seeking to a random point in the file.

Finally, the `StreamTokenizer` class takes an input stream and produces a sequence of tokens. By overriding its various methods in your own subclasses, you can create powerful lexical parsers.

You can learn more about any and all of these other classes from the full (online) API descriptions in your Java release.

Object Serialization (Java 1.1)

A topic to streams, and one that will be available in the core Java library with Java 1.1, is object serialization. *Serialization* is the ability to write a Java object to a stream such as a file or a network connection, and then read it and reconstruct that object on the other side. Object serialization is crucial for the ability to save Java objects to a file (what's called *object persistence*), or to be able to accomplish network-based applications that make use of Remote Method Invocation (RMI)—a capability you'll learn more of on Day 27, "The Standard Extension APIs."

At the heart of object serialization are two streams classes: ObjectInputStream, which inherits from DataInputStream, and ObjectOutputStream, which inherits from DataOutputStream. Both of these classes will be part of the java.io package and will be used much in the same way as the standard input and output streams are. In addition, two interfaces, ObjectOutput and ObjectInput, which inherit from DataInput and DataOutput, respectively, will provide abstract behavior for reading and writing objects.

To use the ObjectInputStream and ObjectOutputStream classes, you create new instances much in the same way you do ordinary streams, and then use the readObject() and writeObject() methods to read and write objects to and from those streams.

ObjectOutputStream's writeObject() method, which takes a single object argument, serializes that object as well as any object it has references to. Other objects written to the same stream are serialized as well, with references to already-serialized objects kept track of and circular references preserved.

ObjectInputStream's readObject() method takes no arguments and reads an object from the stream (you'll need to cast that object to an object of the appropriate class). Objects are read from the stream in the same order in which they are written.

Here's a simple example from the object serialization specification that writes a date to a file (actually, it writes a string label, "Today", and then a Date object):

```
FileOutputStream f = new FileOutputStream("tmp");
ObjectOutput  s  =  new  ObjectOutputStream(f);
s.writeObject("Today");
s.writeObject(new Date());
s.flush();
```

To deserialize the object (read it back in again), use this code:

```
FileInputStream in = new FileInputStream("tmp");
ObjectInputStream s = new ObjectInputStream(in);
String today = (String)s.readObject();
Date date = (Date)s.readObject();
```

One other feature of object serialization to note is the transient modifier. Used in instance variable declarations as other modifiers are, the transient modifier means that the value of that object should not be stored when the object is serialized—that its value is temporary or will need to be re-created from scratch once the object is reconstructed. Use transient variables for environment-specific information (such as file handles that may be different from one side of the serialization to the other) or for values that can be easily recalculated to save space in the final serialized object.

To declare a transient variable, use the transient modifier the way you do other modifiers such as public, private, or abstract:

```
public transient int transientValue = 4;
```

At the time of this writing, object serialization is available as an additional package for Java 1.0.2 as part of the RMI package. You can find out more about it, including full specifications and downloadable software, from the Java RMI Web site at `http://chatsubo.javasoft.com/current/`.

Summary

Today you have learned about the general idea of streams and have met input streams based on byte arrays, files, pipes, sequences of other streams, and string buffers, as well as input filters for buffering, typed data, line numbering, and pushing-back characters.

You have also met the analogous brother output streams for byte arrays, files, and pipes, output filters for buffering and typed data, and the unique output filter used for printing.

Along the way, you have become familiar with the fundamental methods all streams understand (such as `read()` and `write()`), as well as the unique methods many streams add to this repertoire. You have learned about catching `IOExceptions`—especially the most useful of them, `EOFException`.

Finally, the twice-useful `DataInput` and `DataOutput` interfaces formed the heart of `RandomAccessFile`, one of the several utility classes that round out Java's I/O facilities.

Java streams provide a powerful base on which you can build multithreaded, streaming interfaces of the most complex kinds, and the programs (such as HotJava) to interpret them. The higher-level Internet protocols and services of the future that your applets can build on this base are really limited only by your imagination.

19

Q&A

Q In an early `read()` example, you did something with the variable `byteOrMinus1` that seemed a little clumsy. Isn't there a better way? If not, why recommend the cast later?

A Yes, there is something a little odd about those statements. You might be tempted to try something like this instead:

```
while ((b = (byte) s.read()) != -1) {
    . . .    // process the byte b
}
```

The problem with this shortcut occurs if `read()` returns the value `0xFF` (`0377`). Because of the way values are cast, it will appear to be identical to the integer value `-1` that indicates end of stream. Only saving that value in a separate integer variable, and then casting it later, will accomplish the desired result. The cast to `byte` is recommended in the note for slightly different reasons than this, however—storing integer values in correctly sized variables is always good style (and besides, read() really should be returning something of byte size here and throwing an exception for end of stream).

Q **What input streams in java.io actually implement mark(), reset(), and markSupported()?**

A InputStream itself does—and in their default implementations, markSupported() returns false, mark() does nothing, and reset() throws an exception. The only input stream in the current release that correctly supports marking is BufferedInputStream, which overrides these defaults. LineNumberInputStream actually implements mark() and reset(), but in the current release, it doesn't answer markSupported() correctly, so it looks as if it does not.

Q **Why is available() useful, if it sometimes gives the wrong answer?**

A First, for many streams, it gives the right answer. Second, for some network streams, its implementation might be sending a special query to discover some information you couldn't get any other way (for example, the size of a file being transferred by ftp). If you are displaying a "progress bar" for network or file transfers, for example, available() will often give you the total size of the transfer, and when it does not—usually by returning 0—it will be obvious to you (and your users).

Q **What's a good example of the use of the DataInput/DataOutput pair of interfaces?**

A One common use of such a pair is when objects want to "pickle" themselves for storage or movement over a network. Each object implements read and write methods using these interfaces, effectively converting itself to a stream that can later be reconstituted "on the other end" into a copy of the original object.

19

Day **20**

Using Native Methods and Libraries

by Laura Lemay and Charles L. Perkins

Up to this point in the book you've been learning specifically about programming in the Java language and with the Java class libraries. That's why this book is called *Teach Yourself Java,* after all. Today I'm going to digress a little bit and talk about native methods and libraries.

Native methods and libraries are bits of executable code that are written in the traditional way: They are written in a language such as C or C++ and compiled into a platform-specific library such as a DLL or a shared library. Inside your Java applications you can gain access to the functions inside those libraries, allowing you to create a sort of hybrid Java and native code application. Although using native methods can give you some extra benefits Java does not provide (such as faster execution or access to a large body of existing code), there are significant disadvantages in using native methods as well.

Native methods and *native libraries* are bits of platform-specific executable code (written in languages such as C or C++) contained in libraries or DLLs. You can create a hybrid Java application that has access to those native libraries.

Today's lesson covers various topics relating to native methods, including the following:

- [ ] The advantages and disadvantages of using native methods
- [ ] Why using native methods for speed or efficiency is often unnecessary
- [ ] The steps for creating native methods, header and stub files, and native implementations, and linking it all together
- [ ] Various functions and utilities for mapping between Java and C and C++

NOTE

In today's lesson you'll learn the basic techniques for writing native methods in the current version of Java. For the Java 1.1 release, Sun will publish further guidelines for writing native methods to help make sure that native implementations will work between different versions of the Java runtime. These guidelines will be in addition to the technique you will learn in today's lesson, and will build on the skills you learn here.

Why Use Native Methods?

Before I get into the nitty-gritty details of creating native methods, you should first be aware of what native methods give you—and what they take away. Although native methods provide some advantages, those advantages may not appear too exciting when viewed in light of native methods' disadvantages. This section describes both.

Advantages of Using Native Methods

There are several reasons that you might want to consider using native methods in your own Java programs. By far the best of these reasons are

- [ ] Gaining access to special capabilities of your computer or operating system
- [ ] Needing the extra speed that native methods provide
- [ ] Needing access to a large body of existing code

The first, and by far the best, reason to implement native methods is because you need to utilize a special capability of your computer or operating system that the Java class library does not already provide for you. Such capabilities include interfacing to new peripheral devices or plug-in cards, accessing a different type of networking, or using a unique, but valuable feature of your particular operating system. Two more concrete examples are acquiring real-time audio input from a microphone or using 3D "accelerator" hardware in a 3D library. Neither of these is provided to you by the current Java environment, so you must implement them outside Java, in some other language (currently C or any language that can link with C).

The second, and often illusory, reason to use native methods is speed. The argument has been made that because interpreted bytecode is terribly slow in comparison to how quickly native code runs (and it is far slower, as much as 25 times slower), Java code is unsuitable for most applications. In many cases this simply isn't true, or you may be able to extract a fair amount of speed out of your Java program without resorting to native methods (as we'll explore in greater detail later in today's lesson). If, however, your Java application uses very processor-intensive calculations (for example, number crunching or 3D rendering), using native methods for the speed-critical functions and Java for the more general interfaces creates a system with more benefits than a system written in either pure native code or pure Java. In fact, the Java class library uses this approach for many critical system classes to raise the overall level of efficiency in the system. As a user of the Java environment, you don't even know (or see) any side effects of this (except, perhaps, a few classes or methods that are `final` that might not be otherwise).

The third reason to use native classes is if your project has a large body of existing code (what's called *legacy code*, which may be hundreds of lines of code written and maintained by other people over the years). As a good Java programmer and advocate you would, of course, want to port this large body of code to Java. However, real-life considerations of time and resources often don't allow this option. Native methods allow you to write a single interface to that code through Java and link into the existing code as it's needed.

Disadvantages of Native Methods

After reading the advantages of using native methods, you may be all set to jump to the section on how to use them and skip this section. Don't. For every good thing native methods provide in your Java code, they take away a benefit that Java provides in the first place: the ability for your code to run anywhere and be easily ported from one system to another.

Using pure Java, an application or applet can be run on any Java environment in the world by downloading it via the Web or by simply loading the class file on that system. Any new architectures created—or new operating systems written—are irrelevant to your code. All you need is that the (tiny) Java Virtual Machine (or a browser that has one inside it) be available, and it can run anywhere, anytime—now and in the future.

20

With a hybrid Java and native method program, however, you've given up that cross-platform capability. First of all, Java programs that use native methods cannot be applets. Period. For security reasons, applets cannot load native code. So if you use native methods, you've just removed the enormous number of users on the World Wide Web from your market.

Even if you're just creating a Java application, however, and don't intend your code to be run on the Web, using native methods also negates the capability of your program to run on any platform. Native code is, by definition, platform specific. The native code must exist on the platform your Java program is running on for that program to work. For your program to work on different platforms, you'll have to port your native code to that specific platform—which may not be a trivial task. And as new systems or new versions of operating systems appear, you may have to update or re-release new versions of that native code for every system. The write-it-once-run-it-everywhere advantage of Java ceases to exist when you use native methods.

The Illusion of Required Efficiency

Let's digress for a moment and talk about the concept of speed and efficiency of Java programs—or the supposed lack thereof, which may drive you to using native code in your Java programs.

Java bytecode has acquired the reputation of being extraordinarily slow to run in comparison with native executable code. And, examining the benchmarks, Java bytecode is indeed very much slower—as much as 25 times slower. However, that doesn't necessarily make a Java program unbearable to use. Simple applets or applications that rely on user interface elements will appear to run just as fast as their native equivalents. Button clicks are just as fast in Java as they are in native code, and your users are very slow compared to modern computers. It's only in the case of very processor-intensive operations that Java starts to come up short in comparison to native code.

At any rate, worrying over the speed of your Java programs before you write them is often a rathole that can distract you from the larger issues. In this section I'll look at both those larger issues and at the solutions that can make your Java programs run faster.

Design First, Efficiency Later

When you design your program, all your energy and creativity should be directed at the design of a tight, concise, minimal set of classes and methods that are maximally general, abstract, and reusable. (If you think that is easy, look around for a few years and see how bad most software is.) If you spend most of your programming time on thinking and rethinking

20

these fundamental goals and how to achieve them, you are preparing for the future—a future where software is assembled as needed from small components swimming in a sea of network facilities, and anyone can write a component seen by millions (and reused in their programs) in minutes. If, instead, you spend your energy worrying about the speed your software will run *right now* on some computer, your work will be irrelevant after the 18 to 36 months it will take hardware to be fast enough to hide that minor inefficiency in your program.

So you should ignore efficiency altogether? Of course not! Some of the great algorithms of computer science deal with solving hard or "impossible" problems in reasonable amounts of time—and writing your programs carelessly can lead to remarkably slow results. Carelessness, however, can as easily lead to incorrect, fragile, or nonreusable results. If you correct all these latter problems first, the resulting software will be clean, will naturally reflect the structure of the problem you're trying to solve, and thus will be amenable to "speeding up" later.

NOTE

There are always cases where you *must* be fanatical about efficiency in many parts of a set of classes. The Java class library itself is such a case, as is anything that must run in real-time for some critical real-world application (such as flying a plane). Such applications are rare, however.

When speaking of a new kind of programming that must soon emerge, Bill Joy likes to invoke the four S's of Java: small, simple, safe, and secure. The "feel" of the Java language itself encourages the pursuit of clarity and the reduction of complexity. The intense pursuit of efficiency, which increases complexity and reduces clarity, is antithetical to these goals.

Once you build a solid foundation, debug your classes, and your program (or applet) works as you'd like it to, *then* it's time to begin optimizing it.

Just-in-Time Compilers

The first thing to keep in mind about the execution speed of Java is that lots of people are working on fixing it. And the most promising of these technical advancements is the just-in-time (JIT) compiler.

Just-in-time compilers translate Java bytecode into native machine code on-the-fly as the bytecode is running. Depending on how good the JIT compiler is, you can often get very close to native execution speeds out of a standard Java program—without needing to use native code and without needing to make any modifications to your Java program—it just works.

The disadvantage, however, is that to get the speed increase your Java program must be run on a platform that has a JIT compiler installed. At the time of this writing, JIT compilers are still new. Many companies are working on JIT compilers, however, and most of them have versions working or bundled in with development tools so you can experiment with their power. Microsoft's Internet Explorer Web browser, for example, has a JIT compiler built into it. (You'll learn more about the available JIT compilers are expected on Day 22, "Java Programming Tools.") JIT compilers are expected to become much more popular and widespread over the next year.

Simple Optimization Tricks

In addition to relying on JIT technology to speed up your Java programs, there are usually simple optimization tricks you can do to make your programs run more efficiently. Your development environment may even provide a *profiler*, which tells you where the slowest or more frequently run portions of your program are occurring. Even if you don't have a profiler, you can often use debugging tools to find the bottlenecks in your programs and begin to make targeted changes to your classes.

Whole books have been written for optimizing various bits of code in any language, and they can describe it much better than we can. But there are a few simple tricks you can try for the first pass.

First, identify the crucial few methods that take most of the time (there are almost always just a few, and often just one, that take up the majority of your program's time). If those methods contain loops, examine the inner loops to see whether they

- ☐ Call methods that can be made `final`
- ☐ Call a group of methods that can be collapsed into a single method
- ☐ Create objects that can be reused rather than created anew for each loop

If you notice that a long chain of, for example, four or more method calls is needed to reach a destination method's code, *and* this execution path is in one of the critical sections of the program, you can "short-circuit" directly to that destination method in the topmost method. This may require adding a new instance variable to reference the object for that method call directly. This quite often violates layering or encapsulation constraints. This violation, and any added complexity, is the price you pay for efficiency.

Writing Native Methods

If, after all these tricks, your Java code is still *just too slow*, it's time to consider using native methods. In this section you'll learn the steps you must take to write your Java code so that

20

it uses native methods, how to write the native code to implement those native methods, and how to compile and link it all together so it works. This involves four basic steps:

- ☐ Write your Java code so that the methods that will be native have special declarations using the `native` modifier.
- ☐ Compile your Java code and use the `javah` program to generate special header and stub files, which make up the starting point for your native code.
- ☐ Write your native implementations of the native methods.
- ☐ Compile all the native files into a shared library or DLL and run your Java program.

NOTE This discussion—and, in fact, the JDK itself—assumes that you'll be writing your native code in C and C++. Other Java development environments may support other languages.

Write Your Java Code

The first step to implementing native methods is to decide which methods in which classes of your Java program will be native. The mapping between Java and native libraries is through methods (functions), so designing your Java code and keeping track of which methods are native is the most important first step.

To declare that a method will be native inside your Java code, you add the `native` modifier to that method signature, like this:

```
public native void goNative(int x, int y);
```

NOTE The `native` modifier can be used with many of the modifiers you learned about on Day 15, "Modifiers, Access Control, and Class Design," including `public`, `private`, `protected`, `final`, and so on. It cannot be used with `abstract` because abstract methods do not have definitions, native or otherwise.

Note also that the native method in your Java code has no method body. Because this is a native method, its implementation will be provided by the native code, not by Java. Just add a semicolon to the end of the line.

The other change you'll have to make to your Java code is to explicitly load the native library that will contain the native code for these methods. To do this, you add the following boilerplate code to your Java class:

```
static {
    System.loadLibrary("libmynativelibrary.so");
}
```

This bit of code, called a *static initializer*, is used to run code only once when the class is first loaded into the system. In this case, the static initializer executes the System.loadLibrary() method to load in your native library as the class itself is being loaded. If the native library fails to load for some reason, the loading of the Java class fails as well, guaranteeing that no half-set-up version of the class can ever be created.

You can pick any name you want for your native library—here we've used the UNIX convention that libraries start with the word lib and end with the extension .so. For Windows systems, libraries typically end with the extension .DLL.

You can also use the System.load() method to load your native libraries. The difference is that the single argument to load() is the complete pathname to your native library, whereas the argument to loadLibrary() is just the library name, and Java uses the standard way of finding libraries for your system to locate that library (usually environment variables such as LD_LIBRARY_PATH). The latter is more flexible and general-purpose, so it's recommended you use it instead.

And that's all you need to do in your Java code to create native methods and libraries. Subclasses of any class containing your new native methods can still override them, and these new (Java) methods are called for instances of the new subclasses (just as you'd expect).

Listing 20.1 shows an example of a Java program called SimpleFile that was written to use native methods. This program might be used in a version of the Java environment that does not provide file input or output (I/O). Because file I/O is typically system-dependent, native methods must be used to implement those operations.

NOTE

> This example combines simplified versions of two actual Java library classes, java.io.File and java.io.RandomAccessFile.

Listing 20.1. SimpleFile, a Java program that uses native methods.

TYPE

```
1: public class  SimpleFile {
2:     public static final  char     separatorChar = '>';
3:     protected    String  path;
```

20

```
 4:     protected    int     fd;
 5:
 6:     public  SimpleFile(String s) {
 7:         path = s;
 8:     }
 9:
10:     public String  getFileName() {
11:         int  index = path.lastIndexOf(separatorChar);
12:
13:         return (index < 0) ? path : path.substring(index + 1);
14:     }
15:
16:     public String  getPath() {
17:         return path;
18:     }
19:
20:     public native boolean  open();
21:     public native void     close();
22:     public native int      read(byte[]  buffer, int  length);
23:     public native int      write(byte[]  buffer, int  length);
24:
25:     static {
26:         System.loadLibrary("simple");   // runs when class first loaded
27:     }
28: }
```

ANALYSIS   The first thing you notice about `SimpleFile`'s implementation is how unremarkable the first two-thirds of its Java code is! It looks just like any other class, with a class and an instance variable, a constructor, and two normal method implementations (`getFileName()` and `getPath()`). Then, in lines 20 through 23, there are four `native` method declarations, which are just normal method declarations with the code block replaced by a semicolon and the modifier `native` added. These are the methods you have to implement in C code later.

Finally, note the call to `System.loadLibrary()` in line 26, which loads a native library called `simple`. (We've intentionally violated library-naming standards here to make this example simpler.)

NOTE

> The unusual `separatorChar` (`'>'`) is used simply to demonstrate what an implementation might look like on some strange computer whose file system didn't use any of the more common path-separator conventions. Early Xerox computers used `'>'` as a separator, and several existing computer systems still use strange separators today, so this is not all that farfetched.

20

After you write the native part of your Java program, SimpleFile objects can be created and used in the usual way:

```
SimpleFile  f = new SimpleFile(">some>path>and>fileName");

f.open();
f.read(...);
f.write(...);
f.close();
```

Generate Header and Stub Files

The second step to implementing native code is to generate a special set of header and stub files for use by your C or C++ files that implement those native methods. To generate these header and stub files, you use the javah program, which is part of the JDK (it's called JavaH in the Mac JDK).

First, you'll need to compile your Java program as you would any other Java program, using the Java compiler.

Header Files

To generate the headers you need for your native methods, use the javah program. For the SimpleFile class listed in the previous section, use one of the following:

To generate header files for a class, use the javah program with the name of the class file, minus the .class extension. For example, to generate the header file for the SimpleFile class, use this command line:

```
javah SimpleFile
```

To generate the header file for the SimpleFile class, drag-and-drop the class file onto the JavaH icon.

The file SimpleFile.h will be created in the same directory as the SimpleFile.class file.

Note that if the class you've given to javah is inside a package, javah prepends the package's full name to the header filename (and to the structure names it generates inside that file) with all the dots (.) replaced by underscores (_). If SimpleFile had been contained in a hypothetical package called acme.widgets.files, javah would have generated a header file named acme_widgets_files_SimpleFile.h, and the various names within it would have been renamed in a similar manner.

Listing 20.2 shows the header file that is generated by javah.

20

TYPE **Listing 20.2.** `SimpleFile.h` **(a header file).**

```
 1: #include <native.h>
 2: /* Header for class SimpleFile */
 3:
 4: #ifndef _Included_SimpleFile
 5: #define _Included_SimpleFile
 6: struct Hjava_lang_String;
 7:
 8: typedef struct ClassSimpleFile {
 9: #define SimpleFile_separatorChar 62L
10:     struct Hjava_lang_String *path;
11:     long fd;
12: } ClassSimpleFile;
13: HandleTo(SimpleFile);
14:
15: #ifdef __cplusplus
16: extern "C" {
17: #endif
18: extern /*boolean*/ long SimpleFile_open(struct HSimpleFile *);
19: extern void SimpleFile_close(struct HSimpleFile *);
20: extern long SimpleFile_read(struct HSimpleFile *,HArrayOfByte *,long);
21: extern long SimpleFile_write(struct HSimpleFile *,HArrayOfByte *,long);
22: #ifdef __cplusplus
23: }
24: #endif
25: #endif
```

ANALYSIS There are a few things to note about this header file. First, note the struct `ClassSimpleFile`, which contains variables that parallel the instance variables inside your class. Second, note the method signatures at the end of the file; these are the function definitions you'll use in your C or C++ file to implement the actual native methods in the Java code.

Stub Files

To "run interference" between the Java world of objects, arrays, and other high-level constructs and the lower-level world of C, you need stubs, which translate arguments and return values between Java and C.

 Stubs are pieces of "glue" code that tie together Java and C. Stubs translate arguments and values and convert the various constructs in each language to something that can be understood in the other.

Stubs can be automatically generated by `javah`, just like headers. There isn't much you need to know about the stub file, just that it has to be compiled and linked with the C code you write to allow it to interface properly with Java.

To create stub files, you also use the javah program:

WINDOWS Use the javah program with the -stubs option to create the stub file:

```
javah -stubs SimpleFile
```

SOLARIS The file SimpleFile.c will be generated in the same directory as the class file.

MACINTOSH The stub file was generated at the same time you created the header file.

Listing 20.3 shows the result of the stub file for the SimpleFile class.

TYPE   **Listing 20.3.** SimpleFile.c **(a stub file).**

```
 1:/* DO NOT EDIT THIS FILE - it is machine generated */
 2:#include <StubPreamble.h>
 3:
 4:/* Stubs for class SimpleFile */
 5:/* SYMBOL: "SimpleFile/open()Z", Java_SimpleFile_open_stub */
 6:__declspec(dllexport) stack_item *Java_SimpleFile_open_stub(stack_item *_P_,
 7:    struct execenv *_EE_) {
 8:        extern long SimpleFile_open(void *);
 9:        _P_[0].i = (SimpleFile_open(_P_[0].p) ? TRUE : FALSE);
10:        return _P_ + 1;
11:}
12:/* SYMBOL: "SimpleFile/close()V", Java_SimpleFile_close_stub */
13:__declspec(dllexport) stack_item *Java_SimpleFile_close_stub(stack_item *_P_,
14:    struct execenv *_EE_) {
15:        extern void SimpleFile_close(void *);
16:        (void) SimpleFile_close(_P_[0].p);
17:        return _P_;
18:}
19:/* SYMBOL: "SimpleFile/read([BI)I", Java_SimpleFile_read_stub */
20:__declspec(dllexport) stack_item *Java_SimpleFile_read_stub(stack_item *_P_,
21:    struct execenv *_EE_) {
22:        extern long SimpleFile_read(void *,void *,long);
23:        _P_[0].i = SimpleFile_read(_P_[0].p,((_P_[1].p)),((_P_[2].i)));
24:        return _P_ + 1;
25:}
26:/* SYMBOL: "SimpleFile/write([BI)I", Java_SimpleFile_write_stub */
27:__declspec(dllexport) stack_item *Java_SimpleFile_write_stub(stack_item *_P_,
28:    struct execenv *_EE_) {
29:        extern long SimpleFile_write(void *,void *,long);
30:        _P_[0].i = SimpleFile_write(_P_[0].p,((_P_[1].p)),((_P_[2].i)));
31:        return _P_ + 1;
32:}
```

20

Implementing the Native Library

The last step, and the most difficult, is to write the C code for your native methods.

The header file generated by javah gives you the prototypes of the functions you need to implement to make your native code complete. You then write some C code that implements those functions and provides the native facilities that your Java class needs (in the case of SimpleFile, some low-level file I/O routines).

You'll want to include your header file as part of the initial includes for your native implementation:

```
#include <SimpleFile.h>
```

NOTE

> This description glosses over a lot of what you might want to do to actually implement those methods. In particular, Java provides several utility functions that help your native methods interact with Java methods and classes and help map C and C++ constructs to their Java equivalents. We'll describe several of these functions later on in today's lesson in the section "Tools and Techniques for Writing Native Implementations."

Listing 20.4 shows the native implementation of the methods from the SimpleFile class.

TYPE

Listing 20.4. SimpleFileNative.c, **a C implementation of a native method from** SimpleFile.

```
 1: #include "SimpleFile.h"      /* for unhand(), among other things */
 2:
 3: #include <sys/param.h>       /* for MAXPATHLEN */
 4: #include <fcntl.h>           /* for O_RDWR and O_CREAT */
 5:
 6: #define LOCAL_PATH_SEPARATOR  '/'    /* UNIX */
 7:
 8: static void  fixSeparators(char *p) {
 9:     for (; *p != '\0'; ++p)
10:         if (*p == SimpleFile_separatorChar)
11:             *p = LOCAL_PATH_SEPARATOR;
12: }
13:
14: long  SimpleFile_open(struct HSimpleFile  *this) {
15:     int   fd;
16:     char  buffer[MAXPATHLEN];
17:
```

continues

Listing 20.4. continued

```
18:     javaString2CString(unhand(this)->path, buffer, sizeof(buffer));
19:     fixSeparators(buffer);
20:     if ((fd = open(buffer, O_RDWR | O_CREAT, 0664)) < 0)      /* UNIX open */
21:         return(FALSE);   /* or, SignalError() could "throw" an exception */
22:     unhand(this)->fd = fd;          /* save fd in the Java world */
23:     return(TRUE);
24: }
25:
26: void SimpleFile_close(struct HSimpleFile  *this) {
27:     close(unhand(this)->fd);
28:     unhand(this)->fd = -1;
29: }
30:
31: long  SimpleFile_read(struct HSimpleFile  *this,
32:     HArrayOfByte *buffer, _ long  count) {
33:     char  *data      = unhand(buffer)->body;  /* get array data   */
34:     int   len        = obj_length(buffer);    /* get array length */
35:     int   numBytes = (len < count ? len : count);
36:
37:     if ((numBytes = read(unhand(this)->fd, data, numBytes)) == 0)
38:         return(-1);
39:     return(numBytes);          /* the number of bytes actually read */
40: }
41:
42: long  SimpleFile_write(struct HSimpleFile  *this,
43:     HArrayOfByte  *buffer,_ long  count) {
44:     char  *data = unhand(buffer)->body;
45:     int   len  = obj_length(buffer);
46:
47:     return(write(unhand(this)->fd, data, (len < count ? len : count)));
48: }
```

Compile Everything into a Shared Library

The final step is to compile all the .c files, including the stub file and your native method files. Use your favorite C compiler to compile and link those two files into a shared library (a DLL on Windows). On some systems, you may need to specify special compilation flags that mean "make it relocatable and dynamically linkable." (Those flags, if they are required, may vary from system to system; check with your compiler documentation for details.)

TIP

> If you have several classes with native methods, you can include all their stubs in the same .c file, if you like. Of course you might want to name it something else, such as Stubs.c, in that case.

20

The resulting library should be the same name as you gave in your original Java class file as the argument to `System.loadLibrary()`. In the `SimpleFile` class, that library was called `libmynativelibrary.so`. You'll want to name the library that same name and install it wherever your particular system needs libraries to be installed.

Using Your Library

With all the code written and compiled and installed in the right place, all you have to do is run your Java program using the Java bytecode interpreter. When the Java class is loaded, it will also try to load the native library automatically; if it succeeds you should be able to use the classes in your Java class, and they will transparently run the native libraries as they are needed.

If you get an error that the library was not found, the most likely problem is that you do not have your environment set up correctly or that you have not installed your library in the right place.

WINDOWS DLL files are located according to the standard Windows algorithm: the directory the application was located in, the current directory, the System directory in Windows 95 (System32 in NT), the System directory in NT, the Windows directory, and then directories listed in the PATH environment variable.

SOLARIS UNIX systems use the environment variable LD_LIBRARY_PATH to search for libraries. This environment variable should include the standard places shared libraries are stored, as well as the current directory (.). After LD_LIBRARY_PATH has been set, Java will be able to find your library.

MACINTOSH Shared libraries for Java must be stored in the folder System Folder: Extensions:JavaSoft Folder. Rather than copying your native library there, you can also just create an alias to your native library and put it in that folder.

Tools and Techniques for Writing Native Implementations

20

When writing the code for native implementations, a whole set of useful macros and functions is available for mapping between C and C++ and Java, and for accessing Java runtime structures. (Several of them were used in `SimpleFileNative.c`.) In addition, there are several rules and techniques for dealing with the conversion between Java and C. In this section you'll learn about those functions and techniques to make writing your native code easier.

Names

Java names for classes, methods, and variables can be used inside native methods with the following changes (if needed):

- [ ] Any Unicode characters in names are converted to _0dddd, where the ds represent the Unicode number for that character. For example, the Unicode registered trademark symbol, which is Unicode 00ae, would be represented in C as _000ae.

- [ ] Package names are included with all names, with the dots replaced by underscores (_). So, for example, java.Math.pi would be java_Math_pi from the native side.

- [ ] Slashes in package names, if any, are replaced by underscores.

- [ ] Class names are renamed with the word Class prepended to the full name (including package names) For example, the Java class SimpleFile would be ClassSimpleFile (usually, however, you'll refer to classes through handles, which are explained in the next section).

Accessing Java Objects

Java objects are passed to native methods using handles to structures. The handle name is the name of the object (including any package names), prepended with the letter H. So, for example, the class SimpleFile would have a handle called HSimpleFile. The class java.lang.String would convert to Hjava_lang.String (remember, class names have package names included, with underscores to separate them).

 Handles are references to structures that represent Java objects. Each handle has the same name as the class it references, with the letter H prepended.

Each native function automatically gets passed at least one handle in its parameter list. This is called the *automatic parameter*, and it's a handle to the class that contained the original native method. Even if the original name method has no arguments, the C equivalent for that method is passed a handle to the class so it can reference other parts of that object or pass data back to it. In fact, because the handle to the original class behaves as if it were the this object, it's often called this in the native code's method signature as well.

 The *automatic parameter* is a handle to the original Java class that called the native method. Because it is roughly equivalent to this in Java, the automatic parameter is also often called this.

Note the native method signature for the open() method in SimpleFileNative.c, which shows the automatic parameter:

```
long  SimpleFile_open(struct HSimpleFile  *this)
```

To get to the methods or variables inside a class, you must dereference that class's handle. To do this, you can use the macro unhand() (as in "Unhand that object!"). The unhand() macro returns a pointer to a struct. So, for example, to get at the variables inside the `this` handle, you'd reference it like this:

```
unhand(this);
```

After the handle is dereferenced, you can access its variables as if they were normal `struct` elements:

```
unhand(this)->path;
```

References to arrays are slightly different than references to objects, although both are passed as handles, and you can reference their elements by "unhanding" them as well. In the case of arrays, however, the name of the handle includes the words `ArrayOf` prepended to the type of the array, and the letter `H` prepended to that. So, for example, an array of integers, declared like this in Java:

```
int[] lotsOfInts;
```

would look like this on the native side:

```
HArrayOfInt *lotsOfInts;
```

Calling Methods

In the previous section you learned how to deal with references to Java objects as handles. Using `unhand()`, you can dereference those handles and get to the object's variables. But what about methods? From your native code, you can call methods inside Java objects using several utility functions for just that purpose.

In addition, as you pass data back and forth between the Java side and the native side, you'll need to know how data types convert and how to deal with those types in either side.

Functions for Executing Methods

To call methods inside Java objects from within native code, you use special utility functions. To call a regular Java method, use the function `execute_java_dynamic_method()`. To call a class method, use the function `execute_java_static_method()`. Here's the signature for these functions (from the Java `include` file `interpreter.h`, which defines things like this):

```
long execute_java_dynamic_method(ExecEnv *env, HObject *obj,
    char *method_name, char *signature, ...);
long execute_java_static_method(ExecEnv *env, ClassClass *cb,
    char *method_name, char *signature, ...);
```

Both functions take at least four arguments:

☐ An `ExecEnv` structure, which defines the current execution environment. Right now the only possible value for this argument is `0`, which refers to the current execution environment.

☐ For dynamic methods, a reference to the object in which the method you're calling is defined. This would be the left side of the dot in normal Java dot notation. Here, it's a handle to that object.

☐ For static (class) methods, a reference to the class structure in which the method is defined. You can get a hold of a reference to a class using the `FindClass()` and `FindClassFromClass()` functions, described later on in this section.

☐ The method name (as a string).

☐ The method signature.

Any remaining arguments to the `execute_java_static_method()` and `execute_java_dynamic_method()` functions are arguments to the method itself.

Method signatures can be complex, because in this case they are not simply the list of arguments and the return types. Method signatures, for this function, are strings with a set of parentheses containing an argument list, and a return type just after the closing parentheses. Both the argument list and the return type are letters or strings that represent a type.

For the primitive types, use single-letter codes for the argument list and the return type (`B` is byte, `I` is int, `V` is void, and `Z` is boolean). For arrays, use an open square bracket before the type (for example, `[B` denotes a byte array). More letter codes for different types are contained in the Java include file `signature.h`. So, for example, a method that has no arguments and returns void would have a signature of `()V`. One that take three integer arguments and returns an integer would have a signature of `(III)V`.

For object arguments, the code is the letter `L`, then the class name (including the package, with all elements separated by slashes), followed by a semicolon. So, for example, a reference to a `String` object would be `Ljava/lang/String;`.

Got all that? Here are a few examples:

```
execute_java_dynamic_method(0, this, "close", "()Z"
execute_java_static_method(0, MyClass, "reverseString",
    "(Ljava/lang/String;)Ljava/lang/String;", "This is my string");
execute_java_dynamic_method(0, this, "open_speaker()",
    "(Lcom/lne/audio/Device;)Z", theDevice);
```

The `FindClass()` and `FindClassFromClass()` functions can be used to get a reference to a class structure (a pointer of type `ClassClass`) for use with the `execute_java_static_method()` function. Here are their signatures:

```
ClassClass *FindClass(ExecEnv *env,
    char *className, bool_t resolve);
ClassClass *FindClassFromClass(ExecEnv *env,
    char *className, bool_t resolve, ClassClass *from);
```

As with the functions for calling methods, the first argument should be `0` to indicate that this function is to be run in the current environment. The second argument is the class name to find. The `resolve` argument is a boolean which, if `TRUE` or `1`, indicates that the `resolve Class()` method should be called on that class (class resolution is a function of the class loader; it's probably safe to use `TRUE` for this argument in most cases). In the case of `FindClassFromClass`, the fourth argument is an already existing class; the class loader that loaded that class will also be used to find and load the new class.

Passing Parameters Back and Forth

To pass parameters to Java methods from native code or vice versa, you have to understand how data types convert between the two sides of the process.

The primitive data types in Java convert to their nearest equivalents in C. All the Java integer types (`char`, `byte`, `short`, `int`) and `boolean` convert to C `long` types; `long` converts to `int64_t`, and `float` and `double` remain floats and doubles. Keep in mind that because of these conversions, your original native method definitions may need return types that reflect the values sent back from the C side of the native method (for example, all methods that return `integer` types must actually return `long`).

Object types are passed as handles to structures, as you learned earlier, and must be dereferenced using `unhand()` in order to be used.

Creating New Java Objects

Because you can access Java objects and call methods from inside your native code, the one thing left is the capability to create new objects. You can do this too, using the `execute_class_constructor()` function. This function is very similar to the functions for calling methods; in fact, it has the same set of arguments that `execute_java_static_method()` does:

```
HObject *execute_java_constructor(ExecEnv *, char *classname,
    ClassClass *cb, char *signature, ...);
```

The `execute_java_static_method()` function has four arguments, but can have more. The four required arguments are

- [ ] `0`, for the current environment (the only value of this argument currently supported).
- [ ] A string representing the class name that defines this constructor.
- [ ] A class handle such as the one you'd get from `FindClass()`. If you use a class name, this argument should be `NULL`; if you use a class object, the class name should be `NULL` (use one or the other, not both). Using class references over class names can be more efficient if you expect to create lots of objects with the same class, because you can just use the same class reference over and over again (class names must be looked up each time).

20

☐ The signature of the constructor which, as with the functions to execute Java methods, is a string representing the arguments to the method (constructors don't have a return type). As with the functions to call methods, [T is array of type T, B is byte, I is int, and Z is boolean. Other types are defined in signature.h (part of the standard Java include files).

☐ Any other arguments to the constructor are added onto the end of the parameter list.

Here are some examples:

```
execute_java_constructor(0, "MyClass", NULL, "()");
execute_java_constructor(0, "MyOtherClass", NULL, "(II)", 10, 12);
```

The first example creates an instance of the MyClass class, using the constructor with no arguments. The second creates an instance of MyOtherClass, in which the constructor has two integer arguments. Those arguments, 10 and 12, are included at the end of the parameter list.

Handling Exceptions

To handle errors, Java has exceptions. In your native C code, you can set up a Java exception using SignalError, like this:

```
SignalError(0, JAVAPKG "ExceptionClassName", "message");
```

Here, the exception class name is the name of a Java exception class, including its package name, with the separation of package names delineated with a slash rather than a period as in Java. So, for example, the class java.io.IOException would be "java/io/IOException" when used inside SignalError.

The exception will be thrown in Java when your native method returns (which it should immediately after the SignalError). Note that just like regular methods, native methods that throw exceptions must be declared to throw those exceptions using the throw keyword.

Dealing with Strings

Several functions and macros are available in the include file javaString.h to help manage strings. To gain access to these functions, include that header as part of your native code:

```
#include <javaString.h>
```

The makeJavaString() function creates a Java String object out of a C string. To convert a Java String object into a C string, you can use makeCString() or allocCString() (where the former allocates the string from temporary storage and the latter from the heap). Here are their signatures:

```
Hjava_lang_String *makeJavaString(char *string, int length)
```

```
char  *makeCString(Hjava_lang_String *s)
char  *allocCString(Hjava_lang_String *s)
```

To copy Java Strings into preexisting Unicode or ASCII C buffers, you can use javaString2unicode() and javaString2CString():

```
unicode  *javaString2unicode(Hjava_lang_String *s, unicode *buf, int  len)
char     *javaString2CString(Hjava_lang_String *s, char   *buf, int  len)
```

Finally, the javaStringPrint() function prints a Java String object (just like System.out.print()), and the javaStringLength() function gets its length:

```
void  javaStringPrint(Hjava_lang_String *s)
int   javaStringLength(Hjava_lang_String *s)
```

Summary

Today you have learned about the advantages and disadvantages of using native methods, about the many ways that Java (and you) can make your programs run faster, and also about the often illusory need for efficiency.

Finally, you learned the procedure for creating native methods, from both the Java and the C sides, in detail—by generating header files and stubs, and by compiling and linking a full example.

After working your way through today's difficult material, you've mastered one of the most complex parts of the Java language. As a reward, tomorrow we'll look "under the hood" to see some of the hidden power of Java, and you can just sit back and enjoy the ride.

Q&A

Q Your descriptions here are somewhat sparse. What can I use to supplement what I've learned here?

A Look at Sun's Java tutorial (online or on the CD-ROM included with this book) for a more detailed version of how to work with native methods.

Q Does the Java class library need to call System.loadLibrary() to load the built-in classes?

A No, you won't see any loadLibrary() calls in the implementation of any classes in the Java class library. That's because the Java team had the luxury of being able to statically link most of their code into the Java environment, something that really makes sense only when you're in the unique position of providing an entire system, as they are. Your classes must *dynamically* link their libraries into an already-running copy of the Java system. This is, by the way, more flexible than static linking; it allows you to unlink old and relink new versions of your classes at any time, making updating them trivial.

20

Q **Can I statically link my own classes into Java like the Java team did?**

A Yes. You can, if you like, ask Sun Microsystems for the sources to the Java runtime environment itself, and, as long as you obey the (relatively straightforward) legal restrictions on using that code, you can relink the entire Java system plus your classes. Your classes are then statically linked into the system, but you have to give everyone who wants to use your program this special version of the Java environment. Sometimes, if you have strong enough requirements, this is the only way to go, but most of the time, dynamic linking is not only good enough, but preferable.

20

Day 21

Under the Hood

by Charles L. Perkins and Laura Lemay

Today the inner workings of the Java system will be revealed.

You'll find out all about Java's vision, Java's virtual machine, those bytecodes you've heard so much about, that mysterious garbage collector, and why you might worry about security but don't have to.

NOTE The title of this chapter well describes its content; the discussion in today's lesson is quite technical and assumes that you know something about low-level languages (assembly) and compiler/interpreter design concepts.

Let's begin, however, with the big picture.

The Big Picture

The Java team is very ambitious. Their ultimate goal is nothing less than to revolutionize the way software is written and distributed. They've started with the Internet, where they believe much of the interesting software of the future will live.

To achieve such an ambitious goal, a large portion of the Internet programming community itself must be marshaled behind a similar goal and given the tools to help achieve it. The Java language, with its four S's (small, simple, safe, secure) and its flexible, Net-oriented environment, hopes to become the focal point for the rallying of this new legion of programmers.

To this end, Sun Microsystems has done something rather gutsy. What was originally a secret, tens-of-millions-of-dollars research-and-development project, and 100 percent proprietary, has become a free, open, and relatively unencumbered technology standard upon which anyone can build. They are literally *giving it away* and reserving only the rights they need to maintain and grow the standard.

Any truly open standard must be supported by at least one excellent, freely available "demonstration" implementation. Sun has already shipped the 1.0 version of Java as part of the JDK, and has published specifications for the language itself and for the virtual machine and bytecode compilers. In parallel, several universities, companies, and individuals have already expressed their intention to duplicate the Java environment based on the open API that Sun has created.

In addition, the Java runtime environment is being incorporated into a wide variety of operating systems and environments on different platforms. Microsoft and Apple have licensed Java to include the runtime in Windows and the MacOS. A Java runtime will be available on IBM systems (OS/2 and AIX) as well as on nearly every commercial flavor of UNIX. What this means is that applications written in Java will be automatically executable on these systems, without any other software needing to be installed. These steps have been significant in making Java ubiquitous as not only the language for the Internet but also the language for future software development.

> **NOTE**
>
> Throughout this book, the Java runtime and the Java virtual machine are referred to interchangeably. While there are some slight differences between the two, equating them highlights the single *environment* that must be created to support Java.

Several other languages are even contemplating compiling down to Java bytecodes, to help support them in becoming a more robust and widespread standard for moving executable content around on the Net.

Why It's a Powerful Vision

One of the reasons this brilliant move on Sun's part has a real chance of success is the pent-up frustration of literally a whole generation of programmers who desperately want to share their code with one another. Right now, the computer science world is balkanized into factions at universities and companies all over the world, with hundreds of languages, dozens of them widely used, dividing and separating us all. It's the worst sort of Tower of Babel. Java hopes to build some bridges and help tear down that tower. Because it is so simple, because it's so useful for programming over the Internet, and because the Internet is so "hot" right now—this confluence of forces should help propel Java onto center stage.

It deserves to be there. It is the natural outgrowth of ideas that, since the early 1970s inside the Smalltalk group at Xerox PARC, have lain relatively dormant in the mainstream. Smalltalk, in fact, invented the first object-oriented bytecode interpreter and pioneered many of the deep ideas that Java builds on today. Those efforts were not embraced over the intervening decades as a solution to the general problems of software, however. Today, with those problems becoming so much more obvious, and with the Net crying out for a new kind of programming, the soil is fertile to grow something stronger from those old roots, something that just might spread like wildfire. (Is it a coincidence that Java's previous internal names were Green and OAK?)

This new vision of software is one in which the Net becomes an ocean of objects, classes, and the open APIs between them. Traditional applications have vanished, replaced by skeletal frameworks like the Eiffel Tower into which can be fitted any parts from this ocean, on demand, to suit any purpose. User interfaces will be mixed and matched, built in pieces and constructed to taste, whenever the need arises, *by their own users*. Menus of choices will be filled by dynamic lists of *all* the choices available for that function, at that exact moment, across the entire ocean (of the Net).

In such a world, software distribution is no longer an issue. Software will be *everywhere* and will be paid for via a plethora of new micro-accounting models, which charge tiny fractions of cents for the parts as they are assembled and used. Frameworks will come into existence to support entertainment, business, and the social (cyber-)spaces of the near future.

This is a dream that many of us have waited *all our lives* to be a part of. There are tremendous challenges to making it all come true, but the powerful winds of change we all feel must stir us into action because, at last, there is a base on which to build that dream—Java.

The Java Virtual Machine

21

To make visions like this possible, Java must be ubiquitous. It must be able to run on any computer and any operating system—now and in the future. In order to achieve this level of portability, Java must be very precise not only about the language itself, but about the environment in which the language lives. You've seen throughout this book that the Java environment includes a generally useful set of packages of classes and a freely available implementation of them. This takes care of a part of what is needed, but it is crucial also to specify exactly how the runtime environment of Java behaves.

This final requirement is what has stymied many attempts at ubiquity in the past. If you base your system on any assumptions about what is beneath the runtime system, you lose. If you depend in any way on the computer or operating system below, you lose. Java solves this problem by *inventing* an abstract computer of its own and running on that.

This *virtual machine*, as it's called, and which you've used throughout this book as the Java bytecode interpreter, runs a special set of instructions, called *bytecodes*, that are simply a stream of formatted bytes, each of which has a precise specification of exactly what each bytecode does to this virtual machine. The virtual machine is also responsible for certain fundamental capabilities of Java, such as object creation and garbage collection.

Finally, in order to be able to move bytecodes safely across the Internet, you need a bulletproof model of security—and how to maintain it—and a precise format for how this stream of bytecodes can be sent from one virtual machine to another.

Each of these requirements is addressed in today's lesson.

NOTE

> Much of the following description is based closely on the latest "Virtual Machine Specifications" documents (and the 1.0 bytecodes), so if you delve more deeply into the details online, you should cover some familiar ground.

An Overview

It is worth quoting the introduction to the Java virtual machine documentation here, because it is so relevant to the vision outlined earlier:

> The Java virtual machine specification has a purpose that is both like and unlike equivalent documents for other languages and abstract machines. It is intended to present an abstract, logical machine design free from the distraction of inconsequential details of any implementation. It does not anticipate an implementation technology or an implementation host. At the same time it gives a reader sufficient information to allow implementation of the abstract design in a range of technologies.
>
> However, the intent of the [...] Java project is to create a language [...] that will allow the interchange over the Internet of "executable content," which will be embodied by

compiled Java code. The project specifically does not want Java to be a proprietary language and does not want to be the sole purveyor of Java language implementations. Rather, we hope to make documents like this one, and source code for our implementation, freely available for people to use as they choose.

This vision [...] can be achieved only if the executable content can be reliably shared between different Java implementations. These intentions prohibit the definition of the Java virtual machine from being fully abstract. Rather, relevant logical elements of the design have to be made sufficiently concrete to allow the interchange of compiled Java code. This does not collapse the Java virtual machine specification to a description of a Java implementation; elements of the design that do not play a part in the interchange of executable content remain abstract. But it does force us to specify, in addition to the abstract machine design, a concrete interchange format for compiled Java code.

The Java virtual machine specification consists of the following:

- [ ] The bytecode syntax, including opcode and operand sizes, values, and types, and their alignment and endian-ness
- [ ] The values of any identifiers (for example, type identifiers) in bytecodes or in supporting structures
- [ ] The layout of the supporting structures that appear in compiled Java code (for example, the constant pool)
- [ ] The Java `.class` file format

Each of these is covered today.

Despite this degree of specificity, there are still several elements of the design that remain (purposely) abstract, including the following:

- [ ] The layout and management of the runtime data areas
- [ ] The particular garbage-collection algorithms, strategies, and constraints used
- [ ] The compiler, development environment, and runtime extensions (apart from the need to generate and read valid Java bytecodes)
- [ ] Any optimizations performed when valid bytecodes are received

These places are where the creativity of a virtual machine implementor has full rein.

The Fundamental Parts

The Java virtual machine can be divided into five fundamental pieces:

- [ ] A bytecode instruction set
- [ ] A set of registers

- [ ] A stack
- [ ] A garbage-collected heap
- [ ] An area for storing methods

Some of these might be implemented by using an interpreter, a native binary code compiler, or even a hardware chip—but all these logical, abstract components of the virtual machine must be supplied in *some* form in every Java system.

NOTE

> The memory areas used by the Java virtual machine are not required to be at any particular place in memory, to be in any particular order, or even to use contiguous memory. However, all but the method area must be able to represent aligned 32-bit values (for example, the Java stack is 32 bits wide).

The virtual machine, and its supporting code, is often referred to as the *runtime environment*, and when this book refers to something being done at runtime, the virtual machine is what's doing it.

Java Bytecodes

The Java virtual machine instruction set is optimized to be small and compact. It is designed to travel across the Net, and so has traded off speed-of-interpretation for space. (Given that both Net bandwidth and mass storage speeds increase less rapidly than CPU speed, this seems like an appropriate trade-off.)

As mentioned, Java source code is "compiled" into bytecodes and stored in a .class file. On Sun's Java system, this is performed using the Java compiler (javac). The Java compiler is not exactly a traditional "compiler," because it translates source code into bytecodes, a lower-level format that cannot be run directly but must be further interpreted by each computer. Of course, it is exactly this level of indirection that buys you the power, flexibility, and extreme portability of Java code.

NOTE

> Quotation marks are used around the word "compiler" when talking about the Java compiler because later today you will also learn about the "just-in-time" compiler, which acts more like the back end of a traditional compiler. The use of the same word "compiler" for these two different pieces of Java technology is unfortunate, but somewhat reasonable, because each is really one-half (either the front or the back end) of a more traditional compiler.

A bytecode instruction consists of a one-byte opcode that serves to identify the instruction involved and zero or more operands, each of which may be more than one byte long, that encode the parameters the opcode requires.

NOTE

> When operands are more than one byte long, they are stored in big-endian order, high-order byte first. These operands must be assembled from the byte stream at runtime. For example, a 16-bit parameter appears in the stream as two bytes so that its value is `first_byte * 256 + second_byte`. The bytecode instruction stream is only byte-aligned, and alignment of any larger quantities is not guaranteed (except inside the special bytecodes `lookupswitch` and `tableswitch`, which have special alignment rules of their own).

Bytecodes interpret data in the runtime memory areas as belonging to a fixed set of types: the primitive types you've seen several times before, consisting of several signed integer types (8-bit `byte`, 16-bit `short`, 32-bit `int`, 64-bit `long`), one unsigned integer type (16-bit `char`), and two signed floating-point types (32-bit `float`, 64-bit `double`), plus the type "reference to an object" (a 32-bit pointer-like type). Some special bytecodes (for example, the `dup` instructions) treat runtime memory areas as raw data, without regard to type. This is the exception, however—not the rule.

These primitive types are distinguished and managed by the Java compiler, not by the Java runtime environment. These types are not identified in memory, and therefore cannot be distinguished at runtime. Different bytecodes are designed to handle each of the various primitive types uniquely, and the compiler carefully chooses from this palette based on its knowledge of the actual types stored in the various memory areas. For example, when adding two integers, the compiler generates an `iadd` bytecode; for adding two floats, `fadd` is generated.

Specifics about the Java bytecodes themselves are contained in Appendix D, "Bytecodes Reference."

Registers

The registers of the Java virtual machine are just like the registers inside a real computer.

NEW TERM

Registers are used to temporarily store data. In the Java vritual machine registers hold the machine's state, affect its operation, and are updated after each bytecode is executed.

21

The following are the Java registers:

- pc, the program counter, which indicates what bytecode is being executed
- optop, a pointer to the top of the operand stack, which is used to evaluate all arithmetic expressions
- frame, a pointer to the execution environment of the current method, which includes an activation record for this method call and any associated debugging information
- vars, a pointer to the first local variable of the currently executing method

The virtual machine defines these registers to be 32 bits wide.

NOTE

Because the virtual machine is primarily stack-based, it does not use any registers for passing or receiving arguments. This is a conscious choice skewed toward bytecode simplicity and compactness. It also aids efficient implementation on computer systems with fewer registers.

By the way, the pc register is also used when the runtime handles exceptions; catch clauses are (ultimately) associated with ranges of the pc within a method's bytecodes.

The Stack

The Java virtual machine is stack-based. A Java stack frame is similar to the stack frame of a conventional programming language—it holds the state for a single method call. Frames for nested method calls are stacked on top of this frame.

The *stack* is used to supply parameters to bytecodes and methods, and to receive results back from them.

Each stack frame contains three (possibly empty) sets of data: the local variables for the method call, its execution environment, and its operand stack. The sizes of the first two are fixed at the start of a method call, but the operand stack varies in size as bytecodes are executed in the method.

Local variables are stored in an array of 32-bit slots, indexed by the register vars. Most types take up one slot in the array, but the long and double types each take up two slots.

NOTE

Long and double values, stored or referenced via an index N, take up the (32-bit) slots [N] and [N]+1. These 64-bit values are therefore not guaranteed to be 64-bit-aligned. Implementors are free to decide the appropriate way to divide these values between the two slots.

The *execution environment* in a stack frame helps to maintain the stack itself. It contains a pointer to the previous stack frame, a pointer to the local variables of the method call, and pointers to the stack's current "base" and "top." Additional debugging information can also be placed into the execution environment.

The *operand stack*, a 32-bit first-in-first-out (FIFO) stack, is used to store the parameters and return values of most bytecode instructions. For example, the `iadd` bytecode expects two integers to be stored on the top of the stack. It pops them, adds them together, and pushes the resulting sum back onto the stack.

Each primitive data type has unique instructions that know how to extract, operate, and push back operands of that type. For example, `long` and `double` operands take two positions on the stack, and the special bytecodes that handle these operands take this into account. It is illegal for the types on the stack and the instruction operating on them to be incompatible (the Java compiler outputs bytecodes that always obey this rule).

NOTE

> The top of the operand stack and the top of the overall Java stack are almost always the same. Thus, "the stack" refers to both stacks, collectively.

The Heap

The *heap* is that part of memory from which newly created instances (objects) are allocated.

The heap is often assigned a large, fixed size when the Java runtime system is started, but on systems that support virtual memory, it can grow as needed, in a nearly unbounded fashion.

Because objects are automatically garbage-collected in Java, programmers do not have to (and, in fact, *cannot*) manually free the memory allocated to an object when they are finished using it.

Java objects are referenced indirectly in the runtime via *handles,* which are a kind of pointer into the heap.

Because objects are never referenced directly, parallel garbage collectors can be written that operate independently of your program, moving around objects in the heap at will. You'll learn more about garbage collection in the section "The Garbage Collector," later in this lesson.

21

The Method Area

Like the compiled code areas of conventional programming language environments, or the TEXT segment in a UNIX process, the *method area* stores the Java bytecodes that implement almost every method in the Java system. (Remember that some methods might be declared `native`, and thus implemented, for example, in C.) The method area also stores the symbol tables needed for dynamic linking as well as any other additional information debuggers or development environments that might want to associate with each method's implementation.

Because bytecodes are stored as byte streams, the method area is aligned on byte boundaries. (The other areas are all aligned on 32-bit word boundaries.)

The Constant Pool

In the heap, each class has an array of constants, called a *constant pool*, available to it. Usually created by the Java compiler, these constants encode all the names (of variables, methods, and so forth) used by any method in a class. The class contains a count of how many constants there are and an offset that specifies how far into the class description itself the array of constants begins. These constants are typed via specially coded bytes and have a precisely defined format when they appear in the `.class` file for a class. Later today, a little of this file format is covered, but everything is fully specified by the virtual machine specifications in your Java release.

Limitations

The virtual machine, as currently defined, places some restrictions on legal Java programs by virtue of the choices it has made (some were previously described, and more will be detailed later today).

These limitations and their implications are

- [ ] 32-bit pointers, which imply that the virtual machine can address only 4GB of memory (this may be relaxed in later releases)
- [ ] Unsigned 16-bit indices into the exception, line number, and local variable tables, which limits the size of a method's bytecode implementation to 64KB (this limitation may be eliminated in the final release)
- [ ] Unsigned 16-bit indices into the constant pool, which limits the number of constants in a class to 64KB (a limit on the complexity of a class)

In addition, Sun's implementation of the virtual machine uses so-called _quick bytecodes, which further limit the system. Unsigned 8-bit offsets into objects may limit the number of methods in a class to 256 (this limit may not exist in the final release), and unsigned 8-bit argument counts limit the size of the argument list to 255 32-bit words. (Although this means that you can have up to 255 arguments of most types, you can have only 127 of them if they're all `long` or `double`.)

21

The Bytecode Interpreter

A bytecode interpreter examines each opcode byte (bytecode) in a method's bytecode stream, in turn, and executes a unique action for that bytecode. This might consume further bytes for the operands of the bytecode and might affect which bytecode will be examined next. It operates like the hardware CPU in a computer, which examines memory for instructions to carry out in exactly the same manner. It is the software CPU of the Java virtual machine.

Your first, naive attempt to write such a bytecode interpreter will almost certainly be disastrously slow. The inner loop, which dispatches one bytecode each time through the loop, is notoriously difficult to optimize. In fact, smart people have been thinking about this problem, in one form or another, for more than 20 years. Luckily, they've gotten results, all of which can be applied to Java.

The final result is that the interpreter shipped in the current release of Java has an extremely fast inner loop. In fact, on even a relatively slow computer, this interpreter can perform more than 590,000 bytecodes per second! This is really quite good—the CPU in that computer does only about 30 times better, and it has the advantage of using the hardware to do it.

This interpreter is fast enough for most Java programs (and for those *requiring* more speed, they can always use native methods—see yesterday's discussion), but what if a smart implementor wants to do better?

Just-in-Time Compilers

About a decade ago, a really clever trick was discovered by Peter Deutsch while trying to make Smalltalk run faster. He called it dynamic translation during interpretation. Sun calls it "just-in-time" (or JIT) compiling, which, effectively, means converting the relatively slow interpreted bytecode into native machine code just before running it—and therefore getting very close to native performance out of cross-platform Java bytecode.

The trick is to notice that the really fast interpreter you've just written—in C, for example—already has a useful sequence of native binary code for each bytecode that it interprets: *the binary code that the interpreter itself is executing*. Because the interpreter has already been compiled from C into native binary code, for each bytecode that it interprets, it passes through a sequence of native code instructions for the hardware CPU on which it is running. By saving a copy of each binary instruction as it's executed, the interpreter can keep a running log of the binary code it *itself* has run to interpret a bytecode. It can just as easily keep a log of the set of bytecodes that it ran to interpret an entire method.

You take that log of instructions and "peephole-optimize" it, just as a smart compiler does (*peephole optimization* involves taking a short sequence on instructions and replacing them

21

with a shorter or faster set of instructions). This eliminates redundant or unnecessary instructions from the log, and makes it look just like the optimized binary code that a good compiler might have produced.

NOTE This is where the name compiler comes from, in "just-in-time" compiler, but it's really only the back end of a traditional compiler— the part that does code generation. By the way, the front end here is the Java compiler (javac).

Here's where the trick comes in. The next time that method is run (in exactly the same way), the interpreter can now simply execute directly the stored log of binary native code. Because this optimizes the inner-loop overhead of each bytecode, as well as any other redundancies between the bytecodes in a method, it can gain a factor of 10 or more in speed. In fact, an experimental version of this technology at Sun has shown that Java programs using it can run as fast as compiled C programs.

NOTE The parenthetical qualifier in the last paragraph is needed because if anything is different about the input to the method, it takes a different path through the interpreter and must be relogged. (There are sophisticated versions of this technology that solve this, and other, difficulties.) The cache of native code for a method must be invalidated whenever the method has changed, and the interpreter must pay a small cost up front each time a method is run for the first time. However, these small bookkeeping costs are far outweighed by the amazing gains in speed possible.

Just-in-time compilers, often called just JIT compilers, are becoming increasingly popular, and many major vendors (including Microsoft and Symantec) are competing in this realm. Microsoft's Internet Explorer 3.0 ships with a JIT compiler already. You'll learn more about the various JIT compilers available (or soon to be) on Day 28, "Emerging Technologies."

The Class File Format

A Java *class file* is the file generated by the Java compiler with a .class extension. You won't be given the entire .class file format here, only a taste of what it's like. (You can read all about it in the release documentation.) It's mentioned here because it is one of the parts of Java that

21

needs to be specified carefully if all Java implementations are to be compatible with one another, and if Java bytecodes are expected to travel across arbitrary networks—to and from arbitrary computers and operating systems—and yet arrive safely.

The rest of this section paraphrases, and extensively condenses, the latest release of the class file documentation.

Java class files are used to hold the compiled versions of both Java classes and Java interfaces. Compliant Java interpreters must be capable of dealing with all class files that conform to the following specification.

A Java class file consists of a stream of 8-bit bytes. All 16-bit and 32-bit quantities are constructed by reading in two or four 8-bit bytes, respectively. The bytes are joined together in big-endian order. (Use `java.io.DataInput` and `java.io.DataOutput` to read and write class files.)

The class file format is presented below as a series of C-struct-like structures. However, unlike a C struct, there is no padding or alignment between pieces of the structure. Each field of the structure may be of variable size, and an array may be of variable size (in this case, some field prior to the array gives the array's dimension). The types u1, u2, and u4 represent an unsigned 1-, 2-, or 4-byte quantity, respectively.

Attributes are used at several different places in the class file format. All attributes have the following format:

```
GenericAttribute_info {
    u2 attribute_name;
    u4 attribute_length;
    u1 info[attribute_length];
}
```

The `attribute_name` is a 16-bit index into the class's constant pool; the value of `constant_pool[attribute_name]` is a string giving the name of the attribute. The field `attribute_length` gives the length of the subsequent information in bytes. This length does not include the 6 bytes needed to store `attribute_name` and `attribute_length`. In the examples in the rest of this section, whenever an attribute is required, names of all the attributes that are currently understood are listed. In the future, more attributes will be added. Class file readers are expected to skip over and ignore the information in any attributes they do not understand.

The following pseudo-structure gives a top-level description of the format of a class file:

```
ClassFile {
    u4  magic;
    u2  minor_version
    u2  major_version
    u2  constant_pool_count;
    cp_info         constant_pool[constant_pool_count - 1];
    u2  access_flags;
```

21

```
    u2  this_class;
    u2  super_class;
    u2  interfaces_count;
    u2  interfaces[interfaces_count];
    u2  fields_count;
    field_info      fields[fields_count];
    u2  methods_count;
    method_info     methods[methods_count];
    u2  attributes_count;
    attribute_info  attributes[attribute_count];
}
```

Here's one of the smaller structures used:

```
method_info {
    u2  access_flags;
    u2  name_index;
    u2  signature_index;
    u2  attributes_count;
    attribute_info  attributes[attribute_count];
}
```

Finally, here's a sample of one of the later structures in the class file description:

```
Code_attribute {
    u2  attribute_name_index;
    u2  attribute_length;
    u1  max_stack;
    u1  max_locals;
    u2  code_length;
    u1  code[code_length];
    u2  exception_table_length;
    { u2    start_pc;
      u2    end_pc;
      u2    handler_pc;
      u2    catch_type;
    } exception_table[exception_table_length];
    u2  attributes_count;
    attribute_info  attributes[attribute_count];
}
```

None of this is meant to be completely comprehensible (although you might be able to guess at what a lot of the structure members are for), but just suggestive of the sort of structures that live inside class files. Because the compiler and runtime sources are available, you can always begin with them if you actually have to read or write class files yourself. Therefore, you don't need to have a deep understanding of the details, even in that case.

Method Signatures

Because method signatures are used in class files, now is an appropriate time to explore them in the detail promised on earlier days—but they're probably most useful to you when writing the native methods of yesterday's lesson.

21

The *method signature*, in this instance, is a string representing the type of method, field, or array.

A *field signature* represents the value of an argument to a method or the value of a variable and is a series of bytes in the following grammar:

```
<field signature> := <field_type>
<field type>      := <base_type> ¦ <object_type> ¦ <array_type>
<base_type>       := B ¦ C ¦ D ¦ F ¦ I ¦ J ¦ S ¦ Z
<object_type>     := L <full.ClassName> ;
<array_type>      := [ <optional_size> <field_type>
<optional_size>   := [0-9]*
```

Here are the meanings of the base types: B (byte), C (char), D (double), F (float), I (int), J (long), S (short), and Z (boolean).

A *return-type signature* represents the return value from a method and is a series of bytes in the following grammar:

```
<return signature>    := <field type> ¦ V
```

The character V (void) indicates that the method returns no value. Otherwise, the signature indicates the type of the return value. An *argument signature* represents an argument passed to a method:

```
<argument signature>  := <field type>
```

Finally, a *method signature* represents the arguments that the method expects and the value that it returns:

```
<method_signature>    := (<arguments signature>) <return signature>
<arguments signature> := <argument signature>*
```

Let's try out the new rules: A method called `complexMethod()` in the class `my.package.name.ComplexClass` takes three arguments—a `long`, a `boolean`, and a two-dimensional array of `shorts`—and returns `this`. Then its method signature is `(JZ[[S)Lmy.package.name.ComplexClass;`.

A method signature is often prefixed by the name of the method, or by its full package (using an underscore in the place of dots) and its class name followed by a slash (/) and the name of the method, to form a *complete method signature*. (You saw several of these generated in stub comments yesterday.) Now, at last, you have the full story! Thus, the following:

```
my_package_name_ComplexClass/complexMethod(JZ[[S)Lmy.package.name.ComplexClass;
```

is the full, complete method signature of `complexMethod()`. (Phew!)

21

The Garbage Collector

Decades ago, programmers in both the Lisp and Smalltalk communities realized how extremely valuable it is to be able to ignore memory deallocation. They realized that, although allocation is fundamental, deallocation is forced on the programmer by the laziness of the system—*it* should be able to figure out what is no longer useful, and get rid of it. In relative obscurity, these pioneering programmers developed a whole series of garbage collectors to perform this job, each getting more sophisticated and efficient as the years went by. Finally, now that the mainstream programming community has begun to recognize the value of this automated technique, Java can become the first really widespread application of the technology those pioneers developed.

The Problem

Imagine that you're a programmer in a C-like language (probably not too difficult for you, because these languages are the dominant ones right now). Each time you create something, anything, *dynamically* in such a language, you are completely responsible for tracking the life of that object throughout your program and mentally deciding when it will be safe to deallocate it. This can be quite a difficult (sometimes impossible) task, because any of the other libraries or methods you've called might have "squirreled away" a pointer to the object, unbeknownst to you. When it becomes impossible to know, you simply choose *never* to deallocate the object, or at least to wait until every library and method call involved has completed, which could be nearly as long.

The uneasy feeling you get when writing such code is a natural, healthy response to what is inherently an unsafe and unreliable style of programming. If you have tremendous discipline—and so does everyone who writes every library and method you call—you can, in principle, survive this responsibility without too many mishaps. But aren't you human? Aren't they? There must be some small slips in this perfect discipline due to error. What's worse, such errors are virtually undetectable, as anyone who's tried to hunt down a stray pointer problem in C will tell you. What about the thousands of programmers who don't have that sort of discipline?

Another way to ask this question is: Why should any programmers be forced to have this discipline when it is entirely possible for the system to remove this heavy burden from their shoulders?

Software engineering estimates have recently shown that for every 55 lines of production C-like code in the world, there is one bug. This means that your electric razor has about 80 bugs, and your TV, 400. Soon they will have even more, because the size of this kind of embedded computer software is growing exponentially. When you begin to think of how much C-like code is in your car's engine, it should give you pause.

Many of these errors are due to the misuse of pointers, by misunderstanding or by accident, and to the early, incorrect freeing of allocated objects in memory. Java addresses both of these—the former by eliminating explicit pointers from the Java language altogether, and the latter by including, in every Java system, a garbage collector that solves the problem.

The Solution

Imagine a runtime system that tracks each object you create, notices when the last reference to it has vanished, and frees the object for you. How could such a thing actually work?

One brute-force approach, tried early in the days of garbage collecting, is to attach a reference counter to every object. When the object is created, the counter is set to 1. Each time a new reference to the object is made, the counter is incremented, and each time such a reference disappears, the counter is decremented. Because all such references are controlled by the language—as variables and assignments, for example—the compiler can tell whenever an object reference might be created or destroyed, just as it does in handling the scoping of local variables, and thus it can assist with this task. The system itself maintains a set of root objects that are considered too important to be freed. The class Object is one example of such a V.I.P. object. (V.I.O.?) Finally, all that's needed is to test, after each decrement, whether the counter has hit 0. If it has, the object is freed.

If you think carefully about this approach, you will soon convince yourself that it is definitely correct when it decides to free anything. It is so simple that you can immediately tell that it will work. The low-level hacker in you might also feel that if it's *that* simple, it's probably not fast enough to run at the lowest level of the system—and you'd be right.

Think about all the stack frames, local variables, method arguments, return values, and local variables created in the course of even a few hundred milliseconds of a program's life. For each of these tiny, nano-steps in the program, an extra increment (at best) or decrement, test, and deallocation (at worst) will be added to the running time of the program. In fact, the first garbage collectors were slow enough that many predicted they could never be used at all!

Luckily, a whole generation of smart programmers has invented a big bag of tricks to solve these overhead problems. One trick is to introduce special "transient object" areas that don't need to be reference counted. The best of these generational scavenging garbage collectors today can take less than 3 percent of the total time of your program—a remarkable feat if you realize that many other language features, such as loop overheads, can be as large or larger!

There are other problems with garbage collection. If you are constantly freeing and reclaiming space in a program, won't the heap of objects soon become fragmented, with small holes everywhere and no room to create new, large objects? Because the programmer is now free from the chains of manual deallocation, won't he create even more objects than usual?

21

What's worse, there is another way that this simple reference counting scheme is inefficient: in space rather than time. If a long chain of object references eventually comes full circle, back to the starting object, each object's reference count remains at least 1 *forever*. None of these objects will ever be freed!

Together, these problems imply that a good garbage collector must, every once in a while, step back to compact or clean up wasted memory.

Memory compaction occurs when a garbage collector steps back and reorganizes memory, eliminating the holes created by fragmentation. Compacting memory is simply a matter of repositioning objects one by one into a new, compact grouping that places them all in a row, leaving all the free memory in the heap in one big piece.

Cleaning up the circular garbage still lying around after reference counting is called *marking and sweeping*. A mark-and-sweep of memory involves first marking every root object in the system and then following all the object references inside those objects to new objects to mark, and so on, recursively. Then, when you have no more references to follow, you "sweep away" all the unmarked objects and compact memory as before.

The good news is that this solves the space problems you were having. The bad news is that when the garbage collector steps back and does these operations, a nontrivial amount of time passes during which your program is unable to run—all its objects are being marked, swept, rearranged, and so forth, in what seems like an uninterruptible procedure. Your first hint to a solution is the word "seems."

Garbage collecting can actually be done a little at a time, between or in parallel with normal program execution, thus dividing up the large amount of time needed to step back into the numerous so-small-you-don't-notice-them chunks of time that happen between the cracks. (Of course, years of smart thinking went into the abstruse algorithms that make all this possible!)

One final problem that might worry you a little has to do with these object references. Aren't these references scattered throughout your program and not just buried in objects? Even if they're only in objects, don't they have to be changed whenever the object they point to is moved by these procedures? The answer to both of these questions is a resounding *yes*, and overcoming them is the final hurdle to making an efficient garbage collector.

There are really only two choices. The first, brute force, assumes that all the memory containing object references needs to be searched on a regular basis, and whenever the object references found by this search match objects that have moved, the old reference is changed. This assumes that there are "hard" pointers in the heap's memory—ones that point directly to other objects. By introducing various kinds of "soft" pointers, including pointers that are like forwarding addresses, the algorithm improves greatly. Although these brute-force approaches sound slow, it turns out that modern computers can do them fast enough to be useful.

21

NOTE

> You might wonder how the brute-force techniques identify object references. In early systems, references were specially tagged with a *pointer bit* so they could be unambiguously located. Now, so-called conservative garbage collectors simply assume that if it looks like an object reference, it is—at least for the purposes of the mark-and-sweep. Later, when actually trying to update it, they can find out whether it really is an object reference.

The final approach to handling object references, and the one Java currently uses, is also one of the very first ones tried. It involves using 100 percent soft pointers. An object reference is actually a handle, sometimes called an *OOP*, to the real pointer, and a large object table exists to map these handles into the actual object reference. Although this does introduce extra overhead on almost every object reference (some of which can be eliminated by clever tricks, as you might guess), it's not too high a price to pay for this incredibly valuable level of indirection.

This indirection allows the garbage collector, for example, to mark, sweep, move, or examine one object at a time. Each object can be independently moved out from under a running Java program by changing only the object table entries. This not only allows the step-back phase to happen in the tiniest steps, but it makes a garbage collector that runs literally in parallel with your program much easier to write. This is what the Java garbage collector does.

WARNING

> You need to be very careful about garbage collection when you're doing critical, real-time programs (such as those mentioned yesterday that legitimately require native methods)—but how often will your Java code be flying a commercial airliner in real time, anyway?

Java's Parallel Garbage Collector

Java applies almost all these advanced techniques to give you a fast, efficient, parallel garbage collector. Running in a separate thread, it cleans up the Java environment of almost all trash (it is conservative), silently and in the background; is efficient in both space and time; and never steps back for more than a small amount of time. You should never need to know it's there.

21

By the way, if you want to force a full mark-and-sweep garbage collection to happen soon, you can do so simply by calling the `System.gc()` method. You might want to do this if you just freed up a majority of the heap's memory in circular garbage, and want it all taken away quickly. You might also call this whenever you're idle, as a hint to the system about when it would be best to come and collect the garbage.

Ideally, you'll never notice the garbage collector, and all those decades of programmers beating their brains out on your behalf will simply let you sleep better at night—and what's wrong with that?

The Security Story

Speaking of sleeping well at night, if you haven't stepped back yet and said, "My goodness! You mean Java programs will be running rampant on the Internet!?!" you better do so now, for it is a legitimate concern. In fact, it is one of the major technical stumbling blocks (the others being mostly social and economic) to achieving the dream of ubiquity and code sharing for Java mentioned earlier in today's lesson.

Why You Should Worry

Any powerful, flexible technology can be abused. As the Net becomes mainstream and widespread, it, too, will be abused. Already, there have been many blips on the security radar screens of those of us who worry about such things, warning that (at least until today) not enough attention has been paid by the computer industry (or the media) to solving some of the problems that this new world brings with it. One of the benefits of constructively solving security once and for all will be a flowering unseen before in the virtual communities of the Net; whole new economies based on people's attention and creativity will spring to life, rapidly transforming our world in new and positive ways.

The downside to all this new technology is that we (or someone!) must worry long and hard about how to make the playgrounds of the future safe for our children, and for us. Fortunately, Java is a big part of the answer.

Why You Might Not Have To

What gives me any confidence that the Java language and environment will be *safe*, that it will solve the technically daunting and extremely thorny problems inherent in any good form of security, especially for networks?

One simple reason is the history of the people, and the company, who created Java. Many of them are the very smart programmers referred to throughout the book, who helped pioneer

21

many of the ideas that make Java great and who have worked hard over the decades to make techniques such as garbage collection a mainstream reality. They are technically capable of tackling and solving the hard problems that need to be solved.

Sun Microsystems, the company, has been pushing networks as the central theme of all its software for more than a decade. Sun has the engineers and the commitment needed to solve these hard problems, because these same problems are at the very center of both its future business and its vision of the future, in which networking is the center of everything—and global networks are nearly useless without good security. Just this year, Sun has advanced the state of the art in easy-to-use Internet security with its new SunScreen products, and it has assigned Whitfield Diffie to oversee them, who is the man who discovered the underlying ideas on which essentially *all* interesting forms of modern encryption are based.

Enough on deep background. What does the Java environment provide *right now* that helps me feel secure?

Java's Applet Security Model

Java protects you against potential "nasty" Java code via a series of interlocking defenses that, together, form an imposing barrier to any and all such attacks.

WARNING

Of course, no one can protect you from your own ignorance or carelessness. If you're the kind of person who blindly downloads binary executables from your Internet browser and runs them, you need read no farther! You are already in more danger than Java will ever pose.

As a user of this powerful new medium, the Internet, you should educate yourself to the possible threats this new and exciting world entails. In particular, downloading "auto running macros" or reading e-mail with "executable attachments" is just as much a threat as downloading binaries from the Net and running them.

Java does not introduce any new dangers here, but by being the first mainstream use of executable and mobile code on the Net, it is responsible for making people suddenly aware of the dangers that have always been there. Java is already, as you will soon see, much less dangerous than any of these common activities on the Net, and can be made safer still over time. Most of these other (dangerous) activities can never be made safe. So please, do not do them!

A good rule of thumb on the Net is: Don't download anything that you plan to execute (or that will be automatically executed for you) except from someone (or some company) you know well and with

> whom you've had positive, personal experience. If you don't care about losing all the data on your hard drive, or about your privacy, you can do anything you like, but for most of us, this rule should be law.
>
> Fortunately, Java allows you to relax that law. You can run Java applets from anyone, anywhere, in relative safety.

Java's powerful security mechanisms act at four different levels of the system architecture. First, the Java language itself was designed to be safe, and the Java compiler ensures that source code doesn't violate these safety rules. Second, all bytecodes executed by the runtime are screened to be sure that they also obey these rules. (This layer guards against having an altered compiler produce code that violates the safety rules.) Third, the class loader ensures that classes don't violate namespace or access restrictions when they are loaded into the system. Finally, API-specific security prevents applets from doing destructive things. This final layer depends on the security and integrity guarantees from the other three layers.

Let's now examine each of these layers in turn.

The Language and the Compiler

The Java language and its compiler are the first line of defense. Java was designed to be a safe language.

Most other C-like languages have facilities to control access to object-like structures, but also have ways to gain unorthodox access to objects (or to parts of objects), usually by (mis-)using pointers. This introduces two fatal security flaws to any system built on these languages. One is that no object can protect itself from outside modification, duplication, or *spoofing* (other objects pretending to be that object). Another is that a language with powerful pointers is more likely to have serious bugs that compromise security. These pointer bugs, where a pointer starts modifying some other object's memory, were responsible for most of the public (and not-so-public) security problems on the Internet this past decade.

Java eliminates these threats in one stroke by eliminating pointers from the language altogether. There are still pointers of a kind—object references—but these are carefully controlled to be safe: they are unforgeable, and all casts are checked for legality before being allowed. In addition, powerful new array facilities in Java not only help to offset the loss of pointers, but add additional safety by strictly enforcing array bounds, catching more bugs for the programmer (bugs that, in other languages, might lead to unexpected and, therefore, bad-guy-exploitable problems).

The language definition, and the compilers that enforce it, create a powerful barrier to any Java programmer with evil intentions.

Because an overwhelming majority of the Net-savvy software on the Internet may soon be Java, its safe language definition and compilers help to guarantee that most of this software has a solid, secure base. With fewer bugs, Net software will be more predictable—a property that thwarts attacks.

Verifying the Bytecodes

What if that programmer with evil intentions gets a little more determined, and rewrites the Java compiler to suit his nefarious purposes? The Java runtime, getting the lion's share of its bytecodes from the Net, can never tell whether those bytecodes were generated by a trustworthy compiler. Therefore, it must *verify* that they meet all the safety requirements.

Before running any bytecodes, the runtime subjects them to a rigorous series of tests that vary in complexity from simple format checks all the way to running a theorem prover to make certain that they are playing by the rules. These tests verify that the bytecodes do not forge pointers, violate access restrictions, access objects as other than what they are (InputStream objects are always used as InputStream objects, and never as anything else), call methods with inappropriate argument values or types, nor overflow the stack.

Consider the following Java code sample:

```
public class VectorTest {
    public int   array[];

    public int   sum() {
        int[]  localArray = array;
        int    sum        = 0;

        for (int  i = localArray.length;  -i >= 0;  )
            sum += localArray[i];
        return sum;
    }
}
```

The bytecodes generated when this code is compiled look something like the following:

```
        aload_0              Load this
        getfield #10         Load this.array
        astore_1             Store in localArray
        iconst_0             Load 0
        istore_2             Store in sum
        aload_1              Load localArray
        arraylength          Gets its length
        istore_3             Store in i
A:      iinc 3 -1            Subtract 1 from i
        iload_3              Load i
        iflt B               Exit loop if  < 0
        iload_2              Load sum
        aload_1              Load localArray
        iload_3              Load i
        iaload               Load localArray[i]
```

```
        iadd               Add sum
        istore_2           Store in sum
        goto A             Do it again
    B:  iload_2            Load sum
        ireturn            Return it
```

NOTE

> The excellent examples and descriptions in this section of the book are paraphrased from the tremendously informative "Low Level Security in Java" paper by Frank Yellin. You can read this document at `http://java.sun.com:80/sfaq/verifier.html`.

Extra Type Information and Requirements

Java bytecodes encode more type information than is strictly necessary for the interpreter. Even though, for example, the `aload` and `iload` opcodes do exactly the same thing, `aload` is always used to load an object reference and `iload` used to load an integer. Some bytecodes (such as `getfield`) include a symbol table reference—and that symbol table has *even more* type information. This extra type information allows the runtime system to guarantee that Java objects and data aren't illegally manipulated.

Conceptually, before and after each bytecode is executed, every slot in the stack and every local variable has some type. This collection of type information—all the slots and local variables—is called the *type state* of the execution environment. An important requirement of the Java type state is that it must be determinable statically by induction—that is, before any program code is executed. As a result, as the runtime system reads bytecodes, each is required to have the following inductive property: given only the type state before the execution of the bytecode, the type state afterward must be fully determined.

Given *straight-line* bytecodes (no branches) and starting with a known stack state, the state of each slot in the stack is therefore always known. For example, starting with an empty stack:

```
iload_1            Load integer variable. Stack type state is I.
iconst 5           Load integer constant. Stack type state is II.
iadd               Add two integers, producing an integer.
                   Stack type state is I.
```

NOTE

> Smalltalk and PostScript bytecodes do not have this restriction. Their more dynamic type behavior does create additional flexibility in those systems, but Java needs to provide a secure execution environment. It must therefore know all types *at all times* in order to guarantee a certain level of security.

Another requirement made by the Java runtime is that when a set of bytecodes can take more than one path to arrive at the same point, all such paths must arrive there with exactly the same type state. This is a strict requirement, and implies, for example, that compilers cannot generate bytecodes that load all the elements of an array onto the stack. (Because each time through such a loop the stack's type state changes, the start of the loop—"the same point" in multiple paths—would have more than one type state, which is not allowed.)

The Verifier

Bytecodes are checked for compliance with all these requirements, using the extra type information in the class file, by a part of the runtime called the *verifier*. It examines each bytecode in turn, constructing the full type state as it goes, and verifies that all the types of parameters, arguments, and results are correct. Thus, the verifier acts as a gatekeeper to your runtime environment, letting in only those bytecodes that pass muster.

WARNING

The verifier is *the crucial piece* of Java's security, and it depends on your having a correctly implemented (no bugs, intentional or otherwise) runtime system. As of this writing, only Sun is producing Java runtimes (and licensing them to companies such as Netscape and Microsoft for use in their browsers), and they are secure. In the future, however, you should be careful when downloading or buying another company's (or individual's) version of the Java runtime environment. Eventually, Sun will implement validation suites for runtimes, compilers, and so forth to be sure that they are safe and correct. In the meantime, *caveat emptor*! Your runtime is the base on which all the rest of Java's security is built, so make sure it is a good, solid, secure base.

When bytecodes have passed the verifier, they are guaranteed not to do any of the following: cause any operand stack under- or overflows; use parameter, argument, or return types incorrectly; illegally convert data from one type to another (from an integer to a pointer, for example); or access any object's fields illegally (that is, the verifier checks that the rules for `public`, `private`, `package`, and `protected` are obeyed).

As an added bonus, because the interpreter can now count on all these facts being true, it can run much faster than before. All the required checks for safety have been done up front, so it can run at full throttle. In addition, object references can now be treated as capabilities, because they are unforgeable—capabilities allow, for example, advanced security models for file I/O and authentication to be safely built on top of Java.

21

NOTE

Because you can now trust that a `private` variable really is private, and that no bytecode can perform some magic with casts to extract information from it (such as your credit card number), many of the security problems that might arise in other, less safe environments simply vanish! These guarantees also make erecting barriers against destructive applets possible, and easier. Because the Java system doesn't have to worry about dangerous bytecodes, it can get on with creating the other levels of security it wants to provide to you.

The Class Loader

The *class loader* is another kind of gatekeeper, albeit a higher-level one. The verifier is the security of last resort. The class loader is the security of first resort.

When a new class is loaded into the system, it is placed into (lives in) one of several different *realms*. Commonly, there are three possible realms: your local computer, the firewall-guarded local network on which your computer is located, and the Internet (the global Net). Each of these realms is treated differently by the class loader.

NOTE

Actually, there can be as many realms as your desired level of security (or paranoia) requires. This is because the class loader is under your control. As a programmer, you can make your own class loader that implements your own peculiar brand of security. (This is a radical step; you may have to give the users of your program a whole bunch of classes—and they give you a whole lot of trust—to accomplish this.)

In particular, the class loader never allows a class from a less protected realm to replace a class from a more protected realm. The file system's I/O primitives, about which you should be *very* worried (and rightly so), are all defined in a local Java class, which means that they all live in the local-computer realm. Thus, no class from outside your computer (from either the supposedly trustworthy local network or from the Internet) can take the place of these classes and spoof Java code into using nasty versions of these primitives. In addition, classes in one realm cannot call upon the methods of classes in other realms, unless those classes have explicitly declared those methods `public`. This implies that classes from other than your local computer cannot even *see* the file system I/O methods, much less call them, unless you or the system wants them to.

In addition, every new applet loaded from the network is placed into a separate package-like namespace. This means that applets are protected even from each other! No applet can access another's methods (or variables) without its cooperation. Applets from inside the firewall can even be treated differently from those outside the firewall, if you like.

NOTE

> Actually, it's all a little more complex than this. In the current release, an applet is in a package namespace along with any other applets from that *source*. This source, or origin, is most often a host (domain name) on the Internet. This special "subrealm" is used extensively in the next section. Depending on where the source is located, outside the firewall or inside, further restrictions may apply (or be removed entirely). This model is likely to be extended in future releases of Java, providing an even finer degree of control over which classes get to do what.

The class loader essentially partitions the world of Java classes into small, protected little groups, about which you can safely make assumptions that will *always* be true. This type of predictability is the key to well-behaved and secure programs.

You've now seen the full lifetime of a method. It starts as source code on some computer, is compiled into bytecodes on some (possibly different) computer, and can then travel (as a .class file) into any file system or network anywhere in the world. When you run an applet in a Java-enabled browser (or download a class and run it by hand using java), the method's bytecodes are extracted from its .class file and carefully looked over by the verifier. After they are declared safe, the interpreter can execute them for you (or a code generator can generate native binary code for them using either the just-in-time compiler or java2c, and then run that native code directly).

At each stage, more and more security is added. The final level of that security is the Java class library itself, which has several carefully designed classes and APIs that add the final touches to the security of the system.

The Security Manager

SecurityManager is an abstract class that collects, in one place, all the security policy decisions that the system has to make as bytecodes run. You learned before that you can create your own class loader. In fact, you may not have to, because you can subclass SecurityManager to perform most of the same customizations.

An instance of some subclass of SecurityManager is always installed as the current security manager. It has complete control over which of a well-defined set of potentially dangerous

21

methods are allowed to be called by any given class. It takes the realms from the last section into account, the source (origin) of the class, and the type of the class (standalone or loaded by an applet). Each of these can be separately configured to have the effect you (the programmer) like on your Java system. Note that environments such as Web browsers typically already have a security manager in place to handle basic applet security (all the restrictions you've learned about so far in this book), and that security manager cannot be replaced or changed.

What is this "well-defined set" of methods that are protected?

File I/O is a part of the set, for obvious reasons. Applets, by default, can open, read, or write files on the local system.

Also in this protected set are the methods that create and use network connections, both incoming and outgoing.

The final members of the set are those methods that allow one thread to access, control, and manipulate other threads. (Of course, additional methods can be protected as well, by creating a new subclass of SecurityManager that handles them.)

Signed Applets

There is a middle ground between the "sandbox" restrictions that applets always have and an application that can freely run amok on your system. This middle ground involves establishing where an applet comes from, so different applet sources can be allowed different kinds of access.

For example, you might specify different groups of trusted domains (companies), each of which is allowed added privileges when applets from that group are loaded. Applets from systems on an internal network, for example, are more trustworthy than applets from the Internet at large. Some groups can be more trusted than others, and you might even allow groups to grow automatically by allowing existing members to recommend new members for admission. (The Java seal of approval?)

In any case, the possibilities are endless, as long as there is a secure way of recognizing the original creator of an applet.

You might think this problem has already been solved, because classes are tagged with their origin. In fact, the Java runtime goes far out of its way to be sure that that origin information is never lost—any executing method can be dynamically restricted by this information anywhere in the call chain. So why *isn't* this enough?

21

Because what you'd really like to be able to do is permanently "tag" an applet with its original creator (its true origin), and no matter where it has traveled, a browser could verify the integrity and authenticate the creator of that applet.

If somehow those applets were irrevocably tagged with a digital signature by their creator, and that signature could also guarantee that the applet had not been tampered with, you'd be golden.

Luckily, Sun is planning to do exactly that for Java, to have a mechanism for using public key cryptography to "sign" a fragment of code (an applet, an application, a single class) so that you can reliably and securely tell who created or verified that the piece of Java code was trustworthy. With the signature in place, that code could then break out of the sandbox and use the local system more freely. Expect this capability to become more popular and available in the future.

Coming Up in Java 1.1

Promised in Java 1.1 is a set of extension APIs for managing security and encryption in Java. These new classes include support for the digital signature capabilities mentioned in the previous section, as well as general-purpose low-level and high-level cryptography, key management, access control lists, message digest hashes (MD5), and other tools and utilities. On Day 27, "The Standard Extension APIs," you'll learn more about the new security classes in Java.

Summary

Today you have learned about the grand vision that some of us have for Java, and about the exciting future it promises.

Under the hood, the inner workings of the virtual machine, the bytecode interpreter (and all its bytecodes), the garbage collector, the class loader, the verifier, the security manager, and the powerful security features of Java were all revealed.

You now know *almost* enough to write a Java runtime environment of your own—but luckily, you don't have to. You can simply download the latest release of Java—or use a Java-enabled browser to enjoy most of the benefits of Java right away.

21

Q&A

Q I'm still a little unclear about why the Java language and compiler make the Net safer. Can't they just be "side-stepped" by nasty bytecodes?

A Yes, they can—but don't forget that the whole point of using a safe language and compiler was to make the Net *as a whole* safer as more Java code is written. An overwhelming majority of this Java code will be written by honest Java programmers, who will produce safe bytecodes. This makes the Net more predictable over time, and thus more secure.

Q I know you said that garbage collection is something I don't have to worry about, but what if I want (or need) to?

A So, you *are* planning to fly a plane with Java. Cool! For just such cases, there is a way to ask the Java runtime, during startup (`java -noasyncgc`), *not* to run garbage collection unless forced to, either by an explicit call (`System.gc()`) or by running out of memory. (This can be quite useful if you have multiple threads that are messing each other up and want to stop the gc thread from getting in the way while testing them.) Don't forget that turning garbage collection off means that any object you create will live a *long, long time*. If you're real-time, you never want to step back for a full gc—so be sure to reuse objects often, and don't create too many of them!

Q Is there anything else I can do to the garbage collector?

A You can also force the `finalize()` methods of any recently freed objects to be called immediately via `System.runFinalization()`. You might want to do this if you're about to ask for some resources that you suspect might still be tied up by objects that are gone but not forgotten (waiting for `finalize()`). This is even rarer than starting a gc by hand, but it's mentioned here for completeness.

Q I've heard of a tool called `java2c`, which would convert Java code to C code. Does this exist? Where can I get it?

A An experimental `java2c` translator was rumored to exist inside Sun, but was never released. It may be released at a later date.

Q What's the last word on Java?

A Java adds much more than it can ever take away. It has always done so for me, and now, I hope it will for you as well.

The future of the Net is filled with as-yet-undreamt horizons, and the road is long and hard, but Java is a great traveling companion.

BONUS WEEK

At a Glance

- ☐ **Java Programming Tools**

  The runtime interpreter, the compiler, the applet viewer, the debugger, the class file disassembler, the header and stub file generator, and the documentation generator

- ☐ **Working with Data Structures in Java**

  Enumerations, hash tables, and linked lists

- ☐ **Advanced Animation and Media**
- ☐ **Fun with Image Filters**
- ☐ **Client/Server Networking in Java**

☐ **The Standard Extension APIs**

Enterprise, Commerce, Management, Server, Media, Security, Java Beans, and Embedded APIs

☐ **Emerging Technologies**

Java Beans components, JavaOS, Java microprocessors

Day **22**

Java Programming Tools

by Michael Morrison

Trying to perform any craft without the proper tools is a daunting task at best. Java programming is indeed a craft, and like woodworking or engraving, your level of programming success largely depends on your choice of tools as well as your skill in using the tools. You begin this bonus week by looking inside the standard Java programming tools included with the Java Developer's Kit (JDK). Today's lesson isn't just a cursory glance at the Java tools, however. You actually dig into the details of using the tools, including some hidden features and capabilities that seem to have been glossed over in much of the Java documentation. After learning the ins and outs of the standard JDK tools, you'll finish up the lesson by taking a look at some of the more popular Java visual development tools.

Today's lesson covers the following major topics:

☐ The tools included with the JDK and where to get the latest versions

☐ Executing programs with the Java runtime interpreter

☐ Compiling source files with the Java compiler

☐ Debugging programs with the Java debugger

☐ Visual development tools

By the end of today's lesson, you will be well acquainted with the standard JDK tools and how they work. This insight into the standard tools will allow you to use them more effectively in your own projects. Even if you decide to use one of the visual tools highlighted toward the end of the lesson, such as Symantec Café or Visual J++, you may still sometimes find the JDK tools invaluable in certain situations.

Overview of the Standard JDK Tools

The JDK provides a core set of tools necessary for developing programs in Java. Even though the JDK tools aren't particularly fancy in their implementation, they are guaranteed to work with the latest Java release because updated JDK tools are written in Java and are a part of each release. And although third-party add-ons and development environments promise to make Java development smoother and easier, the JDK provides all the essential tools and information necessary to write professional Java applets immediately and at no cost. Because the JDK is Sun's official development kit for Java, you can always count on it to provide the most extensive Java support.

Following is a complete list of the tools that are standard with the JDK:

☐ The runtime interpreter

☐ The compiler

☐ The applet viewer

☐ The debugger

☐ The class file disassembler

☐ The header and stub file generator

☐ The documentation generator

You'll learn about each of these tools in detail in today's lesson. Before you get started, however, it's important to make sure you have the latest version of the JDK. As of this writing, the latest version of the JDK is version 1.02, which is included on the accompanying CD-ROM. This version will probably be around for a while, so you should be okay using it. Just to be sure, you can check Sun's Java Web site at http://www.javasoft.com to see what the latest version is. This Web site provides all the latest news and information

**BD
1**

regarding Java, including the latest release of the JDK. Keep in mind that Java is a new technology that is still in a state of rapid change. Be sure to keep an eye on the Java Web site for the latest information.

The Runtime Interpreter

The Java runtime interpreter is a standalone version of the Java interpreter built into Java-compatible Web browsers, such as Netscape Navigator 3.0 and Microsoft Internet Explorer 3.0. The runtime interpreter provides the support to run Java executable programs in the compiled bytecode class format. Since the interpreter doesn't directly provide any means to view graphical output, you are limited to using it to execute purely textual Java programs and applications that manage their own graphics. If you want to run graphical Java applets, you need to use either the Java applet viewer or a Java-compatible Web browser.

You can think of the runtime interpreter as exposing the bare essentials of the Java runtime system. Even though I use the term *bare essentials*, the interpreter actually lets you do quite a lot. Essentially, you can run any Java programs that don't rely on the `Applet` class. In fact, the statement earlier about not being able to run graphical programs isn't entirely true; you can run graphical Java applications, but you just can't run Java applets. The difference between a Java application and a Java applet is that an application is responsible for creating and maintaining its own window should it require the need for graphical output, whereas an applet relies on a Web browser to provide a window on which to display graphics. So the Java interpreter is capable of executing both textual Java programs and graphical Java applications, but not applets.

Usage

The runtime interpreter is a command-line tool for running Java programs and applications; Java applets require the graphics and display support of a Web browser.

 A *command-line tool* is a tool that is executed at a command prompt, such as a DOS or UNIX shell prompt, with a specified list of arguments.

The syntax for using the Java runtime interpreter follows:

```
java Options Classname Arguments
```

The `Classname` argument specifies the name of the class you want to execute. If the class resides in a package, you must fully qualify the name. For example, if you want to run a class called `SolveIt` that is located in a package called `Equations`, you would execute it in the interpreter like this:

```
java Equations.SolveIt
```

When the Java interpreter executes a class, what it is really doing is executing the main method of the class. The interpreter exits when the main method and any threads created by it are finished executing. The main method accepts a list of arguments that can be used to control the program. Following is the definition of the main method as specified by the Java language:

```
class DoIt {
  public static void main(String argv[]) {
    // do something
  }
}
```

Notice that main has a single parameter, argv, which is an array of String objects. This brings us to the *Arguments* argument for the runtime interpreter, which specifies the arguments passed into the main method. Any arguments passed to the runtime interpreter via *Arguments* are accessible from the argv parameter in main. The following interpreter call passes two numeric arguments to the main method in the DoIt class:

```
java DoIt 8 24
```

TECHNICAL NOTE

> The fact that the Java runtime interpreter actually executes the main method when running a class should give you an idea about one of the reasons why you can't run applets using the runtime interpreter. Give up? The answer is that applets don't even have a main method, so there is no way for the runtime interpreter to know how to begin executing an applet.

The *Options* Argument

The *Options* argument specifies options related to how the runtime interpreter executes the Java program. Following is a list of the most common runtime interpreter options:

```
-debug
-checksource or -cs
-classpath Path
-mx x
-ms x
-noasyncgc
-noverify
-prof
```

22

```
-ss x
-oss x
-t
-verbose or -v
-verbosegc
-verify
-verifyremote
-DPropertyName=NewValue
```

The -debug option starts the interpreter in debugging mode, which allows you to use the Java debugger (jdb) in conjunction with the interpreter. You'll learn more about using the Java debugger a little later in today's lesson.

The -checksource option causes the interpreter to compare the modification dates of the source code files and executable class files. If the source file is more recent, the class is automatically recompiled and the new bytecode executable is loaded.

The Java interpreter uses an environment variable, CLASSPATH, to determine where to look for user-defined classes. The CLASSPATH variable contains a semicolon-delimited list of system paths to user-defined Java classes. Actually, most of the Java tools use the CLASSPATH variable to know where to find user-defined classes. The -classpath option informs the runtime interpreter to override CLASSPATH with the path specified by Path.

The -mx x option allows you to modify the maximum size of the memory allocation pool, or garbage collection heap, used by the interpreter. By default, the pool has a maximum size of 16MB (-mx 16m). x specifies the new maximum size of the pool and is measured in bytes by default. You can also specify x in either kilobytes or megabytes by appending the letter k or m (respectively) onto the value. Also, x must be greater than 1000 bytes, meaning that the pool must have a maximum size of at least 1000 bytes.

The -ms x option is similar to the -mx option, except it allows you to modify the initial size of the memory allocation pool rather than the maximum size. By default, the size of the pool is initially set to 1MB (-ms 1m). x specifies the new initial pool size, and is measured in bytes by default. Similar to the -mx option, you can also specify x in either kilobytes or megabytes by appending the letter k or m (respectively) onto the value. Additionally, x must be greater than 1000 bytes.

The Java runtime system typically performs garbage collection automatically to make sure unneeded memory stays freed up. This takes place in an asynchronous thread that runs alongside other threads in the runtime system. The -noasyncgc option alters this behavior by turning off asynchronous garbage collection. The result is that no garbage collection takes place unless it is explicitly called on or the Java program runs out of memory.

TECHNICAL NOTE

You can force an explicit garbage collection by calling the gc method in the System class.

The -noverify option turns all code verification off, meaning that no bytecodes are processed by the bytecode verifier. Typically, the verifier verifies code loaded into the system using a class loader.

The runtime interpreter includes a built-in profiler, which is invoked using the -prof option. The profiler's job is to report on the amount of time spent in each section of code as a program is executing, which can often be used to find performance bottlenecks in the code. The built-in profiler writes the profile information to a file called java.prof, which is a text file. The profile information consists of how many times each method was called and the relative amount of time spent in the method during each call. The larger the latter number is, the more costly the method in terms of processor overhead. You can easily use this information as a guide to determine the code on which to focus your code optimization efforts.

NOTE

Since the runtime interpreter, and therefore the built-in profiler, can only be used with textual Java programs and standalone applications, you may be wondering how to profile Java applets. Fortunately, you can use the profiler in the runtime interpreter in conjunction with the Java applet viewer. You'll learn how to do this a little later today when you find out about the applet viewer.

Every thread in the Java runtime system is given two stacks: one for Java code and one for C/C++ code. The presence of two stacks reflects the native code support in Java. The -ss x option allows you to alter the maximum stack size used by C code in a thread. The default C stack size is 128KB (-ss 128k). The x parameter specifies the new maximum size in bytes of the C stack, which must be greater than 1000 bytes. You can also specify x in either kilobytes or megabytes by appending the letter k or m (respectively) onto the value. Keep in mind that this option applies to all threads created during program execution.

Similar to the -ss x option, the -oss option allows you to set the maximum stack size that can be used by the Java code in a thread. The default Java code stack size is 400KB (-oss 400k). The x parameter specifies the new maximum size in bytes of the Java stack, which must be greater than 1000 bytes.

22

The -t option prints a trace of the bytecode instructions executed. This option only works with the non-optimized version of the Java interpreter, java_g. (You'll learn about the non-optimized interpreter in a moment.) The -t option generates a great deal of information that can give you a lot of insight into what is happening within a program, provided you are good at following raw bytecodes!

The -verbose option causes the interpreter to print a message to standard output each time a Java class is loaded. Similarly, the -verbosegc option causes the interpreter to print a message each time a garbage collection is performed. A garbage collection is performed by the runtime system to clean up unneeded objects and to free memory.

The opposite of the -noverify option, the -verify option causes the interpreter to run the bytecode verifier on all code loaded into the runtime environment. The default function of the verifier is to only verify code loaded into the system using a class loader. This default behavior can also be explicitly specified using the -verifyremote option.

The -D option allows you to redefine system property values. *PropertyName* specifies the name of the system property you want to change, and *NewValue* specifies the new value you want to assign to it.

 System properties are global system variables that reflect the state of the Java runtime system. For example, the version of the Java runtime system is stored in the java.version system property.

The Non-Optimized Interpreter

Some distributions of the Java Developer's Kit include an alternate Java interpreter called java_g. This is a non-optimized version of the Java interpreter that executes Java bytecodes in a manner more suitable for debugging. If this interpreter is in your JDK distribution, be sure to use it when you are executing code within the Java debugger.

The Compiler

The Java compiler (javac) is used to compile Java source code files into executable Java bytecode classes. In Java, source code files have the extension .java. As you've seen throughout this book, Java source code files are standard ASCII text files, much like the source code files for other popular programming languages like C++. It is the job of the Java compiler to process Java source code files and create executable Java bytecode classes from them. Executable bytecode class files have the extension .class and represent a Java class in its usable form.

Java class files are generated on a one-to-one basis with the classes defined in the source code. In other words, the Java compiler generates exactly one `.class` file for each class you create. Since it is technically possible to define more than one class in a single source file, it is therefore possible for the compiler to generate multiple class files from a single source file. When this happens, it means that the source file contains multiple class definitions.

You may have heard something about just-in-time compilers in relationship to Java. It's important not to get these compilers confused with the Java compiler and the role it plays. The Java compiler is responsible for turning Java source code into Java bytecodes that can be executed within the Java runtime system. The Java virtual machine, which is a component of the runtime system, is responsible for interpreting the bytecodes and making the appropriate system level calls to the native platform. It is at this point where platform independence is achieved by Java; the bytecodes are in a generic form that is only converted to a native form when processed by the virtual machine.

Just-in-time compilers remove the role of the runtime interpreter by converting Java bytecodes to native code on-the-fly before executing a Java program. In this way, just-in-time Java compilers work more like the back end of traditional language compilers in that they generate code for a native platform. Similarly, the Java compiler works more like the front end of a traditional compiler in that it parses Java source code and generates internally useful bytecode classes.

NOTE

> Both Netscape Navigator 3.0 and Microsoft Internet Explorer 3.0 include just-in-time Java compilers.

Keep in mind that Java executables are still centered around the bytecode class format. Even with just-in-time compilers in the picture, all you must be concerned with as a developer is generating the appropriate bytecode classes using the Java compiler. If no just-in-time compiler is present on a user's system, the bytecode classes will be processed and executed by the runtime interpreter. On the other hand, if a just-in-time compiler happens to exist on the system, the bytecode classes will be converted to native code and then executed. Either way, the key to executing Java programs is the bytecode classes, which are created by the Java compiler.

Usage

The Java compiler is a command-line tool whose syntax follows:

```
javac Options Filename
```

The *Filename* argument specifies the name of the source code file you want to compile. The compiler will generate bytecode classes for all classes defined in this file. Likewise, the compiler will also generate bytecode classes for any dependent classes that haven't been compiled yet. In other words, if you are compiling class A, which is derived from class B, and class B has not yet been compiled, the compiler will notice the dependency and go ahead and compile both classes.

The *Options* Argument

The *Options* compiler argument specifies options related to how the compiler creates the executable Java classes. Following is a list of the compiler options:

```
-classpath Path
-d Dir
-g
-nowarn
-O
-verbose
```

The -classpath option tells the compiler to override the CLASSPATH environment variable with the path specified by *Path*. This causes the compiler to look for user-defined classes in the path specified by *Path*. *Path* is a colon-delimited list of directory paths taking the following form:

```
.;YourPath
```

An example of a specific usage of -classpath follows:

```
javac -classpath .;\dev\animate\classes;\dev\render\classes A.java
```

In this case, the compiler is using a user-defined class path to access any classes it needs while compiling the source code file A.java. The -classpath option is sometimes useful when you want to try compiling something without taking the trouble to modify the CLASSPATH environment variable.

The -d option determines the root directory where compiled classes are stored. This is important because many times classes are organized in a hierarchical directory structure. With the -d option, the directory structure will be created beneath the directory specified by *Dir*.

The -g compiler option causes the compiler to generate debugging tables for the Java classes. Debugging tables are used by the Java debugger and contain information such as local variables and line numbers. The default action of the compiler is to only generate line numbers.

A *debugging table* is a collection of information about a program that is used internally by a debugger. Debugging tables are built directly into executable classes during compilation.

Warning

> If you are going to be using the Java debugger to debug the classes generated by the compiler, you must use the -g option. Additionally, for debugging make sure you don't use the -0 option, which optimizes the code.

The -nowarn option turns off compiler warnings. Warnings are printed to standard output during compilation to inform you of potential problems with the source code. It is generally a good idea to keep warnings enabled because they often signal problem areas in your code. However, you may run into a situation where warnings are getting in the way, in which case the -nowarn option might be useful.

The -0 option causes the compiler to optimize the compiled code. In this case, optimization simply means that static, final, and private methods are compiled inline. When a method is compiled inline, it means that the entire body of the method is included in place of each call to the method. This speeds up execution because it eliminates the method call overhead. Optimized classes are usually larger in size to accommodate the duplicate code. The -0 optimization option also suppresses the default creation of line numbers by the compiler. Keep in mind that the -0 option should not be used when you plan on debugging the compiled code using the Java debugger.

 Method inlining is the process of replacing each call to a method with the actual method code. Inlining often increases the size of the resulting class file, but it can help improve performance.

The -verbose option has somewhat of an opposite effect as the -nowarn option—it prints out extra information about the compilation process. You can use -verbose to see exactly what source files are being compiled and what class files are being loaded.

The Non-Optimizing Compiler

Some distributions of the Java Developer's Kit include an alternate Java compiler called javac_g. This version of the Java compiler generates code without some of the internal optimizations performed by the standard javac compiler. If this compiler is in your JDK distribution, be sure to use it when you are compiling code for debugging. Otherwise, stick with the javac compiler for all release code.

The Applet Viewer

The typical method of executing a Java applet is from within a Web browser that has a Web page loaded containing the applet. This is the typical scenario in which most Web users come into contact with Java applets. As a Java developer, you have another option for running Java applets that doesn't involve the use of a Web browser. This option is the Java applet viewer, which serves as a minimal test bed for Java applets. At times you may not want to hassle with using a full-blown Web browser to test an applet, in which case the applet viewer is an ideal alternative.

Even though the applet viewer logically takes the place of a Web browser, it functions very differently from a Web browser. The applet viewer operates on HTML documents, but it only looks for embedded applet tags; it ignores any other HTML code in the document. Each time the applet viewer encounters an applet tag in an HTML document, it launches a separate applet viewer window containing the respective applet.

The only drawback to using the applet viewer is that it doesn't show you how an applet will run within the confines of a real Web setting. Since the applet viewer ignores all HTML codes except applet tags, it doesn't even attempt to display any other information contained in the HTML document. So once you've tested your applet using the applet viewer, be sure to also test it using a Web browser just to make sure it works in the context of a real Web page.

Usage

The Java applet viewer is a command-line tool, meaning that it is invoked from a command prompt. The syntax for the applet viewer follows:

```
appletviewer Options URL
```

The URL argument specifies a document URL containing an HTML page with an embedded Java applet. The applet viewer launches a separate window for each applet embedded in the HTML document. If the document doesn't contain any embedded applets, the applet viewer will simply exit. Figure 22.1 shows the applet viewer in action.

Figure 22.1 shows the Animator demo applet, which comes with the Java Developer's Kit, running in the applet viewer. You run the applet by changing to the directory containing the Animator bytecode class and embedded HTML file and then executing the following statement at the command prompt:

```
appletviewer example1.html
```

example1.html is the HTML file containing the embedded Java applet. As you can see, there's nothing complicated about running Java applets using the applet viewer. The applet viewer is a useful and easy-to-use tool for testing Java applets in a simple environment.

Figure 22.1.

The Animator applet
running in the Java
applet viewer.

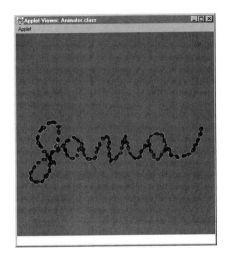

The `Options` **Argument**

The `Options` argument to the applet viewer specifies how to run the Java applet. There is currently only one option supported by the applet viewer, `-debug`. The `-debug` option starts the applet viewer in the Java debugger, which allows you to debug applets. You'll learn more about using the Java debugger a little later in today's lesson.

Commands

The applet viewer has a drop-down menu called Applet containing a group of commands, as shown in Figure 22.2.

Figure 22.2.

The Java applet viewer
with commands available
in the drop-down menu.

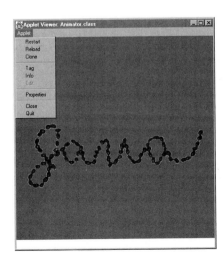

22

The Restart command restarts the currently loaded applet, resulting in a call to the start method for the applet. The Restart command does not reload the applet, however. Similar to Restart, the Reload command reloads the applet and then starts it. Reload is often a better command to use to restart applets as it ensures that an applet is completely reinitialized.

The Clone command launches another instance of the applet viewer executing the same applet. This command is useful when you want to run multiple copies of an applet. For example, a multiuser network applet might support multiple instances that can communicate with each other. You could load one instance of the applet and then use the Clone command to start other instances.

The Tag command displays a window showing the HTML applet tag for the executing applet. The Applet HTML Tag window is shown in Figure 22.3.

Figure 22.3.

The Applet HTML Tag window displayed by the Tag *command.*

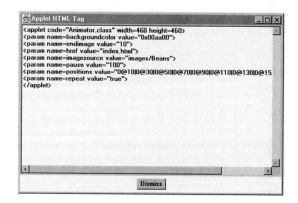

The Info command displays a window showing information about the executing applet, including general applet information and information relating to the parameters used by the applet. This information is returned by the getAppletInfo and getParameterInfo methods of the Applet class. The Applet Info window is shown in Figure 22.4.

Figure 22.4.

The Applet Info window displayed by the Info *command.*

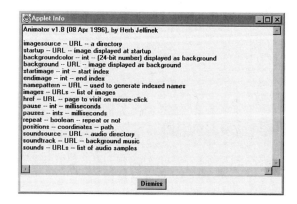

The Edit command is disabled in the current release of the applet viewer. It will presumably be activated in a future release of the applet viewer, in which case it will probably provide a way to alter the applet parameters in the HTML document containing the applet tag.

The Properties command displays a window with access options relating to HTTP and firewall proxies and servers, along with network and class access options. The AppletViewer Properties window is shown in Figure 22.5.

Figure 22.5.

The AppletViewer Properties window displayed by the Properties *command.*

AppletViewer Properties	
Http proxy server:	
Http proxy port:	
Firewall proxy server:	sunweb.ebay
Firewall proxy port:	80
Network access:	Applet Host
Class access:	Restricted
	Apply Reset Cancel

Finally, the Close and Quit commands perform the same function, which is shutting down the applet viewer. It's not clear why there are two different commands for closing the applet viewer—it's presumably an oversight.

Profiling Java Applets

You learned a little earlier today about the profiler built into the Java runtime interpreter. You learned that you can't profile applets using the runtime interpreter alone because you can't even run applets using the interpreter. However, you can profile applets by running the interpreter's profiler in conjunction with the applet viewer. In this case, the applet viewer is launched from within the runtime interpreter, like this:

```
java -prof sun.applet.AppletViewer URL
```

URL specifies the name of the HTML file containing an applet tag (or tags). Notice that the applet viewer is referenced using its fully qualified class name, AppletViewer. When you finish running the applet, the interpreter writes a text file named java.prof to the current directory. This file contains profile information for the applet you just ran. Refer to the earlier discussion of the profiler in the section "The Runtime Interpreter" for information regarding the meaning of the contents of this file.

The Debugger

The Java debugger (jdb) is a command-line utility that enables you to debug Java programs. The Java debugger uses the Java Debugger API to provide debugging support within the Java runtime interpreter. Although the debugger is a command-line tool, it still provides a wide range of standard debugging features such as setting breakpoints and single-stepping through code.

 A *breakpoint* is a line of code you specify that halts the execution of a program.

 Single-stepping is the process of executing your code one line at a time (in single steps).

Before you can use jdb, you must compile your code so that it includes debugging information. The Java compiler switch for doing this is -g, which causes the compiler to generate debugging tables containing information about line numbers and variables.

NOTE

Some distributions of the JDK also include an alternative Java compiler called javac_g. If you have this compiler in your distribution (look in the java/bin directory), use it, because it compiles code without using some of the internal optimizations performed by the javac compiler.

Because debugging is a very broad subject, I've tried to keep this discussion focused on the Java debugger and the basics of how it is used. For a more hands-on look at Java debugging, you may want to check out Sun's online Java debugger tutorials, which are located on Sun's Java Web site at http://www.javasoft.com/products/JDK/debugging/.

Usage

The syntax for using the Java debugger follows:

```
jdb Options <Classname>
```

The Classname argument is optional and specifies the name of the class you want to execute. The fact that Classname is optional brings up an interesting point regarding the usage of the debugger: There are two different ways to go about using the debugger, depending on whether you are debugging an application or an applet. For applications, you simply execute jdb directly and provide the name of the main class in the Classname argument, as the previous syntax shows. If you are debugging an applet, however, you must execute the debugger within the applet viewer, like this:

```
appletviewer -debug URL
```

In this case, *URL* refers to a document URL containing an HTML page with the applet to be debugged. Instead of directly executing the class, the applet viewer launches the debugger and allows you to debug the applet. Technically, there are three ways to use the Java debugger. The third technique involves attaching the debugger to an application that is already running in the interpreter. You'll learn a little more about this debugging approach in the next section.

The *Options* Argument

The *Options* argument is used to specify different settings regarding how a debugging session is started. Following is a list of the debugging options:

```
-host Hostname
-password Password
```

The `-host` option is used to specify the name of the host machine where an existing Java interpreter is running. In this case, the debugger attaches itself to the interpreter so the currently executing application can be debugged. You specify the name of the host machine in the *Hostname* argument.

The `-password` option is also used when attaching the debugger to an existing interpreter session. When the interpreter is started with the `-debug` option, a password is displayed that must be used when initiating the debugging session. You specify this password to the debugger via the `-password` option and the *Password* argument.

Commands

When the debugger is up and running, you control it through commands that are entered at a command-line prompt. The debugger command-line prompt is a > prompt by default, similar to DOS or UNIX shell prompts. This prompt specifies that there is no default thread running. The thread that is currently executing in the debugger is displayed in the command prompt itself, so the > prompt signifies that no thread is currently being debugged. When you are debugging a thread, the command prompt changes to a thread name followed by the current position of the stack frame, which is enclosed in square brackets. An example of a thread prompt is main[1], which signifies that the main thread is running and you are at the topmost position (1) in the stack frame.

Following is a list of some of the most useful debugging commands:

```
help
locals
print Object
dump Object
```

```
methods Class
classes
stop in Classname.Methodname
stop at Classname.LineNumber
step
cont
clear <Classname.LineNumber>
```

Possibly the most important command in jdb is the help command, which prints out a listing of all the available commands and what they do. The next three commands are all related to printing information about objects. The locals command displays the current value of all the objects in the current scope (stack frame). The print and dump commands are both used on objects independent of the current scope. The print command is used to print both entire objects and individual member variables; you simply specify the name of the object or member variable in the *Object* argument. Similar to print, the dump command also prints objects or member variables, but it prints more detailed information such as an object's inheritance.

The methods command is used to list all the methods defined in the class specified by *Class*. The classes command lists all the classes that are currently loaded into memory. The list generated by the classes command is often pretty large since many different classes end up being loaded behind the scenes even in simple Java programs.

Now that you have an idea how to look at the values of different things in the debugger, let's move on to some commands that are a little more exciting. The stop in and stop at commands are used to set breakpoints in methods and at specific lines of source code, respectively. For example, to set a breakpoint in the mouseDown method of an applet called Groovy, you would type the following command at the debugger command line:

```
stop in Groovy.mouseDown
```

When you click the mouse button in the applet window, the debugger will halt the applet at the beginning of the mouseDown method. To begin single-stepping through the method, you use the step command. The debugger executes one line of code for each step command issued. When you find out the information you need and are ready to get things running at full speed again, you use the cont command, which continues the normal execution of the program. Likewise, you can clear any breakpoints you set with the clear command.

That sums up the basics of using the Java debugger. Like any powerful tool, you'll gain confidence with the debugger by simply tinkering with it. I suggest running the debugger on a simple program and getting acquainted with some of the commands before trying to take on a serious debugging project.

The Class File Disassembler

The Java class file disassembler (javap) is used to disassemble a class file, which means the executable class file is resolved into a list of public data, methods, or raw bytecode instructions. The disassembler's default output consists of the public data and methods for a class. The class file disassembler is useful in cases where you don't have the source code for a class but you'd like to know something about how it is implemented.

Usage

The syntax for the disassembler follows:

```
javap Options ClassNames
```

The *ClassNames* argument specifies the names of one or more classes to be disassembled.

The *Options* Argument

The *Options* argument specifies how the classes are to be disassembled. The disassembler supports the following options:

```
-c
-p
-h
-classpath Path
-verify
-version
```

The -c option tells the disassembler to output the actual bytecodes for each method. The -p option tells the disassembler to also include private variables and methods in its output. Without this option, the disassembler only outputs the public member variables and methods. The -h option specifies that information be created that can be used in C header files. This is useful when you are attempting to interface C code to a Java class for which you don't have the source code.

The -classpath option informs the disassembler to override CLASSPATH with the path specified by *Path* when looking for the input class or classes. The -verify option tells the disassembler to run the verifier on the class and output debugging information. Finally, the -version option causes the disassembler to print its version number.

22

The Header and Stub File Generator

The Java header and stub file generator (javah) is used to generate C header and source files for implementing Java methods in C. The files generated can be used to access member variables of an object from C code. The header and stub file generator accomplishes this by generating a C structure whose layout matches that of the corresponding Java class.

NOTE

You learned how to use the javah header and stub file generator on Day 20, "Using Native Methods and Libraries." You can think of today's coverage as more of a reference for the javah tool itself since you learn about all the options supported by javah.

Usage

The syntax for using the header and stub file generator follows:

```
javah Options ClassName
```

The *ClassName* argument is the name of the class to generate C source files from.

The *Options* Argument

The *Options* argument specifies how the source files are to be generated. Following are the options supported by the stub file generator:

```
-o OutputFile
-d Dir
-td Dir
-stubs
-verbose
-classpath Path
```

The -o option is used to concatenate the resulting header and source files when multiple classes are being operated on. When used, the -o option results in the concatenated information being stored in the file specified by *OutputFile*.

The -d option determines the root directory where the generated header and source files are stored. Along with writing the header and source files, the header and stub file generator also writes its own temporary files. The -td option specifies the directory where these temporary files are stored. By default, temporary files are stored in the directory specified by the %TEMP% environment variable; the -td option overrides this directory with *Dir*.

The -stubs option is probably the most important option supported by the header and stub file generator. The -stubs option causes C declarations to be generated from the specified Java class or classes. Without the -stubs option, only header files are generated. When you use the -stubs option, the header and stub file generator creates both header and stub files, which are both typically required to incorporate native C code with Java.

The -verbose option causes the header and stub file generator to print a message to standard output regarding the status of files as they are being generated. Finally, the -classpath option informs the header and stub file generator to override CLASSPATH with the path specified by *Path* when looking for the input class.

The Documentation Generator

The Java documentation generator (javadoc) is a useful tool for generating programming documentation directly from Java source code. The documentation generator parses through Java source files and generates HTML pages based on the declarations and comments. Sun's online Java API documentation was created using the documentation generator, which attests to the practicality of this tool.

Usage

The syntax for using the documentation generator follows:

```
javadoc Options FileName
```

The *FileName* argument specifies either a package or a Java source code file. For source code files, the documentation generator creates HTML pages based on the special documentation comments (/** and */) used throughout the code. The documentation generator reformats and includes all public and protected declarations for classes, interfaces, methods, and variables. You can include special documentation tags within the documentation comments that allow you a little more power and flexibility over the resulting documentation. You'll learn about these tags in a moment.

The *FileName* parameter to the documentation generator can also refer to a package name, in which case documentation is created for all the classes contained in the package. This is an easy way to crank out documentation for a large set of classes with one easy command.

BD 1

The *Options* **Argument**

The *Options* argument enables you to change the default behavior of javadoc. Following are the options supported by the documentation generator:

```
-d Dir
-classpath Path
```

The -d option specifies where the generated HTML documents are stored. The -classpath option informs the documentation generator to override CLASSPATH with the path specified by *Path* when looking for the Java source files.

Documentation Tags

The documentation generator supports special tags for adding extra information to the generated HTML documents. All the tags begin with an @ symbol and must appear at the beginning of a line. Following are the tags related to the generation of class documentation:

```
@see Classname
@see FullyQualifiedClassname
@see Classname.Methodname
@version Version
@author AuthorName
```

The @see tags all add a "see also" hyperlink to the HTML document that refers to a class or method within a class. This is an easy way to provide associations between classes in the documentation. Sun's Java API makes great use of the @see tag to provide cross-references between classes.

The @version tag allows you to include version information with the class, as specified by *Version*. *Version* can contain any text you choose relating to the version of the code. The @author tag lets you provide the name of the author or authors of the source code, as specified by *AuthorName*.

Following is an example of source code making use of the class documentation tags:

```
/**
 * A class for modeling precious gems.
 *
 * @see     Object
 * @see     gemology.Rock
 * @version 2.0  Dec 5, 1996
 * @author  Brett Weir
 */
class Gem extends Rock {
  // class definition
}
```

Notice that the class documentation comment and tags appear just before the class definition. This is important because the documentation generator associates this comment with the Gem class. You can also associate comments with variables and methods in a similar way. For variables, you are limited to using the @see tag. For methods, however, you can use a few other tags:

```
@param ParamName Description
@return Description
@exception Classname Description
```

The @param tag is used to add the method's parameters to the Parameters section generated in the HTML document. The Parameters section is an HTML section that lists the parameters required of a method. ParamName refers to the name of the parameter as defined by the method, and Description is a text description of the parameter.

The @return tag adds a Returns section to the HTML document that brings attention to the return value of the method. You simply provide a description of the return value in Description.

Finally, the @exception tag adds a Throws section to the HTML document, which lists the exceptions potentially thrown by the method. You specify the exception in Classname along with a description of what circumstances result in the exception being thrown in Description. You can use multiple exception tags. The documentation generator automatically creates a hyperlink to the documentation for the exception class referenced.

Following is an example of source code that uses the method tags:

```
/**
 * Determines an estimate of the gem's value.
 *
 * @param      weight   The weight of the gem in carats.
 * @param      color    The color of the gem (0 -> 1.0).
 * @param      clarity  The clarity of the gem (0 -> 1.0).
 * @return     The estimated value of the gem.
 * @exception  NumberFormatException  When the color or clarity isn't
 *             in the range 0 -> 1.0.
 */
public int estimateValue(float weight, float color, float clarity) {
  // method definition
}
```

Visual Development Tools

Even though the JDK tools are powerful and certainly adequate for serious Java programming, few people will argue the benefits of using visual development tools. Along with providing feature-packed source code editors, most visual tools combine many of the standard Java programming tools within one environment. For example, from one development environment you can typically edit, compile, run, and debug Java programs. This seemingly simple merger of tools can really help save precious development time.

Although providing visual versions of the standard Java command-line tools is a benefit in and of itself, visual development tools rarely stop there. Most visual tools also include sophisticated project-management facilities as well as code-generation tools for creating applet templates with complete source code that performs a certain type of core functionality. Some visual tools even go a step further and eliminate much of the programming. These tools focus on harnessing prebuilt components that allow you to develop Java programs without actually writing Java code. These types of tools are typically a little more limited because of their high-level design, but they can save enormous amounts of time and energy in certain cases.

The rest of today's lesson focuses on some of the more popular Java visual development tools that are currently available. My intention isn't to rate the tools or persuade you to try one over another. My goal is simply to let you know what's out there so you can investigate what type of tool might suit your needs. Many of the tools have evaluation versions that you can download for free from an associated Web site, so you can very easily try them out for yourself and come to your own conclusions. Have fun!

Sun's Java WorkShop

Sun's Java WorkShop is a visual development tool written entirely in Java. This is an interesting tool because its design is very Web-centric, meaning that much of the tool itself is comprised of Java applets embedded in HTML pages. Java WorkShop is currently available for Windows and Solaris systems. You can check it out at `http://www.sun.com/sunsoft/Developer-products/java/`, which is Sun's Java WorkShop Web site (see Figure 22.6).

Symantec Café

Symantec Café is a visual Java development environment based on Symantec's popular C++ development environment. It was one of the first visual Java tools available and currently supports both Windows and Macintosh platforms. You can get the latest information about Café at Symantec's Café Web site (see Figure 22.7), which is located at `http://cafe.symantec.com/`.

Figure 22.6.

Sun's Java WorkShop Web site.

Figure 22.7.

The Symantec Café Web site.

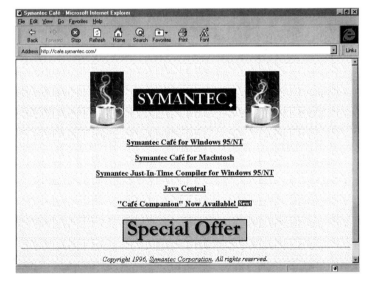

Microsoft Visual J++

Microsoft finally decided to enter the Java development foray in full force with Visual J++, which is a visual Java tool similar to their popular Visual C++ development environment. Visual J++ currently is available only for the Windows platform. You can check out Visual J++ at Microsoft's Visual J++ Web site (see Figure 22.8), which is located at `http://198.105.232.5/visualj/`.

22

Figure 22.8.

The Microsoft Visual J++ Web site.

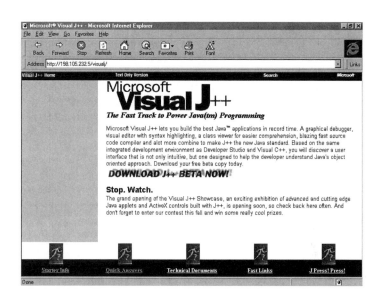

Natural Intelligence's Roaster

Natural Intelligence's Roaster is the first Java development environment targeted specifically for the Macintosh platform. For information about Roaster, check out Natural Intelligence's Roaster Web site (see Figure 22.9) at http://www.natural.com/pages/products/roaster/.

Figure 22.9.

Natural Intelligence's Roaster Web site.

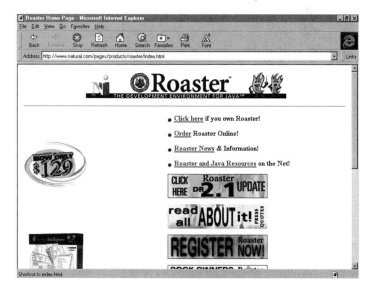

Rogue Wave Software's JFactory

Rogue Wave Software's JFactory Java development tool is aimed more at rapid application development with a minimal amount of programming. This visual application generator is currently available for the Windows platform. You can get more information about JFactory from Rogue Wave Software's JFactory Web site (see Figure 22.10), which is located at `http://www.roguewave.com/products/jfactory/jfactory.html`.

Figure 22.10.

Rogue Wave Software's JFactory Web site.

Penumbra Software's Mojo

Penumbra Software's Mojo development tool offers a programming environment based largely on reusable components. Granted, this is a trend common among many of the visual tools, but Mojo makes a big attempt to minimize custom coding whenever possible. Mojo is currently available for the Windows platform. You can check out Mojo at Penumbra Software's Web site (see Figure 22.11), which is located at `http://www.penumbrasoftware.com/`.

Aimtech's Jamba

Aimtech's Jamba is one of the first offerings in the area of high-level visual Java tools. Jamba is aimed at Internet developers who want to harness the power of Java without any programming or scripting. Jamba is currently available for the Windows platform. You can get the scoop on Jamba by taking a stroll through Aimtech's Jamba Web site (see Figure 22.12), which is located at `http://www.aimtech.com/prodjahome.html`.

Figure 22.11.

Penumbra Software's Mojo Web site.

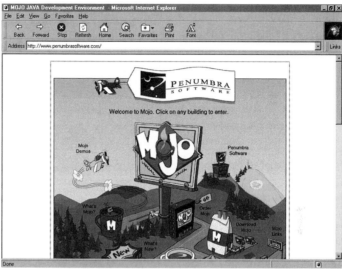

Figure 22.12.

Aimtech's Jamba Web site.

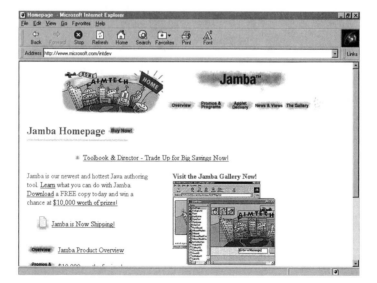

Kinetix's Hyperwire

The last of the visual tools is Kinetix's Hyperwire, which is another high-level tool somewhat similar to Jamba. Unlike Jamba, however, Hyperwire's emphasis is largely placed on creating highly graphical Java applets, including 3D graphics. Hyperwire is currently available for the Windows platform. You can get more information about Hyperwire from Kinetix's

Hyperwire Web site (see Figure 22.13), which is located at http://www.ktx.com/products/hyperwire/.

Figure 22.13.

Kinetix's Hyperwire Web site.

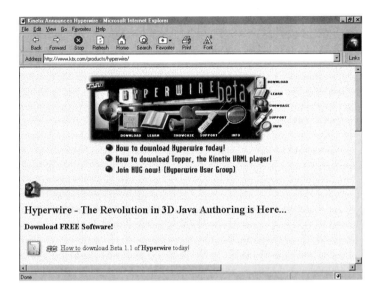

 NOTE

> High-level tools such as Jamba and Hyperwire are sometimes referred to as *authoring tools* because they involve little or no programming.

Summary

Even though Java is easier to use than some other programming languages, becoming a proficient Java programmer still presents a number of hurdles to most of us. One way to lower these hurdles a little is to become well acquainted with the development tools you are using. Possibly even more important is your initial choice of development tools, which can greatly affect your effectiveness as a Java programmer. Today's lesson addresses both of these concerns by presenting you with an in-depth look at the standard JDK tools, along with showing you some other options in the form of visual development tools.

Ultimately, your selection of a development tool or tools will depend on your level of expertise and your development style. Regardless of what type of tool you gravitate toward, be sure to take the time to learn all you can about it. If you are still unsure about what kind of development tool to use, stick with the JDK for a while, since it is guaranteed to meet the basic requirements necessary to build Java programs. Besides, understanding Java programming from the perspective of the standard JDK tools will ultimately give you more insight into the "big picture" of Java development.

You're probably tired of hearing me ramble on about tools by now. That's OK, because tomorrow you shift gears and head straight back into programming by learning about data structures in Java. I'm sure you can't wait!

Q&A

Q What is the significance of the profiler built into the runtime interpreter?

A The profiler is useful in assessing the relative execution times of different parts of a Java program, which is crucial in situations in which you are trying to improve the performance of a Java program. With the information generated by the profiler, you can target specific sections of code to focus optimization efforts.

Q How do I compile multiple classes within a single source code file? I keep getting compiler errors!

A Even though you can compile multiple classes that are defined in one source code file, only one of the classes can be public. Furthermore, the source file must be named after the class that is public. The purpose here is to allow you to include support classes in the same file with public classes. However, you are only allowed one public class per source code file.

Q When do I use the class file disassembler?

A The class file disassembler, although powerful in its own right, isn't necessarily a tool you will find yourself using a lot. Its primary purpose is dissecting Java classes for which you don't have the source code. Using the disassembler, you can look at all the public methods and member variables for a class, which can help a lot when you're trying to figure out how the class works. If you have a knack for details and a lot of Tylenol, you can also use the disassembler to look at the raw bytecodes for classes.

Q I still don't quite understand the distinction between development environments and authoring tools. What's the deal?

A Both of these types of tools qualify as visual tools, but there is a distinct difference between them. Development environments essentially replace the standard command-line JDK tools with integrated visual versions, while sometimes also adding some extra features like project management and simple code generation. Authoring tools, on the other hand, completely move away from the idea of writing source code by providing you with a means to build programs purely by assembling preexisting components. The main difference, then, is that development environments target Java programmers, while authoring tools are readily accessible to nonprogrammers as well.

Day 23

Working with Data Structures in Java

by Michael Morrison

Few programs can be developed without at least some usage of data structures, which are responsible for storing and maintaining information used by a program. Whether you develop your own data structures from scratch or rely on those developed and tested by others, you will undoubtedly need to use data structures at some point in your Java programming endeavors. Today's lesson takes a look at data structures as they relate to Java. It covers the following topics:

☐ Data structure basics

☐ The standard Java data structures

☐ Building your own data structures

By the end of today's lesson, you'll have a good idea of what data structures are readily available in the standard Java packages, along with some data structures you can implement yourself without too much pain. Let's get started!

Data Structure Fundamentals

Like algorithms in general, data structures are one of those general concepts in computer science whose usefulness spreads far and wide. Consequently, a solid understanding of data structures and when to apply certain ones is the trademark of any good programmer. Java programming is no different, and you should take data structures no less seriously in Java than in any other language. Just because many Java programs come in the form of applets, which sound cuter and less auspicious than C or C++ applications, doesn't mean that they don't rely on a solid means of storing and manipulating data.

Almost every Java applet works with information to some extent. Even very simple animation applets that display a series of images must somehow store the images in such a way that the images can be referenced quickly. In this example, a very elementary data structure such as an array might be the best solution, since all that is required of the data structure is the storage of multiple images. Even so, consider the fact that every program has its own set of data requirements that greatly affect the applicability of different data structures. If you don't understand the full range of programming options in terms of data structures, you'll find yourself trying to use an array in every program you write. This tendency to rely on one solution for all your programming problems will end up getting you into trouble. In other words, by understanding how to use a wide variety of data structures, you broaden your perspective on how to solve the inevitable problems arising from new programming challenges.

I mentioned arrays being a very simple data structure. In fact, outside of member variables themselves, arrays are the most simple data structure supported by Java. An array is simply an aggregate series of data elements of the same type. I say that arrays are aggregate because they are treated as a single entity, just like any other member variable. However, they actually contain multiple elements that can be accessed independently. Based on this description, it's logical that arrays are useful any time you need to store and access a group of information that is all of the same type. For example, you could store your picks for a lottery in an array of integers. However, the glaring limitation of arrays is that they can't change in size to accommodate more (or fewer) elements. This means that you can't add new elements to an array that is already full.

It turns out that the data requirements for many practical programs reach far beyond what arrays provide. In other languages, it is often necessary to develop custom data structures

23

whenever the requirements go beyond arrays. However, the Java class library provides a set of data structures in the `java.util` package that give you a lot more flexibility in how to approach organizing and manipulating data. There still may be situations in which these standard data structures don't fit your needs, in which case you'll have to write your own. You'll learn how to implement your own custom data structures later in today's lesson.

TECHNICAL NOTE

Unlike the data structures provided by the `java.util` package, arrays are considered such a core component of the Java language that they are implemented in the language itself. Therefore, you can use arrays in Java without importing any packages.

BD 2

The Standard Java Data Structures

The data structures provided by the Java utility package are very powerful and perform a wide range of functions. These data structures consist of the following interface and five classes:

- ☐ Enumeration
- ☐ BitSet
- ☐ Vector
- ☐ Stack
- ☐ Dictionary
- ☐ Hashtable

The `Enumeration` interface isn't itself a data structure, but it is very important within the context of other data structures. The `Enumeration` interface defines a means to retrieve successive elements from a data structure. For example, `Enumeration` defines a method called `nextElement` that is used to get the next element in a data structure that contains multiple elements.

The `BitSet` class implements a group of bits, or flags, that can be set and cleared individually. This class is very useful in cases where you need to keep up with a set of boolean values; you just assign a bit to each value and set or clear it as appropriate.

 A *flag* is a boolean value that is used to represent one of a group of on/off type states in a program.

The Vector class is similar to a traditional Java array, except that it can grow as necessary to accommodate new elements. Like an array, elements of a Vector object can be accessed via an index into the vector. The nice thing about using the Vector class is that you don't have to worry about setting it to a specific size upon creation; it shrinks and grows automatically when necessary.

The Stack class implements a last-in-first-out (LIFO) stack of elements. You can think of a stack literally as a vertical stack of objects; when you add a new element, it gets stacked on top of the others. When you pull an element off the stack, it comes off the top. In other words, the last element you added to the stack is the first one to come back off.

The Dictionary class is an abstract class that defines a data structure for mapping keys to values. This is useful in cases where you want to be able to access data via a particular key rather than an integer index. Since the Dictionary class is abstract, it provides only the framework for a key-mapped data structure rather than a specific implementation.

NEW TERM A *key* is a numeric identifier used to reference, or look up, a value in a data structure.

An actual implementation of a key-mapped data structure is provided by the Hashtable class. The Hashtable class provides a means of organizing data based on some user-defined key structure. For example, in an address list hash table you could store and sort data based on a key such as ZIP code rather than on a person's name. The specific meaning of keys in regard to hash tables is totally dependent on the usage of the hash table and the data it contains.

That pretty well sums up the data structures provided by the Java utility package. Now that you have a cursory understanding of them, let's dig into each in a little more detail and see how they work.

Enumerations

The Enumeration interface provides a standard means of iterating through a list of sequentially stored elements, which is a common task of many data structures. Even though you can't use the interface outside the context of a particular data structure, understanding how it works will put you well on your way to understanding other Java data structures. With that in mind, take a look at the only two methods defined by the Enumeration interface:

```
public abstract boolean hasMoreElements();
public abstract Object nextElement();
```

The hasMoreElements method is used to determine if the enumeration contains any more elements. You will typically call this method to see if you can continue iterating through an enumeration. An example of this is calling hasMoreElements in the conditional clause of a while loop that is iterating through an enumeration.

The nextElement method is responsible for actually retrieving the next element in an enumeration. If no more elements are in the enumeration, nextElement will throw a NoSuchElementException exception. Since you want to avoid generating exceptions whenever possible, you should always use hasMoreElements in conjunction with nextElement to make sure there is another element to retrieve. Following is an example of a while loop that uses these two methods to iterate through a data structure object that implements the Enumeration interface:

```
// e is an object that implements the Enumeration interface
while (e.hasMoreElements()) {
  Object o = e.nextElement();
  System.out.println(o);
}
```

This sample code prints out the contents of an enumeration using the hasMoreElements and nextElement methods. Pretty simple!

TECHNICAL NOTE

Since Enumeration is an interface, you'll never actually use it as a data structure directly. Rather, you will use the methods defined by Enumeration within the context of other data structures. The significance of this architecture is that it provides a consistent interface for many of the standard data structures, which makes them easier to learn and use.

Bit Sets

The BitSet class is useful whenever you need to represent a group of boolean flags. The nice thing about the BitSet class is that it allows you to use individual bits to store boolean values without the mess of having to extract bit values using bitwise operations; you simply refer to each bit using an index. Another nice feature about the BitSet class is that it automatically grows to represent the number of bits required by a program. Figure 23.1 shows the logical organization of a bit set data structure.

Figure 23.1.

The logical organization of a bit set data structure.

For example, you can use BitSet as an object that has a number of attributes that can easily be modeled by boolean values. Since the individual bits in a bit set are accessed via an index, you can define each attribute as a constant index value:

```
class someBits {
  public static final int readable = 0;
  public static final int writeable = 1;
  public static final int streamable = 2;
  public static final int flexible = 3;
}
```

Notice that the attributes are assigned increasing values, beginning with 0. You can use these values to get and set the appropriate bits in a bit set. But first, you need to create a BitSet object:

```
BitSet bits = new BitSet();
```

This constructor creates a bit set with no specified size. You can also create a bit set with a specific size:

```
BitSet bits = new BitSet(4);
```

This creates a bit set containing four boolean bit fields. Regardless of the constructor used, all bits in new bit sets are initially set to false. Once you have a bit set created, you can easily set and clear the bits using the set and clear methods along with the bit constants you defined:

```
bits.set(someBits.writeable);
bits.set(someBits.streamable);
bits.set(someBits.flexible);
bits.clear(someBits.writeable);
```

In this code, the writeable, streamable, and flexible attributes are set, and then the writeable bit is cleared. Notice that the fully qualified name is used for each attribute, since the attributes are declared as static in the someBits class.

You can get the value of individual bits in a bit set using the get method:

```
boolean canIWrite = bits.get(someBits.writeable);
```

You can find out how many bits are being represented by a bit set using the size method. An example of this follows:

```
int numBits = bits.size();
```

The BitSet class also provides other methods for performing comparisons and bitwise operations on bit sets such as AND, OR, and XOR. All these methods take a BitSet object as their only parameter.

Vectors

The Vector class implements a growable array of objects. Since the Vector class is responsible for growing itself as necessary to support more elements, it has to decide when and by how much to grow as new elements are added. You can easily control this aspect of vectors upon creation. Before getting into that, however, take a look at how to create a basic vector:

```
Vector v = new Vector();
```

That's about as simple as it gets! This constructor creates a default vector containing no elements. Actually, all vectors are empty upon creation. One of the attributes important to how a vector sizes itself is the initial capacity of a vector, which is how many elements the vector allocates memory for by default.

NEW TERM The *size* of a vector is the number of elements currently stored in the vector.

NEW TERM The *capacity* of a vector is the amount of memory allocated to hold elements, and is always greater than or equal to the size.

The following code shows how to create a vector with a specified capacity:

```
Vector v = new Vector(25);
```

This vector is created to immediately support up to 25 elements. In other words, the vector will go ahead and allocate enough memory to support 25 elements. Once 25 elements have been added, however, the vector must decide how to grow itself to accept more elements. You can specify the value by which a vector grows using yet another `Vector` constructor:

```
Vector v = new Vector(25, 5);
```

This vector has an initial size of 25 elements, and will grow in increments of 5 elements whenever its size grows to more than 25 elements. This means that the vector will first jump to 30 elements in size, then 35, and so on. A smaller grow value for a vector results in more efficient memory management, but at the cost of more execution overhead since more memory allocations are taking place. On the other hand, a larger grow value results in fewer memory allocations, but sometimes memory may be wasted if you don't use all the extra space created.

Unlike with arrays, you can't just use square brackets (`[]`) to access the elements in a vector; you have to use methods defined in the `Vector` class. To add an element to a vector, you use the `addElement` method:

```
v.addElement("carrots");
v.addElement("broccoli");
v.addElement("cauliflower");
```

This code shows how to add some vegetable strings to a vector. To get the last string added to the vector, you can use the `lastElement` method:

```
String s = (String)v.lastElement();
```

The `lastElement` method retrieves the last element added to the vector. Notice that you have to cast the return value of `lastElement`, since the `Vector` class is designed to work with the generic `Object` class. Although `lastElement` certainly has its usefulness, you will probably find more use with the `elementAt` method, which allows you to index into a vector to retrieve an element. Following is an example of using the `elementAt` method:

```
String s1 = (String)v.elementAt(0);
String s2 = (String)v.elementAt(2);
```

Since vectors are zero based, the first call to `elementAt` retrieves the `"carrots"` string, and the second call retrieves the `"cauliflower"` string. Just as you can retrieve an element at a particular index, you can also add and remove elements at an index using the `insertElementAt` and `removeElementAt` methods:

```
v.insertElementAt("squash", 1);
v.insertElementAt("corn", 0);
v.removeElementAt(3);
```

The first call to `insertElementAt` inserts an element at index 1, between the `"carrots"` and `"broccoli"` strings. The `"broccoli"` and `"cauliflower"` strings are moved up a space in the vector to accommodate the inserted `"squash"` string. The second call to `insertElementAt` inserts an element at index `0`, which is the beginning of the vector. In this case, all existing elements are moved up a space in the vector to accommodate the inserted `"corn"` string. At this point, the contents of the vector look like this:

```
"corn"
"carrots"
"squash"
"broccoli"
"cauliflower"
```

The call to `removeElementAt` removes the element at index 3, which is the `"broccoli"` string. The resulting contents of the vector consist of the following strings:

```
"corn"
"carrots"
"squash"
"cauliflower"
```

You can use the `setElementAt` method to change a specific element:

```
v.setElementAt("peas", 1);
```

This method replaces the `"carrots"` string with the `"peas"` string, resulting in the following vector contents:

```
"corn"
"peas"
"squash"
"cauliflower"
```

23

If you want to clear out the vector completely, you can remove all the elements with the removeAllElements method:

```
v.removeAllElements();
```

The Vector class also provides some methods for working with elements without using indexes. These methods actually search through the vector for a particular element. The first of these methods is the contains method, which simply checks to see if an element is in the vector:

```
boolean isThere = v.contains("celery");
```

Another method that works in this manner is the indexOf method, which finds the index of an element based on the element itself:

```
int i = v.indexOf("squash");
```

The indexOf method returns the index of the element in question if it is in the vector, or -1 if not. The removeElement method works similarly in that it removes an element based on the element itself rather than on an index:

```
v.removeElement("cauliflower");
```

If you're interested in working with all the elements in a vector sequentially, you can use the elements method, which returns an enumeration of the elements:

```
Enumeration e = v.elements();
```

Recall from earlier in today's lesson that you can use an enumeration to step through elements sequentially. In this example, you can work with the enumeration e using the methods defined by the Enumeration interface.

You may find yourself wanting to work with the size of a vector. Fortunately, the Vector class provides a few methods for determining and manipulating the size of a vector. First, the size method determines the number of elements in the vector:

```
int size = v.size();
```

If you want to explicitly set the size of a vector, you can use the setSize method:

```
v.setSize(10);
```

The setSize method expands or truncates the vector to accommodate the new size specified. If the vector is expanded because of a larger size, null elements are inserted as the newly added elements. If the vector is truncated, any elements at indexes beyond the specified size are discarded.

If you recall, vectors have two different attributes relating to size: size and capacity. The size is the number of elements in the vector and the capacity is the amount of memory allocated to hold all elements. The capacity is always greater than or equal to the size. You can force the capacity to exactly match the size using the `trimToSize` method:

```
v.trimToSize();
```

You can also check to see what the capacity is, using the `capacity` method:

```
int capacity = v.capacity();
```

You'll find that the `Vector` class is one of the most useful data structures provided in the Java API. Hopefully this tour of the class gives you an idea of how powerful vectors are and how easy it is to use them.

Stacks

Stacks are a classic data structure used to model information that is accessed in a specific order. The `Stack` class in Java is implemented as a last-in-first-out (LIFO) stack, which means that the last item added to the stack is the first one to come back off. Figure 23.2 shows the logical organization of a stack.

Figure 23.2.

The logical organization of a stack data structure.

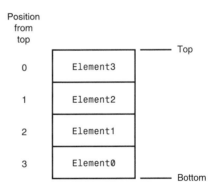

You may be wondering from Figure 23.2 why the numbers of the elements don't match their position from the top of the stack. Keep in mind that elements are added to the top, so `Element0`, which is on the bottom, was the first element added to the stack. Likewise, `Element3`, which is on top, is the last element added to the stack. Also, since `Element3` is at the top of the stack, it will be the first to come back off.

The `Stack` class only defines one constructor, which is a default constructor that creates an empty stack. You use this constructor to create a stack like this:

```
Stack s = new Stack();
```

You add new elements to a stack using the push method, which pushes an element onto the top of the stack:

```
s.push("One");
s.push("Two");
s.push("Three");
s.push("Four");
s.push("Five");
s.push("Six");
```

BD
2

This code pushes six strings onto the stack, with the last string ("Six") remaining on top. You pop elements back off the stack using the pop method:

```
String s1 = (String)s.pop();
String s2 = (String)s.pop();
```

This code pops the last two strings off the stack, leaving the first four strings remaining. This code results in the s1 variable containing the "Six" string and the s2 variable containing the "Five" string.

If you want to get the top element on the stack without actually popping it off the stack, you can use the peek method:

```
String s3 = (String)s.peek();
```

This call to peek returns the "Four" string but leaves the string on the stack. You can search for an element on the stack using the search method:

```
int i = s.search("Two");
```

The search method returns the distance from the top of the stack of the element if it is found, or -1 if not. In this case, the "Two" string is the third element from the top, so the search method returns 2 (zero based).

TECHNICAL NOTE

As in all Java data structures that deal with indexes or lists, the Stack class reports element position in a zero-based fashion. This means that the top element in a stack has a location of 0, and the fourth element down in a stack has a location of 3.

The only other method defined in the Stack class is empty, which determines whether a stack is empty:

```
boolean isEmpty = s.empty();
```

Although maybe not quite as useful as the Vector class, the Stack class provides the functionality for a very common and established data structure.

Dictionaries

The Dictionary class defines a framework for implementing a basic key-mapped data structure. Although you can't actually create Dictionary objects since the class is abstract, you can still learn a lot about key-mapped data modeling by learning how the Dictionary class works. You can put the key-mapped approach to work using the Hashtable class, which is derived from Dictionary, or by deriving your own class from Dictionary. You learn about the Hashtable class in the next section of today's lesson.

The Dictionary class defines a means of storing information based on a key. This is similar in some ways to how the Vector class works, in that elements in a vector are accessed via an index, which is a specific type of key. However, keys in the Dictionary class can be just about anything. You can create your own class to use as the keys for accessing and manipulating data in a dictionary. Figure 23.3 shows how keys map to data in a dictionary.

Figure 23.3.

The logical organization of a dictionary data structure.

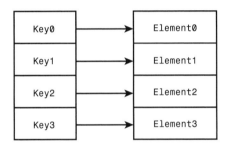

The Dictionary class defines a variety of methods for working with the data stored in a dictionary. All these methods are defined as abstract, meaning that derived classes will have to implement all of them to actually be useful. The put and get methods are used to put objects in the dictionary and get them back. Assuming dict is a Dictionary-derived class that implements these methods, the following code shows how to use the put method to add elements to a dictionary:

```
dict.put("small", new Rectangle(0, 0, 5, 5));
dict.put("medium", new Rectangle(0, 0, 15, 15));
dict.put("large", new Rectangle(0, 0, 25, 25));
```

This code adds three rectangles to the dictionary, using strings as the keys. To get an element from the dictionary, you use the get method and specify the appropriate key:

```
Rectangle r = (Rectangle)dict.get("medium");
```

You can also remove an element from the dictionary with a key using the remove method:

```
dict.remove("large");
```

23

You can find out how many elements are in the dictionary using the `size` method, much as you did with the `Vector` class:

```
int size = dict.size();
```

You can also check whether the dictionary is empty using the `isEmpty` method:

```
boolean isEmpty = dict.isEmpty();
```

Finally, the `Dictionary` class includes two methods for enumerating the keys and values contained within: `keys` and `elements`. The `keys` method returns an enumeration containing all the keys contained in a dictionary, while the `elements` method returns an enumeration of all the key-mapped values contained. Following is an example of retrieving both enumerations:

```
Enumeration keys = dict.keys();
Enumeration elements = dict.elements();
```

Note that since keys are mapped to elements on a one-to-one basis, these enumerations are of equal length.

Hash Tables

The `Hashtable` class is derived from `Dictionary` and provides a complete implementation of a key-mapped data structure. Similar to dictionaries, hash tables allow you to store data based on some type of key. Unlike dictionaries, hash tables have an efficiency associated with them defined by the load factor of the table.

 The *load factor* of a hash table is a number between 0.0 and 1.0 that determines how and when the hash table allocates space for more elements.

Like vectors, hash tables have a capacity, which is the amount of memory allocated for the table. Hash tables allocate more memory by comparing the current size of the table with the product of the capacity and the load factor. If the size of the hash table exceeds this product, the table increases its capacity by rehashing itself.

Load factors closer to 1.0 result in a more efficient use of memory at the expense of a longer look-up time for each element. Similarly, load factors closer to 0.0 result in more efficient look-ups but also tend to be more wasteful with memory. Determining the load factor for your own hash tables is really dependent on the usage of the hash table and whether your priority is on performance or memory efficiency.

You create hash tables using one of three methods. The first method creates a default hash table:

```
Hashtable hash = new Hashtable();
```

The second constructor creates a hash table with the specified initial capacity:

```
Hashtable hash = new Hashtable(20);
```

Finally, the third constructor creates a hash table with the specified initial capacity and load factor:

```
Hashtable hash = new Hashtable(20, 0.75);
```

All the abstract methods defined in Dictionary are implemented in the Hashtable class. Since these methods perform the exact same function in Hashtable, there's no need to cover them again. However, they are listed here just so you'll have an idea of what support Hashtable provides:

```
elements
get
isEmpty
keys
put
remove
size
```

In addition to these methods, the Hashtable class implements a few others that perform functions specific to supporting hash tables. One of these is the clear method, which clears a hash table of all its keys and elements:

```
hash.clear();
```

The contains method is used to see if an object is stored in the hash table. This method searches for an object value in the hash table rather than a key. The following code shows how to use the contains method:

```
boolean isThere = hash.contains(new Rectangle(0, 0, 5, 5));
```

Similar to contains, the containsKey method searches a hash table, but it searches based on a key rather than a value:

```
boolean isThere = hash.containsKey("Small");
```

I mentioned earlier that a hash table will rehash itself when it determines that it must increase its capacity. You can force a rehash yourself by calling the rehash method:

```
hash.rehash();
```

That pretty much sums up the important methods implemented by the Hashtable class. Even though you've seen all the methods, you still may be wondering exactly how the Hashtable class is useful. The practical usage of a hash table is actually in representing data that is too time-consuming to search or reference by value. In other words, hash tables often come in handy when you're working with complex data, where it's much more efficient to access the data using a key rather than by comparing the data objects themselves. Furthermore, hash tables typically compute a key for elements, which is called a hash code. For example, an object such as a string can have an integer hash code computed for it that uniquely represents the string. When a bunch of strings are stored in a hash table, the table can access the strings using integer hash codes as opposed to using the contents of the strings themselves. This results in much more efficient searching and retrieving capabilities.

NEW TERM   A *hash code* is a computed key that uniquely identifies each element in a hash table.

This technique of computing and using hash codes for object storage and reference is exploited heavily throughout the Java system. This is apparent in the fact that the parent of all classes, `Object`, defines a `hashCode` method that is overridden in most standard Java classes. Any class that defines a `hashCode` method can be efficiently stored and accessed in a hash table. A class wishing to be hashed must also implement the `equals` method, which defines a way of telling if two objects are equal. The `equals` method usually just performs a straight comparison of all the member variables defined in a class.

Hash tables are an extremely powerful data structure that you will probably want to integrate into some of your programs that manipulate large amounts of data. The fact that they are so widely supported in the Java API via the `Object` class should give you a clue as to their importance in Java programming.

Building Your Own Data Structures

Even though the Java utility package provides some very powerful and useful data structures, there may be situations in which you need something a little different. I encourage you to make the most of the standard Java data structures whenever possible, since reusing stable code is always a smarter solution than writing your own code. However, in cases where the standard data structures just don't seem to fit, you may need to turn your attention toward other options.

Throughout the rest of today's lesson you'll learn all about one of these other options. More specifically, you'll learn about linked lists, which are a very useful type of data structure not provided in the standard Java data structures. Not only will you learn about linked lists, but you'll also develop your own linked list class that you can reuse in your own Java programs. You'll see that building custom data structures isn't all that difficult. Let's get started!

Linked List Basics

Like vectors and arrays, linked lists are used to store a sequential list of objects. The primary difference between these data structures is that arrays and vectors are better at referencing elements via a numeric index, whereas linked lists are better at accessing data in a purely sequential manner. In other words, linked lists aren't suited for the type of random access provided by arrays and vectors. This may seem like a limitation of linked lists, but it is in fact what makes them unique as a data structure; they are much more efficient when it comes to adding, inserting, and removing elements.

To get a better idea of why linked lists have the properties mentioned, take a look at the logical organization of linked lists shown in Figure 23.4.

Figure 23.4.

*The logical organiza-
tion of a doubly linked
list data structure.*

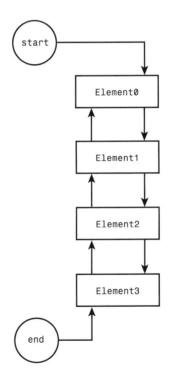

The figure shows the linked list having a distinct start and end, which is somewhat different from arrays and vectors. Sure, arrays and vectors have a first element and a last element, but the elements have no more significance than any other elements. The start and end of linked lists are a strict requirement since linked lists don't hold elements in a fixed amount of memory. This actually touches on the biggest difference between linked lists and vectors/

23

arrays. Linked lists simply hold references to the start and end elements contained within, whereas vectors and arrays contain references to all of their elements.

Another key point to note from Figure 23.4 is that each element in a linked list contains a reference to both the element before and the element after it. This is how elements in linked lists are accessed: by traversing the list through the references to successive elements. In other words, to get the third element in a linked list, you have to start with the first element and follow its reference to the second element, and then repeat the process to get to the third element. This may seem like a tedious process, but it actually works quite well in some situations.

In the discussion thus far, I've glossed over one fine point in regard to linked lists, and that is the two types of linked lists. The type shown in Figure 23.4 is called a *doubly linked list* because it contains references to both the element following and the element preceding a particular element. Another popular type of linked list is the *singly linked list*, where each element contains only a reference to the element following it. Figure 23.5 shows the logical organization of a singly linked list.

Figure 23.5.

The logical organiza-tion of a singly linked list data structure.

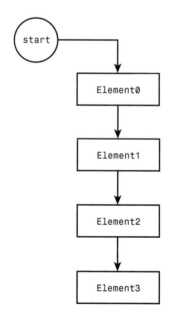

Since doubly linked lists tend to be more general and therefore have a wider range of application, you'll focus on them in today's lesson. Besides, a doubly linked list is really just a singly linked list with more features, which means you can use it just like a singly linked list if you want.

Implementing a Linked List

Now that you have an idea of what a linked list is, let's go ahead and take a stab at developing a fully functioning linked list class. Before jumping into the details of a specific linked list implementation, however, consider the fact that the linked list class you're developing is actually an extension to the standard Java data structures you learned about earlier today. This means that it is to your advantage to design the class to fit in well with the design of the existing data structures. A good approach, then, would be to model the linked list class around the Vector class, at least in regard to some of the basic techniques of manipulating elements through methods. The reason for this is so anyone else using your linked list class can easily see how to use the class based on their understanding of other standard Java classes like Vector. This mindset in terms of extending the standard Java classes is very important when it comes to writing reusable code.

Even though I've been discussing the linked list implementation in terms of a single class, it turns out that it takes a few classes to realistically build a complete linked list. These classes consist of a linked list class, a linked list entry class, and a linked list enumeration class. The linked list class models the list itself and is the only class anyone using the linked list will come into contact with. The other two classes are helper classes that provide some type of behind-the-scenes functionality for the linked list class. The linked list entry class models an individual element within the linked list, and the linked list enumerator class provides support for the Enumeration interface.

Since it is by far the most simple of the three classes, let's start by looking at the linked list entry class, which is called LinkedListEntry:

```
class LinkedListEntry {
  protected Object          val = null;
  protected LinkedListEntry next = null;
  protected LinkedListEntry prev = null;

  public LinkedListEntry(Object obj) {
    // Make sure the object is valid
    if (obj == null)
      throw new NullPointerException();

    val = obj;
  }
}
```

The LinkedListEntry class contains three member variables that keep up with the value of the entry (the element being stored) and a reference to the next and previous elements. This class has a single constructor defined, which simply checks the validity of the object being stored in the entry and assigns it to the entry's val member variable.

Based on the simplicity of LinkedListEntry, you're probably guessing that most of the functionality of the linked list is provided by the main linked list class. You guessed right! This class is called LinkedList and contains a few member variables, which follow:

```
protected LinkedListEntry start = null;
protected LinkedListEntry end = null;
protected int            numElements;
```

The start and end member variables hold references to the beginning and end elements in the list, while the numElements member keeps up with the size of the list. There are also a variety of methods defined in the LinkedList class that resemble methods in the Vector class. One of the most important methods is addElement, which adds a new element to the end of the list. The source code for addElement is shown in Listing 23.1.

TYPE   **Listing 23.1. The LinkedList class's addElement method.**

```
 1: public void addElement(Object obj) {
 2:   // Make sure the object is valid
 3:   if (obj == null)
 4:     throw new NullPointerException();
 5:
 6:   // Create the new entry
 7:   LinkedListEntry newElement = new LinkedListEntry(obj);
 8:   numElements++;
 9:
10:   // See if the new element is the start of the list
11:   if (start == null) {
12:     start = newElement;
13:     end = newElement;
14:   }
15:   else {
16:     end.next = newElement;
17:     newElement.prev = end;
18:     end = newElement;
19:   }
20: }
```

ANALYSIS   The addElement method first checks to make sure the new object is valid. It then creates an entry to hold the object and checks to see if the new element will be placed at the start of the list. addElement then adjusts the references of elements related to the new element so the list's structure is maintained.

Just as the addElement method is important for adding a new element to the end of the list, the insertElementAt method is useful for inserting a new element at any point in the list. Listing 23.2 contains the source code for insertElementAt.

TYPE   **Listing 23.2. The** `LinkedList` **class's** `insertElementAt` **method.**

```
 1: public void insertElementAt(Object obj, Object pos) {
 2:    // Make sure the objects are valid
 3:    if (obj == null || pos == null)
 4:      throw new NullPointerException();
 5:
 6:    // Make sure the position object is in the list
 7:    LinkedListEntry posEntry = find(pos);
 8:    if (posEntry == null)
 9:      throw new NullPointerException();
10:
11:    // Create the new entry
12:    LinkedListEntry newElement = new LinkedListEntry(obj);
13:    numElements++;
14:
15:    // Link in the new entry
16:    newElement.next = posEntry;
17:    newElement.prev = posEntry.prev;
18:    if (posEntry == start)
19:      start = newElement;
20:    else
21:      posEntry.prev.next = newElement;
22:    posEntry.prev = newElement;
23: }
```

ANALYSIS   The `insertElementAt` method takes two parameters that specify the new object to be added to the list, along with the object at the position where the new object is to be inserted. `insertElementAt` first makes sure both objects are valid; then it checks to see if the position object is in the list. If things are okay at this point, a new entry is created to hold the new object, and the references of adjacent elements are adjusted to reflect the insertion.

At this point you have two methods that allow you to add and insert elements to the linked list. However, there still isn't any means to remove elements from the list. Enter the `removeElement` method! Listing 23.3 contains the source code for `removeElement`, which allows you to remove an element by specifying the object itself.

TYPE   **Listing 23.3. The** `LinkedList` **class's** `removeElement` **method.**

```
 1: public boolean removeElement(Object obj) {
 2:    // Make sure the object is valid
 3:    if (obj == null)
 4:      throw new NullPointerException();
 5:
 6:    // Make sure the object is in the list
```

23

```
 7:    LinkedListEntry delEntry = find(obj);
 8:    if (delEntry == null)
 9:      return false;
10:
11:    // Unlink the entry
12:    numElements--;
13:    if (delEntry == start)
14:      start = delEntry.next;
15:    else
16:      delEntry.prev.next = delEntry.next;
17:    if (delEntry == end)
18:      end = delEntry.prev;
19:    else
20:      delEntry.next.prev = delEntry.prev;
21:    return true;
22:  }
```

ANALYSIS The removeElement method first checks to see if the object passed in is valid, and then searches to make sure the object is in the list. It performs the search by calling the find method, which is a private method you'll learn about in just a moment. Upon finding the entry in the list, the removeElement method unlinks the entry by adjusting the references of adjacent entries.

The find method is a private method used internally by the LinkedList class to find entries in the list based on the object they store. Following is the source code for the find method:

```
private LinkedListEntry find(Object obj) {
  // Make sure the list isn't empty and the object is valid
  if (isEmpty() || obj == null)
    return null;

  // Search the list for the object
  LinkedListEntry tmp = start;
  while (tmp != null) {
    if (tmp.val == obj)
      return tmp;
    tmp = tmp.next;
  }
  return null;
}
```

The find method first checks to make sure the list isn't empty and that the object in question is valid. It then traverses the list using a while loop, checking the val member variable of each entry against the object passed in. If there is a match, the entry holding the object is returned; otherwise, null is returned.

The find method isn't public because you don't want outside users of the LinkedList class to know anything about the LinkedListEntry class. In other words, the LinkedListEntry class is a purely internal helper class, so the LinkedListEntry object returned from find wouldn't make any sense to a user of LinkedList. Even though find is private, there is a public method that can be used to see if an object is in the list. This method is called contains; its source code follows:

```
public boolean contains(Object obj) {
  return (find(obj) != null);
}
```

As you can see, all the contains method does is call find and compare the return value to null. Since find only returns a non-null value if an object is found, this little trick works perfectly!

You may have noticed earlier that the find method made a call to the isEmpty method to see if the list was empty. The code for this method follows:

```
public boolean isEmpty() {
  return (start == null);
}
```

Since the start reference in LinkedList only contains a null value if the list is empty, the isEmpty method simply checks to see if it is in fact set to null. This is a very simple and effective way to see if the list is empty.

That pretty much sums up the LinkedList class, except for how it supports the Enumeration interface. In deciding how to support the Enumeration interface, your best bet is to look to the Vector class. The Vector class supports the Enumeration interface through a method called elements. The elements method returns an object of type Enumeration that can be used to enumerate the elements in a vector. Let's use this same approach to add enumeration capabilities to the linked list. Following is the source code for the elements method in the LinkedList class:

```
public Enumeration elements() {
  return new LinkedListEnumerator(this);
}
```

The elements method is probably a lot simpler than you expected. That's because the work of actually supporting the Enumeration interface is left to the LinkedListEnumerator class. Listing 23.4 contains the source code for the LinkedListEnumerator class.

TYPE   **Listing 23.4. The LinkedListEnumerator class.**

```
1: class LinkedListEnumerator implements Enumeration {
2:    protected LinkedListEntry pos;
3:
4:    public LinkedListEnumerator(LinkedList list) {
5:      pos = list.start;
```

```
 6:    }
 7:
 8:    public boolean hasMoreElements() {
 9:      return (pos != null);
10:    }
11:
12:    public Object nextElement() {
13:      // Make sure the current object is valid
14:      if (pos == null)
15:        throw new NoSuchElementException();
16:
17:      // Increment the list and return the object
18:      LinkedListEntry tmp = pos;
19:      pos = pos.next;
20:      return tmp.val;
21:    }
22: }
```

ANALYSIS The first thing to notice in the LinkedListEnumerator class is that it implements the Enumeration interface, which is evident in the class definition. The LinkedListEnumerator class contains one member variable, pos, which keeps up with the current entry in the enumeration. The constructor simply sets the pos member to the start of the list.

Other than saying so in the class definition, implementing the Enumeration interface involves supporting two methods: hasMoreElements and nextElement. The hasMoreElements method simply checks to see if the pos member is non-null, in which case there are more elements to enumerate. The nextElement method makes sure the current entry is valid and then returns the object stored in this entry. And that's really all there is to the LinkedListEnumerator class!

You now have a complete linked list class that is ready to be put to use in a practical Java program. I'll leave it up to you to figure out a neat application of it. Incidentally, all the source code for the linked list classes is located on the accompanying CD-ROM.

Summary

In today's lesson you have learned all about data structures and their relevance to Java programming. You began the lesson with a brief overview of data structures in general and why it is important to have a solid understanding of how to use them. You then moved on to learning about the standard data structures provided in the Java utility package. These standard data structures provide a range of options that cover many practical programming scenarios. However, for those cases where you need something a little different to hold data, you also learned about a type of data structure that isn't provided by the Java utility package: linked lists. You even implemented a linked list class that you can reuse in your own Java programs. This knowledge, combined with an understanding of the standard Java data structures, should serve as a solid foundation for your handling of data in practical programming scenarios.

If you thought the topic of data structures was a little dry, don't worry, because tomorrow's lesson gets much more exciting. Tomorrow you'll learn about advanced animation techniques and the handling of distributed media. You'll even use your newfound understanding of vectors to implement some really neat animation classes!

Q&A

Q If Java arrays are data structures, why aren't they implemented as classes?

A Actually, Java arrays are implemented as classes; they just aren't used as classes in the traditional sense of calling methods, and so on. Even though you won't find a class called Array in the Java API documentation, you can rest assured that under Java's hood there is an array class that is at least vaguely similar to the Vector class.

Q Do all of the standard Java data structures implement the Enumeration interface?

A No, because the design of the Enumeration interface is based on a sequential data structure. For example, the Vector class is sequential and fits in perfectly with supporting the Enumeration interface. However, the BitSet class is very much nonsequential, so supporting the Enumeration interface wouldn't make any sense.

Q I still don't totally see the importance of using a hash table. What gives?

A The concept of calculating a hash code for a complex piece of data is important because it allows you to lessen the overhead involved in searching for the data. The hash code allows you to home in on a particular point in a large set of data before you begin the arduous task of searching based on the data itself, which can greatly improve performance.

Q How are linked lists different from vectors when it comes to the storage of individual elements?

A Vectors manage the memory requirements of all elements by allocating a certain amount of memory upon creation. When a vector is required to grow, it will allocate memory large enough to hold the existing data and the new data, and then copy everything to it. Even if a vector only holds references to objects, it must still manage the memory that holds the references. Linked lists don't manage any of the memory for the elements contained in the list, except for references to the start and end elements.

Day 24

Advanced Animation and Media

by Michael Morrison

A lot of people were stirred when the Web first brought full-color images to the Internet. These days, color images are simply to be expected, while a growing interest is being placed on animation, or moving images. If a picture can tell a thousand words, imagine what a bunch of pictures shown very rapidly can tell!

Today's lesson focuses on how the effect of animated movement is conveyed in Java using a series of images displayed rapidly. This technique is really nothing new to computers or programming, although it is pretty new to the Web. If you're thinking this description of today's lesson sounds awfully familiar, it's because you've already learned about animation in earlier lessons. The difference is that today's lesson is going to take you much further in learning about what animation is and how to do some really powerful things with it.

More specifically, today you'll learn about the following:

- [ ] Animation theory
- [ ] The primary types of animation
- [ ] Transparency, z-order, collision detection, and a few other cool terms you can lay on your friends
- [ ] Tracking images using the Java media tracker
- [ ] Implementing your own sprite animation classes

Although part of today's lesson is theoretical, you'll finish up the lesson by creating a powerful set of reusable sprite animation classes. Don't worry if you don't know what a sprite is yet—you will soon enough!

What Is Animation?

Before getting into animation as it relates to Java, it's important to understand the basics of what animation is and how it works. So let's begin by asking the fundamental question: What is animation? Put simply, animation is the illusion of movement. Am I telling you that every animation you've ever seen is really just an illusion? That's exactly right! And probably the most surprising animated illusion is one that captured our attention long before modern computers—the television. When you watch television, you see lots of things moving around, but what you perceive as movement is really just a trick being played on your eyes.

NEW TERM   *Animation* is the process of simulating movement.

In the case of television, the illusion of movement is created by displaying a rapid succession of images with slight changes in content. The human eye perceives these changes as movement because of its low visual acuity. I'll spare you the biology lesson of why this is so; the point is that our eyes are fairly easy to trick into falling for the illusion of animation. More specifically, the human eye can be tricked into perceiving animated movement with as low as 12 frames of movement per second. Animation speed is measured in frames per second (fps), which is the number of animation frames, or image changes, presented every second.

NEW TERM   *Frames per second* (fps) is the number of animation frames, or image changes, presented every second.

Although 12fps is technically enough to fool our eyes into seeing animation, animations at speeds this low often end up looking somewhat jerky. Most professional animations therefore use a higher frame rate. Television, for example, uses 30fps. When you go to the movies, you see motion pictures at about 24fps. It's pretty apparent that these frame rates are more than enough to captivate our attention and successfully create the illusion of movement.

When programming animation in Java, you typically have the ability to manipulate the frame rate a decent amount. The most obvious limitation on frame rate is the speed at which the computer can generate and display the animation frames. In Java, this is a crucial point because Java applets aren't typically known to be speed demons. However, the recent release of just-in-time Java compilers has helped speed up Java applets, along with alleviating some of the performance concerns associated with animation.

NOTE

> Currently, both Netscape Navigator 3.0 and Microsoft Internet Explorer 3.0 support just-in-time compilation of Java applets.

Types of Animation

I know you're probably itching to see some real animation in Java, but there are a few more issues to cover before getting into the details of animation programming. More specifically, it's important for you to understand the primary types of animation used in Java programming. There are actually a lot of different types of animation, all of which are useful in different instances. However, for the purposes of implementing animation in Java, I've broken animation down into two basic types: frame-based animation and cast-based animation.

Frame-Based Animation

The most simple type of animation is *frame-based* animation, which is the primary type of animation found on the Web. Frame-based animation involves simulating movement by displaying a sequence of pregenerated, static frame images. A movie is a perfect example of frame-based animation; each frame of the film is a frame of animation, and when the frames are shown in rapid succession, they create the illusion of movement.

NEW TERM *Frame-based animation* simulates movement by displaying a sequence of pregenerated, static frame images.

Frame-based animation has no concept of a graphical object distinguishable from the background; everything appearing in a frame is part of that frame as a whole. The result is that each frame image contains all the information necessary for that frame in a static form. This is an important point because it distinguishes frame-based animation from cast-based animation, which you'll learn about next.

Note

Much of the animation used in Web sites is implemented using animated GIF images, which involves storing multiple animation frames in a single GIF image file. Animated GIFs are a very good example of frame-based animation.

Cast-Based Animation

A more powerful animation technique often employed in games and educational software is *cast-based* animation, which is also known as *sprite animation.* Cast-based animation involves graphical objects that move independently of a background. At this point, you may be a little confused by my usage of the term "graphical object" when referring to parts of an animation. In this case, a graphical object is something that logically can be thought of as a separate entity from the background of an animation image. For example, in an animation of the solar system, the planets would be separate graphical objects that are logically independent of the starry background.

Cast-based animation simulates movement using graphical objects that move independently of a background.

Each graphical object in a cast-based animation is referred to as a *sprite* and can have a position that varies over time. In other words, sprites have a velocity associated with them that determines how their position changes over time. Almost every computer game uses sprites to some degree. For example, every object in the classic Asteroids game is a sprite that moves independently of the black background.

A *sprite* is a graphical object that can move independently of a background or other objects.

Note

You may be wondering where the term *cast-based animation* comes from. It comes from the fact that sprites can be thought of as cast members moving around on a stage. This analogy of relating computer animation to theatrical performance is very useful. By thinking of sprites as cast members and the background as a stage, you can take the next logical step and think of an animation as a theatrical performance.

24

> In fact, this isn't far from the mark, because the goal of theatrical performances is to entertain the audience by telling a story through the interaction of the cast members. Likewise, cast-based animations use the interaction of sprites to entertain the user, while often telling a story or at least getting some point across.

Even though the fundamental principle behind sprite animation is the positional movement of a graphical object, there is no reason you can't incorporate frame-based animation into a sprite. Incorporating frame-based animation into a sprite allows you to change the image of the sprite as well as alter its position. This hybrid type of animation is what you will implement later today in the Java sprite classes.

I mentioned in the frame-based animation discussion that television is a good example of frame-based animation. But can you think of something on television that is created in a manner similar to cast-based animation (other than animated movies and cartoons)? Have you ever wondered how weatherpeople magically appear in front of a computer-generated map showing the weather? The news station uses a technique known as *blue-screening*, which enables them to overlay the weatherperson on top of the weather map in real time. It works like this: The person stands in front of a blue backdrop, which serves as a transparent background. The image of the weatherperson is overlaid onto the weather map; the trick is that the blue background is filtered out when the image is overlaid so that it is effectively transparent. In this way, the weatherperson is acting exactly like a sprite!

Transparency

The weatherperson example brings up a very important point regarding sprites: transparency. Because bitmapped images are rectangular by nature, a problem arises when sprite images aren't rectangular in shape. In sprites that aren't rectangular in shape, which is the majority of sprites, the pixels surrounding the sprite image are unused. In a graphics system without transparency, these unused pixels are drawn just like any others. The end result is sprites that have visible rectangular borders around them, which completely destroys the effectiveness of having sprites overlaid on a background image.

What's the solution? Well, one solution is to make all your sprites rectangular. Unless you're planning to write an applet showing dancing boxes, a more realistic solution is transparency, which allows you to define a certain color in an image as unused, or transparent. When pixels of this color are encountered by graphics drawing routines, they are simply skipped, leaving the original background intact. Transparent colors in images act exactly like the weatherperson's blue screen.

 Transparent colors are colors in an image that are unused, meaning that they aren't drawn when the rest of the colors in the image are drawn.

You're probably thinking that implementing transparency involves a lot of low-level bit twiddling and image pixel manipulation. In some programming environments you would be correct in this assumption, but not in Java. Fortunately, transparency is already supported in Java by way of the GIF 89a image format. In the GIF 89a image format, you simply specify a color of the GIF image that serves as the transparent color. When the image is drawn, pixels matching the transparent color are skipped and left undrawn, leaving the background pixels unchanged. No more dancing boxes!

Z-Order

In many instances, you will want some sprites to appear on top of others. For example, in the solar system animation you would want to be able to see some planets passing in front of others. You handle this problem by assigning each planet sprite a screen depth, which is also referred to as *Z-order*.

NEW TERM *Z-order* is the relative depth of sprites on the screen.

The depth of sprites is called *Z-order* because it works sort of like another dimension—like a Z axis. You can think of sprites moving around on the screen in the XY plane. Similarly, the Z axis can be thought of as another axis projected into the screen that determines how the sprites overlap each other. To put it another way, Z-order determines a sprite's depth within the screen. By making use of a Z axis, you might think that Z-ordered sprites are 3D. The truth is that Z-ordered sprites aren't 3D because the Z axis is a hypothetical axis that is used only to determine how sprite objects hide each other. A real 3D sprite would be able to move just as freely in the Z axis as it does in the XY plane.

Just to make sure that you get a clear picture of how Z-order works, let's go back for a moment to the good old days of traditional animation. Traditional animators, such as those at Disney, used celluloid sheets to draw animated objects. They drew on these because they could be overlaid on a background image and moved independently. This was known as *cel animation* and should sound vaguely familiar. (Cel animation is an early version of sprite animation.) Each cel sheet corresponds to a unique Z-order value, determined by where in the pile of sheets the sheet is located. If an image near the top of the pile happens to be in the same location on the cel sheet as any lower images, it conceals them. The location of each image in the stack of cel sheets is its Z-order, which determines its visibility precedence. The same thing applies to sprites in cast-based animations, except that the Z-order is determined by the order in which the sprites are drawn, rather than the cel sheet location. This concept of a pile of cel sheets representing all the sprites in a sprite system will be useful later today when you develop the sprite classes.

Collision Detection

Although collision detection is primarily useful only in games, it is an important component of sprite animation. *Collision detection* is the process of determining whether sprites have collided with each other. Although collision detection doesn't directly play a role in creating the illusion of movement, it is tightly linked to sprite animation and extremely useful in some scenarios, such as games.

NEW TERM   *Collision detection* is the process of determining if sprites have collided with each other.

Collision detection is used to determine when sprites physically interact with each other. In an Asteroids game, for example, if the ship sprite collides with an asteroid sprite, the ship is destroyed. Collision detection is the mechanism employed to find out whether the ship collided with the asteroid. This might not sound like a big deal; just compare their positions and see whether they overlap, right? Correct, but consider how many comparisons must take place when lots of sprites are moving around; each sprite must be compared to every other sprite in the system. It's not hard to see how the overhead of effective collision detection can become difficult to manage.

Not surprisingly, there are many approaches to handling collision detection. The simplest approach is to compare the bounding rectangles of each sprite with the bounding rectangles of all the other sprites. This method is efficient, but if you have objects that are not rectangular, a certain degree of error occurs when the objects brush by each other. This is because the corners might overlap and indicate a collision when really only the transparent areas are overlapping. The more irregular the shape of the sprites, the more errors typically occur. Figure 24.1 shows how simple rectangle collision works.

In Figure 24.1 the areas determining the collision detection are shaded. You can see how simple rectangle collision detection isn't very accurate unless you're dealing with sprites that are rectangular in shape. An improvement on this technique is to shrink the collision rectangles a little, which reduces the corner error. This method improves things a little, but has the potential of causing error in the reverse direction by allowing sprites to overlap in some cases without signaling a collision. Not surprisingly, shrunken rectangle collision works best when you are dealing with sprites that are roughly circular in shape.

Figure 24.1.

Collision detection using simple rectangle collision.

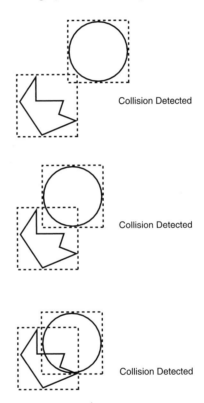

Figure 24.2 shows how shrinking the collision rectangles can improve the error on simple rectangle collision detection. Shrunken rectangle collision is just as efficient as simple rectangle collision because all you are doing is comparing rectangles for intersection.

Figure 24.2.

Collision detection using shrunken rectangle collision.

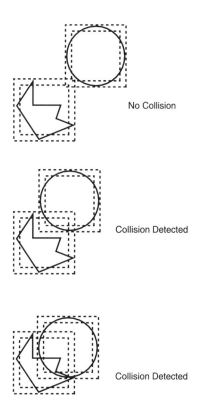

No Collision

Collision Detected

Collision Detected

The most accurate collision detection technique is to detect collision based on the sprite image data, which involves actually checking whether transparent parts of the sprite or the sprite images themselves are overlapping. In this case, you would get a collision only if the actual sprite images are overlapping. This is the ideal technique for detecting collisions because it is exact and allows objects of any shape to move by each other without error. Figure 24.3 shows collision detection using the sprite image data.

Unfortunately, this technique requires far more overhead than the other types of collision detection and is often a major bottleneck in performance. Furthermore, implementing image data collision detection can get very messy. Considering these facts, you'll focus your efforts later today on implementing the first two types of collision detection.

BD
3

Figure 24.3.

*Collision detection using
sprite image data.*

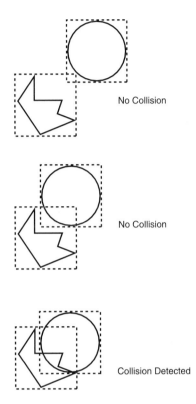

No Collision

No Collision

Collision Detected

Tracking Images

There is one last topic to cover before getting into the details of animation programming in Java: tracking images. Since animations typically require multiple images, the issue of managing images as they are being transferred over a Web connection can't be overlooked. The primary issue with images being transferred is the limited bandwidth many of us have in regard to our Web connections. Since many of us have a limited bandwidth connection (pronounced modem), the speed at which images are transferred over such a Web connection often causes a noticeable delay in a Java applet reliant on them, such as any applet displaying animations.

There is a standard technique for dealing with transfer delay as it affects static images. You've no doubt seen this technique at work in your Web browser when you've viewed images in Web pages. The technique is known as *interlacing* and makes images appear blurry until they have been completely transferred. To use interlacing, images must be stored in an interlaced format (usually GIF version 89a), which means that the image data is arranged such that the image can be displayed before it is completely transmitted. Interlacing is a good approach to dealing with transmission delays for static images because it enables you to see the image as it is being transferred. Without interlacing, you have to wait until the entire image has been transferred before you can see it at all.

Before you get too excited about interlacing, let me point out that it is useful only for static images. You're probably wondering why this is the case. It has to do with the fact that animations (dynamic images) rely on rapidly displaying a sequence of images over time, all of which must be readily available to successfully create the effect of movement. An animation sequence simply wouldn't look right using interlacing because some of the images would be transferred before others.

A good solution to the transfer-delay problem in animated images would be to just wait until all the images have been transferred before displaying the animation. That's fine, but it requires you to know the status of images as they are being transferred. How can you possibly know this? Enter the Java media tracker.

The Java *media tracker* is an object that tracks when media objects, such as images, have been successfully transferred. Using the media tracker, you can keep track of any number of media objects and query to see when they have finished being transmitted. For example, suppose you have an animation with four images. You would register each of these images with the media tracker and then wait until they have all been transferred before displaying the animation. The media tracker keeps up with the load status of each image. When the media tracker reports that all the images have been successfully loaded, you are guaranteed that your animation has all the necessary images to display correctly.

The MediaTracker Class

The Java MediaTracker class is part of the AWT package and contains a variety of members and methods for tracking media objects. Unfortunately, the MediaTracker class that ships with release 1.02 of the Java Developer's Kit supports only image tracking. Future versions of Java are expected to add support for other types of media objects such as sound and music.

The MediaTracker class provides member flags for representing various states associated with tracked media objects. These flags are returned by many of the member functions of MediaTracker, and are the following:

- [ ] LOADING—Indicates that a media object is currently in the process of being loaded.
- [ ] ABORTED—Indicates that the loading of a media object has been aborted.
- [ ] ERRORED—Indicates that some type of error occurred while loading a media object.
- [ ] COMPLETE—Indicates that a media object has been successfully loaded.

The `MediaTracker` class provides a variety of methods for helping to track media objects:

`MediaTracker(Component comp)`—The constructor for `MediaTracker` takes a single parameter of type `Component`. This parameter specifies the `Component` object on which tracked images will eventually be drawn. This parameter reflects the current limitation of being able to track only *images* with the `MediaTracker` class, and not sounds or other types of media.

`void addImage(Image image, int id)`—The `addImage` method adds an image to the list of images currently being tracked. This method takes as its first parameter an `Image` object and as its second parameter an identifier that uniquely identifies the image. If you want to track a group of images together, you can use the same identifier for each image.

`synchronized void addImage(Image image, int id, int w, int h)`—This `addImage` method is similar to the first one, but it has additional parameters for specifying the width and height of a tracked image. This version of `addImage` is used for tracking images that you are going to scale; you pass the width and height to which you are scaling the image.

`boolean checkID(int id)`—After you have added images to the `MediaTracker` object, you are ready to check their status. You use the `checkID` method to check whether images matching the passed identifier have finished loading. The `checkID` method returns `false` if the images have not finished loading, and `true` otherwise. This method returns `true` even if the loading has been aborted or if an error has occurred. You must call the appropriate error-checking methods to see if an error has occurred. (You'll learn about the error-checking methods a little later in this section.) The `checkID` method does not load an image if that image has not already begun loading.

`synchronized boolean checkID(int id, boolean load)`—This `checkID` method is similar to the first one except that it enables you to specify that the image should be loaded even if it hasn't already begun loading, which is carried out by passing `true` in the `load` parameter.

`boolean checkAll()`—The `checkAll` method is similar to the `checkID` methods, except that it applies to all images, not just those matching a certain identifier. The `checkAll` method checks to see if the images have finished loading, but doesn't load any images that haven't already begun loading.

`synchronized boolean checkAll(boolean load)`—This `checkAll` method also checks the status of loading images, but enables you to indicate that images are to be loaded if they haven't started already.

`void waitForID(int id)`—You use the `waitForID` method to begin loading images with a certain identifier. This identifier should match the identifier used when the images were added to the media tracker with the `addImage` method. The `waitForID`

24

method is synchronous, meaning that it does not return until all the specified images have finished loading or an error occurs.

`synchronized boolean waitForID(int id, long ms)`—This `waitForID` method is similar to the first one except that it enables you to specify a timeout period, in which case the load will end and `waitForID` will return `true`. You specify the timeout period in milliseconds by using the `ms` parameter.

`void waitForAll()`—The `waitForAll` method is similar to the `waitForID` methods, except that it operates on all images.

`synchronized boolean waitForAll(long ms)`—This `waitForAll` method is similar to the first one except that it enables you to specify a timeout period, in which case the load will end and `waitForAll` will return `true`. You specify the timeout period in milliseconds by using the `ms` parameter.

`int statusID(int id, boolean load)`—You use the `statusID` method to determine the status of images matching the identifier passed in the `id` parameter. `statusID` returns the bitwise `OR` of the status flags related to the images. The possible flags are `LOADING`, `ABORTED`, `ERRORED`, and `COMPLETE`. The second parameter to `statusID`—`load`—should be familiar to you by now because of its use in the other mediatracker methods. It specifies whether you want the images to begin loading if they haven't begun already. This functionality is similar to that provided by the second versions of the `checkID` and `waitForID` methods.

`int statusAll(boolean load)`—The `statusAll` method is similar to the `statusID` method; the only difference is that `statusAll` returns the status of all the images being tracked rather than just those matching a specific identifier.

`synchronized boolean isErrorID(int id)`—The `isErrorID` method checks the error status of images being tracked, based on the `id` identifier argument. This method basically checks the status of each image for the `ERRORED` flag. Note that this method will return `true` if any of the images have errors; it's up to you to determine which specific images had errors.

`synchronized boolean isErrorAny()`—The `isErrorAny` method is similar to the `isErrorID` method, except that it checks on all images rather than just those matching a certain identifier. Like `isErrorID`, `isErrorAny` will return `true` if any of the images have errors; it's up to you to determine which specific images had errors.

`synchronized Object[] getErrorsID(int id)`—If you use `isErrorID` or `isErrorAny` and find out that there are load errors, you need to figure out which images have errors. You do this by using the `getErrorsID` method. This method returns an array of `Object`s containing the media objects that have load errors. In the current implementation of the `MediaTracker` class, this array is always filled with `Image` objects. If there are no errors, this method returns `null`.

`synchronized Object[] getErrorsAny()`—The `getErrorsAny` method is very similar to `getErrorsID`, except that it returns all errored images.

That wraps up the description of the MediaTracker class. Now that you understand what the class is all about, you're probably ready to see it in action. Don't worry—the Sharks sample applet you'll develop later today will put the media tracker through its paces.

Implementing Sprite Animation

As you learned earlier in today's lesson, sprite animation involves the movement of individual graphic objects called sprites. Unlike simple frame animation, sprite animation involves a decent amount of overhead. More specifically, it is necessary to develop not only a sprite class, but also a sprite management class for keeping up with all the sprites you've created. This is necessary because sprites need to be able to interact with each other through a common mechanism. Besides, it is nice to be able to work with the sprites as a whole when it comes to things like actually drawing the sprites on the screen.

In this section, you'll learn how to implement sprite animation in Java by creating a suite of sprite classes. The primary sprite classes are Sprite and SpriteVector. However, there are also a few support classes that you will learn about as you get into the details of these two primary classes. The Sprite class models a single sprite and contains all the information and methods necessary to get a single sprite up and running. However, the real power of sprite animation is harnessed by combining the Sprite class with the SpriteVector class, which is a container class that manages multiple sprites and their interaction with each other.

The Sprite Class

Although sprites can be implemented simply as movable graphical objects, I mentioned earlier that the sprite class developed today will also contain support for frame animation. A frame-animated sprite is basically a sprite with multiple frame images that can be displayed in succession. Your Sprite class will support frame animation in the form of an array of frame images and some methods for setting the frame image currently being displayed. Using this approach, you'll end up with a Sprite class that supports both fundamental types of animation, which gives you more freedom in creating animated Java applets.

Before jumping into the details of how the Sprite class is implemented, take a moment to think about the different pieces of information that a sprite must keep up with. When you understand the components of a sprite at a conceptual level, it will be much easier to understand the Java code. So exactly what information should the Sprite class maintain? The following list contains the key information that the Sprite class needs to include:

- [ ] An array of frame images
- [ ] The current frame
- [ ] The XY position

☐ The velocity

☐ The Z-order

☐ The boundaries

The first component, an array of frame images, is necessary to carry out the frame animations. Even though this sounds like you are forcing a sprite to have multiple animation frames, a sprite can also use a single image. In this way, the frame animation aspects of the sprite are optional. The current frame keeps up with the current frame of animation. In a typical frame-animated sprite, the current frame is incremented to the next frame when the sprite is updated.

The XY position stores the position of the sprite. You move the sprite simply by altering this position. Alternatively, you can set the velocity and let the sprite alter its position automatically based on the velocity.

The Z-order represents the depth of the sprite in relation to other sprites. Ultimately, the Z-order of a sprite determines its drawing order (you'll learn more on that a little later).

Finally, the boundary of a sprite refers to the bounded region in which the sprite can move. All sprites are bound by some region—usually the size of the applet window. The sprite boundary is important because it determines the limits of a sprite's movement.

Now that you understand the core information required by the Sprite class, it's time to get into the specific Java implementation. Let's begin with the Sprite class's member variables, which follow:

```
public static final int BA_STOP = 0,
                        BA_WRAP = 1,
                        BA_BOUNCE = 2,
                        BA_DIE = 3;
protected Component     component;
protected Image[]       image;
protected int           frame,
                        frameInc,
                        frameDelay,
                        frameTrigger;
protected Rectangle     position,
                        collision;
protected int           zOrder;
protected Point         velocity;
protected Rectangle     bounds;
protected int           boundsAction;
protected boolean       hidden = false;
```

The member variables include the important sprite information mentioned earlier, along with some other useful information. Most notably, you are probably curious about the static final members at the beginning of the listing. These members are constant identifiers that define bounds actions for the sprite. *Bounds actions* are actions that a sprite takes in response to reaching a boundary, such as wrapping to the other side or bouncing. Bounds actions are mutually exclusive, meaning that only one can be set at a time.

The `Component` member variable is necessary because an `ImageObserver` object is required to retrieve information about an image. But what does `Component` have to do with `ImageObserver`? The `Component` class implements the `ImageObserver` interface, and the `Applet` class is derived from `Component`. So a `Sprite` object gets its image information from the Java applet itself, which is used to initialize the `Component` member variable.

NOTE   ImageObserver is an interface defined in the `java.awt.image` package that provides a means for receiving information about an image.

The `image` member variable contains an array of `Image` objects representing the animation frames for the sprite. For sprites that aren't frame animated, this array will simply contain one element.

The `frameInc` member variable is used to provide a means to change the way that the animation frames are updated. For example, in some cases you might want the frames to be displayed in the reverse order. You can easily do this by setting `frameInc` to `-1` (its typical value is `1`). The `frameDelay` and `frameTrigger` member variables are used to provide a means of varying the speed of the frame animation. You'll see how the speed of animation is controlled when you learn about the `incFrame` method later today.

The `position` member variable is a `Rectangle` object representing the current position of the sprite. The `collision` member variable is also a `Rectangle` object and is used to support rectangle collision detection. You'll see how `collision` is used later in today's lesson when you learn about the `setCollision` and `testCollision` methods.

The `zOrder` and `velocity` member variables simply store the Z-order and velocity of the sprite. The `bounds` member variable represents the boundary rectangle to which the sprite is bounded, while the `boundsAction` member variable is the bounds action that is taken when the sprite encounters the boundary.

The last member variable, `hidden`, is a boolean flag that determines whether the sprite is hidden. By setting this variable to `false`, the sprite is hidden from view. Its default setting is `true`, meaning that the sprite is visible.

The `Sprite` class has two constructors. The first constructor creates a `Sprite` without support for frame animation, meaning that it uses a single image to represent the sprite. The code for this constructor follows:

```
public Sprite(Component comp, Image img, Point pos, Point vel, int z,
  int ba) {
  component = comp;
  image = new Image[1];
  image[0] = img;
  setPosition(new Rectangle(pos.x, pos.y, img.getWidth(comp),
```

```
    img.getHeight(comp)));
  setVelocity(vel);
  frame = 0;
  frameInc = 0;
  frameDelay = frameTrigger = 0;
  zOrder = z;
  bounds = new Rectangle(0, 0, comp.size().width, comp.size().height);
  boundsAction = ba;
}
```

This constructor takes an image, a position, a velocity, a Z-order, and a boundary action as parameters. The second constructor takes an array of images and some additional information about the frame animations. The code for the second constructor follows:

```
public Sprite(Component comp, Image[] img, int f, int fi, int fd,
  Point pos, Point vel, int z, int ba) {
  component = comp;
  image = img;
  setPosition(new Rectangle(pos.x, pos.y, img[f].getWidth(comp),
    img[f].getHeight(comp)));
  setVelocity(vel);
  frame = f;
  frameInc = fi;
  frameDelay = frameTrigger = fd;
  zOrder = z;
  bounds = new Rectangle(0, 0, comp.size().width, comp.size().height);
  boundsAction = ba;
}
```

The additional information required of this constructor includes the current frame, frame increment, and frame delay.

WARNING

Because the frame parameter, f, used in the second Sprite constructor is actually used as an index into the array of frame images, make sure you always set it to a valid index when you create sprites using this constructor. In other words, never pass a frame value that is outside the bounds of the image array. In most cases you will use a frame value of 0, which alleviates the potential problem.

The Sprite class contains a number of access methods, which are simply interfaces to get and set certain member variables. These methods consist of one or two lines of code and are pretty self-explanatory. Check out the code for the getVelocity and setVelocity access methods to see what I mean about the access methods being self-explanatory:

```
public Point getVelocity() {
  return velocity;
}
```

```
public void setVelocity(Point vel)
{
  velocity = vel;
}
```

There are more access methods for getting and setting other member variables in Sprite, but they are just as straightforward as getVelocity and setVelocity. Rather than waste time on those, let's move on to some more interesting methods!

The incFrame method is the first Sprite method with any real substance:

```
protected void incFrame() {
  if ((frameDelay > 0) && (--frameTrigger <= 0)) {
    // Reset the frame trigger
    frameTrigger = frameDelay;

    // Increment the frame
    frame += frameInc;
    if (frame >= image.length)
      frame = 0;
    else if (frame < 0)
      frame = image.length - 1;
  }
}
```

incFrame is used to increment the current animation frame. It first checks the frameDelay and frameTrigger member variables to see whether the frame should actually be incremented. This check is what allows you to vary the frame animation speed for a sprite, which is done by changing the value of frameDelay. Larger values for frameDelay result in a slower animation speed. The current frame is incremented by adding frameInc to frame. frame is then checked to make sure that its value is within the bounds of the image array, because it is used later to index into the array when the frame image is drawn.

The setPosition methods set the position of the sprite. Their source code follows:

```
void setPosition(Rectangle pos) {
  position = pos;
  setCollision();
}

public void setPosition(Point pos) {
  position.move(pos.x, pos.y);
  setCollision();
}
```

Even though the sprite position is stored as a rectangle, the setPosition methods allow you to specify the sprite position as either a rectangle or a point. In the latter version, the position rectangle is simply moved to the specified point. After the position rectangle is moved, the collision rectangle is set with a call to setCollision. setCollision is the method that sets the collision rectangle for the sprite. The source code for setCollision follows:

24

```
protected void setCollision() {
  collision = position;
}
```

Notice that `setCollision` sets the collision rectangle equal to the position rectangle, which results in simple rectangle collision detection. Because there is no way to know what sprites will be shaped like, you leave it up to derived sprite classes to implement versions of `setCollision` with specific shrunken rectangle calculations. So to implement shrunken rectangle collision, you just calculate a smaller collision rectangle in `setCollision`.

This `isPointInside` method is used to test whether a point lies inside the sprite. The source code for `isPointInside` follows:

```
boolean isPointInside(Point pt) {
  return position.inside(pt.x, pt.y);
}
```

This method is handy for determining whether the user has clicked on a certain sprite. This is useful in applets where you want to be able to click on objects and move them around, such as a chess game. In a chess game, each piece would be a sprite, and you would use `isPointInside` to find out which piece the user clicked.

The method that does most of the work in `Sprite` is the `update` method, which is shown in Listing 24.1.

TYPE   **Listing 24.1. The `Sprite` class's `update` method.**

```
 1: public boolean update() {
 2:   // Increment the frame
 3:   incFrame();
 4:
 5:   // Update the position
 6:   Point pos = new Point(position.x, position.y);
 7:   pos.translate(velocity.x, velocity.y);
 8:
 9:   // Check the bounds
10:   // Wrap?
11:   if (boundsAction == Sprite.BA_WRAP) {
12:     if ((pos.x + position.width) < bounds.x)
13:       pos.x = bounds.x + bounds.width;
14:     else if (pos.x > (bounds.x + bounds.width))
15:       pos.x = bounds.x - position.width;
16:     if ((pos.y + position.height) < bounds.y)
17:       pos.y = bounds.y + bounds.height;
18:     else if (pos.y > (bounds.y + bounds.height))
19:       pos.y = bounds.y - position.height;
20:   }
21:   // Bounce?
22:   else if (boundsAction == Sprite.BA_BOUNCE) {
```

continues

Listing 24.1. continued

```
23:     boolean bounce = false;
24:     Point   vel = new Point(velocity.x, velocity.y);
25:     if (pos.x < bounds.x) {
26:       bounce = true;
27:       pos.x = bounds.x;
28:       vel.x = -vel.x;
29:     }
30:     else if ((pos.x + position.width) >
31:       (bounds.x + bounds.width)) {
32:       bounce = true;
33:       pos.x = bounds.x + bounds.width - position.width;
34:       vel.x = -vel.x;
35:     }
36:     if (pos.y < bounds.y) {
37:       bounce = true;
38:       pos.y = bounds.y;
39:       vel.y = -vel.y;
40:     }
41:     else if ((pos.y + position.height) >
42:       (bounds.y + bounds.height)) {
43:       bounce = true;
44:       pos.y = bounds.y + bounds.height - position.height;
45:       vel.y = -vel.y;
46:     }
47:     if (bounce)
48:       setVelocity(vel);
49:   }
50:   // Die?
51:   else if (boundsAction == Sprite.BA_DIE) {
52:     if ((pos.x + position.width) < bounds.x || pos.x > bounds.width ||
53:       (pos.y + position.height) < bounds.y || pos.y > bounds.height) {
54:       return true;
55:     }
56:   }
57:   // Stop (default)
58:   else {
59:     if (pos.x  < bounds.x ||
60:       pos.x > (bounds.x + bounds.width - position.width)) {
61:       pos.x = Math.max(bounds.x, Math.min(pos.x,
62:         bounds.x + bounds.width - position.width));
63:       setVelocity(new Point(0, 0));
64:     }
65:     if (pos.y  < bounds.y ||
66:       pos.y > (bounds.y + bounds.height - position.height)) {
67:       pos.y = Math.max(bounds.y, Math.min(pos.y,
68:         bounds.y + bounds.height - position.height));
69:       setVelocity(new Point(0, 0));
70:     }
71:   }
72:   setPosition(pos);
73:
74:   return false;
75: }
```

24

ANALYSIS The `update` method handles the task of updating the animation frame and position of the sprite. `update` begins by updating the animation frame with a call to `incFrame`. The position of the sprite is then updated by translating the position rectangle based on the velocity. You can think of the position rectangle as being slid a distance determined by the velocity.

The rest of the code in `update` is devoted to handling the various bounds actions. The first bounds action flag, `BA_WRAP`, causes the sprite to wrap around to the other side of the bounds rectangle. The `BA_BOUNCE` flag causes the sprite to bounce if it encounters a boundary. The `BA_DIE` flag causes the sprite to die if it encounters a boundary. Finally, the default flag, `BA_STOP`, causes the sprite to stop when it encounters a boundary.

Notice that `update` finishes by returning a boolean value. This boolean value specifies whether the sprite should be killed, which provides a means for sprites to be destroyed when the `BA_DIE` bounds action is defined. If this seems a little strange, keep in mind that the only way to get rid of a sprite is to remove it from the sprite vector. I know, you haven't learned much about the sprite vector yet, but trust me on this one. Since individual sprites know nothing about the sprite vector, they can't directly tell it what to do. So the return value of the `update` method is used to communicate to the sprite vector whether a sprite needs to be killed. A return of `true` means that the sprite is to be killed, and `false` means let it be.

NOTE
> The sprite vector is the list of all sprites currently in the sprite system. It is the sprite vector that is responsible for managing all the sprites, including adding, removing, drawing, and detecting collisions between them.

Judging by its size, it's not hard to figure out that the `update` method is itself the bulk of the code in the `Sprite` class. This is logical, though, because the `update` method is where all the action takes place; `update` handles all the details of updating the animation frame and position of the sprite, along with carrying out different bounds actions.

Another important method in the `Sprite` class is `draw`, whose source code follows:

```
public void draw(Graphics g) {
  // Draw the current frame
  if (!hidden)
    g.drawImage(image[frame], position.x, position.y, component);
}
```

After wading through the `update` method, the `draw` method looks like a piece of cake! It simply uses the `drawImage` method to draw the current sprite frame image to the `Graphics` object that is passed in. Notice that the `drawImage` method requires the image, XY position, and component (`ImageObserver`) to carry this out.

The last method in `Sprite` is `testCollision`, which is used to check for collisions between sprites:

```
protected boolean testCollision(Sprite test) {
  // Check for collision with another sprite
  if (test != this)
    return collision.intersects(test.getCollision());
  return false;
}
```

The sprite to test for collision is passed in the `test` parameter. The test simply involves checking whether the collision rectangles intersect. If so, `testCollision` returns `true`. `testCollision` isn't all that useful within the context of a single sprite, but it is very handy when you put together the `SpriteVector` class, which you are going to do next.

The `SpriteVector` Class

At this point, you have a `Sprite` class with some pretty impressive features, but you don't really have any way to manage it. Of course, you could go ahead and create an applet with some `Sprite` objects, but how would they be able to interact with each other? The answer to this question is the `SpriteVector` class, which handles all the details of maintaining a list of sprites and handling the interactions between them.

The `SpriteVector` class is derived from the `Vector` class, which is a standard class provided in the `java.util` package. The `Vector` class models a growable array of objects. In this case, the `SpriteVector` class is used as a container for a growable array of `Sprite` objects.

The `SpriteVector` class has only one member variable, `background`, which is a `Background` object:

```
protected Background background;
```

This `Background` object represents the background on which the sprites appear. It is initialized in the constructor for `SpriteVector`, like this:

```
public SpriteVector(Background back) {
  super(50, 10);
  background = back;
}
```

The constructor for `SpriteVector` simply takes a `Background` object as its only parameter. You'll learn about the `Background` class a little later today. Notice that the constructor for `SpriteVector` calls the `Vector` parent class constructor and sets the default storage capacity (`50`) and amount to increment the storage capacity (`10`) if the vector needs to grow.

`SpriteVector` contains two access methods for getting and setting the `background` member variable, which follow:

```
public Background getBackground() {
  return background;
}

public void setBackground(Background back) {
  background = back;
}
```

These methods are useful whenever you have an animation that needs to have a changing background. To change the background, you simply call setBackground and pass in the new Background object.

The getEmptyPosition method is used by the SpriteVector class to help position new sprites. Listing 24.2 contains the source code for getEmptyPosition.

TYPE **Listing 24.2. The** SpriteVector **class's** getEmptyPosition **method.**

```
 1: public Point getEmptyPosition(Dimension sSize) {
 2:   Rectangle pos = new Rectangle(0, 0, sSize.width, sSize.height);
 3:   Random    rand = new Random(System.currentTimeMillis());
 4:   boolean   empty = false;
 5:   int       numTries = 0;
 6:
 7:   // Look for an empty position
 8:   while (!empty && numTries++ < 50) {
 9:     // Get a random position
10:     pos.x = Math.abs(rand.nextInt() %
11:       background.getSize().width);
12:     pos.y = Math.abs(rand.nextInt() %
13:       background.getSize().height);
14:
15:     // Iterate through sprites, checking if position is empty
16:     boolean collision = false;
17:     for (int i = 0; i < size(); i++) {
18:       Rectangle testPos = ((Sprite)elementAt(i)).getPosition();
19:       if (pos.intersects(testPos)) {
20:         collision = true;
21:         break;
22:       }
23:     }
24:     empty = !collision;
25:   }
26:   return new Point(pos.x, pos.y);
27: }
```

ANALYSIS getEmptyPosition is a method whose importance might not be readily apparent to you right now; it is used to find an empty physical position in which to place a new sprite in the sprite vector. This doesn't mean the position of the sprite in the array; rather, it means its physical position on the screen. This method is useful when you want to randomly place multiple sprites on the screen. By using getEmptyPosition, you eliminate the possibility of placing new sprites on top of existing sprites.

The isPointInside method in SpriteVector is similar to the version of isPointInside in Sprite, except it goes through the entire sprite vector, checking each sprite. Check out the source code for it:

```
Sprite isPointInside(Point pt) {
  // Iterate backward through the sprites, testing each
  for (int i = (size() - 1); i >= 0; i--) {
    Sprite s = (Sprite)elementAt(i);
    if (s.isPointInside(pt))
      return s;
  }
  return null;
}
```

If the point passed in the parameter pt lies in a sprite, isPointInside returns the sprite. Notice that the sprite vector is searched in reverse, meaning that the last sprite is checked before the first. The sprites are searched in this order for a very important reason: Z-order. The sprites are stored in the sprite vector sorted in ascending Z-order, which specifies their depth on the screen. Therefore, sprites near the beginning of the list are sometimes concealed by sprites near the end of the list. If you want to check for a point lying within a sprite, it makes sense to check the topmost sprites first—that is, the sprites with larger Z-order values. If this sounds a little confusing, don't worry; you'll learn more about Z-order later today when you get to the add method.

As in Sprite, the update method is the key method in SpriteVector because it handles updating all the sprites. Listing 24.3 contains the source code for update.

TYPE   **Listing 24.3. The SpriteVector class's update method.**

```
 1: public void update() {
 2:    // Iterate through sprites, updating each
 3:    Sprite    s, sHit;
 4:    Rectangle lastPos;
 5:    for (int i = 0; i < size(); ) {
 6:      // Update the sprite
 7:      s = (Sprite)elementAt(i);
 8:      lastPos = new Rectangle(s.getPosition().x, s.getPosition().y,
 9:        s.getPosition().width, s.getPosition().height);
10:      boolean kill = s.update();
11:
12:      // Should the sprite die?
13:      if (kill) {
14:        removeElementAt(i);
15:        continue;
16:      }
17:
18:      // Test for collision
19:      int iHit = testCollision(s);
20:      if (iHit >= 0)
21:        if (collision(i, iHit))
```

24

```
22:          s.setPosition(lastPos);
23:      i++;
24:    }
25: }
```

ANALYSIS   The update method iterates through the sprites, calling Sprite's update method on each one. It then checks the return value of update to see if the sprite is to be killed. If the return value is true, the sprite is removed from the sprite vector. Finally, testCollision is called to see whether a collision has occurred between sprites. (You get the whole scoop on testCollision in a moment.) If a collision has occurred, the old position of the collided sprite is restored and the collision method is called.

The collision method is used to handle collisions between two sprites:

```
protected boolean collision(int i, int iHit) {
  // Do nothing
  return false;
}
```

The collision method is responsible for handling any actions that result from a collision between sprites. The action in this case is to simply do nothing, which allows sprites to pass over each other with nothing happening. This method is where you provide specific collision actions in derived sprites. For example, in a weather-simulator animation, you might want clouds to cause lightning when they collide.

The testCollision method is used to test for collisions between a sprite and the rest of the sprites in the sprite vector:

```
protected int testCollision(Sprite test) {
  // Check for collision with other sprites
  Sprite  s;
  for (int i = 0; i < size(); i++)
  {
    s = (Sprite)elementAt(i);
    if (s == test)  // don't check itself
      continue;
    if (test.testCollision(s))
      return i;
  }
  return -1;
}
```

The sprite to be tested is passed in the test parameter. The sprites are then iterated through, and the testCollision method in Sprite is called for each. Notice that testCollision isn't called on the test sprite if the iteration refers to the same sprite. To understand the significance of this code, consider the effect of passing testCollision the same sprite the method is being called on; you would be checking to see if a sprite was colliding with itself, which would always return true. If a collision is detected, the Sprite object that has been hit is returned from testCollision.

The draw method handles drawing the background, as well as drawing all the sprites:

```
public void draw(Graphics g) {
  // Draw the background
  background.draw(g);

  // Iterate through sprites, drawing each
  for (int i = 0; i < size(); i++)
    ((Sprite)elementAt(i)).draw(g);
}
```

The background is drawn with a simple call to the draw method of the Background object. The sprites are then drawn by iterating through the sprite vector and calling the draw method for each.

The add method is probably the trickiest method in the SpriteVector class. Listing 24.4 contains the source code for add.

TYPE **Listing 24.4. The SpriteVector class's add method.**

```
 1: public int add(Sprite s) {
 2:   // Use a binary search to find the right location to insert the
 3:   // new sprite (based on z-order)
 4:   int   l = 0, r = size(), i = 0;
 5:   int   z = s.getZOrder(),
 6:         zTest = z + 1;
 7:   while (r > l) {
 8:     i = (l + r) / 2;
 9:     zTest = ((Sprite)elementAt(i)).getZOrder();
10:     if (z < zTest)
11:       r = i;
12:     else
13:       l = i + 1;
14:     if (z == zTest)
15:       break;
16:   }
17:   if (z >= zTest)
18:     i++;
19:
20:   insertElementAt(s, i);
21:   return i;
22: }
```

ANALYSIS The add method handles adding new sprites to the sprite vector. The catch is that the sprite vector must always be sorted according to Z-order. Why is this? Remember that Z-order is the depth at which sprites appear on the screen. The illusion of depth is established by the order in which the sprites are drawn. This works because sprites drawn later are drawn on top of sprites drawn earlier, and therefore appear to be at a higher depth. Therefore, sorting the sprite vector by ascending Z-order and then drawing them in that order is an effective way to provide the illusion of depth. The add method uses a binary search to find the right spot to add new sprites so that the sprite vector remains sorted by Z-order.

24

That wraps up the SpriteVector class! You now have not only a powerful Sprite class, but also a SpriteVector class for managing and providing interactivity between sprites. All that's left is putting these classes to work in a real applet.

The Background Classes

Actually, there is some unfinished business to deal with before you try out the sprite classes. I'm referring to the Background class used in SpriteVector. While you're at it, let's go ahead and look at a few different background classes that you might find handy.

Background

If you recall, I mentioned earlier today that the Background class provides the overhead of managing a background for the sprites to appear on top of. The source code for the Background class is shown in Listing 24.5.

BD
3

TYPE **Listing 24.5. The Background class.**

```
 1: public class Background {
 2:    protected Component component;
 3:    protected Dimension size;
 4:
 5:    public Background(Component comp) {
 6:       component = comp;
 7:       size = comp.size();
 8:    }
 9:
10:    public Dimension getSize() {
11:       return size;
12:    }
13:
14:    public void draw(Graphics g) {
15:       // Fill with component color
16:       g.setColor(component.getBackground());
17:       g.fillRect(0, 0, size.width, size.height);
18:       g.setColor(Color.black);
19:    }
20: }
```

ANALYSIS As you can see, the Background class is pretty simple. It basically provides a clean abstraction of the background for the sprites. The two member variables maintained by Background are used to keep up with the associated component and dimensions for the background. The constructor for Background takes a Component object as its only parameter. This Component object is typically the applet window, and it serves to provide the dimensions of the background and the default background color.

The getSize method is an access method that simply returns the size of the background. The draw method fills the background with the default background color, as defined by the component member variable.

You're probably thinking that this Background object isn't too exciting. Couldn't you just stick this drawing code directly into SpriteVector's draw method? Yes, you could, but then you would miss out on the benefits provided by the more derived background classes, ColorBackground and ImageBackground, which are explained next. The background classes are a good example of how object-oriented design makes Java code much cleaner and easier to extend.

ColorBackground

The ColorBackground class provides a background that can be filled with any color. Listing 24.6 contains the source code for the ColorBackground class.

TYPE **Listing 24.6. The ColorBackground class.**

```
 1: public class ColorBackground extends Background {
 2:    protected Color color;
 3:
 4:    public ColorBackground(Component comp, Color c) {
 5:       super(comp);
 6:       color = c;
 7:    }
 8:
 9:    public Color getColor() {
10:       return color;
11:    }
12:
13:    public void setColor(Color c) {
14:       color = c;
15:    }
16:
17:    public void draw(Graphics g) {
18:       // Fill with color
19:       g.setColor(color);
20:       g.fillRect(0, 0, size.width, size.height);
21:       g.setColor(Color.black);
22:    }
23: }
```

ANALYSIS ColorBackground adds a single member variable, color, which is a Color object. This member variable holds the color used to fill the background. The constructor for ColorBackground takes Component and Color objects as parameters. There are two access methods for getting and setting the color member variable. The draw method for ColorBackground is very similar to the draw method in Background, except that the color member variable is used as the fill color.

24

ImageBackground

A more interesting Background derived class is ImageBackground, which uses an image as the background. Listing 24.7 contains the source code for the ImageBackground class.

TYPE **Listing 24.7. The ImageBackground class.**

```
 1: public class ImageBackground extends Background {
 2:    protected Image image;
 3:
 4:    public ImageBackground(Component comp, Image img) {
 5:       super(comp);
 6:       image = img;
 7:    }
 8:
 9:    public Image getImage() {
10:       return image;
11:    }
12:
13:    public void setImage(Image img) {
14:       image = img;
15:    }
16:
17:    public void draw(Graphics g) {
18:       // Draw background image
19:       g.drawImage(image, 0, 0, component);
20:    }
21: }
```

ANALYSIS The ImageBackground class adds a single member variable, image, which is an Image object. This member variable holds the image to be used as the background. Not surprisingly, the constructor for ImageBackground takes Component and Image objects as parameters. There are two access methods for getting and setting the image member variable. The draw method for ImageBackground simply draws the background image using the drawImage method of the passed Graphics object.

Sample Applet: Sharks

It's time to take all the hard work that you've put into the sprite classes and see what it amounts to. Figure 24.4 shows a screen shot of the Sharks applet, which shows off the sprite classes you've worked so hard on all day. The complete source code, images, and executable classes for the Sharks applet are on the accompanying CD-ROM.

Figure 24.4.

The Sharks applet.

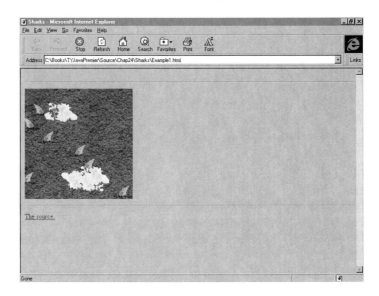

The Sharks applet uses a `SpriteVector` object to manage a group of hungry shark `Sprite` objects. This object, `sv`, is one of the `Shark` applet class's member variables, which follow:

```
private Image          offImage, back;
private Image[]        leftShark = new Image[2];
private Image[]        rightShark = new Image[2];
private Image[]        clouds = new Image[2];
private Graphics       offGrfx;
private Thread         animate;
private MediaTracker   tracker;
private SpriteVector   sv;
private int            delay = 83; // 12 fps
private Random         rand = new Random(System.currentTimeMillis());
```

The `Image` member variables in the `Sharks` class represent the offscreen buffer, the background image, the shark images, and some cloud images. The `Graphics` member variable, `offGrfx`, holds the graphics context for the offscreen buffer image. The `Thread` member variable, `animate`, is used to hold the thread where the animation takes place. The `MediaTracker` member variable, `tracker`, is used to track the various images as they are being loaded. The `SpriteVector` member variable, `sv`, holds the sprite vector for the applet. The integer (`int`) member variable, `delay`, determines the animation speed of the sprites. Finally, the `Random` member variable, `rand`, is used to generate random numbers throughout the applet.

Notice that the `delay` member variable is set to `83`. The `delay` member variable specifies the amount of time (in milliseconds) that elapses between each frame of animation. You can determine the frame rate by inverting the value of `delay`, which results in a frame rate of about 12 frames per second (fps) in this case. This frame rate is pretty much the minimum rate required for fluid animation, such as sprite animation. You'll see how `delay` is used to establish the frame rate in a moment when you get into the details of the `run` method.

The `Sharks` class's `init` method loads all the images and registers them with the media tracker:

```
public void init() {
  // Load and track the images
  tracker = new MediaTracker(this);
  back = getImage(getCodeBase(), "Water.gif");
  tracker.addImage(back, 0);
  leftShark[0] = getImage(getCodeBase(), "LShark0.gif");
  tracker.addImage(leftShark[0], 0);
  leftShark[1] = getImage(getCodeBase(), "LShark1.gif");
  tracker.addImage(leftShark[1], 0);
  rightShark[0] = getImage(getCodeBase(), "RShark0.gif");
  tracker.addImage(rightShark[0], 0);
  rightShark[1] = getImage(getCodeBase(), "RShark1.gif");
  tracker.addImage(rightShark[1], 0);
  clouds[0] = getImage(getCodeBase(), "SmCloud.gif");
  tracker.addImage(clouds[0], 0);
  clouds[1] = getImage(getCodeBase(), "LgCloud.gif");
  tracker.addImage(clouds[1], 0);
}
```

Tracking the images is necessary because you want to wait until all the images have been loaded before you start the animation. The `start` and `stop` methods are standard thread-handler methods:

```
public void start() {
  if (animate == null) {
    animate = new Thread(this);
    animate.start();
  }
}

public void stop() {
  if (animate != null) {
    animate.stop();
    animate = null;
  }
}
```

The `start` method is responsible for initializing and starting the animation thread. Likewise, the `stop` method stops the animation thread and cleans up after it.

WARNING

If for some reason you're thinking that stopping the animation thread in the `stop` method isn't really that big of a deal, think again. The `stop` method is called whenever a user leaves the Web page containing an applet, in which case it is of great importance that you stop all threads executing in the applet. So always make sure to stop threads in the `stop` method of your applets.

The run method is the heart of the animation thread. Listing 24.8 shows the source code for run.

Listing 24.8. The Sharks class's run method.

```
 1: public void run() {
 2:   try {
 3:     tracker.waitForID(0);
 4:   }
 5:   catch (InterruptedException e) {
 6:     return;
 7:   }
 8:
 9:   // Create the sprite vector
10:   sv = new SpriteVector(new ImageBackground(this, back));
11:
12:   // Create and add the sharks
13:   for (int i = 0; i < 8; i++) {
14:     boolean left = (rand.nextInt() % 2 == 0);
15:     Point pos = new Point(Math.abs(rand.nextInt() % size().width),
16:       (i + 1) * 4 + i * leftShark[0].getHeight(this));
17:     Sprite s = new Sprite(this, left ? leftShark : rightShark, 0, 1, 3,
18:       pos, new Point((Math.abs(rand.nextInt() % 3) + 1) * (left ? -1 : 1),
19:       0), 0, Sprite.BA_WRAP);
20:     sv.add(s);
21:   }
22:
23:   // Create and add the clouds
24:   Sprite s = new Sprite(this, clouds[0], new Point(Math.abs(rand.nextInt()
25:     % size().width), Math.abs(rand.nextInt() % size().height)), new
26:     Point(Math.abs(rand.nextInt() % 5) + 1, rand.nextInt() % 3), 1,
27:     Sprite.BA_WRAP);
28:   sv.add(s);
29:   s = new Sprite(this, clouds[1], new Point(Math.abs(rand.nextInt()
30:     % size().width), Math.abs(rand.nextInt() % size().height)), new
31:     Point(Math.abs(rand.nextInt() % 5) - 5, rand.nextInt() % 3), 2,
32:     Sprite.BA_WRAP);
33:   sv.add(s);
34:
35:   // Update everything
36:   long t = System.currentTimeMillis();
37:   while (Thread.currentThread() == animate) {
38:     // Update the sprites
39:     sv.update();
40:     repaint();
41:     try {
42:       t += delay;
43:       Thread.sleep(Math.max(0, t - System.currentTimeMillis()));
44:     }
45:     catch (InterruptedException e) {
46:       break;
47:     }
48:   }
49: }
```

24

ANALYSIS The run method first waits for the images to finish loading by calling the waitForID method of the MediaTracker object. After the images have finished loading, the SpriteVector is created. Eight different shark Sprite objects are then created with varying positions on the screen. Also notice that the direction each shark is moving is chosen randomly, as are the shark images, which also reflect the direction. These shark sprites are then added to the sprite vector.

Once the sharks have been added, a couple cloud sprites are added just to make things a little more interesting. Notice that the Z-order of the clouds is greater than that of the sharks. The Z-order is the next-to-last parameter in the Sprite constructor, and is set to 1 and 2 for the clouds, and 0 for the sharks. This results in the clouds appearing on top of the sharks, as they should. Also, the cloud with a Z-order of 2 will appear to be above the cloud with a Z-order of 1 if they should pass each other.

After creating and adding the clouds, a while loop is entered that handles updating the SpriteVector and forcing the applet to repaint itself. By forcing a repaint, you are causing the applet to redraw the sprites in their newly updated states.

Before you move on, it's important to understand how the frame rate is controlled in the run method. The call to currentTimeMillis returns the current system time in milliseconds. You aren't really concerned with what absolute time this method is returning, because you are only using it here to measure relative time. After updating the sprites and forcing a redraw, the delay value is added to the time you just retrieved. At this point, you have updated the frame and calculated a time value that is delay milliseconds into the future. The next step is to tell the animation thread to sleep an amount of time equal to the difference between the future time value you just calculated and the present time.

This probably sounds pretty confusing, so let me clarify things a little. The sleep method is used to make a thread sleep for a number of milliseconds, as determined by the value passed in its only parameter. You might think that you could just pass delay to sleep and things would be fine. This approach technically would work, but it would have a certain degree of error. The reason is that a finite amount of time passes between updating the sprites and putting the thread to sleep. Without accounting for this lost time, the actual delay between frames wouldn't be equal to the value of delay. The solution is to check the time before and after the sprites are updated, and then reflect the difference in the delay value passed to the sleep method. And that's how the frame rate is managed!

The update method is where the sprites are actually drawn to the applet window:

```
public void update(Graphics g) {
  // Create the offscreen graphics context
  if (offGrfx == null) {
    offImage = createImage(size().width, size().height);
    offGrfx = offImage.getGraphics();
  }
```

```
  // Draw the sprites
  sv.draw(offGrfx);

  // Draw the image onto the screen
  g.drawImage(offImage, 0, 0, null);
}
```

The update method uses double buffering to eliminate flicker in the sprite animation. By using double buffering, you eliminate flicker and allow for speedier animations. The offImage member variable contains the offscreen buffer image used for drawing the next animation frame. The offGrfx member variable contains the graphics context associated with the offscreen buffer image.

In update, the offscreen buffer is first created as an Image object whose dimensions match those of the applet window. It is important that the offscreen buffer be exactly the same size as the applet window. The graphics context associated with the buffer is then retrieved using the getGraphics method of Image. After the offscreen buffer is initialized, all you really have to do is tell the SpriteVector object to draw itself to the buffer. Remember that the SpriteVector object takes care of drawing the background and all the sprites. This is accomplished with a simple call to SpriteVector's draw method. The offscreen buffer is then drawn to the applet window using the drawImage method.

Even though the update method takes care of drawing everything, it is still important to implement the paint method. As a matter of fact, the paint method is very useful in providing the user visual feedback regarding the state of the images used by the applet. Listing 24.9 shows the source code for paint.

TYPE   **Listing 24.9. The Sharks class's paint method.**

```
 1: public void paint(Graphics g) {
 2:   if ((tracker.statusID(0, true) & MediaTracker.ERRORED) != 0) {
 3:     // Draw the error rectangle
 4:     g.setColor(Color.red);
 5:     g.fillRect(0, 0, size().width, size().height);
 6:     return;
 7:   }
 8:   if ((tracker.statusID(0, true) & MediaTracker.COMPLETE) != 0) {
 9:     // Draw the offscreen image
10:     g.drawImage(offImage, 0, 0, null);
11:   }
12:   else {
13:     // Draw the title message (while the images load)
14:     Font        f1 = new Font("TimesRoman", Font.BOLD, 28),
15:                 f2 = new Font("Helvetica", Font.PLAIN, 16);
16:     FontMetrics fm1 = g.getFontMetrics(f1),
17:                 fm2 = g.getFontMetrics(f2);
18:     String      s1 = new String("Sharks"),
19:                 s2 = new String("Loading images...");
20:     g.setFont(f1);
```

24

```
21:       g.drawString(s1, (size().width - fm1.stringWidth(s1)) / 2,
22:         ((size().height - fm1.getHeight()) / 2) + fm1.getAscent());
23:       g.setFont(f2);
24:       g.drawString(s2, (size().width - fm2.stringWidth(s2)) / 2,
25:         size().height - fm2.getHeight() - fm2.getAscent());
26:     }
27: }
```

 Using the media tracker, paint notifies the user that the images are still loading, or that an error has occurred while loading them. Check out Figure 24.5, which shows the Sharks applet while the images are loading.

Figure 24.5.

The Sharks applet while the images are loading.

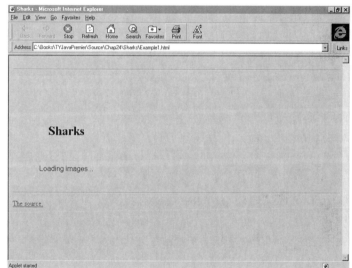

If an error occurs while loading one of the images, the paint method displays a red rectangle over the entire applet window area. If the images have finished loading, paint just draws the latest offscreen buffer to the applet window. If the images haven't finished loading, paint displays the title of the applet and a message stating that the images are still loading (see Figure 24.5). Displaying the title and status message consists of creating the appropriate fonts and centering the text within the applet window.

That's all it takes to get the sprite classes working together. It might seem like a lot of code at first, but think about all that the applet is undertaking. The applet is responsible for loading and keeping track of all the images used by the sprites, as well as the background and offscreen buffer. If the images haven't finished loading, or if an error occurs while loading, the applet has to notify the user accordingly. Additionally, the applet is responsible for maintaining a consistent frame rate and drawing the sprites using double buffering. Even with these responsibilities, the applet is still benefiting a great deal from the functionality provided by the sprite classes.

You can use this applet as a template applet for other applets you create that use the sprite classes. You now have all the functionality required to manage both cast- and frame-based animation, as well as provide support for interactivity among sprites via collision detection.

Summary

In today's lesson you have learned all about animation, including the two major types of animation: frame based and cast based. Adding to this theory, you have learned that sprite animation is where the action really is. You have seen firsthand how to develop a powerful duo of sprite classes for implementing sprite animation, including a few support classes to make things easier. You have put the sprite classes to work in a sample applet that involves relatively little additional overhead.

You now have all you need to start creating your own Java sprite animations with ease. If that's not enough for you, just wait until tomorrow's lesson, which deals with another advanced graphics topic: image filters.

Q&A

Q What's the big deal with sprites?

A The big deal is that sprites provide a very flexible approach to implementing animation. Additionally, using sprites you can take advantage of both fundamental types of animation: frame-based animation and cast-based animation.

Q What exactly is Z-order, and do I really need it?

A Z-order is the depth of a sprite relative to other sprites; sprites with higher Z-order values appear to be on top of sprites with lower Z-order values. You only need Z-order if you have sprites that overlap each other, in which case Z-order will determine which one conceals the other.

Q Why bother with the different types of collision detection?

A The different types of collision detection (rectangle, shrunken rectangle, and image data) provide different trade-offs in regard to performance and accuracy. Rectangle and shrunken rectangle collision detection provide a very high-performance solution, but with moderate to poor accuracy. Image data-collision detection is perfect when it comes to accuracy, but it can bring your applet to its knees in the performance department, not to mention give you a headache trying to make it work.

24

Q Why do I need the `SpriteVector` class? Isn't the `Sprite` class enough?

A The `Sprite` class is nice, but it represents only a single sprite. To enable multiple sprites to interact with each other, you must have a second entity that acts as a storage unit for the sprites. The `SpriteVector` class solves this problem by doubling as a container for all the sprites as well as a means of detecting collisions between sprites.

BD
3

Day **25**

Fun with Image Filters

by Michael Morrison

As you learned both yesterday and earlier in this book, Java provides lots of neat ways to work with graphical images. One of Java's more interesting image-handling features is its support for image filters, which allow you to alter the individual pixels of an image according to a particular algorithm. Image filters can range from simple effects such as adjusting the brightness of an image to more advanced effects such as embossing.

At the heart of Java's graphics and imaging are Java color models. Today's lesson begins by looking into what a color model is, along with how color models affect image handling and Java graphics in general. You'll then move on to learn about Java image filters and how they are used to manipulate graphical images. Java provides a variety of image filter classes that interact together to form a framework for easily filtering graphical images. You can extend the standard Java image filtering classes and build your own image filters to perform just about any type of image processing you can imagine. You'll finish today's lesson by implementing your own image filters.

So today's lesson covers the following primary topics:

- ☐ The basics of color
- ☐ Color models
- ☐ Image filters
- ☐ Writing your own image filters

I think you'll find that image filters are a very interesting and powerful feature of Java that haven't received as much attention as they deserve. Granted, image filters don't share the wide applicability of some other aspects of Java, but they can be fun to tinker with and will inevitably be useful in some specialized applets.

The Basics of Color

Everything graphical in Java, including image filters, begins with the concept of color. I know, you've probably heard something about color before, but maybe not in the way I'm about to describe. You see, when I talk about the notion of color, I mean a computer's notion of color. In other words, I want to briefly take a look at how color is represented on a computer, since it will ultimately give you more insight into how image filters work.

Since modern computer environments are highly graphical, it is imperative that computers know how to process and display information in color. Although most computer operating systems have some degree of platform-dependent handling of color, they all share a common approach to the general representation of colors. Knowing that all data in a computer is ultimately stored in a binary form, it stands to reason that physical colors are somehow mapped to binary values, or numbers, in the computer domain. The question is, how are colors mapped to numbers?

One way to come up with numeric representations of colors would be to start at one end of the color spectrum and assign a number to each color until you reach the other end. This approach solves the problem of representing a color as a number, but it doesn't provide any way to handle the mixing of colors. As anyone who has experienced the joy of Play-Doh can tell you, colors react in different ways when combined with each other. The way colors mix to form other colors goes back to physics, which is a little beyond this discussion. The point is that a computer color system needs to be able to handle mixing colors with accurate, predictable results.

The best place to look for a solution to the color problem is a color computer monitor. A color monitor has three electron guns: red, green, and blue. The output from these three guns converge on each pixel of the screen, exciting phosphors to produce the appropriate color (see

Figure 25.1). The combined intensities of each gun determine the resulting pixel color. This convergence of different colors from the monitor guns is very similar to the convergence of different colored Play-Doh. The primary difference is that monitors use only these three colors (red, green, and blue) to come up with every possible color that can be represented on a computer. (Actually, the biggest difference is that Play-Doh can't display high-resolution computer graphics, but that's another discussion.)

Figure 25.1.

Electron guns in a color monitor converging to create a unique color.

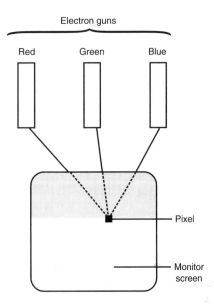

Knowing that monitors form unique colors by using varying intensities of the colors red, green, and blue, you might be thinking that a good solution to the color problem would be to provide an intensity value for each of these primary colors. This is exactly how computers model color. Computers represent different colors by combining the numeric intensities of the primary colors red, green, and blue. This color system is known as RGB (red, green, blue) and is fully supported by Java.

NEW TERM   *RGB* is the primary color system used by Java and stands for red, green, blue.

Although RGB is the most popular computer color system in use, there are others. Another popular color system is HSB, which stands for hue, saturation, brightness. In this system, colors are defined by varying degrees of hue, saturation, and brightness. The HSB color system is also supported by Java.

You already learned about Java's support for color on Day 9, "Graphics, Fonts, and Color." Just so you won't think I'm repeating what you've already learned, understand that this discussion of color is meant to lay more complete groundwork for the advanced issues of using color that are a big part of Java image filtering.

Color Images in Java

Bitmapped color images are composed of pixels that describe the colors at each location of an image. Each pixel in an image has a specific color that is usually described using the RGB color system. Java provides support for working with 32-bit images, which means that each pixel in an image is described using 32 bits. The red, green, and blue components of a pixel's color are stored in these 32 bits, along with an alpha component. The alpha component of a pixel refers to the transparency or opaqueness of the pixel.

 A *pixel* is the smallest graphical component of an image and is assigned a particular color.

 The *alpha component* of a pixel refers to the transparency or opaqueness of the pixel.

A 32-bit Java image pixel is therefore composed of red, green, blue, and alpha components. By default, these four components are packed into a 32-bit pixel value, as shown in Figure 25.2. Notice that each component is described by 8 bits (a byte), yielding possible values between 0 and 255 for each. These components are packed into the 32-bit pixel value from high-order byte to low-order byte in the following order: alpha, red, green, and blue. It is possible for the pixel components to be packed differently, but this is the default pixel storage method used in Java.

Figure 25.2.

The four components of a pixel in a 32-bit Java image.

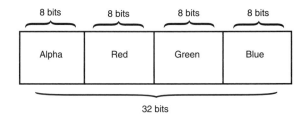

A color component value of 0 means the component is absent, and a value of 255 means it is maxed out. If all three color components are 0, the resulting pixel color is black. Likewise, if all three components are 255, the color is white. If the red component is 255 and the others are 0, the resulting color is pure red.

The alpha component describes the transparency of a pixel, independent of the color components. An alpha value of 0 means a pixel is completely transparent (invisible), and an alpha value of 255 means a pixel is completely opaque. Values between 0 and 255 enable the background color to show through a pixel in varying degrees.

The color components of a Java image are encapsulated in a simple class called Color. The Color class is a member of the java.awt package and represents the three primary color components red, green, and blue. This class is useful because it provides a clean abstraction for representing color, along with useful methods for extracting and modifying the primary components. The Color class also contains predefined constant members representing many popular colors.

Color Models

In Java, pixel colors are managed through color models. Java color models provide an important abstraction that enables Java to work with images of different formats in a similar fashion. More specifically, a color model is a Java object that provides methods for translating from pixel values to the corresponding red, green, and blue color components of an image. At first, this may seem like a trivial chore, knowing that pixel color components are packed neatly into a 32-bit value. However, there are different types of color models reflecting different methods of maintaining pixel colors. The two types of color models supported by Java are direct color models and index color models.

NEW TERM   A *color model* is an abstraction that provides a means to convert pixel color values to absolute colors.

Color models are used extensively in the internal implementations of the various Java image processing classes. What does this mean to you, the ever-practical Java programmer? It means that by understanding color models you know a great deal about the internal workings of color in the Java graphics system. Without fully understanding color models and how they work, you would no doubt run into difficulties when trying to work with the advanced graphics and image-processing classes provided by Java.

Direct Color Models

Direct color models are based on the earlier description of pixels, where each pixel contains specific color and alpha components. Direct color models provide methods for translating these types of pixels into their corresponding color and alpha components. Typically, direct color models extract the appropriate components from the 32-bit pixel value using bit masks.

TECHNICAL NOTE

A *bit mask* is a binary code used to extract specific bits out of a numeric value. The bits are extracted by bitwise ANDing the mask with the value. Masks themselves are typically specified in hexadecimal. For example, to mask out the low-order word of a 32-bit value, you use the mask 0x0000FFFF.

Index Color Models

Index color models work differently than direct color models. In fact, index color models work with pixels containing completely different information than you've learned thus far. Pixels in an image using an index color model don't contain the alpha and RGB components like the pixels used in a direct color model. An index color model pixel contains an index into an array of fixed colors (see Figure 25.3). This array of colors is called a *color map*.

 A *color map* is a list of colors referenced by an image using an index color model. Color maps are also sometimes referred to as *palettes*.

Figure 25.3.

An index color model pixel and its associated color map.

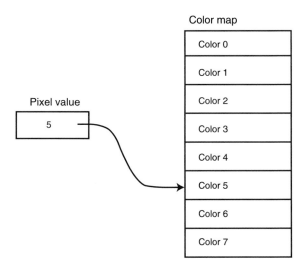

An example of an image that uses an index color model is a 256-color image. 256-color images use 8 bits to describe each pixel, which doesn't leave much room for RGB components, let alone an alpha component. Rather than try to cram these components into 8 bits, 256-color pixels store an 8-bit index into a color map. The color map itself has 256 color entries that each contain RGB and alpha values describing a particular color.

 25

Index color models provide methods for resolving pixels containing color map indexes into alpha, red, green, and blue components. Index color models handle looking up the index of a pixel in the color map and extracting the appropriate components from the color entry.

The Color Model Classes

Java provides standard classes for working with color models in the `java.awt.image` package. At the top of the hierarchy is the `ColorModel` class, which defines the core functionality required of all color models. The `ColorModel` class is an abstract class containing the basic support required to translate pixel values into alpha and color components. Two other classes are derived from `ColorModel`, representing the two types of color models supported by Java: `DirectColorModel` and `IndexColorModel`.

The `DirectColorModel` class is derived from `ColorModel` and provides specific support for direct color models. If you recall, pixels in a direct color model directly contain the alpha and color components in each pixel value.

The `IndexColorModel` class is also derived from `ColorModel` and provides support for index color models. Pixels in an index color model contain indexes into a fixed array of colors known as a color map, or palette. Even though the color model classes are important in understanding the conceptual side of Java graphics, you won't be using them directly when working with image filters, so there's no need to go into any more detail with them here.

Image Filters

Now it's time to move into the meat of today's lesson: image filters. Image filtering is sometimes referred to as *image processing*. Most popular graphical paint programs contain image-processing features, such as sharpening or softening an image. Typically, image processing programs involve the usage of complex libraries of routines for manipulating images. Java provides a simple yet powerful framework for manipulating images. In Java, image processing objects are called image filters, and they serve as a way to abstract the filtering of an image without worrying about the details associated with the source or destination of the image data.

NEW TERM An *image filter* is an object that alters the individual pixels of an image according to a particular algorithm.

A Java image filter can be thought of quite literally as a filter into which all the data for an image must enter and exit on its way from a source to a destination. Take a look at Figure 25.4 to see how image data passes through an image filter.

Figure 25.4.

Image data passing through an image filter.

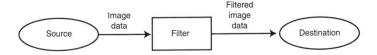

While passing through an image filter, the individual pixels of an image can be altered in any way as determined by the filter. By design, image filters are structured to be self-contained components. The image filter model supported by Java is based on three logical components: an image producer, an image filter, and an image consumer. The image producer makes the raw pixel data for an image available, the image filter in turn filters this data, and the resulting filtered image data is passed on to the image consumer where it has usually been requested. Figure 25.5 shows how these three components interact with each other.

 An *image producer* is an abstract data source that makes available raw pixel data for an image.

 An *image consumer* is an abstract data destination that receives raw pixel data from an image consumer.

Figure 25.5.

The relationship between an image producer, an image filter, and an image consumer.

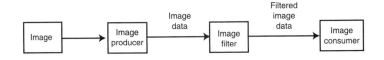

Breaking down the process of filtering images into these three components provides a very powerful object-oriented solution to a complex problem. Different types of image producers can be derived that are able to retrieve image data from a variety of image sources. Likewise, this organization allows filters to ignore the complexities associated with different image sources and focus on the details of manipulating the individual pixels of an image.

The Image Filter Classes

Java's support for image filters is scattered across several classes and interfaces. You don't necessarily have to understand all these classes in detail to work with image filters, but it is important that you understand what functionality they provide and where they fit into the scheme of things. Following are the Java classes and interfaces that provide support for image filtering:

☐ ImageProducer

☐ FilteredImageSource

- ☐ MemoryImageSource
- ☐ ImageConsumer
- ☐ PixelGrabber
- ☐ ImageFilter
- ☐ RGBImageFilter
- ☐ CropImageFilter

The ImageProducer interface describes the methods necessary to extract image pixel data from Image objects. Classes implementing the ImageProducer interface provide implementations of these methods specific to the image source they represent. For example, the MemoryImageSource class implements the ImageProducer interface and produces image pixels from an array of pixel values stored in memory.

The FilteredImageSource class implements the ImageProducer interface and produces filtered image data. The filtered image data produced is based on the image and the filter object passed in the FilteredImageSource class's constructor. FilteredImageSource provides a very simple way to apply image filters to Image objects.

The MemoryImageSource class implements the ImageProducer interface and produces image data based on an array of pixels in memory. This is very useful in cases where you need to build an Image object directly from data in memory.

The ImageConsumer interface describes methods necessary for an object to retrieve image data from an image producer. Objects implementing the ImageConsumer interface are attached to an image producer object when they are interested in its image data. The image producer object delivers the image data by calling methods defined by the ImageConsumer interface.

The PixelGrabber class implements the ImageConsumer interface and provides a way of retrieving a subset of the pixels in an image. A PixelGrabber object can be created based on either an Image object or an object implementing the ImageProducer interface. The constructor for PixelGrabber enables you to specify a rectangular section of the image data to be grabbed. This image data is then delivered by the image producer to the PixelGrabber object.

The ImageFilter class provides the basic functionality of an image filter that operates on image data being delivered from an image producer to an image consumer. ImageFilter objects are specifically designed to be used in conjunction with FilteredImageSource objects. The ImageFilter class is implemented as a null filter, which means that it passes image data unmodified. Nevertheless, it implements the overhead for processing the data in an image. The only thing missing is the actual modification of the pixel data, which is left up to derived filter classes. This is actually a very nice design because it enables you to create new image filters by deriving from ImageFilter and overriding only a few methods.

The ImageFilter class operates on an image using the color model defined by the image producer. The RGBImageFilter class, on the other hand, derives from ImageFilter and implements an image filter specific to the default RGB color model. RGBImageFilter provides the overhead necessary to process image data in a single method that converts pixels one at a time in the default RGB color model. This processing takes place in the default RGB color model regardless of the color model used by the image producer. Like ImageFilter, RGBImageFilter is meant to be used in conjunction with the FilteredImageSource image producer.

The seemingly strange thing about RGBImageFilter is that it is an abstract class, so you can't instantiate objects from it. It is abstract because of a single abstract method, filterRGB. The filterRGB method is used to convert a single input pixel to a single output pixel in the default RGB color model. filterRGB is the workhorse method that handles filtering the image data; each pixel in the image is sent through this method for processing. To create your own RGB image filters, all you must do is derive from RGBImageFilter and implement the filterRGB method. This is the technique you'll use a little later today when you implement your own image filters.

The RGBImageFilter class contains a member variable that is very important in determining how it processes image data: canFilterIndexColorModel. The canFilterIndexColorModel member variable is a boolean that specifies whether the filterRGB method can be used to filter the color map entries of an image using an index color model, rather than the individual pixels themselves. If this member variable is false, each pixel in the image is processed, similar to if it was using a direct color model.

The CropImageFilter class is derived from ImageFilter and provides a means of extracting a rectangular region within an image. Like ImageFilter, the CropImageFilter class is designed to be used with the FilteredImageSource image producer. You may be a little confused by CropImageFilter because it sounds a lot like the PixelGrabber class mentioned earlier. It is important to understand the differences between these two classes because they perform very different functions.

First, remember that PixelGrabber implements the ImageConsumer interface, so it functions as an image consumer. CropImageFilter, on the other hand, is an image filter. This means that PixelGrabber is used as a destination for image data, where CropImageFilter is applied to image data in transit. You use PixelGrabber to extract a region of an image to store in an array of pixels (the destination). You use CropImageFilter to extract a region of an image that is sent along to its destination (usually another Image object).

Writing Your Own Image Filters

Although the standard Java image filter classes are powerful as a framework, they aren't that exciting to work with by themselves. Image filters don't really get interesting until you start implementing your own. Fortunately, the Java classes make it very simple to write your own image filters.

All the image filters you'll develop in today's lesson are derived from RGBImageFilter, which enables you to filter images through a single method, filterRGB. It really is as easy as deriving your class from RGBImageFilter and implementing the filterRGB method. Let's give it a try!

A Color Image Filter

Probably the simplest image filter imaginable is one that filters out the individual color components (red, green, and blue) of an image. The ColorFilter class does exactly that. Listing 25.1 contains the source code for the ColorFilter class. It is located on the CD-ROM in the file ColorFilter.java.

Type **Listing 25.1. The ColorFilter class.**

```
 1: class ColorFilter extends RGBImageFilter {
 2:   boolean red, green, blue;
 3:
 4:   public ColorFilter(boolean r, boolean g, boolean b) {
 5:     red = r;
 6:     green = g;
 7:     blue = b;
 8:     canFilterIndexColorModel = true;
 9:   }
10:
11:   public int filterRGB(int x, int y, int rgb) {
12:     // Filter the colors
13:     int r = red ? 0 : ((rgb >> 16) & 0xff);
14:     int g = green ? 0 : ((rgb >> 8) & 0xff);
15:     int b = blue ? 0 : ((rgb >> 0) & 0xff);
16:
17:     // Return the result
18:     return (rgb & 0xff000000) ¦ (r << 16) ¦ (g << 8) ¦ (b << 0);
19:   }
20: }
```

Analysis The ColorFilter class is derived from RGBImageFilter and contains three boolean member variables that determine which colors are to be filtered out of the image. These member variables are set by the parameters passed into the constructor. The member variable inherited from RGBImageFilter—canFilterIndexColorModel—is set to true to indicate that the color map entries can be filtered using filterRGB if the incoming image is using an index color model.

Beyond the constructor, ColorFilter implements only one method, filterRGB, which is the abstract method defined in RGBImageFilter. filterRGB takes three parameters: the x and y position of the pixel within the image and the 32-bit (integer) color value. The only parameter you are concerned with is the color value, rgb.

Recalling that the default RGB color model places the red, green, and blue components in the lower 24 bits of the 32-bit color value, it is easy to extract each one by shifting out of the rgb parameter. These individual components are stored in the local variables r, g, and b. Notice, however, that each color component is shifted only if it is not being filtered. For filtered colors, the color component is set to 0.

The new color components are then shifted back into a 32-bit color value and returned from filterRGB. Notice that care is taken to ensure that the alpha component of the color value is not altered. The 0xff000000 mask takes care of this because the alpha component resides in the upper byte of the color value.

Congratulations! You've written your first image filter! You have two more to go before you plug them all into a test program.

An Alpha Image Filter

It isn't always apparent to programmers how the alpha value stored in the color value for each pixel affects an image. Remember that the alpha component specifies the transparency or opaqueness of a pixel. By altering the alpha values for an entire image, you can make it appear to fade in and out. This works because the alpha values range from totally transparent (invisible) to totally opaque.

The AlphaFilter class filters the alpha components of an image according to the alpha level you supply in its constructor. Listing 25.2 contains the source code for the AlphaFilter class. It is located on the CD-ROM in the file AlphaFilter.java.

Type | **Listing 25.2. The AlphaFilter class.**

```
1: class AlphaFilter extends RGBImageFilter {
2:     int alphaLevel;
3:
4:     public AlphaFilter(int alpha) {
5:         alphaLevel = alpha;
6:         canFilterIndexColorModel = true;
7:     }
```

25

```
 8:
 9:   public int filterRGB(int x, int y, int rgb) {
10:     // Adjust the alpha value
11:     int alpha = (rgb >> 24) & 0xff;
12:     alpha = (alpha * alphaLevel) / 255;
13:
14:     // Return the result
15:     return ((rgb & 0x00ffffff) ¦ (alpha << 24));
16:   }
17: }
```

ANALYSIS   The AlphaFilter class contains a single member variable, alphaLevel, that keeps up with the alpha level to be applied to the image. This member variable is initialized in the constructor, as is the canFilterIndexModel member variable.

Similar to the ColorFilter class, the filterRGB method is the only other method implemented by AlphaFilter. The alpha component of the pixel is first extracted by shifting it into a local variable, alpha. This value is then scaled according to the alphaLevel member variable initialized in the constructor. The purpose of the scaling is to alter the alpha value based on its current value. If you were to set the alpha component to the alpha level, you wouldn't be taking into account the original alpha component value.

The new alpha component is shifted back into the pixel color value and the result returned from filterRGB. Notice that the red, green, and blue components are preserved by using the 0x00ffffff mask.

A Brightness Image Filter

So far the image filters you've seen have been pretty simple. The last one you create is a little more complex, but it acts as a more interesting filter. The BrightnessFilter class implements an image filter that brightens or darkens an image based on a brightness percentage you provide in the constructor. Listing 25.3 contains the source code for the BrightnessFilter class. It is located on the CD-ROM in the file BrightnessFilter.java.

TYPE   **Listing 25.3. The BrightnessFilter class.**

```
1: class BrightnessFilter extends RGBImageFilter {
2:   int brightness;
3:
4:   public BrightnessFilter(int b) {
5:     brightness = b;
6:     canFilterIndexColorModel = true;
7:   }
8:
```

continues

Listing 25.3. continued

```
 9:    public int filterRGB(int x, int y, int rgb) {
10:        // Get the individual colors
11:        int r = (rgb >> 16) & 0xff;
12:        int g = (rgb >> 8) & 0xff;
13:        int b = (rgb >> 0) & 0xff;
14:
15:        // Calculate the brightness
16:        r += (brightness * r) / 100;
17:        g += (brightness * g) / 100;
18:        b += (brightness * b) / 100;
19:
20:        // Check the boundaries
21:        r = Math.min(Math.max(0, r), 255);
22:        g = Math.min(Math.max(0, g), 255);
23:        b = Math.min(Math.max(0, b), 255);
24:
25:        // Return the result
26:        return (rgb & 0xff000000) ¦ (r << 16) ¦ (g << 8) ¦ (b << 0);
27:    }
28: }
```

ANALYSIS The BrightnessFilter class contains one member variable, brightness, that keeps track of the percentage to alter the brightness of the image. This member variable is set via the constructor, along with the canFilterIndexModel member variable. The brightness member variable can contain values in the range -100 to 100. A value of -100 means the image is darkened by 100 percent, and a value of 100 means the image is brightened by 100 percent. A value of 0 doesn't alter the brightness of the image at all.

It should come as no surprise by now that filterRGB is the only other method implemented by BrightnessFilter. In filterRGB, the individual color components are first extracted into the local variables r, g, and b. The brightness effects are then calculated based on the brightness member variable. The new color components are then checked against the 0 and 255 boundaries and modified if necessary.

Finally, the new color components are shifted back into the pixel color value and returned from filterRGB. Hey, it's not that complicated after all!

Using Image Filters

You put in the time writing some of your own image filters, but you have yet to enjoy the fruit of your labors. It's time to plug the filters into a real Java applet and see how they work. Figure 25.6 shows the FilterTest applet busily at work filtering an image of a pear, quite literally the fruit of your labors!

Figure 25.6.

The FilterTest *applet.*

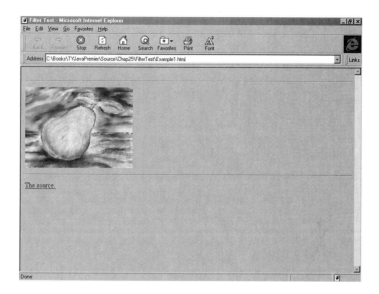

The FilterTest applet uses all three filters you've written to enable you to filter an image of a pear. The R, G, and B keys on the keyboard change the different colors filtered by the color filter. The left and right arrow keys modify the alpha level for the alpha filter. The up and down arrow keys alter the brightness percentage used by the brightness filter. Finally, the Home key restores the image to its unfiltered state.

 Listing 25.4 contains the source code for the FilterTest applet. The complete source code and executables for the FilterTest applet are located on the accompanying CD-ROM.

TYPE **Listing 25.4. The** FilterTest **applet.**

```
 1: public class FilterTest extends Applet {
 2:    Image      src, dst;
 3:    boolean    red, green, blue;
 4:    final int alphaMax = 9;
 5:    int        alphaLevel = alphaMax;
 6:    int        brightness;
 7:
 8:    public void init() {
 9:      src = getImage(getDocumentBase(), "Pear.gif");
10:      dst = src;
11:    }
12:
13:    public void paint(Graphics g) {
```

continues

Listing 25.4. continued

```
14:      g.drawImage(dst, 0, 0, this);
15:    }
16:
17:    public boolean keyDown(Event evt, int key) {
18:      switch (key) {
19:      case Event.HOME:
20:        red = false;
21:        green = false;
22:        blue = false;
23:        alphaLevel = alphaMax;
24:        brightness = 0;
25:        break;
26:      case Event.LEFT:
27:        if (--alphaLevel < 0)
28:          alphaLevel = 0;
29:        break;
30:      case Event.RIGHT:
31:        if (++alphaLevel > alphaMax)
32:          alphaLevel = alphaMax;
33:        break;
34:      case Event.UP:
35:        brightness = Math.min(brightness + 10, 100);
36:        break;
37:      case Event.DOWN:
38:        brightness = Math.max(-100, brightness - 10);
39:        break;
40:      case (int)'r':
41:      case (int)'R':
42:        red = !red;
43:        break;
44:      case (int)'g':
45:      case (int)'G':
46:        green = !green;
47:        break;
48:      case (int)'b':
49:      case (int)'B':
50:        blue = !blue;
51:        break;
52:      default:
53:        return false;
54:      }
55:      filterImage();
56:      return true;
57:    }
58:
59:    void filterImage() {
60:      dst = src;
61:
62:      // Apply the color filter
63:      dst = createImage(new FilteredImageSource(dst.getSource(),
64:        new ColorFilter(red, green, blue)));
65:
66:      // Apply the alpha filter
67:      dst = createImage(new FilteredImageSource(dst.getSource(),
```

25

```
68:        new AlphaFilter((alphaLevel * 255) / alphaMax)));
69:
70:      // Apply the brightness filter
71:      dst = createImage(new FilteredImageSource(dst.getSource(),
72:        new BrightnessFilter(brightness)));
73:
74:      // Redraw the image
75:      repaint();
76:    }
77: }
```

ANALYSIS The FilterTest applet class contains member variables for keeping up with the source and destination images, along with member variables for maintaining the various filter parameters.

The first method implemented by FilterTest is init, which loads the image Pear.gif into the src member variable. It also initializes the dst member variable to the same image. The paint method is implemented next, and simply consists of a call to the drawImage method, which draws the destination (filtered) Image object.

The keyDown method is implemented to handle keyboard events generated by the user. In this case, the keys used to control the image filters are handled in the switch statement. The corresponding member variables are altered according to the keys pressed. Notice the call to the filterImage near the end of keyDown.

The filterImage method is where the actual filtering takes place; it applies each image filter to the image. The dst member variable is first initialized with the src member variable to restore the destination image to its original state. Each filter is then applied using a messy-looking call to createImage. The only parameter to createImage is an ImageProducer object. In this case, you create a FilteredImageSource object to pass into createImage. The constructor for FilteredImageSource takes two parameters: an image producer and an image filter. The first parameter is an ImageProducer object for the source image, which is obtained using the getSource method for the image. The second parameter is an ImageFilter-derived object.

The color filter is first applied to the image by creating a ColorFilter object using the three boolean color value member variables. The alpha filter is applied by creating an AlphaFilter object using the alphaLevel member variable. Rather than allowing 255 different alpha levels, the alpha level is normalized to provide only 10 different alpha levels. This is evident in the equation using alphaMax, which is set to 9. Finally, the brightness filter is applied by creating a BrightnessFilter object and passing in the brightness member variable.

Summary

Although the overall goal of today's lesson is to learn how to use image filters, you also covered a great deal of related material along the way. You first learned about color in general and then about the heart of advanced Java graphics: color models. With color models under your belt, you moved on to image filters. You saw how the Java image filter classes provide a powerful framework for working with images without worrying about unnecessary details. You finished up the lesson by writing three of your own image filters, along with an applet that put them to work filtering a real image.

You're now well versed in one of the more advanced areas of Java graphics programming. Just in case you're starting to burn out on all this graphics stuff, tomorrow's lesson shifts gears dramatically and introduces you to client/server network programming in Java.

Q&A

Q If Java colors are inherently 32 bit, how does Java display color on systems using less than 32 bits to represent color?

A The reality is that there aren't a lot of computer systems out there equipped to fully support 32-bit color. For example, most high-end PCs and Macintoshes only support 24-bit color. Additionally, the average PC only supports 8-bit color. Java handles this internally by mapping 32-bit color values to the underlying system as efficiently as possible, sometimes by using an index color model. In some cases image quality will suffer because the full range of colors in the image can't be displayed.

Q I still don't understand why there is an alpha component in Java colors. What's the deal?

A Strictly speaking, all that is required of Java to support a wide range of colors are the three primary color components: red, green, and blue. However, the alpha component adds the ability to alter the opaqueness of a color, which makes it much easier to implement graphics effects that alter the transparency properties of a color.

Q Is there a situation in which I will ever need to implement my own color model?

A I'm hesitant to say that you'll never need to implement your own color model, but let me say that the situation in which you would need a custom color model is highly unlikely to occur. This is because color models are mainly an internal abstraction used by the Java graphics system itself.

Q **I understand why image filters are useful, but what exactly is the importance of image producers and consumers?**

A Image producers and consumers provide a clean abstraction for the source and destination of raw image data. Without image producers and consumers, you would have to use a custom solution each time you wanted to get data from or write data to an image. By having the source and destination of image data clearly defined, more advanced graphics functions like image filters are much easier to work with.

BD
4

Day 26

Client/Server
Networking in Java

by Michael Morrison

The networking capabilities of Java are perhaps the most powerful component of the Java API because the vast majority of Java programs run in a networked environment. Using the wide range of network features built into Java, you can easily develop Web-based applets that perform a variety of tasks over a network. The network support in Java is particularly well suited to a client/server arrangement where a server marshals information and serves it to clients that handle the details of displaying the information to a user.

In today's lesson you'll learn what Java has to offer in regard to communicating over an Internet network connection using a client/server arrangement. You'll begin the lesson by taking a look at some basic concepts surrounding the structure of the Internet as a network. You'll then move on to what specific support is provided by the standard Java networking API and how it fits in with the client/server paradigm. Finally, you'll conclude the lesson by developing a couple of interesting sample programs demonstrating the different types of client/server approaches available in Java.

The following topics are covered in today's lesson:

- ☐ Internet network basics
- ☐ The client/server paradigm
- ☐ Java sockets
- ☐ Developing a datagram socket applet and server
- ☐ Developing a stream socket applet and server

By the end of this lesson, you'll be ready to build your own Java network client/server programs from scratch. You'll also have a better understanding of one of the reasons Java has become so popular—by virtue of its clean and straightforward support for an otherwise messy and complex area of programming: network programming!

Internet Network Basics

Before you learn about the types of network support Java provides, it's important that you understand some fundamentals about the structure of the Internet as a network. As you are no doubt already aware, the Internet is a global network of many different types of computers connected in various ways. With this wide diversity of both hardware and software all connected together, it's pretty amazing that the Internet is even functional. Trust me, the functionality of the Internet is no accident and has come at no small cost in terms of planning.

The only way to guarantee compatibility and reliable communication across a wide range of different computer systems is to define very strict standards that must be conformed to rigorously. That's exactly the approach taken by the planners of the Internet in determining its communications protocols. Please understand that I'm not the type of person who typically preaches conformity, but conformity in one's personal life is very different from conformity in complex computer networks.

The point is, the only way to allow a wide range of computer systems to coexist and communicate with each other effectively is to hammer out some standards. Fortunately, plenty of standards abound for the Internet, and they share wide support across many different computer systems. Hopefully, I've convinced you of the importance of communication standards on the Internet—let's take a look at a few of them.

Addresses

One of the first areas of standardization on the Internet was in establishing a means to uniquely identify each connected computer. It's not surprising that a technique logically equivalent to traditional mailing addresses is the one that was adopted; each computer physically connected to the Internet is assigned an *address* that uniquely identifies it. These addresses, also referred to as *IP addresses,* come in the form of a 32-bit number that looks like this: 243.37.126.82. You're probably more familiar with the symbolic form of IP addresses, which looks like this: sams.mcp.com.

NEW TERM An *IP address* is a 32-bit number that uniquely identifies each computer physically attached to the Internet.

So addresses provide each computer connected to the Internet with a unique identifier. Each Internet computer has an address for the same reason you have a mailing address and a phone number at your home: to facilitate communication. It might sound simple, and that's because conceptually it is. As long as we can guarantee that each computer is uniquely identifiable, we can easily communicate with any computer without worry. Well, almost. The truth is, addresses are only a small part of the Internet communication equation, but an important part nevertheless. Without addresses, there would be no way to distinguish among different computers.

Protocols

The idea of communicating among different computers on the Internet might not sound like that big a deal now that you understand that they use addresses similar to mailing addresses. The problem is that there are many different types of communication that can take place on the Internet, meaning that there must be an equal number of mechanisms for handling them. It's at this point that the mailing-address comparison to Internet addressing breaks down. The reason for this is that each type of communication taking place on the Internet requires a unique protocol. Your mailing-address essentially revolves around one type of communication: the postal carrier driving up to your mailbox and placing the mail inside.

A *protocol* specifies the format of data being sent over the Internet, along with how and when it is sent. On the other end of the communication, the protocol also defines how the data is received along with its structure and what it means. You've probably heard mention of the Internet being just a bunch of bits flying back and forth in cyberspace. That's a very true statement, and without protocols, those bits wouldn't mean anything.

NEW TERM A *protocol* is a set of rules and standards defining a certain type of Internet communication.

BD
5

The concept of a protocol is not groundbreaking or even new. We use protocols all the time in everyday situations; we just don't call them protocols. Think about how many times you've been involved in this type of dialogue:

"Hi, may I take your order?"

"Yes, I'd like the grilled salmon and a frozen strawberry margarita."

"Thanks, I'll put your order in and bring you your drink."

"Thank you, I'm famished."

Although this conversation might not look like anything special, it is a very definite social protocol used to place orders for food at a restaurant. Conversational protocol is important because it gives us familiarity and confidence in knowing what to do in certain situations. Haven't you ever been nervous when entering a new social situation in which you didn't quite know how to act? In these cases, you didn't really have confidence in the protocol, so you probably worried about a communication problem that could have easily resulted in embarrassment. For computers and networks, protocol breakdown translates into errors and information transfer failure rather than embarrassment.

Now that you understand the importance of protocols, let's take a look at a couple of the more important ones used on the Internet. Without a doubt, the protocol getting the most attention these days is *HTTP*, which stands for Hypertext Transfer Protocol. HTTP is the protocol used to transfer HTML documents on the Web. Another important protocol is *FTP*, which stands for File Transfer Protocol. FTP is a more general protocol used to transfer binary files over the Internet. Each of these protocols has its own unique set of rules and standards defining how information is transferred, and Java provides support for both of them.

 HTTP stands for Hypertext Transfer Protocol, which is the protocol used to transfer HTML documents on the Web.

 FTP stands for File Transfer Protocol, which is the protocol used to transfer files across the Internet.

Ports

Internet protocols make sense only in the context of a service. For example, the HTTP protocol comes into play when you are providing Web content (HTML pages) through an HTTP service. Each computer on the Internet has the capability to provide a variety of services through the various protocols supported. There is a problem, however, in that the type of service must be known before information can be transferred. This is where ports come in. A *port* is a software abstraction that provides a means to differentiate between network services. More specifically, a port is a 16-bit number identifying the different services offered by a network server.

NEW TERM A *port* is a 16-bit number that identifies each service offered by a network server.

Each computer on the Internet has a bunch of ports that can be assigned different services. To use a particular service and therefore establish a line of communication via a particular protocol, you must connect to the correct port. Ports are numbered, and some of the numbers are specifically associated with a type of service. Ports with specific service assignments are known as *standard ports*, meaning that you can always count on a particular port corresponding to a certain service. For example, the FTP service is located on port 21, so any other computer wanting to perform an FTP file transfer would connect to port 21 of the host computer. Likewise, the HTTP service is located on port 80, so any time you access a Web site, you are really connecting to port 80 of the host using the HTTP protocol behind the scenes. Figure 26.1 illustrates how ports and protocols work.

Figure 26.1.

The relationship between protocols and ports.

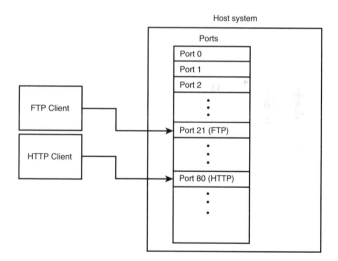

All standard service assignments are given port values below 1024. This means that ports above 1024 are considered available for custom communications, such as those required by a Java client/server program implementing its own protocol. Keep in mind, however, that other types of custom communication also take place above port 1024, so you might have to try a few different ports to find an unused one.

The Client/Server Paradigm

So far I've managed to explain a decent amount of Internet networking fundamentals while dodging a major issue: the client/server paradigm. You've no doubt heard of clients and servers before, but you might not fully understand their importance in regard to the Internet. Well, it's time to remedy that situation, because you won't be able to get much done in Java without understanding how clients and servers work. As a matter of fact, the Java network-programming framework is based on a client/server arrangement.

The client/server paradigm involves thinking of computing in terms of a client, who is essentially in need of some type of information, and a server, who has lots of information and is just waiting to hand it out. Typically, a client will connect to a server and query for certain information. The server will go off and find the information and then return it to the client. It might sound as though I'm oversimplifying things here, but for the most part I'm not; conceptually, client/server computing is as simple as a client asking for information and a server returning it.

In the context of the Internet, clients are typically run on desktop or laptop computers attached to the Internet looking for information, whereas servers are typically run on larger computers with certain types of information available for the clients to retrieve. The Web itself is made up of a bunch of computers that act as Web servers; they have vast amounts of HTML pages and related data available for people to retrieve and browse. Web clients are used by those of us who connect to the Web servers and browse through the Web pages. In this way, Netscape Navigator is considered client Web software. Take a look at Figure 26.2 to get a better idea of the client/server arrangement.

Figure 26.2.

A Web server with multiple clients connected.

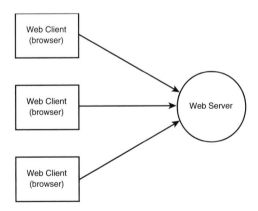

Sockets

One of Java's major strong suits as a programming language is its wide range of network support. Java has this advantage because it was developed with the Internet in mind. The result is that you have lots of options in regard to network programming in Java. Even though there are many network options, most Java network programming uses a particular type of network communication known as *sockets*.

NEW TERM A *socket* is a software abstraction for an input or output medium of communication.

Java performs all of its low-level network communication through sockets. Logically, sockets are one step lower than ports; you use sockets to communicate through a particular port. So a socket is a communication channel that enables you to transfer data through a certain port. Check out Figure 26.3, which shows communication taking place through multiple sockets on a port.

Figure 26.3.

Multiple sockets communicating through a port.

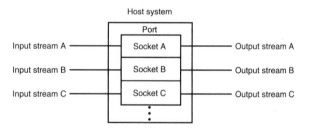

This figure brings up an interesting point about sockets: Data can be transferred through multiple sockets for a single port. This makes sense because it is common for multiple Web users to retrieve Web pages from a server via port 80 (HTTP) at the same time. Java provides basic socket classes to make programming with sockets much easier. Java sockets are broken down into two types: datagram sockets and stream sockets.

Datagram Sockets

A *datagram socket* uses User Datagram Protocol (UDP) to facilitate the sending of *datagrams* (self-contained pieces of information) in an unreliable manner. *Unreliable* means that information sent via datagrams isn't guaranteed to make it to its destination. The trade-off here is that datagram sockets require relatively few resources directly because of this unreliable design. The clients and servers in a datagram scenario don't require a "live" or dedicated network connection, which is sometimes desirable. In this way, a datagram socket is somewhat equivalent to a dial-up network connection, with which you are temporarily connected to a network based on your immediate information needs.

Datagrams are sent as individually bundled packets that may or may not make it to their destination in any particular order or at any particular time. On the receiving end of a datagram system, the packets of information can be received in any order and at any time. For this reason, datagrams sometimes include a sequence number that specifies which piece of the puzzle each bundle corresponds to. The receiver can then wait to receive the entire sequence, in which case it will put them back together to form the original information structure.

 UDP (User Datagram Protocol) is a network broadcast protocol that doesn't guarantee transfer success. In return, UDP relies on few network resources.

 A *datagram* is an independent, self-contained piece of information sent over a network whose arrival, arrival time, and content are not guaranteed.

 A *datagram socket*, or "unconnected" socket, is a socket over which data is bundled into packets and sent without requiring a "live" connection to the destination computer.

The fact that datagram sockets are openly unreliable may lead you to think that they are something to avoid in network programming. However, there are very practical scenarios in which datagram sockets make perfectly acceptable solutions. For example, servers that continually broadcast similar information make great candidates for datagram communication. A stock quote server is a good example since the stock quotes are constantly being spit out with little regard for successful delivery. The fact that stock quotes are highly time-dependent makes it less of an issue if a stock quote never reaches you; you can just wait until a new one is sent.

Java supports datagram socket programming through two classes: `DatagramSocket` and `DatagramPacket`. The `DatagramSocket` class provides an implementation for a basic datagram socket. The `DatagramPacket` class provides the functionality required of a packet of information that is capable of being sent through a datagram socket. These two classes are all you need to get busy writing your own datagram client/server Java programs.

Following is a list of some of the more important methods implemented in the `DatagramSocket` class:

```
DatagramSocket()
DatagramSocket(int port)
void send(DatagramPacket p)
synchronized void receive(DatagramPacket p)
synchronized void close()
```

The first two methods listed are actually constructors for the DatagramSocket class. The first constructor is the default constructor and takes no parameters, and the second constructor creates a datagram socket connected to the specified port. The send and receive methods are very straightforward and provide a means to send and receive datagram packets. The close method simply closes the datagram socket. It doesn't get much simpler than that!

Notice that the DatagramSocket class doesn't distinguish between the socket being a client or server socket. The reason for this is the manner in which datagram communication takes place, which doesn't require that the socket act specifically as a client or server. Rather, Java clients and servers are distinguished by how they use the DatagramSocket class to transmit/receive datagrams.

The other half of the datagram solution is the DatagramPacket class, which models a packet of information sent through a datagram socket. Following are some of the more useful methods in the DatagramPacket class:

```
DatagramPacket(byte ibuf[], int ilength)
DatagramPacket(byte ibuf[], int ilength, InetAddress iaddr, int iport)
byte[] getData()
int getLength()
```

The first two methods are the constructors for DatagramPacket. As you probably guessed from the parameters, you construct datagram packets from byte arrays of data. The first constructor is used for receiving datagrams, as is evident by the absence of an address or port number. The second constructor is used for sending datagrams, which is why you have to specify a destination address and port number for the datagram to be sent. The other two methods return the raw datagram data and the length of the data, respectively.

Other than the constructors, all the methods in DatagramPacket are passive, meaning that they simply return information about the datagram packet and don't actually change anything. This is evidence that the DatagramPacket class is primarily used as a container for data being sent over a datagram socket. In other words, you will typically create a DatagramPacket object as a wrapper for data being sent or received and never call any methods on it.

Stream Sockets

Unlike datagram sockets, in which the communication is roughly akin to that in a dial-up network, a stream socket is more akin to a live network, in which the communication link is continuously active. A stream socket is a "connected" socket through which data is transferred continuously. By *continuously*, I don't necessarily mean that data is being sent all the time, but that the socket itself is active and ready for communication all the time.

A *stream socket*, or connected socket, is a socket through which data can be transmitted continuously.

The benefit of using a stream socket is that information can be sent with less worry about when it will arrive at its destination. Because the communication link is always live, data is generally transmitted immediately after you send it. Of course, this dedicated communication link brings with it the overhead of consuming more resources. However, most network programs benefit greatly from the consistency and reliability of a stream socket.

> **NOTE**
>
> A practical usage of a streaming mechanism is RealAudio, which is a technology that provides a way to listen to audio on the Web as it is being transmitted in real time.

Java supports stream socket programming primarily through two classes: `Socket` and `ServerSocket`. The `Socket` class provides the necessary overhead to facilitate a stream socket client, and the `ServerSocket` class provides the core functionality for a server.

Following is a list of some of the more important methods implemented in the `Socket` class:

```
Socket(String host, int port)
Socket(InetAddress address, int port)
synchronized void close()
InputStream getInputStream()
OutputStream getOutputStream()
```

The first two methods listed are constructors for the `Socket` class. The host computer you are connecting the socket to is specified in the first parameter of each constructor; the difference between the two constructors is whether you specify the host using a string name or an `InetAddress` object. The second parameter is an integer specifying the port you want to connect to. The `close` method is used to close a socket. The `getInputStream` and `getOutputStream` methods are used to retrieve the input and output streams associated with the socket.

The `ServerSocket` class handles the other end of socket communication in a client/server scenario. Following are a few of the more useful methods defined in the `ServerSocket` class:

```
ServerSocket(int port)
ServerSocket(int port, int count)
Socket accept()
void close()
```

The first two methods are the constructors for `ServerSocket`, which both take a port number as the first parameter. The `count` parameter in the second constructor specifies a timeout period for the server to quit automatically "listening" for a client connection. This is the distinguishing factor between the two constructors; the first version doesn't listen for a client connection, whereas the second version does. If you use the first constructor, you must specifically tell the server to wait for a client connection. You do this by calling the `accept` method, which blocks program flow until a connection is made. The `close` method simply closes the server socket.

Like with the datagram socket classes, you might be thinking that the stream socket classes seem awfully simple. In fact, they are simple, which is a good thing. Most of the actual code facilitating communication via stream sockets is handled through the input and output streams connected to a socket. In this way, the communication itself is handled independently of the network socket connection. This might not seem like a big deal at first, but it is crucial in the design of the socket classes; after you've created a socket, you connect an input or output stream to it and then forget about the socket.

Fortune: A Datagram Client and Server

You've now covered the basics of sockets and how they work in Java, but you haven't seen a socket in action. Well, it's time to remedy that situation with a full-blown client/server program that uses datagram sockets. You'll also work through a stream socket example later today, but first things first!

The datagram client/server example is called Fortune and consists of a server that transmits interesting quotes called "fortunes" and a client that receives and displays the fortunes. The Fortune example could also be used to implement a joke-of-the-day server, where users can connect and get the latest joke you have to offer. Since I had more interesting quotes than funny jokes, I decided to stick with a quote server!

The Fortune example works like this: There is a server program that runs on a Web server and waits patiently for clients to connect and ask for a fortune. On the other end, there is a client applet embedded in a Web page that a user accesses with a Java-enabled Web browser. When the user loads the Web page and fires up the applet, the applet connects to the server and asks it for a fortune. The server in turn picks a fortune at random and sends it back to the applet. The applet in return displays the fortune for the user to see. It's that simple!

Designing Fortune

Before jumping into the Java code required to implement the Fortune example, let's briefly take a look at what is required of the design on each side of the client/server fence. On the server side, you need a program that monitors a particular port on the host machine for client connections. When a client is detected, the server picks a random fortune, which is a simple text string, and sends it to the client over the specified port. The server is then free to break

BD
5

the connection and let the client go on its merry way. The server returns to its original wait state, where it looks for other clients to connect. So the server is required to perform the following tasks:

1. Wait for a client to connect.
2. Accept the client connection.
3. Send a random fortune to the client.
4. Go back to step 1.

Now, on to the client. The client side of the Fortune example is an applet that lives in a Web page and has full support for graphical output. The client applet is responsible for connecting to the server and awaiting the server's response. The server's response is the transmission of the fortune string, which the client must receive and display. When the client successfully receives the fortune, it can break the connection with the server. As an added bonus, the client applet is also capable of grabbing another fortune if you click the mouse button. The client's primary tasks follow:

1. Connect to the server.
2. Wait for a fortune to be sent.
3. Display the fortune.
4. Go back to step 1 if the user clicks the mouse button.

Implementing the Fortune Server

You're no doubt itching to see some real code that carries out all these ideas you've been learning. Well, the time has come! Since the Fortune example ultimately begins and ends with the server, let's start by looking at the code for the server. The complete source code for the `FortuneServer` class is located on the accompanying CD-ROM in the file `FortuneServer.java`. Following are the member variables defined in the `FortuneServer` class:

```
private static final int  PORTNUM = 1234;
private String[]          fortunes;
private DatagramSocket     serverSocket;
private Random            rand = new Random(System.currentTimeMillis());
```

The `PORTNUM` member represents the number of the port used by Fortune. The value of `PORTNUM`—1234—is arbitrarily chosen; the important thing is that it is greater than 1024. The `fortunes` member variable is an array of strings that hold the text for the actual fortunes. The `serverSocket` member variable represents the datagram socket used for communication with the client. The `rand` member variable is a `Random` object that is used in determining the random fortune to be sent to the client.

WARNING

> Be sure to always make your port numbers greater than 1024 so that they don't conflict with standard server port assignments.

The constructor for FortuneServer handles creating the server socket:

```java
public FortuneServer() {
  super("FortuneServer");
  try {
    serverSocket = new DatagramSocket(PORTNUM);
    System.out.println("FortuneServer up and running...");
  }
  catch (SocketException e) {
    System.err.println("Exception: couldn't create datagram socket");
    System.exit(1);
  }
}
```

As you can see, the constructor creates a datagram socket using the port number specified by PORTNUM. If the socket cannot be created, an exception is thrown, and the server exits. The server exits because it is pretty much worthless without a socket to communicate through.

The method that does most of the work in the FortuneServer class is the run method, which is shown in Listing 26.1.

TYPE   **Listing 26.1. The run method.**

```java
 1: public void run() {
 2:   if (serverSocket == null)
 3:     return;
 4:
 5:   // Initialize the array of fortunes
 6:   if (!initFortunes()) {
 7:     System.err.println("Error: couldn't initialize fortunes");
 8:     return;
 9:   }
10:
11:   // Look for clients and serve up the fortunes
12:   while (true) {
13:     try {
14:       InetAddress     address;
15:       int             port;
16:       DatagramPacket  packet;
17:       byte[]          data = new byte[256];
18:       int             num = Math.abs(rand.nextInt()) % fortunes.length;
19:
20:       // Wait for a client connection
21:       packet = new DatagramPacket(data, data.length);
```

continues

BD
5

Listing 26.1. continued

```
22:        serverSocket.receive(packet);
23:
24:        // Send a fortune
25:        address = packet.getAddress();
26:        port = packet.getPort();
27:        fortunes[num].getBytes(0, fortunes[num].length(), data, 0);
28:        packet = new DatagramPacket(data, data.length, address, port);
29:        serverSocket.send(packet);
30:      }
31:    catch (Exception e) {
32:        System.err.println("Exception: " + e);
33:        e.printStackTrace();
34:      }
35:    }
36: }
```

ANALYSIS The first thing the run method does is check to make sure the socket is valid. If the socket is okay, run calls initFortunes to initialize the array of fortune strings. You'll learn about the initFortunes method in just a moment. Once the fortunes are initialized, run enters an infinite while loop that waits for a client connection. When a client connection is detected, a datagram packet is created using a random fortune string. This packet is then sent to the client through the socket.

Since you wouldn't want to have to recompile the server application every time you wanted to change the fortunes, the fortunes are read from a text file. Each fortune is stored as a single line of text in the file Fortunes.txt. Following is a listing of the Fortunes.txt file:

```
You can no more win a war than you can win an earthquake.
The highest result of education is tolerance.
The right to be let alone is indeed the beginning of all freedom.
When we lose the right to be different, we lost the right to be free.
The only vice that cannot be forgiven is hypocrisy.
We learn from history that we do not learn from history.
That which we call sin in others is experiment for us.
Few men have virtue to withstand the highest bidder.
```

The initFortunes method is responsible for reading the fortunes from this file and storing them into an array that is more readily accessible. Listing 26.2 contains the source code for the initFortunes method.

TYPE **Listing 26.2. The initFortunes method.**

```
1: private boolean initFortunes() {
2:   try {
3:     File            inFile = new File("Fortunes.txt");
4:     FileInputStream inStream = new FileInputStream(inFile);
5:     byte[]          data = new byte[(int)inFile.length()];
```

26

```
6:
7:      // Read the fortunes into a byte array
8:      if (inStream.read(data) <= 0) {
9:        System.err.println("Error: couldn't read fortunes");
10:       return false;
11:     }
12:
13:     // See how many fortunes there are
14:     int numFortunes = 0;
15:     for (int i = 0; i < data.length; i++)
16:       if (data[i] == (byte)'\n')
17:         numFortunes++;
18:     fortunes = new String[numFortunes];
19:
20:     // Parse the fortunes into an array of strings
21:     int start = 0, index = 0;
22:     for (int i = 0; i < data.length; i++)
23:       if (data[i] == (byte)'\n') {
24:         fortunes[index++] = new String(data, 0, start, i - start - 1);
25:         start = i + 1;
26:       }
27:   }
28:   catch (FileNotFoundException e) {
29:     System.err.println("Exception: couldn't find the fortune file");
30:     return false;
31:   }
32:   catch (IOException e) {
33:     System.err.println("Exception: I/O error trying to read fortunes");
34:     return false;
35:   }
36:
37:   return true;
38: }
```

ANALYSIS The initFortunes method first creates a File object based on the Fortunes.txt file, which is used to initialize a file input stream. The File object is also used to determine the length of the fortunes file. The length of the file is important because it is used to create a byte array large enough to hold all the fortunes that are read.

initFortunes reads the fortunes from the text file with a simple call to the read method of the input stream. The number of fortunes is then determined by counting the number of newline characters ('\n') in the fortune text. This works because each fortune is separated by a newline character in the file. When the number of fortunes has been established, a string array is created that is large enough to hold the fortunes. Using newline characters as separators, the fortune text is then parsed and each fortune stored in the array of strings. The end result is an array of strings that is much more convenient to access than attempting to read a file every time a client wants a fortune.

The last method in the FortuneServer class is main, which is the entry point of the server application:

```
public static void main(String[] args) {
  FortuneServer server = new FortuneServer();
```

BD 5

```
    server.start();
  }
```

As you can see, the `main` method is very simple; it creates a `FortuneServer` object and tells it to start running. That's it for the server side of Fortune!

Implementing the Fortune Client Applet

You might have been surprised by the simplicity of the Fortune server code. If so, then you'll probably be even more surprised by the client side of Fortune. The Fortune client class is simply called `Fortune` and is located on the CD-ROM in the file `Fortune.java`. Following are the member variables defined in the `Fortune` class:

```
private static final int  PORTNUM = 1234;
private String            fortune;
```

The `PORTNUM` member should be very familiar to you. Notice that it is set to the same value as the `PORTNUM` variable defined in `FortuneServer`. This is critical because the port number is what ties the two programs together. The `fortune` member variable simply holds the current fortune being displayed.

WARNING

It is very important that the port numbers for your client and server match exactly, because the port number is how the client and server are linked to each other.

The Fortune applet attempts to grab a fortune from the server as soon as it runs. This is accomplished in the `init` method, whose code follows:

```
public void init() {
  fortune = getFortune();
  if (fortune == null)
    fortune = "Error: No fortunes found!";
}
```

The `init` method calls `getFortune` to get a fortune from the server. If the fortune is invalid, an error message is displayed instead. The `getFortune` method handles the work of actually connecting to and getting a fortune from the server. The code for `getFortune` is shown in Listing 26.3.

TYPE   **Listing 26.3. The `getFortune` method.**

```
1: private String getFortune() {
2:   try {
3:     DatagramSocket  socket;
```

26

```
 4:    DatagramPacket  packet;
 5:    byte[]          data = new byte[256];
 6:
 7:    // Send a fortune request to the server
 8:    socket = new DatagramSocket();
 9:    packet = new DatagramPacket(data, data.length,
10:      InetAddress.getByName(getCodeBase().getHost()), PORTNUM);
11:    socket.send(packet);
12:
13:    // Receive a fortune
14:    packet = new DatagramPacket(data, data.length);
15:    socket.receive(packet);
16:    fortune = new String(packet.getData(), 0);
17:    socket.close();
18:  }
19:  catch (UnknownHostException e) {
20:    System.err.println("Exception: host could not be found");
21:    return null;
22:  }
23:  catch (Exception e) {
24:    System.err.println("Exception: " + e);
25:    e.printStackTrace();
26:    return null;
27:  }
28:  return fortune;
29: }
```

ANALYSIS The getFortune method first creates a request packet and sends it to the server. The contents of this packet are unimportant; the point is to just make contact with the server. After sending the request packet, getFortune creates a new packet and uses it to receive a fortune from the server.

Because Fortune is an applet, the fortunes are displayed graphically via the paint method. Listing 26.4 contains the paint method defined in the Fortune class.

BD 5

TYPE **Listing 26.4. The paint method.**

```
 1: public void paint(Graphics g) {
 2:   // Draw the title and fortune text
 3:   Font          f1 = new Font("TimesRoman", Font.BOLD, 28),
 4:                 f2 = new Font("Helvetica", Font.PLAIN, 16);
 5:   FontMetrics fm1 = g.getFontMetrics(f1),
 6:               fm2 = g.getFontMetrics(f2);
 7:   String      title = new String("Today's Fortune:");
 8:   g.setFont(f1);
 9:   g.drawString(title, (size().width - fm1.stringWidth(title)) / 2,
10:     ((size().height - fm1.getHeight()) / 2) + fm1.getAscent());
```

continues

Listing 26.4. continued

```
11:    g.setFont(f2);
12:    g.drawString(fortune, (size().width - fm2.stringWidth(fortune)) / 2,
13:      size().height - fm2.getHeight() - fm2.getAscent());
14: }
```

ANALYSIS The paint method may look a little complicated, but all it's doing is performing some fancy centering and alignment so that the positioning of the fortune looks good. The paint method also displays the text Today's Fortune: just above the fortune.

The final aspect of the Fortune class that you haven't covered is how to get a new fortune when the user clicks the mouse button. This is handled in the mouseDown method, whose code follows:

```
public boolean mouseDown(Event evt, int x, int y) {
  // Display a new fortune
  getFortune();
  repaint();
  return true;
}
```

Since getFortune already takes care of the details involved in getting a new fortune from the server, all the mouseDown method has to do is call getFortune and update the screen with a call to repaint. That sums up the client side of Fortune, which means you're probably ready to take it for a spin!

Running Fortune

As you already know, the Fortune example is composed of two parts: a client and a server. The Fortune server must be running in order for the client to work. So to get things started, you must first run the server by using the Java interpreter (java); you do this from a command line, like this:

```
java FortuneServer
```

 The other half of Fortune is the client, which is an applet that runs from within a Java-compatible Web browser, like Netscape Navigator or Microsoft Internet Explorer. After you have the server up and running, fire up a browser and load an HTML document including the Fortune client applet. On the CD-ROM, this HTML document is called Example1.html, in keeping with the standard JDK demo applets. After running the Fortune client applet, you should see something similar to what's shown in Figure 26.4. You can click in the applet window to retrieve new fortunes.

Figure 26.4.

The Fortune client applet.

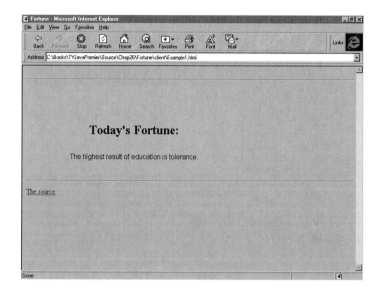

Today's Fortune:

The highest result of education is tolerance.

The source

NOTE

This discussion on running the Fortune example assumes that you either have access to a Web server or can simulate a network connection on your local machine. Since my local Windows 95 system is not part of a physical network, I tested the programs by simulating a network connection. I did this by changing the TCP/IP configuration on my system so that it used a specific IP address (I just made up an address). If you make this change to your network configuration, you won't be able to access a real network using TCP/IP until you set it back, so don't forget to restore things when you're finished.

BD
5

Trivia: A Stream Client and Server

The Fortune programs are a good example of how to use Java's datagram networking facilities. You will probably find, however, that more networking problems require a stream approach. Since I wouldn't want to leave you feeling like half a Java network programmer, let's look at an example that requires a stream socket approach.

The stream client/server example is called Trivia and consists of a server that asks trivia questions and a client that interacts with the server by allowing the user to answer the questions. The Trivia example differs from the Fortune example in that there is an ongoing two-way communication between the client and the server.

The Trivia example works like this: The server program waits patiently for a client to connect. When a client connects, the server sends a question and waits for a response. On the other end, the client receives the question and prompts the user for an answer. The user types in an answer that is sent back to the server. The server then checks to see if the answer is correct and notifies the user. The server follows this up by asking the client if it wants another question. If so, the process repeats.

Designing Trivia

It's important to always perform a brief preliminary design before you start churning out code. With that in mind, let's take a look at what is required of the Trivia server and client. On the server side, you need a program that monitors a particular port on the host machine for client connections, just as you did in Fortune. When a client is detected, the server picks a random question and sends it to the client over the specified port. The server then enters a wait state until it hears back from the client. When it gets an answer back from the client, the server checks it and notifies the client whether it is correct or incorrect. The server then asks the client if it wants another question, upon which it enters another wait state until the client answers. Finally, the server either repeats the process by asking another question, or it terminates the connection with the client. In summary, the server performs the following tasks:

1. Wait for a client to connect.
2. Accept the client connection.
3. Send a random question to the client.
4. Wait for an answer from the client.
5. Check the answer and notify the client.
6. Ask the client if it wants another question.
7. Wait for an answer from the client.
8. Go back to step 3 if necessary.

Unlike Fortune, the client side of the Trivia example is an application that runs from a command line. The client is responsible for connecting to the server and waiting for a question. When it receives a question from the server, the client displays it to the user and allows the user to type in an answer. This answer is sent back to the server, and the client again waits for the server's response. The client displays the server's response to the user and allows the user to confirm whether he wants another question. The client then sends the user's response to the server and exits if the user declined any more questions. The client's primary tasks follow:

26

1. Connect to the server.

2. Wait for a question to be sent.

3. Display the question and input the user's answer.

4. Send the answer to the server.

5. Wait for a reply from the server.

6. Display the server's reply and prompt the user to confirm another question.

7. Send the user's reply to the server.

8. Go back to step 2 if necessary.

Implementing the Trivia Server

Like Fortune, the heart of the Trivia example lies in the server. The Trivia server program is called TriviaServer and is located on the CD-ROM in the file TriviaServer.java. Following are the member variables defined in the TriviaServer class:

```
private static final int  PORTNUM = 1234;

private static final int  WAITFORCLIENT = 0;

private static final int  WAITFORANSWER = 1;

private static final int  WAITFORCONFIRM = 2;

private String[]          questions;

private String[]          answers;

private ServerSocket      serverSocket;

private int               numQuestions;

private int               num = 0;

private int               state = WAITFORCLIENT;

private Random            rand = new Random(System.currentTimeMillis());
```

The WAITFORCLIENT, WAITFORANSWER, and WAITFORCONFIRM members are all state constants that define different states the server can be in. You'll see these constants in action in a moment. The questions and answers member variables are string arrays used to store the questions and corresponding answers. The serverSocket member variable keeps up with the server socket connection. numQuestions is used to store the total number of questions, while num is the number of the current question being asked. The state member variable holds the current state of the server, as defined by the three state constants (WAITFORCLIENT, WAITFORANSWER, and WAITFORCONFIRM). Finally, the rand member variable is used to pick questions at random.

The TriviaServer constructor is very similar to FortuneServer's constructor, except that it creates a ServerSocket rather than a DatagramSocket. Check it out:

BD
5

```
public TriviaServer() {
  super("TriviaServer");
  try {
    serverSocket = new ServerSocket(PORTNUM);
    System.out.println("TriviaServer up and running...");
  }
  catch (IOException e) {
    System.err.println("Exception: couldn't create socket");
    System.exit(1);
  }
}
```

Also like Fortune, the run method in TriviaServer is where most of the action is. The source code for the run method is shown in Listing 26.5.

TYPE | **Listing 26.5. The run method.**

```
 1: public void run() {
 2:    Socket  clientSocket;
 3:
 4:    // Initialize the arrays of questions and answers
 5:    if (!initQnA()) {
 6:      System.err.println("Error: couldn't initialize questions and answers");
 7:      return;
 8:    }
 9:
10:    // Look for clients and ask trivia questions
11:    while (true) {
12:      // Wait for a client
13:      if (serverSocket == null)
14:        return;
15:      try {
16:        clientSocket = serverSocket.accept();
17:      }
18:      catch (IOException e) {
19:        System.err.println("Exception: couldn't connect to client socket");
20:        System.exit(1);
21:      }
22:
23:      // Perform the question/answer processing
24:      try {
25:        DataInputStream is = new DataInputStream(new
26:          BufferedInputStream(clientSocket.getInputStream()));
27:        PrintStream os = new PrintStream(new
28:          BufferedOutputStream(clientSocket.getOutputStream()), false);
29:        String inLine, outLine;
30:
31:        // Output server request
32:        outLine = processInput(null);
33:        os.println(outLine);
34:        os.flush();
35:
36:        // Process and output user input
37:        while ((inLine = is.readLine()) != null) {
```

26

```
38:           outLine = processInput(inLine);
39:           os.println(outLine);
40:           os.flush();
41:           if (outLine.equals("Bye."))
42:             break;
43:         }
44:
45:         // Cleanup
46:         os.close();
47:         is.close();
48:         clientSocket.close();
49:       }
50:       catch (Exception e) {
51:         System.err.println("Exception: " + e);
52:         e.printStackTrace();
53:       }
54:     }
55: }
```

ANALYSIS The run method first initializes the questions and answers by calling `initQnA`. You'll learn about the `initQnA` method in a moment. An infinite `while` loop is then entered that waits for a client connection. When a client connects, the appropriate I/O streams are created, and the communication is handled via the `processInput` method. You'll learn about `processInp ut` next. `processInput` continually processes client responses and handles asking new questions until the client decides not to receive any more questions. This is evidenced by the server sending the string `"Bye."`. The run method then cleans up the streams and client socket.

The `processInput` method keeps up with the server state and manages the logic of the whole question/answer process. The source code for `processInput` is shown in Listing 26.6.

TYPE **Listing 26.6. The `processInput` method.**

```
1: String processInput(String inStr) {
2:   String outStr;
3:
4:   switch (state) {
5:   case WAITFORCLIENT:
6:     // Ask a question
7:     outStr = questions[num];
8:     state = WAITFORANSWER;
9:     break;
10:
11:   case WAITFORANSWER:
12:     // Check the answer
13:     if (inStr.equalsIgnoreCase(answers[num]))
14:       outStr = "That's correct! Want another? (y/n)";
15:     else
```

continues

Listing 26.6. continued

```
16:        outStr = "Wrong, the correct answer is " + answers[num] +
17:           ". Want another? (y/n)";
18:      state = WAITFORCONFIRM;
19:      break;
20:
21:   case WAITFORCONFIRM:
22:      // See if they want another question
23:      if (inStr.equalsIgnoreCase("y")) {
24:        num = Math.abs(rand.nextInt()) % questions.length;
25:        outStr = questions[num];
26:        state = WAITFORANSWER;
27:      }
28:      else {
29:        outStr = "Bye.";
30:        state = WAITFORCLIENT;
31:      }
32:      break;
33:   }
34:   return outStr;
35: }
```

ANALYSIS   The first thing to note about the processInput method is the outStr local variable. The value of this string is sent back to the client in the run method when processInput returns. So keep an eye on how processInput uses outStr to convey information back to the client.

In FortuneServer, the state WAITFORCLIENT represents the server when it is idle and waiting for a client connection. Understand that each case statement in processInput() represents the server leaving the given state. For example, the WAITFORCLIENT case statement is entered when the server has just left the WAITFORCLIENT state. In other words, a client has just connected to the server. When this occurs, the server sets the output string to the current question and sets the state to WAITFORANSWER.

If the server is leaving the WAITFORANSWER state, it means that the client has responded with an answer. processInput checks the client's answer against the correct answer and sets the output string accordingly. It then sets the state to WAITFORCONFIRM.

The WAITFORCONFIRM state represents the server waiting for a confirmation answer from the client. In processInput, the WAITFORCONFIRM case statement indicates that the server is leaving the state because the client has returned a confirmation (yes or no). If the client answered yes with a y, processInput picks a new question and sets the state back to WAITFORANSWER. Otherwise, the server tells the client Bye. and returns the state to WAITFORCLIENT to await a new client connection.

26

Similar to Fortune, the questions and answers in Trivia are stored in a text file. This file is called QnA.txt and is organized with questions and answers on alternating lines. By alternating, I mean that each question is followed by its answer on the following line, which is in turn followed by the next question. Following is a partial listing of the QnA.txt file:

```
What caused the craters on the moon?
meteorites
How far away is the moon (in miles)?
239000
How far away is the sun (in millions of miles)?
93
Is the Earth a perfect spere?
no
What is the internal temperature of the Earth (in degrees F)?
9000
```

The initQnA method handles the work of reading the questions and answers from the text file and storing them in separate string arrays. Listing 26.7 contains the source code for the initQnA method.

TYPE   **Listing 26.7. The initQnA method.**

```
 1: private boolean initQnA() {
 2:   try {
 3:     File            inFile = new File("QnA.txt");
 4:     FileInputStream inStream = new FileInputStream(inFile);
 5:     byte[]          data = new byte[(int)inFile.length()];
 6:
 7:     // Read the questions and answers into a byte array
 8:     if (inStream.read(data) <= 0) {
 9:       System.err.println("Error: couldn't read questions and answers");
10:       return false;
11:     }
12:
13:     // See how many question/answer pairs there are
14:     for (int i = 0; i < data.length; i++)
15:       if (data[i] == (byte)'\n')
16:         numQuestions++;
17:     numQuestions /= 2;
18:     questions = new String[numQuestions];
19:     answers = new String[numQuestions];
20:
21:     // Parse the questions and answers into arrays of strings
22:     int start = 0, index = 0;
23:     boolean isQ = true;
24:     for (int i = 0; i < data.length; i++)
25:       if (data[i] == (byte)'\n') {
26:         if (isQ) {
```

continues

BD
5

Listing 26.7. continued

```
27:              questions[index] = new String(data, 0, start, i - start - 1);
28:              isQ = false;
29:            }
30:            else {
31:              answers[index] = new String(data, 0, start, i - start - 1);
32:              isQ = true;
33:              index++;
34:            }
35:            start = i + 1;
36:          }
37:        }
38:        catch (FileNotFoundException e) {
39:          System.err.println("Exception: couldn't find the fortune file");
40:          return false;
41:        }
42:        catch (IOException e) {
43:          System.err.println("Exception: I/O error trying to read questions");
44:          return false;
45:        }
46:
47:        return true;
48: }
```

ANALYSIS The initQnA method is similar to the initFortunes method in FortuneServer, except that in this case two arrays are being filled with alternating strings. The two arrays are the question and answer string arrays. Rather than repeat the earlier explanation for initFortunes, I'll leave it up to you to compare and contrast the differences between initFortunes and initQnA. You'll find that the differences are very small and have to do with the fact that you are now filling two arrays with alternating strings.

The only remaining method in TriviaServer is main, which follows:

```
public static void main(String[] args) {
  TriviaServer server = new TriviaServer();
  server.start();
}
```

Like the main method in FortuneServer, all this main method does is create the server object and get it started with a call to the start method.

Implementing the Trivia Client Applet

Since the client side of the Trivia example requires the user to type in answers and receive responses back from the server, it is more straightforward to implement as a command-line application. Sure, this may not be as cute as a graphical applet, but it makes it very easy to see the communication events as they unfold. The client application is called Trivia and is located on the CD-ROM in the file Trivia.java.

26

The only member defined in the `Trivia` class is `PORTNUM`, which defines the port number used by both the client and server. There is also only one method defined in the `Trivia` class: `main`. The source code for the `main` method is shown in Listing 26.8.

TYPE **Listing 26.8. The `main` method.**

```
 1: public static void main(String[] args) {
 2:   Socket          socket;
 3:   DataInputStream in;
 4:   PrintStream     out;
 5:   String          address;
 6:
 7:   // Check the command-line args for the host address
 8:   if (args.length != 1) {
 9:     System.out.println("Usage: java Trivia <address>");
10:     return;
11:   }
12:   else
13:     address = args[0];
14:
15:   // Initialize the socket and streams
16:   try {
17:     socket = new Socket(address, PORTNUM);
18:     in = new DataInputStream(socket.getInputStream());
19:     out = new PrintStream(socket.getOutputStream());
20:   }
21:   catch (IOException e) {
22:     System.err.println("Exception: couldn't create stream socket");
23:     System.exit(1);
24:   }
25:
26:   // Process user input and server responses
27:   try {
28:     StringBuffer  str = new StringBuffer(128);
29:     String        inStr;
30:     int           c;
31:
32:     while ((inStr = in.readLine()) != null) {
33:       System.out.println("Server: " + inStr);
34:       if (inStr.equals("Bye."))
35:         break;
36:       while ((c = System.in.read()) != '\n')
37:         str.append((char)c);
38:       System.out.println("Client: " + str);
39:       out.println(str.toString());
40:       out.flush();
41:       str.setLength(0);
42:     }
43:
44:     // Cleanup
45:     out.close();
46:     in.close();
```

continues

Listing 26.8. continued

```
47:     socket.close();
48:     }
49:   catch (IOException e) {
50:     System.err.println("Exception: I/O error trying to talk to server");
51:     }
52: }
```

ANALYSIS The first interesting thing you might notice about the main method is that it looks for a command-line argument. The command-line argument required of the Trivia client is the address of the server, such as thetribe.com. You may be wondering why the Fortune client didn't require you to specify a server address. The reason is that Java applets are accessed via Web pages, which are always associated with a particular server. So Java applets are inherently tied to a server and can therefore query the server for its address. This was accomplished in the Fortune client by calling the getHost method.

With Java applications, you don't have this option because there is no inherent server associated with the application. So you have to either hard-code the server address or ask for it as a command-line argument. I'm not very fond of hard-coding because it requires you to recompile any time you want to change something. Hence the command-line argument!

If the server address command-line argument is valid (not null), the main method creates the necessary socket and I/O streams. It then enters a while loop, where it processes information from the server and transmits user requests back to the server. When the server quits sending information, the while loop falls through, and the main method cleans up the socket and streams. And that's all there is to the Trivia client!

Running Trivia

Like Fortune, the Trivia server must be running in order for the client to work. To get things started, you must first run the server by using the Java interpreter; this is done from a command line, like this:

```
java TriviaServer
```

The Trivia client is also run from a command line, but you must specify a server address as the only argument. Following is an example of running the Trivia client and connecting to the server thetribe.com:

```
java Trivia "thetribe.com"
```

After running the Trivia client and answering a few questions, you should see output similar to this:

```
Server: Is the Galaxy rotating?
yes
Client: yes
Server: That's correct! Want another? (y/n)
y
Client: y
Server: Is the Earth a perfect sphere?
no
Client: no
Server: That's correct! Want another? (y/n)
y
Client: y
Server: What caused the craters on the moon?
asteroids
Client: asteroids
Server: Wrong, the correct answer is meteorites. Want another? (y/n)
n
Client: n
Server: Bye.
```

Summary

Today you have learned a wealth of information about client/server network programming in Java. You began the lesson by learning some fundamental concepts about the Internet and how it is organized as a network. More specifically, you learned about addresses, protocols, and ports, which all play a critical role in Internet communications. From there, you moved on to learning about client/server computing and how Java supports the client/server model through two different types of sockets: datagram sockets and stream sockets.

The last half of today's lesson led you through building two complete client/server programs. These two examples demonstrate the differing approaches to client/server network programming afforded by the Java datagram and stream socket classes. Both of these examples should serve as a solid basis for your own client/server projects.

If all the coding over the past few days has taken its toll on you, relax—tomorrow's lesson involves absolutely no programming. Tomorrow's lesson covers the Java standard extension APIs, which are a new set of API extensions that promise to add all kinds of neat features to Java. Aren't you excited?

Q&A

Q Why is the client/server paradigm so important in Java network programming?

A The client/server model was integrated into Java because it has proved time and again to be superior to other networking approaches. By dividing the process of serving data from the process of viewing and working with data, the client/server approach provides network developers with the freedom to implement a wide range of solutions to common network problems.

Q Why are datagram sockets less suitable for network communications than stream sockets?

A The primary reason is speed, because you have no way of knowing when information transferred through a datagram socket will reach its destination. Admittedly, you don't really know for sure when stream socket data will get to its destination either, but you can rest assured it will be faster than with the datagram socket. Also, datagram socket transfers have the additional complexity of your having to reorganize the incoming data, which is an unnecessary and time-consuming annoyance except in very rare circumstances.

Q How do I incorporate Fortune into a Web site?

A Beyond simply including the client applet in an HTML document that is served up by your Web server, you must also make sure that the Fortune server (FortuneServer) is running on the Web server machine. Without the fortune server, the clients are worthless.

Q How do I change the trivia questions and answers for Trivia?

A You simply edit the QnA.txt text file and add as many questions and answers as you want. Just make sure that each question and answer appears on its own line, and that each answer immediately follows its corresponding question.

Day 27

The Standard Extension APIs

by Michael Morrison

Throughout this book you've learned a lot about the Java programming environment and how it can be used to create interactive Web-based programs. Your knowledge of Java thus far has been entirely based on what is known as the core Java API, or Java Base API. Until recently, this core API comprised the entirety of the Java programming landscape. However, JavaSoft recently announced a broad plan for integrating various new software technologies into the Java API. These new technologies come in the form of extension APIs that integrate with the core Java API, and they are referred to as the *standard extension APIs*. At some point, many of these APIs will merge and become part of the core API, but for now they are all being presented as extensions.

Today's lesson takes a look at these new APIs and discusses what they have to offer, along with exactly how they will integrate with the existing core API. The main topics you cover today are

- [ ] Java software platform overview
- [ ] Enterprise and commerce API extensions
- [ ] Management and server API extensions
- [ ] Media API extensions
- [ ] Security API extensions
- [ ] Component API extensions
- [ ] Embedded systems API extensions

Most of these API extensions are very new and haven't even reached the specification stage. For this reason, today's lesson is only meant to give you an idea of where Java is headed with the standard extension APIs. In other words, you may want to check JavaSoft's Web site (www.javasoft.com) to get the latest scoop on the status of these APIs since they are in a constant state of flux.

Java API Overview

Java release 1.02, which is the latest Java release as of this writing, is now being referred to by JavaSoft as the *core Java API*. The core Java API defines the minimal set of functionality a Java implementation must support to be considered Java compliant. For example, when someone undertakes the job of supporting Java on a particular platform, he must fully implement the core Java API. This guaranteed support for the core API is what allows Java developers the luxury of being able to write Java programs once and have them run on any Java-compliant platform.

In the near future, JavaSoft plans to expand on the core API by introducing new APIs addressing more applied development needs. The new APIs cover a wide range of areas and will ultimately save developers a great deal of time by establishing a consistent approach to certain development issues, thereby reducing the need for custom coding. Some of these new APIs will merge with the core API; others will remain extensions. Regardless of their ultimate relationship to the core API, the new extension APIs are referred to as the standard extension APIs since they extend the current core API as we know it.

The standard extension API is broken up into a set of individual APIs targeting different development needs. Following are the major components of the standard extension APIs:

- [ ] Enterprise API
- [ ] Commerce API

- ☐ Management API
- ☐ Server API
- ☐ Media API
- ☐ Security API
- ☐ Java Beans API
- ☐ Embedded API

The rest of today's lesson focuses on each of these APIs and how they affect the Java software platform.

The Enterprise API

Enterprise computing has become increasingly important in recent years as more and more companies realize the importance of integrating their operations electronically. The unique possibilities afforded by the increased usage of the Internet have served to magnify the popularity of enterprise computing. JavaSoft took note of Java's lack of support for enterprise systems and announced plans for an Enterprise API.

The Java Enterprise API is designed to give Java programs a formal mechanism for connecting to enterprise information systems. This is a much-needed feature in Java since so many corporate computer systems rely heavily on enterprise information sources. In answering this need, the Enterprise API tackles the problem on three fronts. These fronts come in the form of three API subsets:

- ☐ Java Database Connectivity (JDBC)
- ☐ Interface Definition Language (IDL)
- ☐ Remote Method Invocation (RMI)

JavaSoft has recognized the importance of these three API subsets and plans to directly incorporate them into the core Java API at some point in the future.

Java Database Connectivity

The first of these subset APIs, JDBC, defines a structured interface to SQL (Structured Query Language) databases, which is the industry standard approach to accessing relational databases. By supporting SQL, JDBC allows developers to interact and support a wide range of databases. This means that the specifics of the underlying database platform are pretty much irrelevant when it comes to JDBC, which is very good news to Java developers.

BD
6

SQL databases are databases built on the SQL standard, which is a widely accepted standard that defines a strict protocol for accessing and manipulating data.

The JDBC API provides Java developers with a consistent approach to accessing SQL databases that is comparable to existing database development techniques, so interacting with a SQL database using JDBC isn't all that much different than interacting with a SQL database using traditional database tools. This should give Java programmers who already have some database experience confidence that they can hit the ground running with JDBC. The JDBC API has already been widely endorsed by industry leaders, including some development-tool vendors who have announced future support for JDBC in their development products.

The JDBC API includes classes for common SQL database constructs such as database connections, SQL statements, and result sets. JDBC Java programs will be able to use the familiar SQL programming model of issuing SQL statements and processing the resulting data. The JDBC API is largely dependent on a driver manager that supports multiple drivers connecting to different databases. JDBC database drivers can be either written entirely in Java or implemented using native methods to bridge Java applications to existing database access libraries.

 A *result set* is a group data retrieved from a database after a user request.

Interface Definition Language

The IDL subset of the Enterprise API is aimed at providing a way to connect Java client programs to network servers running on other platforms. IDL is an industry standard protocol for client/server communications across different platforms. The primary use of the IDL API is to transparently connect Java client programs to legacy systems.

A *legacy system* is an outdated system that has yet to be reimplemented using current technologies.

The Java IDL API includes the following components:

- A client framework that allows Java IDL clients to be designed as either applets or standalone applications
- A server framework that allows Java applications to act as network servers for IDL clients
- A development tool that automatically generates stub code for specific remote interfaces

27

Remote Method Invocation

The RMI component of the Enterprise API defines an interface for invoking object methods in a distributed environment. The RMI API serves a crucial purpose in the Enterprise API by adding full support for remote object communications. The RMI API makes it straightforward for Java developers to add remote computing support to their classes.

The Commerce API

As the role of the Internet continues to evolve from being just an information source to also being a retail marketplace, the need for a secure commercial transaction protocol is growing to new heights. Both Internet vendors and shoppers alike are eagerly awaiting the inevitable migration of shopping to the Web. JavaSoft has provided an answer to the secure purchasing problem with the Commerce API, which is a Java API extension that provides the overhead for Java programs to support secure purchasing and financial management.

The Java Commerce API aims to provide developers with an elegant solution to the problem of commercial transactions on the Web. The goal is to make purchasing goods a seamless, yet secure, part of the Web experience. To this end, the Commerce API is being pushed by JavaSoft as an open, extensible environment for financial management on the Web. The long-term plan for the Commerce API is for integration into the Java software platform partially with the core API and partially as a standard extension. It isn't clear yet which components will make it into the core API and which will remain separate.

The Commerce API consists of the following primary components:

- An infrastructure
- A database
- Payment cassettes
- Service cassettes
- Administrative interfaces

The infrastructure of the Commerce API is basically the architectural framework that defines the interactions between the other components of the API. This infrastructure is also what gives the API its extensibility to support future commerce extensions.

The database component serves as a repository for user information, such as payment methods and the user's shipping address. The database component contains encryption features so that user information can be kept completely private. Alternately, commerce service providers have the option of sharing user information with one another.

BD
6

The Commerce API makes use of *cassettes*, which are software modules that implement specific financial protocols. The two different types of cassettes supported are payment cassettes and service cassettes. A *payment cassette* defines the protocol for making electronic payments. Examples of payment cassettes are credit cards, debit cards, and eventually digital cash. A user could have multiple payment cassettes that represent different payment instruments, much like we carry different payment instruments in our wallets or purses. In fact, one of the classes in the Commerce API specifically models an electronic wallet.

New Term A *cassette* is a software module that implements a specific payment protocol.

Service cassettes are more general, and they model any type of value-added financial service such as financial analysis or tax preparation modules. For example, you could feasibly purchase a service cassette to help balance your electronic checkbook or assess the value of your stock portfolio.

The last component of the Commerce API includes administrative interfaces, which are dialog boxes and other graphical interfaces used to retrieve information from the user and to configure commerce options.

The Management API

The Management API is designed to answer the needs of integrated network management systems. It includes a wide range of interfaces, classes, and applets to facilitate the development of integrated management solutions. The primary goal of the Management API is to provide a unified approach to handling the complexities involved in developing and maintaining resources and services on a heterogeneous network. Using the Management API, Java developers will be able to rapidly develop network management applications supporting a wide range of systems on large and often complex networks. JavaSoft plans to keep the Management API as a separate extension from the core API.

The Management API includes the following core components:

- ☐ The Admin View Module (AVM)
- ☐ Base object interfaces
- ☐ Managed container interfaces
- ☐ Managed notification interfaces
- ☐ Managed data interfaces
- ☐ Managed protocol interfaces
- ☐ SNMP interfaces
- ☐ Applet integration interfaces

The Admin View Module is an extension of the Java Abstract Windowing Toolkit (AWT) that is enhanced to provide specific support for creating integrated management applications. The classes implemented in the AVM serve as a basis for developing sophisticated graphical user interfaces. For example, the AVM includes support for graphical tables, charts, graphs, and meters.

The base object interfaces define the core object types that are used for distributed resources and services in a management system. Using the base object interfaces, developers can define abstractions for a variety of attributes associated with a managed enterprise environment.

The managed container interfaces define a means for grouping together managed objects for better organization. This organization facilitates a more group-oriented approach to keeping up with managed resources, which can be a great benefit in complex systems.

The managed notification interfaces define a core foundation of managed-event notification services. Developers are free to develop more advanced application-specific notification services by extending these services.

The managed data interfaces provide a means of linking managed object attributes to relational databases via JDBC. In doing so, the managed data interfaces establish a transparent link between management resources and external databases.

The managed protocol interfaces use the Java Security APIs and Java RMI to add secure distributed object support to the core functionality provided by the base object interfaces. In turn, the SNMP interfaces extend the managed protocol interfaces to provide support for SNMP agents. Since SNMP is the most popular management protocol in use, its support via the SNMP interfaces is an important part of the Management API.

 SNMP stands for Simple Network Management Protocol, which is a relatively simple protocol originally developed to solve communication problems between different types of networks and gather network statistics.

Finally, the applet integration interfaces component of the Management API specifies how Java applets can be integrated with the Management API to provide management solutions. Applet developers use the applet integration interfaces to build management support into their applets.

The Server API

After the success of Java and its immediate use for developing client-side applets, JavaSoft decided to take steps to make Java a more viable alternative for server-side applications. The Server API is JavaSoft's answer to the need for more complete server-oriented support in Java. The Server API provides a wide range of server functionality including support for administration, accessibility control, and dynamic resource handling. Also included in the Server API is the Servlet API, which provides a framework for extending servers with servlets. JavaSoft plans to keep the Server API an extension separate from the core API.

 A *servlet* is a Java object that extends the functionality of an information server, such as an HTTP server. You can think of servlets as the server equivalents of client-side Java applets.

The Servlet API provides the overhead necessary for creating servlets and interfacing them with information servers. The Servlet API is equipped to handle the entire servlet/server relationship, with an emphasis on keeping things stable and simple. All that is required to run servlets is a server that supports the Servlet API.

The Media API

Possibly the weakest area of the core Java API as we know it is its support for media. Currently, the Java API supports only static GIF and JPEG images and wave sounds in the AU sound format. This limited media support won't cut it in the long run. Sure, developers can hack their own media implementations to some extent, but they could do that already in a variety of other languages and platforms. Java was supposed to make things easier, right?

JavaSoft realized this weakness and is remedying things with the Media API, which is slated to include support for a dizzying array of media types that will no doubt put Java on the map as a serious multimedia platform. The Media API includes classes that model media types such as full-motion video, audio, 2D and 3D graphics, and telephony. Furthermore, the structure of the API is such that many of these media types will rely on the same underlying facilities. For example, all time-based media like video and audio will use the same underlying timing mechanism, meaning that synchronization won't be a problem.

The Media API is designed to be very open and extensible, which is important considering the fact that the world of multimedia is ever changing. JavaSoft plans to integrate the Media API into the Java platform both as core API additions and as standard extension APIs.

The following API subsets comprise the Media API:

- The Media Framework API
- The 2D Graphics API
- The Animation API
- The 3D Graphics API
- The Video API
- The Audio API

27

☐ The MIDI API
☐ The Share API
☐ The Telephony API

The Media Framework API handles the low-level timing functionality required by many of the other media APIs. This API includes support for timing and synchronization, both of which are critical to media types that must function together in harmony. Also included in the Media Framework API is support for streaming, compression, and live data sources.

NEW TERM *Synchronization* refers to how different time-based media elements agree with each other in time. For example, it is important for the sound track of a movie to remain synchronized with the picture.

NEW TERM *Streaming* is the process of interacting with data while it is still being transferred. For example, a streaming audio player would begin playing audio as soon as a certain minimal amount of data has been transferred.

The 2D Graphics API extends the functionality of the AWT classes to provide wider support for 2D graphics primitives and a variety of different graphical output devices, such as printers. Another important addition to the 2D Graphics API is the definition of a uniform graphical model that brings many graphics functions into one structure. The Animation API uses the 2D Graphics API as a basis for its implementation of animated 2D graphics objects, or sprites. It also relies on the Media Framework API for maintaining timing and synchronization.

The 3D Graphics API provides the overhead necessary to generate high-performance 3D graphics. This API implements 3D graphics by supporting a model of 3D graphical objects that can be rendered at high speeds. The 3D Graphics API also includes support for VRML, which is a popular 3D modeling language. To pull off all this functionality, the 3D Graphics API relies heavily on the functions provided by many of the other media APIs.

The Video API brings full-motion video to Java. The API provides the framework for managing and processing video in either a streaming or stored scenario. Similar to the Video API in some ways, the Audio API also provides support for both streaming and stored media. However, the media supported by the Audio API consists of either sampled or synthesized audio. The Audio API even contains classes for implementing 3D spatial audio.

The MIDI API brings timed musical events to Java by way of the popular MIDI standard. MIDI is an efficient way to represent both musical pieces as well as more general timing resources. Expect to hear the Web much differently once this API catches on!

NEW TERM *MIDI* stands for Musical Instrument Digital Interface. It defines a protocol for communicating and storing time-based events, such as those generated by playing a musical instrument.

BD
6

The Share API is probably the most interesting of the media APIs, simply because it's the least obvious. It defines a means by which live, multiparty communication can take place over a network. The Share API provides support for both synchronization and session management. I wouldn't be surprised to see multiplayer games and "chat" applets take on a new feel once this API is out.

The last of the media APIs is the Telephony API, which gives Java the ability to interact with telephones. Most important telephone functions, including teleconferencing and caller ID, are supported in this API.

The Security API

The eagerly awaited Security API will hopefully remedy one of the biggest limitations of Java applets: the inability to read or write files locally. With full support for cryptography, digital signatures, and authentication, Java developers should be able to leverage security issues to some extent and move away from the seemingly overprotective solution currently in place. The Security API will eventually be incorporated directly into the core Java API.

 Cryptography encompasses the algorithms and techniques used to render data unrecognizable in the hands of unauthorized parties, thereby enforcing information privacy.

 A *digital signature* is an electronic identification technique that serves much the same purpose as a handwritten signature.

 Authentication is the process of verifying an action based on a security check.

The cryptographic functions built into the Security API are isolated from the programmatic interface used by applets wanting to make security decisions. This layering allows the cryptographic functions to be replaced by third-party alternatives without impacting anything at the applet level, thereby giving Java developers more options when it comes to their security needs.

The Java Beans API

The Java Beans API defines an open standard for implementing dynamic Java software components, which are tightly packaged classes designed for reusability. Because the Java Beans API is given prominent coverage in tomorrow's lesson, I'll spare you the juicy details for now. However, I will tell you now that the Java Beans API is planned to merge with the core Java API at some point.

The Embedded API

The last of the standard extension APIs is the Embedded API, which defines a minimal set of Java functionality specifically targeted for embedded systems applications, such as consumer electronics devices. The Embedded API is the only API that doesn't really add anything to the Java core API. In fact, the Embedded API will likely be a subset of the core API since only part of the core functionality is needed in embedded applications. For example, since most embedded systems have no graphical output to speak of, the entire AWT is really unnecessary. Likewise, a network connection is unlikely in an embedded system, so there is no need to include the Java networking package.

 An *embedded system* is a scaled-down computer system programmed to perform a particular function within an electronic device.

It is likely that the Embedded API will consist of the following packages from the core API: language, utilities, and I/O. Beyond those, it's possible that Embedded API extensions could be developed to support specialized networking and output requirements. Since the Embedded API is itself a subset of the core API, it will probably be treated as an extension API.

Summary

Today you have learned about the standard extension APIs that are planned to expand Java in a variety of different directions. These APIs will no doubt boost the appeal of Java to new levels, since developers will have much more reusable code to leverage when building custom applications and applets. Although this will ultimately mean more learning on the part of developers, it will also result in less time spent writing code that is best suited to a standard extension. Knowing this, many developers will be forced to rethink their current plans based on the availability of the standard extension APIs, as there's no need to reinvent the wheel if it's already in the works.

Tomorrow you'll continue to learn about Java extensions by looking at some other technologies that are going to affect Java in the near future.

BD
6

Q&A

Q What exactly is the core Java API and how will it change?

A The core Java API as of Java version 1.02 consists of the eight packages that are shipped with version 1.02 of the Java Developer's Kit. This API will change in future releases to incorporate some of the technologies that are emerging as part of the standard extension APIs. However, not all of the standard extension APIs will make it into the core API; some will remain as extensions.

Q Will the Commerce API help standardize financial transactions on the Web?

A I sure hope so. Considering the large amount of Java development already taking place, combined with JavaSoft's desire to make the Commerce API extensible to a variety of technologies, it stands to reason that the Commerce API will be a major force in shaping the future of financial transactions on the Web.

Q How are servlets developed?

A Servlets are developed in much the same way as applets, except you use the Servlet API instead of the Applet API. Most servlets probably won't have graphical interfaces, but the approach of developing servlets based on an API is still very similar to the current approach to developing applets.

Q How will digital signatures affect Java security?

A It's still not clear what the total impact of digital signatures will be on Java security, but the most likely change will be the removal of the local file access restriction on applets. Using digital signatures, it will be possible to validate the origination of an applet so that users can feel safe allowing the applet more freedom on their system.

Day 28

Emerging Technologies

by Michael Morrison

This last lesson of the bonus week peers into the crystal ball and takes a look at some of the emerging Java technologies. Today you'll learn about a few of the latest groundbreaking Java technologies and what impact they will have on Java as we know it. By looking into the future, you can better gauge where to aim your resources in the present, so today's lesson attempts to give you a rough sketch of a few of the major new and pending products that will no doubt play a significant role in the future of Java.

Today's lesson covers the following major topics:

- ☐ Java Beans components
- ☐ The JavaOS operating system
- ☐ Java microprocessors

The Java technologies you'll learn about today are still in their early stages as of this writing, which means I can give you only a preliminary look at what they have to offer. Nevertheless, you should still be able to take from this lesson a better understanding of where Java is headed and what it might mean to your own development efforts.

Java Beans

For some time now, the software development community has been pushing the idea of reusable components. In case you've missed the hype, a *component* is a reusable piece of software that can be easily assembled to create applications with much greater development efficiency. This notion of reusing carefully packaged software was borrowed to some extent from the assembly-line approach that became so popular in the United States during the industrial revolution, well before the modern computer era. The idea as applied to software is to build small, reusable components once and then reuse them as much as possible, thereby streamlining the entire development process.

 A *software component* is a piece of software isolated into a discrete, easily reusable structure.

Although component software has its merits, fully reusable software has yet to really establish itself; this is so for a variety of reasons, not the least of which is the fact that the software industry is still very young compared to the industries carved out in the industrial revolution. It stands to reason that it should take time to iron out the kinks in the whole software-production process. If you're like me, you'll embrace the rapid changes taking place in the software world and relish the fact that you are a part of a revolution of sorts—an information revolution. But I digress!

Perhaps the largest difficulty component software has had to face is the wide range of disparate microprocessors and operating systems in use today. There have been a variety of reasonable attempts at component software, but they've always been limited to a specific operating system. Microsoft's VBX and OCX component architectures have had great success in the PC world, but they've done little to bridge the gap between other types of operating systems. Weighing in the amount of work required to get an inherently platform-dependent component technology running on a wide range of operating systems, it makes sense that Microsoft has focused solely on the PC market.

 NOTE

Actually, Microsoft's new ActiveX technology, which is based on its OCX technology, aims to provide an all-purpose component technology compatible across a wide range of platforms. However, considering

28

> the dependency of ActiveX on 32-bit Windows code, it has yet to be seen how Microsoft will solve the platform-dependency issue. Maybe they are just waiting around for everyone to switch to Windows 95/NT?

Prior to the explosion of the Internet, the platform-dependency issue wasn't all that big a deal. PC developers didn't necessarily care too much that their products wouldn't run on a Solaris system. Okay, some PC developers hedged their bets and ported their applications to the Macintosh platform, but most with considerable development efforts. The whole scenario changed with the operating system melting pot created by the Internet. The result was a renewed interest in developing software that everyone can use, regardless of which operating system they happen to be running. Java has been a major factor in making truly platform-independent software development a reality. However, until recently Java has not provided an answer to the issue of component software—we'll get to that in just a moment.

As if the platform-dependency issue weren't enough, some existing component technologies also suffer from having to be developed in a particular programming language or for a particular development environment. Just as platform dependency cripples components at runtime, limiting component development to a particular programming language or development environment equally cripples components at the development end. Software developers want to be able to decide for themselves which language is the most appropriate for a particular task. Likewise, developers want to be able to select the development environment that best fits their needs, rather than being forced to use one based on the constraints of a component technology.

So any realistic long-term component technology must deal with both the issue of platform dependency and language dependency. This brings me to the topic at hand: Java Beans. JavaSoft's Java Beans technology is a component technology that answers both of these problems directly. The Java Beans technology promises to take the component software assembly paradigm to a new level. As of this writing, the Java Beans specification is under development with a preliminary release to follow soon after.

Java Beans is being implemented as an architecture- and platform-independent API for creating and using dynamic Java software components. Java Beans picks up where other component technologies have left off, using the portable Java platform as the basis for providing a complete component software solution that is readily applicable to the online world.

BD
7

The Goal of Java Beans

Following the rapid success of the Java runtime system and programming language, JavaSoft realized the importance of developing a complete component technology solution. Its answer is the Java Beans technology, whose design goals can be summarized by the following list of requirements:

- ☐ Compact and easy to create and use
- ☐ Fully portable
- ☐ Built on the inherent strengths of Java
- ☐ Robust distributed computing mechanisms
- ☐ Support for flexible design-time component editors

The first requirement of Java Beans—to be very compact—is based on the fact that the Java Beans components will often be used in distributed environments where entire components may be transferred across a low-bandwidth Internet connection. Clearly, components must be as compact as possible to facilitate a reasonable transfer time. The second part of this goal relates to the ease with which the components are built and used. It's not such a stretch to imagine components that are easy to use, but creating a component architecture that makes it easy to build components is a different issue altogether. Existing attempts at component software have often been plagued by complex programming APIs that make it difficult for developers to create components without chronic headaches. So Java Beans components must be not only easy to use, but also easy to develop. For you and me, this is a critical requirement because it means fewer ulcers and more time to embellish components with frilly features.

Java Beans components are largely based on the class structure already in use with traditional Java applet programming, which is an enormous benefit to those of us heavily investing our time and energy in learning Java. JavaSoft has promised that Java applets designed around the AWT package will easily scale to new Java Beans components. This also has the positive side effect of making Java Beans components very compact, since Java applets are already very efficient in terms of size.

The second major goal of Java Beans is to be fully portable; you learned the importance of this at the beginning of this lesson. JavaSoft is in the process of finalizing a Java Beans API that defines the specific component framework for Java Beans components. The Java Beans API coupled with the platform-independent Java system it is based on will together comprise the platform-independent component solution alluded to earlier. As a result, developers will not need to worry about including platform-specific libraries with their Java applets. The result will be reusable components that will unify the world of computing under one happy, peaceful umbrella. OK, maybe that's asking a little too much—I'll settle for just being able to develop a component and have it run unmodified on any Java-supported system.

The existing Java architecture already offers a wide range of benefits easily applied to components. One of the more important, but rarely mentioned, features of Java is its built-in class discovery mechanism, which allows objects to interact with each other dynamically. This results in a system where objects can be integrated with each other independently of their respective origins or development history. The class discovery mechanism is not just a neat feature of Java; it is a necessary requirement in any component architecture. It is fortunate for Java Beans that this functionality is already provided by Java at no additional cost. Other component architectures have had to implement messy registration mechanisms to achieve the same result.

Another example of Java Beans inheriting existing Java functionality is persistence, which is the capability of an object to store and retrieve its internal state. Persistence is handled automatically in Java Beans by simply using the serialization mechanism already present in Java. Alternately, developers can create customized persistence solutions whenever necessary.

 Persistence is the capability of an object or component to store and retrieve its internal state.

 Serialization is the process of storing or retrieving information through a standard protocol.

Although not a core element of the Java Beans architecture, support for distributed computing is a major issue with Java Beans. Because distributed computing requires relatively complex solutions as a result of the complex nature of distributed systems, Java Beans leverages the usage of external distributed approaches based on need. In other words, Java Beans allows developers to use distributed computing mechanisms whenever necessary, but it doesn't overburden itself with core support for distributed computing. This may seem like the Java Beans architects are being lazy, but in fact it is this very design approach that allows Java Beans components to be very compact, since distributed computing solutions inevitably require much more overhead.

Java Beans component developers have the option of selecting a distributed computing approach that best fits their needs. JavaSoft provides a distributed computing solution in its Remote Method Invocation (RMI) technology, but Java Beans developers are in no way handcuffed to this solution. Other options include CORBA (Common Object Request Broker Architecture) and Microsoft's DCOM (Distributed Component Object Model),

BD 7

among others. The point is that distributed computing has been cleanly abstracted from Java Beans to keep things tight while still allowing developers that require distributed support a wide range of options.

The final design goal of Java Beans deals with design-time issues and how developers build applications using Java Beans components. The Java Beans architecture includes support for specifying design-time properties and editing mechanisms to better facilitate visual editing of Java Beans components. The result is that developers will be able to use visual tools to assemble and modify Java Beans components in a seamless fashion, much the way existing PC visual tools work with components such as VBX or OCX controls. In this way, component developers specify the way in which the components are to be used and manipulated in a development environment. This feature alone will officially usher in the usage of professional visual editors and significantly boost the productivity of applications developers.

How Java Beans Relates to Java

Many developers not completely familiar with the idea of software components will likely be confused by Java Beans's relationship to Java. Hasn't Java been touted as an object-oriented technology capable of serving up reusable objects? Yes and no. Yes, Java provides a means of building reusable objects, but there are few rules or standards governing how objects interact with each other. Java Beans builds on the existing design of Java by specifying a rich set of mechanisms for interaction between objects, along with common actions most objects will need to support, such as persistence and event handling.

The current Java component model, although not bad, is relatively limited when it comes to delivering true reusability and interoperability. At the object level, there is really no straightforward mechanism for creating reusable Java objects that can interact with other objects dynamically in a consistent fashion. The closest thing you can do in Java is to create applets and attempt to allow them to communicate with each other on a Web page, which isn't a very straightforward task. Java Beans provides the framework by which this communication can take place with ease. Even more important is the fact that Java Beans components can be easily tweaked via a standard set of well-defined properties. Basically, Java Beans merges the power of full-blown Java applets with the compactness and reusability of Java AWT components, such as buttons.

Java Beans components aren't limited to visual objects such as buttons, however. You can just as easily develop nonvisual Java Beans components that perform some background function in concert with other components. In this way, Java Beans merges the power of visual Java applets with nonvisual Java applications under a consistent component framework.

NOTE

A nonvisual component is any component that doesn't have visible output. When thinking of components in terms of AWT objects like buttons and menus, this may seem a little strange. However, keep in mind that a component is simply a tightly packaged program and has no specific requirement of being visual. A good example of a nonvisual component is a timer component, which fires timing events at specified intervals. Timer components are very popular in other component development environments, such as Microsoft Visual Basic.

You can use together a variety of Java Beans components without necessarily writing any code by using visual tools. This ability to use a variety of components together regardless of their origin is an enhancement to the current Java model. You can certainly use other prebuilt objects in Java, but you must have an intimate knowledge of the object's interface. Additionally, you must integrate the object into your code programmatically. Java Beans components expose their own interfaces visually, providing a means to edit their properties without programming. Furthermore, using a visual editor, you can simply "drop" a Java Beans component directly into an application without writing any code. This is an entirely new level of flexibility and reuse not previously possible in Java alone.

The Java Beans API

Okay, I've rambled enough about Java Beans from the standpoint of what it does and why it's cool. Let's focus now on some specifics regarding how all this is possible. Keep in mind that Java Beans is ultimately a programming interface, meaning that all its features are implemented as extensions to the standard Java class library. So all the functionality provided by Java Beans is actually implemented in the Java Beans API. The Java Beans API itself is a suite of smaller APIs devoted to specific functions, or services. Following is a list of the main component services in the Java Beans API that are necessary to facilitate all the features you've been learning about today:

- ☐ GUI merging
- ☐ Persistence
- ☐ Event handling
- ☐ Introspection
- ☐ Application builder support

BD
7

By understanding these services and how they work, you'll have much more insight into exactly what type of technology Java Beans is. Each of these services is implemented in the form of smaller APIs contained within the larger Java Beans API. The next few sections are devoted to each of these APIs and why they are necessary elements of the Java Beans architecture.

GUI Merging

The GUI-merging APIs provide a means for a component to merge its GUI elements with the container document, which is usually just the Web page containing the component. Most container documents have menus and toolbars that need to display any special features provided by the component. The GUI-merging APIs allow the component to add features to the container document's menu and toolbar. These APIs also define the mechanism facilitating space negotiations between components and their containers. In other words, the GUI-merging APIs also define the layout properties for components.

NEW TERM A *container document* is a document (typically HTML) containing Java Beans components that serves as a parent for all the components it contains. Container documents typically are responsible for managing the main menu and toolbar, among other things.

Persistence

The persistence APIs specify the mechanism by which components can be stored and retrieved within the context of a containing document. By default, components inherit the automatic serialization mechanism provided by Java. Developers are also free to design more elaborate persistence solutions based on the specific needs of their components.

Event Handling

The event-handling APIs specify an event-driven architecture that defines how components interact with each other. The Java AWT already includes a powerful event-handling model, which serves as the basis for the event-handling component APIs. These APIs are critical in allowing components the freedom to interact with each other in a consistent fashion.

Introspection

The introspection APIs define the techniques by which components make their internal structure readily available at design time. These APIs consist of the functionality necessary to allow development tools to query a component for its internal state, including the interfaces, methods, and member variables that comprise the component. The APIs are divided into two distinct sections, based on the level at which they are being used. For example, the low-level introspection APIs allow development tools direct access to component internals, which is a function you wouldn't necessarily want in the hands of component users. This brings us to the high-level APIs. The high-level APIs use the low-level APIs to determine which parts of a component are exported for user modification. So although development tools will undoubtedly make use of both APIs, they will use the high-level APIs only when providing component information to the user.

Application Builder Support

The application builder support APIs provide the overhead necessary for editing and manipulating components at design time. These APIs are used largely by visual development tools to provide a means to visually lay out and edit components while constructing an application. The section of a component providing visual editing capabilities is specifically designed to be physically separate from the component itself. This is so standalone runtime components can be as compact as possible. In a purely runtime environment, components are transferred with only the necessary runtime component. Developers wanting to use the design-time component facilities can easily acquire the design-time portion of the component.

JavaOS

Even though Java has been touted largely as a neat new programming language, it is in fact much more than that. Java is also a very powerful and compact runtime system that in many ways mimics the facilities provided by a full-blown operating system. Knowing this, it wasn't a complete surprise to some that JavaSoft decided to build a complete operating system around the Java technology. This new operating system is called JavaOS, and is described by JavaSoft as "a highly compact operating system designed to run Java applications directly on microprocessors in anything from net computers to pagers."

The status of the JavaOS project is still largely under wraps as of this writing, but there is enough information out to at least get an idea of where JavaSoft is headed with it. First and foremost, JavaOS is expected to ride the wave created by Java and its insanely rapid success. However, don't let that statement mislead you into thinking that JavaOS is any less legitimate than the technology on which it is built. The idea of building a complete operating system on top of the existing Java technology makes perfect sense. And if JavaSoft puts as much thought into JavaOS as it did into Java, it will no doubt be a very interesting operating system.

BD
7

The applications of a compact, efficient operating system that can natively run Java programs are far and wide. In fact, JavaSoft has already made mention of a variety of devices to which the JavaOS technology could be easily applied. These devices include everything from networked computers to cellular telephones—basically any device that could benefit from a compact operating system and support for a powerful programming language like Java.

Overhead

JavaOS has been described by JavaSoft as just enough of an operating system to run the Java virtual machine. With this minimal design goal, it stands to reason that JavaSoft is largely targeting electronic devices with the JavaOS technology. As part of this approach, JavaOS is specifically designed to be fully ROMable, meaning that it will work well in the embedded systems common to electronic devices.

New Term A *ROMable* software technology is one that can be implemented in read-only memory (ROM). ROM is commonly used in electronic devices to store executable system code, since there is typically no other storage means beyond random access memory (RAM), which is temporary.

New Term An *embedded system* is a scaled-down computer system programmed to perform a particular function within an electronic device.

JavaSoft has made mention of JavaOS being able to run with as little as 512KB of ROM and 256KB of RAM in an embedded environment. Likewise, an entire JavaOS system running on a networked computer requires only 3MB of ROM and 4MB of RAM. These last figures include space for JavaOS, the HotJava Web browser, and a cache for downloading Web content and applets. JavaOS's minimal requirements set the stage for some unique products such as compact personal digital assistants (PDAs) with complete Internet support.

Industry Support

Because of the success of Java, JavaOS is able to enjoy industry support prior to its availability in even a preliminary form. An impressive group of technology companies have already announced plans to license JavaOS. Likewise, an equally important group of software tools companies have announced plans to provide development tools for JavaOS. These two areas of support provide the one-two punch necessary for JavaOS to be a success.

JavaSoft is already working with the software tools companies to define a set of APIs for developing applications for JavaOS. Major players on the Java development scene have already announced intentions to enhance their development environments to support

JavaOS embedded systems development. This is a pretty major step in the embedded programming world, where many development tools are still fairly primitive compared to the visual tools used by computer applications developers.

NOTE

On a similar front, both the Solaris and Windows platforms are slated to include full support for Java at the operating-system level. However, this support will be aimed more at supporting the Java runtime system than serving as an implementation of JavaOS.

Java Microprocessors

As if Sun weren't branching out enough with JavaOS, it recently surprised the microprocessor world by announcing the development of a line of microprocessors that are optimized for Java. Microprocessors aren't new to Sun, whose Sun Microelectronics division is responsible for the popular SPARC line of microprocessors. However, the idea of Sun Microelectronics developing microprocessors specifically to support Java no doubt caught a lot of people off guard, including other microprocessor companies!

NOTE

Just so you don't get confused, both JavaSoft and Sun Microelectronics are divisions of Sun Microsystems. So whenever I refer to Sun I'm referring to the overall company.

Java microprocessors are quite obviously yet another move on Sun's part to capitalize on the success of Java. However, like JavaOS, Sun legitimately has an interesting and potentially lucrative angle in developing Java microprocessors. Also like JavaOS, the primary target application for Java microprocessors is in embedded systems. Speed is a critical factor in embedded systems, primarily due to the limited horsepower available in such small systems. Java microprocessors have the potential to significantly increase performance since they are being designed around the highly efficient Java technology. Contrast this with other embedded microprocessors that typically have a more general design.

Sun is pushing Java microprocessors based on a new microprocessor product paradigm: simple, secure, and small. Add to this Sun's promise of delivering Java microprocessors at a fraction of the cost of traditional microprocessors. Sun is clearly appealing to the consumer

**BD
7**

electronics market, where a compact, low-cost microprocessor would probably rock a lot of boats. Sun has also announced the development of a full range of component- and board-level products to support the microprocessors.

Even though the prospect of a Java microprocessor might seem strange at first, it's not hard to see the motivation. By 1999, the average American home is expected to contain between 50 and 100 microcontrollers. Worldwide, there are also expected to be more than 145 million cellular phone users, with each phone containing at least one microcontroller. And each microcontroller contains at least one microprocessor. Are you starting to get the picture?

 A *microcontroller* is a miniature computer system, usually implemented on a single circuit board, scaled down to support a limited function such as those required by electronic devices.

The Java processor family is slated to consist of three lines of microprocessors:

- [ ] picoJAVA
- [ ] microJAVA
- [ ] UltraJAVA

The next few sections describe these different processor lines and which applications each is targeting.

picoJAVA

The low-end line of Java microprocessors is called picoJAVA and serves as the basic design on which all the microprocessors are based. The picoJAVA core is designed to provide the best price/performance microprocessor that fully supports the Java virtual machine. The picoJAVA line of microprocessors is expected to have a per-processor cost of under $25, establishing it as a prime target for cellular phone applications, among many other consumer electronics products.

microJAVA

The next processor line above picoJAVA is microJAVA, which builds application-specific I/O, memory, communications, and control functions onto the picoJAVA core. microJAVA processors are expected to cost anywhere from $25 to $100, which makes them good candidates for a wide range of network devices such as telecommunications equipment, along with other non-network applications such as printers and video games.

UltraJAVA

The high-end line of Java microprocessors is called UltraJAVA and is designed to be the very fastest Java processors available. The UltraJAVA processor line includes support for advanced graphics by virtue of Sun's Visual Instruction Set (VIS), which defines high-performance hardware graphics extensions. Not surprisingly, the UltraJAVA line of processors is primarily targeting high-end 3D graphics and multimedia applications. With an expected cost starting at $100, the UltraJAVA processor line may still be a bargain.

Summary

Today you have taken stock of the future of Java by learning about some technologies that are built on the stable framework of Java. Although these technologies may not necessarily affect your Java development efforts anytime soon, they will still play a critical role in Java reaching maturity as a stable technology. You began the lesson by learning about Java Beans, which is a new software technology that promises to bring reusable software components to Java. You then moved on to JavaOS, which is a new operating system based entirely on the Java virtual machine. You finished up the lesson with a look at the new Java microprocessors, which aim to be first silicon Java implementation.

This lesson concludes your bonus week. Throughout this week you've learned a great deal of information that isn't entirely related, except for the fact that Java is at the heart of it all. I encourage you to use this information as a foundation to learn more about Java programming and the emerging technologies that will enhance it in the future.

Q&A

Q **What is the difference between a Java Beans component and a regular Java class?**

A A Java Beans component is a regular Java class built on the Java Beans API. More specifically, a Java Beans component adds to the standard Java class structure the ability to interact with other components, a well-defined mechanism for exposing information about itself, and a means by which it can be visually edited.

BD
7

Q What is an example of a container document?

A A good example of a container document is an HTML page. Understand that the role of a container document goes beyond just being a document in the sense that an HTML document consists of HTML code. In regard to Java Beans components, a container document provides much of the overhead of the parent application, such as managing the main menu and toolbar. In this case, the parent application is the Web browser the document is being viewed in.

Q Will JavaOS compete with established desktop operating systems like Windows 95 or the Macintosh OS?

A I'm not going to make any absolute statements here, but it looks extremely unlikely that Sun would ever position JavaOS as an operating system that would compete in the personal computer market—or any desktop computer market, for that matter. By design, JavaOS is targeted toward more compact systems, such as those prevalent in consumer electronics products.

Q Will JavaOS and Java microprocessors change the Java language in any way?

A No. The Java language is frozen as of version 1.02, meaning that any additions to the language must come in the form of new APIs rather than modifications to the core API. It is unlikely that either JavaOS or Java microprocessors would need to modify the design of the Java language, anyway.

28

APPENDIX
A

Language Summary

by Laura Lemay

This appendix contains a summary or quick reference for the Java language, as described in this book.

TECHNICAL NOTE

> This is not a grammar overview, nor is it a technical overview of the language itself. It's a quick reference to be used after you already know the basics of how the language works. If you need a technical description of the language, your best bet is to visit the Java Web site (`http://java.sun.com`) and download the actual specification, which includes a full BNF grammar.

Language keywords and symbols are shown in a monospace font. Arguments and other parts to be substituted are in italic monospace.

Optional parts are indicated by brackets (except in the array syntax section). If there are several options that are mutually exclusive, they are shown separated by pipes (`[ ¦ ]`) like this:

```
[ public ¦ private ¦ protected ] type varname
```

Reserved Words

The following words are reserved for use by the Java language itself (some of them are reserved but not currently used). You cannot use these words to refer to classes, methods, or variable names:

abstract	final	null	transient
boolean	finally	package	try
break	float	private	void
byte	for	protected	volatile
case	goto	public	while
catch	if	return	
char	implements	short	
class	import	static	
const	instanceof	super	
continue	int	switch	
do	interface	synchronized	
double	long	this	
else	native	throw	
extends	new	throws	

Comments

```
/* this is a multiline comment */
// this is a single-line comment
/** Javadoc comment */
```

Literals

number	Type `int`
number[l ¦ L]	Type `long`
0x*hex*	Hex integer
0X*hex*	Hex integer
0*octal*	Octal integer
[*number*].*number*	Type `double`
number[f ¦ f]	Type `float`
number[d ¦ D]	Type `double`
[+ ¦ -] *number*	Signed
*number*e*number*	Exponent
*number*E*number*	Exponent
'*character*'	Single character
"*characters*"	String
" "	Empty string
\b	Backspace
\t	Tab
\n	Line feed
\f	Form feed
\r	Carriage return
\"	Double quote
\'	Single quote
\\	Backslash
\uNNNN	Unicode escape (NNNN is hex)
true	Boolean
false	Boolean

Variable Declaration

[byte ¦ short ¦ int ¦ long] *varname*	Integers (pick one type)
[float ¦ double] *varname*	Floats (pick one type)
char *varname*	Characters
boolean *varname*	Boolean
classname varname	Class types
interfacename varname	Interface types
type *varname*, *varname*, *varname*	Multiple variables

The following options are available only for class and instance variables. Any of these options can be used with a variable declaration:

[static] *variableDeclaration*	Class variable
[final] *variableDeclaration*	Constants
[public ¦ private ¦ protected] *variableDeclaration*	Access control
[volatile] *varname*	Modified asynchronously
[transient] *varname*	Not persistent (not yet implemented)

Variable Assignment

variable = *value*	Assignment
variable++	Postfix increment
++*variable*	Prefix increment
variable--	Postfix decrement
--*variable*	Prefix decrement
variable += *value*	Add and assign
variable -= *value*	Subtract and assign
variable *= *value*	Multiply and assign
variable /= *value*	Divide and assign
variable %= *value*	Modulus and assign
variable &= *value*	AND and assign

`variable |= value`	OR and assign
`variable ^= value`	XOR and assign
`variable <<= value`	Left-shift and assign
`variable >>= value`	Right-shift and assign
`variable >>>= value`	Zero-fill right-shift and assign

Operators

`arg + arg`	Addition
`arg - arg`	Subtraction
`arg * arg`	Multiplication
`arg / arg`	Division
`arg % arg`	Modulus
`arg < arg`	Less than
`arg > arg`	Greater than
`arg <= arg`	Less than or equal to
`arg >= arg`	Greater than or equal to
`arg == arg`	Equal
`arg != arg`	Not equal
`arg && arg`	Logical AND
`arg || arg`	Logical OR
`! arg`	Logical NOT
`arg & arg`	AND
`arg | arg`	OR
`arg ^ arg`	XOR
`arg << arg`	Left-shift
`arg >> arg`	Right-shift
`arg >>> arg`	Zero-fill right-shift
`~ arg`	Complement
`(type)thing`	Casting
`arg instanceof class`	Instance of
`test ? trueOp : falseOp`	Ternary (if) operator

Objects

new *class*()	Creates new instance
new *class*(*arg,arg,arg...*)	New instance with parameters
object.variable	Instance variable
object.classvar	Class variable
Class.classvar	Class variable
object.method()	Instance method (no args)
object.method(*arg,arg,arg...*)	Instance method
object.classmethod()	Class method (no args)
object.classmethod(*arg,arg,arg...*)	Class method
Class.classmethod()	Class method (no args)
Class.classmethod(*arg,arg,arg...*)	Class method

Arrays

NOTE	The brackets in this section are parts of the array creation or access statements. They do not denote optional parts as they do in other parts of this appendix.

type varname[]	Array variable
type[] *varname*	Array variable
new *type*[*numElements*]	New array object
array[*index*]	Element access
array.length	Length of array

Loops and Conditionals

`if ( test) block`	Conditional
`if ( test ) block` `else block`	Conditional with `else`

`switch (test) {`
 	
`    case value : statements`
`    case value : statements`
 	
`    ...`
 	
`    default : statement`
 	
`}`
	`switch` (only with integer or char types)

`for (initializer; test; change ) block`	`for` loop
`while ( test ) block`	`while` loop
`do block` `while (test)`	`do` loop
`break [ label ]`	`break` from loop or `switch`
`continue [ label ]`	`continue` loop
`label:`	Labeled loop

Class Definitions

`class classname block`	Simple class definition

Any of the following optional modifiers can be added to the class definition:

`[ final ] class classname block`	Cannot be subclassed
`[ abstract ] class classname block`	Cannot be instantiated
`[ public ] class classname block`	Accessible outside package
`class classname [ extends Superclass ] block`	Define superclass
`class classname [ implements interfaces ] block`	Implement one or more interfaces

Method and Constructor Definitions

The basic method looks like this, where *returnType* is a type name, a class name, or void.

`returnType methodName() block`	Basic method
`returnType methodName(parameter, parameter, ...) block`	Method with parameters

Method parameters look like this:

`type parameterName`

Method variations can include any of the following optional keywords:

`[ abstract ] returnType methodName() block`	Abstract method
`[ static ] returnType methodName() block`	Class method
`[ native ] returnType methodName() block`	Native method
`[ final ] returnType methodName() block`	`final method`
`[ synchronized ] returnType methodName() block`	Thread lock before executing
`[ public ¦ private ¦ protected ] returnType methodName()`	Access control

Constructors look like this:

`classname() block`	Basic constructor
`classname(parameter, parameter, parameter...) block`	Constructor with parameters
`[ public ¦ private ¦ protected] classname() block`	Access control

In the method/constructor body you can use these references and methods:

`this`	Refers to current object
`super`	Refers to superclass
`super.methodName()`	Calls a superclass's method
`this(...)`	Calls class's constructor
`super(...)`	Calls superclass's constructor
`return [ value ]`	Returns a value

Packages, Interfaces, and Importing

import *package.className*	Imports specific class name
import *package.**	Imports all public classes in package
package *packagename*	Classes in this file belong to this package

interface *interfaceName* [extends *anotherInterface*] *block*

[public] interface *interfaceName* *block*

[abstract] interface *interfaceName* *block*

Exceptions and Guarding

synchronized (*object*) *block*	Waits for lock on *object*

try *block*	Guarded statements
catch (*exception*) *block*	Executed if *exception* is thrown
[finally *block*]	Cleanup code

try *block*	Same as previous example (can
[catch (*exception*) *block*]	use optional catch or finally,
finally *block*	or both)

APPENDIX

B

Class Hierarchy Diagrams

by Charles L. Perkins

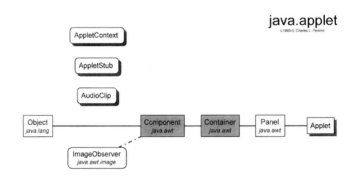

java.applet

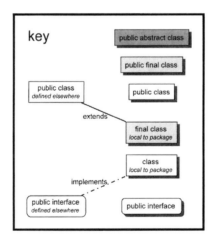

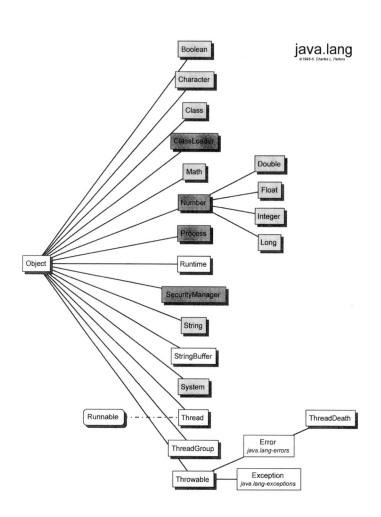

java.lang
©1995-6, Charles L. Perkins

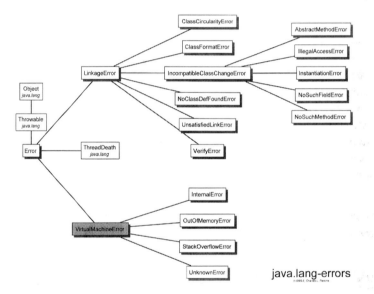

java.lang-errors

B

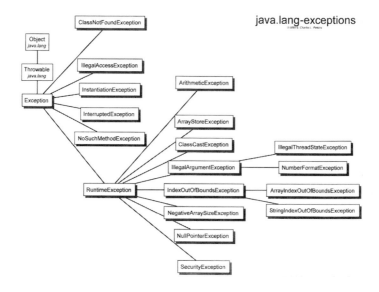

java.lang-exceptions
© 1995 E. Charles L. Perkins

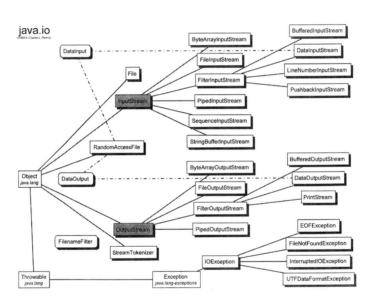

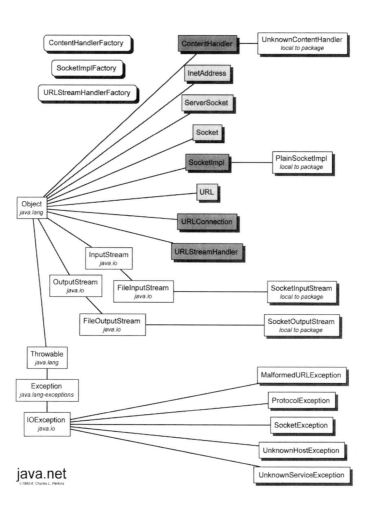

java.net

©1995-6, Charles L. Perkins

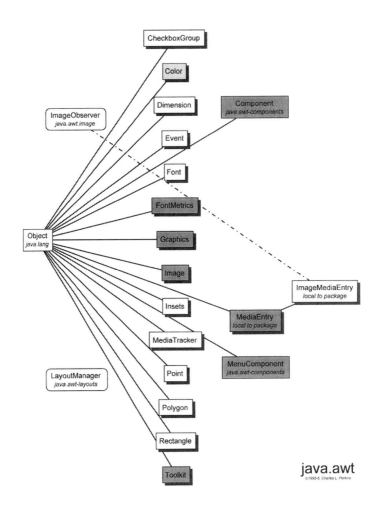

java.awt

©1995-6, Charles L. Perkins

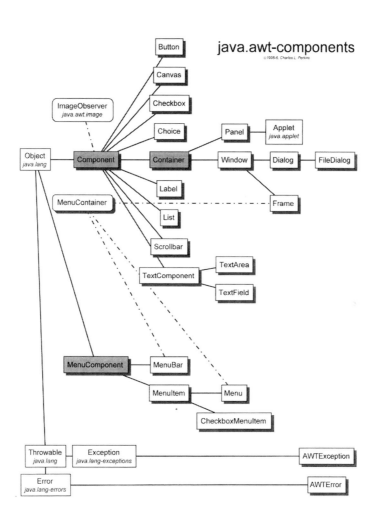

java.awt-components

© 1995-6, Charles L. Perkins

java.awt-layouts

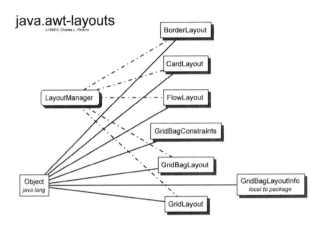

java.awt.image

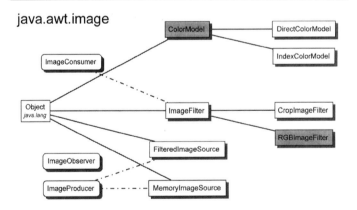

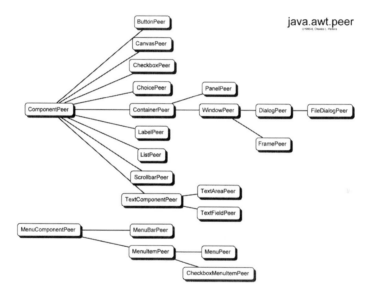

java.awt.peer

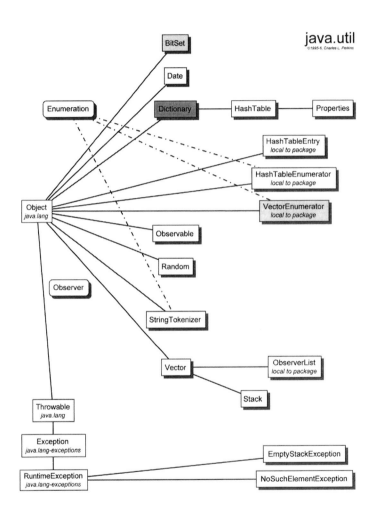

About These Diagrams

The diagrams in this appendix are class hierarchy diagrams for the package java and for all the subpackages recursively below it in the Java 1.0 binary release.

Each page contains the class hierarchy for one package (or a subtree of a particularly large package) with all its interfaces included, and each class in this tree is shown attached to its superclasses, even if they are on another page. A detailed key is located on the first page of this appendix.

I supplemented the API documentation by looking through all the source files to find all the (missing) package classes and their relationships.

I've heard there are various programs that auto-layout hierarchies for you, but I did these the old-fashioned way (in other words, I *earned* it, as J.H. used to say). One nice side effect is that these diagrams should be more readable than a computer would produce, though you will have to live with my aesthetic choices. I chose, for example, to attach lines through the center of each class node, something which I think looks and feels better overall but which on occasion can be a little confusing. Follow lines through the center of the classes (not at the corners, nor along any line not passing through the center) to connect the dots mentally.

APPENDIX C

The Java Class Library

by Laura Lemay

This appendix provides a general overview of the classes available in the standard Java packages (that is, the classes that are guaranteed to be available in any Java implementation). This appendix is intended for general reference; for more information about class inheritance and the exceptions defined for each package, see Appendix B, "Class Hierarchy Diagrams." For more specific information about each class and the methods within each class, see the API documentation from Sun at `http://java.sun.com`. A copy of the 1.0 API documentation is on the CD-ROM included with this book.

java.lang

The `java.lang` package contains the classes and interfaces that make up the core Java language.

Interfaces

Cloneable	Interface indicating that an object may be copied or cloned
Runnable	Methods for classes that want to run as threads

Classes

Boolean	Object wrapper for `boolean` values
Character	Object wrapper for `char` values
Class	Runtime representations of classes
ClassLoader	Abstract behavior for handling loading of classes
Compiler	System class that gives access to the Java compiler
Double	Object wrapper for `double` values
Float	Object wrapper for `float` values
Integer	Object wrapper for `int` values
Long	Object wrapper for `long` values
Math	Utility class for math operations
Number	Abstract superclass of all number classes (`Integer`, `Float`, and so on)
Object	Generic `Object` class, at top of inheritance hierarchy

Process	Abstract behavior for processes such as those spawned using methods in the System class
Runtime	Access to the Java runtime
SecurityManager	Abstract behavior for implementing security policies
String	Character strings
StringBuffer	Mutable strings
System	Access to Java's system-level behavior, provided in a platform-independent way
Thread	Methods for managing threads and classes that run in threads
ThreadDeath	Class of object thrown when a thread is asynchronously terminated
ThreadGroup	A group of threads
Throwable	Generic exception class; all objects thrown must be a Throwable

java.util

The java.util package contains various utility classes and interfaces, including random numbers, system properties, and other useful classes.

Interfaces

Enumeration	Methods for enumerating sets of values
Observer	Methods for allowing classes to observe Observable objects

Classes

BitSet	A set of bits
Date	The current system date, as well as methods for generating and parsing dates
Dictionary	An abstract class that maps between keys and values (superclass of HashTable)
HashTable	A hash table

Observable	An abstract class for observable objects
Properties	A hash table that contains behavior for setting and retrieving persistent properties of the system or of a class
Random	Utilities for generating random numbers
Stack	A stack (a last-in-first-out queue)
StringTokenizer	Utilities for splitting strings into a sequence of individual "tokens"
Vector	A growable array of Objects

java.io

The java.io package provides input and output classes and interfaces for streams and files.

Interfaces

DataInput	Methods for reading machine-independent typed input streams
DataOutput	Methods for writing machine-independent typed output streams
FilenameFilter	Methods for filtering filenames

Classes

BufferedInputStream	A buffered input stream
BufferedOutputStream	A buffered output stream
ByteArrayInputStream	An input stream from a byte array
ByteArrayOutputStream	An output stream to a byte array
DataInputStream	Enables you to read primitive Java types (ints, chars, booleans, and so on) from a stream in a machine-independent way
DataOutputStream	Enables you to write primitive Java data types (ints, chars, booleans, and so on) to a stream in a machine-independent way
File	Represents a file on the host's file system
FileDescriptor	Holds onto the UNIX-like file descriptor of a file or socket

`FileInputStream`	An input stream from a file, constructed using a filename or descriptor
`FileOutputStream`	An output stream to a file, constructed using a filename or descriptor
`FilterInputStream`	Abstract class that provides a filter for input streams (and for adding stream functionality such as buffering)
`FilterOutputStream`	Abstract class that provides a filter for output streams (and for adding stream functionality such as buffering)
`InputStream`	An abstract class representing an input stream of bytes; the parent of all input streams in this package
`LineNumberInputStream`	An input stream that keeps track of line numbers
`OutputStream`	An abstract class representing an output stream of bytes; the parent of all output streams in this package
`PipedInputStream`	A piped input stream, which should be connected to a `PipedOutputStream` to be useful
`PipedOutputStream`	A piped output stream, which should be connected to a `PipedInputStream` to be useful (together they provide safe communication between threads)
`PrintStream`	An output stream for printing (used by `System.out.println(...)`)
`PushbackInputStream`	An input stream with a 1-byte push-back buffer
`RandomAccessFile`	Provides random access to a file, constructed from filenames, descriptors, or objects
`SequenceInputStream`	Converts a sequence of input streams into a single input steam
`StreamTokenizer`	Converts an input stream into a sequence of individual tokens
`StringBufferInputStream`	An input stream from a `String` object

java.net

The java.net package contains classes and interfaces for performing network operations, such as sockets and URLs.

Interfaces

ContentHandlerFactory	Methods for creating ContentHandler objects
SocketImplFactory	Methods for creating socket implementations (instance of the SocketImpl class)
URLStreamHandlerFactory	Methods for creating URLStreamHandler objects

Classes

ContentHandler	Abstract behavior for reading data from a URL connection and constructing the appropriate local object, based on MIME types
DatagramPacket	A datagram packet (UDP)
DatagramSocket	A datagram socket
InetAddress	An object representation of an Internet host (host name, IP address)
ServerSocket	A server-side socket
Socket	A socket
SocketImpl	An abstract class for specific socket implementations
URL	An object representation of a URL
URLConnection	Abstract behavior for a socket that can handle various Web-based protocols (http, ftp, and so on)
URLEncoder	Turns strings into x-www-form-urlencoded format
URLStreamHandler	Abstract class for managing streams to object referenced by URLs

java.awt

The `java.awt` package contains the classes and interfaces that make up the Abstract Windowing Toolkit (AWT).

Interfaces

LayoutManager	Methods for laying out containers
MenuContainer	Methods for menu-related containers

Classes

BorderLayout	A layout manager for arranging items in border formation
Button	A UI pushbutton
Canvas	A canvas for drawing and performing other graphics operations
CardLayout	A layout manager for HyperCard-like metaphors
Checkbox	A check box
CheckboxGroup	A group of exclusive check boxes (radio buttons)
CheckboxMenuItem	A toggle menu item
Choice	A pop-up menu of choices
Color	An abstract representation of a color
Component	The abstract generic class for all UI components
Container	Abstract behavior for a component that can hold other components or containers
Dialog	A window for brief interactions with users
Dimension	An object representing width and height
Event	An object representing events caused by the system or based on user input
FileDialog	A dialog for getting filenames from the local file system
FlowLayout	A layout manager that lays out objects from left to right in rows
Font	An abstract representation of a font

FontMetrics	Abstract class for holding information about a specific font's character shapes and height and width information
Frame	A top-level window with a title
Graphics	Abstract behavior for representing a graphics context, and for drawing and painting shapes and objects
GridBagConstraints	Constraints for components laid out using GridBagLayout
GridBagLayout	A layout manager that aligns components horizontally and vertically based on their values from GridBagConstraints
GridLayout	A layout manager with rows and columns; elements are added to each cell in the grid
Image	An abstract representation of a bitmap image
Insets	Distances from the outer border of the window; used to lay out components
Label	A text label for UI components
List	A scrolling list
MediaTracker	A way to keep track of the status of media objects being loaded over the Net
Menu	A menu, which can contain menu items and is a container on a menu bar
MenuBar	A menu bar (container for menus)
MenuComponent	The abstract superclass of all menu elements
MenuItem	An individual menu item
Panel	A container that is displayed
Point	An object representing a point (x and y coordinates)
Polygon	An object representing a set of points
Rectangle	An object representing a rectangle (x and y coordinates for the top corner, plus width and height)
Scrollbar	A UI scrollbar object
TextArea	A multiline, scrollable, editable text field

TextComponent	The superclass of all editable text components
TextField	A fixed-size editable text field
Toolkit	Abstract behavior for binding the abstract AWT classes to a platform-specific toolkit implementation
Window	A top-level window, and the superclass of the Frame and Dialog classes

java.awt.image

The java.awt.image package is a subpackage of the AWT that provides classes for managing bitmap images.

Interfaces

ImageConsumer	Methods for receiving image data created by an ImageProducer
ImageObserver	Methods to track the loading and construction of an image
ImageProducer	Methods for producing image data received by an ImageConsumer

Classes

ColorModel	An abstract class for managing color information for images
CropImageFilter	A filter for cropping images to a particular size
DirectColorModel	A specific color model for managing and translating pixel color values
FilteredImageSource	An ImageProducer that takes an image and an ImageFilter object and produces an image for an ImageConsumer
ImageFilter	A filter that takes image data from an ImageProducer, modifies it in some way, and hands it off to a ImageConsumer
IndexColorModel	A specific color model for managing and translating color values in a fixed-color map

MemoryImageSource	An image producer that gets its image from memory; used after constructing an image by hand
PixelGrabber	An `ImageConsumer` that retrieves a subset of the pixels in an image
RGBImageFilter	Abstract behavior for a filter that modifies the RGB values of pixels in RGB images

java.awt.peer

The `java.awt.peer` package is a subpackage of AWT that provides the (hidden) platform-specific AWT classes (for example, for Motif, Macintosh, or Windows 95) with platform-independent interfaces to implement. Thus, callers using these interfaces need not know which platform's window system these hidden AWT classes are currently implementing.

Each class in the AWT that inherits from either `Component` or `MenuComponent` has a corresponding peer class. Each of those classes is the name of the `Component` with `-Peer` added (for example, `ButtonPeer`, `DialogPeer`, and `WindowPeer`). Because each one provides similar behavior, they are not enumerated here.

java.applet

The `java.applet` package provides applet-specific behavior.

Interfaces

AppletContext	Methods to refer to the applet's context
AppletStub	Methods for implementing applet viewers
AudioClip	Methods for playing audio files

Classes

Applet	The base applet class

APPENDIX
D

Bytecodes Reference

Let's look at a (progressively less and less) detailed description of each class of bytecodes.

For each bytecode, some brief text describes its function and a textual "picture" of the stack, both before and after the bytecode has been executed, is shown. This text picture will look like the following:

```
..., value1, value2 => ..., value3
```

This means that the bytecode expects two operands—value1 and value2—to be on the top of the stack, pops them both off the stack, operates on them to produce value3, and pushes value3 back onto the top of the stack. You should read each stack from right to left, with the rightmost value being the top of the stack. The ... is read as "the rest of the stack below," which is irrelevant to the current bytecode. All operands on the stack are 32 bits wide.

Because most bytecodes take their arguments from the stack and place their results back there, the brief text descriptions that follow only say something about the source or destination of values if they are *not* on the stack. For example, the description "Load integer from local variable." means that the integer is loaded onto the stack, and "Integer add." intends its integers to be taken from—and the result returned to—the stack.

Bytecodes that don't affect control flow simply move the pc onto the next bytecode that follows in sequence. Those that do affect the pc say so explicitly. Whenever you see byte1, byte2, and so forth, it refers to the first byte, second byte, and so on, that follow the opcode byte itself. After such a bytecode is executed, the pc automatically advances over these operand bytes to start the next bytecode in sequence.

NOTE

> The next few sections are in "reference manual style," presenting each bytecode separately in all its (often redundant) detail; each bytecode is presented as an operation followed by an explanation. Later sections begin to collapse and coalesce this verbose style into something shorter and more readable. The verbose form is shown at first because the online reference manuals will look more like it, and because it drives home the point that each bytecode "function" comes in many, nearly identical bytecodes, one for each primitive type in Java.

Pushing Constants onto the Stack

```
bipush          ... => ..., value
```

Push 1-byte signed integer. byte1 is interpreted as a signed 8-bit value. This value is expanded to an int and pushed onto the operand stack.

```
sipush          ... => ..., value
```

Push 2-byte signed integer. `byte1` and `byte2` are assembled into a signed 16-bit value. This `value` is expanded to an `int` and pushed onto the operand stack.

```
ldc1            ... => ..., item
```

Push `item` from constant pool. `byte1` is used as an unsigned 8-bit index into the constant pool of the current class. The `item` at that index is resolved and pushed onto the stack.

```
ldc2            ... => ..., item
```

Push `item` from constant pool. `byte1` and `byte2` are used to construct an unsigned 16-bit index into the constant pool of the current class. The `item` at that index is resolved and pushed onto the stack.

```
ldc2w           ... => ..., constant-word1, constant-word2
```

Push `long` or `double` from constant pool. `byte1` and `byte2` are used to construct an unsigned 16-bit index into the constant pool of the current class. The two-word constant at that index is resolved and pushed onto the stack.

```
aconst_null     ... => ..., null
```

Push the `null` object reference onto the stack.

```
iconst_m1       ... => ..., -1
```

Push the `int` `-1` onto the stack.

```
iconst_<I>      ... => ..., <I>
```

Push the `int` `<I>` onto the stack. There are six of these bytecodes, one for each of the integers 0–5: `iconst_0`, `iconst_1`, `iconst_2`, `iconst_3`, `iconst_4`, and `iconst_5`.

```
lconst_<L>      ... => ..., <L>-word1, <L>-word2
```

Push the `long` `<L>` onto the stack. There are two of these bytecodes, one for each of the integers 0 and 1: `lconst_0` and `lconst_1`.

```
fconst_<F>      ... => ..., <F>
```

Push the `float` `<F>` onto the stack. There are three of these bytecodes, one for each of the integers 0–2: `fconst_0`, `fconst_1`, and `fconst_2`.

```
dconst_<D>      ... => ..., <D>-word1, <D>-word2
```

Push the `double` `<D>` onto the stack. There are two of these bytecodes, one for each of the integers 0 and 1: `dconst_0`, and `dconst_1`.

D

Loading Local Variables onto the Stack

```
iload          ... => ..., value
```

Load `int` from local variable. Local variable `byte1` in the current Java frame must contain an `int`. The `value` of that variable is pushed onto the operand stack.

```
iload_<I>      ... => ..., value
```

Load `int` from local variable. Local variable `<I>` in the current Java frame must contain an `int`. The `value` of that variable is pushed onto the operand stack. There are four of these bytecodes, one for each of the integers 0–3: `iload_0`, `iload_1`, `iload_2`, and `iload_3`.

```
lload          ... => ..., value-word1, value-word2
```

Load `long` from local variable. Local variables `byte1` and `byte1 + 1` in the current Java frame must together contain a long integer. The values contained in those variables are pushed onto the operand stack.

```
lload_<L>      ... => ..., value-word1, value-word2
```

Load `long` from local variable. Local variables `<L>` and `<L> + 1` in the current Java frame must together contain a long integer. The value contained in those variables is pushed onto the operand stack. There are four of these bytecodes, one for each of the integers 0–3: `lload_0`, `lload_1`, `lload_2`, and `lload_3`.

```
fload          ... => ..., value
```

Load `float` from local variable. Local variable `byte1` in the current Java frame must contain a single-precision floating-point number. The `value` of that variable is pushed onto the operand stack.

```
fload_<F>      ... => ..., value
```

Load `float` from local variable. Local variable `<F>` in the current Java frame must contain a single-precision floating-point number. The value of that variable is pushed onto the operand stack. There are four of these bytecodes, one for each of the integers 0–3: `fload_0`, `fload_1`, `fload_2`, and `fload_3`.

```
dload          ... => ..., value-word1, value-word2
```

Load `double` from local variable. Local variables `byte1` and `byte1 + 1` in the current Java frame must together contain a double-precision floating-point number. The value contained in those variables is pushed onto the operand stack.

```
dload_<D>      ... => ..., value-word1, value-word2
```

Load `double` from local variable. Local variables `<D>` and `<D> + 1` in the current Java frame must together contain a double-precision floating-point number. The value contained in those variables is pushed onto the operand stack. There are four of these bytecodes, one for each of the integers 0–3: `dload_0`, `dload1`, `dload_2`, and `dload_3`.

```
aload          ... => ..., value
```

Load object reference from local variable. Local variable `byte1` in the current Java frame must contain a return address or reference to an object or array. The value of that variable is pushed onto the operand stack.

```
aload_<A>      ... => ..., value
```

Load object reference from local variable. Local variable `<A>` in the current Java frame must contain a return address or reference to an object. The value of that variable is pushed onto the operand stack. There are four of these bytecodes, one for each of the integers 0–3: `aload_0`, `aload_1`, `aload_2`, and `aload_3`.

Storing Stack Values into Local Variables

```
istore         ..., value => ...
```

Store `int` into local variable. `value` must be an `int`. Local variable `byte1` in the current Java frame is set to `value`.

```
istore_<I>     ..., value => ...
```

Store `int` into local variable. `value` must be an `int`. Local variable `<I>` in the current Java frame is set to `value`. There are four of these bytecodes, one for each of the integers 0–3: `istore_0`, `istore_1`, `istore_2`, and `istore_3`.

```
lstore         ..., value-word1, value-word2 => ...
```

Store `long` into local variable. `value` must be a long integer. Local variables `byte1` and `byte1` + 1 in the current Java frame are set to `value`.

```
lstore_<L>     ..., value-word1, value-word2 => ...
```

Store `long` into local variable. `value` must be a long integer. Local variables `<L>` and `<L>` + 1 in the current Java frame are set to `value`. There are four of these bytecodes, one for each of the integers 0–3: `lstore_0`, `lstore_1`, `lstore_2`, and `lstore_3`.

```
fstore         ..., value => ...
```

Store `float` into local variable. `value` must be a single-precision floating-point number. Local variable `byte1` in the current Java frame is set to `value`.

```
fstore_<F>     ..., value => ...
```

Store `float` into local variable. `value` must be a single-precision floating-point number. Local variable `<F>` in the current Java frame is set to `value`. There are four of these bytecodes, one for each of the integers 0–3: `fstore_0`, `fstore_1`, `fstore_2`, and `fstore_3`.

```
dstore          ..., value-word1, value-word2 => ...
```

Store `double` into local variable. `value` must be a double-precision floating-point number. Local variables `byte1` and `byte1 + 1` in the current Java frame are set to `value`.

```
dstore_<D>      ..., value-word1, value-word2 => ...
```

Store `double` into local variable. `value` must be a double-precision floating-point number. Local variables `<D>` and `<D> + 1` in the current Java frame are set to `value`. There are four of these bytecodes, one for each of the integers 0–3: `dstore_0`, `dstore_1`, `dstore_2`, and `dstore_3`.

```
astore          ..., handle => ...
```

Store object reference into local variable. `handle` must be a return address or a reference to an object. Local variable `byte1` in the current Java frame is set to `value`.

```
astore_<A>      ..., handle => ...
```

Store object reference into local variable. `handle` must be a return address or a reference to an object. Local variable `<A>` in the current Java frame is set to `value`. There are four of these bytecodes, one for each of the integers 0–3: `astore_0`, `astore_1`, `astore_2`, and `astore_3`.

```
iinc            -no change-
```

Increment local variable by constant. Local variable `byte1` in the current Java frame must contain an `int`. Its value is incremented by the value `byte2`, where `byte2` is treated as a signed 8-bit quantity.

Managing Arrays

```
newarray        ..., size => result
```

Allocate new array. `size` must be an `int`; it represents the number of elements in the new array. `byte1` is an internal code that indicates the type of array to allocate. Possible values for `byte1` are as follows: `T_BOOLEAN` (4), `T_CHAR` (5), `T_FLOAT` (6), `T_DOUBLE` (7), `T_BYTE` (8), `T_SHORT` (9), `T_INT` (10), and `T_LONG` (11).

An attempt is made to allocate a new array of the indicated type, capable of holding `size` elements. This will be the `result`. If `size` is less than zero, a `NegativeArraySizeException` is thrown. If there is not enough memory to allocate the array, an `OutOfMemoryError` is thrown. All elements of the array are initialized to their default values.

```
anewarray       ..., size => result
```

Allocate new array of objects. `size` must be an `int`; it represents the number of elements in the new array. `byte1` and `byte2` are used to construct an index into the constant pool of the current class. The item at that index is resolved. The resulting entry must be a class.

An attempt is made to allocate a new array of the indicated class type, capable of holding size elements. This will be the result. If size is less than 0, a NegativeArraySizeException is thrown. If there is not enough memory to allocate the array, an OutOfMemoryError is thrown. All elements of the array are initialized to null.

NOTE

anewarray is used to create a single dimension of an array of objects. For example, the request new Thread[7] generates the following bytecodes:

```
bipush 7
anewarray <Class "java.lang.Thread">
```

anewarray can also be used to create the outermost dimension of a multidimensional array. For example, the array declaration new int[6][] generates this:

```
bipush 6
anewarray <Class "[I">
```

(See the section "Method Signatures" for more information on strings such as "[I".)

```
multianewarray  ..., size1 size2...sizeN => result
```

Allocate new multidimensional array. Each size<I> must be an int; each represents the number of elements in a dimension of the array. byte1 and byte2 are used to construct an index into the constant pool of the current class. The item at that index is resolved. The resulting entry must be an array class of one or more dimensions.

byte3 is a positive integer representing the number of dimensions being created. It must be less than or equal to the number of dimensions of the array class. byte3 is also the number of elements that are popped off the stack. All must be ints greater than or equal to zero. These are used as the sizes of the dimensions. An attempt is made to allocate a new array of the indicated class type, capable of holding size<1> * size<2> * ... * <sizeN> elements. This will be the result. If any of the size<I> arguments on the stack is less than zero, a NegativeArraySizeException is thrown. If there is not enough memory to allocate the array, an OutOfMemoryError is thrown.

NOTE

new int[6][3][] generates these bytecodes:

```
bipush 6
bipush 3
multianewarray <Class "[[[I"> 2
```

It's more efficient to use newarray or anewarray when creating arrays of single dimension.

D

```
arraylength      ..., array => ..., length
```

Get length of array. array must be a reference to an array object. The length of the array is determined and replaces array on the top of the stack. If array is null, a NullPointerException is thrown.

```
iaload          ..., array, index => ..., value
laload          ..., array, index => ..., value-word1, value-word2
faload          ..., array, index => ..., value
daload          ..., array, index => ..., value-word1, value-word2
aaload          ..., array, index => ..., value
baload          ..., array, index => ..., value
caload          ..., array, index => ..., value
saload          ..., array, index => ..., value
```

Load <type> from array. array must be an array of <type>s. index must be an int. The <type> value at position number index in array is retrieved and pushed onto the top of the stack. If array is null, a NullPointerException is thrown. If index is not within the bounds of array, an ArrayIndexOutOfBoundsException is thrown. <type> is, in turn, int, long, float, double, object reference, byte, char, and short. <type>s long and double have two word values, as you've seen in previous load bytecodes.

```
iastore         ..., array, index, value => ...
lastore         ..., array, index, value-word1, value-word2 => ...
fastore         ..., array, index, value => ...
dastore         ..., array, index, value-word1, value-word2 => ...
aastore         ..., array, index, value => ...
bastore         ..., array, index, value => ...
castore         ..., array, index, value => ...
sastore         ..., array, index, value => ...
```

Store into <type> array. array must be an array of <type>s, index must be an int, and value a <type>. The <type> value is stored at position index in array. If array is null, a NullPointerException is thrown. If index is not within the bounds of array, an ArrayIndexOutOfBoundsException is thrown. <type> is, in turn, int, long, float, double, object reference, byte, char, and short. <type>s long and double have two word values, as you've seen in previous store bytecodes.

Stack Operations

```
nop         -no change-
```

Do nothing.

```
pop         ..., any => ...
```

Pop the top word from the stack.

```
pop2        ..., any2, any1 => ...
```

Pop the top two words from the stack.

```
dup            ..., any => ..., any, any
```

Duplicate the top word on the stack.

```
dup2           ..., any2, any1 => ..., any2, any1, any2,any1
```

Duplicate the top two words on the stack.

```
dup_x1         ..., any2, any1 => ..., any1, any2,any1
```

Duplicate the top word on the stack and insert the copy two words down in the stack.

```
dup2_x1        ..., any3, any2, any1 => ..., any2, any1, any3,any2,any1
```

Duplicate the top two words on the stack and insert the copies two words down in the stack.

```
dup_x2         ..., any3, any2, any1 => ..., any1, any3,any2,any1
```

Duplicate the top word on the stack and insert the copy three words down in the stack.

```
dup2_x2        ..., any4, any3, any2, any1 => ..., any2, any1, any4,any3,any2,any1
```

Duplicate the top two words on the stack and insert the copies three words down in the stack.

```
swap           ..., any2, any1 => ..., any1, any2
```

Swap the top two elements on the stack.

Arithmetic Operations

```
iadd           ..., v1, v2 => ..., result
ladd           ..., v1-word1, v1-word2, v2-word1, v2-word2 => ..., r-word1, r-word2
fadd           ..., v1, v2 => ..., result
dadd           ..., v1-word1, v1-word2, v2-word1, v2-word2 => ..., r-word1, r-word2
```

v1 and v2 must be <type>s. The vs are added and are replaced on the stack by their <type> sum. <type> is, in turn, int, long, float, and double.

```
isub           ..., v1, v2 => ..., result
lsub           ..., v1-word1, v1-word2, v2-word1, v2-word2 => ..., r-word1, r-word2
fsub           ..., v1, v2 => ..., result
dsub           ..., v1-word1, v1-word2, v2-word1, v2-word2 => ..., r-word1, r-word2
```

v1 and v2 must be <type>s. v2 is subtracted from v1, and both vs are replaced on the stack by their <type> difference. <type> is, in turn, int, long, float, and double.

```
imul           ..., v1, v2 => ..., result
lmul           ..., v1-word1, v1-word2, v2-word1, v2-word2 => ..., r-word1, r-word2
fmul           ..., v1, v2 => ..., result
dmul           ..., v1-word1, v1-word2, v2-word1, v2-word2 => ..., r-word1, r-word2
```

v1 and v2 must be <type>s. Both vs are replaced on the stack by their <type> product. <type> is, in turn, int, long, float, and double.

```
idiv          ..., v1, v2 => ..., result
ldiv          ..., v1-word1, v1-word2, v2-word1, v2-word2 => ..., r-word1, r-word2
fdiv          ..., v1, v2 => ..., result
ddiv          ..., v1-word1, v1-word2, v2-word1, v2-word2 => ..., r-word1, r-word2
```

v1 and v2 must be *<type>*s. v2 is divided by v1, and both vs are replaced on the stack by their *<type>* quotient. An attempt to divide by zero results in an `ArithmeticException` being thrown. *<type>* is, in turn, int, long, `float`, and `double`.

```
irem          ..., v1, v2 => ..., result
lrem          ..., v1-word1, v1-word2, v2-word1, v2-word2 => ..., r-word1, r-word2
frem          ..., v1, v2 => ..., result
drem          ..., v1-word1, v1-word2, v2-word1, v2-word2 => ..., r-word1, r-word2
```

v1 and v2 must be *<type>*s. v2 is divided by v1, and both vs are replaced on the stack by their *<type>* remainder. An attempt to divide by zero results in an `ArithmeticException` being thrown. *<type>* is, in turn, int, long, `float`, and `double`.

```
ineg          ..., value => ..., result
lneg          ..., value-word1, value-word2 => ..., result-word1, result-word2
fneg          ..., value => ..., result
dneg          ..., value-word1, value-word2 => ..., result-word1, result-word2
```

value must be a *<type>*. It is replaced on the stack by its arithmetic negation. *<type>* is, in turn, int, long, `float`, and `double`.

NOTE Now that you're familiar with the look of the bytecodes, the summaries that follow will become shorter and shorter (for space reasons). You can always get any desired level of detail from the full virtual machine specification in the latest Java release.

Logical Operations

```
ishl          ..., v1, v2 => ..., result
lshl          ..., v1-word1, v1-word2, v2 => ..., r-word1, r-word2
ishr          ..., v1, v2 => ..., result
lshr          ..., v1-word1, v1-word2, v2 => ..., r-word1, r-word2
iushr         ..., v1, v2 => ..., result
lushr         ..., v1-word1, v1-word2, v2-word1, v2-word2 => ..., r-word1, r-word2
```

For types int and long: arithmetic shift left, shift right, and logical shift right.

```
iand          ..., v1, v2 => ..., result
land          ..., v1-word1, v1-word2, v2-word1, v2-word2 => ..., r-word1, r-word2
ior           ..., v1, v2 => ..., result
lor           ..., v1-word1, v1-word2, v2-word1, v2-word2 => ..., r-word1, r-word2
ixor          ..., v1, v2 => ..., result
lxor          ..., v1-word1, v1-word2, v2-word1, v2-word2 => ..., r-word1, r-word2
```

For types int and long: bitwise AND, OR, and XOR.

Conversion Operations

```
i2l        ..., value => ..., result-word1, result-word2
i2f        ..., value => ..., result
i2d        ..., value => ..., result-word1, result-word2
l2i        ..., value-word1, value-word2 => ..., result
l2f        ..., value-word1, value-word2 => ..., result
l2d        ..., value-word1, value-word2 => ..., result-word1, result-word2
f2i        ..., value => ..., result
f2l        ..., value => ..., result-word1, result-word2
f2d        ..., value => ..., result-word1, result-word2
d2i        ..., value-word1, value-word2 => ..., result
d2l        ..., value-word1, value-word2 => ..., result-word1, result-word2
d2f        ..., value-word1, value-word2 => ..., result

int2byte   ..., value => ..., result
int2char   ..., value => ..., result
int2short  ..., value => ..., result
```

These bytecodes convert from a value of type <lhs> to a result of type <rhs>. <lhs> and <rhs> can be any of i, l, f, and d, which represent int, long, float, and double, respectively. The final three bytecodes convert types that are self-explanatory.

Transfer of Control

```
ifeq       ..., value => ...
ifne       ..., value => ...
iflt       ..., value => ...
ifgt       ..., value => ...
ifle       ..., value => ...
ifge       ..., value => ...

if_icmpeq  ..., value1, value2 => ...
if_icmpne  ..., value1, value2 => ...
if_icmplt  ..., value1, value2 => ...
if_icmpgt  ..., value1, value2 => ...
if_icmple  ..., value1, value2 => ...
if_icmpge  ..., value1, value2 => ...

ifnull     ..., value => ...
ifnonnull  ..., value => ...
```

When value <rel> 0 is true in the first set of bytecodes, value1 <rel> value2 is true in the second set, or value is null (or not null) in the third, byte1 and byte2 are used to construct a signed 16-bit offset. Execution proceeds at that offset from the pc. Otherwise, execution proceeds at the bytecode following. <rel> is one of eq, ne, lt, gt, le, and ge, which represent equal, not equal, less than, greater than, less than or equal, and greater than or equal, respectively.

```
lcmp       ..., v1-word1, v1-word2, v2-word1, v2-word2 => ..., result

fcmpl      ..., v1, v2 => ..., result
dcmpl      ..., v1-word1, v1-word2, v2-word1, v2-word2 => ..., result
```

```
fcmpg         ..., v1, v2 => ..., result
dcmpg         ..., v1-word1, v1-word2, v2-word1, v2-word2 => ..., result
```

v1 and v2 must be long, float, or double. They are both popped from the stack and compared. If v1 is greater than v2, the int value 1 is pushed onto the stack. If v1 is equal to v2, 0 is pushed onto the stack. If v1 is less than v2, -1 is pushed onto the stack. For floating-point, if either v1 or v2 is NaN, -1 is pushed onto the stack for the first pair of bytecodes, +1 for the second pair.

```
if_acmpeq     ..., value1, value2 => ...
if_acmpne     ..., value1, value2 => ...
```

Branch if object references are equal/not equal. value1 and value2 must be references to objects. They are both popped from the stack. If value1 is equal/not equal to value2, byte1 and byte2 are used to construct a signed 16-bit offset. Execution proceeds at that offset from the pc. Otherwise, execution proceeds at the bytecode following.

```
goto          -no change-
goto_w        -no change-
```

Branch always. byte1 and byte2 (plus byte3 and byte4 for goto_w) are used to construct a signed 16-bit (32-bit) offset. Execution proceeds at that offset from the pc.

```
jsr           ... => ..., return-address
jsr-w         ... => ..., return-address
```

Jump subroutine. The address of the bytecode immediately following the jsr is pushed onto the stack. byte1 and byte2 (plus byte3 and byte4 for goto_w) are used to construct a signed 16-bit (32-bit) offset. Execution proceeds at that offset from the pc.

```
ret           -no change-
ret2_w        -no change-
```

Return from subroutine. Local variable byte1 (plus byte2 for ret_w are assembled into a 16-bit index) in the current Java frame must contain a return address. The contents of that local variable are written into the pc.

NOTE   jsr pushes the address onto the stack, and ret gets it out of a local variable. This asymmetry is intentional. The jsr and ret bytecodes are used in the implementation of Java's finally keyword.

Method Return

```
return        ... => [empty]
```

Return (void) from method. All values on the operand stack are discarded. The interpreter then returns control to its caller.

```
ireturn      ..., value => [empty]
lreturn      ..., value-word1, value-word2 => [empty]
freturn      ..., value => [empty]
dreturn      ..., value-word1, value-word2 => [empty]
areturn      ..., value => [empty]
```

Return <*type*> from method. `value` must be a <*type*>. The value is pushed onto the stack of the previous execution environment. Any other values on the operand stack are discarded. The interpreter then returns control to its caller. <*type*> is, in turn, `int`, `long`, `float`, `double`, and object reference.

NOTE

> The stack behavior of the "return" bytecodes may be confusing to anyone expecting the Java operand stack to be just like the C stack. Java's operand stack actually consists of a number of noncontiguous segments, each corresponding to a method call. A return bytecode empties the Java operand stack segment corresponding to the frame of the returning call, but does not affect the segment of any parent calls.

Table Jumping

```
tableswitch     ..., index => ...
```

`tableswitch` is a variable-length bytecode. Immediately after the `tableswitch` opcode, zero to three `0` bytes are inserted as padding so that the next byte begins at an address that is a multiple of four. After the padding are a series of signed 4-byte quantities: `default-offset`, `low`, `high`, and then (`high - low + 1`) further signed 4-byte offsets. These offsets are treated as a `0`-based jump table.

The `index` must be an `int`. If `index` is less than `low` or `index` is greater than `high`, `default-offset` is added to the `pc`. Otherwise, the (`index - low`)th element of the jump table is extracted and added to the `pc`.

```
lookupswitch    ..., key => ...
```

`lookupswitch` is a variable-length bytecode. Immediately after the `lookupswitch` opcode, zero to three `0` bytes are inserted as padding so that the next byte begins at an address that is a multiple of four. Immediately after the padding is a series of pairs of signed 4-byte quantities. The first pair is special; it contains the `default-offset` and the number of pairs that follow. Each subsequent pair consists of a `match` and an `offset`.

The `key` on the stack must be an `int`. This `key` is compared to each of the `matches`. If it is equal to one of them, the corresponding `offset` is added to the `pc`. If the `key` does not match any of the `matches`, the `default-offset` is added to the `pc`.

Manipulating Object Fields

```
putfield       ..., handle, value => ...
putfield       ..., handle, value-word1, value-word2 => ...
```

Set field in object. byte1 and byte2 are used to construct an index into the constant pool of the current class. The constant pool item is a field reference to a class name and a field name. The item is resolved to a field block pointer containing the field's width and offset (both in bytes).

The field at that offset from the start of the instance pointed to by handle will be set to the value on the top of the stack. The first stack picture is for 32-bit, and the second for 64-bit-wide fields. This bytecode handles both. If handle is null, a NullPointerException is thrown. If the specified field is a static field, an IncompatibleClassChangeError is thrown.

```
getfield       ..., handle => ..., value
getfield       ..., handle => ..., value-word1, value-word2
```

Fetch field from object. byte1 and byte2 are used to construct an index into the constant pool of the current class. The constant pool item will be a field reference to a class name and a field name. The item is resolved to a field block pointer containing the field's width and offset (both in bytes).

handle must be a reference to an object. The value at offset into the object referenced by handle replaces handle on the top of the stack. The first stack picture is for 32-bit, and the second for 64-bit-wide fields. This bytecode handles both. If the specified field is a static field, an IncompatibleClassChangeError is thrown.

```
putstatic      ..., value => ...
putstatic      ..., value-word1, value-word2 => ...
```

Set static field in class. byte1 and byte2 are used to construct an index into the constant pool of the current class. The constant pool item will be a field reference to a static field of a class. That field will be set to have the value on the top of the stack. The first stack picture is for 32-bit, and the second for 64-bit-wide fields. This bytecode handles both. If the specified field is not a static field, an IncompatibleClassChangeError is thrown.

```
getstatic      ..., => ..., value_
getstatic      ..., => ..., value-word1, value-word2
```

Get static field from class. byte1 and byte2 are used to construct an index into the constant pool of the current class. The constant pool item will be a field reference to a static field of a class. The value of that field is placed on the top of the stack. The first stack picture is for 32-bit, and the second for 64-bit-wide fields. This bytecode handles both. If the specified field is not a static field, an IncompatibleClassChangeError is thrown.

Method Invocation

```
invokevirtual    ..., handle, [arg1, [arg2, ...]], ... => ...
```

Invoke instance method based on runtime type. The operand stack must contain a reference to an object and some number of arguments. byte1 and byte2 are used to construct an index into the constant pool of the current class. The item at that index in the constant pool contains the complete method signature. A pointer to the object's method table is retrieved from the object reference. The method signature is looked up in the method table. The method signature is guaranteed to exactly match one of the method signatures in the table.

The result of the lookup is an index into the method table of the named class that's used to look in the method table of the object's runtime type, where a pointer to the method block for the matched method is found. The method block indicates the type of method (native, synchronized, and so on) and the number of arguments (nargs) expected on the operand stack.

If the method is marked synchronized, the monitor associated with handle is entered.

The base of the local variables array for the new Java stack frame is set to point to handle on the stack, making handle and the supplied arguments (arg1, arg2, and so on) the first nargs local variables of the new frame. The total number of local variables used by the method is determined, and the execution environment of the new frame is pushed after leaving sufficient room for the locals. The base of the operand stack for this method invocation is set to the first word after the execution environment. Finally, execution continues with the first bytecode of the matched method.

If handle is null, a NullPointerException is thrown. If during the method invocation a stack overflow is detected, a StackOverflowError is thrown.

```
invokenonvirtual  ..., handle, [arg1, [arg2, ...]], ... => ...
```

Invoke instance method based on compile-time type. The operand stack must contain a reference (handle) to an object and some number of arguments. byte1 and byte2 are used to construct an index into the constant pool of the current class. The item at that index in the constant pool contains the complete method signature and class. The method signature is looked up in the method table of the class indicated. The method signature is guaranteed to exactly match one of the method signatures in the table.

The result of the lookup is a method block. The method block indicates the type of method (native, synchronized, and so on) and the number of arguments (nargs) expected on the operand stack. (The last three paragraphs are identical to the previous bytecode.)

```
invokestatic      ..., , [arg1, [arg2, ...]], ... => ...
```

Invoke class (static) method. The operand stack must contain some number of arguments. byte1 and byte2 are used to construct an index into the constant pool of the current class. The item at that index in the constant pool contains the complete method signature and class. The method signature is looked up in the method table of the class indicated. The method signature is guaranteed to match one of the method signatures in the class's method table exactly.

The result of the lookup is a method block. The method block indicates the type of method (native, synchronized, and so on) and the number of arguments (nargs) expected on the operand stack.

If the method is marked synchronized, the monitor associated with the class is entered. (The last two paragraphs are identical to those in invokevirtual, except that no NullPointerException can be thrown.)

```
invokeinterface   ..., handle, [arg1, [arg2, ...]], ...=> ...
```

Invoke interface method. The operand stack must contain a reference (handle) to an object and some number of arguments. byte1 and byte2 are used to construct an index into the constant pool of the current class. The item at that index in the constant pool contains the complete method signature. A pointer to the object's method table is retrieved from the object reference. The method signature is looked up in the method table. The method signature is guaranteed to exactly match one of the method signatures in the table.

The result of the lookup is a method block. The method block indicates the type of method (native, synchronized, and so on) but, unlike the other "invoke" bytecodes, the number of available arguments (nargs) is taken from byte3; byte4 is reserved for future use. (The last three paragraphs are identical to those in invokevirtual.)

Exception Handling

```
athrow            ..., handle => [undefined]
```

Throw exception. handle must be a handle to an exception object. That exception, which must be an instance of Throwable (or a subclass), is thrown. The current Java stack frame is searched for the most recent catch clause that handles the exception. If a matching "catch list" entry is found, the pc is reset to the address indicated by the catch-list pointer, and execution continues there.

If no appropriate catch clause is found in the current stack frame, that frame is popped and the exception is rethrown, starting the process all over again in the parent frame. If handle is null, a NullPointerException is thrown instead.

Miscellaneous Object Operations

new   ... => ..., handle

Create new object. byte1 and byte2 are used to construct an index into the constant pool of the current class. The item at that index should be a class name that can be resolved to a class pointer. A new instance of that class is then created and a reference (handle) for the instance is placed on the top of the stack.

checkcast   ..., handle => ..., [handle ¦ ...]

Make sure object is of given type. handle must be a reference to an object. byte1 and byte2 are used to construct an index into the constant pool of the current class. The string at that index of the constant pool is presumed to be a class name that can be resolved to a class pointer.

checkcast determines whether handle can be cast to a reference to an object of that class. (A null handle can be cast to any class.) If handle can be legally cast, execution proceeds at the next bytecode, and the handle remains on the stack. If not, a ClassCastException is thrown and the stack is emptied.

instanceof   ..., handle => ..., result

Determine whether object is of given type. handle must be a reference to an object. byte1 and byte2 are used to construct an index into the constant pool of the current class. The string at that index of the constant pool is presumed to be a class name that can be resolved to a class pointer.

If handle is null, the result is 0 (false). Otherwise, instanceof determines whether handle can be cast to a reference to an object of that class. The result is 1 (true) if it can, and 0 (false) otherwise.

Monitors

monitorenter   ..., handle => ...

Enter monitored region of code. handle must be a reference to an object. The interpreter attempts to obtain exclusive access via a lock mechanism to handle. If another thread already has handle locked, the current thread waits until the handle is unlocked. If the current thread already has handle locked, execution continues normally. If handle has no lock on it, this bytecode obtains an exclusive lock. (A null in either bytecode throws NullPointerException.)

monitorexit   ..., handle => ...

Exit monitored region of code. handle must be a reference to an object. The lock on handle is released. If this is the last lock that this thread has on that handle (one thread is allowed to have multiple locks on a single handle), other threads that are waiting for handle are allowed to proceed. (A null in either bytecode throws NullPointerException.)

Debugging

```
breakpoint        -no change-
```

Call breakpoint handler. The breakpoint bytecode is used to overwrite a bytecode to force control temporarily back to the debugger prior to the effect of the overwritten bytecode. The original bytecode's operands (if any) are not overwritten, and the original bytecode is restored when the breakpoint bytecode is removed.

The _quick Bytecodes

The following discussion, straight out of the Java virtual machine documentation, shows you an example of the cleverness mentioned earlier that's needed to make a bytecode interpreter fast:

> The following set of pseudo-bytecodes, suffixed by _quick, are all variants of standard Java bytecodes. They are used by the runtime to improve the execution speed of the bytecode interpreter. They aren't officially part of the virtual machine specification and are invisible outside a Java virtual machine implementation. However, inside that implementation they have proven to be an effective optimization.
>
> First, you should know that the javac Java compiler still generates only non-_quick bytecodes. Second, all bytecodes that have a _quick variant reference the constant pool. When _quick optimization is turned on, each non-_quick bytecode (that has a _quick variant) resolves the specified item in the constant pool, signals an error if the item in the constant pool could not be resolved for some reason, turns itself into the _quick variant of itself, and then performs its intended operation.
>
> This is identical to the actions of the non-_quick bytecode, except for the step of overwriting itself with its _quick variant. The _quick variant of a bytecode assumes that the item in the constant pool has already been resolved, and that this resolution did not produce any errors. It simply performs the intended operation on the resolved item.

Thus, as your bytecodes are being interpreted, they are automatically getting faster and faster! Here are all the _quick variants in the current Java runtime:

```
ldc1_quick
ldc2_quick
ldc2w_quick
```

```
anewarray_quick
multinewarray_quick

putfield_quick
putfield2_quick
getfield_quick
getfield2_quick
putstatic_quick
putstatic2_quick
getstatic_quick
getstatic2_quick

invokevirtual_quick
invokevirtualobject_quick
invokenonvirtual_quick
invokestatic_quick
invokeinterface_quick

new_quick
checkcast_quick
instanceof_quick
```

If you'd like to go back in this appendix and look at what each of these does, you can find the name of the original bytecode on which a _quick variant is based simply by removing the _quick from its name. The bytecodes putstatic, getstatic, putfield, and getfield have two _quick variants each, one for each stack picture in their original descriptions. invokevirtual has two variants: one for objects and one for arrays (to do fast lookups in java.lang.Object).

D

NOTE

One last note on the _quick optimization, regarding the unusual handling of the constant pool (for detail fanatics only): When a class is read in, an array constant_pool[] of size nconstants is created and assigned to a field in the class. constant_pool[0] is set to point to a dynamically allocated array that indicates which fields in the constant_pool have already been resolved. constant_pool[1] through constant_pool[nconstants - 1] are set to point at the "type" field that corresponds to this constant item.

When a bytecode is executed that references the constant pool, an index is generated, and constant_pool[0] is checked to see whether the index has already been resolved. If so, the value of constant_pool[index] is returned. If not, the value of constant_pool[index] is resolved to be the actual pointer or data, and overwrites whatever value was already in constant_pool[index].

APPENDIX

E

java.applet
Package Reference

The java.applet package contains the necessary support for graphical Java applets that execute within the confines of a Web page.

AppletContext

The AppletContext interface is provided to give information on an applet's environment. An AppletContext interface can be obtained by calling the Applet class's getAppletContext method.

getAudioClip

```
public abstract AudioClip getAudioClip(URL url)
```

getAudioClip retrieves an AudioClip based on the URL input parameter.

Parameters: url—a URL object containing location information for the clip to be retrieved.

Returns: An AudioClip object that can be played at a later time.

getImage

```
public abstract Image getImage(URL url)
```

getImage retrieves image information based on the URL input parameter. Note that this function returns immediately and does not retrieve the entire image. This image will not be retrieved until the Image object is actually needed.

Parameters: url—a URL object containing location information for the image to be retrieved.

Returns: An Image object containing information about the URL passed in.

getApplet

```
public abstract Applet getApplet(String name)
```

getApplet returns an Applet object from the current AppletContext based on the input name argument.

Parameters: name—a String object representing an applet's name. This name should correspond to the applet's HTML name attribute.

Returns: An Applet object or null if no applet exists with the designated name.

getApplets

`public abstract Enumeration getApplets()`

getApplets returns an Enumeration interface for all the applets on the current AppletContext.

Returns: An Enumeration interface that can be used to retrieve all the applets on the current applet context.

showDocument

`public abstract void showDocument(URL url)`

showDocument will load the URL argument into the current AppletContext if it is a valid URL. This method may be ignored, depending on the applet context.

Parameters: url—a URL object containing location information for the image to be retrieved.

showDocument

`public abstract void showDocument(URL url, String target)`

This showDocument method will load the URL argument into a target window or frame depending on the target string. This method may be ignored, depending on the applet context.

Parameters:

url—a URL object containing location information for the image to be retrieved.

target—the target string, which can be one of the following values:

- ☐ "_self"—show in current frame.
- ☐ "_parent"—show in parent frame.
- ☐ "_top"—show in top-most frame.
- ☐ "_blank"—show in new unnamed top-level window.
- ☐ <other>—show in new top-level window named <other>.

showStatus

`public abstract void showStatus(String status)`

showStatus shows a status message using the applet's context.

Parameters: msg—a string containing the message to be displayed.

E

AppletStub

The `java.applet.AppletStub` interface is most often used as an interface to build applet viewers, browsers, or other tools that want to display applets within them. This interface is not normally implemented by Java applet developers.

isActive

`public abstract boolean isActive()`

isActive is used to determine whether this applet is currently active.

Returns: `true` if the applet is active, `false` if not.

getDocumentBase

`public abstract URL getDocumentBase()`

getDocumentBase returns the URL of the current page that this applet is embedded in.

Returns: A `URL` object containing information about the current URL.

getCodeBase

`public abstract URL getCodeBase()`

getCodeBase returns the URL of the applet itself.

Returns: A `URL` object containing information about the applet's URL.

getParameter

`public abstract String getParameter(String name)`

getParameter returns the `String` value of the parameter passed in using the HTML `<PARAM>` tag.

getAppletContext

`public abstract AppletContext getAppletContext()`

getAppletContext returns an `AppletContext` object. This object can be used to determine information about the applet's runtime environment.

Returns: An `AppletContext` object.

appletResize

`public abstract void appletResize(int width, int height)`

`appletResize` is called when the applet wants to be resized.

Parameters:

`width`—an integer value specifying the applet's new width.

`height`—an integer value specifying the applet's new height.

AudioClip

The `AudioClip` interface is used to provide high-level access to sound playback capabilities. This interface, like `AppletContext` and `AppletStub`, is usually implemented only by applet viewers.

play

`public abstract void play()`

The `play` method plays audio files from the beginning until the end or `stop` method is called.

loop

`public abstract void loop()`

The `loop` method plays audio files in a loop continuously.

stop

`public abstract void stop()`

The `stop` method stops the playing of an audio file.

Applet

Extends: `Panel`

This implies that every applet has some visual component. The basic visual component is a panel in an HTML page.

Applet

```
public Applet()
```

This is the default constructor for the Applet class. This function creates a new applet. Each applet should implement at a minimum the init or start methods to display themselves on the screen and for initial setup.

setStub

```
public final void setStub(AppletStub stub)
```

setStub sets the AppletStub to the stub passed in. This function is called automatically by the underlying system and usually is not called directly. The only time AppletStub methods need to be implemented is if you are writing your own applet viewer or browser.

Parameters: stub—the underlying stub used to implement an applet viewer.

isActive

```
public boolean isActive()
```

isActive is used to determine whether this applet is currently active. An applet is set Active just before the Start method is called.

getDocumentBase

```
public URL getDocumentBase()
```

getDocumentBase returns the URL of the current page that this applet is embedded in.

Returns: A URL object containing information about the current URL.

getCodeBase

```
public URL getCodeBase()
```

getCodeBase returns the URL of the applet itself.

Returns: A URL object containing information about the applet's URL.

getParameter

```
public String getParameter(String name)
```

getParameter returns the String value of the parameter passed in using the HTML <PARAM> tag.

Parameters: name—a case-sensitive string that matches (exactly!) the parameter name passed in using the HTML PARAM tag.

Returns: A string value representing the PARAM tag's VALUE attribute.

getAppletContext

```
public AppletContext getAppletContext()
```

getAppletContext returns an AppletContext object. This object can be used to determine information about the applet's runtime environment.

Returns: An AppletContext object.

resize

```
public void resize(int width, int height)
```

resize makes use of the Applet class's inheritance from the Panel class to resize the applet based on the input values.

Parameters:

width—an integer value specifying the applet's new width.

height—an integer value specifying the applet's new height.

resize

```
public void resize(Dimension d)
```

This resize function accepts a Dimension object as its argument.

Parameters: d—a Dimension object that specifies the new size of the applet.

showStatus

```
public void showStatus(String msg)
```

showStatus shows a status message using the applet's context.

Parameters: msg—a string containing the message to be displayed.

getImage

```
public Image getImage(URL url)
```

getImage retrieves image information based on the URL input parameter. Note that this function returns immediately and does not retrieve the entire image. This image will not be retrieved until the Image object is actually needed.

Parameters: url—a URL object containing location information for the image to be retrieved.

Returns: An Image object containing information about the URL passed in.

getImage

```
public Image getImage(URL url, String name)
```

This getImage function accepts both the URL input parameter containing base location information as well as a String input parameter containing the filename.

Parameters:

url—a URL object containing base location information for the image to be retrieved.

name—a string object containing a filename relative to the base URL passed using the url argument.

Returns: An Image object containing information about the URL passed in.

getAudioClip

```
public AudioClip getAudioClip(URL url)
```

getAudioClip retrieves an AudioClip based on the URL input parameter.

Parameters: url—a URL object containing location information for the clip to be retrieved.

Returns: An AudioClip object that can be played at a later time.

getAudioClip

```
public AudioClip getAudioClip(URL url, String name)
```

This getAudioClip function accepts both the URL input parameter containing base location information as well as a String input parameter containing the filename.

Parameters:

url—a URL object containing base location information for the AudioClip to be retrieved.

name—a string object containing a filename relative to the base URL passed using the url argument.

Returns: An AudioClip object that can be played at a later time.

getAppletInfo

```
public String getAppletInfo()
```

getAppletInfo is provided for applet authors to return name, copyright, and version information for their applets. The default implementation returns null.

Returns: A String containing author, version, and copyright information (or anything else) for the applet.

getParameterInfo

```
public String[][] getParameterInfo()
```

getParameterInfo is provided for applet authors to provide information on any parameters that the applet may take as input. Conventional return values have the following information: name, type, and comments. The default implementation returns a null String array.

Returns: A String array where each element contains, by Java conventions, three values: name, type, and comments. Each of these elements represent a parameter that the applet takes as input.

play

```
public void play(URL url)
```

play is used to play an AudioClip at the location given by the URL input parameter.

Parameters: url—a URL object containing location information for the clip to be retrieved.

play

```
public void play(URL url, String name)
```

This play method is used to play an AudioClip given a base URL and a filename for input parameters.

Parameters:

url—a URL object containing base location information for the AudioClip to be retrieved.

name—a string object containing a filename relative to the base URL passed using the url argument.

init

`public void init()`

The `init` method is called automatically after the applet is created. This function never needs to be called directly.

start

`public void start()`

The `start` method is called automatically to start the applet after it has been initialized. This function never needs to be called directly. `start` is called when an applet is first displayed on a screen, or when a page is revisited within a Web browser.

stop

`public void stop()`

The `stop` method is called automatically to stop an applet from running. This function never needs to be called directly unless the applet knows that it needs to stop executing. `stop` is called when the Web page containing the applet is replaced by another Web page.

destroy

`public void destroy()`

The `destroy` method is called automatically when the applet's system resources are being reclaimed. This function never needs to be called directly. `destroy` is called after the `stop` method has finished.

APPENDIX

F

java.awt **Package Reference**

The `java.awt` package contains what is known as the Java Abstract Windowing Toolkit. The classes within this package make up the prebuilt graphical user interface components that are available to Java developers through the Java Developer's Kit. Classes defined within this package include such useful components as colors, fonts, and widgets such as buttons and scrollbars.

LayoutManager

The `LayoutManager` interface is provided so that it can be implemented by objects that know how to lay out containers.

addLayoutComponent

```
void addLayoutComponent(String name, Component comp)
```

The `addLayoutComponent` method lays out the specified component within the layout manager.

Parameters:

name—the name of the component to be laid out.

comp—the `Component` object to be laid out within the layout manager.

removeLayoutComponent

```
void removeLayoutComponent(Component comp)
```

The `removeLayoutComponent` method removes a specified component from the layout manager.

Parameters: comp—the `Component` object that is to be removed from within the layout manager.

preferredLayoutSize

```
Dimension preferredLayoutSize(Container parent)
```

The `preferredLayoutSize` method determines the preferred layout size for a specified container.

Parameters: parent—a `Container` object that is to be laid out using the layout manager.

Returns: A `Dimension` object containing the preferred size of the `Container` parameter.

minimumLayoutSize

`Dimension minimumLayoutSize(Container parent)`

The `minimumLayoutSize` method determines the minimum layout size for a specified container.

Parameters: parent—a `Container` object that is to be laid out using the layout manager.

Returns: A `Dimension` object containing the minimum size of the `Container` parameter.

layoutContainer

`void layoutContainer(Container parent)`

The `layoutContainer` method will lay out the specified `Container` object within the layout manager.

Parameters: parent—a `Container` object that is to be laid out using the layout manager.

MenuContainer

The `MenuContainer` is an interface that is implemented by all menu-related containers.

getFont

`Font getFont()`

The `getFont` method returns the current font of the menu container.

Returns: The current `Font` object.

postEvent

`boolean postEvent(Event evt)`

The `postEvent` method posts the specified event to the `MenuContainer`.

Parameters: evt—the `Event` object to be posted to the menu container.

Returns: A boolean value containing `true` if the event was handled, `false` if not.

remove

`void remove(MenuComponent comp)`

The `remove` method removes the specified `MenuComponent` object from the `MenuContainer`.

Parameters: comp—the `MenuComponent` class to be removed from the `MenuContainer`.

BorderLayout

Extends: Object

Implements: LayoutManager

A BorderLayout is used to lay out components on a panel by implementing the LayoutManager interface. Components are laid out using members named North, South, East, West, and Center.

BorderLayout **Constructor**

```
public BorderLayout()
```

This BorderLayout constructor constructs a BorderLayout layout manager.

BorderLayout **Constructor**

```
public BorderLayout(int hgap, int vgap)
```

This BorderLayout constructor constructs a BorderLayout layout manager using the hgap and vgap values to set the horizontal and vertical gap sizes.

Parameters:

hgap—an integer value used to set the horizontal gap size.

vgap—an integer value used to set the vertical gap size.

addLayoutComponent

```
public void addLayoutComponent(String name, Component comp)
```

addLayoutComponent adds a component to the border layout according to that component's name (North, South, East, West, or Center). The component's preferred size is used for all layout types except Center.

Parameters:

name—a string value that must correspond to one of the following names: North, South, East, West, or Center.

comp—a Component object to be added to this layout manager.

removeLayoutComponent

```
public void removeLayoutComponent(Component comp)
```

removeLayoutComponent removes the specified component from the layout manager.

Parameters: comp—the Component object to be removed

minimumLayoutSize

public Dimension minimumLayoutSize(Container target)

minimumLayoutSize returns the minimum dimension needed to lay out the components contained in the target parameter. Note that this function only determines the required size based on visible components.

Parameters: target—a Container class containing components to be laid out.

preferredLayoutSize

public Dimension preferredLayoutSize(Container target)

preferredLayoutSize returns the preferred dimension needed to lay out the components contained in the target parameter. This dimension is based on the individual component's preferred sizes. Note that this function only determines the required size based on visible components.

Parameters: target—a Container class containing components to be laid out.

layoutContainer

public void layoutContainer(Container target)

layoutContainer will lay out the components contained in the target Container parameter. This method will reshape the components in the container based on the requirements of the border layout itself.

Parameters: target—a Container class containing components to be laid out.

toString

public String toString()

toString returns a string representation of the BorderLayout class.

Returns: A String value containing the BorderLayout class's name plus its hgap and vgap values.

Button

Extends: Component

A button can be placed on any type of layout because it derives directly from Component.

Button **Constructor**

public Button()

This BUTTON constructor constructs a simple button with no text label.

Button **Constructor**

public Button(String label)

This Button constructor constructs a simple button with a text label.

Parameters: label—a String value used to set the button's label.

addNotify

public synchronized void addNotify()

addNotify sets the peer of the button using the function getToolkit.createButton. Using peer interfaces allows the user interface of the button to be changed without changing its functionality.

getLabel

public String getLabel()

getLabel returns the button's label string.

Returns: A String value representing the button's label string.

setLabel

public void setLabel(String label)

setLabel modifies the button's label string.

Parameters: label—a String value representing the button's new label string.

Canvas

Extends: Component

A Canvas is used as a drawing surface for GUI applications.

addNotify

```
public synchronized void addNotify()
```

addNotify sets the peer of the canvas using the function getToolkit.createCanvas. Using peer interfaces allows the user interface of the canvas to be changed without changing its functionality.

paint

```
public void paint(Graphics g)
```

The paint method paints the canvas using the default background color (determine by calling getBackground).

CardLayout

Extends: Object

Implements: LayoutManager

The CardLayout class is a layout manager that allows the addition of "cards," only one of which may be visible at any given time. The user can "flip" through the cards.

CardLayout **Constructor**

```
public CardLayout()
```

This CardLayout constructor creates a new CardLayout layout manager.

CardLayout **Constructor**

```
public CardLayout(int hgap, int vgap)
```

This CardLayout constructor constructs a CardLayout layout manager using the hgap and vgap values to set the horizontal and vertical gap sizes.

Parameters:

hgap—an integer value used to set the horizontal gap size.

vgap—an integer value used to set the vertical gap size.

addLayoutComponent

public void addLayoutComponent(String name, Component comp)

addLayoutComponent adds a component to the card layout.

Parameters:

name—a string value that corresponds to the component's name.

comp—a Component object to be added to this layout manager.

removeLayoutComponent

public void removeLayoutComponent(Component comp)

removeLayoutComponent removes the specified component from the layout manager.

Parameters: comp—the Component object to be removed.

minimumLayoutSize

public Dimension minimumLayoutSize(Container target)

minimumLayoutSize returns the minimum dimension needed to lay out the components contained in the target parameter. Note that this function only determines the required size based on visible components.

Parameters: target—a Container class containing components to be laid out.

preferredLayoutSize

public Dimension preferredLayoutSize(Container target)

preferredLayoutSize returns the preferred dimension needed to lay out the components contained in the target parameter. This dimension is based on the individual component's preferred sizes. Note that this function only determines the required size based on visible components.

Parameters: target—a Container class containing components to be laid out.

layoutContainer

`public void layoutContainer(Container parent)`

layoutContainer will lay out the components contained in the target Container parameter. This method will reshape the components in the container based on the requirements of the border layout itself.

Parameters: target—a Container class containing components to be laid out.

first

`public void first(Container parent)`

The first method shows the first component in the card layout (the first card).

Parameters: parent—the parent Container class containing the components to be flipped through.

next

`public void next(Container parent)`

The next method shows the next component in the card layout (the next card).

Parameters: parent—the parent Container class containing the components to be flipped through.

previous

`public void previous (Container parent)`

The previous method shows the previous component in the card layout (the previous card).

Parameters: parent—the parent Container class containing the components to be flipped through.

last

`public void last(Container parent)`

The last method shows the last component in the card layout (the last card).

Parameters: parent—the parent Container class containing the components to be flipped through.

show

`public void show(Container parent, String name)`

The show method flips to the component specified in the name parameter.

Parameters:

parent—the parent Container class containing the components to be flipped through.

name—a string value representing the name of the component to be displayed.

toString

`public String toString()`

toString returns a string representation of the card layout class.

Returns: A String value containing the card layout class's name plus its hgap and vgap values.

Checkbox

Extends: Component

A Checkbox is a user interface component that is used to represent a true/false (or on/off) value.

Checkbox **Constructor**

`public Checkbox()`

This Checkbox constructor constructs the simplest of all check boxes: one with no label, no group, and a false state value.

Checkbox **Constructor**

`public Checkbox(String label)`

This Checkbox constructor constructs a check box using the label parameter to set the check box's label. This check box will belong to no group and will be set to a false state value.

Parameters: label—a string value representing the check box's label.

Checkbox **Constructor**

`public Checkbox(String label, CheckboxGroup group, boolean state)`

This Checkbox constructor constructs a check box including the label, group, and initial value.

Parameters:

label—a string value representing the check box's label.

group—a CheckboxGroup object that this check box will be a member of.

state—the initial state value for this check box.

addNotify

```
public synchronized void addNotify()
```

addNotify sets the peer of the check box using the function getToolkit.createCheckbox. Using peer interfaces allows the user interface of the check box to be changed without changing its functionality.

getLabel

```
public String getLabel()
```

getLabel returns the check box's label string.

Returns: A String value representing the check box's label string.

setLabel

```
public void setLabel(String label)
```

setLabel modifies the check box's label string.

Parameters: label—a String value representing the check box's new label string.

getState

```
public boolean getState()
```

getState returns the check box's current state value.

Returns: A boolean value representing the check box's current state.

setState

```
public void setState(boolean state)
```

setState sets the check box to the value represented by the state parameter.

Parameters: state—a boolean value containing the new value of the check box's state.

getCheckboxGroup

`public CheckboxGroup getCheckboxGroup()`

The `getCheckboxGroup` method returns the `CheckboxGroup` that this check box is a member of.

Returns: A `CheckboxGroup` class that this check box is a member of.

setCheckboxGroup

`public void setCheckboxGroup(CheckboxGroup g)`

The `setCheckboxGroup` method is used to add this check box to a `CheckboxGroup`.

Parameters: g—a `CheckboxGroup` class to which this check box is to be added.

CheckboxGroup

Extends: `Object`

A `CheckboxGroup` is used to group a set of `Checkbox` classes. When check boxes are created within a `CheckboxGroup`, only one check box may be selected at one time.

CheckboxGroup **Constructor**

`public CheckboxGroup()`

This `CheckboxGroup` constructor constructs a `CheckboxGroup` instance with no check box members.

getCurrent

`public Checkbox getCurrent()`

The `getCurrent` method returns the current check box.

Returns: A `Checkbox` object representing the currently selected check box.

setCurrent

`public synchronized void setCurrent(Checkbox box)`

The `setCurrent` method sets the current check box in this `CheckboxGroup`.

Parameters: box—the `Checkbox` object that is to be made current.

toString

`public String toString()`

toString returns a string containing Checkboxgroup information.

Returns: A string value containing the CheckboxGroup's name as well as the name of the currently selected check box.

CheckboxMenuItem

Extends: MenuItem

A CheckboxMenuItem is a user interface component that can be added to a menu to represent a boolean value selection.

CheckboxMenuItem **Constructor**

`public CheckboxMenuItem(String label)`

This CheckboxMenuItem constructor creates a CheckboxMenuItem with a text label containing the string passed in.

Parameters: label—a string value representing the label of the CheckboxMenuItem to be displayed.

addNotify

`public synchronized void addNotify()`

addNotify sets the peer of the CheckboxMenuItem using the function getToolkit.createCheckboxMenuItem. Using peer interfaces allows the user interface of the CheckboxMenuItem to be changed without changing its functionality.

getState

`public boolean getState()`

getState returns the state value of the CheckboxMenuItem's check box.

Returns: A boolean value representing the CheckboxMenuItem's check box state.

setState

`public void setState(boolean t)`

setState is used to set the CheckboxMenuItem's check box state value.

Parameters: t—a boolean value representing the CheckboxMenuItem's check box state value.

paramString

`public String paramString()`

paramString returns a string containing CheckboxMenuItem information

Returns: A string value containing the CheckboxMenuItem's label as well as the state value of the CheckboxMenuItem's check box.

Choice

Extends: Component

A Choice is a user interface component that displays a pop-up menu. The current selection is displayed as the pop-up menu's title.

Choice **Constructor**

`public Choice()`

This Choice constructor creates a default Choice object that contains no information.

addNotify

`public synchronized void addNotify()`

addNotify sets the peer of the Choice using the function getToolkit.createChoice. Using peer interfaces allows the user interface of the Choice to be changed without changing its functionality.

countItems

`public int countItems()`

countItems returns the number of items (or choices) that are available in this Choice object.

Returns: An integer value containing the number of items stored in this Choice object.

getItem

```
public String getItem(int index)
```

The getItem method returns the choice string at the index represented by the index value passed in.

Parameters: index—an integer value representing the index of the string item to be returned.

Returns: A String value representing the string at the index passed into this method.

addItem

```
public synchronized void addItem(String item)
```

addItem is used to add a String to a Choice object's internal list. The currently selected item will be displayed in the Choice object's pop-up menu.

Parameters: item—a String object containing a string to be added to the choice list.

Throws: NullPointerException if the string item to be added is null.

getSelectedItem

```
public String getSelectedItem()
```

getSelectedItem returns the string value of the currently selected item.

Returns: A String value containing the currently selected item's string.

getSelectedIndex

```
public int getSelectedIndex()
```

getSelectedIndex returns the index of the currently selected item.

Returns: An integer value containing the index of the currently selected item.

select

```
public synchronized void select(int pos)
```

This select method selects the item at the position represented by the pos parameter.

Parameters: pos—an integer value representing the position of the item to be selected

Throws: IllegalArgumentException if the position value passed in is invalid.

select

```
public void select(String str)
```

This select method selects the item represented by the String parameter.

Parameters: str—a String value representing the string value of the choice to be selected.

Color

Extends: Object

The Color class is provided to encapsulate RGB (red-green-blue) color values.

Member Constants

```
public final static Color white
```

Static value representing the color white.

```
public final static Color lightGray
```

Static value representing the color light gray.

```
public final static Color gray
```

Static value representing the color gray.

```
public final static Color darkGray
```

Static value representing the color dark gray.

```
public final static Color black
```

Static value representing the color black.

```
public final static Color red
```

Static value representing the color red.

```
public final static Color pink
```

Static value representing the color pink.

```
public final static Color orange
```

Static value representing the color orange.

```
public final static Color yellow
```

Static value representing the color yellow.

```
public final static Color green
```

Static value representing the color green.

```
public final static Color magenta
```

Static value representing the color magenta.

```
public final static Color cyan
```

Static value representing the color cyan.

```
public final static Color blue
```

Static value representing the color blue.

Color **Constructor**

```
public Color(int r, int g, int b)
```

This Color constructor accepts as arguments individual red, green, and blue color values. These values must be in the range 0–255.

Parameters:

r—the red color value.

g—the green color value.

b—the blue color value.

Color **Constructor**

```
public Color(int rgb)
```

This Color constructor creates a Color object based on the RGB color value passed in.

Parameters: rgb—an integer value containing the red, green, and blue color values that will be used to create this Color object.

Color **Constructor**

```
public Color(float r, float g, float b)
```

This Color constructor create a Color object based on the color values passed in. This constructor is similar to the Color constructor that accepts integer red, green, and blue inputs except that this Color constructor accepts float values. These values must be in the range 0–1.0.

Parameters:

r—the red color value.

g—the green color value.

b—the blue color value.

getRed

```
public int getRed()
```

The getRed method returns the red component of this color.

Returns: An integer value representing this color's red component.

getGreen

```
public int getGreen()
```

The getGreen method returns the green component of this color.

Returns: An integer value representing this color's green component.

getBlue

```
public int getBlue()
```

The getBlue method returns the blue component of this color.

Returns: An integer value representing this color's blue component.

getRGB

```
public int getRGB()
```

The getRGB method returns the RGB value of this color.

Returns: An integer value representing this color's RGB value in the default RGB color model.

brighter

```
public Color brighter()
```

The brighter method brightens this color by modifying the RGB color value. This method increases the individual red, green, and blue color components by a factor of approximately 1.4.

Returns: A Color object representing a brighter version of the current color.

darker

```
public Color darker()
```

The darker method darkens this color by modifying the RGB color value. This method decreases the individual red, green, and blue color components by a factor of approximately 1.4.

Returns: A Color object representing a darker version of the current color.

hashCode

```
public int hashCode()
```

hashCode returns this color's hash code. This is useful when storing colors in a hash table.

Returns: An integer value representing this color's hash code.

equals

```
public boolean equals(Object obj)
```

The equals method compares the Object parameter with this Color object. It returns a boolean value representing the result of this comparison.

Parameters: obj—an Object object to be compared with this color.

Returns: A boolean value representing the result of the comparison of the Object parameter to this color.

toString

```
public String toString()
```

toString returns a string representation of the Color class.

Returns: A String value containing the Color class's name plus its red, green, and blue values.

getColor

```
public static Color getColor(String nm)
```

getColor returns the specified color property based on the name that is passed in.

Parameters: nm—the name of the color property.

Returns: A Color value representing the desired color property.

getColor

`public static Color getColor(String nm, Color v)`

getColor returns the specified `Color` property of the specified color.

Parameters:

nm—the name of the color property.

v—the specified color to be examined.

Returns: A `Color` value representing the desired color property.

getColor

`public static Color getColor(String nm, int v)`

getColor returns the specified `Color` property of the color value that is passed in.

Parameters:

nm—the name of the color property.

v—the color value.

Returns: A `Color` value representing the desired color property.

HSBtoRGB

`public static int HSBtoRGB(float hue, float saturation, float brightness)`

HSB stands for hue, saturation, and brightness. To convert from an HSB value to an RGB value, simply call this function with the appropriate arguments.

Parameters:

hue—the color's hue component.

saturation—the color's saturation component.

brightness—the color's brightness component.

Returns: An RGB value that corresponds to the HSB inputs.

RGBtoHSB

`public static float[] RGBtoHSB(int r, int g, int b, float[] hsbvals)`

HSB stands for hue, saturation, and brightness. To convert from an RGB value to an HSB value, simply call this function with the appropriate arguments.

Parameters:

r—the color's red component.

g—the color's green component.

b—the color's blue component.

hsbvals—an array that will be used to store the HSB result values.

Returns: An array containing the resultant HSB values.

getHSBColor

```
public static Color getHSBColor(float h, float s, float b)
```

The getHSBColor method returns a Color object representing the RGB value of the input HSB parameters.

Parameters:

h—the color's hue component.

s—the color's saturation component.

b—the color's brightness component.

Returns: A Color object representing the RGB value of the input hue, saturation, and brightness.

Component

Extends: Object

Implements: ImageObserver

The Component class is used to represent a generic user interface component. All AWT UI components derive from the Component class.

getParent

```
public Container getParent()
```

getParent returns this component's parent (a Container class).

Returns: A Container class representing the component's parent.

getPeer

```
public ComponentPeer getPeer()
```

getPeer returns this component's peer (A ComponentPeer interface).

Returns: A ComponentPeer interface representing the component's peer.

getToolkit

```
public Toolkit getToolkit()
```

getToolkit returns the toolkit of this component. The toolkit is used to create the peer for the component.

Returns: A Toolkit class. A toolkit is required to bind the abstract AWT classes to a native toolkit implementation.

isValid

```
public boolean isValid()
```

isValid determines whether this component is valid. A component is considered to be invalid when it is first shown on the screen.

Returns: A boolean value representing the valid state of this component.

isVisible

```
public boolean isVisible()
```

isVisible determines whether this component is visible. A component is, by default, visible until told otherwise. A component can be visible yet not show on the screen if the component's container is invisible.

Returns: A boolean value representing the visible state of this component.

isShowing

```
public boolean isShowing()
```

isShowing determines whether this component is shown on the screen. A component can be visible yet not show on the screen if the component's container is invisible.

Returns: A boolean value representing the show state of this component.

isEnabled

```
public boolean isEnabled()
```

isEnabled determines whether this component is currently enabled. By default, components are enabled until told otherwise.

Returns: A boolean value representing the enabled state of this component.

location

```
public Point location()
```

location returns the location of this component in its parent's coordinate space. Note that the Point object returned contains the top-left corner coordinates of this component.

Returns: A Point object containing the location of the component.

size

```
public Dimension size()
```

size returns the current size of the component.

Returns: A Dimension object containing the size of the component.

bounds

```
public Rectangle bounds()
```

bounds returns the bounding rectangle of the component.

Returns: A Rectangle object containing the boundaries for the component.

enable

```
public synchronized void enable()
```

The enable method is used to enable a component. When a component is disabled, it may be "grayed out" or simply not respond to user inputs.

enable

```
public void enable(boolean cond)
```

This enable method is used to conditionally enable a component. When a component is disabled, it may be "grayed out" or simply not respond to user inputs.

Parameters: cond—a boolean value representing the new enabled state of the component.

disable

`public synchronized void disable()`

The `disable` method disables a component. When a component is disabled, it may be "grayed out" or simply not respond to user inputs.

show

`public synchronized void show()`

`show` shows the component.

show

`public void show(boolean cond)`

This `show` method conditionally shows the component. If the input parameter is `true`, the component will be shown. If the input parameter is `false`, the component will be hidden.

Parameters: cond—a boolean value representing the new visible state of the component.

hide

`public synchronized void hide()`

The `hide` method hides the component from view.

getForeground

`public Color getForeground()`

`getForeground` returns the foreground color of the component. If the component's foreground color has not been set, the foreground color of its parent is returned.

Returns: A `Color` object representing the foreground color of this component.

setForeground

`public synchronized void setForeground(Color c)`

`setForeground` sets the foreground color of the component.

Parameters: c—the new foreground color of this component.

getBackground

`public Color getBackground()`

getBackground returns the background color of the component. If the component's background color has not been set, the background color of its parent is returned.

Returns: A Color object representing the background color of this component.

setBackground

```
public synchronized void setBackground(Color c)
```

setBackground sets the background color of the component.

Parameters: c—the new background color of this component.

getFont

```
public Font getFont()
```

getFont returns the font of the component. If the component's font has not been set, the font of its parent is returned.

setFont

```
public synchronized void setFont(Font f)
```

setFont sets the font of the component.

Parameters: f—the new font of this component.

getColorModel

```
public synchronized ColorModel getColorModel()
```

getColorModel gets the color model that will be used to display this component on an output device.

Returns: A ColorModel object representing the color model used by this component.

move

```
public void move(int x, int y)
```

The move method moves a component to a new location within its parent's coordinate space.

Parameters:

x—the new x coordinate of the component within its parent's coordinate space.

y—the new y coordinate of the component within its parent's coordinate space.

resize

`public void resize(int width, int height)`

`resize` resizes the component to the specified width and height.

Parameters:

`width`—the new width size of the component.

`height`—the new height size of the component.

resize

`public void resize(Dimension d)`

`resize` resizes the component to the specified dimension.

Parameters: `d`—a `Dimension` object representing the new size of the component.

reshape

`public synchronized void reshape(int x, int y, int width, int height)`

`reshape` completely changes the bounding box of the component by changing its size and location.

Parameters:

`x`—the new x coordinate of the component within its parent's coordinate space.

`y`—the new y coordinate of the component within its parent's coordinate space.

`width`—the new width size of the component.

`height`—the new height size of the component.

preferredSize

`public Dimension preferredSize()`

The `preferredSize` method returns the preferred size of the component.

Returns: A `Dimension` object representing the preferred size of the component.

minimumSize

`public Dimension minimumSize()`

`minimumSize` returns the minimum size of the component.

Returns: A `Dimension` object representing the minimum size of the component.

layout

```
public void layout()
```

The layout method is called when the component needs to be laid out.

validate

```
public void validate()
```

validate validates a component by calling its layout method.

invalidate

```
public void invalidate()
```

invalidate invalidates a component, forcing the component and all parents above it to be laid out.

getGraphics

```
public Graphics getGraphics()
```

getGraphics returns a Graphics context for the component. If the component is not currently on the screen, this function will return null.

Returns: A Graphics object representing the component's graphics context.

getFontMetrics

```
public FontMetrics getFontMetrics(Font font)
```

getFontMetrics returns the current font metrics for a specified font. If the component is not currently on the screen, this function will return null.

Parameters: font—a Font object to be examined.

Returns: A FontMetrics object representing the component's font metrics.

paint

```
public void paint(Graphics g)
```

The paint method paints the component on the screen using the Graphics context parameter.

Parameters: g—the Graphics context that the component will paint itself onto.

update

`public void update(Graphics g)`

The `update` method repaints the component in response to a call to the `repaint` method.

Parameters: g—the `Graphics` context that the component will paint itself onto.

paintAll

`public void paintAll(Graphics g)`

The `paintAll` method is used to paint the component along with all of its subcomponents.

Parameters: g—the `Graphics` context that the component will paint itself onto.

repaint

`public void repaint()`

`repaint` is used to force a component to repaint itself. Calling this function will result in a call to `repaint`.

repaint

`public void repaint(long tm)`

This repaint method is used to force a component to repaint itself in `tm` milliseconds.

Parameters: tm—the time span, in milliseconds, from the time this function was called that the component will repaint itself.

repaint

`public void repaint(int x, int y, int width, int height)`

This `repaint` method will force the component to repaint part of its surface area based on the input coordinates.

Parameters:

x—the x coordinate marking the surface area to be repainted.

y—the y coordinate marking the surface area to be repainted.

width—the width of the surface area to be repainted.

height—the height of the surface area to be repainted.

repaint

```
public void repaint(long tm, int x, int y, int width, int height)
```

This repaint method will force the component to repaint part of its surface area based on the input coordinates at a specified time in the future.

Parameters:

tm—the time, in milliseconds, from the time this method was called that the component will need to repaint itself.

x—the x coordinate marking the surface area to be repainted.

y—the y coordinate marking the surface area to be repainted.

width—the width of the surface area to be repainted.

height—the height of the surface area to be repainted.

print

```
public void print(Graphics g)
```

print prints the component using the Graphics context. The default implementation of this method calls paint.

Parameters: g—the Graphics context to be printed on.

printAll

```
public void printAll(Graphics g)
```

printAll prints the component and all of its subcomponents using the Graphics context.

Parameters: g—the Graphics context to be printed on.

imageUpdate

```
public boolean imageUpdate(Image img, int flags, int x, int y, int w, int h)
```

imageUpdate repaints the component when the specified image has changed.

Parameters:

img—an Image object to be examined for changes.

flags—a flags parameter contains imaging flags such as FRAMEBITS, ALLBITS, and SOMEBITS.

x—the x coordinate marking the surface area to be repainted.

y—the y coordinate marking the surface area to be repainted.

width—the width of the surface area to be repainted.

height—the height of the surface area to be repainted.

Returns: A boolean value that is `true` if the image has changed, `false` if not.

createImage

```
public Image createImage(ImageProducer producer)
```

`createImage` creates an `Image` using the specified image producer.

Parameters: producer—an `ImageProducer` interface that will be used to produce a new image.

Returns: An `Image` object.

createImage

```
public Image createImage(int width, int height)
```

This `createImage` creates an offscreen `Image` object using the specified width and height. This `Image` object can be used for things like double buffering.

Parameters:

width—the width of the `Image` object to be created.

height—the height of the `Image` object to be created.

Returns: An `Image` object.

prepareImage

```
public boolean prepareImage(Image image, ImageObserver observer)
```

`prepareImage` prepares an image for rendering on this component. Because the `Image` is downloaded using a separate thread, the `ImageObserver` interface is notified when the image is ready to be rendered.

Parameters:

image—an `Image` object that will be rendered on this component.

observer—an `Observer` interface that will be notified when the `Image` is ready to be rendered.

Returns: A boolean value that is `true` if the image has been prepared, `false` if not.

prepareImage

```
public boolean prepareImage(Image image, int width, int height,
  ImageObserver observer)
```

This prepareImage method is similar to the prepareImage method documented previously except that this method scales the image based on the width and height parameters.

Parameters:

image—an Image object that will be rendered on this component.

width—the width of the image to be rendered.

height—the height of the image to be rendered.

observer—an Observer interface that will be notified when the Image is ready to be rendered.

Returns: A boolean value that is true if the image has been prepared, false if not.

checkImage

```
public int checkImage(Image image, ImageObserver observer)
```

checkImage checks the status of the construction of the image to be rendered.

Parameters:

image—an Image object that will be rendered on this component.

observer—an Observer interface that will be notified when the Image is ready to be rendered.

Returns: An integer value that is the boolean OR of the ImageObserver flags for the data that is currently available.

checkImage

```
public int checkImage(Image image, int width, int height, ImageObserver
  observer)
```

This checkImage method checks the status of the construction of a scaled representation of this image.

Parameters:

image—an Image object that will be rendered on this component.

width—the width of the image to be checked.

height—the height of the image to be checked.

observer—an Observer interface that will be notified when the image is ready to be rendered.

Returns: An integer value that is the boolean OR of the ImageObserver flags for the data that is currently available.

inside

```
public synchronized boolean inside(int x, int y)
```

The inside method determines whether the x and y coordinates are within the bounding rectangle of the component.

Parameters:

x—the x coordinate to be examined.

y—the y coordinate to be examined.

Returns: A boolean value representing the result of the coordinate check.

locate

```
public Component locate(int x, int y)
```

locate returns the Component at the specified x and y coordinates.

Parameters:

x—the x coordinate to be examined.

y—the y coordinate to be examined.

Returns: The Component that is found at the specified x and y coordinates.

deliverEvent

```
public void deliverEvent(Event e)
```

deliverEvent delivers an event to the component.

Parameters: e—an Event object encapsulating the event.

postEvent

```
public boolean postEvent(Event e)
```

postEvent posts an event to the component resulting in a call to handleEvent.

Parameters: e—an Event object encapsulating the event.

Returns: A boolean value that is true if the event was handled, false if not.

handleEvent

`public boolean handleEvent(Event evt)`

`handleEvent` is used to handle individual events by the component.

Parameters: evt—an Event object encapsulating the event.

Returns: A boolean value that is true if the event was handled, false if not.

mouseDown

`public boolean mouseDown(Event evt, int x, int y)`

The `mouseDown` method is called if the mouse is down.

Parameters:

evt—an Event object encapsulating the event.

x—the x coordinate of the mouse down click point.

y—the y coordinate of the mouse down click point.

Returns: A boolean value that is true if the event was handled, false if not.

mouseDrag

`public boolean mouseDrag(Event evt, int x, int y)`

The `mouseDrag` method is called if the mouse is dragged.

Parameters:

evt—an Event object encapsulating the event.

x—the x coordinate of the current mouse point coordinate.

y—the y coordinate of the current mouse point coordinate.

Returns: A boolean value that is true if the event was handled, false if not.

mouseUp

`public boolean mouseUp(Event evt, int x, int y)`

The `mouseUp` method is called when the mouse button is let up.

Parameters:

evt—an Event object encapsulating the event.

x—the x coordinate of the mouse up point.

y—the y coordinate of the mouse up point.

Returns: A boolean value that is `true` if the event was handled, `false` if not.

mouseMove

```
public boolean mouseMove(Event evt, int x, int y)
```

The `mouseMove` method is called if the mouse is moved.

Parameters:

evt—an `Event` object encapsulating the event.

x—the x coordinate of the current mouse point coordinate.

y—the y coordinate of the current mouse point coordinate.

Returns: A boolean value that is `true` if the event was handled, `false` if not.

mouseEnter

```
public boolean mouseEnter(Event evt, int x, int y)
```

The `mouseEnter` method is called if the mouse enters the component.

Parameters:

evt—an `Event` object encapsulating the event.

x—the x coordinate of the current mouse point coordinate.

y—the y coordinate of the current mouse point coordinate.

Returns: A boolean value that is `true` if the event was handled, `false` if not.

mouseExit

```
public boolean mouseExit(Event evt, int x, int y)
```

The `mouseExit` method is called if the mouse exits the component.

Parameters:

evt—an `Event` object encapsulating the event.

x—the x coordinate of the mouse exit point.

y—the y coordinate of the mouse exit point.

Returns: A boolean value that is `true` if the event was handled, `false` if not.

keyDown

```
public boolean keyDown(Event evt, int key)
```

The keyDown method is called when a key is pressed.

Parameters:

evt—an Event object encapsulating the event.

key—an integer value representing the code of the key that was pressed.

Returns: A boolean value that is true if the event was handled, false if not.

keyUp

```
public boolean keyUp(Event evt, int key)
```

The keyUp method is called when a key is let up.

Parameters:

evt—an Event object encapsulating the event.

key—an integer value representing the code of the key that was pressed.

Returns: A boolean value that is true if the event was handled, false if not.

action

```
public boolean action(Event evt, Object what)
```

The action method is called if an action occurs within the component.

Parameters:

evt—an Event object encapsulating the event.

what—an object representing the action that is occurring.

Returns: A boolean value that is true if the event was handled, false if not.

addNotify

```
public void addNotify()
```

addNotify notifies a component to create a peer object.

removeNotify

```
public synchronized void removeNotify()
```

removeNotify notifies a component to destroy the peer object.

gotFocus

```
public boolean gotFocus(Event evt, Object what)
```

The gotFocus method is called when the component receives the input focus.

Parameters:

evt—an Event object encapsulating the event.

what—an object representing the action that is occurring.

Returns: A boolean value that is true if the event was handled, false if not.

lostFocus

```
public boolean lostFocus(Event evt, Object what)
```

The lostFocus method is called when the component loses the input focus.

Parameters:

evt—an Event object encapsulating the event.

what—an object representing the action that is occurring.

Returns: A boolean value that is true if the event was handled, false if not.

requestFocus

```
public void requestFocus()
```

The requestFocus method requests the current input focus. If this method is successful, gotFocus will then be called.

nextFocus

```
public void nextFocus()
```

The nextFocus method switches the focus to the next component. The next component can be determined by examining the tab order of the components on a form.

toString

`public String toString()`

toString returns a string representation of the Component class.

Returns: A String value containing the Component class's name plus its x, y, height, and width values.

list

`public void list()`

The list method prints a listing of the component to the print stream.

list

`public void list(PrintStream out)`

This list method prints a listing of the component to the specified output stream.

Parameters: out—a PrintStream object.

list

`public void list(PrintStream out, int indent)`

This list method prints a listing of the component to the specified output stream at the specified indention.

Parameters:

out—a PrintStream object.

indent—an integer value representing the amount to be indented.

Container

Extends: Component

A Container class is defined as a class that can contain other components.

countComponents

`public int countComponents()`

countComponents returns the number of components contained within the container.

Returns: An integer value representing the number of components within the container.

getComponent

```
public synchronized Component getComponent(int n)
```

The getComponent method returns the component at the specified index.

Parameters: n—an integer value representing the index at which to retrieve a component.

Returns: A Component object within the container.

getComponents

```
public synchronized Component[] getComponents()
```

getComponents returns an array of Component objects contained within the Container.

Returns: An array of Component objects contained within the container.

insets

```
public Insets insets()
```

The insets methods returns the borders of this container.

Returns: An Insets object representing the insets of the container.

add

```
public Component add(Component comp)
```

The add method adds a Component to the container at the end of the container's array of components.

Parameters: comp—the component to be added.

Returns: The Component object that was added to the container's list.

add

```
public synchronized Component add(Component comp, int pos)
```

This add method adds a Component to the container at the specified index in the container's array of components.

Parameters:

comp—the component to be added.

pos—the position the component is to be added at.

Returns: The Component object that was added to the container's list.

add

`public synchronized Component add(String name, Component comp)`

This add method adds a Component using the Component argument and that Component's name.

Parameters:

name—a String representing the name of the component.

comp—the component to be added.

Returns: The Component object that was added to the container's list.

remove

`public synchronized void remove(Component comp)`

The remove method removes the specified component from the Container's list.

Parameters: comp—the component to be removed.

removeAll

`public synchronized void removeAll()`

The removeAll method removes all components from within the Container.

getLayout

`public LayoutManager getLayout()`

getLayout returns this container's layout manager.

Returns: A layout manager interface representing the container's LayoutManager.

setLayout

`public void setLayout(LayoutManager mgr)`

setLayout sets the current layout manager of the container.

Parameters: mgr—the layout manager that will control the layouts of this Container's components.

layout

`public synchronized void layout()`

The layout method is called to perform a layout on this component.

validate

```
public synchronized void validate()
```

The validate method refreshes the container and all of the components within it by validating the container and all of its components.

preferredSize

```
public synchronized Dimension preferredSize()
```

preferredSize returns the preferred size of this container.

Returns: A Dimension object representing the preferred size of this Container.

minimumSize

```
public synchronized Dimension minimumSize()
```

minimumSize returns the minimum size of this container.

Returns: A Dimension object representing the minimum size of this Container.

paintComponents

```
public void paintComponents(Graphics g)
```

The paintComponents method is used to paint each of the components within the container.

Parameters: g—the Graphics context that the container's components will be painted on.

printComponents

```
public void printComponents(Graphics g)
```

The printComponents method is used to print each of the components within the container.

Parameters: g—the Graphics context that the container's components will be printed on.

deliverEvent

```
public void deliverEvent(Event e)
```

deliverEvent locates the appropriate component within the container that the event applies to and delivers the event to that component.

Parameters: e—the event to be delivered.

locate

`public Component locate(int x, int y)`

The `locate` method locates and returns the component that lies at the specified x and y coordinates within the container.

Parameters:

x—the x coordinate of the component to be located.

y—the y coordinate of the component to be located.

addNotify

`public synchronized void addNotify()`

`addNotify` notifies the container to create a peer interface. This method will also notify each of the container's components to do likewise.

removeNotify

`public synchronized void removeNotify()`

`removeNotify` notifies the container to remove its peer. This method will also notify each of the container's components to do likewise.

list

`public void list(PrintStream out, int indent)`

The `list` method prints a list for each component within the container to the specified output stream at the specified indentation.

Parameters:

out—a `PrintStream` object.

indent—an integer amount representing the value to indent the list.

Dialog

Extends: Window

The `Dialog` class is used to create a window that can be closed by the user. Dialogs are normally temporary windows that are used for inputting information.

`Dialog` **Constructor**

`public Dialog(Frame parent, boolean modal)`

This `Dialog` constructor constructs a `Dialog` object from a parent `Frame` object. This dialog is initially invisible.

Parameters:

`parent`—the parent frame of the dialog.

`modal`—a boolean value designating this dialog to be either modal or nonmodal.

`Dialog` **Constructor**

`public Dialog(Frame parent, String title, boolean modal)`

This `Dialog` constructor constructs a `Dialog` object from a parent `Frame` object. This dialog is initially invisible.

Parameters:

`parent`—the parent frame of the dialog.

`title`—a `String` value representing the title to be displayed for this dialog.

`modal`—a boolean value designating this dialog to be either modal or nonmodal.

addNotify

`public synchronized void addNotify()`

The `addNotify` method creates the dialog's peer. Making use of a peer interface allows the dialog's appearance to be changed without changing its functionality.

isModal

`public boolean isModal()`

`isModal` returns the modal status of the dialog.

Returns: A boolean value representing the dialog's modal status. If this is `true`, the dialog is modal. If `false`, the dialog is nonmodal.

getTitle

`public String getTitle()`

`getTitle` returns the dialog's title string.

Returns: A `String` value representing the title string of the dialog.

setTitle

`public void setTitle(String title)`

The setTitle method sets the dialog's title string.

Parameters: title—a String value representing the dialog's new title.

isResizable

`public boolean isResizable()`

The isResizable method is called to determine whether or not this dialog can be resized.

Returns: A boolean value that is true if the dialog is resizable, false if it is not.

setResizable

`public void setResizable(boolean resizable)`

The setResizable method is used to change whether a dialog can be resized.

Parameters: resizable—a boolean value that is true if the dialog is to be resizable and false if not.

Dimension

Extends: Object

A Dimension class is used to encapsulate an object's height and width.

Member Variables

`public int width`

The width instance variable contains the integer value representing the Dimension's width value.

`public int height`

The height instance variable contains the integer value representing the Dimension's height value.

Dimension Constructor

`public Dimension()`

This Dimension constructor constructs an empty Dimension object.

Dimension **Constructor**

`public Dimension(Dimension d)`

This `Dimension` constructor constructs a `Dimension` object from an existing `Dimension` object.

Parameters: d—a `Dimension` object whose values will be used to create the new dimension.

Dimension **Constructor**

`public Dimension(int width, int height)`

This `Dimension` constructor constructs a `Dimension` object based on the `width` and `height` input parameters.

Parameters:

width—an integer value representing the width of the new dimension.

height—an integer value representing the height of the new dimension.

toString

`public String toString()`

The `toString` method is used to return a string representation of this `Dimension` object.

Returns: A `String` containing this dimension's height and width values.

Event

Extends: `Object`

The `Event` class is used to encapsulate GUI event's in a platform-independent manner.

Member Constants

`public static final int SHIFT_MASK`

The `SHIFT_MASK` value represents the Shift Modifier constant.

`public static final int CTRL_MASK`

The `CTRL_MASK` value represents the Control Modifier constant.

`public static final int META_MASK`

The `META_MASK` value represents the Meta Modifier constant.

```
public static final int ALT_MASK
```

The ALT_MASK value represents the Alt Modifier constant.

```
public static final int HOME
```

The HOME value represents the Home key.

```
public static final int END
```

The END value represents the End key.

```
public static final int PGUP
```

The PGUP value represents the Page Up key.

```
public static final int PGDN
```

The PGDN value represents the Page Down key.

```
public static final int UP
```

The UP value represents the up-arrow key.

```
public static final int DOWN
```

The DOWN value represents the down-arrow key.

```
public static final int LEFT
```

The LEFT value represents the left-arrow key.

```
public static final int RIGHT
```

The RIGHT value represents the right-arrow key.

```
public static final int F1
```

The F1 value represents the F1 key.

```
public static final int F2
```

The F2 value represents the F2 key.

```
public static final int F3
```

The F3 value represents the F3 key.

```
public static final int F4
```

The F4 value represents the F4 key.

```
public static final int F5
```

The F5 value represents the F5 key.

```
public static final int F6
```

The F6 value represents the F6 key.

```
public static final int F7
```

The F7 value represents the F7 key.

```
public static final int F8
```

The F8 value represents the F8 key.

```
public static final int F9
```

The F9 value represents the F9 key.

```
public static final int F10
```

The F10 value represents the F10 key.

```
public static final int F11
```

The F11 value represents the F11 key.

```
public static final int F12
```

The F12 value represents the F12 key.

```
public static final int WINDOW_DESTROY
```

The WINDOW_DESTROY value represents the destroy window event.

```
public static final int WINDOW_EXPOSE
```

The WINDOW_EXPOSE value represents the expose window event.

```
public static final int WINDOW_ICONIFY
```

The WINDOW_ICONIFY value represents the iconify window event.

```
public static final int WINDOW_DEICONIFY
```

The DEICONIFY_WINDOW value represents the deiconify window event.

```
public static final int WINDOW_MOVED
```

The WINDOW_MOVED value represents the window moved event.

```
public static final int KEY_PRESS
```

The KEY_PRESS value represents the keypress event.

```
public static final int KEY_RELEASE
```

The KEY_RELEASE value represents the key release event.

```
public static final int KEY_ACTION
```

The KEY_ACTION value represents the key action keyboard event.

```
public static final int KEY_ACTION_RELEASE
```

The KEY_ACTION_RELEASE value represents the key action release keyboard event.

```
public static final int MOUSE_DOWN
```

The MOUSE_DOWN value represents the mouse down event.

```
public static final int MOUSE_UP
```

The MOUSE_UP value represents the mouse up event.

```
public static final int MOUSE_MOVE
```

The MOUSE_MOVE value represents the mouse move event.

```
public static final int MOUSE_ENTER
```

The MOUSE_ENTER value represents the mouse enter event.

```
public static final int MOUSE_EXIT
```

The MOUSE_EXIT value represents the mouse exit event.

```
public static final int MOUSE_DRAG
```

The MOUSE_DRAG value represents the mouse drag event.

```
public static final int SCROLL_LINE_UP
```

The SCROLL_LINE_UP value represents the line up scroll event.

```
public static final int SCROLL_LINE_DOWN
```

The SCROLL_LINE_DOWN value represents the line down scroll event.

```
public static final int SCROLL_PAGE_UP
```

The SCROLL_PAGE_UP value represents the page up scroll event.

```
public static final int SCROLL_PAGE_DOWN
```

The SCROLL_PAGE_DOWN value represents the page down scroll event.

```
public static final int SCROLL_ABSOLUTE
```

The SCROLL_ABSOLUTE value represents the absolute scroll event.

F

```
public static final int LIST_SELECT
```

The LIST_SELECT value represents the select list event.

```
public static final int LIST_DESELECT
```

The LIST_DESELECT value represents the deselect list event.

```
public static final int ACTION_EVENT
```

The ACTION_EVENT value represents an action event.

```
public static final int LOAD_FILE
```

The LOAD_FILE value represents a file load event.

```
public static final int SAVE_FILE
```

The SAVE_FILE value represents a file save event.

```
public static final int GOT_FOCUS
```

The GOT_FOCUS value represents a got focus event.

```
public static final int LOST_FOCUS
```

The LOST_FOCUS value represents a lost focus event.

Member Variables

```
public Object target
```

The target instance variable represents the object that is the target of the event.

```
public long when
```

The when instance variable represents the time stamp of the event.

```
public int id
```

The id instance variable represents the type of the event.

```
public int x
```

The x instance variable represents the x coordinate of the event.

```
public int y
```

The y instance variable represents the y coordinate of the event.

```
public int key
```

The key instance variable represents the key that was pressed to trigger the keyboard event.

```
public int modifiers
```

The `modifiers` instance variable represents the state of the modifier keys.

```
public int clickCount
```

The `clickCount` instance variable represents the number of clicks during the mouse down event. If this event wasn't triggered by a mouse down action, this value will be 0. It will be 1 for a single click, and 2 for a double click.

```
public Object arg
```

The `arg` instance variable represents an arbitrary argument.

```
public Event evt
```

The evt instance variable represents the next event. This is useful when multiple events will be stored in an array or linked list.

Event **Constructor**

```
public Event(Object target, long when, int id, int x, int y, int key, int
modifiers, Object arg)
```

This Event constructor constructs an event using the target, current time, event ID, location, key pressed and modifiers, and some argument.

Parameters:

target—the target object for the event.

when—the time stamp for the event.

id—the event type.

x—the x coordinate of the event.

y—the y coordinate of the event.

key—the key pressed that triggered a keyboard event.

modifiers—the state of the modifier keys.

arg—an arbitrary argument.

F

Event **Constructor**

```
public Event(Object target, long when, int id, int x, int y, int key, int
modifiers)
```

This Event constructor constructs an event using the target, current time, event ID, location, key pressed, and modifiers.

Parameters:

target—the target object for the event.

when—the time stamp for the event.

id—the event type.

x—the x coordinate of the event.

y—the y coordinate of the event.

key—the key pressed that triggered a keyboard event.

Event **Constructor**

```
public Event(Object target, int id, Object arg)
```

This Event constructor constructs an event using the target, event ID, and some argument.

Parameters:

target—the target object for the event.

id—the event type.

arg—an arbitrary argument.

translate

```
public void translate(int x, int y)
```

The translate method translates coordinates for a given component. If the object sending this event has targeted a certain component, this method will translate the coordinates to make sense for that particular component.

Parameters:

x—the x coordinate.

y—the y coordinate.

shiftDown

`public boolean shiftDown()`

The `shiftDown` method returns the current state of the Shift key.

Returns: A boolean value that is `true` if the Shift key is down, `false` if it is up.

controlDown

`public boolean controlDown()`

The `controlDown` method returns the current state of the Ctrl key.

Returns: A boolean value that is `true` if the Ctrl key is down, `false` if it is up.

metaDown

`public boolean metaDown()`

The `metaDown` method returns the current state of the Meta key.

Returns: A boolean value that is `true` if the meta key is down, `false` if it is up.

toString

`public String toString()`

The `toString` method returns the string representation of the current event.

Returns: A `String` value containing information on the event, including the `id`, `x`, `y`, `key`, `shiftDown`, `controlDown`, and `metaDown` values.

FileDialog

Extends: `Dialog`

A `FileDialog` is presented to a user in order for that user to select a file. This dialog is a modal dialog, therefore the calling thread will be blocked until this dialog exits.

Member Constants

`public static final int LOAD`

The `LOAD` static value represents the file load variable.

`public static final int SAVE`

The `SAVE` static value represents the file save variable.

FileDialog **Constructor**

```
public FileDialog(Frame parent, String title)
```

This FileDialog constructor constructs a file dialog using a parent frame and a title string.

Parameters:

parent—the parent frame of the file dialog.

title—a String containing the dialog's title.

FileDialog **Constructor**

```
public FileDialog(Frame parent, String title, int mode)
```

This FileDialog constructor constructs a file dialog using a parent frame, a title string, and a mode value representing either a load or save dialog.

Parameters:

parent—the parent frame of the file dialog.

title—a String containing the dialog's title.

mode—an integer value representing the dialog mode (LOAD or SAVE).

addNotify

```
public synchronized void addNotify()
```

addNotify notifies FileDialog to create a peer. Using a peer interface allows the user interface of the file dialog to be changed without changing its functionality.

getMode

```
public int getMode()
```

getMode returns the current mode of the file dialog.

Returns: An integer value representing the current mode (LOAD or SAVE) of the file dialog.

getDirectory

```
public String getDirectory()
```

The getDirectory method returns the current directory of the file dialog.

Returns: A String value representing FileDialog's current directory.

setDirectory

`public void setDirectory(String dir)`

The `setDirectory` method is used to set the current directory of the `FileDialog`.

Parameters: `dir`—a `String` value representing the directory to be set.

getFile

`public String getFile()`

The `getFile` method returns the currently selected file within `FileDialog`.

Returns: A `String` value representing the file dialog's current file.

setFile

`public void setFile(String file)`

The `setFile` method is used to set the current file of the file dialog.

Parameters: `file`—a `String` value representing the file to be set.

FlowLayout

Extends: `Object`

Implements: `LayoutManager`

A `FlowLayout` implements the `LayoutManager` interface. This class is used to lay out buttons from left to right until no more buttons fit on the `Panel`.

Member Constants

`public static final int LEFT`

The `LEFT` static value represents the left alignment variable.

`public static final int CENTER`

The `CENTER` static value represents the center alignment variable.

`public static final int RIGHT`

The `RIGHT` static value represents the right alignment variable.

FlowLayout **Constructor**

public FlowLayout()

This FlowLayout constructor constructs a default FlowLayout class with a centered alignment.

FlowLayout **Constructor**

public FlowLayout(int align)

This FlowLayout constructor constructs a FlowLayout class using the specified alignment.

Parameters: align—the alignment value (LEFT, CENTER, or RIGHT).

FlowLayout **Constructor**

public FlowLayout(int align, int hgap, int vgap)

This FlowLayout constructor constructs a FlowLayout class using the specified alignment and gap values.

Parameters:

align—the alignment value (LEFT, CENTER, or RIGHT).

hgap—the horizontal gap value.

vgap—the vertical gap value.

addLayoutComponent

public void addLayoutComponent(String name, Component comp)

The addLayoutComponent method adds a component to the FlowLayout class.

Parameters:

name—a String value representing the name of the Component to be added.

comp—the Component object to be added to FlowLayout.

removeLayoutComponent

public void removeLayoutComponent(Component comp)

removeLayoutComponent removes a component from the FlowLayout class.

Parameters: comp—a Component object to be removed from FlowLayout.

preferredLayoutSize

`public Dimension preferredLayoutSize(Container target)`

The `preferredLayoutSize` method returns the preferred size for this `FlowLayout` given the components in the specified container.

Parameters: `target`—a `Container` object that will be examined to determine the preferred layout size for this `FlowLayout`.

Returns: A `Dimension` class containing the preferred size of the `FlowLayout`.

minimumLayoutSize

`public Dimension minimumLayoutSize(Container target)`

The `minimumLayoutSize` method returns the minimum size for this `FlowLayout` given the components in the specified container.

Parameters: `target`—a `Container` object that will be examined to determine the minimum layout size for this `FlowLayout`.

Returns: A `Dimension` class containing the minimum size of the `FlowLayout`.

layoutContainer

`public void layoutContainer(Container target)`

The `layoutContainer` method lays out the components within the specified container.

Parameters: `target`—a `Container` class containing a set of components that will be laid out according to the `FlowLayout` rules.

toString

`public String toString()`

The `toString` method returns a string representation of the `FlowLayout` class.

Returns: A `String` containing information about the `FlowLayout`, including the `FlowLayout`'s name, alignment, hgap, and vgap values.

Font

Extends: `Object`

This class is used to encapsulate a font.

Member Constants

`public static final int PLAIN`

The PLAIN static value represents the plain style constant.

`public static final int BOLD`

The BOLD static value represents the bold style constant.

`public static final int ITALIC`

The ITALIC static value represents the italic style constant.

Font **Constructor**

`public Font(String name, int style, int size)`

The Font constructor constructs a font of the specified name, style, and size.

Parameters:

name—the name of the font to be created.

style—the style (PLAIN and/or BOLD and/or ITALIC) of the font to be created.

size—the size of the font to be created.

getFamily

`public String getFamily()`

getFamily returns the font family that this font belongs to.

Returns: A String value representing the font's family name.

getName

`public String getName()`

getName returns the name of the Font object.

Returns: A String value representing the name of the font.

getStyle

`public int getStyle()`

getStyle returns the style of the Font object.

Returns: An integer value representing the style of the font.

getSize

```
public int getSize()
```

getSize returns the size of the Font object.

Returns: An integer value representing the point size of the font.

isPlain

```
public boolean isPlain()
```

isPlain returns the plain style state of the Font.

Returns: A boolean value that is true if the font is plain, false if not.

isBold

```
public boolean isBold()
```

isBold returns the bold style state of the Font.

Returns: A boolean value that is true if the font is bold, false if not.

isItalic

```
public boolean isItalic()
```

isItalic returns the italic style state of the Font.

Returns: A boolean value that is true if the font is italic, false if not.

getFont

```
public static Font getFont(String nm)
```

getFont returns a Font based on the system properties list and the name passed in.

Parameters: nm—the name of the font to be returned from the system properties list.

Returns: A Font object based on the system properties list.

getFont

```
public static Font getFont(String nm, Font font)
```

This getFont method returns a Font based on the system properties list, the name passed in, and a default font in case the specified name is not found.

Parameters:

nm—the name of the font to be returned from the system properties list.

font—the default font to be returned if the font specified by the nm variable is not found.

Returns: A Font object based on the system properties list.

hashCode

public int hashCode()

hashCode returns a hash code for this font.

Returns: An integer value representing the hash code for the font.

equals

public boolean equals(Object obj)

equals compares an object with the Font object.

Parameters: obj—the object to compare the font with.

Returns: A boolean value that is true if the objects are equal, false if not.

toString

public String toString()

The toString method is used to return a string representation of the font.

Returns: A String value containing the font family, name, style, and size values.

FontMetrics

Extends: Object

The FontMetrics class is used to encapsulate a FontMetrics object containing font information.

getFont

public Font getFont()

The getFont method returns the font that these FontMetrics refer to.

Returns: A Font object.

getLeading

```
public int getLeading()
```

The getLeading method gets the line spacing of the font.

Returns: An integer value containing the standard leading, or line spacing, of the font. The line spacing of a font is the space reserved between the descent of a text character and the ascent of a text character below it.

getAscent

```
public int getAscent()
```

The getAscent method gets the ascent value for a font.

Returns: An integer value containing the ascent value for a font. This value is the distance from the bottom of a character to its top.

getDescent

```
public int getDescent()
```

The getDescent method gets the descent value for a font.

Returns: An integer value containing the descent value for a font. This value is the bottom coordinate of a character.

getHeight

```
public int getHeight()
```

The getHeight method gets the height of a line of text using the current Font.

Returns: An integer value containing the height of a line of text. This value is calculated by adding the ascent, descent, and leading values.

getMaxAscent

```
public int getMaxAscent()
```

getMaxAscent returns the maximum value of a font's ascent.

Returns: An integer value containing the maximum value of a font's ascent for all of that font's characters.

getMaxDescent

`public int getMaxDescent()`

getMaxDescent returns the maximum value of a font's descent.

Returns: An integer value containing the maximum value of a font's descent for all of that font's characters.

getMaxDecent

`public int getMaxDecent()`

The getMaxDecent method is provided only for backward compatibility. It simply calls the getMaxDescent method.

Returns: An integer value containing the maximum value of a font's descent for all of that font's characters.

getMaxAdvance

`public int getMaxAdvance()`

The getMaxAdvance method gets the maximum amount for a character's advance value. The advance is the amount that is advanced from the beginning of one character to the next character.

charWidth

`public int charWidth(int ch)`

charWidth returns the width of a particular character for the current font.

Parameters: ch—an integer value representing the character to be checked.

Returns: An integer value representing the width of the specified character.

charWidth

`public int charWidth(char ch)`

This charWidth method returns the width of a particular character for the current font.

Parameters: ch—a string value representing the character to be checked.

Returns: An integer value representing the width of the specified character.

stringWidth

```
public int stringWidth(String str)
```

The stringWidth method returns the width of a specified string using the current font.

Parameters: str—a string representing the characters to be checked.

Returns: An integer value representing the advance width of the specified string.

charsWidth

```
public int charsWidth(char data[], int off, int len)
```

The charsWidth method returns the width of a specified string of characters using the current font.

Parameters:

data—an array of characters to be checked.

off—an integer value representing the offset into the array where the string will start.

len—the number of characters to be measured.

Returns: An integer value representing the advance width of the specified string.

bytesWidth

```
public int bytesWidth(byte data[], int off, int len)
```

The bytesWidth method returns the width of a specified array of bytes

Parameters:

data—an array of bytes to be checked.

off—an integer value representing the offset into the array where the string will start.

len—the number of bytes to be measured.

Returns: An integer value representing the advance width of the specified string.

getWidths

```
public int[] getWidths()
```

The getWidths method gets the advance widths of the first 256 characters of the font.

Returns: An integer array containing the advance widths of the first 256 characters of the font.

toString

```
public String toString()
```

The toString method is used to return a string representation of the FontMetrics class.

Returns: A String value containing the font metrics' name, font, ascent, descent, and height.

Frame

Extends: Window

Implements: MenuContainer

A Frame class represents a basic window.

Member Constants

```
public static final int      DEFAULT_CURSOR
```

The DEFAULT_CURSOR static value represents the default cursor.

```
public static final int      CROSSHAIR_CURSOR
```

The CROSSHAIR_CURSOR static value represents the crosshair cursor.

```
public static final int      TEXT_CURSOR
```

The TEXT_CURSOR static value represents the text cursor.

```
public static final int      WAIT_CURSOR
```

The WAIT_CURSOR static value represents the wait cursor.

```
public static final int      SW_RESIZE_CURSOR
```

The SW_RESIZE_CURSOR static value represents the southwest resize cursor.

```
public static final int      SE_RESIZE_CURSOR
```

The SE_RESIZE_CURSOR static value represents the southeast resize cursor.

```
public static final int      NW_RESIZE_CURSOR
```

The NW_RESIZE_CURSOR static value represents the northwest resize cursor.

```
public static final int      NE_RESIZE_CURSOR
```

The NE_RESIZE_CURSOR static value represents the northeast resize cursor.

```
public static final int      N_RESIZE_CURSOR
```

The N_RESIZE_CURSOR static value represents the north resize cursor.

```
public static final int      S_RESIZE_CURSOR
```

The S_RESIZE_CURSOR static value represents the south resize cursor.

```
public static final int      W_RESIZE_CURSOR
```

The W_RESIZE_CURSOR static value represents the west resize cursor.

```
public static final int      E_RESIZE_CURSOR
```

The E_RESIZE_CURSOR static value represents the east resize cursor.

```
public static final int      HAND_CURSOR
```

The HAND_CURSOR static value represents the hand cursor.

```
public static final int      MOVE_CURSOR
```

The MOVE_CURSOR static value represents the move cursor.

Frame **Constructor**

```
public Frame()
```

The Frame constructor constructs a default frame that is invisible and that uses the BorderLayout layout manager.

Frame **Constructor**

```
public Frame(String title)
```

This Frame constructor constructs a default frame using the specified title that is invisible and that uses the BorderLayout layout manager.

Parameters: title—a String value containing the frame's title string.

addNotify

```
public synchronized void addNotify()
```

The addNotify method creates a peer interface for the frame. Peer interfaces allow the user interface of the frame to be changed without changing its functionality.

getTitle

`public String getTitle()`

getTitle returns the frame's title.

Returns: A String value representing the title of the frame.

setTitle

`public void setTitle(String title)`

setTitle sets the frame's title.

Parameters: title—a String value representing the title of the frame.

getIconImage

`public Image getIconImage()`

The getIconImage method returns an image representing the iconized image of the frame.

Returns: An Image class representing the iconized image of the frame.

setIconImage

`public void setIconImage(Image image)`

setIconImage is used to set the image that will be used when the frame is iconized.

Parameters: image—an Image class that will be displayed when the frame is iconized.

getMenuBar

`public MenuBar getMenuBar()`

The getMenuBar method returns the MenuBar object that is contained within this frame.

Returns: A MenuBar class that is displayed within this frame.

setMenuBar

`public synchronized void setMenuBar(MenuBar mb)`

setMenuBar sets the MenuBar class to be displayed within the frame.

Parameters: mb—a MenuBar object to be used for the frame's menu bar.

remove

```
public synchronized void remove(MenuComponent m)
```

The remove method removes the specified MenuComponent from the frame.

Parameters: A MenuComponent object that is to be removed from the frame.

dispose

```
public synchronized void dispose()
```

The dispose method disposes of the frame. This method first disposes of the frame's menu bar, and then disposes of the frame itself.

isResizable

```
public boolean isResizable()
```

The isResizable method returns the frame's resizable state.

Returns: A boolean value that is true if the frame can be resized, false if not.

setResizable

```
public void setResizable(boolean resizable)
```

The setResizable method sets the frame's resizable state.

Returns: A boolean value that is true if the frame can be resized, false if not.

setCursor

```
public void setCursor(int cursorType)
```

The setCursor method sets the cursor to be displayed within the frame.

Returns: An integer value representing the cursor to be displayed, which can be any of the frame's static values such as WAIT_CURSOR, MOVE_CURSOR, and so on.

getCursorType

```
public int getCursorType()
```

The getCursorType method returns the frame's current cursor type.

Returns: An integer value representing the current cursor type for the frame.

Graphics

Extends: Object

The Graphics class represents the base class for all types of graphics contexts.

create

`public abstract Graphics create()`

This abstract function creates a new Graphics object.

create

`public Graphics create(int x, int y, int width, int height)`

The create method creates a new Graphics object using the specified parameters.

Parameters:

x—the x coordinate of the graphics context.

y—the y coordinate of the graphics context.

width—the width of the graphics context.

height—the height of the graphics context.

Returns: A Graphics class corresponding to the create method's specifications.

translate

`public abstract void translate(int x, int y)`

The translate method translates the Graphics object to the new x and y origin coordinates.

Parameters:

x—the new x origin coordinate.

y—the new y origin coordinate.

getColor

`public abstract Color getColor()`

The getColor method returns the current color.

Returns: A Color object representing the current color used for drawing operations.

setColor

`public abstract void setColor(Color c)`

The `setColor` method sets the current color.

Parameters: c—a `Color` object to be used for graphics drawing operations.

setPaintMode

`public abstract void setPaintMode()`

The `setPaintMode` method sets the paint mode to overwrite the destination with the current color.

setXORMode

`public abstract void setXORMode(Color c1)`

The `setXORMode` method sets the paint mode to XOR the current colors with the specified color. This means that when redrawing over an existing area, colors that match the current color will be changed to the specified color c1 and vice versa.

Parameters: c1—the `Color` object specified to be XOR'd with the current color.

getFont

`public abstract Font getFont()`

The `getFont` method returns the current font used for the graphics context.

Returns: A `Font` object representing the graphics context's current font.

setFont

`public abstract void setFont(Font font)`

The `setFont` method sets the graphics context's font.

Parameters: A `Font` object that will be used as the current font.

getFontMetrics

`public FontMetrics getFontMetrics()`

The `getFontMetrics` method will return the font metrics for the current font.

Returns: A `FontMetrics` object representing the font metrics for the current font.

getFontMetrics

`public abstract FontMetrics getFontMetrics(Font f)`

This `getFontMetrics` method will return the font metrics for the specified font.

Returns: A `FontMetrics` object representing the font metrics for the specified font.

getClipRect

`public abstract Rectangle getClipRect()`

The `getClipRect` method will return the current clipping rectangle for the `Graphics` class.

Returns: A `Rectangle` object representing the current clipping rectangle.

clipRect

`public abstract void clipRect(int x, int y, int width, int height)`

The `clipRect` method will set the current clipping rectangle for the `Graphics` class.

Parameters:

`x`—the x coordinate of the clipping rectangle.

`y`—the y coordinate of the clipping rectangle.

`width`—the width of the clipping rectangle.

`height`—the height of the clipping rectangle.

copyArea

`public abstract void copyArea(int x, int y, int width, int height, int dx, int dy)`

The `copyArea` method copies a specified section of the screen to another location.

Parameters:

`x`—the x coordinate of the region to be copied.

`y`—the y coordinate of the region to be copied.

`width`—the width of the region to be copied.

`height`—the height of the region to be copied.

`dx`—the horizontal distance of the region to be copied to.

`dy`—the vertical distance of the region to be copied to.

drawLine

`public abstract void drawLine(int x1, int y1, int x2, int y2)`

The `drawLine` method will draw a line on the graphics context from one point to another point specified by the input parameters.

Parameters:

x1—the x coordinate of the line's starting point.

y1—the y coordinate of the line's starting point.

x2—the x coordinate of the line's ending point.

y2—the y coordinate of the line's ending point.

fillRect

`public abstract void fillRect(int x, int y, int width, int height)`

The `fillRect` method fills the specified rectangular region with the current color.

Parameters:

x—the x coordinate of the rectangle to be filled.

y—the y coordinate of the rectangle to be filled.

width—the width of the rectangle to be filled.

height—the height of the rectangle to be filled.

drawRect

`public void drawRect(int x, int y, int width, int height)`

The `drawRect` method draws the outline of a rectangle using the current color and the specified dimensions.

Parameters:

x—the x coordinate of the rectangle to be drawn.

y—the y coordinate of the rectangle to be drawn.

width—the width of the rectangle to be drawn.

height—the height of the rectangle to be drawn.

clearRect

`public abstract void clearRect(int x, int y, int width, int height)`

The `clearRect` method clears a rectangle by filling it with the current background color of the current drawing surface.

Parameters:

x—the x coordinate of the rectangle to be cleared.

y—the y coordinate of the rectangle to be cleared.

width—the width of the rectangle to be cleared.

height—the height of the rectangle to be cleared.

drawRoundRect

`public abstract void drawRoundRect(int x, int y, int width, int height,`
`  int arcWidth, int arcHeight)`

The `drawRoundRect` method draws the outline of a rectangle with rounded edges using the current color and the specified coordinates.

Parameters:

x—the x coordinate of the rectangle to be drawn.

y—the y coordinate of the rectangle to be drawn.

width—the width of the rectangle to be drawn.

height—the height of the rectangle to be drawn.

arcWidth—the horizontal diameter of the arc at the four corners.

arcHeight—the vertical diameter of the arc at the four corners.

fillRoundRect

`public abstract void fillRoundRect(int x, int y, int width, int height, int`
`arcWidth, int arcHeight)`

The `fillRoundRect` method fills a rectangle with rounded edges using the current color and the specified coordinates.

Parameters:

x—the x coordinate of the rectangle to be drawn.

y—the y coordinate of the rectangle to be drawn.

width—the width of the rectangle to be drawn.

height—the height of the rectangle to be drawn.

arcWidth—the horizontal diameter of the arc at the four corners.

arcHeight—the vertical diameter of the arc at the four corners.

draw3DRect

`public void draw3DRect(int x, int y, int width, int height, boolean raised)`

The draw3DRect method draws a highlighted 3D rectangle at a default viewing angle.

Parameters:

x—the x coordinate of the rectangle to be drawn.

y—the y coordinate of the rectangle to be drawn.

width—the width of the rectangle to be drawn.

height—the height of the rectangle to be drawn.

raised—a boolean value determining whether the rectangle is raised.

fill3DRect

`public void fill3DRect(int x, int y, int width, int height, boolean raised)`

The fill3DRect method fills a highlighted 3D rectangle using the current color and specified coordinates at a default viewing angle.

Parameters:

x—the x coordinate of the rectangle to be drawn.

y—the y coordinate of the rectangle to be drawn.

width—the width of the rectangle to be drawn.

height—the height of the rectangle to be drawn.

raised—a boolean value determining whether the rectangle is raised.

drawOval

`public abstract void drawOval(int x, int y, int width, int height)`

The drawOval method draws the outline of an oval shape using the current color and the specified coordinates. The oval is drawn inside the rectangle represented by the input coordinates.

Parameters:

x—the x coordinate of the rectangle to draw the oval within.

y—the y coordinate of the rectangle to draw the oval within.

width—the width of the rectangle to draw the oval within.

height—the height of the rectangle to draw the oval within.

fillOval

```
public abstract void fillOval(int x, int y, int width, int height)
```

The fillOval method fills an oval using the current color and the specified coordinates. The oval is drawn inside the rectangle represented by the input coordinates.

Parameters:

x—the x coordinate of the rectangle to draw the oval within.

y—the y coordinate of the rectangle to draw the oval within.

width—the width of the rectangle to draw the oval within.

height—the height of the rectangle to draw the oval within.

drawArc

```
public abstract void drawArc(int x, int y, int width, int height, int
startAngle, int arcAngle)
```

The drawArc method draws an arc outline using the current color and bounded by the specified input coordinates. Note that 0 degrees represents the three o'clock position and that positive angles are measured going counterclockwise.

Parameters:

x—the x coordinate of the rectangle to draw the arc within.

y—the y coordinate of the rectangle to draw the arc within.

width—the width of the rectangle to draw the arc within.

height—the height of the rectangle to draw the arc within.

startAngle—the starting angle of the arc to be drawn.

arcAngle—the angle of the arc relative to the start angle.

fillArc

```
public abstract void fillArc(int x, int y, int width, int height, int
startAngle, int arcAngle)
```

The fillArc method fills an arc using the current color and bounded by the specified input coordinates. Note that 0 degrees represents the three o'clock position and that positive angles are measured going counterclockwise.

Parameters:

x—the x coordinate of the rectangle to draw the arc within.

y—the y coordinate of the rectangle to draw the arc within.

width—the width of the rectangle to draw the arc within.

height—the height of the rectangle to draw the arc within.

startAngle—the starting angle of the arc to be drawn.

arcAngle—the angle of the arc relative to the start Angle.

drawPolygon

```
public abstract void drawPolygon(int xPoints[], int yPoints[], int nPoints)
```

The drawPolygon method draws a polygon using the current color and the specified coordinates.

Parameters:

xPoints—an array of integers containing the starting x coordinates for each edge of the polygon.

yPoints—an array of integers containing the starting y coordinates for each edge of the polygon.

nPoints—an integer value representing the number of edges of the polygon.

drawPolygon

```
public void drawPolygon(Polygon p)
```

This drawPolygon method draws a polygon using the specified Polygon class.

Parameters: p—a Polygon object containing the coordinates for the polygon to be drawn.

fillPolygon

```
public abstract void fillPolygon(int xPoints[], int yPoints[], int nPoints)
```

The fillPolygon method fills a polygon using the current color and the specified coordinates.

Parameters:

xPoints—an array of integers containing the starting x coordinates for each edge of the polygon.

yPoints—an array of integers containing the starting y coordinates for each edge of the polygon.

nPoints—an integer value representing the number of edges of the polygon.

fillPolygon

```
public void fillPolygon(Polygon p)
```

This fillPolygon method fills a polygon using the specified Polygon object and the current color.

Parameters: p—a Polygon object containing the coordinates for the polygon to be drawn.

drawString

```
public abstract void drawString(String str, int x, int y)
```

The drawString method will draw a string using the current font at the specified coordinates.

Parameters:

str—the string to be displayed.

x—the x coordinate to draw the string at.

y—the y coordinate to draw the string at.

drawChars

```
public void drawChars(char data[], int offset, int length, int x, int y)
```

The drawChars method will draw a string using the current font at the specified coordinates.

Parameters:

data—an array of characters.

offset—the offset within the array of characters that the displayed string will start at.

length—the number of characters to draw.

x—the x coordinate to draw the string at.

y—the y coordinate to draw the string at.

drawBytes

```
public void drawBytes(byte data[], int offset, int length, int x, int y)
```

The drawChars method will draw a string using the current font at the specified coordinates.

Parameters:

data—an array of bytes.

offset—the offset within the array of bytes that the displayed string will start at.

length—the number of bytes to draw.

x—the x coordinate to draw the string at.

y—the y coordinate to draw the string at.

drawImage

```
public abstract boolean drawImage(Image img, int x, int y, ImageObserver ob-
server)
```

The drawImage method will draw an image at a specified location.

Parameters:

img—an Image class to be drawn using the graphics context.

x—the x coordinate to draw the image at.

y—the y coordinate to draw the image at.

observer—an ImageObserver interface that will be used to notify when the drawing is done.

Returns: A boolean value indicating the success/failure of the draw operation.

drawImage

```
public abstract boolean drawImage(Image img, int x, int y, int width,
  int height, ImageObserver observer)
```

This drawImage method will draw an image at a specified location within the specified bounding rectangle.

Parameters:

img—an Image class to be drawn using the graphics context.

x—the x coordinate to draw the image at.

y—the y coordinate to draw the image at.

width—the width of the rectangle to draw the image within.

height—the height of the rectangle to draw the image within.

observer—an ImageObserver interface that will be used to notify when the drawing is done.

Returns: A boolean value indicating the success/failure of the draw operation.

drawImage
```
public abstract boolean drawImage(Image img, int x, int y, Color bgcolor,
    ImageObserver observer)
```
This drawImage method will draw an image at a specified location using the specified background color.

Parameters:

img—an Image class to be drawn using the graphics context.

x—the x coordinate to draw the image at.

y—the y coordinate to draw the image at.

bgcolor—the background color to be used.

observer—an ImageObserver derived object that will be used to notify when the drawing is done.

Returns: A boolean value indicating the success/failure of the draw operation.

drawImage
```
public abstract boolean drawImage(Image img, int x, int y, int width,
    int height, Color bgcolor, ImageObserver observer)
```
The drawImage method will draw an image at a specified location within a specified bounding rectangle using a specified background color.

Parameters:

img—an Image class to be drawn using the graphics context.

x—the x coordinate to draw the image at.

y—the y coordinate to draw the image at.

width—the width of the bounding rectangle.

height—the height of the bounding rectangle.

bgcolor—the background color to be used.

observer—an ImageObserver interface that will be used to notify when the drawing is done.

Returns: A boolean value indicating the success/failure of the draw operation.

dispose
```
public abstract void dispose()
```
The dispose method disposes of the Graphics object.

finalize
```
public void finalize()
```
The finalize method disposes of the Graphics object once it is no longer referenced.

toString
```
public String toString()
```
The toString method returns a string representation of the Graphics object.

Returns: A String containing the Graphics class name, current color, and current font.

GridBagConstraints

Extends: Object

Implements: Cloneable

A GridBagConstraints class is used in conjunction with a GridBagLayout in order to specify the constraints of the objects being laid out.

Member Constants
```
public static final int RELATIVE
```
A public static value representing the relative constraint.
```
public static final int REMAINDER
```
A public static value representing the remainder constraint.
```
public static final int NONE
```
A public static value representing the none constraint.

```
public static final int BOTH
```

A public static value representing the both constraint.

```
public static final int HORIZONTAL
```

A public static value representing the horizontal constraint.

```
public static final int VERTICAL
```

A public static value representing the vertical constraint.

```
public static final int CENTER
```

A public static value representing the center constraint.

```
public static final int NORTH
```

A public static value representing the north constraint.

```
public static final int NORTHEAST
```

A public static value representing the northeast constraint.

```
public static final int EAST
```

A public static value representing the east constraint.

```
public static final int SOUTHEAST
```

A public static value representing the southeast constraint.

```
public static final int SOUTH
```

A public static value representing the south constraint.

```
public static final int SOUTHWEST
```

A public static value representing the southwest constraint.

```
public static final int WEST
```

A public static value representing the west constraint.

```
public static final int NORTHWEST
```

A public static value representing the northwest constraint.

Member Variables

```
public int gridx
```

The gridx variable is used to store the grid x coordinate.

`public int gridy`

The `gridy` variable is used to store the grid y coordinate.

`public int gridwidth`

The `gridwidth` variable is used to store the grid bounding rectangle width.

`public int gridheight`

The `gridheight` variable is used to store the grid bounding rectangle height.

`public double weightx`

The `weightx` variable is used to store the horizontal space for a component to reserve for itself. If this is set to `0` (the default), all components within a row will be bunched together in the center of the row.

`public double weighty`

The `weighty` variable is used to store the vertical space for a component to reserve for itself. If this is set to `0` (the default), all components within a column will be bunched together in the center of the column.

`public int anchor`

The `anchor` variable is used to determine how to display a component when it is smaller than its display area. Valid values for this variable are CENTER (the default), NORTH, NORTHEAST, EAST, SOUTHEAST, SOUTH, SOUTHWEST, WEST, and NORTHWEST.

`public int fill`

The `fill` variable is used to determine how to display a component when it is larger than its display area. Valid values for this variable are NONE, HORIZONTAL, VERTICAL, and BOTH.

`public Insets insets`

The `insets` variable is used to determine the space between the component and its bounding area.

`public int ipadx`

The `ipadx` variable is used to determine the amount of padding to always add to the component on its left and right sides.

`public int ipady`

The `ipady` variable is used to determine the amount of padding to always add to the component on its top and bottom sides.

GridBagConstraints **Constructor**

`public GridBagConstraints ()`

The GridBagConstraints constructor creates a GridBagConstraints class containing default values.

clone

`public Object clone()`

The clone method creates a clone of this GridBagConstraints object.

Returns: An Object object representing a clone of this GridBagConstraints object.

GridBagLayout

Extends: Object

Implements: LayoutManager

The GridBagLayout implements the LayoutManager interface. This class uses a rectangular grid of cells to lay out components within the cells. Each component is associated with a GridBagConstraints object that controls how the component is actually laid out within the grid.

Member Variables

`public int columnWidths[]`

The columnWidths variable is an array of integers representing the widths of each column used by GridBagLayout.

`public int rowHeights[]`

The rowHeights variable is an array of integers representing the heights of each column used by GridBagLayout.

`public double columnWeights[]`

The columnWeights variable is an array of doubles representing the space to be distributed for each column.

`public double rowWeights[]`

The rowWeights variable is an array of doubles representing the space to be distributed for each row.

GridBagLayout **Constructor**

`public GridBagLayout()`

The GridBagLayout constructor constructs a GridBagLayout class for use in laying out components on a form.

setConstraints

`public void setConstraints(Component comp, GridBagConstraints constraints)`

The setConstraints method sets GridBagConstraints for the specified component.

Parameters:

comp—a component to be modified within GridBagLayout.

constraints—the GridBagConstraints that will be applied to the component.

getConstraints

`public GridBagConstraints getConstraints(Component comp)`

The getConstraints method returns the constraints currently applied to the specified component.

Parameters: comp—a component managed by GridBagLayout.

Returns: A GridBagConstraints class representing the constraints placed upon the specified component.

getLayoutOrigin

`public Point getLayoutOrigin ()`

The getLayoutOrigin method returns the origin of the layout manager.

Returns: A Point class representing the origin of GridBagLayout.

getLayoutDimensions

`public int [][] getLayoutDimensions ()`

The getLayoutDimensions method returns an array of dimensions with an element for each component.

Returns: An array containing layout dimensions for components managed by the GridBagLayout.

getLayoutWeights

`public double [][] getLayoutWeights()`

The `getLayoutWeights` method returns an array of weights with an element for each component.

Returns: An array containing layout weights for components managed by `GridBagLayout`.

location

`public Point location(int x, int y)`

The `location` method returns a `Point` object representing the point within the layout manager corresponding to the specified coordinates.

Parameters:

x—the x coordinate.

y—the y coordinate.

Returns: A `Point` object.

addLayoutComponent

`public void addLayoutComponent(String name, Component comp)`

The `addLayoutComponent` method adds a component to `GridBagLayout`.

Parameters:

name—the name of the component to be added.

comp—the component to be added.

removeLayoutComponent

`public void removeLayoutComponent(Component comp)`

The `removeLayoutComponent` method removes a component from the `GridBagLayout`.

Parameters: comp—the component to be removed.

preferredLayoutSize

`public Dimension preferredLayoutSize(Container parent)`

The `preferredLayoutSize` method returns the preferred size for the layout manager given the specified container and the components within it.

Parameters: parent—a Container object containing components.

Returns: A Dimension object specifying the preferred size of the layout manager.

minimumLayoutSize
`public Dimension minimumLayoutSize(Container parent)`

The minimum `preferredLayoutSize` method returns the minimum size for the layout manager given the specified container and the components within it.

Parameters: parent—a Container object containing components.

Returns: A Dimension object specifying the minimum size of the layout manager.

layoutContainer
`public void layoutContainer(Container parent)`

The `layoutContainer` method lays out the specified container within the layout manager.

Parameters: parent—a Container object containing components.

toString
`public String toString()`

The `toString` method returns a string containing information about the GridBagLayout.

Returns: A String containing the name of GridBagLayout.

GridLayout

Extends: Object

Implements: LayoutManager

The GridLayout class implements the LayoutManager interface. It is used to lay out grid objects.

GridLayout **Constructor**
`public GridLayout(int rows, int cols)`

The GridLayout constructor constructs a grid layout manager using the specified number of rows and columns.

Parameters:

rows—the number of rows to be laid out.

cols—the number of columns to be laid out.

GridLayout **Constructor**

public GridLayout(int rows, int cols, int hgap, int vgap)

This GridLayout constructor constructs a grid layout manager using the specified number of rows and columns as well as the horizontal and vertical gaps to be used.

Parameters:

rows—the number of rows to be laid out.

cols—the number of columns to be laid out.

hgap—the horizontal gap value.

vgap—the vertical gap value.

addLayoutComponent

public void addLayoutComponent(String name, Component comp)

The addLayoutComponent method adds a component to GridLayout.

Parameters:

name—the name of the component to be added.

comp—the component to be added.

removeLayoutComponent

public void removeLayoutComponent(Component comp)

The removeLayoutComponent method removes a component from the GridBagLayout.

Parameters: comp—the component to be removed.

preferredLayoutSize

public Dimension preferredLayoutSize(Container parent)

The preferredLayoutSize method returns the preferred size for the layout manager given the specified container and the components within it.

Parameters: parent—a Container object containing components.

Returns: A Dimension object specifying the preferred size of the layout manager.

minimumLayoutSize

`public Dimension minimumLayoutSize(Container parent)`

The minimum `preferredLayoutSize` method returns the minimum size for the layout manager given the specified container and the components within it.

Parameters: parent—a Container object containing components.

Returns: A Dimension object specifying the minimum size of the layout manager.

layoutContainer

`public void layoutContainer(Container parent)`

The `layoutContainer` method lays out the specified container within the layout manager.

Parameters: parent—a Container object containing components.

toString

`public String toString()`

The `toString` method returns a string containing information about the GridLayout.

Returns: A String containing the grid layout's name, hgap, vgap, rows, and cols values.

Image

Extends: Object

An Image class is actually an abstract class. A platform-specific implementation must be provided for it to be used.

getWidth

`public abstract int getWidth(ImageObserver observer)`

The `getWidth` method returns the width of the image. If the width of the image is not yet known, ImageObserver will be notified at a later time and -1 will be returned.

Parameters: observer—an ImageObserver-derived object that will be notified if the image is not yet available.

Returns: An integer value representing the width of the image, or -1 if the image is not yet available.

getHeight

```
public abstract int getHeight(ImageObserver observer)
```

The getWidth method returns the height of the image. If the height of the image is not yet known, ImageObserver will be notified at a later time and -1 will be returned.

Parameters: observer—an ImageObserver-derived object that will be notified if the image is not yet available.

Returns: An integer value representing the height of the image, or -1 if the image is not yet available.

getSource

```
public abstract ImageProducer getSource()
```

The getSource method returns the ImageProducer interface responsible for producing the Image's pixels.

Returns: An ImageProducer interface used by the image-filtering classes in package java.awt.Image.

getGraphics

```
public abstract Graphics getGraphics()
```

The getGraphics method is used to return a graphics context for drawing into. This function is used for offscreen image operations such as double buffering of an image.

Returns: A Graphics object used for image-drawing purposes.

getProperty

```
public abstract Object getProperty(String name, ImageObserver observer)
```

The getProperty method is used to return image property information (each image type has its own set of properties).

Parameters:

name—the image property name to be returned.

observer—an ImageObserver-derived object that will be notified if the image is not yet ready.

Returns: The Property object that corresponds with the property requested. If the image is not yet available, this method returns null. If the property was undefined, an UndefinedProperty object is returned.

flush

```
public abstract void flush()
```

The `flush` method flushes all image data. Calling this method returns the image to its initial empty state; therefore, the image will need to be re-created after calling this method.

Insets

Extends: Object

Implements: Cloneable

The `Insets` class encapsulate the insets of a container.

Member Variables

```
public int top
```

An integer value representing the inset from the top.

```
public int left
```

An integer value representing the inset from the left.

```
public int bottom
```

An integer value representing the inset from the bottom.

```
public int right
```

An integer value representing the inset from the right.

Insets **Constructor**

```
public Insets(int top, int left, int bottom, int right)
```

This `Insets` constructor creates an `Insets` object from the specified values.

Parameters:

top—an integer value representing the inset from the top.

left—an integer value representing the inset from the left.

bottom—an integer value representing the inset from the bottom.

right—an integer value representing the inset from the right.

F

toString

`public String toString()`

The `toString` method provides a string representation of the `Insets` class.

Returns: A `String` value containing the `Insets`'s name, top, left, bottom, and right values.

clone

`public Object clone()`

The `clone` method creates and returns a clone of the `Insets` object.

Returns: An `Object` class representing a clone of the current `Insets`.

Label

Extends: `Component`

A `Label` is a component used to display a single line of text on the screen.

Member Constants

`public static final int LEFT`

A static integer value representing left alignment.

`public static final int CENTER`

A static integer value representing center alignment.

`public static final int RIGHT`

A static integer value representing right alignment.

Label **Constructor**

`public Label()`

The `Label` constructor constructs a label with no string.

Label **Constructor**

`public Label(String label)`

This `Label` constructor constructs a label using the specified string.

Parameters: `label`—a `String` that will be displayed as the label.

Label **Constructor**

`public Label(String label, int alignment)`

This `Label` constructor constructs a label using the specified string and alignment.

Parameters:

`label`—a `String` that will be displayed as the label.

`alignment`—an alignment value (CENTER, LEFT, or RIGHT).

addNotify

`public synchronized void addNotify()`

The `addNotify` method creates the peer interface for the label. Using a peer interface allows the user interface of the label to be modified without changing the functionality.

getAlignment

`public int getAlignment()`

The `getAlignment` method returns the label's current alignment.

Returns: An integer value representing the label's current alignment (LEFT, RIGHT, or CENTER).

setAlignment

`public void setAlignment(int alignment)`

The `setAlignment` method sets the label's current alignment.

Parameters: `alignment`—an integer value representing the label's new alignment (LEFT, RIGHT, or CENTER).

getText

`public String getText()`

The `getText` method returns the label's current text string.

Returns: A `String` value representing the label's current text.

setText

```
public void setText(String label)
```

The setText method sets the label's current text string.

Parameters: label—a String value representing the label's new text.

List

Extends: Component

A List component is a scrolling list of text items. Lists can allow multiple selection and visible lines.

List **Constructor**

```
public List()
```

The List constructor creates a List object with no lines or multiple selection capability.

List **Constructor**

```
public List(int rows, boolean multipleSelections)
```

This List constructor constructs a List object with the specified lines and multiple selection capability.

Parameters:

rows—the number of items in the list.

multipleSelections—a boolean value that is true if multiple selections are allowed, false if not.

addNotify

```
public synchronized void addNotify()
```

The addNotify method creates the peer interface for the list. Using a peer interface allows the user interface of the list to be modified without changing the functionality.

removeNotify

```
public synchronized void removeNotify()
```

The removeNotify method removes the peer for the list.

countItems

`public int countItems()`

The `countItems` method returns the number of items in the list.

Returns: An integer value representing the number of items in the list.

getItem

`public String getItem(int index)`

The `getItem` method returns the item at the specified list index.

Parameters: `index`—an integer value representing the index into the list's string elements.

Returns: The `String` value stored at the specified list index.

addItem

`public synchronized void addItem(String item)`

The `addItem` method adds a `String` item to the end of the list.

Parameters: `item`—a `String` item to be added to the end of the list.

addItem

`public synchronized void addItem(String item, int index)`

This `addItem` method adds a `String` item at the specified index within the list.

Parameters:

`item`—a `String` item to be added to the list.

`index`—an integer value representing the index within the list to add the `String` to (if this value is -1 or greater than the number of items within the list, the `String` item will be added to the end of the list).

replaceItem

`public synchronized void replaceItem(String newValue, int index)`

The `replaceItems` method replaces the current item at the specified index with the new `String` item.

Parameters:

newValue—a String value representing the new String to be used to modify the list.

index—an integer value representing the index within the list to be replaced with the new string (if this value is -1 or greater than the number of items within the list, the String item will be added to the end of the list).

clear

```
public synchronized void clear()
```

The clear method will clear the list's string of items.

delItem

```
public synchronized void delItem(int position)
```

The delItem method will delete the String item stored at the specified position within the list.

Parameters: position—an integer value representing the position of the string to be deleted.

delItems

```
public synchronized void delItems(int start, int end)
```

The delItems method will delete a sequence of String items stored at the specified positions within the list.

Parameters:

start—an integer value representing the first position containing a string to be deleted.

end—an integer value representing the last position containing a string to be deleted.

getSelectedIndex

```
public synchronized int getSelectedIndex()
```

The getSelectedIndex method returns the index of the currently selected position within the list.

Returns: An integer value representing the currently selected position within the list.

getSelectedIndexes

```
public synchronized int[] getSelectedIndexes()
```

The getSelectedIndexes method returns an array containing all of the currently selected positions within the list.

Returns: An array of integers containing the currently selected positions within the list.

getSelectedItem

`public synchronized String getSelectedItem()`

The getSelectedItem method returns the string at the currently selected position within the list.

Returns: The String value that is at the currently selected position within the list.

getSelectedItems

`public synchronized String[] getSelectedItems()`

The getSelectedItems method returns an array of Strings that are at the currently selected positions within the list.

Returns: An array of strings that are at the currently selected positions within the list.

select

`public synchronized void select(int index)`

The select method selects the item in the list at the specified index position.

Parameters: index—an integer value representing the position to be selected within the list.

deselect

`public synchronized void deselect(int index)`

The deselect method deselects the item in the list at the specified index position.

Parameters: index—an integer value representing the position to be deselected within the list.

isSelected

`public synchronized boolean isSelected(int index)`

The isSelected method checks the specified index position to see wether it is currently selected.

Parameters: index—an integer value representing the position to be checked within the list.

Returns: A boolean value that will be true if the specified index position is selected, false if not.

getRows

`public int getRows()`

The `getRows` method returns the number of rows within the list.

Returns: An integer value representing the number of rows currently in the list.

allowsMultipleSelections

`public boolean allowsMultipleSelections()`

The `allowsMultipleSelections` method returns the multiple selection state of the `List` object.

Returns: A boolean value that will be `true` if multiple selections are allowed, `false` if not.

setMultipleSelections

`public void setMultipleSelections(boolean v)`

The `setMultipleSelections` method sets the multiple selection state of the `List` object.

Parameters: v—a boolean value that will be `true` if multiple selections are to be allowed, `false` if not.

getVisibleIndex

`public int getVisibleIndex()`

The `getVisibleIndex` method returns the index of the item that was last made visible by the `makeVisible` method.

Returns: An integer value representing the index of the item that was just made visible by the `makeVisible` method.

makeVisible

`public void makeVisible(int index)`

The `makeVisible` method forces the list item at the specified index position to be visible.

Parameters: index—the index position of the item that is to be made visible.

preferredSize

`public Dimension preferredSize(int rows)`

The `preferredSize` method returns the preferred size of the `List` object based on the specified number of rows.

Parameters: rows—the number of rows used to determine the list's preferred size.

Returns: A Dimension object representing the preferred size of the list.

preferredSize
```
public Dimension preferredSize()
```
This preferredSize method returns the preferred size of the List object based on its current number of rows.

Returns: A Dimension object representing the preferred size of the list.

minimumSize
```
public Dimension minimumSize(int rows)
```
The minimumSize method returns the minimum size of the List object based on the specified number of rows.

Parameters: rows—the number of rows used to determine the list's minimum size.

Returns: A Dimension object representing the minimum size of the list.

minimumSize
```
public Dimension minimumSize()
```
This minimumSize method returns the minimum size of the List object based on its current number of rows.

Returns: A Dimension object representing the minimum size of the list.

MediaTracker

Extends: Object

The MediaTracker class is provided to track the status of media objects. At the current time, only images are supported, but this functionality could be extended to support audio and video as well.

Member Constants
```
public static final int LOADING
```
A static integer value representing the LOADING status.

```
public static final int ABORTED
```

A static integer value representing the ABORTED status.

```
public static final int ERRORED
```

A static integer value representing the ERRORED status.

```
public static final int COMPLETE
```

A static integer value representing the COMPLETE status.

MediaTracker **Constructor**

```
public MediaTracker(Component comp)
```

The MediaTracker constructor creates a MediaTracker object to track images for the specified component.

Parameters: comp—a component that will use a MediaTracker object to track images.

addImage

```
public void addImage(Image image, int id)
```

The addImage method will add the specified Image to the list of images being tracked by the MediaTracker. The Image will be rendered at its default size.

Parameters:

image—the Image object to be added to the list.

id—an identification used to reference the Image object.

addImage

```
public synchronized void addImage(Image image, int id, int w, int h)
```

This addImage method will add the specified Image to the list of images being tracked by the MediaTracker. The image will be rendered at its specified size.

Parameters:

image—the Image object to be added to the list.

id—an ID used to reference the Image object.

w—the width the image will be rendered at.

h—the height the image will be rendered at.

checkAll

```
public boolean checkAll()
```

The checkAll method is used to check if all of the images have been loaded.

Returns: A boolean value that is true if all of the images have been loaded, false if not.

checkAll

```
public synchronized boolean checkAll(boolean load)
```

This checkAll method is used to check whether all of the images have been loaded. The load parameter forces the MediaTracker to load any images that are not currently being loaded.

Parameters: load—a boolean value that, if true, will force the MediaTracker to load any images that are not currently being loaded.

Returns: A boolean value that is true if all of the images have been loaded, false if not.

isErrorAny

```
public synchronized boolean isErrorAny()
```

The isErrorAny method checks the status of all images being tracked by the MediaTracker.

Returns: A boolean value that will be true if any image loaded had an error value, false if not.

getErrorsAny

```
public synchronized Object[] getErrorsAny()
```

The getErrorsAny method checks the status of all images being tracked by the MediaTracker and returns an array of all media objects that have generated an error.

Returns: An array of media objects that have encountered an error. This array will be null if no objects have encountered an error.

waitForAll

```
public void waitForAll() throws InterruptedException
```

The waitForAll method begins to load all Images without being interrupted. If there is an error, the InterruptedException is thrown.

Throws: InterruptedException if another thread has interrupted this thread.

waitForAll

`public synchronized boolean waitForAll(long ms) throws InterruptedException`

This `waitForAll` method begins to load all images without being interrupted. This method will continue to load images until there is an error or until the specified timeout has elapsed. If there is an error, the `InterruptedException` is thrown.

Parameters: `ms`—a long integer value representing the timeout value (in milliseconds) to wait before halting the loading of images.

Returns: A boolean value that will return `true` if all of the images were successfully loaded before timing out, `false` if not.

Throws: `InterruptedException` if another thread has interrupted this thread.

statusAll

`public int statusAll(boolean load)`

The `statusAll` method returns the boolean OR of all of the media objects being tracked.

Parameters: `load`—a boolean value that specifies whether to start the image loading.

Returns: The boolean OR of all of the media objects being tracked. This value can be `LOADED`, `ABORTED`, `ERRORED`, or `COMPLETE`.

checkID

`public boolean checkID(int id)`

The `checkID` method checks to see if all images tagged with the specified ID have been loaded.

Parameters: `id`—an integer tag used to identify a media object or objects.

Returns: A boolean value that is `true` if all objects with the specified ID have been loaded, `false` if not.

checkID

`public synchronized boolean checkID(int id, boolean load)`

The `checkID` method checks to see whether all images tagged with the specified `id` have been loaded. These images will be loaded based on the value of the `load` parameter.

Parameters:

`id`—an integer tag used to identify a media object or objects.

load—a boolean value that is true if all objects with the specified identifier are to be loaded, false if not.

Returns: A boolean value that is true if all objects with the specified identifier have been loaded, false if not.

isErrorID

```
public synchronized boolean isErrorID(int id)
```

The isErrorID method checks the error status of all media objects with the specified id.

Parameters: id—an integer tag used to identify a media object or objects.

Returns: A boolean value that is true if all objects were loaded without error, false if not.

getErrorsID

```
public synchronized Object[] getErrorsID(int id)
```

The getErrorsAny method checks the status of all images being tracked by the MediaTracker whose id match the specified id. It returns an array of all media objects that have generated an error.

Parameters: id—an integer tag used to identify a media object or objects.

Returns: An array of media objects that have encountered an error. This array will be null if no objects have encountered an error.

waitForID

```
public void waitForID(int id) throws InterruptedException
```

The waitForID method begins to load all images with the specified id without being interrupted. If there is an error, the InterruptedException is thrown.

Parameters: id—an integer tag used to identify a media object or objects.

Throws: InterruptedException if another thread has interrupted this thread.

waitForID

```
public synchronized boolean waitForID(int id, long ms) throws
  InterruptedException
```

This waitForID method begins to load all images with the specified ID without being interrupted. This method will continue to load images until there is an error or until the specified timeout has elapsed. If there is an error, the InterruptedException is thrown.

Parameters:

id—an integer tag used to identify a media object or objects.

ms—a long integer value representing the timeout value (in milliseconds) to wait before halting the loading of images.

Returns: A boolean value that will return true if all of the images were successfully loaded before timing out, false if not.

Throws: InterruptedException if another thread has interrupted this thread.

statusID

```
public int statusID(int id, boolean load)
```

The statusID method returns the boolean OR of all of the media objects being tracked with the specified id.

Parameters:

id—an integer tag used to identify a media object or objects.

load—a boolean value that specifies whether to start the image loading.

Returns: The boolean OR of all the media objects being tracked. This value can be LOADED, ABORTED, ERRORED, or COMPLETE.

Menu

Extends: MenuItem

Implements: MenuContainer

A Menu is a component of a menu bar.

Menu **Constructor**

```
public Menu(String label)
```

The Menu constructor constructs a menu using the specified label string.

Parameters: label—a String value that will be displayed as the menu's label.

Menu **Constructor**

```
public Menu(String label, boolean tearOff)
```

This Menu constructor constructs a menu using the specified label string and tear-off option.

Parameters:

label—a String value that will be displayed as the menu's label.

tearOff—a boolean value that is true if this menu is to be a tear-off menu, false if not.

addNotify

```
public synchronized void addNotify()
```

The addNotify method creates the peer interface for the menu. Using a peer interface allows the user interface of the menu to be modified without changing the functionality.

removeNotify

```
public synchronized void removeNotify()
```

The removeNotify method removes the peer for the menu.

isTearOff

```
public boolean isTearOff()
```

The isTearOff method returns the tear-off status of the menu.

Returns: A boolean value that will be true if the menu is a tear-off menu, false if not.

countItems

```
public int countItems()
```

The countItems method returns the number of items in this menu.

Returns: An integer value representing the number of items that have been added to this menu.

getItem

```
public MenuItem getItem(int index)
```

The getItem method returns the MenuItem object at the specified index in the menu list.

Parameters: index—an integer value representing the position of the menu item to be returned.

Returns: A MenuItem object at the specified position.

add

```
public synchronized MenuItem add(MenuItem mi)
```

The add method adds the specified menu item to the menu's list.

Parameters: mi—the MenuItem object to be added to the list.

Returns: A MenuItem object that was added to the list.

add

```
public void add(String label)
```

This add method adds a MenuItem with the specified label to the menu.

Parameters: label—a String value representing the label to be added to the menu's list.

addSeparator

```
public void addSeparator()
```

The addSeparator method adds a separator menu item to the menu.

remove

```
public synchronized void remove(int index)
```

The remove method removes the menu item at the specified index.

Parameters: index—the position within the menu's item list to be removed from the list.

remove

```
public synchronized void remove(MenuComponent item)
```

This remove method removes the menu item specified in the item parameter.

Parameters: item—the MenuComponent object to be removed from the menu's item list.

MenuBar

Extends: MenuComponent

Implements: MenuContainer

A MenuBar object represents a menu bar on a frame. A MenuBar object attaches to a Frame object using the method Frame.setMenuBar.

MenuBar **Constructor**

```
public MenuBar()
```

The MenuBar constructor constructs an empty MenuBar object.

addNotify

```
public synchronized void addNotify()
```

The addNotify method creates the peer interface for the menu bar. Using a peer interface allows the user interface of the menu bar to be modified without changing the functionality.

removeNotify

```
public synchronized void removeNotify()
```

The removeNotify method removes the peer for the menu bar.

getHelpMenu

```
public Menu getHelpMenu()
```

The getHelpMenu method returns the help menu on the menu bar.

Returns: A Menu object representing the menu bar's help menu.

setHelpMenu

```
public synchronized void setHelpMenu(Menu m)
```

The setHelpMenu method sets the help menu for the menu bar.

Parameters: m—a Menu object representing the menu bar's help menu.

add

```
public synchronized Menu add(Menu m)
```

The add method adds the specified menu to the menu bar.

Parameters: m—a Menu object that is to be added to the menu bar.

Returns: The Menu object that was added to the menu bar.

remove

`public synchronized void remove(int index)`

The `remove` method removes the menu located at the specified index on the menu bar.

Parameters: index—the position of the menu to be removed within the menu bar's list of menus.

remove

`public synchronized void remove(MenuComponent m)`

This `remove` method removes the specified menu component from the menu bar.

Parameters: m—a `MenuComponent` object to be removed from the menu bar.

countMenus

`public int countMenus()`

The `countMenus` method returns the number of menus located on this menu bar.

Returns: An integer value representing the number of menus located on this menu bar.

getMenu

`public Menu getMenu(int i)`

The `getMenu` method returns the `Menu` object at the specified location within the menu bar's list of menus.

Parameters: i—an integer value representing the position of the menu to be retrieved from the menu bar's list.

Returns: A `Menu` object returned from the menu bar's list.

MenuComponent

Extends: `Object`

The `MenuComponent` class serves as the base class for all menu-type components such as `Menu`, `MenuBar`, and `MenuItem`.

getParent

`public MenuContainer getParent()`

The getParent method returns the parent menu container of the menu component.

Returns: A MenuContainer object that is the parent of the menu component.

getPeer

```
public MenuComponentPeer getPeer()
```

The getPeer method returns the MenuComponentPeer interface for the MenuComponent object. The MenuComponentPeer interface allows the user interface of a MenuComponent to be changed without changing its functionality.

Returns: A MenuComponentPeer interface.

getFont

```
public Font getFont()
```

The getFont method returns the current default font for the MenuComponent.

Returns: A Font object.

setFont

```
public void setFont(Font f)
```

The setFont method is used to set the display font for the MenuComponent.

Parameters: f—the Font object representing the menu component's new font.

removeNotify

```
public void removeNotify()
```

The removeNotify removes the peer for this menu component.

postEvent

```
public boolean postEvent(Event evt)
```

The postEvent method posts the specified event to the menu component.

Parameters: evt—the Event object containing the current event that applies to the menu component.

toString

`public String toString()`

The `toString` method returns a string representation of the `MenuComponent` object.

Returns: A `String` containing the menu component's name.

MenuItem

Extends: `MenuComponent`

A `MenuItem` represents a choice in a menu.

MenuItem **Constructor**

`public MenuItem(String label)`

The `MenuItem` constructor constructs a menu item using the specified label string.

Parameters: `label`—the `String` that will be displayed as the menu item's label.

addNotify

`public synchronized void addNotify()`

The `addNotify` method creates the peer interface for the menu item. Using a peer interface allows the user interface of the menu item to be modified without changing the functionality.

getLabel

`public String getLabel()`

The `getLabel` method returns the label string for the menu item.

Returns: A `String` value representing the menu item's displayed label.

setLabel

`public void setLabel(String label)`

The `setLabel` method is used to change the string label of the menu item.

Parameters: `label`—a `String` value representing the menu item's displayed label.

isEnabled

`public boolean isEnabled()`

The `isEnabled` method can be called to determine whether the menu item is enabled.

Returns: A boolean value that will be `true` if the menu item is enabled, `false` if not.

enable

`public void enable()`

The `enable` method enables the menu item.

enable

`public void enable(boolean cond)`

This `enable` method enables the menu item based on the specified condition.

Parameters: cond—a boolean value that will conditionally enable the menu item.

disable

`public void disable()`

The `disable` method disables the menu item, making it unselectable by the user.

paramString

`public String paramString()`

The `paramString` method returns a string representation of the menu item.

Returns: A `String` value containing the menu item's label string.

Panel

Extends: Container

The `Panel` class represents a generic container for graphical elements.

Panel **Constructor**

`public Panel()`

The `Panel` constructor constructs a default `Panel` object that will use the `FlowLayout` layout manager.

addNotify

```
public synchronized void addNotify()
```

The addNotify method creates the peer interface for the panel. Using a peer interface allows the user interface of the panel to be modified without changing the functionality.

Point

Extends: Object

A Point class encapsulates an x,y coordinate.

Member Variables

```
public int x
```

The x variable represents the x coordinate of the point.

```
public int y
```

The y variable represents the y coordinate of the point.

Point Constructor

```
public Point(int x, int y)
```

The Point constructor constructs a Point object using the specified coordinates.

Parameters:

x—the x coordinate of the point.

y—the y coordinate of the point.

move

```
public void move(int x, int y)
```

The move method moves the point to the new specified coordinates.

Parameters:

x—the new x coordinate of the point.

y—the new y coordinate of the point.

translate

```
public void translate(int x, int y)
```

The `translate` method translates the point by the specified coordinates.

Parameters:

x—the x amount to transfer the point.

y—the y amount to transfer the point.

hashCode

```
public int hashCode()
```

The `hashCode` method returns a hash code for the point.

Returns: An integer value that represents the point's hash code.

equals

```
public boolean equals(Object obj)
```

The `equals` method compares the `Point` object to the specified object.

Parameters: `obj`—the object to compare the point to.

Returns: A boolean value representing the result of the comparison (`true` or `false`).

toString

```
public String toString()
```

The `toString` method returns a string representation of the `Point` object.

Returns: A `String` containing the point's name and x and y values.

Polygon

Extends: `Object`

A `Polygon` contains a list of x,y coordinates, unlike a `Point` class, which contains only one coordinate set.

Member Variables

```
public int npoints
```

The `npoint` variable represents the total number of points within the Polygon.

```
public int xpoints[]
```

The `xpoints` variable is an integer array of all of the x coordinate points.

```
public int ypoints[]
```

The ypoints variable is an integer array of all of the y coordinate points.

Polygon **Constructor**

```
public Polygon()
```

The Polygon constructor constructs an empty Polygon object.

Polygon

```
public Polygon(int xpoints[], int ypoints[], int npoints)
```

This Polygon constructor constructs a Polygon object using the specified coordinates.

Parameters:

xpoints—an array of integers representing the x coordinate points of the polygon.

ypoints—an array of integers representing the y coordinate points of the polygon.

npoints—an integer value representing the number of points in the polygon.

addPoint

```
public void addPoint(int x, int y)
```

The addPoint method adds a point to the polygon.

Parameters:

x—the x coordinate of the point to be added.

y—the y coordinate of the point to be added.

getBoundingBox

```
public Rectangle getBoundingBox()
```

The getBoundingBox returns the rectangular bounding box for the polygon.

Returns: A Rectangle object representing the bounding box for the polygon.

inside

```
public boolean inside(int x, int y)
```

The inside method determines whether the specified coordinates are inside the polygon's bounding rectangle.

Parameters:

x—the x coordinate to check.

y—the y coordinate to check.

Returns: A boolean value that is true if the coordinates are inside the polygon's bounding rectangle, false if not.

Rectangle

Extends: Object

A Rectangle class specifies the dimensions of a rectangle using x, y, height, and width values.

Member Variables

`public int x`

The x variable stores the rectangle's x coordinate.

`public int y`

The y variable stores the rectangle's y coordinate.

`public int width`

The width variable stores the rectangle's width.

`public int height`

The height variable stores the rectangle's height.

Rectangle **Constructor**

`public Rectangle()`

The Rectangle constructor constructs a rectangle of zero size.

Rectangle **Constructor**

`public Rectangle(int x, int y, int width, int height)`

This Rectangle constructor constructs a rectangle using the specified coordinates.

Parameters:

x—the x coordinate of the rectangle.

y—the y coordinate of the rectangle.

width—the width of the rectangle.

height—the height of the rectangle.

Rectangle **Constructor**

public Rectangle(int width, int height)

This Rectangle constructor constructs a rectangle using the specified width and height.

Parameters:

width—the width of the rectangle.

height—the height of the rectangle.

Rectangle **Constructor**

public Rectangle(Point p, Dimension d)

This Rectangle constructor constructs a rectangle using the specified coordinates and size.

Parameters:

p—a Point object containing the rectangle's x and y coordinates.

d—a Dimension object containing the rectangle's size.

Rectangle **Constructor**

public Rectangle(Point p)

This Rectangle constructor constructs a rectangle using the specified point.

Parameters: p—a Point object containing the rectangle's x and y coordinates.

Rectangle **Constructor**

public Rectangle(Dimension d)

This Rectangle constructor constructs a rectangle using the specified Dimension.

Parameters: d—a Dimension object containing the rectangle's size.

reshape

`public void reshape(int x, int y, int width, int height)`

The reshape method resizes the rectangle's coordinates and size.

Parameters:

x—the x coordinate of the rectangle.

y—the y coordinate of the rectangle.

width—the width of the rectangle.

height—the height of the rectangle.

move

`public void move(int x, int y)`

The move method moves the rectangle to the specified coordinates.

Parameters:

x—the x coordinate of the rectangle.

y—the y coordinate of the rectangle.

translate

`public void translate(int x, int y)`

The translate method translates the rectangle by the specified coordinates.

Parameters:

x—the x translation amount of the rectangle's coordinates.

y—the y translation amount of the rectangle's coordinates.

resize

`public void resize(int width, int height)`

The resize method changes the rectangle's size to the specified parameters.

Parameters:

width—the width of the rectangle.

height—the height of the rectangle.

inside

`public boolean inside(int x, int y)`

The `inside` method determines whether the specified coordinates are inside the rectangle's bounding rectangle.

Parameters:

x—the x coordinate to be checked.

y—the y coordinate to be checked.

Returns: A boolean value that is `true` if the coordinates are within the bounding rectangle, `false` if not.

intersects

`public boolean intersects(Rectangle r)`

The `intersects` method determines whether the specified rectangle intersects the rectangle's bounding rectangle.

Parameters: r—a `Rectangle` object to be checked for intersection with the rectangle.

Returns: A boolean value that is `true` if the objects intersect, `false` if not.

intersection

`public Rectangle intersection(Rectangle r)`

The `intersection` computes the intersection rectangle (if any) of the two rectangles.

Parameters: r—a `Rectangle` object to be tested for intersection with the rectangle.

Returns: A `Rectangle` object that is the intersection of the two `Rectangle` objects.

union

`public Rectangle union(Rectangle r)`

The `union` method returns the union of the two rectangles.

Parameters: r—a `Rectangle` object that will be used to determine the union rectangle.

Returns: A `Rectangle` object representing the union of the two rectangles.

add

```
public void add(int newx, int newy)
```

The add method adds a new point to the rectangle using the specified coordinates. This results in the smallest possible rectangle that contains the current rectangle and the coordinates.

Parameters:

newx—an integer value representing the x coordinate of the point.

newy—an integer value representing the y coordinate of the point.

add

```
public void add(Point pt)
```

This add method adds a new point to the rectangle using the specified Point object. This results in the smallest possible rectangle that contains the current rectangle and the point's coordinates.

Parameters: pt—a Point object representing the point's coordinates.

add

```
public void add(Rectangle r)
```

This add method adds a new rectangle to the existing rectangle. This results in the union of the two rectangles (current and new).

Parameters: r—a Rectangle object that will be used to perform a union with the rectangle.

grow

```
public void grow(int h, int v)
```

The grow method grows the Rectangle object by the specified horizontal and vertical amounts. The x and y coordinates will be shifted by the specified amounts, and the height and width sizes will also be increased by the specified amounts.

Parameters:

h—an integer amount representing the amount to grow the rectangle by in the horizontal direction.

v—an integer amount representing the amount to grow the rectangle by in the vertical direction.

isEmpty

```
public boolean isEmpty()
```

The isEmpty method is used to determine whether the rectangle's width and height are less than or equal to zero.

Returns: A boolean value that will be true if the rectangle is empty, false if not.

hashCode

```
public int hashCode()
```

The hashCode method returns the hash code for the rectangle.

Parameters: An integer value representing the rectangle's hash code.

equals

```
public boolean equals(Object obj)
```

The equals method compares the specified object with the rectangle.

Parameters: obj—an object to be compared with the rectangle.

Returns: A boolean value that is true if the two objects are equal, false if they are not.

toString

```
public String toString()
```

The toString method returns a String representation of the rectangle's contents.

Returns: A String containing the rectangle's name, x, y, height, and width values.

Scrollbar

Extends: Component

A Scrollbar component can be added to a frame or other object to provide scrolling capabilities.

Member Constants

```
public static final int HORIZONTAL
```

The HORIZONTAL static int value represents the horizontal scrollbar orientation variable.

```
public static final int VERTICAL
```

The VERTICAL static int value represents the vertical scrollbar orientation variable.

Scrollbar **Constructor**

```
public Scrollbar()
```

The Scrollbar constructor constructs a default scrollbar.

Scrollbar **Constructor**

```
public Scrollbar(int orientation)
```

This Scrollbar constructor constructs a scrollbar with the specified orientation.

Parameters: orientation—an integer value that can be either HORIZONTAL or VERTICAL.

Scrollbar **Constructor**

```
public Scrollbar(int orientation, int value, int visible, int minimum,
  int maximum)
```

This Scrollbar constructor constructs a complete scrollbar using the specified orientation and properties.

Parameters:

orientation—an integer value that can be either HORIZONTAL or VERTICAL.

value—an integer value representing the scrollbar's value.

visible—an integer value representing the size of the scrollbar's visible portion.

minimum—an integer value representing the scrollbar's minimum value.

maximum—an integer value representing the scrollbar's maximum value.

addNotify

```
public synchronized void addNotify()
```

The addNotify method creates the peer interface for the scrollbar. Using a peer interface allows the user interface of the scrollbar to be modified without changing the functionality.

getOrientation

```
public int getOrientation()
```

The getOrientation method returns the orientation value of the scrollbar.

Returns: An integer value that can be either HORIZONTAL or VERTICAL.

getValue

```
public int getValue()
```

The getValue method returns the current value of the scrollbar.

Returns: An integer value representing the value of the scrollbar.

setValue

```
public void setValue(int value)
```

The setValue method set the value of the scrollbar to the specified value.

Parameters: value—An integer value representing the new value of the scrollbar.

getMinimum

```
public int getMinimum()
```

The getMinimum method returns the minimum value of the scrollbar.

Returns: An integer value representing the scrollbar's minimum value.

getMaximum

```
public int getMaximum()
```

The getMaximum method returns the maximum value of the scrollbar.

Returns: An integer value representing the scrollbar's maximum value.

getVisible

```
public int getVisible()
```

The getVisible portion returns the visible amount of the scrollbar.

Returns: An integer value representing the scrollbar's visible amount.

setLineIncrement

```
public void setLineIncrement(int 1)
```

The setLineIncrement method sets the line increment for the scrollbar.

Parameters: 1—an integer value representing the line increment for the scrollbar, which is the amount that the scrollbar's position increases or decreases when the user clicks its up or down widgets.

getLineIncrement

```
public int getLineIncrement()
```

The getLineIncrement method returns the line increment for the scrollbar.

Returns: An integer value representing the line increment for the scrollbar, which is the amount that the scrollbar's position increases or decreases when the user clicks its up or down widgets.

setPageIncrement

```
public void setPageIncrement(int 1)
```

The setPageIncrement method sets the page increment for the scrollbar.

Parameters: 1—an integer value representing the page increment for the scrollbar, which is the amount that the scrollbar's position increases or decreases when the user clicks its page up or page down widgets.

getPageIncrement

```
public int getPageIncrement()
```

The getPageIncrement method returns the page increment for the scrollbar.

Returns: An integer value representing the page increment for the scrollbar, which is the amount that the scrollbar's position increases or decreases when the user clicks its page up or page down widgets.

setValues

```
public void setValues(int value, int visible, int minimum, int maximum)
```

The setValues method sets the scrollbar's properties based on the specified values.

Parameters:

value—an integer value representing the current value of the scrollbar.

visible—an integer value representing the visible amount of the scrollbar.

minimum—an integer value representing the scrollbar's minimum value.

maximum—an integer value representing the scrollbar's maximum value.

TextArea

Extends: TextComponent

A TextArea class represents a multiline component that can be used for text display or editing.

TextArea **Constructor**

```
public TextArea()
```

The TextArea constructor constructs a TextArea object.

TextArea

```
public TextArea(int rows, int cols)
```

This TextArea constructor constructs a TextArea object using the specified row and column values.

Parameters:

rows—an integer value specifying the number of rows to use.

cols—an integer value specifying the number of columns to use.

TextArea **Constructor**

```
public TextArea(String text)
```

This TextArea constructor constructs a TextArea object using the specified text.

Parameters: text—a String value containing the text to be displayed in the text area.

TextArea **Constructor**

```
public TextArea(String text, int rows, int cols)
```

This TextArea constructor constructs a TextArea object using the specified row, column, and text values.

Parameters:

text—a `String` value containing the text to be displayed in the text area.

rows—an integer value specifying the number of rows to use.

cols—an integer value specifying the number of columns to use.

addNotify

```
public synchronized void addNotify()
```

The `addNotify` method creates the peer interface for the text area. Using a peer interface allows the user interface of the text area to be modified without changing the functionality.

insertText

```
public void insertText(String str, int pos)
```

The `insertText` method inserts a text string into the text area's text at the specified position.

Parameters:

str—a `String` value containing the text to be inserted in the text area.

pos—an integer value specifying the position to insert the text string into.

appendText

```
public void appendText(String str)
```

The `appendText` method appends a text string onto the text area's text.

Parameters: str—a `String` value containing the text to be appended in the text area.

replaceText

```
public void replaceText(String str, int start, int end)
```

The `replaceText` method replaces a section of the text area's text at the specified positions with the specified text string.

Parameters:

str—a `String` value containing the text that will replace the text area's current text.

start—the starting position of the text to be replaced within the text area.

end—the ending position of the text to be replaced within the text area.

getRows

`public int getRows()`

The `getRows` method returns the number of rows within the text area.

Returns: An integer value representing the number of rows within the text area.

getColumns

`public int getColumns()`

The `getColumns` method returns the number of columns within the text area.

Returns: An integer value representing the number of rows within the text area.

preferredSize

`public Dimension preferredSize(int rows, int cols)`

The `preferredSize` method returns the preferred size of a text area comprising the specified rows and columns.

Parameters:

rows—the number of rows in the text area.

cols—the number of columns in the text area.

Returns: A `Dimension` object representing the preferred size of the specified text area.

preferredSize

`public Dimension preferredSize()`

This `preferredSize` method returns the preferred size dimension of a `TextArea` object.

Returns: A `Dimension` object representing the preferred size of a text area.

minimumSize

`public Dimension minimumSize(int rows, int cols)`

The `minimumSize` method returns the minimum size of a text area comprised of the specified rows and columns.

Parameters:

rows—the number of rows in the text area.

cols—the number of columns in the text area.

Returns: A Dimension object representing the minimum size of the specified text area.

minimumSize

```
public Dimension minimumSize()
```

This minimumSize method returns the minimum size dimension of a TextArea object.

Returns: A Dimension object representing the minimum size of a text area.

TextComponent

Extends: Component

The TextComponent class is a component that provides some text for display or editing. It serves as the base class for the TextArea and TextField classes.

removeNotify

```
public synchronized void removeNotify()
```

The removeNotify method removes the text component's peer interface. A peer interface can be used to modify the text component's user interface without changing its functionality.

setText

```
public void setText(String t)
```

The setText method sets the text component's displayed text to the specified String value.

Parameters: t—a String value representing the string to be stored in the text component's text value.

getText

```
public String getText()
```

The getText method returns the text component's text value.

Returns: A String value representing the text component's text value.

getSelectedText

`public String getSelectedText()`

The `getSelectedText` method returns the selected text contained in this text component.

Returns: A `String` value representing the text component's text value.

isEditable

`public boolean isEditable()`

The `isEditable` method is used to determine whether the text component's text can be edited.

Returns: A boolean value that is `true` if the text can be edited, `false` if not.

setEditable

`public void setEditable(boolean t)`

The `setEditable` method is used to set the text component's edit property.

Parameters: t—a boolean value that is `true` if the text can be edited, `false` if not.

getSelectionStart

`public int getSelectionStart()`

The `getSelectionStart` method returns the starting position of the selected text in the text component.

Returns: An integer value representing the position of the first selected character in the text component.

getSelectionEnd

`public int getSelectionEnd()`

The `getSelectionEnd` method returns the ending position of the selected text in the text component.

Returns: An integer value representing the position of the last selected character in the text component.

select

`public void select(int selStart, int selEnd)`

The `select` method selects a portion of the text component's text based on the specified position.

Parameters:

`selStart`—an integer value representing the position of the first character to be selected in the text component.

`selEnd`—an integer value representing the position of the last character to be selected in the text component.

selectAll

```
public void selectAll()
```

The `selectAll` method selects all of the text component's text.

TextField

Extends: `TextComponent`

The `TextField` class provides a single line of text for display or editing.

TextField **Constructor**

```
public TextField()
```

The `TextField` constructor constructs a text field of default size.

TextField **Constructor**

```
public TextField(int cols)
```

This `TextField` constructor constructs a text field using the specified column size.

Parameters: `cols`—the number of characters that can be entered into the text field.

TextField **Constructor**

```
public TextField(String text)
```

This `TextField` constructor constructs a text field using the specified input string.

Parameters: `text`—the default text to be displayed within the text field.

`TextField` **Constructor**

`public TextField(String text, int cols)`

This TextField constructor constructs a text field using the specified input string and column values.

Parameters:

text—the default text to be displayed within the text field.

Cols—the number of columns to display.

`addNotify`

`public synchronized void addNotify()`

The addNotify method creates the peer interface for the text field. Using a peer interface allows the user interface of the text field to be modified without changing the functionality.

`getEchoChar`

`public char getEchoChar()`

The getEchoChar method retrieves the character that will be used for echoing.

Returns: A character value that represents the character that will be used for echoing.

`echoCharIsSet`

`public boolean echoCharIsSet()`

The echoCharIsSet method is used to determine whether the echo character has been set.

Returns: A boolean value that is true if the echo character has been set, false if not.

`getColumns`

`public int getColumns()`

The getColumns method returns the number of columns used in the display area of this text field.

Returns: An integer value representing the number of columns (characters) that will be displayed by the text field.

`setEchoCharacter`

`public void setEchoCharacter(char c)`

The setEchoCharacter method is used to set the character that will be used for echoing. Echoing is often used on password fields so that the actual characters entered won't be echoed to the screen.

Parameters: c—a character value representing the character to be echoed to the screen.

preferredSize

```
public Dimension preferredSize(int cols)
```

This preferredSize method returns the preferred size dimension of a text field object.

Returns: A Dimension object representing the preferred size of a text field.

minimumSize

```
public Dimension minimumSize(int cols)
```

The minimumSize method returns the minimum size of a text field comprised of the specified number of columns.

Parameters: cols—the number of columns in the text field.

Returns: A Dimension object representing the minimum size of the specified text field.

minimumSize

```
public Dimension minimumSize()
```

This minimumSize method returns the minimum size dimension of a TextField object.

Returns: A Dimension object representing the minimum size of a text field.

Toolkit

Extends: Object

The Toolkit class is used to bind a native toolkit to the AWT classes.

getScreenSize

```
public abstract Dimension getScreenSize()
```

The getScreenSize method returns the size of the screen.

Returns: A Dimension object containing the size of the screen.

getScreenResolution

```
public abstract int getScreenResolution()
```

The getScreenResolution method returns the current screen resolution in units of dots per inch.

Returns: An integer value representing the current screen resolution in dots per inch.

getColorModel

```
public abstract ColorModel getColorModel()
```

The getColorModel method returns the current color model being used.

Returns: A ColorModel object representing the current color model.

getFontList

```
public abstract String[] getFontList()
```

The getFontList method returns a list of the fonts available.

Returns: An array of strings containing the names of all fonts available to the system.

getFontMetrics

```
public abstract FontMetrics getFontMetrics(Font font)
```

The getFontMetrics method returns the font metrics for a specified font.

Parameters: A Font object.

Returns: A FontMetrics object containing information on the specified font.

sync

```
public abstract void sync()
```

The sync method syncs the graphics state. This is useful when doing animation.

getDefaultToolkit

```
public static synchronized Toolkit getDefaultToolkit()
```

The getDefaultToolkit method returns a Toolkit object that is used as the default toolkit.

Returns: A Toolkit object representing the default system toolkit.

getImage

```
public abstract Image getImage(String filename)
```

The getImage method returns an Image object that corresponds with the specified Image filename.

Parameters: filename—a String value containing the filename of the image to be loaded.

Returns: An Image object.

getImage

```
public abstract Image getImage(URL url)
```

The getImage method retrieves an Image object that corresponds with the specified URL.

Parameters: url—the uniform resource locator (URL) of the specified image object.

Returns: An Image object.

prepareImage

```
public abstract boolean prepareImage(Image image, int width, int height,
  ImageObserver observer)
```

The prepareImage method prepares an image for rendering on the screen based on the specified image sizes.

Parameters:

image—an Image object.

width—an integer value representing the width of the image when displayed.

height—an integer value representing the height of the image when displayed.

observer—an ImageObserver object that will be notified when the image is prepared.

Returns: A boolean value that is true if the image was prepared successfully, false if not.

checkImage

```
public abstract int checkImage(Image image, int width, int height,
  ImageObserver observer)
```

The checkImage method checks the status of the image construction.

Parameters:

image—an Image object.

width—an integer value representing the width of the image when displayed.

height—an integer value representing the height of the image when displayed.

observer—an ImageObserver object that will be notified when the image is prepared.

Returns: An integer value representing the status of the image construction.

createImage

```
public abstract Image createImage(ImageProducer producer)
```

The createImage method creates an image using the ImageProducer interface.

Parameters: producer—an ImageProducer object that will be notified when the image is prepared.

Returns: An Image object.

Window

Extends: Container

The Window class is defined as a top-level window with no borders and no menu bar.

Window Constructor

```
public Window(Frame parent)
```

The Window constructor constructs a window whose parent is specified by the parent parameter. This window will be invisible after creation and will act as a modal dialog when initially shown.

Parameters: parent—a Frame object that is the parent of this window.

addNotify

```
public synchronized void addNotify()
```

The addNotify method creates the peer interface for the window. Using a peer interface allows the user interface of the window to be modified without changing the functionality.

pack

`public synchronized void pack()`

The pack method packs the components within the window based on the components' preferred sizes.

show

`public void show()`

The show method shows the window after it has been constructed. If the window is already visible, the show method will bring the window to the front.

dispose

`public synchronized void dispose()`

The dispose method disposes of the window and all of its contents. This method must be called to release the window's resources.

toFront

`public void toFront()`

The toFront method brings the parent frame to the front of the window.

toBack

`public void toBack()`

The toBack method sends the parent frame to the back of the window.

getToolkit

`public Toolkit getToolkit()`

The getToolkit method returns the current toolkit for the window.

Returns: A Toolkit object.

getWarningString

`public final String getWarningString()`

The getWarningString method returns a string that is used to warn users. This string typically displays a security warning and is displayed in an area of the window visible to users.

Returns: A String value containing a warning string for users to read.

AWTException

Extends: Exception

The AWTException class is used to signal that an AWT exception has occurred.

AWTError

Extends: Error

The AWTError encapsulates an AWT error.

APPENDIX

G

java.awt.image
Package Reference

While nearly all of the java.awt package consists of graphical user interface components to be used for screen layout, the java.awt.image package contains classes that provide functionality for various image transformations and operations.

ImageConsumer

The ImageConsumer interface is implemented by objects interested in acquiring data provided by the ImageProducer interface.

Member Variables

int RANDOMPIXELORDER

The pixels will be delivered in a random order.

int TOPDOWNLEFTRIGHT

The pixels will be delivered in top-down, left-right order.

int COMPLETESCANLINES

The pixels will be delivered in complete scan lines.

int SINGLEPASS

The pixels will be delivered in a single pass.

int SINGLEFRAME

The pixels will be delivered in a single frame.

int IMAGEERROR

An error occurred during image processing.

int SINGLEFRAMEDONE

A single frame is complete, but the overall operation has not been completed.

int STATICIMAGEDONE

The image construction is complete.

int IMAGEABORTED

The image creation was aborted.

setDimensions

```
void setDimensions(int width, int height)
```

The setDimensions method is used to report the dimensions of the source image to the image consumer.

Parameters:

width—the width of the source image.

height—the height of the source image.

setProperties

```
void setProperties(Hashtable props)
```

The setProperties method is used to report the properties of the source image to the image consumer.

Parameters: props—a Hashtable object containing the image properties.

setColorModel

```
void setColorModel(ColorModel model)
```

The setColorModel method is used to report the color model of the source image to the image consumer.

Parameters: model—the color model used by the source image.

setHints

```
void setHints(int hintflags)
```

The setHints method is used to report hints to the image consumer.

Parameters: hintflags—an integer value containing hints about the manner in which the pixels will be delivered.

setPixels

```
void setPixels(int x, int y, int w, int h, ColorModel model, byte pixels[],
  int off, int scansize)
```

The setPixels method is used to deliver the pixels to the ImageConsumer. Note: Pixel (x,y) is stored in the pixels array at index (y * scansize + x + off).

Parameters:

x—the x coordinate.

y—the y coordinate.

w—the width of the image.

h—the height of the image.

model—the color model used.

pixels—an array of bytes containing pixel information.

off—the offset value.

scansize—the scansize value.

setPixels
```
void setPixels(int x, int y, int w, int h, ColorModel model, int pixels[],
  int off, int scansize)
```
The setPixels method is used to deliver the pixels to the ImageConsumer. Note: Pixel (x,y) is stored in the pixels array at index (y * scansize + x + off).

Parameters:

x—the x coordinate.

y—the y coordinate.

w—the width of the image.

h—the height of the image.

model—the color model used.

pixels—an array of integers containing pixel information.

off—the offset value.

scansize—the scansize value.

imageComplete
```
void imageComplete(int status)
```
The imageComplete method is called when the image producer is finished delivering an image frame. The image consumer should remove itself from the image producer's list at this time.

ImageObserver

The ImageObserver interface is an asynchronous update interface used to receive information on the status of image construction.

Member Constants

`public static final int WIDTH`

The width of the base image is now available.

`public static final int HEIGHT`

The height of the base image is now available.

`public static final int PROPERTIES`

The properties of the base image are now available.

`public static final int SOMEBITS`

Some bits of the image for drawing are now available.

`public static final int FRAMEBITS`

Another complete frame of a multiframe image is now available.

`public static final int ALLBITS`

A static image that was previously drawn is now complete and can be drawn again.

`public static final int ERROR`

An image that was being tracked asynchronously has encountered an error.

`public static final int ABORT`

An image that was being tracked was aborted before production was completed.

imageUpdate
```
public boolean imageUpdate(Image img, int infoflags, int x, int y, int width,
  int height)
```

The imageUpdate method is called every time image information becomes available. The recipients of the update messages are ImageObserver objects that have requested information about an image using asynchronous interfaces.

Parameters:

img—the image of interest.

infoflags—status flags indicating the progress of the image process.

x—the x coordinate that applies (if necessary).

y—the y coordinate that applies (if necessary).

width—the width of the image (if necessary).

height—the height of the image (if necessary).

ImageProducer

The ImageProducer interface is implemented by objects that produce images. Each image contains an image producer.

addConsumer

```
public void addConsumer(ImageConsumer ic)
```

The addConsumer method adds the image consumer to a list to receive image data during reconstruction of the image.

Parameters: ic—an ImageConsumer-derived object.

isConsumer

```
public boolean isConsumer(ImageConsumer ic)
```

The isConsumer method determines whether the specified image consumer is currently on the image producer's list of recipients.

Parameters: ic—an ImageConsumer-derived object

Returns: A boolean value that is true if the image consumer is registered, false if not.

removeConsumer

```
public void removeConsumer(ImageConsumer ic)
```

The removeConsumer method removes the specified image consumer from the internal list.

Parameters: ic—an ImageConsumer-derived object.

startProduction

`public void startProduction(ImageConsumer ic)`

The `startProduction` method adds the specified image consumer to the list of image data recipients and immediately begins production of the image data.

Parameters: `ic`—an `ImageConsumer`-derived object.

requestTopDownLeftRightResend

`public void requestTopDownLeftRightResend(ImageConsumer ic)`

The `requestTopDownLeftRightResend` method is used to deliver the image data to the specified image consumer in top-down, left-right order.

Parameters: `ic`—an `ImageConsumer`-derived object.

ColorModel

Extends: `Object`

The `ColorModel` class is an abstract class that provides functions for translating pixel values into RGB color values.

ColorModel **Constructor**

`public ColorModel(int bits)`

The `ColorModel` constructor constructs a color model that describes a pixel of the specified number of bits.

Parameters: `bits`—an integer value containing the number of bits that will describe a pixel using this color model.

getRGBdefault

`public static ColorModel getRGBdefault()`

The `getRGBdefault` method returns the default color model that is used throughout all AWT image interfaces. This default color model uses a pixel format that encapsulates alpha, red, green, and blue color values (8 bits each) using the following methodology: `0xAARRGGBB`.

Returns: A `ColorModel` object representing the default color model for all AWT image interfaces.

G

getPixelSize

`public int getPixelSize()`

The `getPixelSize` method returns the size of the color model's pixel.

Returns: An integer value representing the number of bits that make up a pixel in this color model.

getRed

`public abstract int getRed(int pixel)`

The `getRed` method returns the red component of the specified pixel.

Parameters: `pixel`—an integer containing the pixel representation for this color model.

Returns: An integer value representing the red component of the pixel.

getGreen

`public abstract int getGreen(int pixel)`

The `getGreen` method returns the green component of the specified pixel.

Parameters: `pixel`—an integer containing the pixel representation for this color model.

Returns: An integer value representing the green component of the pixel.

getBlue

`public abstract int getBlue(int pixel)`

The `getBlue` method returns the blue component of the specified pixel.

Parameters: `pixel`—an integer containing the pixel representation for this color model.

Returns: An integer value representing the blue component of the pixel.

getAlpha

`public abstract int getAlpha(int pixel)`

The `getAlpha` method returns the alpha component of the specified pixel.

Parameters: `pixel`—an integer containing the pixel representation for this color model.

Returns: An integer value representing the alpha component of the pixel.

getRGB

```
public int getRGB(int pixel)
```

The getRGB method returns the RGB value of the pixel using the default color model.

Parameters: pixel—an integer containing the pixel representation for this color model.

Returns: An integer value representing the RGB value of the pixel using the default color model.

finalize

```
public void finalize()
```

The finalize method is used to clean up internal data allocated by the ColorModel.

CropImageFilter

Extends: ImageFilter

The CropImageFilter class provides the capability to extract a rectangular subset of a given image (that is, crop it). This class is used in conjunction with a FilteredImageSource class to provide a source for the cropped image.

CropImageFilter **Constructor**

```
public CropImageFilter(int x, int y, int w, int h)
```

The CropImageFilter constructor constructs a CropImageFilter to crop an image using the specified parameters.

Parameters:

x—the x coordinate of the image to be cropped.

y—the y coordinate of the image to be cropped.

w—the width of the image to be cropped.

h—the height of the image to be cropped.

setProperties

```
public void setProperties(Hashtable props)
```

The setProperties method takes the props parameter from a source object and adds the croprect property to it to identify the region being cropped.

Parameters: props—a Hashtable object containing properties from the source object.

setDimensions

```
public void setDimensions(int w, int h)
```

The setDimensions method overrides the source's dimensions and passes the dimensions of the cropped region to the ImageConsumer interface.

Parameters:

w—the width value.

h—the height value.

setPixels

```
public void setPixels(int x, int y, int w, int h, ColorModel model,
  int pixels[], int off, int scansize)
```

The setPixels method filters the pixels array by determining which pixels lie in the cropped region. Those that do are passed on to the Consumer interface.

Parameters:

x—the x coordinate of the image.

y—the y coordinate of the image.

w—the width of the image.

h—the height of the image.

model—the color model to which the pixels array conforms.

pixels—an array of integers containing pixels to be examined.

off—a variable that is passed on to the image consumer class's setPixels method.

scansize—an integer value representing the scansize of the operation.

DirectColorModel

Extends: ColorModel

The DirectColorModel class specifies translations from pixel values to RGB color values for pixels that have the colors embedded directly in the pixel bits.

DirectColorModel **Constructor**

public DirectColorModel(int bits, int rmask, int gmask, int bmask)

The DirectColorModel constructor constructs a direct color model using the specified parameters. DirectColorModels built using this constructor have a default alphamask value of 255.

Parameters:

bits—the number of bits used to represent a pixel.

rmask—the number of bits required to represent the red component.

gmask—the number of bits required to represent the green component.

bmask—the number of bits required to represent the blue component.

DirectColorModel **Constructor**

public DirectColorModel(int bits, int rmask, int gmask, int bmask, int amask)

The DirectColorModel constructor constructs a direct color model using the specified parameters.

Parameters:

bits—the number of bits used to represent a pixel.

rmask—the number of bits required to represent the red component.

gmask—the number of bits required to represent the green component.

bmask—the number of bits required to represent the blue component.

amask—the number of bits required to represent the alpha component.

getRedMask

```
final public int getRedMask()
```

The getRedMask method returns the current red mask value.

Returns: An integer value representing the red mask value.

getGreenMask

```
final public int getGreenMask()
```

The getGreenMask method returns the current green mask value.

Returns: An integer value representing the green mask value.

getBlueMask

```
final public int getBlueMask()
```

The getBlueMask method returns the current blue mask value.

Returns: An integer value representing the blue mask value.

getAlphaMask

```
final public int getAlphaMask()
```

The getAlphaMask method returns the current alpha mask value.

Returns: An integer value representing the alpha mask value.

getRed

```
final public int getRed(int pixel)
```

The getRed method returns the red component for the specified pixel in the range 0–255.

Parameters: pixel—an integer value representing a pixel under the direct color model.

Returns: An integer value representing the red component of the pixel.

getGreen

```
final public int getGreen(int pixel)
```

The getGreen method returns the green component for the specified pixel in the range 0–255.

Parameters: `pixel`—an integer value representing a pixel under the direct color model.

Returns: An integer value representing the green component of the pixel.

getBlue

`final public int getBlue(int pixel)`

The `getBlue` method returns the blue component for the specified pixel in the range 0–255.

Parameters: `pixel`—an integer value representing a pixel under the direct color model.

Returns: An integer value representing the blue component of the pixel.

getAlpha

`final public int getAlpha(int pixel)`

The `getAlpha` method returns the alpha component for the specified pixel in the range 0–255.

Parameters: `pixel`—an integer value representing a pixel under the direct color model.

Returns: An integer value representing the alpha component of the pixel.

getRGB

`final public int getRGB(int pixel)`

The `getRGB` method returns the RGB color value for the specified pixel in the range 0–255.

Parameters: `pixel`—an integer value representing a pixel under the direct color model.

Returns: An integer value representing the RGB color value of the pixel using the default RGB color model.

FilteredImageSource

Extends: `Object`

Implements: `ImageProducer`

`FilteredImageSource` takes as input an existing image and a filter object. It applies the filter to the image to produce a new version of the original image. The `FilteredImageSource` class implements the `ImageProducer` interface.

FilteredImageSource **Constructor**

```
public FilteredImageSource(ImageProducer orig, ImageFilter imgf)
```

The `FilteredImageSource` constructor constructs a `FilteredImageSource` object that takes a producer source and an image filter to produce a filtered version of the image.

Parameters:

`orig`—an `ImageProducer`-derived object that supplies the image source.

`imgf`—an `ImageFilter` object that filters the image to produce a new image.

addConsumer

```
public synchronized void addConsumer(ImageConsumer ic)
```

The `addConsumer` method adds an `ImageConsumer` interface to a list of consumers interested in image data.

Parameters: `ic`—an `ImageConsumer`-derived object to be added to a list of image consumers.

isConsumer

```
public synchronized boolean isConsumer(ImageConsumer ic)
```

The `isConsumer` method determines whether the specified image consumer is currently on the list of image consumers for the image data.

Parameters: `ic`—an image consumer derived object to be used for the check.

Returns: A boolean value that is `true` if the specified image consumer is on the list, `false` if not.

removeConsumer

```
public synchronized void removeConsumer(ImageConsumer ic)
```

The `removeConsumer` method removes the specified image consumer from the list of image consumers.

Parameters: `ic`—the image consumer to be removed from the list.

startProduction

```
public void startProduction(ImageConsumer ic)
```

The startProduction method adds the specified image consumer to the list of image consumers and immediately starts delivery of the image data to the interface.

Parameters: ic—the image consumer that will be used to produce new image data.

requestTopDownLeftRightResend

public void requestTopDownLeftRightResend(ImageConsumer ic)

The requestTopDownLeftRightResend method is used to deliver the image data to the specified image consumer in top-down, left-right order.

Parameters: ic—the image consumer that will be the recipient of the image data when it is present.

ImageFilter

Extends: Object

Implements: ImageConsumer, Cloneable

The ImageFilter class acts as a base class for all image-filtering classes. It implements the ImageConsumer and Cloneable interfaces.

getFilterInstance

public ImageFilter getFilterInstance(ImageConsumer ic)

The getFilterInstance method returns an ImageFilter object that will be used to perform the filtering for the specified image consumer.

Parameters: ic—the image consumer that requires the image filtering.

Returns: An ImageFilter object to be used to perform the image filtering.

setDimensions

public void setDimensions(int width, int height}

The setDimensions method filters the information provided in the setDimensions method of the ImageConsumer interface.

Parameters:

width—the filter width.

height—the filter height.

setProperties

```
public void setProperties(Hashtable props)
```

The setProperties method passes the props value along after a property is added that identifies which filters have been applied to the image.

Parameters: props—a Hashtable object containing a set of properties.

setColorModel

```
public void setColorModel(ColorModel model)
```

The setColorModel method filters the information provided in the setColorModel method of the ImageConsumer interface.

Parameters: model—a ColorModel object.

setHints

```
public void setHints(int hints)
```

The setHints method filters the information provided in the setHints method of the Image ImageConsumer interface.

Parameters: hints—an integer value containing hints.

setPixels

```
public void setPixels(int x, int y, int w, int h, ColorModel model,
  byte pixels[], int off, int scansize)
```

The setPixels method filters the pixels array. The pixels that pass through the filter are passed onto the ImageConsumer interface.

Parameters:

x—the x coordinate of the image.

y—the y coordinate of the image.

w—the width of the image.

h—the height of the image.

model—the ColorModel to which the pixels array conforms.

pixels—a byte array containing pixels to be examined.

off—a variable that is passed on to the image consumer's setPixels method.

scansize—an integer value representing the scansize of the operation.

imageComplete

```
public void imageComplete(int status)
```

The imageComplete method filters the information provided by the imageComplete method in the ImageConsumer interface.

Parameters: status—an integer value representing the status of the filter operation

resendTopDownLeftRight

```
public void resendTopDownLeftRight(ImageProducer ip)
```

The resendTopDownLeftRight method is used to deliver the image data to the specified image consumer in top-down, left-right order.

Parameters: ip—the image producer that is responsible for production of the image data.

clone

```
public Object clone()
```

The clone method returns a clone of the image filter.

Returns: An object that is identical to the image filter.

IndexColorModel

Extends: ColorModel

This class translates from pixel values to RGB color values for pixels that represent indexes into a color map.

IndexColorModel **Constructor**

```
public IndexColorModel(int bits, int size, byte r[], byte g[], byte b[])
```

The IndexColorModel constructor constructs a color model from the specified information.

Parameters:

bits—the number of bits required to represent a pixel.

size—the size of the color arrays.

r—the red color array.

g—the green color array.

b—the blue color array.

`IndexColorModel` **Constructor**

```
public IndexColorModel(int bits, int size, byte r[], byte g[], byte b[],
  int trans)
```

The `IndexColorModel` constructor constructs a color model from the specified information.

Parameters:

bits—the number of bits required to represent a pixel.

size—the size of the color arrays.

r—the red color array.

g—the green color array.

b—the blue color array.

trans—an integer value representing the index that identifies the transparent pixel.

`IndexColorModel` **Constructor**

```
public IndexColorModel(int bits, int size, byte r[], byte g[], byte b[],
  byte a[])
```

The `IndexColorModel` constructor constructs a color model from the specified information.

Parameters:

bits—the number of bits required to represent a pixel.

size—the size of the color arrays.

r—the red color array.

g—the green color array.

b—the blue color array.

a—the alpha color array.

IndexColorModel **Constructor**

```
public IndexColorModel(int bits, int size, byte cmap[], int start,
  boolean hasalpha)
```

The IndexColorModel constructor constructs a color model from the specified information.

Parameters:

bits—the number of bits required to represent a pixel.

size—the size of the color arrays.

cmap—a byte array representing the color map array.

start—the index representing the first color component within the color array.

hasalpha—a boolean value indicating whether alpha values are contained within the color map.

IndexColorModel **Constructor**

```
public IndexColorModel(int bits, int size, byte cmap[], int start,
  boolean hasalpha, int trans)
```

The IndexColorModel constructor constructs a color model from the specified information.

Parameters:

bits—the number of bits required to represent a pixel.

size—the size of the color arrays.

cmap—a byte array representing the color map array.

start—the index representing the first color component within the color array.

hasalpha—a boolean value indicating whether alpha values are contained within the color map.

trans—an integer value representing the index of the transparent pixel.

getMapSize

```
final public int getMapSize()
```

The getMapSize method returns the size of the color map used by the IndexColorModel.

Returns: An integer value representing the size of the color map used by the index color model.

getTransparentPixel

`final public int getTransparentPixel()`

The `getTransparentPixel` method returns the index into the color map of the transparent pixel.

Returns: An integer value representing the index into the color map of the transparent pixel. If there is no transparent pixel, this method returns -1.

getReds

`final public void getReds(byte r[])`

The `getReds` method fills the byte array with the red color components.

Parameters: r—a byte array that is filled by the `getReds` method with the red color components.

getGreens

`final public void getGreens(byte g[])`

The `getGreens` method fills the byte array with the green color components.

Parameters: g—a byte array that is filled by the `getGreens` method with the green color components.

getBlues

`final public void getBlues(byte b[])`

The `getBlues` method fills the byte array with the blue color components.

Parameters: b—a byte array that is filled by the `getBlues` method with the blue color components.

getAlphas

`final public void getAlphas(byte a[])`

The `getAlphas` method fills the byte array with the alpha components.

Parameters: a—a byte array that is filled by the `getAlphas` method with the alpha components.

getRed

```
final public int getRed(int pixel)
```

The getRed method returns the red color component for the specified pixel using the index color model.

Parameters: pixel—an integer value representing a pixel.

Returns: An integer value in the range 0–255 representing the red component for the specified pixel.

getGreen

```
final public int getGreen(int pixel)
```

The getGreen method returns the green color component for the specified pixel using the index color model.

Parameters: pixel—an integer value representing a pixel.

Returns: An integer value in the range 0–255 representing the green component for the specified pixel.

getBlue

```
final public int getBlue(int pixel)
```

The getBlue method returns the blue color component for the specified pixel using the index color model.

Parameters: pixel—an integer value representing a pixel.

Returns: An integer value in the range 0–255 representing the blue component for the specified pixel.

getAlpha

```
final public int getAlpha(int pixel)
```

The getAlpha method returns the alpha color component for the specified pixel using the index color model.

Parameters: pixel—an integer value representing a pixel.

Returns: An integer value in the range 0–255 representing the alpha component for the specified pixel.

getRGB

```
final public int getRGB(int pixel)
```

The getRGB method returns the RGB color value for the specified pixel using the default RGB color model.

Parameters: pixel—an integer value representing a pixel.

Returns: An integer value in the range 0–255 representing the RGB color value for the specified pixel.

MemoryImageSource

Extends: Object

Implements: ImageProducer

This class uses an array to produce image pixel values.

MemoryImageSource **Constructor**

```
public MemoryImageSource(int w, int h, ColorModel cm, byte[] pix, int off,
  int scan)
```

The MemoryImageSource constructor uses an array of bytes to produce image data for an Image object.

Parameters:

w—the width of the image to be created in pixels.

h—the height of the image to be created in pixels.

cm—the color model used to translate the pixel values.

pix—a byte array containing the image data.

off—the offset into the array to begin reading.

scan—the scan value.

MemoryImageSource **Constructor**

```
public MemoryImageSource(int w, int h, ColorModel cm, byte[] pix, int off,
   int scan, Hashtable props)
```

The MemoryImageSource constructor uses an array of bytes to produce image data for an Image object.

Parameters:

w—the width of the image to be created in pixels.

h—the height of the image to be created in pixels.

cm—the color model used to translate the pixel values.

pix—a byte array containing the image data.

off—the offset into the array to begin reading.

scan—the scan value.

props—a Hashtable object containing properties to be used by the image producer.

MemoryImageSource **Constructor**

```
public MemoryImageSource(int w, int h, ColorModel cm, int[] pix, int off,
   int scan)
```

The MemoryImageSource constructor uses an array of bytes to produce image data for an Image object.

Parameters:

w—the width of the image to be created in pixels.

h—the height of the image to be created in pixels.

cm—the color model used to translate the pixel values.

pix—an integer array containing the image data.

off—the offset into the array to begin reading.

scan—the scan value.

MemoryImageSource **Constructor**

```
public MemoryImageSource(int w, int h, ColorModel cm, int[] pix, int off,
  int scan, Hashtable props)
```

The MemoryImageSource constructor uses an array of bytes to produce image data for an Image object.

Parameters:

w—the width of the image to be created in pixels.

h—the height of the image to be created in pixels.

cm—the color model used to translate the pixel values.

pix—an integer array containing the image data.

off—the offset into the array to begin reading.

scan—the scan value.

props—a Hashtable object containing properties to be used by the image producer.

MemoryImageSource **Constructor**

```
public MemoryImageSource(int w, int h, int pix[], int off, int scan)
```

The MemoryImageSource constructor uses an array of bytes to produce image data for an Image object.

Parameters:

w—the width of the image to be created in pixels.

h—the height of the image to be created in pixels.

pix—an integer array containing the image data.

off—the offset into the array to begin reading.

scan—the scan value.

MemoryImageSource **Constructor**

```
public MemoryImageSource(int w, int h, int pix[], int off, int scan,
  Hashtable props)
```

The MemoryImageSource constructor uses an array of bytes to produce image data for an Image object.

Parameters:

w—the width of the image to be created in pixels.

h—the height of the image to be created in pixels.

pix—an integer array containing the image data.

off—the offset into the array to begin reading.

scan—the scan value.

props—a Hashtable object containing properties to be used by the image producer.

addConsumer

```
public synchronized void addConsumer(ImageConsumer ic)
```

The addConsumer method adds an ImageConsumer interface to a list of image consumers who are interested in data for the image.

Parameters: ic—an ImageConsumer-derived object.

isConsumer

```
public synchronized boolean isConsumer(ImageConsumer ic)
```

The isConsumer method determines if the specified image consumer is currently in the list.

Parameters: ic—an ImageConsumer-derived object.

Returns: A boolean value that is true if the ImageConsumer object is already in the list, false if not.

removeConsumer

```
public synchronized void removeConsumer(ImageConsumer ic)
```

The removeConsumer method removes the specified image consumer from the list of image consumers interested in receiving image data.

Parameters: ic—an ImageConsumer-derived object.

startProduction

```
public void startProduction(ImageConsumer ic)
```

The startProduction method adds the specified image consumer to a list of image consumers interested in receiving image data. This method also immediately starts production of image data to be sent to the ImageConsumer interfaces.

Parameters: ic—an ImageConsumer-derived object.

requestTopDownLeftRightResend

```
public void requestTopDownLeftRightResend(ImageConsumer ic)
```

The requestTopDownLeftRightResend method is used to deliver the image data to the specified image consumer in top-down, left-right order.

Parameters: ic—an ImageConsumer-derived object.

PixelGrabber

Extends: Object

Implements: ImageConsumer

The PixelGrabber class implements the ImageConsumer interface to retrieve a subset of pixels from an image.

PixelGrabber **Constructor**

```
public PixelGrabber(Image img, int x, int y, int w, int h, int[] pix, int off,
  int scansize)
```

The PixelGrabber constructor constructs a PixelGrabber object to retrieve a subset of pixels from the image. In this case, the PixelGrabber will grab a rectangular section of pixels.

Parameters:

img—an Image object to be "grabbed."

x—the x coordinate from which to begin grabbing pixels.

y—the y coordinate from which to begin grabbing pixels.

w—the width of the PixelGrabber bounding rectangle.

h—the height of the PixelGrabber bounding rectangle.

pix—an array of integers used to store the grabbed pixels.

off—the offset into the image to begin calculations.

scan—an integer value used to represent the scansize.

PixelGrabber **Constructor**

```
public PixelGrabber(ImageProducer ip, int x, int y, int w, int h, int[] pix,
  int off, int scansize)
```

The PixelGrabber constructor constructs a PixelGrabber object to retrieve a subset of pixels from the image. In this case, the PixelGrabber will grab a rectangular section of pixels.

Parameters:

ip—an ImageProducer object to be grabbed.

x—the x coordinate from which to begin grabbing pixels.

y—the y coordinate from which to begin grabbing pixels.

w—the width of the PixelGrabber bounding rectangle.

h—the height of the PixelGrabber bounding rectangle.

pix—an array of integers used to store the grabbed pixels.

off—the offset into the image to begin calculations.

scan—an integer value used to represent the scansize.

grabPixels

```
public boolean grabPixels() throws InterruptedException
```

The grabPixels method notifies the pixel grabber to begin grabbing pixels and wait until all of the pixels to be grabbed have been delivered.

Returns: A boolean value that is true if the operation was successful, false if not.

Throws: InterruptedException if the process was interrupted.

grabPixels

```
public synchronized boolean grabPixels(long ms) throws InterruptedException
```

This grabPixels method notifies the pixel grabber to begin grabbing pixels at some specified time in the future and wait until all of the pixels to be grabbed have been delivered.

Parameters: ms—a long integer value representing the start time in milliseconds.

Returns: A boolean value that is true if the operation was successful, false if not.

Throws: InterruptedException if the process was interrupted.

status

```
public synchronized int status()
```

The status method returns a value representing the status of the grab operation.

Returns: An integer value representing the operation's status. This value will be a bitwise OR of all relevant image observer flags.

setDimensions

```
public void setDimensions(int width, int height)
```

The setDimensions method must be implemented by this class to fulfill its interface with the ImageConsumer interface.

Parameters: width—the width parameter.

Parameters: height—the height parameter.

setHints

```
public void setHints(int hints)
```

The setHints method must be implemented by this class to fulfill its interface with the ImageConsumer interface.

Parameters: hints—the hints parameter.

setProperties

```
public void setProperties(Hashtable props)
```

The setProperties method must be implemented by this class to fulfill its interface with the ImageConsumer interface.

Parameters: props—a Hashtable object.

setColorModel

```
public void setColorModel(ColorModel model)
```

The setColorModel method must be implemented by this class to fulfill its interface with the ImageConsumer interface.

Parameters: model—a ColorModel object.

setPixels

```
public void setPixels(int srcX, int srcY, int srcW, int srcH,
  ColorModel model, byte pixels[], int srcOff, int srcScan)
```

The setPixels method must be implemented by this class to fulfill its interface with the ImageConsumer interface.

Parameters:

srcX—an integer value representing the source x coordinate.

srcY—an integer value representing the source y coordinate.

srcW—an integer value representing the source width.

srcH—an integer value representing the source height.

model—the color model to be used.

pixels—a byte array of pixel values.

srcOff—the offset into the source array.

srcScan—the source scan value.

imageComplete

```
public synchronized void imageComplete(int status)
```

The imageComplete method must be implemented by this class to fulfill its interface with the ImageConsumer interface.

Parameters: status—an integer value representing the status of the pixel grab operation.

RGBImageFilter

Extends: ImageFilter

The RGBImageFilter abstract class provides the functionality to process image data within a single method which converts pixels in the default RGB ColorModel.setColorModel

SetColorModel

```
public void setColorModel(ColorModel model)
```

The setColorModel method checks the type of the specified color model. If it is an IndexColorModel and the protected canFilterIndexColorModel variable is true, the color model will be set to the IndexColorModel. Otherwise, the default RGB color model will be used for all filtering operations.

Parameters: Model—the color model to be used for filtering.

substituteColorModel

```
public void substituteColorModel(ColorModel oldcm, ColorModel newcm)
```

The substituteColorModel method allows color models to be interchanged on-the-fly. If the old color model is encountered during a setPixels method call, the new color model will be used instead.

Parameters:

oldcm—the old color model to be replaced.

newcm—the new color model.

filterIndexColorModel

```
public IndexColorModel filterIndexColorModel(IndexColorModel icm)
```

The filterIndexColorModel method runs each entry in the specified IndexColorModel through the filterRGB method and returns a new color model.

Parameters: icm—the IndexColorModel object to be filtered.

Returns: An IndexColorModel object that has been filtered by the RGBImageFilter class.

filterRGBPixels

```
public void filterRGBPixels(int x, int y, int w, int h, int pixels[], int off,
  int scansize)
```

The `filterRGBPixels` method filters an array of pixels through the `filterRGB` method.

Parameters:

x—the x coordinate from which to start the filtering.

y—the y coordinate from which to start the filtering.

w—the width of the image to be filtered.

h—the height of the image to be filtered.

pixels—an array of integers representing pixel values.

off—the offset used.

scansize—the scansize used.

setPixels

```
public void setPixels(int x, int y, int w, int h, ColorModel model,
  int pixels[], int off, int scansize)
```

The `setPixels` method converts the pixels and color model before passing them on. If the color model has already been converted, the pixels are passed through with the converted color model. If not, then the pixel array is converted to the default RGB color model using the `filterRGBPixels` method.

Parameters:

x—the x coordinate from which to start the filtering.

y—the y coordinate from which to start the filtering.

w—the width of the image to be filtered.

h—the height of the image to be filtered.

model—the color model with which the pixels comply.

pixels—an array of integers representing pixel values.

off—the offset used.

scansize—the scansize used.

filterRGB

```
public abstract int filterRGB(int x, int y, int rgb)
```

The `filterRGB` method allows subclasses to specify a method that converts an input pixel using the default RGB color model to an output pixel.

Parameters:

x—the x coordinate of the pixel.

y—the y coordinate of the pixel.

rgb—the pixel value using the default RGB color model.

Returns: An integer value representing the filtered pixel value.

APPENDIX H

java.awt.peer
Package Reference

The java.awt.peer package is interesting because it contains no classes. Every object defined within the java.awt.peer package is an interface. By examining the contents of the classes in the java.awt package, you will find that all the GUI components in that package implement the interfaces found in the java.awt.peer package. Nearly all the methods defined in the java.awt.peer interfaces are *friendly* methods, meaning that they can only be accessed from within java.awt package classes.

ButtonPeer

Extends: ComponentPeer

The ButtonPeer interface extends interface java.awt.peer.ComponentPeer. The ButtonPeer interface provides the basic structure required for button component functionality.

setLabel

void setLabel(String label)

The setLabel method should set the displayed label for the button using the specified label string.

Parameters: label—a string that will be displayed as the button's label.

CanvasPeer

Extends: ComponentPeer

The CanvasPeer interface extends interface java.awt.peer.ComponentPeer. The CanvasPeer interface provides the basic structure required for canvas component functionality.

CheckboxMenuItemPeer

Extends: MenuItemPeer

The CheckboxMenuItemPeer interface extends interface java.awt.peer.MenuItemPeer. The CheckboxMenuItemPeer interface provides the basic structure required for check box menu item component functionality.

setState

```
void setState(boolean t)
```

The setState method sets the checked state of a check box menu item.

Parameters: t—a boolean value that will be true if the check box is to be checked, false if not.

CheckboxPeer

Extends: ComponentPeer

The CheckboxPeer interface extends interface java.awt.peer.ComponentPeer. The CheckboxPeer interface provides the basic structure required for check box component functionality.

setState

```
void setState(boolean state)
```

The setState method sets the checked state of a check box.

Parameters: t—a boolean value that will be true if the check box is to be checked, false if not.

setCheckboxGroup

```
void setCheckboxGroup(CheckboxGroup g)
```

The setCheckboxGroup method should set which check box group the check box belongs to, using the specified check box group.

Parameters: g—a CheckboxGroup object that this check box will be a member of.

setLabel

```
void setLabel(String label)
```

The setLabel method should set the displayed label for the check box using the specified label string.

Parameters: label—a String that will be displayed as the check box's label.

ChoicePeer

Extends: ComponentPeer

The ChoicePeer interface extends interface java.awt.peer.ComponentPeer. The ChoicePeer interface provides the basic structure required for Choice component functionality.

addItem

void addItem(String item, int index)

The addItem method adds the specified item to the choice list at the specified list index.

Parameters: item—a string value representing the item to be added to the choice list.

Parameters: index—the integer index into the choice list where the item parameter is to be added.

select

void select(int index)

The select method selects the choice list item at the specified index.

Parameters: index—the index into the choice list to be selected.

ComponentPeer

The ComponentPeer interface extends class java.lang.Object. The ComponentPeer interface provides the basic structure required for component functionality.

show

void show()

The show method should be implemented to make the Component object visible.

hide

void hide()

The hide method should hide the component so that is not visible.

enable

```
void enable()
```

The enable method should enable the component so that it can be selected by the user.

disable

```
void disable()
```

The disable method should disable the component (gray it out, and so on) so that it cannot be selected by the user.

paint

```
void paint(Graphics g)
```

The paint method should display the component using the specified Graphics context.

Parameters: g—a Graphics object used for drawing purposes.

repaint

```
void repaint(long tm, int x, int y, int width, int height)
```

The repaint method repaints a part of the component at some specified time in the future.

Parameters:

tm—maximum time in milliseconds before the update.

x—the x coordinate of the component's bounding rectangle to repaint.

y—the y coordinate of the component's bounding rectangle to repaint.

width—the width of the component's bounding rectangle to repaint.

height—the height of the component's bounding rectangle to repaint.

print

```
void print(Graphics g)
```

The print method should print the component using the specified Graphics object.

Parameters: g—a Graphics object used for drawing purposes.

reshape

```
void reshape(int x, int y, int width, int height)
```

The reshape method reshapes the component to the specified bounding rectangle.

Parameters:

x—the x coordinate of the component's new bounding rectangle.

y—the y coordinate of the component's new bounding rectangle.

width—the width of the component's new bounding rectangle.

height—the height of the component's new bounding rectangle.

handleEvent

```
boolean handleEvent(Event e)
```

The handleEvent method should handle the specified event for the component.

Parameters: e—an Event object encapsulating some system event.

minimumSize

```
Dimension minimumSize()
```

The minimumSize method returns the minimum size allowable for the component.

Returns: A Dimension object containing the component's minimum size.

preferredSize

```
Dimension preferredSize()
```

The preferredSize method returns the preferred size allowable for the component.

Returns: A Dimension object containing the component's preferred size.

getColorModel

```
ColorModel getColorModel()
```

The getColorModel method returns the color model used for this component.

Returns: A ColorModel object that contains the component's color model information.

getToolkit

```
Toolkit getToolkit()
```

The getToolkit method returns the component's managing tool kit.

Returns: A Toolkit object.

getGraphics

```
Graphics getGraphics()
```

The getGraphics method returns a Graphics context for the component.

Returns: A Graphics object used for drawing purposes.

getFontMetrics

```
FontMetrics getFontMetrics(Font font)
```

The getFontMetrics method returns the font metrics information for the specified Font.

Parameters: font—a Font object.

Returns: A FontMetrics object containing metrics information on the specified font.

dispose

```
void dispose()
```

The dispose method disposes of a component's resources and the component itself.

setForeground

```
void setForeground(Color c)
```

The setForeground method sets the foreground color for the component using the specified color.

Parameters: c—a Color object specifying which color to use for the foreground color.

setBackground

```
void setBackground(Color c)
```

The setBackground method sets the background color for the component using the specified color.

Parameters: c—a Color object specifying which color to use for the background color.

setFont

`void setFont(Font f)`

The `setFont` method sets the font to use for this component using the specified font.

Parameters: f—a `Font` object specifying which font to use for the component.

requestFocus

`void requestFocus()`

The `requestFocus` method requests the input focus for the component.

nextFocus

`void nextFocus()`

The `nextFocus` method shifts the focus to the next component on the screen.

createImage

`Image createImage(ImageProducer producer)`

The `createImage` method creates an `Image` object using the specified `ImageProducer` interface.

Parameters: producer—an `ImageProducer` derived object used to produce an image.

Returns: An `Image` object.

createImage

`Image createImage(int width, int height)`

This `createImage` method creates an image for offscreen use using the specified sizes.

Parameters:

width—the width of the image to be created.

height—the height of the image to be created.

Returns: An `Image` object.

prepareImage

`boolean prepareImage(Image img, int w, int h, ImageObserver o)`

The `prepareImage` method prepares the image for rendering on this component using the specified parameters.

Parameters:

img—an Image object to be rendered.

w—the width of the rectangle to render the image in.

h—the height of the rectangle to render the image in.

o—the image observer used to monitor the image rendering.

Returns: A boolean value that is true if the image was rendered successfully, false if not.

checkImage

```
int checkImage(Image img, int w, int h, ImageObserver o)
```

The checkImage method returns the status of a scaled rendering of a specified Image.

Parameters:

img—an Image object to be rendered.

w—the width of the rectangle to render the image in.

h—the height of the rectangle to render the image in.

o—the image observer used to monitor the image rendering.

Returns: An integer value containing the boolean OR of the image observer status flags.

ContainerPeer

Extends: ComponentPeer

The ContainerPeer interface extends interface java.awt.peer.ComponentPeer. The ContainerPeer interface provides the basic structure required for container component functionality.

insets

```
Insets insets()
```

The insets method returns an Insets object representing the insets of the container.

Returns: An Insets object.

DialogPeer

Extends: WindowPeer

The DialogPeer interface extends interface java.awt.peer.WindowPeer. The DialogPeer interface provides the basic structure required for dialog box component functionality.

setTitle

void setTitle(String title)

The setTitle method sets the title to be displayed on the dialog's title bar.

Parameters: title—a string value that will be used as the dialog's title.

setResizable

void setResizable(boolean resizeable)

The setResizable method determines the dialog's resize state.

Parameters: resizeable—a boolean value that is true if the dialog can be resized, false if not.

FileDialogPeer

Extends: DialogPeer

The FileDialogPeer interface extends interface java.awt.peer.DialogPeer. The FileDialogPeer interface provides the basic structure required for file selection dialog component functionality.

setFile

void setFile(String file)

The setFile method sets the filename to be displayed in the file dialog.

Parameters: file—a string value representing a filename.

setDirectory

void setDirectory(String dir)

The setDirectory method sets the directory to be selected in the file dialog.

Parameters: dir—a string value representing the directory name.

setFilenameFilter

void setFilenameFilter(FilenameFilter filter)

The setFilenameFilter() sets the filter to be used in the file dialog.

Parameters: filter—a FilenameFilter object used to filter filenames.

FramePeer

Extends: WindowPeer

The FramePeer interface extends interface java.awt.peer.WindowPeer. The FramePeer interface provides the basic structure required for frame component functionality.

setTitle

void setTitle(String title)

The setTitle method sets the title of the frame to the specified title string.

Parameters: title—a string value representing the frame's title.

setIconImage

void setIconImage(Image im)

The setIconImage method sets the image to be used when the frame is iconized.

Parameters: im—an Image object.

setMenuBar

void setMenuBar(MenuBar mb)

The setMenuBar method sets the menu bar to be used for the frame.

Parameters: mb—A MenuBar object.

setResizable

void setResizable(boolean resizeable)

The setResizable method determines the resize state of the frame.

Parameters: resizeable—a boolean value that is true if the frame can be resized, false if not.

setCursor

```
void setCursor(int cursorType)
```

The setCursor method sets the cursor type for the frame.

Parameters: cursorType—an integer value representing the cursor type.

LabelPeer

Extends: ComponentPeer

The LabelPeer interface extends interface java.awt.peer.ComponentPeer. The LabelPeer interface provides the basic structure required for label component functionality.

setText

```
void setText(String label)
```

The setText method sets the text to be displayed on the label.

Parameters: label—a string value that is used as the label string.

setAlignment

```
void setAlignment(int alignment)
```

The setAlignment method sets the alignment type of the label.

Parameters: alignment—an integer value that determines the alignment of the label (LEFT, RIGHT, or CENTER).

ListPeer

Extends: ComponentPeer

The ListPeer interface extends interface java.awt.peer.ComponentPeer. The ListPeer interface provides the basic structure required for list component functionality.

getSelectedIndexes

`int[] getSelectedIndexes()`

The `getSelectedIndexes` method returns an array containing the selected indexes in the list.

Returns: An integer array containing the indexes that are currently selected in the list.

addItem

`void addItem(String item, int index)`

The `addItem` method adds a `String` item at the specified index.

Parameters:

`item`—a string value to be added to the list.

`index`—an integer value representing the index into the list.

delItems

`void delItems(int start, int end)`

The `delItems` method deletes a range of values from the list using the specified range values.

Parameters:

`start`—an integer value marking the start of the deletion range.

`end`—an integer value marking the end of the deletion range.

clear

`void clear()`

The `clear` method clears all elements from the list.

select

`void select(int index)`

This `select` method selects the specified index.

Parameters: `index`—an integer value specifying the item in the list to be selected.

deselect

`void deselect(int index)`

The `deselect` method deselects an item within the list.

Parameters: index—an integer value specifying the item in the list to be deselected.

makeVisible

`void makeVisible(int index)`

The `makeVisible` method forces the list to scroll, if necessary, so that the specified index will be made visible to the user.

Parameters: index—an integer value representing the index to be made visible.

setMultipleSelections

`void setMultipleSelections(boolean v)`

The `setMultipleSelections` method specifies whether the list should allow multiple selections or not.

Parameters: v—a boolean value that is `true` if multiple selections are to be allowed, `false` if not.

preferredSize

`Dimension preferredSize(int v)`

The `preferredSize` method sets the preferred size for a list of the specified number of items.

Parameters: v—an integer value specifying the number of items within the list.

Returns: A `Dimension` object containing the preferred size of the list.

minimumSize

`Dimension minimumSize(int v)`

The `minimumSize` method sets the minimum size for a list of the specified number of items.

Parameters: v—an integer value specifying the number of items within the list.

Returns: A `Dimension` object containing the minimum size of the list.

MenuBarPeer

Extends: MenuComponentPeer

The MenuBarPeer interface extends interface java.awt.peer.MenuComponentPeer. The MenuBarPeer interface provides the basic structure required for menu bar component functionality.

addMenu

void addMenu(Menu m)

The addMenu method adds the specified Menu to the menu bar.

Parameters: m—the Menu object to be added to the menu bar.

delMenu

void delMenu(int index)

The delMenu method deletes the menu at the specified index from the menu bar.

Parameters: index—an integer value representing the index to be deleted from the menu bar.

addHelpMenu

void addHelpMenu(Menu m)

The addHelpMenu adds a help menu to the menu bar.

Parameters: m—the Menu object to be added to the menu bar.

MenuComponentPeer

Extends: MenuComponentPeer

The MenuComponentPeer interface extends interface java.awt.peer.MenuComponentPeer. The MenuComponentPeer interface provides the basic structure required for menu component functionality.

dispose

void dispose()

The dispose method disposes of a MenuComponent's allocated resources.

MenuItemPeer

Extends: MenuComponentPeer

The MenuItemPeer interface extends interface java.awt.peer.MenuComponentPeer. The MenuItemPeer interface provides the basic structure required for menu item component functionality.

setLabel

void setLabel(String label)

The setLabel method sets the label string that will be displayed on the menu item.

Parameters: label—a string value that will be displayed as the menu item's label.

enable

void enable()

The enable method enables the menu item for user selection.

disable

void disable()

The disable method disables the menu item for user selection.

MenuPeer

Extends: MenuItemPeer

The MenuPeer interface extends interface java.awt.peer.MenuItemPeer. The MenuPeer interface provides the basic structure required for menu component functionality.

addSeparator

void addSeparator()

The addSeparator method adds a separator element to the menu. A separator is an item like a line that cannot be selected by the user and that will not trigger a menu selection event.

addItem

`void addItem(MenuItem item)`

The `addItem` method adds a menu item to the menu.

Parameters: item—a `MenuItem` object.

delItem

`void delItem(int index)`

The `delItem` method deletes the menu item at the specified index.

Parameters: index—an integer value representing the index on the menu to be deleted.

PanelPeer

Extends: `ContainerPeer`

The `PanelPeer` interface extends interface `java.awt.peer.ContainerPeer`. The `PanelPeer` interface provides the basic structure required for panel component functionality.

ScrollbarPeer

Extends: `ComponentPeer`

The `ScrollbarPeer` interface extends interface `java.awt.peer.ComponentPeer`. The `ScrollbarPeer` interface provides the basic structure required for scrollbar component functionality.

setValue

`void setValue(int value)`

The `setValue` method sets the value of the scrollbar.

Parameters: value—an integer value representing the value (position) of the scrollbar.

setValues

`void setValues(int value, int visible, int minimum, int maximum)`

The `setValues` method sets the specified properties of the scrollbar.

Parameters:

value—the new value of the scrollbar.

visible—the number of units to be displayed by the scrollbar.

Parameters:

minimum—the minimum value of the scrollbar.

maximum—the maximum value of the scrollbar.

setLineIncrement

void setLineIncrement(int 1)

The setLineIncrement method sets the increment value represented by a user clicking on a scrollbar line up/down widget.

Parameters: 1—an integer value representing the line increment value.

setPageIncrement

void setPageIncrement(int 1)

The setPageIncrement method sets the increment value represented by a user clicking on a scrollbar page up/down widget.

Parameters: 1—an integer value representing the page increment value.

TextAreaPeer

Extends: TextComponentPeer

The TextAreaPeer interface extends interface java.awt.peer.TextAreaPeer. The TextAreaPeer interface provides the basic structure required for text area component functionality.

insertText

void insertText(String txt, int pos)

The insertText method inserts the specified text at the specified position within the text area.

Parameters:

txt—a string value representing the text to be inserted.

pos—an integer value representing the position within the text area to insert the text at.

replaceText

```
void replaceText(String txt, int start, int end)
```

The replaceText method replaces text at the specified positions with the new text.

Parameters:

txt—a string value representing the text to be inserted into the text area.

start—an integer value containing the start position of the text to be replaced.

end—an integer value containing the end position of the text to be replaced.

preferredSize

```
Dimension preferredSize(int rows, int cols)
```

The preferredSize method returns the preferred size of a text area of the specified dimensions.

Parameters:

rows—the number of rows in the text area.

cols—the number of columns in the text area.

Returns: A Dimension object containing the preferred size of the text area.

minimumSize

```
Dimension minimumSize(int rows, int cols)
```

The minimumSize method returns the minimum size of a text area of the specified dimensions.

Parameters:

rows—the number of rows in the text area.

cols—the number of columns in the text area.

Returns: A Dimension object containing the minimum size of the text area.

TextComponentPeer

Extends: ComponentPeer

The TextComponentPeer interface extends interface java.awt.peer.ComponentPeer. The TextComponentPeer interface provides the basic structure required for text component functionality.

setEditable

void setEditable(boolean editable)

The setEditable method is used to set the text component's editable state.

Parameters: A boolean value that is true if the text can be edited, false if not.

getText

String getText()

The getText method returns the text component's displayed text.

Returns: A string value representing the text contained in the text component.

setText

void setText(String 1)

The setText method sets the text to be displayed in the text component.

Parameters: 1—a string value to be displayed by the text component.

getSelectionStart

int getSelectionStart()

The getSelectionStart method returns the position of the first selected character in the text component.

Returns: An integer value specifying the position of the first selected character in the text component.

getSelectionEnd

int getSelectionEnd()

The getSelectionEnd method returns the position of the last selected character in the text component.

Returns: An integer value specifying the position of the last selected character in the text component.

select

void select(int selStart, int selEnd)

The `select` method selects the specified text within the `TextComponent`.

Parameters:

`selStart`—an integer value representing the starting character to be selected.

`selEnd`—an integer value representing the ending character to be selected.

TextFieldPeer

Extends: `TextComponentPeer`

The `TextFieldPeer` interface extends `class java.lang.Object`. The `TextFieldPeer` interface provides the basic structure required for text field component functionality.

setEchoCharacter

`void setEchoCharacter(char c)`

The `setEchoCharacter` method sets the echo character to be echoed to the screen as the user types.

Parameters: c—a character value to be displayed no matter what character the user types.

preferredSize

`Dimension preferredSize(int cols)`

The `preferredSize` method returns the preferred size of the text field based on the specified number of characters.

Parameters: cols—an integer value containing the number of characters in the text field.

Returns: A `Dimension` object containing the preferred size of the text field.

minimumSize

`Dimension minimumSize(int cols)`

The `minimumSize` method returns the minimum size of the text field based on the specified number of characters.

Parameters: cols—an integer value containing the number of characters in the text field.

Returns: A `Dimension` object containing the minimum size of the text field.

WindowPeer

Extends: ContainerPeer

The WindowPeer interface extends interface java.awt.peer.ContainerPeer. The WindowPeer interface provides the basic structure required for window component functionality.

toFront

void toFront()

The toFront method moves the window to the front of the display.

toBack

void toBack()

The toBack method moves the window to the back of the display.

APPENDIX I

java.io **Package Reference**

The java.io package provides classes with support for reading and writing data to and from different input and output devices, including files, strings, and other data sources. The I/O package includes classes for inputting streams of data, outputting streams of data, working with files, and tokenizing streams of data.

DataInput

This interface describes an input stream that can read input data in a platform-independent manner.

readBoolean

```
public abstract boolean readBoolean() throws IOException
```

This method reads a boolean value (byte) from the input stream. A value of 0 is interpreted as false, while all other values are interpreted as true.

Returns: The boolean value read.

Throws: EOFException if the end of the stream is reached before reading the value.

Throws: IOException if an I/O error occurs.

readByte

```
public abstract byte readByte() throws IOException
```

This method reads a signed byte (8-bit) value from the input stream.

Returns: The byte value read.

Throws: EOFException if the end of the stream is reached before reading the value.

Throws: IOException if an I/O error occurs.

readChar

```
public abstract char readChar() throws IOException
```

This method reads a Unicode character (16-bit) value from the input stream.

Returns: The Unicode character value read.

Throws: EOFException if the end of the stream is reached before reading the value.

Throws: IOException if an I/O error occurs.

readDouble

```
public abstract double readDouble() throws IOException
```

This method reads a double (64-bit) value from the input stream.

Returns: The double value read.

Throws: EOFException if the end of the stream is reached before the value is read.

Throws: IOException if an I/O error occurs.

readFloat

```
public abstract float readFloat() throws IOException
```

This method reads a float (32-bit) value from the input stream.

Returns: The float value read.

Throws: EOFException if the end of the stream is reached before reading the value.

Throws: IOException if an I/O error occurs.

readFully

```
public abstract void readFully(byte b[]) throws IOException
```

This method reads up to b.length bytes from the input stream into the byte array b, blocking until all bytes are read.

Parameters: b—the byte array into which the data is read.

Throws: EOFException if the end of the stream is reached before the specified number of bytes is read.

Throws: IOException if an I/O error occurs.

readFully

```
public abstract void readFully(byte b[], int off, int len) throws IOException
```

This method reads up to len bytes from the input stream into the byte array b beginning off bytes into the array, blocking until all bytes are read.

Parameters:

b—the byte array into which the data is read.

off—the starting offset into the array for the data to be written to.

len—the maximum number of bytes to read.

Throws: EOFException if the end of the stream is reached before the specified number of bytes is read.

Throws: IOException if an I/O error occurs.

readInt

```
public abstract int readInt() throws IOException
```

This method reads an integer (32-bit) value from the input stream.

Returns: The integer value read.

Throws: EOFException if the end of the stream is reached before the value is read.

Throws: IOException if an I/O error occurs.

readLine

```
public abstract String readLine() throws IOException
```

This method reads a line of text from the input stream.

Returns: A string containing the line of text read.

Throws: EOFException if the end of the stream is reached before the line of text is read.

Throws: IOException if an I/O error occurs.

readLong

```
public abstract long readLong() throws IOException
```

This method reads a long (64-bit) value from the input stream.

Returns: The long value read.

Throws: EOFException if the end of the stream is reached before the value is read.

Throws: IOException if an I/O error occurs.

readShort

```
public abstract short readShort() throws IOException
```

This method reads a short (16-bit) value from the input stream.

Returns: The short value read.

Throws: EOFException if the end of the stream is reached before the value is read.

Throws: IOException if an I/O error occurs.

readUnsignedByte

```
public abstract int readUnsignedByte() throws IOException
```

This method reads an unsigned byte (8-bit) value from the input stream.

Returns: The unsigned byte value read.

Throws: EOFException if the end of the stream is reached before the value is read.

Throws: IOException if an I/O error occurs.

readUnsignedShort

```
public abstract int readUnsignedShort() throws IOException
```

This method reads an unsigned short (16-bit) value from the input stream.

Returns: The short value read.

Throws: EOFException if the end of the stream is reached before the value is read.

Throws: IOException if an I/O error occurs.

readUTF

```
public abstract String readUTF() throws IOException
```

This method reads a string that has been encoded using a modified UTF-8 format from the input stream.

Returns: The string read.

Throws: EOFException if the end of the stream is reached before the string is read.

Throws: UTFDataFormatException if the bytes read do not represent a valid UTF-8 encoding of a string.

Throws: IOException if an I/O error occurs.

skipBytes

```
public abstract int skipBytes(int n) throws IOException
```

This method skips n bytes of data in the input stream, blocking until all bytes are skipped.

Parameters: n—the number of bytes to skip.

Returns: The actual number of bytes skipped.

Throws: EOFException if the end of the stream is reached before skipping the specified number of bytes.

Throws: IOException if an I/O error occurs.

DataOutput

This interface describes an output stream that can write output data in a platform-independent manner.

write

```
public abstract void write(byte b[]) throws IOException
```

This method writes b.length bytes to the output stream from the byte array b, blocking until all bytes are written.

Parameters: b—the byte array from which the data is written.

Throws: IOException if an I/O error occurs.

write

```
public abstract void write(byte b[], int off, int len) throws IOException
```

This method writes len bytes to the output stream from the byte array b beginning off bytes into the array, blocking until all bytes are written.

Parameters:

b—the byte array from which the data is written.

off—the starting offset into the array for the data to be read from.

len—the number of bytes to write.

Throws: IOException if an I/O error occurs.

write

```
public abstract void write(int b) throws IOException
```

This method writes a byte value to the output stream, blocking until the byte is written.

Parameters: b—the byte value to be written.

Throws: IOException if an I/O error occurs.

writeBoolean

```
public abstract void writeBoolean(boolean v) throws IOException
```

This method writes a boolean value to the output stream. The boolean value true is written as the byte value 1, whereas false is written as the byte value 0.

Parameters: v—the boolean value to be written.

Throws: IOException if an I/O error occurs.

writeByte

```
public abstract void writeByte(int v) throws IOException
```

This method writes a byte (8-bit) value to the output stream.

Parameters: v—the byte value to be written.

Throws: IOException if an I/O error occurs.

writeBytes

```
public abstract void writeBytes(String s) throws IOException
```

This method writes a string to the output stream as a sequence of bytes.

Parameters: s—the string to be written as bytes.

Throws: IOException if an I/O error occurs.

writeChar

```
public abstract void writeChar(int v) throws IOException
```

This method writes a character (16-bit) value to the output stream.

Parameters: v—the character value to be written.

Throws: IOException if an I/O error occurs.

writeChars

```
public abstract void writeChars(String s) throws IOException
```

This method writes a string to the output stream as a sequence of characters.

Parameters: s—the string to be written as characters.

Throws: IOException if an I/O error occurs.

writeDouble

```
public abstract void writeDouble(double v) throws IOException
```

This method writes a double (64-bit) value to the output stream.

Parameters: v—the double value to be written.

Throws: IOException if an I/O error occurs.

writeFloat

```
public abstract void writeFloat(float v) throws IOException
```

This method writes a float (32-bit) value to the output stream.

Parameters: v—the float value to be written.

Throws: IOException if an I/O error occurs.

writeInt

```
public abstract void writeInt(int v) throws IOException
```

This method writes an integer (32-bit) value to the output stream.

Parameters: v—the integer value to be written.

Throws: IOException if an I/O error occurs.

writeLong

```
public abstract void writeLong(long v) throws IOException
```

This method writes a long (64-bit) value to the output stream.

Parameters: v—the long value to be written.

Throws: IOException if an I/O error occurs.

writeShort

```
public abstract void writeShort(int v) throws IOException
```

This method writes a short (16-bit) value to the output stream.

Parameters: v—the short value to be written.

Throws: IOException if an I/O error occurs.

writeUTF

```
public abstract void writeUTF(String str) throws IOException
```

This method encodes a string using a modified UTF-8 format and writes it to the output stream.

Parameters: str—the string to be written.

Throws: IOException if an I/O error occurs.

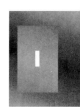

FilenameFilter

This interface describes a filename filter used to filter directory listings. Filename filters are used by the list method defined in the File class, as well as the AWT's FileDialog component.

accept

```
public abstract boolean accept(File dir, String name)
```

This method determines whether a file should be included in a directory listing.

Parameters:

dir—the directory in which the file is located.

name—the filename.

Returns: true if the file should be included in the directory list; false otherwise.

BufferedInputstream

Extends: FilterInputStream

This class implements a buffered input stream, which allows you to read data from a stream without causing a call to the underlying system for each byte read. This is accomplished by reading blocks of data into a buffer, where the data is readily accessible, independent of the underlying stream. Subsequent reads are much faster since they read from the buffer rather than the underlying input stream.

Member Variables

`protected byte buf[]`

This is the buffer where data is stored.

`protected int count`

This is the number of bytes of data currently in the buffer.

`protected int marklimit`

This is the maximum number of bytes that can be read before the marked position (`markpos`) is invalidated.

`protected int markpos`

This is the position in the buffer of the current mark, which provides a means to return to a particular location in the buffer via the `mark` and `reset` methods. The mark position is set to `-1` if there is no current mark.

`protected int pos`

This is the current read position in the buffer.

`BufferedInputStream` **Constructor**

`public BufferedInputStream(InputStream in)`

This constructor creates a new buffered input stream with a default buffer size of 512 bytes to read data from the `in` input stream.

Parameters: in—the input stream to read data from.

`BufferedInputStream` **Constructor**

`public BufferedInputStream(InputStream in, int size)`

This constructor creates a new buffered input stream with a buffer size of `size` bytes to read data from the `in` input stream.

Parameters: in—the input stream to read data from.

Parameters: size—the buffer size.

`availableBufferedInputStream`

`public int available() throws IOException`

This method determines the number of bytes that can be read from the input stream without blocking. This value is calculated by adding the number of free bytes in the buffer and the number of bytes available in the input stream.

Returns: The number of available bytes.

Throws: IOException if an I/O error occurs.

markBufferedInputStream

`public void mark(int readlimit)`

This method marks the current read position in the input stream. The reset method can be used to reset the read position to this mark; subsequent reads will read data beginning at the mark position. The mark position is invalidated after readlimit bytes have been read.

Parameters: readlimit—the maximum number of bytes that can be read before the mark position becomes invalid.

markSupportedBufferedInputStream

`public boolean markSupported()`

This method determines if the input stream supports the mark and reset methods.

Returns: true if the mark and reset methods are supported; false otherwise.

readBufferedInputStream

`public int read() throws IOException`

This method reads a byte value from the buffered input stream, blocking until the byte is read.

Returns: An integer representing the byte value read, or -1 if the end of the stream is reached.

Throws: IOException if an I/O error occurs.

readBufferedInputStream

`public int read(byte b[], int off, int len) throws IOException`

This method reads up to len bytes from the buffered input stream into the byte array b beginning off bytes into the array, blocking until all bytes are read.

Parameters:

b—the byte array into which the data is read.

off—the starting offset into the array for the data to be written to.

len—the maximum number of bytes to read.

Returns: The actual number of bytes read, or -1 if the end of the stream is reached.

Throws: IOException if an I/O error occurs.

resetBufferedInputStream

public void reset() throws IOException

This method resets the read position in the input stream to the current mark position, as set by the mark method.

Throws: IOException if the stream has not been marked or if the mark is invalid.

skipBufferedInputStream

public long skip(long n) throws IOException

This method skips n bytes of data in the input stream.

Parameters: n—the number of bytes to skip.

Returns: The actual number of bytes skipped.

Throws: IOException if an I/O error occurs.

BufferedOutputStream

Extends: FilterOutputStream

This class implements a buffered output stream, which allows you to write data to a stream without causing a call to the underlying system for each byte written. This is accomplished by writing blocks of data into a buffer rather than directly to the underlying output stream. The buffer is then written to the underlying output stream when the buffer fills up or is flushed, or the stream is closed.

Member Variables

protected byte buf[]

This is the buffer where data is stored.

protected int count

This is the number of bytes of data currently in the buffer.

BufferedOutputStream **Constructor**

`public BufferedOutputStream(OutputStream out)`

This constructor creates a new buffered output stream with a default buffer size of 512 bytes to write data to the out output stream.

Parameters: out—the output stream to write data to.

BufferedOutputStream **Constructor**

`public BufferedOutputStream(OutputStream out, int size)`

This constructor creates a new buffered output stream with a buffer size of size bytes to write data to the out output stream.

Parameters:

out—the output stream to write data to.

size—the buffer size.

flushBufferedOutputStream

`public void flush() throws IOException`

This method flushes the output stream, resulting in any buffered data being written to the underlying output stream.

Throws: IOException if an I/O error occurs.

writeBufferedOutputStream

`public void write(byte b[], int off, int len) throws IOException`

This method writes len bytes to the buffered output stream from the byte array b beginning off bytes into the array.

Parameters:

b—the byte array from which the data is written.

off—the starting offset into the array for the data to be read from.

len—the number of bytes to write.

Throws: IOException if an I/O error occurs.

writeBufferedOutputStream

```
public void write(int b) throws IOException
```

This method writes a byte value to the buffered output stream.

Parameters: b—the byte value to be written.

Throws: IOException if an I/O error occurs.

ByteArrayInputStream

Extends: InputStream

This class implements an input stream whose data is read from an array of bytes.

Member Variables

```
protected byte buf[]
```

This is the buffer where data is stored.

```
protected int count
```

This is the number of bytes of data currently in the buffer.

```
protected int pos
```

This is the current read position in the buffer.

ByteArrayInputStream Constructor

```
public ByteArrayInputStream(byte b[])
```

This constructor creates a new input stream from the byte array b. Note that the byte array is not copied to create the stream.

Parameters: b—the byte array from which the data is read.

ByteArrayInputStream Constructor

```
public ByteArrayInputStream(byte b[], int off, int len)
```

This constructor creates a new input stream of size len from the byte array b beginning off bytes into the array. Note that the byte array is not copied to create the stream.

Parameters:

b—the byte array from which the data is read.

off—the starting offset into the array for the data to be read from.

len—the maximum number of bytes to read.

availableByteArrayInputStream

`public int available()`

This method determines the number of bytes that can be read from the input stream.

Returns: The number of available bytes.

readByteArrayInputStream

`public int read()`

This method reads a byte value from the input stream.

Returns: An integer representing the byte value read, or -1 if the end of the stream is reached.

readByteArrayInputStream

`public int read(byte b[], int off, int len)`

This method reads up to len bytes from the input stream into the byte array b beginning off bytes into the array.

Parameters:

b—the byte array into which the data is read.

off—the starting offset into the array for the data to be written to.

len—the maximum number of bytes to read.

Returns: The actual number of bytes read, or -1 if the end of the stream is reached.

resetByteArrayInputStream

`public void reset()`

This method resets the read position to the beginning of the input stream.

skipByteArrayInputStream

`public long skip(long n)`

This method skips n bytes of data in the input stream.

Parameters: n—the number of bytes to skip.

Returns: The actual number of bytes skipped.

ByteArrayOutputStream

Extends: `OutputStream`

This class implements an output stream whose data is written to an array of bytes. The byte array automatically grows as data is written to it.

Member Variables

`protected byte buf[]`

This is the buffer where data is stored.

`protected int count`

This is the number of bytes of data currently in the buffer.

ByteArrayOutputStream **Constructor**

`public ByteArrayOutputStream()`

This constructor creates a new output stream with a default buffer size of 32 bytes. The size of the buffer automatically grows as data is written to it.

ByteArrayOutputStream **Constructor**

`public ByteArrayOutputStream(int size)`

This constructor creates a new output stream with an initial size of size bytes. The size of the buffer automatically grows as data is written to it.

Parameters: size—the initial size of the buffer.

resetByteArrayOutputStream

`public void reset()`

This method resets the contents of the underlying byte array by setting the `count` member variable to zero, resulting in the accumulated data being discarded.

sizeByteArrayOutputStream

`public int size()`

This method returns the current size of the buffer, which is stored in the `count` member variable.

Returns: The current size of the buffer.

toByteArrayByteArrayOutputStream

`public byte[] toByteArray()`

This method creates a new byte array containing the data currently stored in the underlying byte array associated with the output stream.

Returns: A byte array containing the current data stored in the output stream.

toStringByteArrayOutputStream

`public String toString()`

This method creates a new string containing the data currently stored in the underlying byte array associated with the output stream.

Returns: A string containing the current data stored in the output stream.

toStringByteArrayOutputStream

`public String toString(int hibyte)`

This method creates a new string containing the data currently stored in the underlying byte array associated with the output stream, with the top 8 bits of each string character set to `hibyte`.

Parameters: `hibyte`—the high byte value for each character.

Returns: A string containing the current data stored in the output stream, with the high byte of each character set to `hibyte`.

writeByteArrayOutputStream

`public void write(byte b[], int off, int len)`

This method writes `len` bytes to the output stream from the byte array `b` beginning `off` bytes into the array.

Parameters:

`b`—the byte array from which the data is written.

`off`—the starting offset into the array for the data to be read from.

`len`—the number of bytes to write.

writeByteArrayOutputStream

`public void write(int b)`

This method writes a byte value to the output stream.

Parameters: `b`—the byte value to be written.

writeToByteArrayOutputStream

`public void writeTo(OutputStream out) throws IOException`

This method writes the contents of the underlying byte array to another output stream.

Parameters: `out`—the output stream to write to.

Throws: `IOException` if an I/O error occurs.

DataInputStream

Extends: `FilterInputStream`

Implements: `DataInput`

This class implements an input stream that can read Java primitive data types in a platform-independent manner.

DataInputStream **Constructor**

`public DataInputStream(InputStream in)`

This method creates a new data input stream to read data from the `in` input stream.

Parameters: `in`—the input stream to read data from.

read

```
public final int read(byte b[]) throws IOException
```

This method reads up to b.length bytes from the data input stream into the byte array b, blocking until all bytes are read.

Parameters: b—the byte array into which the data is read.

Returns: The actual number of bytes read, or -1 if the end of the stream is reached.

Throws: IOException if an I/O error occurs.

read

```
public final int read(byte b[], int off, int len) throws IOException
```

This method reads up to len bytes from the data input stream into the byte array b beginning off bytes into the array, blocking until all bytes are read.

Parameters:

b—the byte array into which the data is read.

off—the starting offset into the array for the data to be written to.

len—the maximum number of bytes to read.

Returns: The actual number of bytes read, or -1 if the end of the stream is reached.

Throws: IOException if an I/O error occurs.

readBoolean

```
public final boolean readBoolean() throws IOException
```

This method reads a boolean value (byte) from the data input stream, blocking until the byte is read. A value of 0 is interpreted as false, and all other values are interpreted as true.

Returns: The boolean value read.

Throws: EOFException if the end of the stream is reached before reading the value.

Throws: IOException if an I/O error occurs.

readByte

```
public final byte readByte() throws IOException
```

This method reads a signed byte (8-bit) value from the data input stream, blocking until the byte is read.

Returns: The byte value read.

Throws: EOFException if the end of the stream is reached before reading the value.

Throws: IOException if an I/O error occurs.

readChar

```
public final char readChar() throws IOException
```

This method reads a character (16-bit) value from the data input stream, blocking until both bytes are read.

Returns: The character value read.

Throws: EOFException if the end of the stream is reached before reading the value.

Throws: IOException if an I/O error occurs.

readDouble

```
public final double readDouble() throws IOException
```

This method reads a double (64-bit) value from the data input stream, blocking until all eight bytes are read.

Returns: The double value read.

Throws: EOFException if the end of the stream is reached before reading the value.

Throws: IOException if an I/O error occurs.

readFloat

```
public final float readFloat() throws IOException
```

This method reads a float (32-bit) value from the data input stream, blocking until all four bytes are read.

Returns: The float value read.

Throws: EOFException if the end of the stream is reached before reading the value.

Throws: IOException if an I/O error occurs.

readFully

```
public final void readFully(byte b[]) throws IOException
```

This method reads up to b.length bytes from the data input stream into the byte array b, blocking until all bytes are read.

Parameters: b—the byte array into which the data is read.

Throws: EOFException if the end of the stream is reached before reading the specified number of bytes.

Throws: IOException if an I/O error occurs.

readFully

```
public final void readFully(byte b[], int off, int len) throws IOException
```

This method reads up to len bytes from the data input stream into the byte array b beginning off bytes into the array, blocking until all bytes are read.

Parameters:

b—the byte array into which the data is read.

off—the starting offset into the array for the data to be written to.

len—the maximum number of bytes to read.

Throws: EOFException if the end of the stream is reached before reading the specified number of bytes.

Throws: IOException if an I/O error occurs.

readInt

```
public final int readInt() throws IOException
```

This method reads an integer (32-bit) value from the data input stream, blocking until all four bytes are read.

Returns: The integer value read.

Throws: EOFException if the end of the stream is reached before reading the value.

Throws: IOException if an I/O error occurs.

readLine

```
public final String readLine() throws IOException
```

This method reads a line of text from the data input stream, blocking until either a newline character ('\n') or a carriage return character ('\r') is read.

Returns: A string containing the line of text read.

Throws: EOFException if the end of the stream is reached before reading the line of text.

Throws: IOException if an I/O error occurs.

readLong

```
public final long readLong() throws IOException
```

This method reads a long (64-bit) value from the data input stream, blocking until all eight bytes are read.

Returns: The long value read.

Throws: EOFException if the end of the stream is reached before reading the value.

Throws: IOException if an I/O error occurs.

readShort

```
public final short readShort() throws IOException
```

This method reads a signed short (16-bit) value from the data input stream, blocking until both bytes are read.

Returns: The short value read.

Throws: EOFException if the end of the stream is reached before reading the value.

Throws: IOException if an I/O error occurs.

readUnsignedByte

```
public final int readUnsignedByte() throws IOException
```

This method reads an unsigned byte (8-bit) value from the data input stream, blocking until the byte is read.

Returns: The unsigned byte value read.

Throws: EOFException if the end of the stream is reached before reading the value.

Throws: IOException if an I/O error occurs.

readUnsignedShort

```
public final int readUnsignedShort() throws IOException
```

This method reads an unsigned short (16-bit) value from the data input stream, blocking until both bytes are read.

Returns: The unsigned short value read.

Throws: EOFException if the end of the stream is reached before reading the value.

Throws: IOException if an I/O error occurs.

readUTF

`public final String readUTF() throws IOException`

This method reads a string that has been encoded using a modified UTF-8 format from the data input stream, blocking until all bytes are read.

Returns: The string read.

Throws: EOFException if the end of the stream is reached before reading the string.

Throws: UTFDataFormatException if the bytes read do not represent a valid UTF-8 encoding of a string.

Throws: IOException if an I/O error occurs.

readUTF

`public final static String readUTF(DataInput in) throws IOException`

This method reads a string from the in data input stream that has been encoded using a modified UTF-8 format, blocking until all bytes are read.

Parameters: in—the data input stream to read the string from.

Returns: The string read.

Throws: EOFException if the end of the stream is reached before reading the string.

Throws: UTFDataFormatException if the bytes read do not represent a valid UTF-8 encoding of a string.

Throws: IOException if an I/O error occurs.

skipBytes

`public final int skipBytes(int n) throws IOException`

This method skips n bytes of data in the data input stream, blocking until all bytes are skipped.

Parameters: n—the number of bytes to skip.

Returns: The actual number of bytes skipped.

Throws: EOFException if the end of the stream is reached before skipping the specified number of bytes.

Throws: IOException if an I/O error occurs.

DataOutputStream

Extends: `FilterOutputStream`

Implements: `DataOutput`

This class implements an output stream that can write Java primitive data types in a platform-independent manner.

Member Variables

`protected int written`

This is the number of bytes written to the output stream thus far.

DataOutputStream **Constructor**

`public DataOutputStream(OutputStream out)`

This method creates a new data output stream to write data to the out output stream.

Parameters: out—the output stream to write data to.

flush

`public void flush() throws IOException`

This method flushes the data output stream, resulting in any buffered data being written to the underlying output stream.

Throws: IOException if an I/O error occurs.

size

`public final int size()`

This method returns the number of bytes written to the data output stream thus far, which is stored in the written member variable.

Returns: The number of bytes written to the data output stream thus far.

write

`public void write(byte b[], int off, int len) throws IOException`

This method writes len bytes to the data output stream from the byte array b beginning off bytes into the array.

Parameters:

b—the byte array from which the data is written.

off—the starting offset into the array for the data to be read from.

len—the number of bytes to write.

Throws: IOException if an I/O error occurs.

write

```
public void write(int b) throws IOException
```

This method writes a byte value to the data output stream.

Parameters:

b—the byte value to be written.

IOException if an I/O error occurs.

writeBoolean

```
public final void writeBoolean(boolean v) throws IOException
```

This method writes a boolean value to the data output stream. The boolean value true is written as the byte value 1, where false is written as the byte value 0.

Parameters: v—the boolean value to be written.

Throws: IOException if an I/O error occurs.

writeByte

```
public final void writeByte(int v) throws IOException
```

This method writes a byte (8-bit) value to the data output stream.

Parameters: v—the byte value to be written.

Throws: IOException if an I/O error occurs.

writeBytes

```
public final void writeBytes(String s) throws IOException
```

This method writes a string to the data output stream as a sequence of bytes.

Parameters: s—the string to be written as bytes.

Throws: IOException if an I/O error occurs.

writeChar

```
public final void writeChar(int v) throws IOException
```

This method writes a character (16-bit) value to the data output stream.

Parameters: v—the character value to be written.

Throws: IOException if an I/O error occurs.

writeChars

```
public final void writeChars(String s) throws IOException
```

This method writes a string to the data output stream as a sequence of characters.

Parameters: s—the string to be written as characters.

Throws: IOException if an I/O error occurs.

writeDouble

```
public final void writeDouble(double v) throws IOException
```

This method writes a double (64-bit) value to the data output stream.

Parameters: v—the double value to be written.

Throws: IOException if an I/O error occurs.

writeFloat

```
public final void writeFloat(float v) throws IOException
```

This method writes a float (32-bit) value to the data output stream.

Parameters: v—the float value to be written.

Throws: IOException if an I/O error occurs.

writeInt

```
public final void writeInt(int v) throws IOException
```

This method writes an integer (32-bit) value to the data output stream.

Parameters: v—the integer value to be written.

Throws: IOException if an I/O error occurs.

writeLong

```
public final void writeLong(long v) throws IOException
```

This method writes a long (64-bit) value to the data output stream.

Parameters: v—the long value to be written.

Throws: IOException if an I/O error occurs.

writeShort

```
public final void writeShort(int v) throws IOException
```

This method writes a short (16-bit) value to the data output stream.

Parameters: v—the short value to be written.

Throws: IOException if an I/O error occurs.

writeUTF

```
public final void writeUTF(String str) throws IOException
```

This method encodes a string using a modified UTF-8 format and writes it to the data output stream.

Parameters: str—the string to be written.

Throws: IOException if an I/O error occurs.

File

Extends: Object

This class implements a filename in a platform-independent manner. The File class provides the functionality necessary to work with filenames and directories without having to deal with the complexities associated with filenames on a particular platform.

Member Variables

```
public final static String pathSeparator
```

This is the platform-specific path separator string.

```
public final static char pathSeparatorChar
```

This is the platform-specific path separator character, which separates filenames in a path list.

```
public final static String separator
```

This is the platform-specific file separator string.

```
public final static char separatorChar
```

This is the platform-specific file separator character, which separates the file and directory components in a filename.

File **Constructor**

```
public File(File dir, String name)
```

This constructor creates a filename of an underlying file based on the specified directory and filename. If no directory is specified in the dir argument, the constructor assumes the file is in the current directory.

Parameters:

dir—the directory where the file is located.

name—the filename.

File **Constructor**

```
public File(String path)
```

This constructor creates a filename of an underlying file based on the specified file path.

Parameters: path—the file path.

Throws: NullPointerException if the file path is null.

File **Constructor**

```
public File(String path, String name)
```

This constructor creates a filename of an underlying file based on the specified path and filename.

Parameters: path—the path where the file is located.

Parameters: name—the filename.

canRead

```
public boolean canRead()
```

This method determines if the underlying file can be read from. In other words, if the file is readable canRead determines if the file exists.

Returns: `true` if the file can be read from; `false` otherwise.

Throws: `SecurityException` if the application doesn't have read access to the file.

canWrite

`public boolean canWrite()`

This method determines if the underlying file can be written to. In other words, if the file is writable `canWrite` determines if the file exists.

Returns: `true` if the file can be written to; `false` otherwise.

Throws: `SecurityException` if the application doesn't have write access to the file.

delete

`public boolean delete()`

This method deletes the underlying file.

Returns: `true` if the file is deleted; `false` otherwise.

Throws: `SecurityException` if the application doesn't have access to delete the file.

equals

`public boolean equals(Object obj)`

This method compares the pathname of the `obj` `File` object to the pathname of the underlying file.

Parameters: `obj`—the object to compare with.

Returns: `true` if the pathnames are equal; `false` otherwise.

exists

`public boolean exists()`

This method determines if the underlying file exists by opening it for reading and then closing it.

Returns: `true` if the file exists; `false` otherwise.

Throws: `SecurityException` if the application doesn't have read access to the file.

getAbsolutePath

```
public String getAbsolutePath()
```

This method determines the platform-specific absolute pathname of the underlying file.

Returns: The absolute pathname of the file.

getName

```
public String getName()
```

This method determines the filename of the underlying file, which doesn't include any path information.

Returns: The filename of the file.

getParent

```
public String getParent()
```

This method determines the parent directory of the underlying file, which is the immediate directory where the file is located.

Returns: The parent directory of the file, or null if the file is located in the root directory.

getPath

```
public String getPath()
```

This method determines the pathname of the underlying file.

Returns: The pathname of the file.

hashCode

```
public int hashCode()
```

This method calculates a hash code for the underlying file.

Returns: A hash code for the file.

isAbsolute

```
public boolean isAbsolute()
```

This method determines if this object represents an absolute pathname for the underlying file. Note that absolute pathnames are platform specific.

Returns: true if the pathname for the file is absolute; false otherwise.

isDirectory

```
public boolean isDirectory()
```

This method determines if the underlying file is actually a directory.

Returns: true if the file is actually a directory; false otherwise.

Throws: SecurityException if the application doesn't have read access to the file.

isFile

```
public boolean isFile()
```

This method determines if the underlying file is a normal file; i.e. not a directory.

Returns: true if the file is a normal file; false otherwise.

Throws: SecurityException if the application doesn't have read access to the file.

lastModified

```
public long lastModified()
```

This method determines the last modification time of the underlying file. Note that this time is system-specific and is not absolute; in other words, only use the time to compare against other times retrieved using this method.

Returns: The last modification time of the file, or 0 if the file doesn't exist.

Throws: SecurityException if the application doesn't have read access to the file.

length

```
public long length()
```

This method determines the length in bytes of the underlying file.

Returns: The length of the file in bytes.

Throws: SecurityException if the application doesn't have read access to the file.

list

```
public String[] list()
```

This method builds a list of the filenames located in the directory represented by this object. Note that the underlying file must actually be a directory for this method to work.

Returns: An array containing the filenames located in the directory.

Throws: SecurityException if the application doesn't have read access to the file.

list

```
public String[] list(FilenameFilter filter)
```

This method builds a list of the filenames located in the directory represented by this object using the specified filename filter. Note that the underlying file must actually be a directory for this method to work.

Parameters: filter—the filename filter used to select the filenames.

Returns: An array containing the filtered filenames located in the directory.

Throws: SecurityException if the application doesn't have read access to the file.

mkdir

```
public boolean mkdir()
```

This method creates a directory based on the pathname specified by this object.

Returns: true if the directory is created; false otherwise.

Throws: SecurityException if the application doesn't have write access to the file.

mkdirs

```
public boolean mkdirs()
```

This method creates a directory based on the pathname specified by this object, including all necessary parent directories.

Returns: true if the directory (or directories) is created; false otherwise.

Throws: SecurityException if the application doesn't have write access to the file.

renameTo

```
public boolean renameTo(File dest)
```

This method renames the underlying file to the filename specified by the dest file object.

Parameters: dest—the new filename.

Returns: true if the file is renamed; false otherwise.

Throws: SecurityException if the application doesn't have write access to both the underlying file and the file represented by the dest file object.

toString

```
public String toString()
```

This method determines a string representation of the pathname for the underlying file.

Returns: A string representing the pathname of the file.

FileDescriptor

Extends: Object

This class implements a handle to a platform-specific file or socket structure. FileDescriptor objects are primarily used internally by the Java system and are never created by an application directly.

Member Variables

```
public final static FileDescriptor err
```

This is a handle to the standard error stream.

```
public final static FileDescriptor in
```

This is a handle to the standard input stream.

```
public final static FileDescriptor out
```

This is a handle to the standard output stream.

FileDescriptor Constructor

```
public FileDescriptor()
```

This constructor creates a default FileDescriptor object.

valid

```
public boolean valid()
```

This method determines whether this object represents a valid open file or socket.

Returns: true if the underlying file or socket is valid; false otherwise.

FileInputStream

Extends: InputStream

This class implements an input stream for reading data from a file or file descriptor.

FileInputStream **Constructor**

public FileInputStream(File file) throws FileNotFoundException

This constructor creates a file input stream to read data from the specified file.

Parameters: file—the file to be opened for reading.

Throws: FileNotFoundException if the file is not found.

Throws: SecurityException if the application doesn't have read access to the file.

FileInputStream **Constructor**

public FileInputStream(FileDescriptor fdObj)

This constructor creates a file input stream to read data from the file represented by the specified file descriptor.

Parameters: fdObj—the file descriptor representing the file to be opened for reading.

Throws: SecurityException if the application doesn't have read access to the file.

FileInputStream **Constructor**

public FileInputStream(String name) throws FileNotFoundException

This constructor creates a file input stream to read data from the file with the specified filename.

Parameters: name—the filename of the file to be opened for reading.

Throws: FileNotFoundException if the file is not found.

Throws: SecurityException if the application doesn't have read access to the file.

available

public int available() throws IOException

This method determines the number of bytes that can be read from the file input stream without blocking.

Returns: The number of available bytes.

Throws: IOException if an I/O error occurs.

close

```
public void close() throws IOException
```

This method closes the file input stream, releasing any resources associated with the stream.

Throws: IOException if an I/O error occurs.

finalize

```
protected void finalize() throws IOException
```

This method makes sure the close method is called when the file input stream is cleaned up by the Java garbage collector.

Throws: IOException if an I/O error occurs.

getFD

```
public final FileDescriptor getFD() throws IOException
```

This method determines the file descriptor associated with the file input stream.

Returns: The file descriptor associated with the stream.

Throws: IOException if an I/O error occurs.

read

```
public int read() throws IOException
```

This method reads a byte value from the file input stream, blocking until the byte is read.

Returns: An integer representing the byte value read, or -1 if the end of the stream is reached.

Throws: IOException if an I/O error occurs.

read

```
public int read(byte b[]) throws IOException
```

This method reads up to b.length bytes from the file input stream into the byte array b, blocking until all bytes are read.

Parameters: b—the byte array into which the data is read.

Returns: The actual number of bytes read, or -1 if the end of the stream is reached.

Throws: IOException if an I/O error occurs.

read

```
public int read(byte b[], int off, int len) throws IOException
```

This method reads up to len bytes from the file input stream into the byte array b beginning off bytes into the array, blocking until all bytes are read.

Parameters:

b—the byte array into which the data is read.

off—the starting offset into the array for the data to be written to.

len—the maximum number of bytes to read.

Returns: The actual number of bytes read, or -1 if the end of the stream is reached.

Throws: IOException if an I/O error occurs.

skip

```
public long skip(long n) throws IOException
```

This method skips n bytes of data in the file input stream.

Parameters: n—the number of bytes to skip.

Returns: The actual number of bytes skipped.

Throws: IOException if an I/O error occurs.

FileOutputStream

Extends: OutputStream

This class implements an output stream for writing data to a file or file descriptor.

FileOutputStream

```
public FileOutputStream(File file) throws IOException
```

This constructor creates a file output stream to write data to the specified file.

FilterInputStream

Extends: `InputStream`

This class defines an input stream filter that can be used to filter data on an underlying input stream. Most of the methods defined in `FilterInputStream` simply call corresponding methods in the underlying input stream. You simply override appropriate methods to provide the filtering functionality. `FilterInputStream` serves as the basis for all other input stream filter implementations. Derived filtered input streams can be chained together to provide complex filtering operations.

Member Variables

`protected InputStream in`

This is the underlying input stream that is being filtered.

FilterInputStream **Constructor**

`protected FilterInputStream(InputStream in)`

This constructor creates a filtered input stream based on the specified underlying input stream.

Parameters: in—the input stream to be filtered.

available

`public int available() throws IOException`

This method determines the number of bytes that can be read from the filtered input stream without blocking.

Returns: The number of available bytes.

Throws: `IOException` if an I/O error occurs.

close

`public void close() throws IOException`

This method closes the filtered input stream, releasing any resources associated with the stream.

Throws: `IOException` if an I/O error occurs.

mark

`public void mark(int readlimit)`

This method marks the current read position in the filtered input stream. The `reset` method can be used to reset the read position to this mark; subsequent reads will read data beginning at the mark position. The mark position is invalidated after `readlimit` bytes have been read.

Parameters: `readlimit`—the maximum number of bytes that can be read before the mark position becomes invalid.

markSupported

`public boolean markSupported()`

This method determines if the filtered input stream supports the `mark` and `reset` methods.

Returns: `true` if the `mark` and `reset` methods are supported; `false` otherwise.

read

`public int read() throws IOException`

This method reads a byte value from the filtered input stream, blocking until the byte is read.

Returns: An integer representing the byte value read, or `-1` if the end of the stream is reached.

Throws: `IOException` if an I/O error occurs.

read

`public int read(byte b[]) throws IOException`

This method reads up to `b.length` bytes from the filtered input stream into the byte array `b`, blocking until all bytes are read.

Parameters: `b`—the byte array into which the data is read.

Returns: The actual number of bytes read, or `-1` if the end of the stream is reached.

Throws: `IOException` if an I/O error occurs.

read

`public int read(byte b[], int off, int len) throws IOException`

This method reads up to `len` bytes from the filtered input stream into the byte array `b` beginning `off` bytes into the array, blocking until all bytes are read.

Parameters:

b—the byte array into which the data is read.

off—the starting offset into the array for the data to be written to.

len—the maximum number of bytes to read.

Returns: The actual number of bytes read, or -1 if the end of the stream is reached.

Throws: IOException if an I/O error occurs.

reset

```
public void reset() throws IOException
```

This method resets the read position in the input stream to the current mark position, as set by the mark method.

Throws: IOException if the stream has not been marked or if the mark is invalid.

skip

```
public long skip(long n) throws IOException
```

This method skips n bytes of data in the input stream.

Parameters: n—the number of bytes to skip.

Returns: The actual number of bytes skipped.

Throws: IOException if an I/O error occurs.

FilterOutputStream

Extends: OutputStream

This class defines an output stream filter that can be used to filter data on an underlying output stream. Most of the methods defined in FilterOutputStream simply call corresponding methods in the underlying output stream. You simply override appropriate methods to provide the filtering functionality. FilterOutputStream serves as the basis for all other output stream filter implementations. Derived filtered output streams can be chained together to provide complex filtering operations.

Member Variables

`protected OutputStream out`

This is the underlying output stream that is being filtered.

FilterOutputStream

`public FilterOutputStream(OutputStream out)`

This constructor creates a filtered output stream based on the specified underlying output stream.

Parameters: out—the output stream to be filtered.

close

`public void close() throws IOException`

This method closes the filtered output stream, releasing any resources associated with the stream.

Throws: IOException if an I/O error occurs.

flush

`public void flush() throws IOException`

This method flushes the filtered output stream, resulting in any buffered data being written to the underlying output stream.

Throws: IOException if an I/O error occurs.

write

`public void write(byte b[]) throws IOException`

This method writes b.length bytes to the filtered output stream from the byte array b.

Parameters: b—the byte array from which the data is written.

Throws: IOException if an I/O error occurs.

write

`public void write(byte b[], int off, int len) throws IOException`

This method writes len bytes to the filtered output stream from the byte array b beginning off bytes into the array, blocking until all bytes are written.

Parameters:

b—the byte array from which the data is written.

off—the starting offset into the array for the data to be read from.

len—the number of bytes to write.

Throws: IOException if an I/O error occurs.

write

```
public void write(int b) throws IOException
```

This method writes a byte value to the buffered output stream.

Parameters: b—the byte value to be written.

Throws: IOException if an I/O error occurs.

InputStream

Extends: Object

This class is an abstract class representing an input stream of bytes. All input streams are based on InputStream.

InputStream **Constructor**

```
public InputStream()
```

This constructor creates a default input stream.

available

```
public int available() throws IOException
```

This method determines the number of bytes that can be read from the input stream without blocking. This method should be overridden in all subclasses, as it returns 0 in InputStream.

Returns: The number of available bytes.

Throws: IOException if an I/O error occurs.

close

`public void close() throws IOException`

This method closes the input stream, releasing any resources associated with the stream. This method should usually be overridden in subclasses, as it does nothing in InputStream.

Throws: IOException if an I/O error occurs.

mark

`public void mark(int readlimit)`

This method marks the current read position in the input stream. The reset method can be used to reset the read position to this mark; subsequent reads will read data beginning at the mark position. The mark position is invalidated after readlimit bytes have been read. This method should usually be overridden in subclasses, as it does nothing in InputStream.

Parameters: readlimit—the maximum number of bytes that can be read before the mark position becomes invalid.

markSupported

`public boolean markSupported()`

This method determines if the input stream supports the mark and reset methods. This method should usually be overridden in subclasses, as it always returns false in InputStream.

Returns: true if the mark and reset methods are supported; false otherwise.

read

`public abstract int read() throws IOException`

This method reads a byte value from the input stream, blocking until the byte is read. This method must be overridden in all subclasses, as it is defined as abstract in InputStream.

Returns: An integer representing the byte value read, or -1 if the end of the stream is reached.

Throws: IOException if an I/O error occurs.

read

`public int read(byte b[]) throws IOException`

This method reads up to b.length bytes from the input stream into the byte array b, blocking until all bytes are read. This method actually calls the three-parameter version of read passing b, 0, and b.length as the parameters.

Parameters: b—the byte array into which the data is read.

Returns: The actual number of bytes read, or -1 if the end of the stream is reached.

Throws: IOException if an I/O error occurs.

read

```
public int read(byte b[], int off, int len) throws IOException
```

This method reads up to len bytes from the input stream into the byte array b beginning off bytes into the array, blocking until all bytes are read. This method actually reads each byte by calling the read method that takes no parameters. Subclasses should provide a more efficient implementation of this method that isn't reliant on the other read method if possible.

Parameters:

b—the byte array into which the data is read.

off—the starting offset into the array for the data to be written to.

len—the maximum number of bytes to read.

Returns: The actual number of bytes read, or -1 if the end of the stream is reached.

Throws: IOException if an I/O error occurs.

reset

```
public void reset() throws IOException
```

This method resets the read position in the input stream to the current mark position, as set by the mark method. This method should be overridden in subclasses requiring mark/reset functionality, as it always throws an IOException in InputStream; this is a result of the fact that input streams don't support mark/reset functionality by default.

Throws: IOException if the stream has not been marked or if the mark is invalid.

skip

```
public long skip(long n) throws IOException
```

This method skips n bytes of data in the input stream. This method should usually be overridden with a more efficient version in subclasses, as it reads skipped data into a temporary byte array in InputStream.

Parameters: n—the number of bytes to skip.

Returns: The actual number of bytes skipped.

Throws: IOException if an I/O error occurs.

LineNumberInputStream

Extends: FilterInputStream

This class implements an input stream that keeps track of how many lines have passed through the stream. A line is defined as a sequence of bytes followed by either a carriage return character (`'\r'`), a newline character (`'\n'`), or a carriage return character immediately followed by a newline character. In all three cases, the new line is interpreted as a single character.

LineNumberInputStream **Constructor**

```
public LineNumberInputStream(InputStream in)
```

This constructor creates a line number input stream that counts lines based on the specified input stream.

Parameters: in—the input stream to count lines from.

available

```
public int available() throws IOException
```

This method determines the number of bytes that can be read from the input stream without blocking. Note that this number could be as little as half as large as that of the underlying stream, since LineNumberInputStream combines carriage return/newline character pairs into a single new line byte.

Returns: The number of available bytes.

getLineNumber

```
public int getLineNumber()
```

This method determines the current line number for the input stream, which is the count of how many lines the stream has processed.

Returns: The current line number.

mark

```
public void mark(int readlimit)
```

This method marks the current read position in the input stream. The reset method can be used to reset the read position to this mark; subsequent reads will read data beginning at the mark position. The mark position is invalidated after readlimit bytes have been read. mark makes sure to store away the current line number so it isn't invalidated by a subsequent call to reset.

Parameters: readlimit—the maximum number of bytes that can be read before the mark position becomes invalid.

read

```
public int read() throws IOException
```

This method reads a byte value from the input stream, blocking until the byte is read.

Returns: An integer representing the byte value read, or -1 if the end of the stream is reached.

Throws: IOException if an I/O error occurs.

read

```
public int read(byte b[], int off, int len) throws IOException
```

This method reads up to len bytes from the input stream into the byte array b beginning off bytes into the array, blocking until all bytes are read.

Parameters:

b—the byte array into which the data is read.

off—the starting offset into the array for the data to be written to.

len—the maximum number of bytes to read.

Returns: The actual number of bytes read, or -1 if the end of the stream is reached.

Throws: IOException if an I/O error occurs.

reset

```
public void reset() throws IOException
```

This method resets the read position in the input stream to the current mark position, as set by the mark method. The current line number is reset to the value it held when the mark method was called.

setLineNumber

`public void setLineNumber(int lineNumber)`

This method sets the current line number to the specified line number.

Parameters: lineNumber—the new line number to be set.

skip

`public long skip(long n) throws IOException`

This method skips n bytes of data in the input stream.

Parameters: n—the number of bytes to skip.

Returns: The actual number of bytes skipped.

Throws: IOException if an I/O error occurs.

OutputStream

Extends: Object

This class is an abstract class representing an output stream of bytes. All output streams are based on OutputStream.

OutputStream **Constructor**

`public OutputStream()`

This constructor creates a default output stream.

close

`public void close() throws IOException`

This method closes the output stream, releasing any resources associated with the stream. This method should usually be overridden in subclasses, as it does nothing in OutputStream.

Throws: IOException if an I/O error occurs.

flush

```
public void flush() throws IOException
```

This method flushes the output stream, resulting in any buffered data being written to the underlying output stream. This method should usually be overridden in subclasses, as it does nothing in OutputStream.

Throws: IOException if an I/O error occurs.

write

```
public void write(byte b[]) throws IOException
```

This method writes b.length bytes to the output stream from the byte array b. This method actually calls the three-parameter version of write passing b, 0, and b.length as the parameters.

Parameters: b—the byte array from which the data is written.

Throws: IOException if an I/O error occurs.

write

```
public void write(byte b[], int off, int len) throws IOException
```

This method writes len bytes to the output stream from the byte array b beginning off bytes into the array. This method actually writes each byte by calling the write method that takes one parameter. Subclasses should provide a more efficient implementation of this method that isn't reliant on the other write method if possible.

Parameters:

b—the byte array from which the data is written.

off—the starting offset into the array for the data to be read from.

len—the number of bytes to write.

Throws: IOException if an I/O error occurs.

write

```
public abstract void write(int b) throws IOException
```

This method writes a byte value to the output stream. This method must be overridden in all subclasses, as it is defined as abstract in OutputStream.

Parameters: b—the byte value to be written.

Throws: IOException if an I/O error occurs.

PipedInputStream

Extends: InputStream

This class implements a piped input stream, which acts as the receiving end of a communications pipe. Piped input streams must be connected to a piped output stream to receive data. In other words, a piped output stream must be used to send the data received by a piped input stream.

PipedInputStream **Constructor**

public PipedInputStream()

This constructor creates a piped input stream that isn't connected to anything. The stream must be connected to a piped output stream via the connect method before it can be used.

PipedInputStream **Constructor**

public PipedInputStream(PipedOutputStream src) throws IOException

This constructor creates a piped input stream that is connected to the specified piped output stream.

Parameters: src—the piped output stream to connect to.

Throws: IOException if an I/O error occurs.

close

public void close() throws IOException

This method closes the piped input stream, releasing any resources associated with the stream.

Throws: IOException if an I/O error occurs.

connect

public void connect(PipedOutputStream src) throws IOException

This method connects the input stream to the specified piped output stream.

Parameters: src—the piped output stream to connect to.

Throws: IOException if an I/O error occurs.

read

```
public int read() throws IOException
```

This method reads a byte value from the piped input stream, blocking until the byte is read.

Returns: An integer representing the byte value read, or -1 if the end of the stream is reached.

Throws: IOException if an I/O error occurs.

read

```
public int read(byte b[], int off, int len) throws IOException
```

This method reads up to len bytes from the piped input stream into the byte array b beginning off bytes into the array, blocking until all bytes are read.

Parameters:

b—the byte array into which the data is read.

off—the starting offset into the array for the data to be written to.

len—the maximum number of bytes to read.

Returns: The actual number of bytes read, or -1 if the end of the stream is reached.

Throws: IOException if an I/O error occurs.

PipedOutputStream

Extends: OutputStream

This class implements a piped output stream, which acts as the sending end of a communications pipe. Piped output streams must be connected to a piped input stream to send data. In other words, a piped input stream must be used to receive the data sent by a piped output stream.

PipedOutputStream **Constructor**

```
public PipedOutputStream()
```

This constructor creates a piped output stream that isn't connected to anything. The stream must be connected to a piped input stream via the connect method before it can be used.

`PipedOutputStream` **Constructor**

`public PipedOutputStream(PipedInputStream snk) throws IOException`

This constructor creates a piped output stream that is connected to the specified piped input stream.

Parameters: snk—the piped input stream to connect to.

Throws: IOException if an I/O error occurs.

close

`public void close() throws IOException`

This method closes the piped output stream, releasing any resources associated with the stream.

Throws: IOException if an I/O error occurs.

connect

`public void connect(PipedInputStream snk) throws IOException`

This method connects the output stream to the specified piped input stream.

Parameters: snk—the piped input stream to connect to.

Throws: IOException if an I/O error occurs.

write

`public void write(byte b[], int off, int len) throws IOException`

This method writes len bytes to the piped output stream from the byte array b beginning off bytes into the array.

Parameters:

b—the byte array from which the data is written.

off—the starting offset into the array for the data to be read from.

len—the number of bytes to write.

Throws: IOException if an I/O error occurs.

write

```
public void write(int b) throws IOException
```

This method writes a byte value to the piped output stream.

Parameters: b—the byte value to be written.

Throws: IOException if an I/O error occurs.

PrintStream

Extends: FilterOutputStream

This class implements an output stream that has additional methods for printing basic types of data. You can set up the stream so that it is flushed every time a newline character ('\n') is written. Note that only the lower 8 bits of any 16-bit value are printed to the stream.

PrintStream **Constructor**

```
public PrintStream(OutputStream out)
```

This constructor creates a print stream that writes data to the specified underlying output stream.

Parameters: out—the output stream to be written to.

PrintStream **Constructor**

```
public PrintStream(OutputStream out, boolean autoflush)
```

This constructor creates a print stream that writes data to the specified underlying output stream, with an option of flushing its output each time a newline character ('\n') is encountered.

Parameters:

out—the output stream to be written to.

autoflush—a boolean value specifying whether the stream is flushed when a newline character is encountered.

checkError

```
public boolean checkError()
```

This method flushes the underlying output stream and determines whether an error has occurred on the stream. Note that errors are cumulative, meaning that once an error is encountered, checkError will continue to return true on all successive calls.

Returns: true if the print stream has ever encountered an error on the underlying output stream; false otherwise.

```
public void close()
```

This method closes the print stream, releasing any resources associated with the underlying output stream.

flush

```
public void flush()
```

This method flushes the print stream, resulting in any buffered data being written to the underlying output stream.

print

```
public void print(boolean b)
```

This method prints the string representation of a boolean value to the underlying output stream. If the boolean value is true, the string "true" is printed; otherwise, the string "false" is printed.

Parameters: b—the boolean value to be printed.

print

```
public void print(char c)
```

This method prints the lower 8 bits of a character value to the underlying output stream.

Parameters: c—the character value to be printed.

print

```
public void print(char s[])
```

This method prints the lower 8 bits of each character value in an array of characters to the underlying output stream.

Parameters: s—the array of characters to be printed.

print

`public void print(double d)`

This method prints the string representation of a double value to the underlying output stream. Note that the string representation is the same as that returned by the toString method of the Double class.

Parameters: d—the double value to be printed.

print

`public void print(float f)`

This method prints the string representation of a float value to the underlying output stream. Note that the string representation is the same as that returned by the toString method of the Float class.

Parameters: f—the float value to be printed.

print

`public void print(int i)`

This method prints the string representation of an integer value to the underlying output stream. Note that the string representation is the same as that returned by the toString method of the Integer class.

Parameters: i—the integer value to be printed.

print

`public void print(long l)`

This method prints the string representation of a long value to the underlying output stream. Note that the string representation is the same as that returned by the toString method of the Long class.

Parameters: l—the long value to be printed.

print

`public void print(Object obj)`

This method prints the string representation of an object to the underlying output stream. Note that the string representation is the same as that returned by the toString method of the object.

Parameters: obj—the object to be printed.

print

`public void print(String s)`

This method prints the lower 8 bits of each character in a string to the underlying output stream. If the string is null, the string `"null"` is printed.

Parameters: s—the string to be printed.

println

`public void println()`

This method prints the newline character (`'\n'`) to the underlying output stream.

println

`public void println(boolean b)`

This method prints the string representation of a boolean value to the underlying output stream, followed by a newline character (`'\n'`). If the boolean value is true, the string `"true"` is printed; otherwise, the string `"false"` is printed.

Parameters: b—the boolean value to be printed.

println

`public void println(char c)`

This method prints the lower 8 bits of a character value to the underlying output stream, followed by a newline character.

Parameters: c—the character value to be printed

println

`public void println(char s[])`

This method prints the lower 8 bits of each character value in an array of characters to the underlying output stream, followed by a newline character.

Parameters: s—the array of characters to be printed.

println

```
public void println(double d)
```

This method prints the string representation of a double value to the underlying output stream, followed by a newline character. Note that the string representation is the same as that returned by the toString method of the Double class.

Parameters: d—the double value to be printed.

println

```
public void println(float f)
```

This method prints the string representation of a float value to the underlying output stream, followed by a newline character. Note that the string representation is the same as that returned by the toString method of the Float class.

Parameters: f—the float value to be printed.

println

```
public void println(int i)
```

This method prints the string representation of an integer value to the underlying output stream, followed by a newline character. Note that the string representation is the same as that returned by the toString method of the Integer class.

Parameters: i—the integer value to be printed.

println

```
public void println(long l)
```

This method prints the string representation of a long value to the underlying output stream, followed by a newline character. Note that the string representation is the same as that returned by the toString method of the Long class.

Parameters: l—the long value to be printed.

println

```
public void println(Object obj)
```

This method prints the string representation of an object to the underlying output stream, followed by a newline character. Note that the string representation is the same as that returned by the toString method of the object.

Parameters: obj—the object to be printed.

println

```
public void println(String s)
```

This method prints the lower 8 bits of each character in a string to the underlying output stream, followed by a newline character. If the string is null, the string "null" is printed.

Parameters: s—the string to be printed.

write

```
public void write(byte b[], int off, int len)
```

This method writes len bytes to the underlying output stream from the byte array b beginning off bytes into the array.

Parameters:

b—the byte array from which the data is written.

off—the starting offset into the array for the data to be read from.

len—the number of bytes to write.

write

```
public void write(int b)
```

This method writes a byte value to the underlying output stream. The write method of the underlying output stream is actually called to write the byte value. Additionally, if the byte represents the newline character ('\n') and autoflush is turned on, the flush method is called.

If an IOException is thrown while writing the byte, the exception is caught and an internal error flag is set; this flag can be checked by calling the checkError method. This technique is used to alleviate having to use a try-catch clause every time you want to print something.

Parameters: b—the byte value to be written.

Throws: IOException if an I/O error occurs.

PushbackInputStream

Extends: FilterInputStream

This class implements a input stream filter that provides a one byte push back buffer. Using the PushbackInputStream class, an application can push the last byte read back into the stream so it will be re-read the next time the read method is called. This functionality is sometimes useful in situations where byte-delimited data is being read; the delimited bytes can be pushed back into the stream so the next read operation will read them.

Member Variables

`protected int pushBack`

This is the push back buffer containing the character that was pushed back. A value of -1 indicates that the push back buffer is empty.

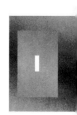

PushbackInputStream **Constructor**

`public PushbackInputStream(InputStream in)`

This constructor creates a push back input stream using the specified underlying input stream.

Parameters: in—the input stream to use the push back filter on.

available

`public int available() throws IOException`

This method determines the number of bytes that can be read from the push back input stream without blocking.

Returns: The number of available bytes.

Throws: IOException if an I/O error occurs.

markSupported

`public boolean markSupported()`

This method determines if the push back input stream supports the mark and reset methods.

Returns: true if the mark and reset methods are supported; false otherwise.

read

`public int read() throws IOException`

This method reads a byte value from the push back input stream, blocking until the byte is read. The read method actually returns the push back character if there is one, and calls the underlying input stream's read method if not.

Returns: An integer representing the byte value read, or -1 if the end of the stream is reached.

Throws: IOException if an I/O error occurs.

read

```
public int read(byte bytes[], int off, int len) throws IOException
```

This method reads up to `len` bytes from the buffered input stream into the byte array `bytes` beginning `off` bytes into the array, blocking until all bytes are read.

Parameters:

`bytes`—the byte array into which the data is read.

`off`—the starting offset into the array for the data to be written to.

`len`—the maximum number of bytes to read.

Returns: The actual number of bytes read, or `-1` if the end of the stream is reached.

Throws: `IOException` if an I/O error occurs.

unread

```
public void unread(int ch) throws IOException
```

This method pushes a character back into the stream so that it is read the next time the `read` method is called. Note that there can only be one push back character, meaning that multiple calls to `unread` without matching calls to `read` will result in an `IOException` being thrown.

Parameters: `ch`—the character to push back into the stream.

Throws: `IOException` if an attempt is made to push back more than one character.

RandomAccessFile

Extends: `Object`

Implements: `DataOutput`, `DataInput`

This class implements a random access file stream, providing functionality for both reading from and writing to random access files.

RandomAccessFile **Constructor**

```
public RandomAccessFile(String name, String mode) throws IOException
```

This constructor creates a random access file stream based on the file with the specified filename and access mode. There are two supported access modes: Mode `"r"` is for read-only files and mode `"rw"` is for read/write files.

Parameters:

name—the filename of the file to access.

mode—the access mode.

Throws: IOException if an I/O error occurs.

Throws: IllegalArgumentException if the access mode is not equal to "r" or "rw".

Throws: SecurityException if the access mode is "r" and the application doesn't have read access to the file, or if the access mode is "rw" and the application doesn't have both read and write access to the file.

RandomAccessFile **Constructor**

```
public RandomAccessFile(File file, String mode) throws IOException
```

This constructor creates a random access file stream based on the specified file and access mode. There are two supported access modes: mode "r" is for read-only files and mode "rw" is for read/write files.

Parameters:

file—the file to access.

mode—the access mode.

Throws: IOException if an I/O error occurs.

Throws: IllegalArgumentException if the access mode is not equal to "r" or "rw".

Throws: SecurityException if the access mode is "r" and the application doesn't have read access to the file, or if the access mode is "rw" and the application doesn't have both read and write access to the file.

close

```
public void close() throws IOException
```

This method closes the random access file stream, releasing any resources associated with the stream.

Throws: IOException if an I/O error occurs.

getFD

`public final FileDescriptor getFD() throws IOException`

This method determines the file descriptor associated with the random access file stream.

Returns: The file descriptor associated with the stream.

Throws: IOException if an I/O error occurs.

getFilePointer

`public long getFilePointer() throws IOException`

This method determines the current read/write position in bytes of the random access file stream, which is the offset of the read/write position from the beginning of the stream.

Returns: The current read/write position of the stream.

Throws: IOException if an I/O error occurs.

length

`public long length() throws IOException`

This method determines the length in bytes of the underlying file.

Returns: The length of the underlying file.

Throws: IOException if an I/O error occurs.

read

`public int read() throws IOException`

This method reads a byte value from the random access file stream, blocking until the byte is read.

Returns: An integer representing the byte value read, or -1 if the end of the stream is reached.

Throws: IOException if an I/O error occurs.

read

`public int read(byte b[]) throws IOException`

This method reads up to b.length bytes from the random access file stream into the byte array b, blocking until at least one byte is available.

Parameters: b—the byte array into which the data is read.

Returns: The total number of bytes read, or -1 if the end of the stream is reached.

Throws: IOException if an I/O error occurs.

read

`public int read(byte b[], int off, int len) throws IOException`

This method reads up to len bytes from the random access file stream into the byte array b beginning off bytes into the array, blocking until at least one byte is available.

Parameters:

b—the byte array into which the data is read.

off—the starting offset into the array for the data to be written to.

len—the maximum number of bytes to read.

Returns: The total number of bytes read, or -1 if the end of the stream is reached.

Throws: IOException if an I/O error occurs.

readBoolean

`public final boolean readBoolean() throws IOException`

This method reads a boolean value (byte) from the random access file stream. A value of 0 is interpreted as false, while all other values are interpreted as true.

Returns: The boolean value read.

Throws: EOFException if the end of the stream is reached before reading the value.

Throws: IOException if an I/O error occurs.

readByte

`public final byte readByte() throws IOException`

This method reads a signed byte (8-bit) value from the random access file stream, blocking until the byte is read.

Returns: The byte value read.

Throws: EOFException if the end of the stream is reached before reading the value.

Throws: IOException if an I/O error occurs.

readChar

```
public final char readChar() throws IOException
```

This method reads a character (16-bit) value from the random access file stream, blocking until both bytes are read.

Returns: The character value read.

Throws: EOFException if the end of the stream is reached before reading the value.

Throws: IOException if an I/O error occurs.

readDouble

```
public final double readDouble() throws IOException
```

This method reads a double (64-bit) value from the random access file stream, blocking until all eight bytes are read.

Returns: The double value read.

Throws: EOFException if the end of the stream is reached before reading the value.

Throws: IOException if an I/O error occurs.

readFloat

```
public final float readFloat() throws IOException
```

This method reads a float (32-bit) value from the random access file stream, blocking until all four bytes are read.

Returns: The float value read.

Throws: EOFException if the end of the stream is reached before reading the value.

Throws: IOException if an I/O error occurs.

readFully

```
public final void readFully(byte b[]) throws IOException
```

This method reads up to b.length bytes from the random access file stream into the byte array b, blocking until all bytes are read.

Parameters: b—the byte array into which the data is read.

Throws: EOFException if the end of the stream is reached before reading the value.

Throws: IOException if an I/O error occurs.

readFully

```
public final void readFully(byte b[], int off, int len) throws IOException
```

This method reads up to len bytes from the random access file stream into the byte array b beginning off bytes into the array, blocking until all bytes are read.

Parameters:

b—the byte array into which the data is read.

off—the starting offset into the array for the data to be written to.

len—the maximum number of bytes to read.

Throws: EOFException if the end of the stream is reached before reading the value.

Throws: IOException if an I/O error occurs.

readInt

```
public final int readInt() throws IOException
```

This method reads an integer (32-bit) value from the random access file stream, blocking until all four bytes are read.

Returns: The integer value read.

Throws: EOFException if the end of the stream is reached before reading the value.

Throws: IOException if an I/O error occurs.

readLine

```
public final String readLine() throws IOException
```

This method reads a line of text from the random access file stream, blocking until either a newline character ('\n') or a carriage return character ('\r') is read.

Returns: A string containing the line of text read.

Throws: IOException if an I/O error occurs.

readLong

```
public final long readLong() throws IOException
```

This method reads a long (64-bit) value from the random access file stream, blocking until all eight bytes are read.

Returns: The long value read.

Throws: EOFException if the end of the stream is reached before reading the value.

Throws: IOException if an I/O error occurs.

readShort

`public final short readShort() throws IOException`

This method reads a short (16-bit) value from the random access file stream, blocking until both bytes are read.

Returns: The short value read.

Throws: EOFException if the end of the stream is reached before reading the value.

Throws: IOException if an I/O error occurs.

readUnsignedByte

`public final int readUnsignedByte() throws IOException`

This method reads an unsigned byte (8-bit) value from the random access file stream, blocking until the byte is read.

Returns: The unsigned byte value read.

Throws: EOFException if the end of the stream is reached before reading the value.

Throws: IOException if an I/O error occurs.

readUnsignedShort

`public final int readUnsignedShort() throws IOException`

This method reads an unsigned short (16-bit) value from the random access file stream, blocking until both bytes are read.

Returns: The unsigned short value read.

Throws: EOFException if the end of the stream is reached before reading the value.

Throws: IOException if an I/O error occurs.

readUTF

`public final String readUTF() throws IOException`

This method reads a string that has been encoded using a modified UTF-8 format from the random access file stream, blocking until all bytes are read.

Returns: The string read.

Throws: EOFException if the end of the stream is reached before reading the string.

Throws: UTFDataFormatException if the bytes read do not represent a valid UTF-8 encoding of a string.

Throws: IOException if an I/O error occurs.

seek

```
public void seek(long pos) throws IOException
```

This method sets the current stream position to the specified absolute position. The position is absolute because it is always relative to the beginning of the stream.

Parameters: pos—the absolute position to seek to.

Throws: IOException if an I/O error occurs.

skipBytes

```
public int skipBytes(int n) throws IOException
```

This method skips n bytes of data in the random access file stream, blocking until all bytes are skipped.

Parameters: n—the number of bytes to skip.

Returns: The actual number of bytes skipped.

Throws: EOFException if the end of the stream is reached before skipping the specified number of bytes.

Throws: IOException if an I/O error occurs.

write

```
public void write(byte b[]) throws IOException
```

This method writes b.length bytes to the random access file stream from the byte array b.

Parameters: b—the byte array from which the data is written.

Throws: IOException if an I/O error occurs.

write

```
public void write(byte b[], int off, int len) throws IOException
```

This method writes len bytes to the random access file stream from the byte array b beginning off bytes into the array.

Parameters:

b—the byte array from which the data is written.

off—the starting offset into the array for the data to be read from.

len—the number of bytes to write.

Throws: IOException if an I/O error occurs.

write

```
public void write(int b) throws IOException
```

This method writes a byte value to the random access file stream.

Parameters: b—the byte value to be written.

Throws: IOException if an I/O error occurs.

writeBoolean

```
public final void writeBoolean(boolean v) throws IOException
```

This method writes a boolean value to the random access file stream. The boolean value true is written as the byte value 1, where false is written as the byte value 0.

Parameters: v—the boolean value to be written.

Throws: IOException if an I/O error occurs.

writeByte

```
public final void writeByte(int v) throws IOException
```

This method writes a byte (8-bit) value to the random access file stream.

Parameters: v—the byte value to be written.

Throws: IOException if an I/O error occurs.

writeBytes

`public final void writeBytes(String s) throws IOException`

This method writes a string to the random access file stream as a sequence of bytes.

Parameters: s—the string to be written as bytes.

Throws: IOException if an I/O error occurs.

writeChar

`public final void writeChar(int v) throws IOException`

This method writes a character (16-bit) value to the random access file stream.

Parameters: v—the character value to be written.

Throws: IOException if an I/O error occurs.

writeChars

`public final void writeChars(String s) throws IOException`

This method writes a string to the random access file stream as a sequence of characters.

Parameters: s—the string to be written as characters.

Throws: IOException if an I/O error occurs.

writeDouble

`public final void writeDouble(double v) throws IOException`

This method writes a double (64-bit) value to the random access file stream.

Parameters: v—the double value to be written.

Throws: IOException if an I/O error occurs.

writeFloat

`public final void writeFloat(float v) throws IOException`

This method writes a float (32-bit) value to the random access file stream.

Parameters: v—the float value to be written.

Throws: IOException if an I/O error occurs.

writeInt

```
public final void writeInt(int v) throws IOException
```

This method writes an integer (32-bit) value to the random access file stream.

Parameters: v—the integer value to be written.

Throws: IOException if an I/O error occurs.

writeLong

```
public final void writeLong(long v) throws IOException
```

This method writes a long (64-bit) value to the random access file stream.

Parameters: v—the long value to be written.

Throws: IOException if an I/O error occurs.

writeShort

```
public final void writeShort(int v) throws IOException
```

This method writes a short (16-bit) value to the random access file stream.

Parameters: v—the short value to be written.

Throws: IOException if an I/O error occurs.

writeUTF

```
public final void writeUTF(String str) throws IOException
```

This method encodes a string using a modified UTF-8 format and writes it to the random access file stream.

Parameters: str—the string to be written.

Throws: IOException if an I/O error occurs.

SequenceInputStream

Extends: InputStream

This class implements an input stream that can combine several input streams in a serial manner so that they function together like a single input stream. Each input stream comprising the sequence is read from in turn; the sequence input stream handles closing streams as they finish and switching to the next one.

SequenceInputStream **Constructor**

```
public SequenceInputStream(Enumeration e)
```

This constructor creates a sequence input stream containing the specified enumerated list of input streams.

Parameters: e—the list of input streams for the sequence.

SequenceInputStream **Constructor**

```
public SequenceInputStream(InputStream s1, InputStream s2)
```

This constructor creates a sequence input stream containing the two specified input streams.

Parameters:

s1—the first input stream in the sequence.

s2—the second input stream in the sequence.

close

```
public void close() throws IOException
```

This method closes the sequence input stream, releasing any resources associated with the stream. Additionally, this close method calls the close method for the substream currently being read from as well as the substreams that have yet to be read from.

Throws: IOException if an I/O error occurs.

read

```
public int read() throws IOException
```

This method reads a byte value from the currently active substream in the sequence input stream, blocking until the byte is read. If the end of the substream is reached, the close method is called on the substream and read begins reading from the next substream.

Returns: An integer representing the byte value read, or -1 if the end of the stream is reached.

read

```
public int read(byte b[], int pos, int len) throws IOException
```

This method reads up to len bytes from the currently active substream in the sequence input stream into the byte array b beginning off bytes into the array, blocking until all bytes are read. If the end of the substream is reached, the close method is called on the substream and read begins reading from the next substream.

Parameters:

b—the byte array into which the data is read.

off—the starting offset into the array for the data to be written to.

len—the maximum number of bytes to read.

Returns: The actual number of bytes read, or -1 if the end of the stream is reached.

Throws: IOException if an I/O error occurs.

StreamTokenizer

Extends: Object

This class implements a string tokenizer stream, which parses an input stream into a stream of tokens. The StreamTokenizer class provides a variety of methods for establishing how the tokens are parsed. Each character read from the stream is evaluated as having zero or more of the following attributes: whitespace, alphabetic, numeric, string quote, or comment.

Member Variables

public double nval

This member variable holds a numeric token value whenever the ttype member variable is set to TT_NUMBER.

public String sval

This member variable holds a string representation of a word token whenever the ttype member variable is set to TT_WORD, or it holds the body of a quoted string token when ttype is set to a quote character.

public int ttype

This is the type of the current token, which can be one of the following:

- ☐ Integer representation of a character for single character tokens.
- ☐ Quote character for quoted string tokens.
- ☐ TT_WORD for word tokens.
- ☐ TT_NUMERIC for numeric tokens.
- ☐ TT_EOL if the end of a line has been reached on the input stream.
- ☐ TT_EOF if the end of the stream has been reached.

public final static int TT_EOF

This is a constant token type representing the end-of-file token.

```
public final static int TT_EOL
```

This is a constant token type representing the end-of-line token.

```
public final static int TT_NUMBER
```

This is a constant token type identifying a numeric token; the actual numeric value is stored in nval.

```
public final static int TT_WORD
```

This is a constant token type identifying a word token; the actual word value is stored in sval.

StreamTokenizer **Constructor**

```
public StreamTokenizer(InputStream I)
```

This constructor creates a string tokenizer stream that parses the specified input stream. By default, the string tokenizer stream recognizes numbers, strings quoted with single and double quotes, all alphabetic characters, and comments preceded by a '/' character.

Parameters: I—the input stream to be parsed.

commentChar

```
public void commentChar(int ch)
```

This method establishes the specified character as starting single line comments.

Parameters: ch—the new single line comment character.

eolIsSignificant

```
public void eolIsSignificant(boolean flag)
```

This method establishes whether end-of-line characters are recognized as tokens.

Parameters: flag—a boolean value specifying whether end-of-line characters are treated as tokens; a value of true means end-of-line characters are treated as tokens, whereas a value of false means they are treated as whitespace.

lineno

```
public int lineno()
```

This method determines the current line number of the string tokenizer stream.

Returns: The current line number of the stream.

lowerCaseMode

```
public void lowerCaseMode(boolean flag)
```

This method establishes whether word tokens (TT_WORD) are forced to lowercase when they are parsed.

Parameters: flag—a boolean value specifying whether word tokens are forced to lowercase; a value of true means word tokens are forced to lowercase, whereas a value of false means they are left unmodified.

nextToken

```
public int nextToken() throws IOException
```

This method parses the next token from the underlying input stream. After the token is parsed, the ttype member variable is set to the type of the token, while the value of some tokens is contained in either the nval or sval member variables, depending on the token type.

Returns: The type of the token.

Throws: IOException if an I/O error occurs.

ordinaryChar

```
public void ordinaryChar(int ch)
```

This method establishes that the specified character is handled as an ordinary character by the tokenizer, meaning that the character is not interpreted as a comment character, word component, string delimiter, whitespace, or numeric character. Ordinary characters are parsed as single character tokens.

Parameters: ch—the character to be set as ordinary.

ordinaryChars

```
public void ordinaryChars(int low, int hi)
```

This method establishes that the characters in the specified range are handled as ordinary characters by the tokenizer, meaning that the characters are not interpreted as comment characters, word components, string delimiters, whitespace, or numeric characters. Ordinary characters are parsed as single character tokens.

Parameters:

low—the low end of the ordinary character range.

hi—the high end of the ordinary character range.

parseNumbers

`public void parseNumbers()`

This method establishes that numbers should be parsed. When a number is parsed, the `ttype` member variable is set to `TT_NUMBER`, with the corresponding numeric value stored in `nval`.

pushBack

`public void pushBack()`

This method pushes the current token back into the string tokenizer stream, meaning that the next call to `nextToken` will result in this token being handled.

quoteChar

`public void quoteChar(int ch)`

This method establishes that matching pairs of the specified character be used to delimit string constants. When a string constant is parsed, the `ttype` member variable is set to the delimiting character, with the corresponding string body stored in `sval`.

Parameters: ch—the new string delimiter character.

resetSyntax

`public void resetSyntax()`

This method resets the syntax table so that all characters are considered ordinary. An ordinary character is a character that isn't interpreted as a comment character, word component, string delimiter, whitespace, or numeric character. Ordinary characters are parsed as single character tokens.

slashSlashComments

`public void slashSlashComments(boolean flag)`

This method establishes whether C++ style comments (//) are recognized by the parser. A C++ style comment is defined by two consecutive forward slash characters, which starts a comment that extends to the end of the line.

Parameters: flag—a boolean value specifying whether C++ style comments are recognized; a value of `true` means C++ style comments are recognized, whereas a value of `false` means they are not treated specially.

slashStarComments

`public void slashStarComments(boolean flag)`

This method establishes whether C style comments (/*...*/) are recognized by the parser. A C style comment is defined by a forward slash character followed by an asterisk, which starts a comment. The comment continues until a corresponding asterisk followed by a forward slash character is reached.

Parameters: flag—a boolean value specifying whether C style comments are recognized; a value of true means C style comments are recognized, whereas a value of false means they are not treated specially.

toString

`public String toString()`

This method determines the string representation of the current token in the string tokenizer stream.

Returns: The string representation of the current token.

whitespaceChars

`public void whitespaceChars(int low, int hi)`

This method establishes that the characters in the specified range are handled as whitespace by the tokenizer, meaning that the characters serve only to separate tokens.

Parameters:

low—the low end of the whitespace character range.

hi—the high end of the whitespace character range.

wordChars

`public void wordChars(int low, int hi)`

This method establishes that the characters in the specified range are handled as words by the tokenizer.

Parameters: low—the low end of the word character range.

Parameters: hi—the high end of the word character range.

StringBufferInputStream

Extends: InputStream

This class implements an input stream whose data is fed by a string. Note that only the lower 8 bits of each character in the string are used by this class.

Member Variables

protected String buffer

This is the string buffer from which the data is read.

protected int count

This is the number of characters currently in the buffer.

protected int pos

This is the current read position in the buffer.

StringBufferInputStream Constructor

public StringBufferInputStream(String s)

This constructor creates a string buffer input stream based on the specified string. Note that the string buffer is not copied to create the input stream.

Parameters: s—the input string buffer.

available

public int available()

This method determines the number of bytes that can be read from the string buffer input stream without blocking.

Returns: The number of available bytes.

read

public int read()

This method reads a byte value from the string buffer input stream, which is the lower 8 bits of the next character in the underlying string buffer.

Returns: An integer representing the byte value read, or -1 if the end of the stream is reached.

read

```
public int read(byte b[], int off, int len)
```

This method reads up to `len` bytes from the string buffer input stream into the byte array `b` beginning `off` bytes into the array. Note that each byte is actually the lower 8 bits of the corresponding character in the underlying string buffer.

Parameters:

`b`—the byte array into which the data is read.

`off`—the starting offset into the array for the data to be written to.

`len`—the maximum number of bytes to read.

Returns: The actual number of bytes read, or `-1` if the end of the stream is reached.

reset

```
public void reset()
```

This method resets the read position to the beginning of the string buffer input stream.

skip

```
public long skip(long n)
```

This method skips `n` bytes of data in the string buffer input stream.

Parameters: `n`—the number of bytes to skip.

Returns: The actual number of bytes skipped.

EOFException

Extends: `IOException`

This exception class signals that an end-of-file (EOF) has been reached unexpectedly during an input operation. This exception is primarily used by data input streams, which typically expect a binary file in a specific format, in which case an end-of-file is an unusual condition.

FileNotFoundException

Extends: `IOException`

This exception class signals that a file could not be found.

IOException

Extends: Exception

This exception class signals that some kind of input/output (I/O) exception has occurred.

InterruptedIOException

Extends: IOException

This exception class signals that an input/output (I/O) operation has been interrupted.

UTFDataFormatException

Extends: IOException

This exception class signals that a malformed UTF-8 string has been read in a data input stream.

APPENDIX

J

java.lang Package Reference

The java.lang package provides the core classes that make up the Java programming environment. The language package includes classes representing numbers, strings, and objects, as well as classes for handling compilation, the runtime environment, security, and threaded programming. The java.lang package is automatically imported into every Java program.

Cloneable

This interface indicates that an object may be cloned using the clone method defined in Object. The clone method clones an object by copying each of its member variables. Attempts to clone an object that doesn't implement the Cloneable interface result in a CloneNotSupportedException being thrown.

Runnable

This interface provides a means for an object to be executed within a thread without having to be derived from the Thread class. Classes implementing the Runnable interface supply a run method that defines the threaded execution for the class.

run

```
public abstract void run()
```

This method is executed when a thread associated with an object implementing the Runnable interface is started. All of the threaded execution for the object takes place in the run method, which means you should place all threaded code in this method.

Boolean

Extends: Object

This class implements an object type wrapper for boolean values. Object type wrappers are useful because many Java classes operate on objects rather than primitive data types.

Member Constants

```
public final static Boolean FALSE
```

This is a constant Boolean object representing the primitive boolean value false.

```
public final static Boolean TRUE
```

This is a constant Boolean object representing the primitive boolean value true.

Boolean **Constructor**

public Boolean(boolean value)

This constructor creates a boolean wrapper object representing the specified primitive boolean value.

Parameters: value—the boolean value to be wrapped.

Boolean **Constructor**

public Boolean(String s)

This constructor creates a boolean wrapper object representing the specified string. If the string is set to "true", the wrapper represents the primitive boolean value true; otherwise, the wrapper represents false.

Parameters: s—the string representation of a boolean value to be wrapped.

booleanValue

public boolean booleanValue()

This method determines the primitive boolean value represented by this object.

Returns: The boolean value represented.

equals

public boolean equals(Object obj)

This method compares the boolean value of the specified object to the boolean value of this object. The equals method returns true only if the specified object is a Boolean object representing the same primitive boolean value as this object.

Parameters: obj—the object to compare.

Returns: true if the specified object is a Boolean object representing the same primitive boolean value as this object; false otherwise.

getBoolean

public static boolean getBoolean(String name)

This method determines the boolean value of the system property with the specified name.

Parameters: name—the system property name to check the boolean value of.

Returns: The boolean value of the specified system property.

hashCode

`public int hashCode()`

This method calculates a hash code for this object.

Returns: A hash code for this object.

toString

`public String toString()`

This method determines a string representation of the primitive boolean value for this object. If the boolean value is `true`, the string `"true"` is returned; otherwise, the string `"false"` is returned.

Returns: A string representing the boolean value of this object.

valueOf

`public static Boolean valueOf(String s)`

This method creates a new boolean wrapper object based on the boolean value represented by the specified string. If the string is set to `"true"`, the wrapper represents the primitive boolean value `true`; otherwise, the wrapper represents `false`.

Parameters: s—the string representation of a boolean value to be wrapped.

Returns: A boolean wrapper object representing the specified string.

Character

Extends: `Object`

This class implements an object type wrapper for character values. Object type wrappers are useful because many Java classes operate on objects rather than primitive data types.

Member Constants

`public final static int MAX_RADIX`

This is a constant representing the maximum radix value allowed for conversion between numbers and strings. This constant is set to `36`.

```
public final static int MAX_VALUE
```

This is a constant representing the largest character value supported. This constant is set to
`'\uffff'`.

```
public final static int MIN_RADIX
```

This is a constant representing the minimum radix value allowed for conversion between
numbers and strings. This constant is set to 2.

```
public final static int MIN_VALUE
```

This is a constant representing the smallest character value supported. This constant is set to
`'\u0000'`.

Character **Constructor**

```
public Character(char value)
```

This constructor creates a character wrapper object representing the specified primitive
character value.

Parameters: value—the character value to be wrapped.

charValue

```
public char charValue()
```

This method determines the primitive character value represented by this object.

Returns: The character value represented.

digit

```
public static int digit(char ch, int radix)
```

This method determines the numeric value of the specified character digit using the specified
radix.

Parameters:

ch—the character to be converted to a number.

radix—the radix to use in the conversion.

Returns: The numeric value of the specified character digit using the specified radix, or -1
if the character isn't a valid numeric digit.

equals

`public boolean equals(Object obj)`

This method compares the character value of the specified object to the character value of this object. The `equals` method returns `true` only if the specified object is a `Character` object representing the same primitive character value as this object.

Parameters: `obj`—the object to compare.

Returns: `true` if the specified object is a `Character` object representing the same primitive character value as this object; `false` otherwise.

forDigit

`public static char forDigit(int digit, int radix)`

This method determines the character value of the specified numeric digit using the specified radix.

Parameters:

`digit`—the numeric digit to be converted to a character.

`radix`—the radix to use in the conversion.

Returns: The character value of the specified numeric digit using the specified radix, or `0` if the number isn't a valid character.

hashCode

`public int hashCode()`

This method calculates a hash code for this object.

Returns: A hash code for this object.

isDefined

`public static boolean isDefined(char ch)`

This method determines if the specified character has a defined Unicode meaning. A character is defined if it has an entry in the Unicode attribute table.

Parameters: `ch`—the character to be checked.

Returns: `true` if the character has a defined Unicode meaning; `false` otherwise.

isDigit

```
public static boolean isDigit(char ch)
```

This method determines if the specified character is a numeric digit. A character is a numeric digit if its Unicode name contains the word DIGIT.

Parameters: ch—the character to be checked.

Returns: true if the character is a numeric digit; false otherwise.

isJavaLetter

```
public static boolean isJavaLetter(char ch)
```

This method determines if the specified character is permissible as the leading character in a Java identifier. A character is considered a Java letter if it is a letter, the ASCII dollar sign character ($), or the underscore character (_).

Parameters: ch—the character to be checked.

Returns: true if the character is a Java letter; false otherwise.

isJavaLetterOrDigit

```
public static boolean isJavaLetterOrDigit(char ch)
```

This method determines if the specified character is permissible as a non-leading character in a Java identifier. A character is considered a Java letter or digit if it is a letter, a digit, the ASCII dollar sign character ($), or the underscore character (_).

Parameters: ch—the character to be checked.

Returns: true if the character is a Java letter or digit; false otherwise.

isLetter

```
public static boolean isLetter(char ch)
```

This method determines if the specified character is a letter.

Parameters: ch—the character to be checked.

Returns: true if the character is a letter; false otherwise.

isLetterOrDigit

`public static boolean isLetterOrDigit(char ch)`

This method determines if the specified character is a letter or digit.

Parameters: ch—the character to be checked.

Returns: true if the character is a letter or digit; false otherwise.

isLowerCase

`public static boolean isLowerCase(char ch)`

This method determines if the specified character is a lowercase character.

Parameters: ch—the character to be checked.

Returns: true if the character is a lowercase character; false otherwise.

isSpace

`public static boolean isSpace(char ch)`

This method determines if the specified character is a whitespace character.

Parameters: ch—the character to be checked.

Returns: true if the character is a whitespace character; false otherwise.

isTitleCase

`public static boolean isTitleCase(char ch)`

This method determines if the specified character is a titlecase character. Titlecase characters are those whose printed representations look like pairs of Latin letters.

Parameters: ch—the character to be checked.

Returns: true if the character is a titlecase character; false otherwise.

isUpperCase

`public static boolean isUpperCase(char ch)`

This method determines if the specified character is an uppercase character.

Parameters: ch—the character to be checked.

Returns: true if the character is an uppercase character; false otherwise.

toLowerCase

`public static char toLowerCase(char ch)`

This method converts the specified character to a lowercase character, if the character isn't already lowercase and a lowercase equivalent exists.

Parameters: ch—the character to be converted.

Returns: The lowercase equivalent of the specified character, if one exists; otherwise, the original character.

toString

`public String toString()`

This method determines a string representation of the primitive character value for this object; the resulting string is one character in length.

Returns: A string representing the character value of this object.

toTitleCase

`public static char toTitleCase(char ch)`

This method converts the specified character to a titlecase character, if the character isn't already titlecase and a titlecase equivalent exists. Titlecase characters are those whose printed representations look like pairs of Latin letters.

Parameters: ch—the character to be converted.

Returns: The titlecase equivalent of the specified character, if one exists; otherwise, the original character.

toUpperCase

`public static char toUpperCase(char ch)`

This method converts the specified character to an uppercase character, if the character isn't already uppercase and an uppercase equivalent exists.

Parameters: ch—the character to be converted.

Returns: The uppercase equivalent of the specified character, if one exists; otherwise, the original character.

Class

Extends: Object

This class implements a runtime descriptor for classes and interfaces in a running Java program. Instances of Class are automatically constructed by the Java virtual machine when classes are loaded, which explains why there are no public constructors for the class.

forName

`public static Class forName(String className) throws ClassNotFoundException`

This method determines the runtime class descriptor for the class with the specified name.

Parameters: className—the fully qualified name of the desired class.

Returns: The runtime class descriptor for the class with the specified name.

Throws: ClassNotFoundException if the class could not be found.

getClassLoader

`public ClassLoader getClassLoader()`

This method determines the class loader for this object.

Returns: The class loader for this object, or null if the class wasn't created by a class loader.

getInterfaces

`public Class[] getInterfaces()`

This method determines the interfaces implemented by the class or interface represented by this object.

Returns: An array of interfaces implemented by the class or interface represented by this object, or an array of length 0 if no interfaces are implemented.

getName

`public String getName()`

This method determines the fully qualified name of the class or interface represented by this object.

Returns: The fully qualified name of the class or interface represented by this object.

getSuperclass

`public Class getSuperclass()`

This method determines the superclass of the class represented by this object.

Returns: The superclass of the class represented by this object, or null if this object represents the Object class.

isInterface

`public boolean isInterface()`

This method determines if the class represented by this object is actually an interface.

Returns: true if the class is an interface; false otherwise.

newInstance

`public Object newInstance() throws InstantiationException,`
`IllegalAccessException`

This method creates a new default instance of the class represented by this object.

Returns: A new default instance of the class represented by this object.

Throws: InstantiationException if you try to instantiate an abstract class or an interface, or if the instantiation fails for some other reason.

Throws: IllegalAccessException if the class is not accessible.

toString

`public String toString()`

This method determines the name of the class or interface represented by this object, with the string "class" or the string "interface" prepended appropriately.

Returns: The name of the class or interface represented by this object, with a descriptive string prepended indicating whether the object represents a class or interface.

ClassLoader

Extends: Object

This class is an abstract class that defines a mechanism for dynamically loading classes into the Java runtime system.

ClassLoader **Constructor**

`protected ClassLoader()`

This constructor creates a default class loader. If a security manager is present, it is checked to see if the current thread has permission to create the class loader. If not, a SecurityException is thrown.

Throws: SecurityException if the current thread doesn't have permission to create the class loader.

defineClass

`protected final Class defineClass(byte b[], int off, int len)`

This method converts an array of bytes into an instance of class Class by reading len bytes from the array b beginning off bytes into the array.

Parameters:

b—the byte array containing the class data.

off—the starting offset into the array for the data.

len—the length in bytes of the class data.

Returns: A Class object created from the class data.

Throws: ClassFormatError if the class data does not define a valid class.

findSystemClass

`protected final Class findSystemClass(String name) throws ClassNotFoundException`

This method finds the system class with the specified name, loading it if necessary. A system class is a class loaded from the local file system with no class loader in a platform-specific manner.

Parameters: name—the name of the system class to find.

Returns: A Class object representing the system class.

Throws: ClassNotFoundException if the class is not found.

Throws: NoClassDefFoundError if a definition for the class is not found.

loadClass

```
protected abstract Class loadClass(String name, boolean resolve)
throws ClassNotFoundException
```

This method loads the class with the specified name, resolving it if the resolve parameter is set to true. This method must be implemented in all derived class loaders, because it is defined as abstract.

Parameters:

name—the name of the desired class.

resolve—a boolean value specifying whether the class is to be resolved; a value of true means the class is resolved, whereas a value of false means the class isn't resolved.

Returns: The loaded Class object, or null if the class isn't found.

Throws: ClassNotFoundException if the class is not found.

resolveClass

```
protected final void resolveClass(Class c)
```

This method resolves the specified class so that instances of it can be created or so that its methods can be called.

Parameters: c—the class to be resolved.

Compiler

Extends: Object

This class provides the framework for native Java code compilers and related services. The Java runtime system looks for a native code compiler on startup, in which case the compiler is called to compile Java bytecode classes into native code.

command

```
public static Object command(Object any)
```

This method performs some compiler-specific operation based on the type of specified object and its related state.

Parameters: any—the object to perform an operation based on.

Returns: A compiler-specific value, or null if no compiler is available.

compileClass

```
public static boolean compileClass(Class clazz)
```

This method compiles the specified class.

Parameters: clazz—the class to compile.

Returns: true if the compilation was successful, false if the compilation failed or if no compiler is available.

compileClasses

```
public static boolean compileClasses(String string)
```

This method compiles all classes whose names match the specified string name.

Parameters: string—a string containing the name of the classes to compile.

Returns: true if the compilation was successful, false if the compilation failed or if no compiler is available.

disable

```
public static void disable()
```

This method disables the compiler.

enable

```
public static void enable()
```

This method enables the compiler.

Double

Extends: Number

This class implements an object type wrapper for double values. Object type wrappers are useful because many Java classes operate on objects rather than primitive data types.

Member Constants

```
public final static double MAX_VALUE
```

This is a constant representing the maximum value allowed for a double. This constant is set to 1.79769313486231570e+308d.

```
public final static double MIN_VALUE
```

This is a constant representing the minimum value allowed for a double. This constant is set to `4.94065645841246544e-324d`.

```
public final static double NaN
```

This is a constant representing the not-a-number value for double types, which is not equal to anything, including itself.

```
public final static double NEGATIVE_INFINITY
```

This is a constant representing negative infinity for double types.

```
public final static double POSITIVE_INFINITY
```

This is a constant representing positive infinity for double types.

Double **Constructor**

```
public Double(double value)
```

This constructor creates a double wrapper object representing the specified primitive double value.

Parameters: value—the double value to be wrapped.

Double **Constructor**

```
public Double(String s) throws NumberFormatException
```

This constructor creates a double wrapper object representing the specified string. The string is converted to a double using a similar technique as the valueOf method.

Parameters: s—the string representation of a double value to be wrapped.

Throws: NumberFormatException if the string does not contain a parsable double.

doubleToLongBits

```
public static long doubleToLongBits(double value)
```

This method determines the IEEE 754 floating-point double precision representation of the specified double value. The IEEE 754 floating-point double precision format specifies the following bit layout:

- ☐ 63 represents the sign of the number.
- ☐ 62–52 represent the exponent of the number.
- ☐ 51–0 represent the mantissa of the number.

Parameters: `value`—the double value to convert to the IEEE 754 format.

Returns: The IEEE 754 floating-point representation of the specified double value.

doubleValue

```
public double doubleValue()
```

This method determines the primitive double value represented by this object.

Returns: The double value represented.

equals

```
public boolean equals(Object obj)
```

This method compares the double value of the specified object to the double value of this object. The `equals` method only returns `true` if the specified object is a `Double` object representing the same primitive double value as this object. Note that to be useful in hash tables, this method considers two `NaN` double values to be equal, even though `NaN` technically is not equal to itself.

Parameters: `obj`—the object to compare.

Returns: `true` if the specified object is a `Double` object representing the same primitive double value as this object; `false` otherwise.

floatValue

```
public float floatValue()
```

This method converts the primitive double value represented by this object to a float.

Returns: A float conversion of the double value represented.

hashCode

```
public int hashCode()
```

This method calculates a hash code for this object.

Returns: A hash code for this object.

intValue

```
public int intValue()
```

This method converts the primitive double value represented by this object to an integer.

Returns: An integer conversion of the double value represented.

isInfinite

`public boolean isInfinite()`

This method determines if the primitive double value represented by this object is positive or negative infinity.

Returns: `true` if the double value is positive or negative infinity; `false` otherwise.

isInfinite

`public static boolean isInfinite(double v)`

This method determines if the specified double value is positive or negative infinity.

Parameters: v—the double value to be checked.

Returns: `true` if the double value is positive or negative infinity; `false` otherwise.

isNaN

`public boolean isNaN()`

This method determines if the primitive double value represented by this object is not a number (NaN).

Returns: `true` if the double value is not a number; `false` otherwise.

isNaN

`public static boolean isNaN(double v)`

This method determines if the specified double value is not a number (NaN).

Parameters: v—the double value to be checked.

Returns: `true` if the double value is not a number; `false` otherwise.

longBitsToDouble

`public static double longBitsToDouble(long bits)`

This method determines the double representation of the specified IEEE 754 floating-point double precision value. The IEEE 754 floating-point double precision format specifies the following bit layout:

- 63 represents the sign of the number.
- 62–52 represent the exponent of the number.
- 51–0 represent the mantissa of the number.

Parameters: bits—the IEEE 754 floating-point value to convert to a double.

Returns: The double representation of the specified IEEE 754 floating-point value.

longValue

```
public long longValue()
```

This method converts the primitive double value represented by this object to a long.

Returns: A long conversion of the double value represented.

toString

```
public String toString()
```

This method determines a string representation of the primitive double value for this object.

Returns: A string representing the double value of this object.

toString

```
public static String toString(double d)
```

This method determines a string representation of the specified double value.

Parameters: d—the double value to be converted.

Returns: A string representing the specified double value.

valueOf

```
public static Double valueOf(String s) throws NumberFormatException
```

This method creates a new double wrapper object based on the double value represented by the specified string.

Parameters: s—the string representation of a double value to be wrapped.

Returns: A double wrapper object representing the specified string.

Throws: NumberFormatException if the string does not contain a parsable double.

Float

Extends: `Number`

This class implements an object type wrapper for float values. Object type wrappers are useful because many Java classes operate on objects rather than primitive data types.

Member Constants

`public final static float MAX_VALUE`

This is a constant representing the maximum value allowed for a float. This constant is set to `3.40282346638528860e+38`.

`public final static float MIN_VALUE`

This is a constant representing the minimum value allowed for a float. This constant is set to `1.40129846432481707e-45`.

`public final static float NaN`

This is a constant representing the not-a-number value for float types, which is not equal to anything, including itself.

`public final static float NEGATIVE_INFINITY`

This is a constant representing negative infinity for float types.

`public final static float POSITIVE_INFINITY`

This is a constant representing positive infinity for float types.

Float **Constructor**

`public Float(double value)`

This constructor creates a float wrapper object representing the specified primitive double value.

Parameters: `value`—the double value to be wrapped.

Float **Constructor**

`public Float(float value)`

This constructor creates a float wrapper object representing the specified primitive float value.

Parameters: `value`—the float value to be wrapped.

Float **Constructor**

```
public Float(String s) throws NumberFormatException
```

This constructor creates a float wrapper object representing the specified string. The string is converted to a float using a similar technique as the valueOf method.

Parameters: s—the string representation of a float value to be wrapped.

Throws: NumberFormatException if the string does not contain a parsable float.

doubleValue

```
public double doubleValue()
```

This method converts the primitive float value represented by this object to a double.

Returns: A double conversion of the float value represented.

equals

```
public boolean equals(Object obj)
```

This method compares the float value of the specified object to the float value of this object. The equals method only returns true if the specified object is a Float object representing the same primitive float value as this object. Note that to be useful in hash tables, this method considers two NaN float values to be equal, even though NaN technically is not equal to itself.

Parameters: obj—the object to compare.

Returns: true if the specified object is a Float object representing the same primitive float value as this object; false otherwise.

floatToIntBits

```
public static int floatToIntBits(float value)
```

This method determines the IEEE 754 floating-point single precision representation of the specified float value. The IEEE 754 floating-point single precision format specifies the following bit layout:

- ☐ 31 represents the sign of the number.
- ☐ 30–23 represent the exponent of the number.
- ☐ 22–0 represent the mantissa of the number.

Parameters: value—the float value to convert to the IEEE 754 format.

Returns: The IEEE 754 floating-point representation of the specified float value.

floatValue

`public float floatValue()`

This method determines the primitive float value represented by this object.

Returns: The float value represented.

hashCode

`public int hashCode()`

This method calculates a hash code for this object.

Returns: A hash code for this object.

intBitsToFloat

`public static float intBitsToFloat(int bits)`

This method determines the float representation of the specified IEEE 754 floating-point single precision value. The IEEE 754 floating-point single precision format specifies the following bit layout:

- ☐ 31 represents the sign of the number.
- ☐ 30–23 represent the exponent of the number.
- ☐ 22–0 represent the mantissa of the number.

Parameters: `bits`—the IEEE 754 floating-point value to convert to a float.

Returns: The float representation of the specified IEEE 754 floating-point value.

intValue

`public int intValue()`

This method converts the primitive float value represented by this object to an integer.

Returns: An integer conversion of the float value represented.

isInfinite

`public boolean isInfinite()`

This method determines if the primitive float value represented by this object is positive or negative infinity.

Returns: `true` if the float value is positive or negative infinity; `false` otherwise.

isInfinite

`public static boolean isInfinite(float v)`

This method determines if the specified float value is positive or negative infinity.

Parameters: v—the float value to be checked.

Returns: true if the float value is positive or negative infinity; false otherwise.

isNaN

`public boolean isNaN()`

This method determines if the primitive float value represented by this object is not a number (NaN).

Returns: true if the float value is not a number; false otherwise.

isNaN

`public static boolean isNaN(float v)`

This method determines if the specified float value is not a number (NaN).

Parameters: v—the float value to be checked.

Returns: true if the float value is not a number; false otherwise.

longValue

`public long longValue()`

This method converts the primitive float value represented by this object to a long.

Returns: A long conversion of the float value represented.

toString

`public String toString()`

This method determines a string representation of the primitive float value for this object.

Returns: A string representing the float value of this object.

toString

`public static String toString(float f)`

This method determines a string representation of the specified float value.

Parameters: f—the float value to be converted.

Returns: A string representing the specified float value.

valueOf

`public static Float valueOf(String s) throws NumberFormatException`

This method creates a new float wrapper object based on the float value represented by the specified string.

Parameters: s—the string representation of a float value to be wrapped.

Returns: A float wrapper object representing the specified string.

Throws: NumberFormatException if the string does not contain a parsable float.

Integer

Extends: Number

This class implements an object type wrapper for integer values. Object type wrappers are useful because many Java classes operate on objects rather than primitive data types.

Member Constants

`public final static int MAX_VALUE`

This is a constant representing the maximum value allowed for an integer. This constant is set to 0x7fffffff.

`public final static int MIN_VALUE`

This is a constant representing the minimum value allowed for an integer. This constant is set to 0x80000000.

Integer **Constructor**

`public Integer(int value)`

This constructor creates an integer wrapper object representing the specified primitive integer value.

Parameters: value—the integer value to be wrapped.

Integer **Constructor**

`public Integer(String s) throws NumberFormatException`

This constructor creates an integer wrapper object representing the specified string. The string is converted to an integer using a similar technique as the valueOf method.

Parameters: s—the string representation of an integer value to be wrapped.

Throws: NumberFormatException if the string does not contain a parsable integer.

doubleValue

`public double doubleValue()`

This method converts the primitive integer value represented by this object to a double.

Returns: A double conversion of the integer value represented.

equals

`public boolean equals(Object obj)`

This method compares the integer value of the specified object to the integer value of this object. The equals method returns true only if the specified object is an Integer object representing the same primitive integer value as this object.

Parameters: obj—the object to compare.

Returns: true if the specified object is an Integer object representing the same primitive integer value as this object; false otherwise.

floatValue

`public float floatValue()`

This method converts the primitive integer value represented by this object to a float.

Returns: A float conversion of the integer value represented.

getInteger

`public static Integer getInteger(String name)`

This method determines an Integer object representing the value of the system property with the specified name. If the system property doesn't exist, null is returned.

Parameters: name—the system property name to check the integer value of.

Returns: An Integer object representing the value of the specified system property, or null if the property doesn't exist.

getInteger

```
public static Integer getInteger(String name, int val)
```

This method determines an Integer object representing the value of the system property with the specified name. If the system property doesn't exist, an Integer object representing the specified default property value is returned.

Parameters: name—the system property name to check the integer value of.

Parameters: val—the default integer property value.

Returns: An Integer object representing the value of the specified system property, or an Integer object representing val if the property doesn't exist.

getInteger

```
public static Integer getInteger(String name, Integer val)
```

This method determines an Integer object representing the value of the system property with the specified name. In addition, this version of getInteger includes support for reading hexadecimal and octal property values. If the system property doesn't exist, the specified default property value is returned.

Parameters:

name—the system property name to check the integer value of.

val—the default integer property value object.

Returns: An Integer object representing the value of the specified system property, or val if the property doesn't exist.

hashCode

```
public int hashCode()
```

This method calculates a hash code for this object.

Returns: A hash code for this object.

intValue

```
public int intValue()
```

This method determines the primitive integer value represented by this object.

Returns: The integer value represented.

longValue

```
public long longValue()
```

This method converts the primitive integer value represented by this object to a long.

Returns: A long conversion of the integer value represented.

parseInt

```
public static int parseInt(String s) throws NumberFormatException
```

This method parses a signed decimal integer value from the specified string. Note that all the characters in the string must be decimal digits, with the exception that the first character can be a minus character (-) to denote a negative number.

Parameters: s—the string representation of an integer value.

Returns: The integer value represented by the specified string.

Throws: NumberFormatException if the string does not contain a parsable integer.

parseInt

```
public static int parseInt(String s, int radix) throws NumberFormatException
```

This method parses a signed integer value in the specified radix from the specified string. Note that all the characters in the string must be digits in the specified radix, with the exception that the first character can be a minus character (-) to denote a negative number.

Parameters:

s—the string representation of an integer value.

radix—the radix to use for the integer.

Returns: The integer value represented by the specified string.

Throws: NumberFormatException if the string does not contain a parsable integer.

toBinaryString

```
public static String toBinaryString(int i)
```

This method determines a string representation of the specified unsigned base 2 integer value.

Parameters: i—the unsigned base 2 integer value to be converted.

Returns: A string representing the specified unsigned base 2 integer value.

toHexString

```
public static String toHexString(int i)
```

This method determines a string representation of the specified unsigned base 16 integer value.

Parameters: i—the unsigned base 16 integer value to be converted.

Returns: A string representing the specified unsigned base 16 integer value.

toOctalString

```
public static String toOctalString(int i)
```

This method determines a string representation of the specified unsigned base 8 integer value.

Parameters: i—the unsigned base 8 integer value to be converted.

Returns: A string representing the specified unsigned base 8 integer value.

toString

```
public String toString()
```

This method determines a string representation of the primitive decimal integer value for this object.

Returns: A string representing the decimal integer value of this object.

toString

```
public static String toString(int i)
```

This method determines a string representation of the specified decimal integer value.

Parameters: i—the decimal integer value to be converted.

Returns: A string representing the specified decimal integer value.

toString

`public static String toString(int i, int radix)`

This method determines a string representation of the specified integer value in the specified radix.

Parameters:

i—the integer value to be converted.

radix—the radix to use for the conversion.

Returns: A string representing the specified integer value in the specified radix.

valueOf

`public static Integer valueOf(String s) throws NumberFormatException`

This method creates a new integer wrapper object based on the decimal integer value represented by the specified string.

Parameters: s—the string representation of a decimal integer value to be wrapped.

Returns: An integer wrapper object representing the specified string.

Throws: NumberFormatException if the string does not contain a parsable integer.

valueOf

`public static Integer valueOf(String s, int radix) throws NumberFormatException`

This method creates a new integer wrapper object based on the integer value in the specified radix represented by the specified string.

Parameters:

s—the string representation of an integer value to be wrapped.

radix—the radix to use for the integer.

Returns: An integer wrapper object in the specified radix representing the specified string.

Throws: NumberFormatException if the string does not contain a parsable integer.

Long

Extends: Number

This class implements an object type wrapper for long values. Object type wrappers are useful because many Java classes operate on objects rather than primitive data types.

Member Constants

`public final static int MAX_VALUE`

This is a constant representing the maximum value allowed for a long. This constant is set to `0x7fffffffffffffff`.

`public final static int MIN_VALUE`

This is a constant representing the minimum value allowed for a long. This constant is set to `0x8000000000000000`.

Long **Constructor**

`public Long(long value)`

This constructor creates a long wrapper object representing the specified primitive long value.

Parameters: value—the long value to be wrapped.

Long **Constructor**

`public Long(String s) throws NumberFormatException`

This constructor creates a long wrapper object representing the specified string. The string is converted to a long using a similar technique as the `valueOf` method.

Parameters: s—the string representation of a long value to be wrapped.

Throws: `NumberFormatException` if the string does not contain a parsable long.

doubleValue

`public double doubleValue()`

This method converts the primitive long value represented by this object to a double.

Returns: A double conversion of the long value represented.

equals

`public boolean equals(Object obj)`

This method compares the long value of the specified object to the long value of this object. The `equals` method returns `true` only if the specified object is a `Long` object representing the same primitive long value as this object.

Parameters: obj—the object to compare.

Returns: true if the specified object is a Long object representing the same primitive long value as this object; false otherwise.

floatValue

`public float floatValue()`

This method converts the primitive long value represented by this object to a float.

Returns: A float conversion of the long value represented.

getLong

`public static Long getLong(String name)`

This method determines a Long object representing the value of the system property with the specified name. If the system property doesn't exist, null is returned.

Parameters: name—the system property name to check the long value of.

Returns: A Long object representing the value of the specified system property, or null if the property doesn't exist.

getLong

`public static Long getLong(String name, long val)`

This method determines a Long object representing the value of the system property with the specified name. If the system property doesn't exist, a Long object representing the specified default property value is returned.

Parameters: name—the system property name to check the long value of.

Parameters: val—the default long property value.

Returns: A Long object representing the value of the specified system property, or a long object representing val if the property doesn't exist.

getLong

`public static Long getLong(String name, Long val)`

This method determines a Long object representing the value of the system property with the specified name. In addition, this version of getLong includes support for reading hexadecimal and octal property values. If the system property doesn't exist, the specified default property value is returned.

Parameters:

name—the system property name to check the long value of.

val—the default long property value object.

Returns: A Long object representing the value of the specified system property, or val if the property doesn't exist.

hashCode

```
public int hashCode()
```

This method calculates a hash code for this object.

Returns: A hash code for this object.

intValue

```
public int intValue()
```

This method converts the primitive long value represented by this object to an integer.

Returns: An integer conversion of the long value represented.

longValue

```
public long longValue()
```

This method determines the primitive long value represented by this object.

Returns: The long value represented.

parseLong

```
public static long parseLong(String s) throws NumberFormatException
```

This method parses a signed decimal long value from the specified string. Note that all the characters in the string must be decimal digits, with the exception that the first character can be a minus character (-) to denote a negative number.

Parameters: s—the string representation of a long value.

Returns: The long value represented by the specified string.

Throws: NumberFormatException if the string does not contain a parsable long.

parseLong

`public static long parseLong(String s, int radix) throws NumberFormatException`

This method parses a signed long value in the specified radix from the specified string. Note that all the characters in the string must be digits in the specified radix, with the exception that the first character can be a minus character (-) to denote a negative number.

Parameters:

s—the string representation of a long value.

radix—the radix to use for the long.

Returns: The long value represented by the specified string.

Throws: `NumberFormatException` if the string does not contain a parsable long.

toBinaryString

`public static String toBinaryString(long l)`

This method determines a string representation of the specified unsigned base 2 long value.

Parameters: l—the unsigned base 2 long value to be converted.

Returns: A string representing the specified unsigned base 2 long value.

toHexString

`public static String toHexString(long l)`

This method determines a string representation of the specified unsigned base 16 long value.

Parameters: l—the unsigned base 16 long value to be converted.

Returns: A string representing the specified unsigned base 16 long value.

toOctalString

`public static String toOctalString(long l)`

This method determines a string representation of the specified unsigned base 8 long value.

Parameters: l—the unsigned base 8 long value to be converted.

Returns: A string representing the specified unsigned base 8 long value.

toString

```
public String toString()
```

This method determines a string representation of the primitive decimal long value for this object.

Returns: A string representing the decimal long value of this object.

toString

```
public static String toString(long l)
```

This method determines a string representation of the specified decimal long value.

Parameters: l—the decimal long value to be converted.

Returns: A string representing the specified decimal long value.

toString

```
public static String toString(long l, int radix)
```

This method determines a string representation of the specified long value in the specified radix.

Parameters:

i—the long value to be converted.

radix—the radix to use for the conversion.

Returns: A string representing the specified long value in the specified radix.

valueOf

```
public static Long valueOf(String s) throws NumberFormatException
```

This method creates a new long wrapper object based on the decimal long value represented by the specified string.

Parameters: s—the string representation of a decimal long value to be wrapped.

Returns: A long wrapper object representing the specified string.

Throws: NumberFormatException if the string does not contain a parsable long.

valueOf

`public static Long valueOf(String s, int radix) throws NumberFormatException`

This method creates a new long wrapper object based on the long value in the specified radix represented by the specified string.

Parameters:

s—the string representation of a long value to be wrapped.

radix—the radix to use for the long.

Returns: A long wrapper object in the specified radix representing the specified string.

Throws: `NumberFormatException` if the string does not contain a parsable long.

Math

Extends: `Object`

This class implements a library of common math functions, including methods for performing basic numerical operations such as elementary exponential, logarithm, square root, and trigonometric functions.

Member Constants

`public final static double E`

This is a constant representing the double value of `E`, which is the base of the natural logarithms. This constant is set to `2.7182818284590452354`.

`public final static double PI`

This is a constant representing the double value of `PI`, which is the ratio of the circumference of a circle to its diameter. This constant is set to `3.14159265358979323846`.

abs

`public static double abs(double a)`

This method calculates the absolute value of the specified double value.

Parameters: a—the double value to calculate the absolute value of.

Returns: The absolute value of the double value.

abs

```
public static float abs(float a)
```

This method calculates the absolute value of the specified float value.

Parameters: a—the float value to calculate the absolute value of.

Returns: The absolute value of the float value.

abs

```
public static int abs(int a)
```

This method calculates the absolute value of the specified integer value.

Parameters: a—the integer value to calculate the absolute value of.

Returns: The absolute value of the integer value.

abs

```
public static long abs(long a)
```

This method calculates the absolute value of the specified long value.

Parameters: a—the long value to calculate the absolute value of.

Returns: The absolute value of the long value.

acos

```
public static double acos(double a)
```

This method calculates the arc cosine of the specified double value.

Parameters: a—the double value to calculate the arc cosine of.

Returns: The arc cosine of the double value.

asin

```
public static double asin(double a)
```

This method calculates the arc sine of the specified double value.

Parameters: a—the double value to calculate the arc sine of.

Returns: The arc sine of the double value.

atan

`public static double atan(double a)`

This method calculates the arc tangent of the specified double value.

Parameters: a—the double value to calculate the arc tangent of.

Returns: The arc tangent of the double value.

atan2

`public static double atan2(double x, double y)`

This method calculates the theta component of the polar coordinate (r,theta) corresponding to the rectangular coordinate (x y) specified by the double values.

Parameters:

x—the x component value of the rectangular coordinate.

y—the y component value of the rectangular coordinate.

Returns: The theta component of the polar coordinate corresponding to the rectangular coordinate specified by the double values.

ceil

`public static double ceil(double a)`

This method determines the smallest double whole number that is greater than or equal to the specified double value.

Parameters: a—the double value to calculate the ceiling of.

Returns: The smallest double whole number that is greater than or equal to the specified double value.

cos

`public static double cos(double a)`

This method calculates the cosine of the specified double value, which is specified in radians.

Parameters: a—the double value to calculate the cosine of, in radians.

Returns: The cosine of the double value.

exp

```
public static double exp(double a)
```

This method calculates the exponential value of the specified double value, which is E raised to the power of a.

Parameters: a—the double value to calculate the exponential value of.

Returns: The exponential value of the specified double value.

floor

```
public static double floor(double a)
```

This method determines the largest double whole number that is less than or equal to the specified double value.

Parameters: a—the double value to calculate the floor of.

Returns: The largest double whole number that is less than or equal to the specified double value.

IEEEremainder

```
public static double IEEEremainder(double f1, double f2)
```

This method calculates the remainder of f1 divided by f2 as defined by the IEEE 754 standard.

Parameters:

f1—the dividend for the division operation.

f2—the divisor for the division operation.

Returns: The remainder of f1 divided by f2 as defined by the IEEE 754 standard.

log

```
public static double log(double a) throws ArithmeticException
```

This method calculates the natural logarithm (base E) of the specified double value.

Parameters: a—the double value, which is greater than 0.0, to calculate the natural logarithm of.

Returns: The natural logarithm of the specified double value.

Throws: ArithmeticException if the specified double value is less than 0.0.

max

```
public static double max(double a, double b)
```

This method determines the larger of the two specified double values.

Parameters:

a—the first double value to be compared.

b—the second double value to be compared.

Returns: The larger of the two specified double values.

max

```
public static float max(float a, float b)
```

This method determines the larger of the two specified float values.

Parameters:

a—the first float value to be compared.

b—the second float value to be compared.

Returns: The larger of the two specified float values.

max

```
public static int max(int a, int b)
```

This method determines the larger of the two specified integer values.

Parameters:

a—the first integer value to be compared.

b—the second integer value to be compared.

Returns: The larger of the two specified integer values.

max

```
public static long max(long a, long b)
```

This method determines the larger of the two specified long values.

Parameters:

a—the first long value to be compared.

b—the second long value to be compared.

Returns: The larger of the two specified long values.

min

`public static double min(double a, double b)`

This method determines the smaller of the two specified double values.

Parameters:

a—the first double value to be compared.

b—the second double value to be compared.

Returns: The smaller of the two specified double values.

min

`public static float min(float a, float b)`

This method determines the smaller of the two specified float values.

Parameters:

a—the first float value to be compared.

b—the second float value to be compared.

Returns: The smaller of the two specified float values.

min

`public static int min(int a, int b)`

This method determines the smaller of the two specified integer values.

Parameters:

a—the first integer value to be compared.

b—the second integer value to be compared.

Returns: The smaller of the two specified integer values.

min

`public static long min(long a, long b)`

This method determines the smaller of the two specified long values.

Parameters:

a—the first long value to be compared.

b—the second long value to be compared.

Returns: The smaller of the two specified long values.

pow

```
public static double pow(double a, double b) throws ArithmeticException
```

This method calculates the double value a raised to the power of b.

Parameters:

a—a double value to be raised to a power specified by b.

b—the power to raise a to.

Returns: The double value a raised to the power of b.

Throws: ArithmeticException if a equals 0.0 and b is less than or equal to 0.0, or if a is less than or equal to 0.0 and b is not a whole number.

random

```
public static double random()
```

This method generates a pseudo-random double between 0.0 and 1.0.

Returns: A pseudo-random double between 0.0 and 1.0.

rint

```
public static double rint(double a)
```

This method determines the closest whole number to the specified double value. If the double value is equally spaced between two whole numbers, rint will return the even number.

Parameters: a—the double value to determine the closest whole number.

Returns: The closest whole number to the specified double value.

round

```
public static long round(double a)
```

This method rounds off the specified double value by determining the closest long value.

Parameters: a—the double value to round off.

Returns: The closest long value to the specified double value.

round

```
public static int round(float a)
```

This method rounds off the specified float value by determining the closest integer value.

Parameters: a—the float value to round off.

Returns: The closest integer value to the specified float value.

sin

```
public static double sin(double a)
```

This method calculates the sine of the specified double value, which is specified in radians.

Parameters: a—the double value to calculate the sine of, in radians.

Returns: The sine of the double value.

sqrt

```
public static double sqrt(double a) throws ArithmeticException
```

This method calculates the square root of the specified double value.

Parameters: a—the double value, which is greater than 0.0, to calculate the square root for.

Returns: The square root of the double value.

Throws: ArithmeticException if the specified double value is less than 0.0.

tan

```
public static double tan(double a)
```

This method calculates the tangent of the specified double value, which is specified in radians.

Parameters: a—the double value to calculate the tangent of, in radians.

Returns: The tangent of the double value.

Number

Extends: Object

This class is an abstract class that provides the basic functionality required of a numeric object. All specific numeric objects are derived from Number.

doubleValue

```
public abstract double doubleValue()
```

This method determines the primitive double value represented by this object. Note that this may involve rounding if the number is not already a double.

Returns: The double value represented.

floatValue

```
public abstract float floatValue()
```

This method determines the primitive float value represented by this object. Note that this may involve rounding if the number is not already a float.

Returns: The float value represented.

intValue

```
public abstract int intValue()
```

This method determines the primitive integer value represented by this object.

Returns: The integer value represented.

longValue

```
public abstract long longValue()
```

This method determines the primitive long value represented by this object.

Returns: The long value represented.

Object

This class is the root of the Java class hierarchy, providing the core functionality required of all objects. All classes have Object as a superclass, and all classes implement the methods defined in Object.

Object Constructor

```
public Object()
```

This constructor creates a default object.

clone

```
protected Object clone() throws CloneNotSupportedException
```

This method creates a clone of this object by creating a new instance of the class and copying each of the member variables of this object to the new object. To be cloneable, derived classes must implement the `Cloneable` interface.

Returns: A clone of this object.

Throws: `OutOfMemoryError` if there is not enough memory.

Throws: `CloneNotSupportedException` if the object doesn't support the `Cloneable` interface or if it explicitly doesn't want to be cloned.

equals

```
public boolean equals(Object obj)
```

This method compares this object with the specified object for equality. The `equals` method is used by the `Hashtable` class to compare objects stored in the hash table.

Parameters: `obj`—the object to compare.

Returns: `true` if this object is equivalent to the specified object; `false` otherwise.

finalize

```
protected void finalize() throws Throwable
```

This method is called by the Java garbage collector when an object is being destroyed. The default behavior of `finalize` is to do nothing. Derived classes can override `finalize` to include cleanup code that is to be executed when the object is destroyed.

getClass

```
public final Class getClass()
```

This method determines the runtime class descriptor for this object.

Returns: The runtime class descriptor for this object.

hashCode

```
public int hashCode()
```

This method calculates a hash code for this object, which is a unique integer identifying the object. Hash codes are used by the `Hashtable` class.

Returns: A hash code for this object.

notify

```
public final void notify()
```

This method wakes up a single thread that is waiting on this object's monitor. A thread is set to wait on an object's monitor when the wait method is called. The notify method should only be called by a thread that is the owner of this object's monitor. Note that the notify method can only be called from within a synchronized method.

Throws: IllegalMonitorStateException if the current thread is not the owner of this object's monitor.

notifyAll

```
public final void notifyAll()
```

This method wakes up all threads that are waiting on this object's monitor. A thread is set to wait on an object's monitor when the wait method is called. The notifyAll method should only be called by a thread that is the owner of this object's monitor. Note that the notifyAll method can only be called from within a synchronized method.

Throws: IllegalMonitorStateException if the current thread is not the owner of this object's monitor.

toString

```
public String toString()
```

This method determines a string representation of this object. It is recommended that all derived classes override toString.

Returns: A string representing this object.

wait

```
public final void wait() throws InterruptedException
```

This method causes the current thread to wait forever until it is notified via a call to the notify or notifyAll methods. The wait method should only be called by a thread that is the owner of this object's monitor. Note that the wait method can only be called from within a synchronized method.

Throws: IllegalMonitorStateException if the current thread is not the owner of this object's monitor.

Throws: InterruptedException if another thread has interrupted this thread.

wait

```
public final void wait(long timeout) throws InterruptedException
```

This method causes the current thread to wait until it is notified via a call to the notify or notifyAll method, or until the specified timeout period has elapsed. The wait method should only be called by a thread that is the owner of this object's monitor. Note that the wait method can only be called from within a synchronized method.

Parameters: timeout—the maximum timeout period to wait, in milliseconds.

Throws: IllegalMonitorStateException if the current thread is not the owner of this object's monitor.

Throws: InterruptedException if another thread has interrupted this thread.

wait

```
public final void wait(long timeout, int nanos) throws InterruptedException
```

This method causes the current thread to wait until it is notified via a call to the notify or notifyAll method, or until the specified timeout period has elapsed. The timeout period in this case is the addition of the timeout and nanos parameters, which provide finer control over the timeout period. The wait method should only be called by a thread that is the owner of this object's monitor. Note that the wait method can only be called from within a synchronized method.

Parameters:

timeout—the maximum timeout period to wait, in milliseconds.

nanos—the additional time for the timeout period, in nanoseconds.

Throws: IllegalMonitorStateException if the current thread is not the owner of this object's monitor.

Throws: InterruptedException if another thread has interrupted this thread.

Process

Extends: Object

This class is an abstract class that provides the basic functionality required of a system process. Derived Process objects (subprocesses) are returned from the exec methods defined in the Runtime class.

Process **Constructor**

`public Process()`

This constructor creates a default process.

destroy

`public abstract void destroy()`

This method kills the subprocess.

exitValue

`public abstract int exitValue()`

This method determines the exit value of the subprocess.

Returns: The integer exit value for the subprocess.

Throws: `IllegalThreadStateException` if the subprocess has not yet terminated.

getErrorStream

`public abstract InputStream getErrorStream()`

This method determines the error stream associated with the subprocess.

Returns: The error stream associated with the subprocess.

getInputStream

`public abstract InputStream getInputStream()`

This method determines the input stream associated with the subprocess.

Returns: The input stream associated with the subprocess.

getOutputStream

`public abstract OutputStream getOutputStream()`

This method determines the output stream associated with the subprocess.

Returns: The output stream associated with the subprocess.

waitFor

```
public abstract int waitFor() throws InterruptedException
```

This method waits for the subprocess to finish executing. When the subprocess finishes executing, the integer exit value is returned.

Returns: The integer exit value for the subprocess.

Throws: InterruptedException if another thread has interrupted this thread.

Runtime

Extends: Object

This class provides a mechanism for interacting with the Java runtime environment. Each running Java application has access to a single instance of the Runtime class, which it can use to query and modify the runtime environment.

exec

```
public Process exec(String command) throws IOException
```

This method executes the system command represented by the specified string in a separate subprocess.

Parameters: command—a string representing the system command to execute.

Returns: The subprocess that is executing the system command.

Throws: SecurityException if the current thread cannot create the subprocess.

exec

```
public Process exec(String command, String envp[]) throws IOException
```

This method executes the system command represented by the specified string in a separate subprocess with the specified environment.

Parameters:

command—a string representing the system command to execute.

envp—an array of strings representing the environment.

Returns: The subprocess that is executing the system command.

Throws: SecurityException if the current thread cannot create the subprocess.

exec

`public Process exec(String cmdarray[]) throws IOException`

This method executes the system command with arguments represented by the specified string array in a separate subprocess.

Parameters: `cmdarray`—an array of strings representing the system command to execute along with its arguments.

Returns: The subprocess that is executing the system command.

Throws: `SecurityException` if the current thread cannot create the subprocess.

exec

`public Process exec(String cmdarray[], String envp[]) throws IOException`

This method executes the system command with arguments represented by the specified string array in a separate subprocess with the specified environment.

Parameters:

`cmdarray`—an array of strings representing the system command to execute along with its arguments.

`envp`—an array of strings representing the environment.

Returns: The subprocess that is executing the system command.

Throws: `SecurityException` if the current thread cannot create the subprocess.

exit

`public void exit(int status)`

This method exits the Java runtime system (virtual machine) with the specified integer exit status. Note that since `exit` kills the runtime system, it never returns.

Parameters: `status`—the integer exit status; this should be set to nonzero if this is an abnormal exit.

Throws: `SecurityException` if the current thread cannot exit with the specified exit status.

freeMemory

```
public long freeMemory()
```

This method determines the approximate amount of free memory available in the runtime system, in bytes.

Returns: Approximate amount of free memory available, in bytes.

gc

```
public void gc()
```

This method invokes the Java garbage collector to clean up any objects that are no longer needed, usually resulting in more free memory.

getLocalizedInputStream

```
public InputStream getLocalizedInputStream(InputStream in)
```

This method creates a localized input stream based on the specified input stream. A localized input stream is a stream whose local characters are mapped to Unicode characters as they are read.

Parameters: in—the input stream to localize.

Returns: A localized input stream based on the specified input stream.

getLocalizedOutputStream

```
public OutputStream getLocalizedOutputStream(OutputStream out)
```

This method creates a localized output stream based on the specified output stream. A localized output stream is a stream whose Unicode characters are mapped to local characters as they are written.

Parameters: out—the output stream to localize.

Returns: A localized output stream based on the specified output stream.

getRuntime

```
public static Runtime getRuntime()
```

This method gets the runtime environment object associated with the current Java program.

Returns: The runtime environment object associated with the current Java program.

load

`public void load(String pathname)`

This method loads the dynamic library with the specified complete pathname.

Parameters: pathname—the path name of the library to load.

Throws: UnsatisfiedLinkError if the library doesn't exist.

Throws: SecurityException if the current thread can't load the library.

loadLibrary

`public void loadLibrary(String libname)`

This method loads the dynamic library with the specified library name. Note that the mapping from library name to a specific filename is performed in a platform-specific manner.

Parameters: libname—the name of the library to load.

Throws: UnsatisfiedLinkError if the library doesn't exist.

Throws: SecurityException if the current thread can't load the library.

runFinalization

`public void runFinalization()`

This method explicitly causes the finalize methods of any discarded objects to be called.

totalMemory

`public long totalMemory()`

This method determines the total amount of memory in the runtime system, in bytes.

Returns: The total amount of memory, in bytes.

traceInstructions

`public void traceInstructions(boolean on)`

This method is used to determine whether the Java virtual machine prints out a detailed trace of each instruction executed.

Parameters: on—a boolean value specifying whether the Java virtual machine prints out a detailed trace of each instruction executed; a value of true means the instruction trace is printed, whereas a value of false means the instruction trace isn't printed.

traceMethodCalls

`public void traceMethodCalls(boolean on)`

This method is used to determine whether the Java virtual machine prints out a detailed trace of each method that is called.

Parameters: on—a boolean value specifying whether the Java virtual machine prints out a detailed trace of each method that is called; a value of `true` means the method call trace is printed, whereas a value of `false` means the method call trace isn't printed.

SecurityManager

Extends: `Object`

This class is an abstract class that defines a security policy that can be used by Java programs to check for potentially unsafe operations.

Member Variables

`protected boolean inCheck`

This member variable specifies whether a security check is in progress. A value of `true` indicates that a security check is in progress, where a value of `false` means no check is taking place.

SecurityManager Constructor

`protected SecurityManager()`

This constructor creates a default security manager. Note that only one security manager is allowed for each Java program.

Throws: `SecurityException` if the security manager cannot be created.

checkAccept

`public void checkAccept(String host, int port)`

This method checks to see if the calling thread is allowed to establish a socket connection to the specified port on the specified host.

Parameters:

host—the host name to connect the socket to.

port—the number of the port to connect the socket to.

Throws: SecurityException if the calling thread doesn't have permission to establish the socket connection.

checkAccess

```
public void checkAccess(Thread g)
```

This method checks to see if the calling thread is allowed access to the specified thread.

Parameters: g—the thread to check for access.

Throws: SecurityException if the calling thread doesn't have access to the specified thread.

checkAccess

```
public void checkAccess(ThreadGroup g)
```

This method checks to see if the calling thread is allowed access to the specified thread group.

Parameters: g—the thread group to check for access.

Throws: SecurityException if the calling thread doesn't have access to the specified thread group.

checkConnect

```
public void checkConnect(String host, int port)
```

This method checks to see if the calling thread has established a socket connection to the specified port on the specified host.

Parameters:

host—the host name to check the connection for.

port—the number of the port to check the connection for.

Throws: SecurityException if the calling thread doesn't have permission to establish the socket connection.

checkConnect

```
public void checkConnect(String host, int port, Object context)
```

This method checks to see if the specified security context has established a socket connection to the specified port on the specified host.

Parameters:

host—the host name to check the connection for.

port—the number of the port to check the connection for.

context—the security context for the check.

Throws: SecurityException if the specified security context doesn't have permission to establish the socket connection.

checkCreateClassLoader

public void checkCreateClassLoader()

This method checks to see if the calling thread is allowed access to create a new class loader.

Throws: SecurityException if the calling thread doesn't have permission to create a new class loader.

checkDelete

public void checkDelete(String file)

This method checks to see if the calling thread is allowed access to delete the file with the specified platform-specific filename.

Parameters: file—the platform-specific filename for the file to be checked.

Throws: SecurityException if the calling thread doesn't have permission to delete the file.

checkExec

public void checkExec(String cmd)

This method checks to see if the calling thread is allowed access to create a subprocess to execute the specified system command.

Parameters: cmd—a string representing the system command to be checked.

Throws: SecurityException if the calling thread doesn't have permission to create a subprocess to execute the system command.

checkExit

```
public void checkExit(int status)
```

This method checks to see if the calling thread is allowed access to exit the Java runtime system with the specified exit status.

Parameters: status—the integer exit status to be checked.

Throws: SecurityException if the calling thread doesn't have permission to exit with the specified exit status.

checkLink

```
public void checkLink(String libname)
```

This method checks to see if the calling thread is allowed access to dynamically link the library with the specified name.

Parameters: libname—the name of the library to be checked.

Throws: SecurityException if the calling thread doesn't have permission to dynamically link the library.

checkListen

```
public void checkListen(int port)
```

This method checks to see if the calling thread is allowed to wait for a connection request on the specified port.

Parameters: port—the number of the port to check the connection for.

Throws: SecurityException if the calling thread doesn't have permission to wait for a connection request on the specified port.

checkPackageAccess

```
public void checkPackageAccess(String pkg)
```

This method checks to see if the calling thread is allowed access to the package with the specified name.

Parameters: pkg—the name of the package to be checked.

Throws: SecurityException if the calling thread doesn't have permission to access the package.

checkPackageDefinition

`public void checkPackageDefinition(String pkg)`

This method checks to see if the calling thread is allowed to define classes in the package with the specified name.

Parameters: pkg—the name of the package to be checked.

Throws: SecurityException if the calling thread doesn't have permission to define classes in the package.

checkPropertiesAccess

`public void checkPropertiesAccess()`

This method checks to see if the calling thread is allowed access to the system properties.

Throws: SecurityException if the calling thread doesn't have permission to access the system properties.

checkPropertyAccess

`public void checkPropertyAccess(String key)`

This method checks to see if the calling thread is allowed access to the system property with the specified key name.

Parameters: key—the key name for the system property to check.

Throws: SecurityException if the calling thread doesn't have permission to access the system property with the specified key name.

checkRead

`public void checkRead(FileDescriptor fd)`

This method checks to see if the calling thread is allowed access to read from the file with the specified file descriptor.

Parameters: fd—the file descriptor for the file to be checked.

Throws: SecurityException if the calling thread doesn't have permission to read from the file.

checkRead

`public void checkRead(String filename)`

This method checks to see if the calling thread is allowed access to read from the file with the specified platform-specific filename.

Parameters: `file`—the platform-specific filename for the file to be checked.

Throws: `SecurityException` if the calling thread doesn't have permission to read from the file.

checkRead

`public void checkRead(String file, Object context)`

This method checks to see if the specified security context is allowed access to read from the file with the specified platform-specific filename.

Parameters:

`file`—the platform-specific filename for the file to be checked.

`context`—the security context for the check.

Throws: `SecurityException` if the specified security context doesn't have permission to read from the file.

checkSetFactory

`public void checkSetFactory()`

This method checks to see if the calling thread is allowed access to set the socket or stream handler factory used by the URL class.

Throws: `SecurityException` if the calling thread doesn't have permission to set the socket or stream handler factory.

checkTopLevelWindow

`public boolean checkTopLevelWindow(Object window)`

This method checks to see if the calling thread is trusted to show the specified top-level window.

Parameters: `window`—the top-level window to be checked.

Returns: `true` if the calling thread is trusted to show the top-level window; `false` otherwise.

checkWrite

`public void checkWrite(FileDescriptor fd)`

This method checks to see if the calling thread is allowed access to write to the file with the specified file descriptor.

Parameters: fd—the file descriptor for the file to be checked.

Throws: SecurityException if the calling thread doesn't have permission to write to the file.

checkWrite

`public void checkWrite(String file)`

This method checks to see if the calling thread is allowed access to write to the file with the specified platform-specific filename.

Parameters: file—the platform-specific filename for the file to be checked.

Throws: SecurityException if the calling thread doesn't have permission to write to the file.

classDepth

`protected int classDepth(String name)`

This method determines the stack depth of the class with the specified name.

Parameters: name—the fully qualified name of the class to determine the stack depth of.

Returns: The stack depth of the class, or -1 if the class can't be found in any stack frame.

classLoaderDepth

`protected int classLoaderDepth()`

This method determines the stack depth of the most recently executing method of a class defined using a class loader.

Returns: The stack depth of the most recently executing method of a class defined using a class loader, or -1 if no method is executing within a class defined by a class loader.

currentClassLoader

`protected ClassLoader currentClassLoader()`

This method determines the current class loader on the stack.

Returns: The current class loader on the stack, or null if no class loader exists on the stack.

getClassContext

```
protected Class[] getClassContext()
```

This method determines the current execution stack, which is an array of classes corresponding to each method call on the stack.

Returns: An array of classes corresponding to each method call on the stack.

getInCheck

```
public boolean getInCheck()
```

This method determines whether there is a security check in progress.

Returns: true if a security check is in progress; false otherwise.

getSecurityContext

```
public Object getSecurityContext()
```

This method creates a platform-specific security context based on the current runtime environment.

Returns: A platform-specific security context based on the current runtime environment.

inClass

```
protected boolean inClass(String name)
```

This method determines if a method in the class with the specified name is on the execution stack.

Parameters: name—the name of the class to check.

Returns: true if a method in the class is on the execution stack; false otherwise.

inClassLoader

```
protected boolean inClassLoader()
```

This method determines if a method in a class defined using a class loader is on the execution stack.

Returns: true if a method in a class defined using a class loader is on the execution stack; false otherwise.

String

Extends: Object

This class implements a constant string of characters. The String class provides a wide range of support for working with strings of characters. Note that literal string constants are automatically converted to String objects by the Java compiler.

String **Constructor**

```
public String()
```

This constructor creates a default string containing no characters.

String **Constructor**

```
public String(byte ascii[], int hibyte)
```

This constructor creates a string from the specified array of bytes, with the top 8 bits of each string character set to hibyte.

Parameters:

ascii—the byte array that is to be converted to string characters.

hibyte—the high byte value for each character.

String **Constructor**

```
public String(byte ascii[], int hibyte, int off, int count)
```

This constructor creates a string of length count from the specified array of bytes beginning off bytes into the array, with the top 8 bits of each string character set to hibyte.

Parameters:

ascii—the byte array that is to be converted to string characters.

hibyte—the high byte value for each character.

off—the starting offset into the array of bytes.

count—the number of bytes from the array to convert.

Throws: StringIndexOutOfBoundsException if the offset or count for the byte array is invalid.

String **Constructor**

`public String(char value[])`

This constructor creates a string from the specified array of characters.

Parameters: value—the character array to initialize the string with.

String **Constructor**

`public String(char value[], int off, int count)`

This constructor creates a string of length count from the specified array of characters beginning off bytes into the array.

Parameters:

value—the character array to initialize the string with.

off—the starting offset into the array of characters.

count—the number of characters from the array to use in initializing the string.

Throws: StringIndexOutOfBoundsException if the offset or count for the character array is invalid.

String **Constructor**

`public String(String value)`

This method creates a new string that is a copy of the specified string.

Parameters: value—the string to initialize this string with.

String **Constructor**

`public String(StringBuffer buffer)`

This method creates a new string that is a copy of the contents of the specified string buffer.

Parameters: buffer—the string buffer to initialize this string with.

charAt

`public char charAt(int index)`

This method determines the character at the specified index. Note that string indexes are zero based, meaning that the first character is located at index 0.

Parameters: index—the index of the desired character.

Returns: The character at the specified index.

Throws: StringIndexOutOfBoundsException if the index is out of range.

compareTo

```
public int compareTo(String anotherString)
```

This method compares this string with the specified string lexicographically.

Parameters: anotherString—the string to be compared with.

Returns: If this string is equal to the specified string, a value less than 0 if this string is lexicographically less than the specified string, or a value greater than 0 if this string is lexicographically greater than the specified string.

concat

```
public String concat(String str)
```

This method concatenates the specified string onto the end of this string.

Parameters: str—the string to concatenate.

Returns: This string, with the specified string concatenated onto the end.

copyValueOf

```
public static String copyValueOf(char data[])
```

This method converts a character array to an equivalent string by creating a new string and copying the characters into it.

Parameters: data—the character array to convert to a string.

Returns: A string representation of the specified character array.

copyValueOf

```
public static String copyValueOf(char data[], int off, int count)
```

This method converts a character array to an equivalent string by creating a new string and copying count characters into it beginning at off.

Parameters:

data—the character array to convert to a string.

off—the starting offset into the character array.

count—the number of characters from the array to use in initializing the string.

Returns: A string representation of the specified character array beginning at off and of length count.

endsWith

```
public boolean endsWith(String suffix)
```

This method determines whether this string ends with the specified suffix.

Parameters: suffix—the suffix to check.

Returns: true if this string ends with the specified suffix; false otherwise.

equals

```
public boolean equals(Object obj)
```

This method compares the specified object to this string. The equals method returns true only if the specified object is a String object of the same length and contains the same characters as this string.

Parameters: obj—the object to compare.

Returns: true if the specified object is a String object of the same length and contains the same characters as this string; false otherwise.

equalsIgnoreCase

```
public boolean equalsIgnoreCase(String anotherString)
```

This method compares the specified string to this string, ignoring case.

Parameters: anotherString—the string to compare.

Returns: true if the specified string is of the same length and contains the same characters as this string, ignoring case; false otherwise.

getBytes

```
public void getBytes(int srcBegin, int srcEnd, byte dst[], int dstBegin)
```

This method copies the lower 8 bits of each character in this string beginning at srcBegin and ending at srcEnd into the byte array dst beginning at dstBegin.

Parameters:

srcBegin—index of the first character in the string to copy.

srcEnd—index of the last character in the string to copy.

dst—the destination byte array.

dstBegin—the starting offset into the byte array.

getChars

```
public void getChars(int srcBegin, int srcEnd, char dst[], int dstBegin)
```

This method copies each character in this string beginning at srcBegin and ending at srcEnd into the character array dst beginning at dstBegin.

Parameters:

srcBegin—index of the first character in the string to copy.

srcEnd—index of the last character in the string to copy.

dst—the destination character array.

dstBegin—the starting offset into the character array.

Throws: StringIndexOutOfBoundsException if there is an invalid index into the buffer.

hashCode

```
public int hashCode()
```

This method calculates a hash code for this object.

Returns: A hash code for this object.

indexOf

```
public int indexOf(int ch)
```

This method determines the index of the first occurrence of the specified character in this string.

Parameters: ch—the character to search for.

Returns: The index of the first occurrence of the specified character, or -1 if the character doesn't occur.

indexOf

`public int indexOf(int ch, int fromIndex)`

This method determines the index of the first occurrence of the specified character in this string beginning at `fromIndex`.

Parameters:

`ch`—the character to search for.

`fromIndex`—the index to start the search from.

Returns: The index of the first occurrence of the specified character beginning at `fromIndex`, or `-1` if the character doesn't occur.

indexOf

`public int indexOf(String str)`

This method determines the index of the first occurrence of the specified substring in this string.

Parameters: `str`—the substring to search for.

Returns: The index of the first occurrence of the specified substring, or `-1` if the substring doesn't occur.

indexOf

`public int indexOf(String str, int fromIndex)`

This method determines the index of the first occurrence of the specified substring in this string, beginning at `fromIndex`.

Parameters:

`str`—the substring to search for.

`fromIndex`—the index to start the search from.

Returns: The index of the first occurrence of the specified substring beginning at `fromIndex`, or `-1` if the substring doesn't occur.

intern

`public String intern()`

This method determines a string that is equal to this string, but is guaranteed to be from a pool of unique strings.

Returns: A string that is equal to this string, but is guaranteed to be from a pool of unique strings.

lastIndexOf

```
public int lastIndexOf(int ch)
```

This method determines the index of the last occurrence of the specified character in this string.

Parameters: ch—the character to search for.

Returns: The index of the last occurrence of the specified character, or -1 if the character doesn't occur.

lastIndexOf

```
public int lastIndexOf(int ch, int fromIndex)
```

This method determines the index of the last occurrence of the specified character in this string, beginning at fromIndex.

Parameters:

ch—the character to search for.

fromIndex—the index to start the search from.

Returns: The index of the last occurrence of the specified character beginning at fromIndex, or -1 if the character doesn't occur.

lastIndexOf

```
public int lastIndexOf(String str)
```

This method determines the index of the last occurrence of the specified substring in this string.

Parameters: str—the substring to search for.

Returns: The index of the last occurrence of the specified substring, or -1 if the substring doesn't occur.

lastIndexOf

```
public int lastIndexOf(String str, int fromIndex)
```

This method determines the index of the last occurrence of the specified substring in this string beginning at fromIndex.

Parameters:

str—the substring to search for.

fromIndex—the index to start the search from.

Returns: The index of the last occurrence of the specified substring beginning at fromIndex, or -1 if the substring doesn't occur.

length

```
public int length()
```

This method determines the length of this string, which is the number of Unicode characters in the string.

Returns: The length of this string.

regionMatches

```
public boolean regionMatches(boolean ignoreCase, int toffset, String other,
int ooffset, int len)
```

This method determines whether a substring of this string matches a substring of the specified string, with an option for ignoring case.

Parameters:

ignoreCase—a boolean value specifying whether case is ignored; a value of true means case is ignored, where a value of false means case isn't ignored.

toffset—the index to start the substring for this string.

other—the other string to compare.

ooffset—the index to start the substring for the string to compare.

len—the number of characters to compare.

Returns: true if the substring of this string matches the substring of the specified string; false otherwise.

regionMatches

```
public boolean regionMatches(int toffset, String other, int ooffset, int len)
```

This method determines whether a substring of this string matches a substring of the specified string.

Parameters:

toffset—the index to start the substring for this string.

other—the other string to compare.

ooffset—the index to start the substring for the string to compare.

len—the number of characters to compare.

Returns: true if the substring of this string matches the substring of the specified string; false otherwise.

replace

```
public String replace(char oldChar, char newChar)
```

This method replaces all occurrences of oldChar in this string with newChar.

Parameters:

oldChar—the old character to replace.

newChar—the new character to take its place.

Returns: This string, with all occurrences of oldChar replaced with newChar.

startsWith

```
public boolean startsWith(String prefix)
```

This method determines whether this string starts with the specified prefix.

Parameters: prefix—the prefix to check.

Returns: true if this string starts with the specified prefix; false otherwise.

startsWith

```
public boolean startsWith(String prefix, int fromIndex)
```

This method determines whether this string starts with the specified prefix beginning at fromIndex.

Parameters:

prefix—the prefix to check.

fromIndex—the index to start the search from.

Returns: true if this string starts with the specified prefix beginning at fromIndex; false otherwise.

substring

`public String substring(int beginIndex)`

This method determines the substring of this string beginning at `beginIndex`.

Parameters: `beginIndex`—the beginning index of the substring, inclusive.

Returns: The substring of this string beginning at `beginIndex`.

Throws: `StringIndexOutOfBoundsException` if `beginIndex` is out of range.

substring

`public String substring(int beginIndex, int endIndex)`

This method determines the substring of this string beginning at `beginIndex` and ending at `endIndex`.

Parameters:

`beginIndex`—the beginning index of the substring, inclusive.

`endIndex`—the end index of the substring, exclusive.

Returns: The substring of this string beginning at `beginIndex` and ending at `endIndex`.

Throws: `StringIndexOutOfBoundsException` if `beginIndex` or `endIndex` is out of range.

toCharArray

`public char[] toCharArray()`

This method converts this string to a character array by creating a new array and copying each character of the string to it.

Returns: A character array representing this string.

toLowerCase

`public String toLowerCase()`

This method converts all the characters in this string to lowercase.

Returns: This string, with all the characters converted to lowercase.

toString

`public String toString()`

This method returns this string.

Returns: This string itself.

toUpperCase

```
public String toUpperCase()
```

This method converts all the characters in this string to uppercase.

Returns: This string, with all the characters converted to uppercase.

trim

```
public String trim()
```

This method trims leading and trailing whitespace from this string.

Returns: This string, with leading and trailing whitespace removed.

valueOf

```
public static String valueOf(boolean b)
```

This method creates a string representation of the specified boolean value. If the boolean value is true, the string "true" is returned; otherwise, the string "false" is returned.

Parameters: b—the boolean value to get the string representation of.

Returns: A string representation of the specified boolean value.

valueOf

```
public static String valueOf(char c)
```

This method creates a string representation of the specified character value.

Parameters: c—the character value to get the string representation of.

Returns: A string representation of the specified character value.

valueOf

```
public static String valueOf(char data[])
```

This method creates a string representation of the specified character array.

Parameters: data—the character array to get the string representation of.

Returns: A string representation of the specified character array.

valueOf

```
public static String valueOf(char data[], int off, int count)
```

This constructor creates a string representation of length `count` from the specified array of characters beginning `off` bytes into the array.

Parameters:

`data`—the character array to get the string representation of.

`off`—the starting offset into the array of characters.

`count`—the number of characters from the array to use in initializing the string.

Returns: A string representation of the specified character array.

valueOf

```
public static String valueOf(double d)
```

This method creates a string representation of the specified double value.

Parameters: `d`—the double value to get the string representation of.

Returns: A string representation of the specified double value.

valueOf

```
public static String valueOf(float f)
```

This method creates a string representation of the specified float value.

Parameters: `f`—the float value to get the string representation of.

Returns: A string representation of the specified float value.

valueOf

```
public static String valueOf(int i)
```

This method creates a string representation of the specified integer value.

Parameters: `i`—the integer value to get the string representation of.

Returns: A string representation of the specified integer value.

valueOf

```
public static String valueOf(long l)
```

This method creates a string representation of the specified long value.

Parameters: l—the long value to get the string representation of.

Returns: A string representation of the specified long value.

valueOf

```
public static String valueOf(Object obj)
```

This method creates a string representation of the specified object. Note that the string representation is the same as that returned by the toString method of the object.

Parameters: obj—the object to get the string representation of.

Returns: A string representation of the specified object value, or the string "null" if the object is null.

StringBuffer

Extends: Object

This class implements a variable string of characters. The StringBuffer class provides a wide range of append and insert methods, along with some other support methods for getting information about the string buffer.

StringBuffer **Constructor**

```
public StringBuffer()
```

This constructor creates a default string buffer with no characters.

StringBuffer **Constructor**

```
public StringBuffer(int length)
```

This constructor creates a string buffer with the specified length.

Parameters: length—the initial length of the string buffer.

StringBuffer **Constructor**

```
public StringBuffer(String str)
```

This constructor creates a string buffer with the specified initial string value.

Parameters: str—the initial string value of the string buffer.

append

```
public StringBuffer append(boolean b)
```

This method appends the string representation of the specified boolean value to the end of this string buffer.

Parameters: b—the boolean value to be appended.

Returns: This string buffer, with the boolean appended.

append

```
public StringBuffer append(char c)
```

This method appends the string representation of the specified character value to the end of this string buffer.

Parameters: c—the character value to be appended.

Returns: This string buffer, with the character appended.

append

```
public StringBuffer append(char str[])
```

This method appends the string representation of the specified character array to the end of this string buffer.

Parameters: str—the character array to be appended.

Returns: This string buffer, with the character array appended.

append

```
public StringBuffer append(char str[], int off, int len)
```

This method appends the string representation of the specified character subarray to the end of this string buffer.

Parameters:

str—the character array to be appended.

off—the starting offset into the character array to append.

len—the number of characters to append.

Returns: This string buffer, with the character subarray appended.

append

`public StringBuffer append(double d)`

This method appends the string representation of the specified double value to the end of this string buffer.

Parameters: d—the double value to be appended.

Returns: This string buffer, with the double appended.

append

`public StringBuffer append(float f)`

This method appends the string representation of the specified float value to the end of this string buffer.

Parameters: f—the float value to be appended.

Returns: This string buffer, with the float appended.

append

`public StringBuffer append(int i)`

This method appends the string representation of the specified integer value to the end of this string buffer.

Parameters: i—the integer value to be appended.

Returns: This string buffer, with the integer appended.

append

`public StringBuffer append(long l)`

This method appends the string representation of the specified long value to the end of this string buffer.

Parameters: l—the long value to be appended.

Returns: This string buffer, with the long appended.

append

`public StringBuffer append(Object obj)`

This method appends the string representation of the specified object to the end of this string buffer.

Parameters: obj—the object to be appended.

Returns: This string buffer, with the object appended.

append

`public StringBuffer append(String str)`

This method appends the specified string to the end of this string buffer.

Parameters: str—the string to be appended.

Returns: This string buffer, with the string appended.

capacity

`public int capacity()`

This method determines the capacity of this string buffer, which is the amount of character storage currently allocated in the string buffer.

Returns: The capacity of this string buffer.

charAt

`public char charAt(int index)`

This method determines the character at the specified index. Note that string buffer indexes are zero based, meaning that the first character is located at index 0.

Parameters: index—the index of the desired character.

Returns: The character at the specified index.

Throws: `StringIndexOutOfBoundsException` if the index is out of range.

ensureCapacity

`public void ensureCapacity(int minimumCapacity)`

This method ensures that the capacity of this string buffer is at least equal to the specified minimum.

Parameters: minimumCapacity—the minimum desired capacity.

getChars

```
public void getChars(int srcBegin, int srcEnd, char dst[], int dstBegin)
```

This method copies each character in this string buffer beginning at srcBegin and ending at srcEnd into the character array dst beginning at dstBegin.

Parameters:

srcBegin—index of the first character in the string buffer to copy.

srcEnd—index of the last character in the string buffer to copy.

dst—the destination character array.

dstBegin—the starting offset into the character array.

Throws: StringIndexOutOfBoundsException if there is an invalid index into the buffer.

insert

```
public StringBuffer insert(int off, boolean b)
```

This method inserts the string representation of the specified boolean value at the specified offset of this string buffer.

Parameters:

off—the offset at which to insert the boolean.

b—the boolean value to be inserted.

Returns: This string buffer, with the boolean inserted.

Throws: StringIndexOutOfBoundsException if the offset is invalid.

insert

```
public StringBuffer insert(int off, char c)
```

This method inserts the string representation of the specified character value at the specified offset of this string buffer.

Parameters:

off—the offset at which to insert the character.

c—the character value to be inserted.

Returns: This string buffer, with the character inserted.

Throws: StringIndexOutOfBoundsException if the offset is invalid.

insert

`public StringBuffer insert(int off, char str[])`

This method inserts the string representation of the specified character array at the specified offset of this string buffer.

Parameters:

off—the offset at which to insert the character array.

str—the character array to be inserted.

Returns: This string buffer, with the character array inserted.

Throws: StringIndexOutOfBoundsException if the offset is invalid.

insert

`public StringBuffer insert(int off, double d)`

This method inserts the string representation of the specified double value at the specified offset of this string buffer.

Parameters:

off—the offset at which to insert the double.

d—the double value to be inserted.

Returns: This string buffer, with the double inserted.

Throws: StringIndexOutOfBoundsException if the offset is invalid.

insert

`public StringBuffer insert(int off, float f)`

This method inserts the string representation of the specified float value at the specified offset of this string buffer.

Parameters:

off—the offset at which to insert the float.

f—the float value to be inserted.

Returns: This string buffer, with the float inserted.

Throws: StringIndexOutOfBoundsException if the offset is invalid.

insert

`public StringBuffer insert(int off, int i)`

This method inserts the string representation of the specified integer value at the specified offset of this string buffer.

Parameters:

off—the offset at which to insert the integer.

i—the integer value to be inserted.

Returns: This string buffer, with the integer inserted.

Throws: `StringIndexOutOfBoundsException` if the offset is invalid.

insert

`public StringBuffer insert(int off, long l)`

This method inserts the string representation of the specified long value at the specified offset of this string buffer.

Parameters:

off—the offset at which to insert the long.

l—the long value to be inserted.

Returns: This string buffer, with the long inserted.

Throws: `StringIndexOutOfBoundsException` if the offset is invalid.

insert

`public StringBuffer insert(int off, Object obj)`

This method inserts the string representation of the specified object at the specified offset of this string buffer.

Parameters:

off—the offset at which to insert the object.

obj—the object to be inserted.

Returns: This string buffer, with the object inserted.

Throws: `StringIndexOutOfBoundsException` if the offset is invalid.

insert

`public StringBuffer insert(int off, String str)`

This method inserts the specified string at the specified offset of this string buffer.

Parameters:

off—the offset at which to insert the string.

str—the string to be inserted.

Returns: This string buffer, with the string inserted.

Throws: `StringIndexOutOfBoundsException` if the offset is invalid.

length

`public int length()`

This method determines the length of this string buffer, which is the actual number of characters stored in the buffer.

Returns: The length of this string buffer.

reverse

`public StringBuffer reverse()`

This method reverses the character sequence in this string buffer.

Returns: This string buffer, with the characters reversed.

setCharAt

`public void setCharAt(int index, char ch)`

This method changes the character at the specified index in this string to the specified character.

Parameters:

index—the index of the character to change.

ch—the new character.

Throws: `StringIndexOutOfBoundsException` if the index is invalid.

setLength

`public void setLength(int newLength)`

This method explicitly sets the length of this string buffer. If the length is reduced, characters are lost; if the length is increased, new characters are set to 0 (null).

Parameters: newLength—the new length of the string buffer.

Throws: StringIndexOutOfBoundsException if the length is invalid.

toString

`public String toString()`

This method determines a constant string representation of this string buffer.

Returns: The constant string representation of this string buffer.

System

Extends: Object

This class provides a platform-independent means of interacting with the Java runtime system. The System class provides support for standard input, standard output, and standard error streams, along with providing access to system properties, among other things.

Member Variables

`public static PrintStream err`

This is the standard error stream, which is used for printing error information. Typically this stream corresponds to display output since it is important that the user see the error information.

`public static InputStream in`

This is the standard input stream, which is used for reading character data. Typically this stream corresponds to keyboard input or another input source specified by the host environment or user.

`public static PrintStream out`

This is the standard output stream, which is used for printing character data. Typically this stream corresponds to display output or another output destination specified by the host environment or user.

arraycopy

```
public static void arraycopy(Object src, int src_position, Object dst,
int dst_position, int len)
```

This method copies `len` array elements from the `src` array beginning at `src_position` to the `dst` array beginning at `dst_position`. Both `src` and `dst` must be array objects. Note that `arraycopy` does not allocate memory for the destination array; the memory must already be allocated.

Parameters:

`src`—the source array to copy data from.

`src_position`—the start position in the source array.

`dst`—the destination array to copy data to.

`dst_position`—the start position in the destination array.

`len`—the number of array elements to be copied.

Throws: `ArrayIndexOutOfBoundsException` if the copy would cause data to be accessed outside of array bounds.

Throws: `ArrayStoreException` if an element in the source array could not be stored in the destination array due to a type mismatch.

currentTimeMillis

```
public static long currentTimeMillis()
```

This method determines the current UTC time relative to midnight, January 1, 1970 UTC, in milliseconds.

Returns: The current UTC time relative to midnight, January 1, 1970 UTC, in milliseconds.

exit

```
public static void exit(int status)
```

This method exits the Java runtime system (virtual machine) with the specified integer exit status. Note that since `exit` kills the runtime system, it never returns.

Parameters: `status`—the integer exit status; this should be set to nonzero if this is an abnormal exit.

Throws: `SecurityException` if the current thread cannot exit with the specified exit status.

gc

```
public static void gc()
```

This method invokes the Java garbage collector to clean up any objects that are no longer needed, usually resulting in more free memory.

getProperties

```
public static Properties getProperties()
```

This method determines the current system properties. Following is a list of all the system properties guaranteed to be supported:

- ☐ `java.version`—the Java version number.
- ☐ `java.vendor`—the Java vendor-specific string.
- ☐ `java.vendor.url`—the Java vendor URL.
- ☐ `java.home`—the Java installation directory.
- ☐ `java.class.version`—the Java class format version number.
- ☐ `java.class.path`—the Java CLASSPATH environment variable.
- ☐ `os.name`—the operating system name.
- ☐ `os.arch`—the operating system architecture.
- ☐ `os.version`—the operating system version.
- ☐ `file.separator`—the file separator.
- ☐ `path.separator`—the path separator.
- ☐ `line.separator`—the line separator.
- ☐ `user.name`—the user's account name.
- ☐ `user.home`—the user's home directory.
- ☐ `user.dir`—the user's current working directory.

Returns: The current system properties.

Throws: `SecurityException` if the current thread cannot access the system properties.

getProperty

```
public static String getProperty(String key)
```

This method determines the system property with the specified key name.

Parameters: key—the key name of the system property.

Returns: The system property with the specified key name.

Throws: `SecurityException` if the current thread cannot access the system property.

getProperty

```
public static String getProperty(String key, String def)
```

This method determines the system property with the specified key name; it returns the specified default property value if the key isn't found.

Parameters:

key—the key name of the system property.

def—the default property value to use if the key isn't found.

Returns: The system property with the specified key name, or the specified default property value if the key isn't found.

Throws: SecurityException if the current thread cannot access the system property.

getSecurityManager

```
public static SecurityManager getSecurityManager()
```

This method gets the security manager for the Java program, or null if none exists.

Returns: The security manager for the Java program, or null if none exists.

load

```
public static void load(String pathname)
```

This method loads the dynamic library with the specified complete path name. This method simply calls the load method in the Runtime class.

Parameters: pathname—the path name of the library to load.

Throws: UnsatisfiedLinkError if the library doesn't exist.

Throws: SecurityException if the current thread can't load the library.

loadLibrary

```
public static void loadLibrary(String libname)
```

This method loads the dynamic library with the specified library name. Note that the mapping from library name to a specific filename is performed in a platform-specific manner.

Parameters: libname—the name of the library to load.

Throws: UnsatisfiedLinkError if the library doesn't exist.

Throws: SecurityException if the current thread can't load the library.

runFinalization

```
public static void runFinalization()
```

This method explicitly causes the finalize methods of any discarded objects to be called. Typically, the finalize methods of discarded objects are automatically called asynchronously when the garbage collector cleans up the objects. You can use runFinalization to have the finalize methods called synchronously.

setProperties

```
public static void setProperties(Properties props)
```

This method sets the system properties to the specified properties.

Parameters: props—the new properties to be set.

setSecurityManager

```
public static void setSecurityManager(SecurityManager s)
```

This method sets the security manager to the specified security manager. Note that the security manager can be set only once for a Java program.

Parameters: s—the new security manager to be set.

Throws: SecurityException if the security manager has already been set.

Thread

Extends: Object

Implements: Runnable

This class provides the overhead necessary to manage a single thread of execution within a process. The Thread class is the basis for multithreaded programming in Java.

Member Constants

```
public final static int MAX_PRIORITY
```

This is a constant representing the maximum priority a thread can have, which is set to 10.

```
public final static int MIN_PRIORITY
```

This is a constant representing the minimum priority a thread can have, which is set to 1.

```
public final static int NORM_PRIORITY
```

This is a constant representing the normal (default) priority for a thread, which is set to 5.

Thread **Constructor**

`public Thread()`

This constructor creates a default thread. Note that threads created with this constructor must have overridden their run method to actually do anything.

Thread **Constructor**

`public Thread(Runnable target)`

This constructor creates a thread that uses the run method of the specified runnable.

Parameters: target—the object whose run method is used by the thread.

Thread **Constructor**

`public Thread(ThreadGroup group, Runnable target)`

This constructor creates a thread belonging to the specified thread group that uses the run method of the specified runnable.

Parameters:

group—the thread group the thread is to be a member of.

target—the object whose run method is used by the thread.

Thread **Constructor**

`public Thread(String name)`

This constructor creates a thread with the specified name.

Parameters: name—the name of the new thread.

Thread **Constructor**

`public Thread(ThreadGroup group, String name)`

This constructor creates a thread belonging to the specified thread group with the specified name.

Parameters:

group—the thread group the thread is to be a member of.

name—the name of the new thread.

Thread **Constructor**

```
public Thread(Runnable target, String name)
```

This constructor creates a thread with the specified name that uses the run method of the specified runnable.

Parameters:

target—the object whose run method is used by the thread.

name—the name of the new thread.

Thread **Constructor**

```
public Thread(ThreadGroup group, Runnable target, String name)
```

This constructor creates a thread belonging to the specified thread group with the specified name that uses the run method of the specified runnable.

Parameters:

group—the thread group the thread is to be a member of.

target—the object whose run method is used by the thread.

name—the name of the new thread.

activeCount

```
public static int activeCount()
```

This method determines the number of active threads in this thread's thread group.

Returns: The number of active threads in this thread's thread group.

checkAccess

```
public void checkAccess()
```

This method checks to see if the currently running thread is allowed access to this thread.

Throws: SecurityException if the calling thread doesn't have access to this thread.

countStackFrames

```
public int countStackFrames()
```

This method determines the number of stack frames in this thread. Note that the thread must be suspended to use this method.

Returns: The number of stack frames in this thread.

Throws: `IllegalThreadStateException` if the thread is not suspended.

currentThread

```
public static Thread currentThread()
```

This method determines the currently running thread.

Returns: The currently running thread.

destroy

```
public void destroy()
```

This method destroys this thread without performing any cleanup, meaning that any monitors locked by the thread remain locked. Note that this method should only be used as a last resort for destroying a thread.

dumpStack

```
public static void dumpStack()
```

This method prints a stack trace for this thread. Note that this method is useful only for debugging.

enumerate

```
public static int enumerate(Thread list[])
```

This method fills the specified array with references to every active thread in this thread's thread group.

Parameters: `list`—an array to hold the enumerated threads.

Returns: The number of threads added to the array.

getName

```
public final String getName()
```

This method determines the name of this thread.

Returns: The name of this thread.

getPriority

`public final int getPriority()`

This method determines the priority of this thread.

Returns: The priority of this thread.

getThreadGroup

`public final ThreadGroup getThreadGroup()`

This method determines the thread group for this thread.

Returns: The thread group for this thread.

interrupt

`public void interrupt()`

This method interrupts this thread.

interrupted

`public static boolean interrupted()`

This method determines if this thread has been interrupted.

Returns: `true` if the thread has been interrupted; `false` otherwise.

isAlive

`public final boolean isAlive()`

This method determines if this thread is active. An active thread is a thread that has been started and has not yet stopped.

Returns: `true` if the thread is active; `false` otherwise.

isDaemon

`public final boolean isDaemon()`

This method determines if this thread is a daemon thread. A daemon thread is a background thread that is owned by the runtime system rather than a specific process.

Returns: `true` if the thread is a daemon thread; `false` otherwise.

isInterrupted

`public boolean isInterrupted()`

This method determines if this thread has been interrupted.

Returns: `true` if the thread has been interrupted; `false` otherwise.

join

`public final void join() throws InterruptedException`

This method causes the current thread to wait indefinitely until it dies.

Throws: `InterruptedException` if another thread has interrupted this thread.

join

`public final void join(long timeout) throws InterruptedException`

This method causes the current thread to wait until it dies, or until the specified timeout period has elapsed.

Parameters: `timeout`—the maximum timeout period to wait, in milliseconds.

Throws: `InterruptedException` if another thread has interrupted this thread.

join

`public final void join(long timeout, int nanos) throws InterruptedException`

This method causes the current thread to wait until it dies, or until the specified timeout period has elapsed. The timeout period in this case is the addition of the `timeout` and `nanos` parameters, which provide finer control over the timeout period.

Parameters:

`timeout`—the maximum timeout period to wait, in milliseconds.

`nanos`—the additional time for the timeout period, in nanoseconds.

Throws: `InterruptedException` if another thread has interrupted this thread.

resume

`public final void resume()`

This method resumes this thread's execution if it has been suspended.

Throws: `SecurityException` if the current thread doesn't have access to this thread.

run

`public void run()`

This method is the body of the thread, which performs the actual work of the thread. The run method is called when the thread is started. The run method is either overridden in a derived Thread class or implemented in a class implementing the Runnable interface.

setDaemon

`public final void setDaemon(boolean daemon)`

This method sets this thread as either a daemon thread or a user thread based on the specified boolean value. Note that the thread must be inactive to use this method.

Parameters: daemon—a boolean value that determines whether the thread is a daemon thread.

Throws: IllegalThreadStateException if the thread is active.

setName

`public final void setName(String name)`

This method sets the name of this thread.

Parameters: name—the new name of the thread.

Throws: SecurityException if the current thread doesn't have access to this thread.

setPriority

`public final void setPriority(int newPriority)`

This method sets the priority of this thread.

Parameters: newPriority—the new priority of the thread.

Throws: IllegalArgumentException if the priority is not within the range MIN_PRIORITY to MAX_PRIORITY.

Throws: SecurityException if the current thread doesn't have access to this thread.

sleep

`public static void sleep(long millis) throws InterruptedException`

This method causes the current thread to sleep for the specified length of time, in milliseconds.

Parameters: `millis`—the length of time to sleep, in milliseconds.

Throws: `InterruptedException` if another thread has interrupted this thread.

sleep

`public static void sleep(long millis, int nanos) throws InterruptedException`

This method causes the current thread to sleep for the specified length of time. The length of time in this case is the addition of the `millis` and `nanos` parameters, which provide finer control over the sleep time.

Parameters:

`millis`—the length of time to sleep, in milliseconds.

`nanos`—the additional time for the sleep time, in nanoseconds.

Throws: `InterruptedException` if another thread has interrupted this thread.

start

`public void start()`

This method starts this thread, causing the `run` method to be executed.

Throws: `IllegalThreadStateException` if the thread was already running.

stop

`public final void stop()`

This method abnormally stops this thread, causing it to throw a `ThreadDeath` object. You can catch the `ThreadDeath` object to perform cleanup, but there is rarely a need to do so.

Throws: `SecurityException` if the current thread doesn't have access to this thread.

stop

`public final synchronized void stop(Throwable o)`

This method abnormally stops this thread, causing it to throw the specified object. Note that this version of stop should be used only in very rare situations.

Parameters: o—the object to be thrown.

Throws: `SecurityException` if the current thread doesn't have access to this thread.

suspend

```
public final void suspend()
```

This method suspends the execution of this thread.

Throws: SecurityException if the current thread doesn't have access to this thread.

toString

```
public String toString()
```

This method determines a string representation of this thread, which includes the thread's name, priority, and thread group.

Returns: A string representation of this thread.

yield

```
public static void yield()
```

This method causes the currently executing thread to yield so that other threads can execute.

ThreadGroup

Extends: Object

This class implements a thread group, which is a set of threads that can be manipulated as one. Thread groups can also contain other thread groups, resulting in a thread hierarchy.

ThreadGroup **Constructor**

```
public ThreadGroup(String name)
```

This constructor creates a thread group with the specified name. The newly created thread group belongs to the thread group of the current thread.

Parameters: name—the name of the new thread group.

ThreadGroup **Constructor**

```
public ThreadGroup(ThreadGroup parent, String name)
```

This constructor creates a thread group with the specified name and belonging to the specified parent thread group.

Parameters:

parent—the parent thread group.

name—the name of the new thread group.

Throws: NullPointerException if the specified thread group is null.

Throws: SecurityException if the current thread cannot create a thread in the specified thread group.

activeCount

```
public int activeCount()
```

This method determines the number of active threads in this thread group or in any other thread group that has this thread group as an ancestor.

Returns: The number of active threads in this thread group or in any other thread group that has this thread group as an ancestor.

activeGroupCount

```
public int activeGroupCount()
```

This method determines the number of active thread groups that have this thread group as an ancestor.

Returns: The number of active thread groups that have this thread group as an ancestor.

checkAccess

```
public final void checkAccess()
```

This method checks to see if the currently running thread is allowed access to this thread group.

Throws: SecurityException if the calling thread doesn't have access to this thread group.

destroy

```
public final void destroy()
```

This method destroys this thread group and all of its subgroups.

Throws: IllegalThreadStateException if the thread group is not empty or if it was already destroyed.

Throws: SecurityException if the calling thread doesn't have access to this thread group.

enumerate

```
public int enumerate(Thread list[])
```

This method fills the specified array with references to every active thread in this thread group.

Parameters: list—an array to hold the enumerated threads.

Returns: The number of threads added to the array.

enumerate

```
public int enumerate(Thread list[], boolean recurse)
```

This method fills the specified array with references to every active thread in this thread group. If the recurse parameter is set to true, all the active threads belonging to subgroups of this thread are also added to the array.

Parameters:

list—an array to hold the enumerated threads.

recurse—a boolean value specifying whether to recursively enumerate active threads in subgroups.

Returns: The number of threads added to the array.

enumerate

```
public int enumerate(ThreadGroup list[])
```

This method fills the specified array with references to every active subgroup in this thread group.

Parameters: list—an array to hold the enumerated thread groups.

Returns: The number of thread groups added to the array.

enumerate

```
public int enumerate(ThreadGroup list[], boolean recurse)
```

This method fills the specified array with references to every active subgroup in this thread group. If the recurse parameter is set to true, all the active thread groups belonging to subgroups of this thread are also added to the array.

Parameters:

list—an array to hold the enumerated thread groups.

recurse—a boolean value specifying whether to recursively enumerate active thread groups in subgroups.

Returns: The number of thread groups added to the array.

getMaxPriority

```
public final int getMaxPriority()
```

This method determines the maximum priority of this thread group. Note that threads in this thread group cannot have a higher priority than the maximum priority.

Returns: The maximum priority of this thread group.

getName

```
public final String getName()
```

This method determines the name of this thread group.

Returns: The name of this thread group.

getParent

```
public final ThreadGroup getParent()
```

This method determines the parent of this thread group.

Returns: The parent of this thread group.

isDaemon

```
public final boolean isDaemon()
```

This method determines if this thread group is a daemon thread group. A daemon thread group is automatically destroyed when all its threads finish executing.

Returns: true if the thread group is a daemon thread group; false otherwise.

list

```
public void list()
```

This method prints information about this thread group to standard output, including the active threads in the group. Note that this method is useful only for debugging.

parentOf

```
public final boolean parentOf(ThreadGroup g)
```

This method checks to see if this thread group is a parent or ancestor of the specified thread group.

Parameters: g—the thread group to be checked.

Returns: true if this thread group is the parent or ancestor of the specified thread group; false otherwise.

resume

```
public final void resume()
```

This method resumes execution of all the threads in this thread group that have been suspended.

Throws: SecurityException if the current thread doesn't have access to this thread group or any of its threads.

setDaemon

```
public final void setDaemon(boolean daemon)
```

This method sets this thread group as either a daemon thread group or a user thread group based on the specified boolean value. A daemon thread group is automatically destroyed when all its threads finish executing.

Parameters: daemon—a boolean value that determines whether the thread group is a daemon thread group.

Throws: SecurityException if the current thread doesn't have access to this thread group.

setMaxPriority

```
public final void setMaxPriority(int pri)
```

This method sets the maximum priority of this thread group.

Parameters: pri—the new maximum priority of the thread group.

Throws: SecurityException if the current thread doesn't have access to this thread group.

stop

```
public final synchronized void stop()
```

This method stops all the threads in this thread group and in all of its subgroups.

Throws: SecurityException if the current thread doesn't have access to this thread group, any of its threads, or threads in subgroups.

suspend

```
public final synchronized void suspend()
```

This method suspends all the threads in this thread group and in all of its subgroups.

Throws: SecurityException if the current thread doesn't have access to this thread group, any of its threads, or threads in subgroups.

toString

```
public String toString()
```

This method determines a string representation of this thread group.

Returns: A string representation of this thread group.

uncaughtException

```
public void uncaughtException(Thread t, Throwable e)
```

This method is called when a thread in this thread group exits because of an uncaught exception. You can override this method to provide specific handling of uncaught exceptions.

Parameters:

t—the thread that is exiting.

e—the uncaught exception.

Throwable

Extends: Object

This class provides the core functionality for signaling when exceptional conditions occur. All errors and exceptions in the Java system are derived from Throwable. The Throwable class contains a snapshot of the execution stack for helping to track down why exceptional conditions occur.

Throwable **Constructor**

`public Throwable()`

This constructor creates a default throwable with no detail message; the stack trace is automatically filled in.

Throwable **Constructor**

`public  constructorhrowable constructor ( constructortring  constructormessage)`

This constructor creates a throwable with the specified detail message; the stack trace is automatically filled in.

Parameters: message—the detail message.

fillInStackTrace

`public Throwable fillInStackTrace()`

This method fills in the execution stack trace. Note that this method is only useful when rethrowing this throwable.

Returns: This throwable.

getMessage

`public String getMessage()`

This method determines the detail message of this throwable.

Returns: The detail message of this throwable.

printStackTrace

`public void printStackTrace()`

This method prints this throwable and its stack trace to the standard error stream.

printStackTrace

`public void printStackTrace(PrintStream s)`

This method prints this throwable and its stack trace to the specified print stream.

Parameters: s—the print stream to print the stack to.

toString

```
public String toString()
```

This method determines a string representation of this throwable.

Returns: A string representation of this throwable.

RuntimeException

This exception class signals that an invalid cast has occurred.

ClassNotFoundException

Extends: Exception

This exception class signals that a class could not be found.

CloneNotSupportedException

Extends: Exception

This exception class signals that an attempt has been made to clone an object that doesn't support the Cloneable interface.

Exception

Extends: Throwable

This throwable class indicates exceptional conditions that a Java program might want to know about.

IllegalAccessException

Extends: Exception

This exception class signals that the current thread doesn't have access to a class.

IllegalArgumentException

Extends: RuntimeException

This exception class signals that a method has been passed an illegal argument.

IllegalMonitorStateException

Extends: RuntimeException

This exception class signals that a thread has attempted to access an object's monitor without owning the monitor.

IllegalThreadStateException

Extends: IllegalArgumentException

This exception class signals that a thread is not in the proper state for the requested operation.

IndexOutOfBoundsException

Extends: RuntimeException

This exception class signals that an index of some sort is out of bounds.

InstantiationException

Extends: Exception

This exception class signals that an attempt has been made to instantiate an abstract class or an interface.

InterruptedException

Extends: Exception

This exception class signals that a thread has been interrupted that is already waiting or sleeping.

NegativeArraySizeException

Extends: RuntimeException

This exception class signals that an attempt has been made to create an array with a negative size.

NullPointerException

Extends: RuntimeException

This exception class signals an attempt to access a null pointer as an object.

NumberFormatException

Extends: IllegalArgumentException

This exception class signals an attempt to convert a string to an invalid number format.

RuntimeException

Extends: Exception

This exception class signals an exceptional condition that can reasonably occur in the Java runtime system.

SecurityException

Extends: RuntimeException

This exception class signals that a security violation has occurred.

StringIndexOutOfBoundsException

Extends: IndexOutOfBoundsException

This exception class signals that an invalid string index has been used.

AbstractMethodError

Extends: IncompatibleClassChangeError

This error class signals an attempt to call an abstract method.

ClassFormatError

Extends: LinkageError

This error class signals an attempt to read a file in an invalid format.

Error

Extends: Throwable

This throwable class indicates a serious problem beyond the scope of what a Java program can fix.

IllegalAccessError

Extends: IncompatibleClassChangeError

This error class signals an attempt to access a member variable or call a method without proper access.

IncompatibleClassChangeError

Extends: LinkageError

This error class signals that an incompatible change has been made to some class definition.

InstantiationError

Extends: IncompatibleClassChangeError

This error class signals an attempt to instantiate an abstract class or an interface.

InternalError

Extends: VirtualMachineError

This error class signals that some unexpected internal error has occurred.

LinkageError

Extends: Error

This error class signals that a class has some dependency on another class, but that the latter class has incompatibly changed after the compilation of the former class.

NoClassDefFoundError

Extends: LinkageError

This error class signals that a class definition could not be found.

NoSuchFieldError

Extends: IncompatibleClassChangeError

This error class signals an attempt to access a member variable that doesn't exist.

NoSuchMethodError

Extends: IncompatibleClassChangeError

This error class signals an attempt to call a method that doesn't exist.

OutOfMemoryError

Extends: VirtualMachineError

This error class signals that the Java runtime system is out of memory.

StackOverflowError

Extends: VirtualMachineError

This error class signals that a stack overflow has occurred.

ThreadDeath

Extends: Error

This error class signals that a thread is being abnormally stopped via the stop method.

UnknownError

Extends: VirtualMachineError

This error class signals that an unknown but serious error has occurred.

UnsatisfiedLinkError

Extends: LinkageError

This error class signals that a native implementation of a method declared as native cannot be found.

VerifyError

Extends: LinkageError

This error class signals that a class has failed the runtime verification test.

VirtualMachineError

Extends: Error

This error class signals that the Java virtual machine is broken or has run out of resources necessary for it to continue operating.

APPENDIX

K

java.net **Package Reference**

The java.net package contains classes and interfaces used for networking. This includes classes to create and manipulate sockets, data packets, and URLs.

ContentHandlerFactory

This interface signals when an unknown service exception has occurred.

createContentHandler

`public abstract ContentHandler createContentHandler(String mimetype)`

The createContentHandler method creates a new content handler to read the content from a URLStreamHandler using the specified MIME type.

Parameters: mimetype—a String object containing the MIME type of the content.

Returns: A ContentHandler object that will read data from a URL connection and construct an object.

SocketImplFactory

This interface is used by the socket class to specify socket implementations.

createSocketImpl

`SocketImpl createSocketImpl()`

The createSocketImple method creates a SocketImpl instance that is an implementation of a socket.

Returns: A SocketImpl object that provides a socket implementation.

URLStreamHandlerFactory

This interface is used by the URL class to create stream handlers for various stream types.

createURLStreamHandler

`URLStreamHandler createURLStreamHandler(String protocol)`

The createURLStreamHandler method creates a URLStreamHandler instance for use by the URL class based on the specified protocol.

Parameters: protocol—a String object that specifies the protocol to be used by the URLStreamHandler class.

Returns: A URLStreamHandler object that is created with the protocol specified in the input parameter.

ContentHandler

Extends: Object

The ContentHandler class is used as a base class for classes that will handle specific MIME content types.

getContent

abstract public Object getContent(URLConnection urlc)

The getContent method accepts a URLConnection argument positioned at the beginning of an input stream and constructs an object from the input stream.

Parameters: urlc—a URLConnection object representing the input stream to be read in by the content handler.

Returns: An object that was constructed from the specified URL connection.

Throws: IOException if the input stream could not be read.

DatagramPacket

Extends: Object

The DatagramPacket class is used to store packet data such as data, length, Internet address, and port.

DatagramPacket **Constructor**

public DatagramPacket(byte ibuf[], int ilength)

This DatagramPacket constructor constructs a DatagramPacket object to be used for receiving datagrams.

Parameters:

ibuf—an array of bytes that will be used to store the datagram packet.

ilength—an integer value specifying the size of the datagram packet.

DatagramPacket **Constructor**

`public DatagramPacket(byte ibuf[], int ilength, InetAddress iaddr, int iport)`

This `DatagramPacket` constructor constructs a `DatagramPacket` object to be sent.

Parameters:

ibuf—an array of bytes that will be used to store the datagram packet.

ilength—an integer value specifying the size of the datagram packet.

iaddr—the destination IP address.

iport—the destination port.

getAddress

`public InetAddress getAddress()`

The `getAddress` method returns the IP address value of the `DatagramPacket`.

Returns: An `InetAddress` object containing the IP address of the datagram packet.

getPort

`public int getPort()`

The `getPort` method returns the port value of the `DatagramPacket`.

Returns: An integer value containing the port address of the datagram packet.

getData

`public byte[] getData()`

The `getData` method returns the array of datagram packet values.

Returns: An array of bytes containing the contents of the datagram packet.

getLength

`public int getLength()`

The `getLength` method returns the length of the datagram packet.

Returns: An integer value containing the length of the datagram packet.

DatagramSocket

Extends: Object

The DatagramSocket class is used to designate a dedicated socket for implementing unreliable datagrams.

DatagramSocket **Constructor**

`public DatagramSocket() throws SocketException`

The DatagramSocket constructor is used to implement an unreliable Datagram connection.

Throws: SocketException if the socket could not be created.

DatagramSocket **Constructor**

`public DatagramSocket(int port) throws SocketException`

This DatagramSocket constructor implements an unreliable datagram connection using the specified port value.

Parameters: port—an integer value specifying the port to be used for the socket.

Throws: SocketException if the socket could not be created.

send

`public void send(DatagramPacket p) throws IOException`

The send method sends a datagram packet to the destination address specified in the datagram packet's address value.

Parameters: p—a DatagramPacket object containing data to be sent through the socket.

Throws: IOException if an I/O exception has occurred.

receive

`public synchronized void receive(DatagramPacket p) throws IOException`

The receive method receives a datagram packet. This method will block until the datagram packet has been received.

Parameters: p—the datagram packet to be received.

Throws: IOException if an I/O exception has occurred.

getLocalPort

```
public int getLocalPort()
```

The getLocalPort method returns the port on the local machine that this socket is bound to.

Returns: An integer value containing the port value that this socket is bound to.

close

```
public synchronized void close()
```

The close method closes the datagram socket.

InetAddress

Extends: Object

The InetAddress class is used to represent Internet addresses.

getHostName

```
public String getHostName()
```

The getHostName method returns the name of the host for this InetAddress. If the host is null, the returned string will contain any of the local machine's available network addresses.

Returns: A String object containing the name of the host for this InetAddress.

getAddress

```
public byte[] getAddress()
```

The getAddress method returns an array of bytes containing the raw IP address in network byte order.

Returns: A byte array containing the raw IP address of this InetAddress in network byte order.

getHostAddress

```
public String getHostAddress()
```

The getHostAddress method returns the IP address string %d.%d.%d.%d.

Returns: A String value containing the raw IP address using the standard IP address format.

hashCode

`public int hashCode()`

The `hashCode` method returns a hash code for this `InetAddress`.

Returns: An integer value representing this `InetAddress`'s hash code.

equals

`public boolean equals(Object obj)`

The `equals` method is used to compare this `InetAddress` object to the specified object.

Parameters: `obj`—the object to be compared with the address.

Returns: A boolean value that will be `true` if the objects are equal; `false` if not.

toString

`public String toString()`

The `toString` method is used to return a string representation of the `InetAddress`.

Returns: A `String` value containing information about the `InetAddress`.

getByName

```
public static synchronized InetAddress getByName(String host)
  throws UnknownHostException
```

The `getByName` method returns an `InetAddress` object based on the specified hostname.

Parameters: `host`—a string object specifying the name of the host.

Returns: An `InetAddress` object containing the Internet address information for the specified host.

Throws: `UnknownHostException` if the specified host is invalid or unknown.

getAllByName

```
public static synchronized InetAddress getAllByName(String host)[]
  throws UnknownHostException
```

The `getAllByName` method returns an array of `InetAddress` objects representing all of the addresses for the specified host.

Parameters: `host`—a `String` object specifying the name of the host.

Returns: An array of all corresponding `InetAddresses` for the specified host.

Throws: `UnknownHostException` if the specified host is invalid or unknown.

getLocalHost

`public static InetAddress getLocalHost() throws UnknownHostException`

The `getLocalHost()` returns an `InetAddress` object representing the address of the local host.

Returns: An `InetAddress` object containing the Internet address information for the local host.

ServerSocket

Extends: `Object`

The `ServerSocket` class is used to encapsulate a server socket.

ServerSocket **Constructor**

`public ServerSocket(int port) throws IOException`

The `ServerSocket` constructor creates a server socket on the specified port.

Parameters: port—an integer value specifying the port to create the socket on.

Throws: `IOException` if an I/O exception has occurred.

ServerSocket **Constructor**

`public ServerSocket(int port, int backlog) throws IOException`

This `ServerSocket` constructor creates a server socket on the specified port and listens to it for a specified time.

Parameters: port—an integer value specifying the port to create the socket on.

Throws: `IOException` if an I/O exception has occurred.

getInetAddress

`public InetAddress getInetAddress()`

The `getInetAddress` method returns an `InetAddress` object specifying the address to which this socket is connected.

Returns: An `InetAddress` object containing the address information to which the socket is connected.

getLocalPort

```
public int getLocalPort()
```

The getLocalPort method returns the local port on which the socket is currently listening.

Returns: An integer value representing the port on the local machine which the server socket is listening to.

accept

```
public Socket accept() throws IOException
```

The accept method is used to accept a connection. This method will block all others until a connection is made.

Returns: A Socket object after the connection has been accepted.

Throws: IOException if an I/O error occurred when waiting for the connection.

close

```
public void close() throws IOException
```

The close method closes the socket's connection.

Throws: IOException if an I/O error occurred while closing the server socket.

toString

```
public String toString()
```

The toString method returns a string representation of the ServerSocket.

Returns: A String object containing the implementation address and implementation port of the server socket.

setSocketFactory

```
public static synchronized void setSocketFactory(SocketImplFactory fac)
  throws IOException, SocketException
```

The setSocketFactory method sets the server SocketImplFactory for use by this ServerSocket. This factory can only be set once.

Parameters: fac—a SocketImplFactory derived object to be used by this server socket.

Throws: IOException if there was an I/O error when setting the SocketImplFactory.

A SocketException if the SocketImplFactory has already been set.

Socket

Extends: Object

The Socket class is used to implement socket functionality. The setSocketImplFactory method is used to change the socket's implementation based on specific firewalls.

Socket **Constructor**

public Socket(String host, int port) throws UnknownHostException, IOException

This Socket constructor creates a stream socket to the specified port on the specified host.

Parameters:

host—a String object containing the hostname to create the socket on.

port—an integer value representing the port to create the socket on.

Throws: UnknownHostException if the hostname is unrecognized or invalid.

An IOException if an I/O error occurred while creating the socket.

Socket **Constructor**

public Socket(String host, int port, boolean stream) throws IOException

This Socket constructor creates a stream socket to the specified port on the specified host. The boolean stream value can be used to specify a stream socket or a datagram socket.

Parameters:

host—a String object containing the hostname to create the socket on.

port—an integer value representing the port to create the socket on.

stream—a boolean value that is true if a stream socket is to be created; false if a datagram socket is to be created.

Throws: IOException if an I/O error occurred while creating the socket.

Socket **Constructor**

public Socket(InetAddress address, int port) throws IOException

This Socket constructor creates a stream socket to the specified port at the specified InetAddress.

Parameters:

address—an InetAddress object specifying the address to create the socket at.

port—an integer value representing the port to create the socket on.

Throws: IOException if an I/O error occurred while creating the socket.

Socket **Constructor**

```
public Socket(InetAddress address, int port, boolean stream) throws IOException
```

This Socket constructor creates a stream socket to the specified port at the specified address. The boolean stream value can be used to specify a stream socket or a datagram socket.

Parameters:

address—an InetAddress object specifying the address to create the socket at.

port—an integer value representing the port to create the socket on.

stream—a boolean value that is true if a stream socket is to be created; false if a datagram socket is to be created.

Throws: IOException if an I/O error occurred while creating the socket.

getInetAddress

```
public InetAddress getInetAddress()
```

The getInetAddress method is used to return the address to which the socket is connected.

Returns: An InetAddress object containing information about the address to which the socket is connected.

getPort

```
public int getPort()
```

The getPort method returns the remote port to which the socket is connected.

Returns: An integer value representing the remote port number that the socket is connected to.

getLocalPort

```
public int getLocalPort()
```

The getLocalPort method returns the local port to which the socket is connected.

Returns: An integer value representing the local port number that the socket is connected to.

getInputStream

```
public InputStream getInputStream() throws IOException
```

The getInputStream method returns an input stream for this socket.

Returns: An InputStream object to be used as the socket's input stream.

Throws: IOException if an I/O error occurred while retrieving the input stream.

getOutputStream

```
public OutputStream getOutputStream() throws IOException
```

The getOutputStream method returns an output stream for this socket.

Returns: An OutputStream object to be used as the socket's output stream.

Throws: IOException if an I/O error occurred while retrieving the output stream.

close

```
public synchronized void close() throws IOException
```

The close method closes the socket's connection.

Throws: IOException if an I/O error occurred while closing the socket.

toString

```
public String toString()
```

The toString method returns a string representation of the socket.

Returns: A String object containing the socket information.

setSocketImplFactory

```
public static synchronized void setSocketImplFactory(SocketImplFactory fac)
  throws IOException
```

The setSocketImplFactory method sets the SocketImplFactory interface for this socket. The factory can only be specified once.

Parameters: fac—a SocketImplFactory derived object to be used by this socket.

Throws: IOException if an I/O error occurred while setting the SocketImplFactory.

SocketImpl

Extends: Object

The SocketImpl class is an abstract base class provided as a template for socket implementations.

toString

```
public String toString()
```

The toString method returns a string representation of the SocketImpl class.

Returns: A String object containing the port and address of this socket.

URL

Extends: Object

The URL class is used to represent a uniform resource locator. URL is a reference to an object on the Web such as an FTP site, an e-mail address, or an HTML page on a Web server.

URL **Constructor**

```
public URL(String protocol, String host, int port, String file) throws
    MalformedURLException
```

This URL constructor creates a URL using the specified protocol, host, port, and host filename.

Parameters:

protocol—a String object specifying the protocol to be used.

host—a String object specifying the hostname.

port—an integer value specifying the port.

file—a String object specifying the file name on the host.

Throws: MalformedURLException if the protocol was unknown or invalid.

URL **Constructor**

```
public URL(String protocol, String host, String file) throws
    MalformedURLException
```

This URL constructor creates a URL using the specified protocol, host, and host file name. The port number will be the default port used for the specified protocol.

Parameters:

protocol—a String object specifying the protocol to be used.

host—a String object specifying the hostname.

file—a String object specifying the file name on the host.

Throws: MalformedURLException if the protocol was unknown or invalid.

URL **Constructor**

public URL(String spec) throws MalformedURLException

This URL constructor creates a URL using the specified unparsed URL.

Parameters: spec—a String object containing an unparsed URL string.

Throws: MalformedURLException if the specified unparsed URL was invalid.

URL **Constructor**

public URL(URL context, String spec) throws MalformedURLException

This URL constructor creates a URL using the specified context and unparsed URL. If the unparsed URL is an absolute URL it is used as is, otherwise it is used in combination with the specified context.

Parameters:

context—a URL object specifying the context to be used in combination with the unparsed URL string.

spec—a String object containing an unparsed URL string.

Throws: MalformedURLException if the specified unparsed URL was invalid.

getPort

public int getPort()

The getPort method returns the port number for this URL.

Returns: An integer value representing the port number for this URL, which is -1 if the port has not been set.

getProtocol

```
public String getProtocol()
```

The getProtocol method returns a string representing the protocol used by this URL.

Returns: A String object containing the protocol name.

getHost

```
public String getHost()
```

The getHost method returns a string containing the hostname.

Returns: A String object containing the hostname.

getFile

```
public String getFile()
```

The getFile method returns a string containing the host filename.

Returns: A String object containing the name of the file on the host.

getRef

```
public String getRef()
```

The getRef method returns the ref (if any) that was specified in the unparsed string used to create this URL.

Returns: A String object containing the URL's ref.

equals

```
public boolean equals(Object obj)
```

The equals method can be used to compare this URL to another object.

Parameters: obj—an object that will be compared with this URL.

Returns: A boolean value that will be true if the objects are equal, false if not.

hashCode

```
public int hashCode()
```

The hashCode method will return a hash code value for the URL.

Returns: An integer value representing the hash code value of this URL.

sameFile

```
public boolean sameFile(URL other)
```

The sameFile method can be used to determine if the specified file is the same file used to create this URL.

Parameters: other—a URL object specifying the location of another file.

Returns: A boolean value that will be true if the files are equal; false if not.

toString

```
public String toString()
```

The toString method returns a string representation of the URL.

Returns: A String object containing a textual representation of the URL including the protocol, host, port, and filename.

toExternalForm

```
public String toExternalForm()
```

The toExternalForm method is used to reverse the parsing of the URL.

Returns: A String object containing the textual representation of the fully qualified URL.

openConnection

```
public URLConnection openConnection() throws java.io.IOException
```

The openConnection method will open a URLConnection to the object specified by the URL.

Returns: A URLConnection object that represents a connection to the URL.

Throws: IOException if an I/O error occurred while creating the URL connection.

openStream

```
public final InputStream openStream() throws java.io.IOException
```

The openStream method opens an InputStream.

Returns: An InputStream representing an input stream for the URL.

Throws: IOException if an I/O error occurred while creating the input stream.

getContent

`public final Object getContent() throws java.io.IOException`

The `getContent` method retrieves the contents from the opened connection.

Returns: An object representing the contents that are retrieved from the connection.

Throws: `IOException` if an I/O error occurred while retrieving the content.

setURLStreamHandlerFactory

`public static synchronized void setURLStreamHandlerFactory(`
`  URLStreamHandlerFactory fac)`

The `setURLStreamHandlerFactory` method sets the `URLStreamHandlerFactory` interface for this URL. The factory can only be specified once.

Parameters: `fac`—a `URLStreamHandlerFactory` interface to be used by this URL.

Throws: `Error` if this factory has already been specified.

URLConnection

Extends: `Object`

The `URLConnection` class is an abstract base class used to represent a URL connection. It must be subclassed in order to provide true functionality.

connect

`abstract public void connect() throws IOException`

The `connect` method is used to connect the `URLConnection` after it has been created. Operations that depend on being connected will call this method to automatically connect.

Throws: `IOException` if an I/O error occurred while the connection was attempted.

getURL

`public URL getURL()`

The `getURL` method returns the URL for this URL connection.

Returns: A `URL` object.

getContentLength

```
public int getContentLength()
```

The getContentLength method returns the length of the content.

Returns: An integer value containing the length of the content, which is -1 if the length is not known.

getContentType

```
public String getContentType()
```

The getContentType method returns the type of the content.

Returns: A String object containing the type of the content, which is null if the type is not known.

getContentEncoding

```
public String getContentEncoding()
```

The getContentEncoding method returns the encoding of the content.

Returns: A String object containing the encoding of the content, which is null if the encoding is not known.

getExpiration

```
public long getExpiration()
```

The getExpiration method will return the expiration of the object.

Returns: A long value containing the expiration of the object. This value will be 0 if the expiration is not known.

getDate

```
public long getDate()
```

The getDate method will return the date of the object.

Returns: A long value containing the date of the object. This value will be 0 if the date is not known.

getLastModified

```
public long getLastModified()
```

The getLastModified() will return the last modified date of the object.

Returns: A long value containing the last modified date of the object. This value will be 0 if the last modified date is not known.

getHeaderField

```
public String getHeaderField(String name)
```

The getHeaderField method returns the contents of the header field based on the specified field name.

Parameters: name—a String object specifying the name of the header field to be returned.

Returns: A String object containing the contents of the specified header field. This value will be null if the contents are not known.

getHeaderFieldInt

```
public int getHeaderFieldInt(String name, int Default)
```

The getHeaderFieldInt method returns the pre-parsed contents of the specified header field.

Parameters:

name—a String object specifying the name of the header field to be returned.

Default—an integer value containing the value to be returned if the field is missing.

Returns: An integer value containing the preparsed header field value.

getHeaderFieldDate

```
public long getHeaderFieldDate(String name, long Default)
```

The getHeaderFieldDate method returns the contents of the specified header field parsed as a date.

Parameters:

name—a String object specifying the name of the header field to be returned.

Default—an integer value containing the value to be returned if the field is missing.

Returns: A long value containing the header field value parsed as a date.

getHeaderFieldKey

```
public String getHeaderFieldKey(int n)
```

The getHeaderFieldKey method returns the key for the specified header field.

Parameters: n—the position of the header field to be returned.

Returns: A String object containing the key for the specified header field. This value will be null if there are fewer than *n* header fields.

getHeaderField

```
public String getHeaderField(int n)
```

The getHeaderField method returns the specified header field value.

Parameters: n—the position of the header field to be returned.

Returns: A String object containing the contents of the specified header field. This value will be null if there are fewer than *n* header fields.

getContent

```
public Object getContent() throws IOException
```

The getContent method returns the object referred to by this URLConnection.

Returns: An Object object that was referred to by this URL.

Throws: IOException if an I/O error occurred while retrieving the content.

getInputStream

```
public InputStream getInputStream() throws IOException
```

The getInputStream method returns an InputStream object to be used as an input stream to read from the object.

Returns: An InputStream object to be used to read from the object.

Throws: IOException if an I/O error occurred while creating the input stream.

getOutputStream

```
public OutputStream getOutputStream() throws IOException
```

The getOutputStream method returns an OutputStream object to be used as an output stream to write to the object.

Returns: An `OutputStream` object to be used to write to the object.

Throws: `IOException` if an I/O error occurred while creating the output stream.

toString

```
public String toString()
```

The `toString` method returns a string representation of the `URLConnection`.

Returns: A `String` object containing a textual representation of the `URLConnection` object.

setDoInput

```
public void setDoInput(boolean doinput)
```

The `setDoInput` method sets the functionality of the URL connection. If the parameter is `true`, the URL connection will be used for input. If it is `false`, it will be used for output.

Parameters: `doinput`—a boolean value that will be `true` if the URL connection is to be used for input; `false` if for output.

setDoOutput

```
public void setDoOutput(boolean dooutput)
```

The `setDoOutput` method sets the functionality of the URL connection. If the parameter is `true`, the URL connection will be used for output. If it is `false`, it will be used for input.

Parameters: `dooutput`—a boolean value that will be `true` if the URL connection is to be used for output; `false` if for input.

getDoOutput

```
public boolean getDoOutput()
```

The `getDoOutput` method returns the input/output functionality of the `URLConnection`.

Returns: A boolean value that will be `true` if the URL connection is used for output; `false` if it is used for input.

setAllowUserInteraction

```
public void setAllowUserInteraction(boolean allowuserinteraction)
```

The `setAllowUserInteraction` method allows the protocol to interact with the user.

Parameters: `allowuserinteraction`—a boolean value that should be `true` if user interaction is allowed; `false` if not.

getAllowUserInteraction

`public boolean getAllowUserInteraction()`

The `getAllowUserInteraction` method can be called to determine if user interaction is allowed.

Returns: A boolean value that will be `true` if user interaction is allowed; `false` if not.

setDefaultAllowUserInteraction

`public static void setDefaultAllowUserInteraction(`
`  boolean defaultallowuserinteraction)`

The `setDefaultAllowUserInteraction` method allows the default user interaction value to be set for all URL connections because it is a static method.

Parameters: `defaultallowuserinteraction`—a boolean value that should be `true` if user interaction is allowed; `false` if not.

getDefaultAllowUserInteraction

`public static boolean getDefaultAllowUserInteraction()`

The `getDefaultAllowUserInteraction` static method returns the default user interaction value.

Returns: A boolean value that will be `true` if user interaction is allowed; `false` if not.

setUseCaches

`public void setUseCaches(boolean usecaches)`

The `setUseCaches` method is used to control the use of caching by the protocol. Some protocols allow files to be cached.

Parameters: `usecaches`—a boolean value that will be `true` if caching is to be used by the protocol; `false` if not.

getUseCaches

`public boolean getUseCaches()`

The `getUseCaches` method can be called to determine if caching is to be used by the protocol.

Returns: A boolean value that will be `true` if caching is to be used by the protocol; `false` if not.

setIfModifiedSince

`public void setIfModifiedSince(long ifmodifiedsince)`

The `setIfModifiedSince` method is provided to set the internal `ifmodifiedsince` variable of the `URLConnection` class. Because some protocols allow caching of files, if the file to be retrieved is newer than `ifmodifiedsince`, it will need to retrieved from the URL (rather than the cache).

Parameters: `ifmodifiedsince`—a long value used to represent the `ifmodifiedsince` date.

getIfModifiedSince

`public long getIfModifiedSince()`

The `getIfModifiedSince` method returns the internal `ifmodifiedsince` date value. See the `setIfModifiedSince` method documentation.

Returns: A long value representing the `ifmodifiedsince` date value.

getDefaultUseCaches

`public boolean getDefaultUseCaches()`

The `getDefaultUseCaches` method can be called to determine if caches are used by default.

Returns: A boolean value that will be `true` if caches are used by default; `false` if not.

setDefaultUseCaches

`public void setDefaultUseCaches(boolean defaultusecaches)`

The `setDefaultUseCaches` method can be used to force all `URLConnections` to use caching by default because it is a static value.

Parameters: `defaultusecaches`—a boolean value that should be `true` if caches are to be used by default; `false` if not.

setRequestProperty

`public void setRequestProperty(String key, String value)`

The `setRequestProperty` method is used to set `URLConnection` properties.

Parameters:

`key`—a `String` object containing the key by which the property is known.

`value`—a `String` object containing the property value.

getRequestProperty

`public String getRequestProperty(String key)`

The getRequestProperty method returns the value for the specified property key.

Parameters: key—a String object containing the key by which the property is known.

Returns: A String object containing the specified property's value.

setDefaultRequestProperty

`public static void setDefaultRequestProperty(String key, String value)`

The setDefaultRequestProperty method sets the default value of a specified property. All current and future URL connections will be initialized with these properties.

Parameters:

key—a String object containing the key by which the property is known.

value—a String object containing the specified property's value.

getDefaultRequestProperty

`public static String getDefaultRequestProperty(String key)`

The getDefaultRequestProperty method gets the default value of a specified property.

Parameters: key—a String object containing the key by which the property is known.

Returns: A String object containing the specified property's value.

setContentHandlerFactory

`public static synchronized void setContentHandlerFactory(`
`  ContentHandlerFactory fac)`

The setContentHandlerFactory method is used to set the ContentHandlerFactory interface for this URL connection. The factory can only be set once.

Parameters: fac—a ContentHandlerFactory-derived object.

Throws: Error if the ContentHandlerFactory has already been defined.

URLEncoder

Extends: Object

The URLEncoder class is used to encode text into *x-www-form-urlencoded* format.

encode

`public static String encode(String s)`

The encode method is used to translate a string into *x-www-form-urlencoded* format.

Parameters: s—a `String` object to be translated.

Returns: A `String` object in *x-www-form-urlencoded* format.

MalformedURLException

Extends: `IOException`

The `MalformedURLException` class is used to signal a malformed URL.

ProtocolException

Extends: `IOException`

This exception signals when a connect receives an `EPROTO` message. This exception is used by the `Socket` class.

SocketException

Extends: `IOException`

This exception signals when an error has occurred while trying to use a socket. This exception is used by the `Socket` class.

UnknownHostException

Extends: `IOException`

This exception signals that the host address specified by the client cannot be resolved.

UnknownServiceException

Extends: `IOException`

This exception signals when an unknown service exception has occurred.

APPENDIX

L

java.util **Package Reference**

The java.util package contains a variety of classes representing data structures and other miscellaneous features such as support for date and time.

Enumeration

The Enumeration interface defines methods that can be used to iterate through a set of objects.

hasMoreElements

```
public abstract boolean hasMoreElements()
```

Can be used to determine if the enumeration has more elements.

Returns: true if there are more elements, false if not.

nextElement

```
public abstract Object nextElement()
```

This method returns the next element in the enumeration. Calling it repeatedly will move through the enumeration.

Returns: The next element in the enumeration.

Throws: NoSuchElementException if there are no more elements in the enumeration.

Observer

The Observer interface defines an update method that is invoked by an Observable object whenever the Observable object has changed and wants to notify its observers.

update

```
public abstract void update(Observable o, Object arg)
```

This method is called whenever an Observable instance that is being observed invokes either of its notifyObservers methods.

Parameters:

o—the Observable object that is generating this message.

arg—any additional information passed by the Observable object's notifyObservers method.

BitSet

Extends: Object

Implements: Cloneable

This class represents a dynamically sized set of bits. Two constructors are provided, one that creates an empty set of unspecified size and one that creates a set of a specified size. The set method can be used to set an individual bit, or clear can be used to clear an individual bit.

BitSet **Constructor**

public BitSet()

This constructor creates an empty bit set.

BitSet **Constructor**

public BitSet(int nbits)

This constructor creates an empty bit set with the specified number of bits.

Parameters: nbits—the number of bits in the set.

and

public void and(BitSet set)

This method logically ANDs the bit set with another bit set.

Parameters: set—the bit set to AND with the current set.

clear

public void clear(int bit)

Clears the specified bit.

Parameters: bit—the bit to clear.

clone

public Object clone()

This method overrides the clone method in Object. It can be used to clone the bit set.

equals

`public boolean equals(Object obj)`

This method can be used to compare the contents of two bit sets. If the same bits are set in the two bit sets, they are considered equal.

Parameters: `obj`—the bit set to compare against.

Returns: `true` if the set bits are the same, `false` otherwise.

get

`public boolean get(int bit)`

Gets the value of a specified bit in the set.

Parameters: `bit`—the bit to get.

Returns: `true` if the bit is set; `false` if it is clear.

hashCode

`public int hashCode()`

This method overrides the `hashCode` method in `Object` and can be used to get a hash code for the instance.

Returns: A hash code for the instance.

or

`public void or(BitSet set)`

This method logically ORs the bit set with another.

Parameters: `set`—the bit set to OR with the current set.

set

`public void set(int bit)`

Sets the specified bit.

Parameters: `bit`—the bit to set.

size

`public int size()`

This method returns the amount of space, in bits, used to store the set. Space for a bit set is allocated in 64-bit increments.

Returns: The amount of space, in bits, used to store the bit set.

toString

`public String toString()`

This method formats the bit set as a string. The string will consist of an opening curly brace, comma-separated values representing each set bit, and a closing curly brace.

Returns: A string representing the bits in the bit set that are set.

xor

`public void xor(BitSet set)`

This method logically XORs the bit set with another bit set.

Parameters: set—the bit set to XOR with the current set.

Date

Extends: Object

The Date class stores a representation of a date and time and provides methods for manipulating the date and time components. Constructors are provided that will create a new Date instance based on the current date and time, the UNIX-standard milliseconds since midnight on January 1, 1970, a string, or from integers representing the year, month, day, hours, minutes, and seconds.

Date **Constructor**

`public Date()`

This method creates a new Date object using today's date.

Date **Constructor**

```
public Date(long date)
```

This method creates a date from a `long` that represents the number of milliseconds since January 1, 1970.

Parameters: date—the number of milliseconds since January 1, 1970.

Date **Constructor**

```
public Date(int year, int month, int date)
```

This method creates a new `Date` object that corresponds to the year, month, and day passed to it. The first month of the year is month zero. The day of the month is normalized so that impossible dates become real dates.

Parameters:

year—the number of years since 1900.

month—the zero-based month, from 0 to 11.

date—the day of the month.

Date **Constructor**

```
public Date(int year, int month, int date, int hrs, int min)
```

This method creates a new `Date` object that corresponds to the year, month, day, hours, and minutes passed to it. As with the prior constructor, the day of the month is normalized so that impossible dates become real dates.

Parameters:

year—the number of years since 1900.

month—the zero-based month, from 0 to 11.

date—the day of the month.

hrs—the zero-based number of hours (0–23).

min—the zero-based number of minutes (0–59).

Date **Constructor**

```
public Date(int year, int month, int date, int hrs, int min, int sec)
```

This method creates a new Date object that corresponds to the year, month, day, hour, minute, and seconds passed to it. As with the other constructors, the day of the month is normalized so that impossible dates become real dates.

Parameters:

year—the number of years since 1900.

month—the zero-based month, from 0 to 11.

date—the day of the month.

hrs—the zero-based number of hours (0–23).

min—the zero-based number of minutes (0–59).

sec—the zero-based number of seconds (0–59).

Date **Constructor**

```
public Date(String s)
```

This method creates a new date based on the date string passed to it.

Parameters: s—a time string in the format passed to java.util.Date.Parse, as described later in this appendix.

UTC

```
public static long UTC(int year, int month, int date, int hrs, int min, int sec)
```

This method calculates the time in UTC (Coordinated Universal Time) format based on the specified parameters. Parameters are expected to be given in UTC values, not the time in the local time zone.

Parameters:

year—the number of years since 1900.

month—the zero-based month, from 0 to 11.

date—the day of the month.

hrs—the zero-based number of hours (0–23).

min—the zero-based number of minutes (0–59).

sec—the zero-based number of seconds (0–59).

Returns: A UTC time value.

parse

`public static long parse(String s)`

This method calculates the time in UTC format based on the string passed to it.

Parameters: s—a formatted time string such as `Mon, 8 Apr 1996 21:32:PM PST`.

Returns: A UTC time value.

after

`public boolean after(Date when)`

Determines whether the `Date` occurs after the specified date.

Parameters: when—the date to compare against.

Returns: `true` if the object's date occurs after the specified date; `false` otherwise.

before

`public boolean before(Date when)`

This method determines whether the `Date` occurs before the specified date.

Parameters: when—the date to compare against.

Returns: `true` if the object's date occurs before the specified date; `false` otherwise.

equals

`public boolean equals(Object obj)`

This method determines whether two `Date` objects are the same by comparing the dates represented by each object.

Parameters: obj—the object to compare against.

Returns: `true` if the dates are the same; `false` otherwise.

getDate

`public int getDate()`

This method returns the day (or date) portion of a `Date` object.

Returns: The day of the month, from 1 to 31.

getDay

```
public int getDay()
```

This method returns the day of the week. Sunday is assigned a value of 0.

Returns: The day of the week from 0 (Sunday) to 6 (Saturday).

getHours

```
public int getHours()
```

This method returns the hour.

Returns: The hour from 0 to 23.

getMinutes

```
public int getMinutes()
```

This method returns the minutes.

Returns: The minutes from 0 to 59.

getMonth

```
public int getMonth()
```

This method returns the month.

Returns: The month from 0 (January) to 11 (December).

getSeconds

```
public int getSeconds()
```

This method returns the seconds.

Returns: The seconds from 0 to 59.

getTime

```
public long getTime()
```

This method returns the number of milliseconds since midnight on January 1, 1970.

Returns: The time expressed in elapsed milliseconds.

getTimezoneOffset

```
public int getTimezoneOffset()
```

This method returns the offset in minutes of the current time zone from the UTC.

Returns: The number of minutes difference between the time zone of the object and UTC.

getYear

```
public int getYear()
```

This method returns the year after 1900.

Returns: The year after 1900.

hashCode

```
public int hashCode()
```

This method overrides the hashCode method in Object and can be used to get a hash code for the instance.

Returns: A hash code for the instance.

setDate

```
public void setDate(int date)
```

This method sets the day of the month portion of a Date object.

Parameters: date—the day value.

setHours

```
public void setHours(int hours)
```

This method sets the hours portion of a Date object.

Parameters: hours—the hour from 0 (midnight) to 23.

setMinutes

```
public void setMinutes(int minutes)
```

This method sets the minutes portion of a Date object.

Parameters: minutes—the minutes from 0 to 59.

setMonth

`public void setMonth(int month)`

This method sets the month portion of a `Date` object.

Parameters: `month`—the zero-based month from 0 (January) to 11 (December).

setSeconds

`public void setSeconds(int seconds)`

This method sets the seconds portion of a `Date` object.

Parameters: `seconds`—the seconds from 0 to 59.

setTime

`public void setTime(long time)`

This method sets the time to the time represented by the number of milliseconds in the `time` parameter. It is frequently used in conjunction with the `getTime` method that returns a number of milliseconds.

Parameters: `time`—the new time in milliseconds since January 1, 1970.

setYear

`public void setYear(int year)`

This method sets the year portion of a `Date` instance.

Parameters: `year`—the year after 1900 (for 1996, use 96).

toGMTString

`public String toGMTString()`

This method creates a string that contains the date and time formatted according to GMT (Greenwich Mean Time) conventions.

Returns: A string representing the date in GMT format, such as `14 Nov 1995 08:00:00 GMT`.

toLocaleString

`public String toLocaleString()`

This method creates a string that contains the date and time in the format of the current locale.

Returns: A string representing the date as formatted for the locale of the instance, such as `11/14/95 00:00:00`.

toString

`public String toString()`

This method creates a string that contains the day of the week, the date, and the time.

Returns: A string representing the day of the week, date and time of the instance, such as `Tue Nov 14 00:00:00 1995`.

Dictionary

Extends: `Object`

The `Dictionary` class is an abstract class. Each element in a `Dictionary` consists of a key and value. Elements are added to a `Dictionary` using `put` and are retrieved using `get`. Elements may be deleted with `remove`. The methods `elements` and `keys` each return an enumeration of the values and keys, respectively, stored in the `Dictionary`.

Dictionary **Constructor**

`public Dictionary()`

This is a default constructor that will create an empty dictionary.

elements

`public abstract Enumeration elements()`

This abstract method returns an enumeration of all elements in a dictionary.

Returns: An enumeration of each of the elements in the dictionary. The methods of `Enumeration` can be used to iterate through the elements.

get

`public abstract Object get(Object key)`

This abstract method retrieves an object from a dictionary based on its key.

Parameters: `key`—the key of the object to be retrieved.

Returns: The value associated with the key, if found; null if not.

isEmpty

`public abstract boolean isEmpty()`

This abstract method can be used to determine if the dictionary is empty.

Returns: `true` if the dictionary is empty; `false` if not.

keys

`public abstract Enumeration keys()`

This abstract method returns an enumeration of all keys in a dictionary.

Returns: An enumeration of each of the keys in the dictionary. The methods of `Enumeration` can be used to iterate through the keys.

put

`public abstract Object put(Object key, Object value)`

This abstract method inserts a new element into the dictionary. To retrieve an element, use the `get` method.

Parameters:

key—the key to be added.

value—the value associated with the key.

Returns: If the key was already in the dictionary, the old value associated with it is returned. If not, null is returned.

Throws: `NullPointerException` if the value is null.

remove

`public abstract Object remove(Object key)`

This abstract method removes an object from a dictionary.

Parameters: key—the key of the element to be removed.

Returns: If the key is found, the value associated with it is returned; if not, null is returned.

size

`public abstract int size()`

This abstract method returns the number of elements in the dictionary.

Returns: The number of items stored in the dictionary.

Hashtable

Extends: Dictionary

The Hashtable class is used for mapping keys to values. Each element in a hash table consists of a key and a value. Elements are added to a hash table using the put method and are retrieved using get. Elements may be deleted from a hash table with remove. A hash table will expand in size as elements are added to it. When creating a new hash table, you can specify an initial capacity and a load factor. The hash table will increase in size whenever adding a new element would move the hash table past its threshold. A hash table's *threshold* is its capacity multiplied by its load factor. For example, a hash table with a capacity of 100 and a load factor of 0.75 would have a threshold of 75 items.

Hashtable **Constructor**

```
public Hashtable(int initialCapacity, float loadFactor)
```

This constructor creates a new instance of a hash table with the specified initial capacity and load factor. Although an initial capacity is specified, the hash table will grow as needed when new items are added. The initial capacity specifies how many elements could be stored in the hash table if the load factor is 1.0. The load factor is a number between 0.0 and 1.0 and specifies the percentage of the hash table that must be full before the size is automatically increased.

Parameters:

initialCapacity—the initial capacity of the hash table.

loadFactor—a value between 0.0 and 1.0 that specifies the percent of available hash slots that can be filled before the table is automatically rehashed into a large hash table.

Hashtable **Constructor**

```
public Hashtable(int initialCapacity)
```

This constructor creates a new hash table with the specified initial capacity and a default load factor of 0.75.

Parameters: initialCapacity—the initial capacity of the hash table.

Hashtable **Constructor**

```
public Hashtable()
```

This constructor creates a new hash table using default values for the initial capacity and the load factor. A default of 101 is used for the initial capacity, and 0.75 is used for the load factor.

clear

`public synchronized void clear()`

This method will remove all elements from a hash table.

clone

`public synchronized Object clone()`

This method clones the hash table into a new hash table. The keys and values themselves are not cloned.

Returns: A cloned hash table.

contains

`public synchronized boolean contains(Object value)`

This method searches the hash table to determine if a specific value is stored.

Parameters: value—the value to search for.

Returns: true if the value is found; false if not.

Throws: NullPointerException if the value is null.

containsKey

`public synchronized boolean containsKey(Object key)`

This method searches the hash table to determine if a specific key occurs.

Parameters: key—the key to search for.

Returns: true if the key is found; false if not.

elements

`public synchronized Enumeration elements()`

This method returns an enumeration of all of the element values in the instance.

Returns: An enumeration of each of the keys in the hash table. The methods of Enumeration can be used to iterate through the keys.

get

```
public synchronized Object get(Object key)
```

This method retrieves the object associated with the specified key.

Parameters: key—the key of the object to be retrieved.

Returns: The value associated with the key, if found; null if not.

isEmpty

```
public boolean isEmpty()
```

This method can be used to determine if the hash table is empty.

Returns: true if the hash table is empty; false if not.

keys

```
public synchronized Enumeration keys()
```

This method returns an enumeration of all the keys in the instance.

Returns: An enumeration of each of the keys in the hash table. The methods of Enumeration can be used to iterate through the keys.

put

```
public synchronized Object put(Object key, Object value)
```

This method inserts a new element into the hash table. To retrieve an element, use the get method.

Parameters:

key—the key to be added.

value—the value associated with the key.

Returns: If the key was already in the hash table, the old value associated with it is returned. If not, null is returned.

Throws: NullPointerException if the value is null.

rehash

```
protected void rehash()
```

This method rehashes the hash table into a larger hash table. It is not normally necessary to call this method directly because it is invoked automatically based on the capacity and load factor of the hash table.

remove

```
public synchronized Object remove(Object key)
```

This method removes an object from a hash table.

Parameters: key—the key of the element to be removed.

Returns: If the key is found, the value associated with it is returned; if not, null is returned.

size

```
public int size()
```

This method returns the number of elements in the hash table.

Returns: The number of items stored in the hash table.

toString

```
public synchronized String toString()
```

This method overrides the toString method in Object and formats the contents of the hash table as a string.

Returns: A string representation of the hash table.

Observable

Extends: Object

An Observable class is a class that can be watched or monitored by another class that implements the Observer interface. Associated with an Observable instance is a list of observers. Whenever the Observable instance changes it can notify each of its observers. By using Observable and Observer classes you can achieve a better partitioning of your code by decreasing the reliance of one class on another.

Observable **Constructor**

```
public Observable()
```

This is an empty, default constructor.

addObserver

```
public synchronized void addObserver(Observer o)
```

This method will add an observer to the list of objects that are observing this instance. The observer must implement the Observer interface.

Parameters: o—the observer to add.

clearChanged

```
protected synchronized void clearChanged()
```

This method clears the internal flag that indicates an Observable instance has changed.

countObservers

```
public synchronized int countObservers()
```

This method counts the numbers of observers who are observing the instance.

Returns: The number of observers for the instance.

deleteObserver

```
public synchronized void deleteObserver(Observer o)
```

This method will delete an observer from the list of observers that are monitoring an Observable object. The observer must have been previously added with addObserver.

Parameters: o—the observer to delete.

deleteObservers

```
public synchronized void deleteObservers()
```

This method will delete all observers of the Observable instance.

hasChanged

```
public synchronized boolean hasChanged()
```

This method can be used to query if an Observable has changed.

Returns: true if an observable change has occurred; false otherwise.

notifyObservers

```
public void notifyObservers()
```

This method will notify all observers that a change has occurred in the Observable object. This will result in a call to the update method in each observer.

notifyObservers

```
public synchronized void notifyObservers(Object arg)
```

This method will notify all observers that a change has occurred in the Observable object. This will result in a call to the update method in each observer to which arg will be passed.

Parameters: arg—any object that can be used to convey information to the observers.

setChanged

```
protected synchronized void setChanged()
```

This method sets an internal flag to indicate that an observable change has occurred within the instance.

Properties

Extends: Hashtable

The Properties class can be used to store keys and associated values. Through its save and load methods, Properties can be written to disk. This makes this class an excellent mechanism for storing configuration information between runs of a program.

Member Variables

```
protected Properties defaults
```

This member stores the default property values.

Properties **Constructor**

```
public Properties()
```

This constructor is used to create an empty, new instance of Properties.

Properties **Constructor**

```
public Properties(Properties defaults)
```

This constructor will create a new instance of `Properties` and will establish a set of default properties.

getProperty

```
public String getProperty(String key)
```

This method is used to retrieve a property based on its key. If no matching key is found, the defaults are searched. If no match is found there either, null is returned.

Parameters: key—the key of the property to retrieve.

Returns: The property associated with the key or null if there is no matching key.

getProperty

```
public String getProperty(String key, String defaultValue)
```

This method is used to retrieve a property based on its key. If no match is found, `defaultValue` is returned.

Parameters:

key—the key of the property to retrieve.

defaultValue—the value to use if no matching key is found.

Returns: The property associated with the key or the `defaultValue` if there is no matching key.

list

```
public void list(PrintStream out)
```

This method will list all of the properties to the specified `PrintStream`. It is useful mainly while debugging.

Parameters: out—the `PrintStream` where the properties are to be printed.

load

```
public synchronized void load(InputStream in) throws IOException
```

This method reads a set of properties from the specified `InputStream`. Used in conjunction with the save method, `Properties` can be written to disk at the end of a program run and then reloaded at the start of the next run.

Parameters: `in`—the input stream from which the properties are to be read.

Throws: `IOException` if the specified file is not found or cannot be read.

propertyNames

`public Enumeration propertyNames()`

This method returns an enumeration of all of the property names in the instance.

Returns: An enumeration of each of the property names. The methods of `Enumeration` can be used to iterate through the property names.

save

`public synchronized void save(OutputStream out, String header)`

This method saves the properties to an output stream. Since `FileOutputStream` is a subclass of `OutputStream`, this method can be used to write to a file.

Parameters:

`out`—the output stream to which the properties are to be written.

`header`—a header that will be sent to the output stream before the properties.

Random

Extends: `Object`

The `Random` class represents a pseudo-random number generator. Two constructors are provided, one taking a seed value as a parameter and the other taking no parameters and using the current time as a seed.

random **Constructor**

`public random()`

This constructor creates a new random number generator that is seeded based on the current time.

random **Constructor**

```
public random(long seed)
```

This constructor creates a new random number generator based on the specified seed value. A program can reset the seed of an already created instance by using the setSeed method.

Parameters: seed—the seed value.

nextDouble

```
public double nextDouble()
```

This method retrieves the next number from the random number generator. The number will be a pseudo-random, uniformly distributed double between 0.0D and 1.0D.

Returns: A randomly distributed double between 0.0D and 1.0D.

nextFloat

```
public float nextFloat()
```

This method retrieves the next number from the random number generator. The number will be a pseudo-random, uniformly distributed float between 0.0F and 1.0F.

Returns: A randomly distributed float between 0.0F and 1.0F.

nextGaussian

```
public synchronized double nextGaussian()
```

This method retrieves the next value from the pseudo-random number generator. The value will be returned as a Gaussian-distributed double that has a mean of 0 and a standard deviation of 1.

Returns: A Gaussian-distributed double.

nextInt

```
public int nextInt()
```

This method retrieves the next number from the random number generator. The number will be a pseudo-random int with a value that is uniformly distributed among all possible int values.

Returns: A randomly distributed int.

nextLong

```
public long nextLong()
```

This method retrieves the next number from the random number generator. The number will be a pseudo-random `long` with a value that is uniformly distributed among all possible `long` values.

Returns: A randomly distributed `long`.

setSeed

```
public synchronized void setSeed(long seed)
```

This method sets a seed value for the pseudo-random number generator. The seed value is used to determine the values that are generated. By setting a specific seed value, the random number generator can be coerced into generating a specific sequence of values.

Parameters: seed—the seed value.

Stack

Extends: Vector

The `Stack` class implements a simple last-in-first-out stack. An item is stored on a stack by "pushing" it onto the stack. An item may subsequently be "popped" off the stack and used. The item popped off a stack will always be the most recently pushed item.

Stack **Constructor**

```
public Stack()
```

This is the default constructor.

empty

```
public boolean empty()
```

This method can be used to determine if the stack contains items.

Returns: `true` if the stack is empty; `false` otherwise.

peek

```
public Object peek()
```

This method can be used to peek at the top item on the stack. It is similar to `pop` but does not remove the item from the stack.

Returns: The item at the top of the stack.

Throws: EmptyStackException if the stack is empty.

pop

```
public Object pop()
```

This method retrieves the last item added to the stack. To examine, but not remove, the top item in the stack use the peek method.

Returns: The item at the top of the stack.

Throws: EmptyStackException if the stack is empty.

push

```
public Object push(Object item)
```

This method adds a new item to the stack.

Parameters: item—the item to push onto the stack.

Returns: The item that was pushed onto the stack.

search

```
public int search(Object o)
```

This method examines the stack to see if the specified object is in the stack.

Parameters: o—the object to search for.

Returns: The distance from the top of the stack, or -1 if the item is not in the stack.

StringTokenizer

Extends: Object

Implements: Enumeration

A StringTokenizer can be used to parse a string into its constituent tokens. For example, each word in a sentence could be considered a token. However, the StringTokenizer class goes beyond the parsing of sentences. You can create a fully customized tokenizer by specifying the set of token delimiters when the string tokenizer is created.

StringTokenizer **Constructor**

`public StringTokenizer(String str, String delim, boolean returnTokens)`

This constructor creates a new instance based on the string to be tokenized, the set of delimiters, and a flag indicating if delimiters should be returned as tokens.

Parameters:

str—the string to be tokenized.

delim—a string containing the delimiters to use when tokenizing the string.

returnTokens—true if the string tokenizer should return delimiters as tokens; false if not.

StringTokenizer **Constructor**

`public StringTokenizer(String str, String delim)`

This constructor creates a new instance based on the string to be tokenized and a set of delimiters.

Parameters:

str—the string to be tokenized.

delim—a string containing the delimiters to use when tokenizing the string.

StringTokenizer **Constructor**

`public StringTokenizer(String str)`

This constructor creates a new instance based on the string to be tokenized and the default set of delimiters. The default delimiters are the space, tab, newline, and carriage-return characters.

countTokens

`public int countTokens()`

This method returns the number of remaining tokens.

Returns: The quantity of tokens remaining in the string being tokenized.

hasMoreElements

```
public boolean hasMoreElements()
```

This method can be used to determine if the string tokenizer contains more elements (tokens). This method is identical to hasMoreTokens and is a member of StringTokenizer because StringTokenizer implements the Enumeration interface.

Returns: true if there are more elements; false otherwise.

hasMoreTokens

```
public boolean hasMoreTokens()
```

This method can be used to determine if the string tokenizer contains more tokens. It is identical to hasMoreElements.

Returns: true if there are more tokens; false otherwise.

nextElement

```
public Object nextElement()
```

This method overrides nextElement in the Enumeration interface and exists because StringTokenizer implements that interface. It is identical to nextToken and returns the next token in the enumeration.

Returns: The next token in the enumeration.

Throws: NoSuchElementException if there are no more elements.

nextToken

```
public String nextToken()
```

This method returns the next token in the string that is being tokenized. It is typically used inside a loop that processes each token.

Returns: The next token in the string being tokenized.

Throws: NoSuchElementException if there are no more tokens.

nextToken

```
public String nextToken(String delim)
```

This method changes the set of delimiter characters and then returns the next token. The new delimiter set will remain in effect after this method completes.

Parameters: delim—a string containing the new set of delimiters.

Returns: The next token in the string being tokenized.

Throws: `NoSuchElementException` if there are no more tokens.

Vector

Extends: `Object`

Implements: `Cloneable`

A vector is analogous to a linked list in other languages or class libraries. A vector stores items of type `Object` so it can be used to store instances of any Java class. A single vector may store different elements that are instances of different classes.

Vector **Constructor**

```
public Vector(int initialCapacity, int capacityIncrement)
```

This constructor will create a new instance of a vector with space for `initialCapacity` elements initially. Memory for additional elements will be allocated in blocks that will each hold `capacityIncrement` elements.

Parameters:

`initialCapacity`—the number of elements to allocate space for when the object is created.

`capacityIncrement`—the number of additional elements to allocate space for whenever additional space is needed.

Vector **Constructor**

```
public Vector(int initialCapacity)
```

This constructor will create a new instance of a vector with space for `initialCapacity` elements initially. Whenever a new element is added that would have exceeded this capacity, the size of the vector is doubled.

Parameters: `initialCapacity`—the number of elements to allocate space for when the object is created.

Vector **Constructor**

```
public constructorVector()
```

This constructor will create a new instance of a vector. Initially, the vector will have room for storing 10 elements, but this will increase automatically to accommodate new elements. Whenever a new element is added that would have exceeded this capacity, the size of the vector is doubled.

Member Variables

`protected int capacityIncrement`

This member stores the amount by which the vector will be incremented each time it needs to grow. If capacityIncrement is 0, the buffer does not grow by a fixed amount but instead doubles whenever it needs to grow.

`protected int elementCount`

This member stores the number of elements in the vector.

`protected Object elementData[]`

This member is the array where the Vector elements are stored.

addElement

`public final synchronized void addElement(Object obj)`

This method is used to insert new elements into the vector; a vector can store objects of different types.

Parameters: obj—the object to add to the vector.

capacity

`public final int capacity()`

This method returns the number of elements that will fit in the vector before more space is allocated.

Returns: The number of elements that will fit in the currently allocated portion of the vector.

clone

`public synchronized Object clone()`

This method overrides clone in Object and will clone the vector. Only the vector itself is cloned; the elements of the vector are not cloned.

Returns: A cloned copy of the vector.

contains

`public final boolean contains(Object elem)`

This method determines if an object is stored in a vector.

Returns: true if the object is stored in the vector; false otherwise.

copyInto

`public final synchronized void copyInto(Object anArray[])`

This method copies the elements of the vector into an array.

Parameters: `anArray`—the array into which the vector elements will be copied.

elementAt

`public final synchronized Object elementAt(int index)`

This method retrieves the element located at the specified index within the vector.

Parameters: `index`—the zero-based index number of the element to retrieve.

Returns: The element at the specified zero-based index.

Throws: `ArrayIndexOutOfBoundsException` if an invalid index is specified.

elements

`public final synchronized Enumeration elements()`

This method returns an `Enumeration` of the elements in the vector, making it easy to iterate through the elements.

Returns: An `Enumeration` consisting of all the elements in the vector.

ensureCapacity

`public final synchronized void ensureCapacity(int minCapacity)`

This method ensures that the vector has at least the specified minimum capacity. If the current capacity of the vector is less than `minCapacity`, the size of the vector is increased to hold at least `minCapacity`.

Parameters: `minCapacity`—the minimum capacity of the vector.

firstElement

`public final synchronized Object firstElement()`

This method retrieves the first element in the vector. If the vector is empty, an exception is thrown. It performs the same function as `elementAt(0)`.

Returns: The element at the specified zero-based index.

Throws: `NoSuchElementException` if the vector is empty.

indexOf

```
public final int indexOf(Object elem)
```

This method searches the vector and returns the zero-based index number of the first matching object.

Parameters: elem—the element to find the index of.

Returns: The element number of the first element that matches elem, or -1 if no match is found.

indexOf

```
public final synchronized int indexOf(Object elem, int index)
```

This method finds the first element in the vector that matches elem starting at the element given by index. It is very useful for traversing a vector searching for all elements matching a specific object.

Parameters:

elem—the element to find the index of.

index—the index number at which to start the search.

Returns: The element number of the first element that matches elem, or -1 if no match is found.

insertElementAt

```
public final synchronized void insertElementAt(Object obj, int index)
```

This method, like addElement, is used to add a new element to a vector. However, this method can be used to specify where in the vector the new element should be added. All Vector elements with index numbers greater than or equal to index are moved to make room for the new element.

Parameters:

obj—the object to add to the vector.

index—the zero-based index at which the object is to be inserted.

Throws: ArrayIndexOutOfBoundsException if the specified index is invalid.

isEmpty

```
public final boolean isEmpty()
```

This method is used to determine if the vector contains any elements.

Returns: `true` if the vector has no elements; `false` otherwise.

lastElement

`public final synchronized Object lastElement()`

This method retrieves the last element in the vector. If the vector is empty an exception is thrown.

Returns: The element at the specified zero-based index.

Throws: `NoSuchElementException` if the vector is empty.

lastIndexOf

`public final int lastIndexOf(Object elem)`

This method searches the vector and returns the zero-based index number of the last matching object.

Parameters: `elem`—the element to find the index of.

Returns: The element number of the last element that matches `elem`, or `-1` if no match is found.

lastIndexOf

`public final synchronized int lastIndexOf(Object elem, int index)`

This method finds the last element in the vector that matches `elem` starting at the element given by `index`. It is very useful for traversing a vector backward searching for all elements matching a specific object.

Parameters:

`elem`—the element to find the last index of.

`index`—the index number at which to start the search.

Returns: The element number of the last element that matches `elem`, or `-1` if no match is found.

removeAllElements

`public final synchronized void removeAllElements()`

This method can be used to remove all elements from the vector.

removeElement

`public final synchronized boolean removeElement(Object obj)`

This method can be used to remove a specific element from the vector. Only the first element that matches `obj` is removed.

Parameters: `obj`—the object to remove.

Returns: `true` if the element was found and deleted; `false` otherwise.

removeElementAt

`public final synchronized void removeElementAt(int index)`

This method removes the element at the specified zero-based index.

Parameters: `index`—the index number of the element to remove from the vector.

Throws: `ArrayIndexOutOfBoundsException` if the specified index is invalid.

setElementAt

`public final synchronized void setElementAt(Object obj, int index)`

This method replaces an element in the vector with another element.

Parameters:

`obj`—the object to be placed in the vector.

`index`—the index number of the element to be replaced.

Throws: `ArrayIndexOutOfBoundsException` if the specified index is invalid.

setSize

`public final synchronized void setSize(int newSize)`

This method sets the size of the vector. If the specified size makes the vector too small to hold its current elements, elements from the end of the vector are removed. If the new size is larger than the current size, empty elements are added at the end of the vector.

Parameters: `newSize`—the desired size of the vector.

size

`public final int size()`

The method returns the number of elements currently in the vector.

Returns: The number of elements in the vector.

toString

```
public final synchronized String toString()
```

This method overrides the toString method in Object and formats the contents of the vector as a string.

Returns: A string representation of the vector.

trimToSize

```
public final synchronized void trimToSize()
```

This method will remove any excess capacity from the vector by resizing it to hold only the quantity of elements it currently holds. If new items are added, the size of the vector will be increased.

EmptyStackException

Extends: RuntimeException

This exception signals when the stack is empty.

NoSuchElementException

Extends: RuntimeException

This exception signals when an enumeration is empty.

L

APPENDIX

M

What's on the CD-ROM

On the *Teach Yourself Java in 21 Days, Professional Reference Edition* CD you will find all the sample files that have been presented in this book along with a wealth of other applications and utilities.

NOTE

> Please refer to the `readme.wri` file on the CD-ROM (Windows) or the Guide to the CD-ROM (Macintosh) for the latest listing of software.

Windows Software

Java

- ☐ Sun's Java Developer's Kit for Windows 95/NT, version 1.0.2
- ☐ Sample Java applets
- ☐ Sample JavaScripts
- ☐ Jamba Integrated Development Environment (IDE)
- ☐ Javelin IDE
- ☐ JDesigner Pro Database Wizard
- ☐ JFactory IDE
- ☐ JPad IDE
- ☐ JPad Pro IDE
- ☐ Kawa IDE
- ☐ Studio J++ Applet Creator

HTML Tools

- ☐ Microsoft Internet Assistants for Access, Excel, PowerPoint, Schedule+, and Word
- ☐ W3e HTML Editor
- ☐ CSE 3310 HTML Validator
- ☐ Hot Dog 32-bit HTML editor
- ☐ HoTMetaL HTML editor
- ☐ HTMLed HTML editor
- ☐ HTML Assistant for Windows

- [ ] WebEdit Pro HTML editor
- [ ] Web Weaver HTML editor
- [ ] ImageGen

Graphics, Video, and Sound Applications

- [ ] Goldwave sound editor, player, and recorder
- [ ] MapThis image map utility
- [ ] Paint Shop Pro 3.12 graphics editor and graphic file format converter for Windows
- [ ] SnagIt screen capture utility
- [ ] ThumbsPlus image viewer and browser

Utilities

- [ ] Microsoft Viewers for Excel, PowerPoint, and Word
- [ ] Adobe Acrobat viewer
- [ ] Microsoft PowerPoint Animation Player & Publisher
- [ ] WinZip for Windows NT/95
- [ ] WinZip Self-Extractor

Macintosh Software

Java

- [ ] Sun's Java Developer's Kit for Macintosh v1.0.2
- [ ] Sample applets
- [ ] Sample JavaScripts

HTML and Graphics Applications

- [ ] BBEdit Light 3.5.1
- [ ] BBEdit 4.0 demo
- [ ] HTML Web Weaver
- [ ] HTML Markup
- [ ] Web Painter

M

Utilities

- [ ] Adobe Acrobat reader
- [ ] ScrapIt Pro 5.13
- [ ] ZipIt for Macintosh

About Shareware

Shareware is not free. Please read all documentation associated with a third-party product (usually contained in files named `readme.txt` or `license.txt`) and follow all guidelines.

Index

Symbols

A

Laura Lemay's Web Workshop: Netscape Navigator Gold 3

—Laura Lemay & Ned Snell

Netscape Gold and JavaScript are two powerful tools to create and design effective Web pages. This book details not only design elements, but also how to use the Netscape Gold WYSIWYG editor. The included CD-ROM contains editors and code from the book, making the reader's learning experience a quick and effective one.

Price: $39.99 USA/$53.99 CDN   User level: Casual—Accomplished
ISBN: 1-57521-128-9   400 pages

Laura Lemay's Web Workshop: 3D Graphics and VRML 2

—Laura Lemay & Karl Jacobs

This is the easiest way for readers to learn how to add three-dimensional virtual worlds to Web pages. It describes the new VRML 2 specification, explores the wide array of existing VRML sites on the Web, and steps the readers through the process of creating his own 3D Web environments. The CD-ROM contains the book in HTML format, a hand-picked selection of the best VRML and 3D graphics tools, plus a collection of ready-to-use virtual worlds.

Price: $39.99 USA/$56.95 CDN   User level: Casual—Accomplished
ISBN: 1-57521-143-2   400 pages

Laura Lemay's Web Workshop: Graphics and Web Page Design

—Laura Lemay, Jon Duff, and James L. Mohler

With the number of Web pages increasing daily, only the well-designed will stand out and grab the attention of those browsing the Web. This book illustrates, in classic Laura Lemay style, how to design attractive Web pages that will be visited over and over again. The CD-ROM contains HTML editors, graphics software, and royalty-free graphics and sound files.

Price: $55.00 USA/$77.95 CDN   User level: Accomplished
ISBN: 1-57521-125-4   500 pages

Laura Lemay's Web Workshop: JavaScript

—Laura Lemay

Readers will explore various aspects of Web publishing—whether CGI scripting and interactivity or graphics design or Netscape Gold—in greater depth than in the *Teach Yourself* books. The CD-ROM includes the complete book in HTML format, publishing tools, templates, graphics, backgrounds, and more.

Price: $39.99 USA/$56.95 CDN   User level: Casual—Accomplished
ISBN: 1-57521-141-6   400 pages

Laura Lemay's Web Workshop: Microsoft FrontPage

—Laura Lemay & Denise Tyler

This is a clear hands-on guide to maintaining Web pages with Microsoft's FrontPage. Written in the clear, conversational style of Laura Lemay, it is packed with many interesting, colorful examples that demonstrate specific tasks of interest to the reader.

Price: $39.99 USA/$56.95 CDN   User level: Casual —Accomplished
ISBN: 1-57521-149-1   400 pages

Laura Lemay's Web Workshop: Creating Commercial Web Pages

—Laura Lemay & Daniel Bishop

Filled with sample Web pages, this book shows how to create commercial-grade Web pages using HTML, CGI, and Java. In the classic clear style of Laura Lemay, author of the best-selling *Teach Yourself Java*, this book details not only how to create the page, but how to apply proven principles of design that will make the Web page a marketing tool.

Price: $39.99 USA/$56.95 CDN   User level: Accomplished
ISBN: 1-57521-126-2   400 pages

Teach Yourself Web Publishing with HTML 3.2 in 14 Days, Professional Reference Edition

—Laura Lemay

This is the updated edition of Lemay's previous bestseller, *Teach Yourself Web Publishing with HTML in 14 Days, Premier Edition*. In it readers will find all the advanced topics and updates—including adding audio, video, and animation—to Web page creation.

Price: $59.99 USA/$81.95 CDN   User level: New—Casual—Accomplished
ISBN: 1-57521-096-7   1,104 pages

Teach Yourself SunSoft Java WorkShop in 21 Days

—Rogers Cadenhead, Laura Lemay, and Charles L. Perkins

Written in Java itself, the Java WorkShop included with this book works as a cross-platform tool that provides a rich set of tools for the beginner or professional Java programmer. The WorkShop combines with the book to provide the most comprehensive way to learn SunSoft Java WorkShop.

Price: $39.99 USA/$56.95 CDN   User level: Casual—Accomplished
ISBN: 1-57521-159-9   600 pages

Add to Your Sams.net Library Today
with the Best Books for Internet Technologies

ISBN	Quantity	Description of Item	Unit Cost	Total Cost
1-57521-126-2		Laura Lemay's Web Workshop: Creating Commercial Web Pages (book/CD-ROM)	$39.99	
1-57521-128-9		Laura Lemay's Web Workshop: Netscape Navigator Gold 3 (book/ CD-ROM)	$39.99	
1-57521-125-4		Laura Lemay's Web Workshop: Graphics and Web Page Design (book/CD-ROM)	$55.00	
1-57521-141-6		Laura Lemay's Web Workshop: JavaScript (book/CD-ROM)	$39.99	
1-57521-149-1		Laura Lemay's Web Workshop: Microsoft FrontPage (book/CD-ROM)	$39.99	
1-57521-141-6		Laura Lemay's Web Workshop: 3D Graphics and VRML 2 (book/CD-ROM)	$39.99	
1-57521-096-7		Teach Yourself Web Publishing with HTML 3.2 in 14 days, Professional Reference Edition (book/CD-ROM)	$59.99	
1-57521-159-9		Teach Yourself SunSoft Java WorkShop in 21 Days (book/CD-ROM)	$39.99	
		Shipping and Handling: See information below.		
		TOTAL		

Shipping and Handling: $4.00 for the first book, and $1.75 for each additional book. If you need to have it NOW, we can ship product to you in 24 hours for an additional charge of approximately $18.00, and you will receive your item overnight or in two days. Overseas shipping and handling adds $2.00. Prices subject to change. Call between 9:00 a.m. and 5:00 p.m. EST for availability and pricing information on latest editions.

201 W. 103rd Street, Indianapolis, Indiana 46290

1-800-428-5331 — Orders   1-800-835-3202 — FAX   1-800-858-7674 — Customer Service

Book ISBN 1-57521-183-1

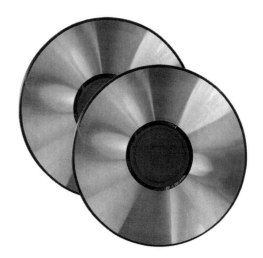

NOTE

Windows NT 3.51 users will be unable to access the \WIN95NT4 directory because it was left in its original long filename state with a combination of upper- and lowercases. This was done to allow Windows 95 and Windows NT 4 users direct access to those files on the CD. All other directories were translated in compliance with the Windows NT 3.51 operating system and may be accessed without trouble. (Note that attempting to access the \WIN95NT4 directory will cause no harm; you simply will be unable to read the contents.)

Macintosh Installation Instructions

1. Insert the CD-ROM into your CD-ROM drive.
2. When an icon for the CD appears on your desktop, open the disc by double-clicking on its icon.
3. Double-click on the icon named Guide to the CD-ROM and follow the directions that appear.

Installing the CD-ROM

The companion CD-ROM contains all the source code and project files developed by the authors, plus an assortment of evaluation versions of third-party products. To install, please follow these steps.

Windows 95/NT 4 Installation Instructions

1. Insert the CD-ROM into your CD-ROM drive.
2. From the Windows 95 desktop, double-click on the My Computer icon.
3. Double-click on the icon representing your CD-ROM drive.
4. Double-click on the icon titled `setup.exe` to run the CD-ROM installation program.

Windows NT 3.51 Installation Instructions

1. Insert the CD-ROM into your CD-ROM drive.
2. From File Manager or Program Manager, choose Run from the File menu.
3. Type `<drive>\SETUP` and press Enter, where `<drive>` corresponds to the drive letter of your CD-ROM. For example, if your CD-ROM is drive `D:`, type `D:\SETUP` and press Enter.
4. Follow the onscreen instructions.